EU Competition Law, Data Protection and Online Platforms

International Competition Law Series

VOLUME 68

Editor

In its series editor, Alastair Sutton, Kluwer is fortunate to engage and benefit from the experience and expertise of one of the world's outstanding authorities on European Union and international economic law.

Introduction

In their efforts to regulate competition in an increasingly complex business environment, competition authorities face a daunting task. The European Commission and Courts, as well as national courts and legislatures, policymakers, and regulators, are constantly proposing, enacting, reviewing, and enforcing new legal measures, often addressing novel situations. Every industry and service is affected.

Contents/Subjects

With many titles currently available and new ones appearing regularly, the series' coverage includes detailed analyses of relevant legislation and case law in major global trading jurisdictions, defences used in cases involving the digital network economy, state aid cases, enforcement methodologies and a great deal more.

Objective & Readership

The purpose of Kluwer's International Competition Law Series is to follow the ever-changing contours of this dynamic area of the law, keeping the practice in sharp focus so that practising lawyers (including in-house counsel) and academics can be assured of the most up-to-date guidance and sources, in the widest possible range of applications.

The titles published in this series are listed at the end of this volume.

EU Competition Law, Data Protection and Online Platforms

Data as Essential Facility

Inge Graef

 Wolters Kluwer

Published by:
Kluwer Law International B.V.
PO Box 316
2400 AH Alphen aan den Rijn
The Netherlands
Website: www.wklawbusiness.com

Sold and distributed in North, Central and South America by:
Wolters Kluwer Legal & Regulatory U.S.
7201 McKinney Circle
Frederick, MD 21704
United States of America
Email: customer.service@wolterskluwer.com

Sold and distributed in all other countries by:
Turpin Distribution Services Ltd
Stratton Business Park
Pegasus Drive, Biggleswade
Bedfordshire SG18 8TQ
United Kingdom
Email: kluwerlaw@turpin-distribution.com

Printed on acid-free paper.

ISBN 978-90-411-8324-8

e-Book: 978-90-411-8325-5
web-PDF: 978-90-411-8326-2

© 2016 Kluwer Law International BV, The Netherlands

Printed in the United Kingdom.

Table of Contents

Table of Contents

Acknowledgements

This book forms the result of a doctoral research project conducted at the Centre for IT & IP Law (CiTiP) of the Faculty of Law of KU Leuven. Its publication is a good occasion to express my gratitude to several people and institutions who have provided their support along the writing process.

At CiTiP, I found a very stimulating working environment made up of a dynamic bunch of researchers with different backgrounds and interests. It has been a privilege to be a part of such a vibrant research group. Over the years, I have benefited from invaluable discussions with colleagues who have widened my horizon to 'exotic' topics that I was not yet familiar with such as data protection, e-health and cyber security. I am grateful to all my colleagues who make CiTiP such an enjoyable place to work. Notably, I would like to mention my roommates over the past years, Björn, Ellen, Valerie and Stephanie in particular, who brightened up my day on many occasions by providing welcome distractions from the PhD writing. In addition, I would like to say a word of thanks to the 'admin team', Shuki, Carmen and Edith, for the excellent administrative support.

During my PhD studies, I have benefited from a scholarship from the Research Foundation Flanders (FWO) which gave me the freedom and opportunities to participate in conferences and workshops in Belgium and abroad. At these occasions, I have met many fellow researchers who have often provided renewed inspiration and motivation for the thesis. Special thanks go out to Dr. Yuli Wahyuningtyas with whom I had the pleasure to work on a number of papers and who joined me in attending many competition law events. I would also like to thank FWO for funding my research stay at the Max Planck Institute for Innovation and Competition in Munich in Fall 2014 where I benefited from useful exchanges with Dr. Beatriz Conde Gallego and Dr. Gintaré Surblyté.

The members of my PhD examination committee deserve particular mention here. Before all others, I am grateful to Prof. Dr. Peggy Valcke for being a most inspiring supervisor and for being there whenever I needed advice or guidance. For the encouragement she offered and for the opportunities she created for me over the years, I will always be thankful. I am also much indebted to my co-supervisor Prof. Dr. Wouter Devroe for introducing me to the exciting field of competition law when I was a master student in Maastricht, for supporting me and following my work ever since, and for stimulating me to form my own opinion on the PhD topic. I would also like to thank Prof. Dr. Pierre Larouche and Prof. Dr. Alexandre de Streel for their commitment to the PhD project as members of my supervisory committee and for providing detailed comments and suggestions on draft chapters along the way. In addition, I wish to express my gratitude to Em. Prof. Dr. Jules Stuyck for kindly accepting to read the manuscript and to act as a member of the examination committee at the end of the project.

Finally, a very special thanks go to my parents and sister for their continued support and encouragement without which I would not have reached this far.

CHAPTER 1

Introduction

1.1 BACKGROUND

The digital economy has brought about new market developments which have impacted society as a whole. Online services bring many benefits to consumers in the form of new types of social interaction and other innovative functionalities. At the same time, the use of digital processes has enabled market players to increase their productivity, resulting into lower prices and intensified competition in many sectors. The advent of the digital economy also transformed commercial behaviour and led to new business models. While digitalisation continues to contribute to a dynamic evolution of markets and competition, concerns are increasingly being raised about the alleged powerful market positions of a number of key players.[1]

The significance of data for digital markets and digital business models plays a key role in this regard. Innovative products and services are increasingly being offered online which enables providers to collect information about the profile, behaviour and interests of users. The knowledge that can be extracted from this data forms the basis for the competitiveness and growth of individual players in digital markets. Datasets built on the basis of the information that individuals disclose when using online services have become an economic asset in the digital economy.[2] In general, the increasing collection and use of data has positive welfare effects. The greater knowledge about the interests of users may lead to better quality of services and enable companies to cut costs, for example, because of more precise advertisement targeting possibilities. However, the increased collection and use of data can also result in

---

1. MONOPOLKOMMISSION, 'Competition policy: The challenge of digital markets', Special report No. 68, July 2015, par. S3 and S4, available at http://www.monopolkommission.de/images/PDF/SG/s 68_fulltext_eng.pdf.
2. WORLD ECONOMIC FORUM, 'Personal Data: The Emergence of a New Asset Class', January 2011, available at http://www3.weforum.org/docs/WEF_ITTC_PersonalDataNewAsset_Report_2011. pdf.

1

negative welfare effects. In particular, having control over and being able to analyse large volumes of data may form a source of power for incumbent market players.[3]

It is instructive to note that as early as 2010 Tim Berners-Lee, known as the inventor of the world wide web, identified several trends which in his view threaten the internet as we know it. One of the referred threats concerns the walling off by large social networking sites of information posted by users from the rest of the web. By assembling information disclosed by users into databases and reusing the information to provide value-added services only within their own sites, providers create closed silos which may, in the view of Berners-Lee, lead to the fragmentation of the web and threaten its existence as a single, universal information space.[4] Such developments also raise questions about the role of competition law in addressing potential forms of abuse of dominance relating to data. In this regard, the Competition Commissioner recognised in a January 2016 speech that there is scope for competition enforcement in cases where only a few companies control the data needed to satisfy customers and cut costs because this could give them the power to drive their rivals out of the market.[5]

1.2   FOCUS OF THE BOOK

Against this background, the book explores how existing competition tools and concepts can be applied to data-related competition concerns in digital markets. The key focus of the book is on potential refusals of dominant firms to give access to data on online platforms such as search engines, social networks and e-commerce platforms. Even though the analysis may also be applicable to other online services, particular attention is paid to the three latter types of online platforms because of the importance of data for their business models and the fact that they are commonly referred to as 'gatekeepers' of the internet. In line with its significance in the digital economy, data is becoming a necessary input of production for a variety of products and services competing with or complementary to the services offered by incumbent providers of online search engines, social networks and e-commerce platforms. By refusing to share information with potential competitors or new entrants, incumbents may limit effective competition to the detriment of consumers.

In this context, the question rises whether the denial of a dominant firm to grant competitors access to its dataset could constitute a refusal to deal under Article 102 of the Treaty on the Functioning of the European Union (TFEU)[6] and lead to competition law liability under the so-called essential facilities doctrine. This doctrine attacks a particular form of exclusionary anticompetitive conduct by which a dominant

---

3. MONOPOLKOMMISSION, 'Competition policy: The challenge of digital markets', Special report No. 68, July 2015, par. S3 and S10.
4. T. BERNERS-LEE, 'Long Live the Web: A Call for Continued Open Standards and Neutrality', *Scientific American* December 2010, vol. 303, no. 6, (80).
5. Speech of Competition Commissioner Vestager, 'Competition in a big data world', DLD 16 Munich, 17 January 2016, available at https://ec.europa.eu/commission/2014-2019/vestager/announcements/competition-big-data-world_en.
6. Consolidated version of the TFEU [2012] OJ C 326/47.

undertaking refuses to give access to a type of infrastructure or other form of facility to which rivals need access in order to be able to compete.

The main research question addressed in the book revolves around the issue of whether and to what extent data may constitute an essential facility. While scholars have pointed to the probability of competitors asking access to data stored on online platforms,[7] it is not clear how an obligation of dominant firms to give access to the data on their platforms would fit with earlier decisions and judgments. The essential facilities doctrine has already been applied to physical infrastructures including ports and tunnels as well as to intangible assets protected by intellectual property rights. Because of the particular nature of data collected by providers of online platforms and the new business models that are employed, potential refusals to share data give rise to new competition concerns and may require a different analysis under the essential facilities doctrine.

The focus on the issue of when refusals to give access to data may constitute abusive behaviour under Article 102 TFEU also enables an analysis of how existing competition tools for market definition and assessment of dominance can be applied to online platforms. In addition, the imposition of a duty to share data with competitors raises questions about the interaction of competition law with data protection legislation considering that the information collected by providers of online platforms may also include personal data of individuals. So even though the book mainly deals with the specific question of how the essential facilities doctrine should be applied to data, a broader analysis of other related issues is required in order to give an adequate answer to the research question. This ensures that the findings have a wider relevance beyond the reach of the essential facilities doctrine and also allow for more general conclusions about how competition law can be adequately applied to new developments in digital markets.

1.3 STRUCTURE AND METHODOLOGY

The book consists of three self-standing parts which each have a different angle and approach. Part I outlines the economic characteristics of search engines, social networks and e-commerce platforms, including their multi-sided nature, with the aim of analysing how relevant markets can be defined and dominance can be assessed of providers of online platforms. A law and economics methodology is used to this end. Findings from economic literature about multi-sided businesses are integrated into the analysis of how existing competition tools can be applied to online platforms. In this regard, guidance is taken from previous decisions of the European Commission and judgments of the EU Courts as well as, to a more limited extent, from relevant cases in other jurisdictions. Attention is also paid to economic literature examining the

---

7. D.S. EVANS, 'Antitrust Issues Raised by the Emerging Global Internet Economy', *Northwestern University Law Review Colloquy* 2008, vol. 102, (285), p. 304; C.S. YOO, 'When Antitrust Met Facebook', *George Mason Law Review* 2012, vol. 19, no. 5, (1147), pp. 1154-1158; S.W. WALLER, 'Antitrust and Social Networking', *North Carolina Law Review* 2012, vol. 90, no. 5, (1771), pp. 1799-1800.

relationship between competition and innovation, and to business literature which distinguishes between different types of competition and innovation. Findings from the business literature form the basis for the normative analysis of the essential facilities doctrine in Part II.

Part II revolves around the application of the essential facilities doctrine to data. Next to refusals to deal, two other potential competition problems involving access to data and online platforms can be identified, namely restrictions on data portability and interoperability as imposed by providers of online platforms. Before engaging in an in-depth analysis of the essential facilities doctrine, attention is paid to these possible competition issues as well as to the question of whether user data as collected by providers of online platforms can be protected under data protection and intellectual property regimes. Even though the analysis mainly focuses on EU competition law, the development of the essential facilities doctrine under US antitrust law[8] is also discussed because the concept originated at that side of the Atlantic. In this regard, relevant EU and US decision-making practice, case law, policy documents and literature are studied. In addition, by building on the findings from the business literature analysed in Part I, the trade-off between different economic interests to be made in refusal to deal cases is discussed. While this trade-off remains a choice between two valid policy options (i.e., to intervene or not to intervene), a need for a more coherent application of the essential facilities doctrine that is in line with the underlying economics can be identified. To this end, insights are drawn from the economic trade-off which form the principles on which a proposed framework for the application of the essential facilities doctrine is built. Afterwards, it is analysed how the essential facilities doctrine can be applied to potential refusals of dominant firms to give access to data on online platforms. In that context, regard is also had to the role of data as a competitive advantage or entry barrier in digital markets and to market definition and dominance with respect to data.

Because the data to be shared by a dominant provider of an online platform may also include personal data, possible limitations that data protection legislation puts to the imposition of a duty to deal under competition law also have to be assessed. In addition, dominant firms may rely on their obligations under data protection law as an objective justification for refusing to supply data to competitors. Against this background, the role of data protection interests in competition enforcement is explored in Part III. In particular, it is analysed to what extent data protection may constitute a non-price parameter of competition. Furthermore, the more controversial issue of whether competition enforcement can be used to promote data protection interests is examined. To this end, the inherent limitations of competition enforcement as a body of law mainly concerned with economic efficiency are outlined, while also providing suggestions for better aligning the enforcement of the two regimes in the context of merger and abuse of dominance cases. A doctrinal legal research methodology is applied in Part III relying on an analysis of relevant EU legislation, policy documents, case law and literature in the field of data protection and competition law.

---

8. While the term 'antitrust' is mostly used in the US, it is more common to refer to 'competition' in the EU. In this book, both terms are used interchangeably.

Developments in the decision-making practice of the US Federal Trade Commission and in US legal doctrine are also covered where appropriate.

By relying on a variety of approaches, the book aims to contribute to ongoing academic and policy discussions about how data-related competition concerns should be addressed under competition law. At the same time, the analysis conducted in the three parts has a wider relevance for competition enforcement in digital markets that is outlined in the conclusion.

Part I
Competition and Innovation on Online Platforms

The evolution of the internet has led to the rise of different types of platforms that bring two or more groups of customers together. By focusing on online platforms, this book intends to concentrate on internet services that act as an intermediary or a platform between users and advertisers.[9] Web-based businesses such as search engines and social networks aim to build an audience for advertisers. In order to attract users, these platforms provide users a service like search functionality (Google) or social networking possibilities (Facebook). Access to the user traffic is sold to advertisers who generate the money for the platform. Although transaction or e-commerce platforms such as Amazon and eBay still mainly rely on income from fees they charge the sellers on their platforms, the provision of advertising services also starts to raise a considerable amount of revenue.[10] For the purposes of this book e-commerce platforms will therefore also be considered as online intermediaries.

The goal of the first part of the book is to study the economic characteristics of online platforms and to analyse how current competition tools for market definition and assessment of dominance may be applied to search engines, social networks and e-commerce platforms. In addition, economic and empirical literature on the link between competition and innovation is examined in order to consider the effect of changes in market structure resulting from competition law interventions on the level of innovation in a market. Attention is also paid to the role of innovation as a parameter for competition in dynamic industries such as the online intermediary sector.

---

9. Content providers and application developers can be considered as the third customer group on some online platforms.
10. In addition to the fees it charges sellers, Amazon receives income from its own sales as a retailer. Amazon's revenues from its ad business in 2013 were estimated to amount to $835 million, placing it ahead of Twitter that accounted for USD 583 million in advertising revenues. See R. Hof, 'Amazon's Ad Business Suddenly Looks Real', *Forbes*, 5 June 2013, available at http://www.forbes.com/sites/roberthof/2013/06/05/amazons-ad-business-suddenly-looks-real/.

CHAPTER 2

Business Models and Economic Characteristics of Online Platforms

2.1 INTRODUCTION

Online platforms have several characteristics which distinguish them from other businesses. In addition to operating solely on the internet, these platforms act as intermediaries between different customer groups and form part of the so-called network economy. In this chapter, the economic features of online intermediaries are discussed with a focus on search engines, social networks and e-commerce platforms.

In section 2.2, the business models of these platforms are analysed. This is followed by a description of their multi-sided nature in section 2.3 and a discussion on the extent to which network economy characteristics are present in each of the respective types of platforms in section 2.4.

2.2 DESCRIBING THE ONLINE INTERMEDIARY ENVIRONMENT

While search engine and social network providers mainly rely on advertising to fund their respective platforms to which they offer users access free of charge, advertising services constitute only an additional revenue source for e-commerce platforms.[11] The functionalities of these three types of online platforms are discussed below as well as the business models that the leading firms in these industries employ.

---

11. It was reported that Amazon made USD 187 million in ad revenues in the US in the first quarter of 2015, while its total US revenues amounted to USD 1 billion that quarter. See K. LIYAKASA, 'Amazon's Q1 Sheds (More) Light On Ad Revenues', *AdExchanger*, 23 April 2015, available at http://adexchanger.com/ad-exchange-news/amazons-q1-reveals-ads-business-may-bank-1-bil lion-a-year/.

2.2.1 Search Engines

The online search business has seen rapid growth after the emergence of the first search engine Archie, which was only used by academics, in 1990. Along with the development of the internet that became accessible to the general public in the mid-1990s, the search engine business flourished as the need for a good search engine rose that could help users to navigate through the wealth of information. Despite the emergence of several search engines in the mid-1990s such as AltaVista, Lycos and Yahoo, Google, which entered the market only in 1998, was able to take the leading position in the industry. Google's eventual success is said to be due to its PageRank algorithm which ranks search results according to their relative importance instead of on the basis of the number of times a search query is displayed on a certain web page. The latter was how existing search engines ranked search results at that time.[12]

The main classification used for search engines is based on the distinction between general or horizontal search engines like Google and specialised or vertical search engines which only cover a particular type of service or content such as shopping (Ciao), travel (TripAdvisor) and maps (Euro-Cities). Google provides a horizontal search engine but also operates many different vertical search engines including Google Shopping, Google Images, Google Scholar, Google Books, Google News, etc. By bringing order to publicly available web pages, Google aims to organise the world's information and make it universally accessible and useful.[13] The search results page that Google displays consists of a combination of web results from its horizontal search engine and listings from its vertical search engines. This service that merges search results composed of links to websites with the display of search results consisting of maps, pictures, news, etc. is referred to as 'universal search'.

The main search engines such as Google, Bing and Yahoo provide users access to their service free of charge and use contextual advertising to finance their business. They sell advertising space by letting companies bid on keywords that they deem relevant to their business. An auction determines the rank of the advertisements in the search results taking into account the maximum bid of the advertiser for the keyword and the relevance of its advertisement to the user's search query. Pay-per-click is the most commonly used advertising model and implies that the advertiser pays every time a user clicks on its advertisement and thus effectively visits its website. A search query leads to the display of two types of search results. The advertisements tailored to the search query are displayed as sponsored results at the top or right side of the page. For the non-sponsored or organic search results that are displayed under the sponsored ones, the search engines use 'robots', 'spiders' or 'crawlers' to explore the web in order to find and index relevant content.[14]

---

12. For a more elaborate overview of the development of the search engine industry, see A.D. VANBERG, 'From Archie to Google - Search Engine Providers and Emergent Challenges in Relation to EU Competition Law', *European Journal of Law and Technology*, vol. 3, no. 1, (1), pp. 2-4.
13. See https://www.google.com/intl/en/about/company/.
14. J. GRIMMELMANN, 'The Structure of Search Engine Law', *Iowa Law Review* 2007, vol. 93, no. 1, (1), pp. 7 and 11-12. For a description of the working of a web crawler, see also Case No COMP/M.6281 – *Microsoft/Skype*, 7 October 2011, footnote 10: '*A web crawler is a software*

Search engine providers rely on an algorithm to return relevant results to the search queries of users. In order to improve their search algorithm and the performance of the search functionality delivered to users, well-known search engines including Google, Yahoo and Bing collect information such as the date and time of the search and the location of the user (based on the Internet Protocol (IP) address) and store data about the search queries that users have looked for as well as the links that are subsequently clicked on. These query logs or search logs (hereafter: search data) are used by the search engines to improve the relevance of their search results in the future by looking at, for example in which language, from which geographical location, and at what time of the day a user enters a particular search query.[15] In addition to search data which cannot lead to the identification of a specific user and which enables a search engine to improve its search results on the basis of these general indicators, the prevailing search engines create profiles of each individual user by combining information about earlier search preferences and behaviour of the specific user on the platform. When a user is logged in on the search service, the provider is able to combine data about that user's search history and other information which is collected in the context of the use of additional services that the search engine might offer such as maps, video search and email.[16]

Although alternative search engines such as Ixquick (also referred to as Startpage)[17] and DuckDuckGo also rely (partly) on advertising to fund their business,[18] they do not track users and therefore call themselves 'privacy-friendly'.[19] The

---

application that downloads web pages. Typically web crawlers have the ability to determine the addresses of more web pages to download by extracting the links contained on already downloaded web pages. Web crawlers are used by search engines to build their indexes of web content. For this purpose the content of the downloaded pages is further analysed and indexed (for example, the language of the page and when it was last changed is determined). The resulting index is a database that is searched when the user enters a query into the search box. Web crawlers have to work continuously in order to keep the index "fresh", i.e. to ensure that the indexed content to the largest possible extent equals the actual content of the web pages'.

15. See, for example F. SILVESTRI, 'Mining Query Logs: Turning Search Usage Data into Knowledge', Foundation and Trends in Information Retrieval 2010, vol. 4, no. 1-2, (1).

16. N. ZINGALES, 'Regulating Search: Competition Policy and Data Protection at the Crossroad', Media Laws 10 September 2012, available at http://www.medialaws.eu/regulating-search-competition-policy-and-data-protection-at-the-crossroad/. Google, for example, states in its privacy policy that it 'may combine personal information from one service with information, including personal information, form other Google services'. See Google, 'Privacy Policy', 19 August 2015, available at http://www.google.com/intl/en-GB/policies/privacy/.

17. Ixquick is a so-called metasearch engine that sends user queries to several search engines and aggregates the results into a single list: 'When you search with Ixquick search engine, you are searching many popular search engines simultaneously and anonymously. Combined, these engines cover more of the Internet than any one search engine alone'. See Ixquick, 'Ixquick Protects Your Privacy!', available at https://www.ixquick.com/eng/what-makes-ixquick-special.html.

18. Ixquick relies solely on advertising for its income. See Ixquick, 'FAQ. Q: Is Ixquick free? How does Ixquick generate its income?', available at https://ixquick.com/eng/company-faq.html. DuckDuckGo funds its search engine by way of advertising as well as through the commission that it receives from Amazon and eBay when searchers visit their websites via DuckDuckGo and subsequently make a purchase. See DuckDuckGo, 'Advertising and affiliates', available at https://duck.co/help/company/advertising-and-affiliates.

19. Ixquick was awarded the European Privacy Seal for its search engine that can be accessed through ixquick.com or startpage.com in 2011. This seal certifies that IT products or services

privacy-friendly search engines either do not collect personal data from searchers at all or retain this data for only a few days.[20] While user traffic to privacy-friendly search engines is increasing,[21] the collection of user data seems vital for a search engine to keep attracting users and advertisers. Since users are not charged a monetary fee for access to the search service, quality and in particular the relevance of the search results is an important parameter of competition.[22] Personalisation of search results therefore improves the attributes of a search engine that users deem important and helps the search engine to keep attracting users. The availability of personal data of users also enables the search engine to better target advertisements which gives advertisers a better chance to reach interested buyers.[23] For this reason, the search engine will attract more advertisers if the ads are well-targeted to users. More effective targeting also enables the search engine provider to charge more for its advertising services. Furthermore, under the pay-per-click advertising model that is most commonly employed in search engines, the advertiser only pays when a user clicks on its advertisement. To gain revenue, the search engine thus has to ensure that the advertisements displayed in the search results are so relevant for the user that it clicks on them.[24] The accumulation of user information is vital in this perspective.

2.2.2 Social Networks

Social networks, understood in this book as services enabling users to create a public or semi-public profile and a list of friends or contacts,[25] started to emerge on the

---

facilitate their use in a way compliant with European regulations on privacy and data protection. See EuroPriSe, 'European Privacy Seal for Ixquick and Startpage', available at https://www.european-privacy-seal.eu/EPS-en/Ixquick-startpage.

20. Both DuckDuckGo and Ixquick do not collect or share personal information. See DuckDuckGo, 'Privacy', available at https://duckduckgo.com/privacy and Ixquick, 'Our Privacy Policy', available at https://ixquick.com/eng/privacy-policy.html.

21. See C. Farivar, 'Fueled by Snowden and Apple, Private Search Engine DuckDuckGo Rapidly Grows', *Ars Technica*, 25 June 2015, available at http://arstechnica.com/business/2015/06/fueled-by-snowden-and-apple-private-search-engine-duckduckgo-rapidly-growing/.

22. See Case No COMP/M.5727 - *Microsoft/Yahoo! Search Business*, 18 February 2010, par. 100 and Case No COMP/M.6281 - *Microsoft/Skype*, 7 October 2011, par. 81.

23. In addition, targeted advertising is beneficial for users who get to see ads that fit their interests. See UK Office of Fair Trading, 'Online Targeting of Advertising and Prices - A market study', May 2010, p. 5, available at http://webarchive.nationalarchives.gov.uk/20140402142426/http:/www.oft.gov.uk/shared_oft/business_leaflets/659703/OFT1231.pdf: '*Improving the targeting of advertising decreases suppliers' advertising costs and increases revenues for web-publishers. This increased efficiency feeds through to reduced costs for consumers for example by enabling free access to content. Consumers are also less likely to receive adverts that are not of interest to them*'.

24. See D. Geradin and M. Kuschewsky, 'Competition Law and Personal Data: Preliminary Thoughts on a Complex Issue', *SSRN Working Paper* February 2013, pp. 3-4, available at http://papers.ssrn.com/sol3/papers.cfm?abstract_id = 2216088.

25. These are the two essential functionalities of a social networking service according to the, in the European Commission's words, '*overwhelming majority of respondents to the market investigation*' conducted in the context of the review of Facebook's acquisition of WhatsApp. Other important features which, however, do not all have to be present for a service to be qualified as a social network include exchanging messages, sharing information, commenting on postings and recommending friends (Case No COMP/M.7217 – *Facebook/WhatsApp*, 3 October 2014,

internet in the late 1990s. SixDegrees.com was the first website that enabled users to create profiles, list their friends and browse through their list of contacts and those drawn up by others on the same platform. Before the launch of SixDegrees.com in 1997, each of these three features existed separately on other websites but they were never combined in one service. Although SixDegrees attracted a lot of users, it did not succeed in achieving a sustainable business and therefore had to shut down its website in 2000. Several new social networks came and went afterwards with Friendster and Myspace being the most successful ones. Facebook started to compete with Myspace in 2005 and has meanwhile established itself as the leader of the social network industry. Although it was designed to support Harvard students only, Facebook expanded its audience to include eventually everyone.[26]

Next to social networks that target the general public, specialised social networks exist that focus on a particular type of user such as LinkedIn which is a business network aimed at people in professional occupations and Research Gate which is dedicated to scientists and researchers. In addition, websites that initially focused on sharing of media content started to implement social network features and have become social networks themselves. In this context, a distinction has been made between 'user-oriented' and 'content-oriented' social networks separating social networks that focus on social relationships and communities from social networks in which the networks of users are not determined by their underlying social relationships but instead by their common interests. YouTube is an illustration of the latter.[27] Other social networks like Twitter centre around microblogging, a feature that Facebook, Google + and others have integrated into their service in the form of status updates.

Unlike other advertising-based platforms, social networks do not offer content themselves but provide the means for users to interact and create content in the form of profiles, messages, photos and videos. Similar to search engine providers, the prevailing online social network providers give users access to their service free of charge and rely on advertising to finance their business.[28] Facebook gets additional revenue from fees related to payments that take place on the social network. Facebook gives developers free access to the application programming interfaces (APIs) that

---

par. 51). A definition of social networks commonly used in literature is that of Boyd and Ellison: 'web-based services that allow individuals to (1) construct a public or semi-public profile within a bounded system, (2) articulate a list of other users with whom they share a connection, and (3) view and traverse their list of connections and those made by others within the system' (D.M. BOYD AND N.B. ELLISON, 'Social Network Sites: Definition, History, and Scholarship', *Journal of Computer-Mediated Communication* 2008, vol. 13, no. 1, (210), p. 211).

26. For a more elaborate overview of the development of the online social network industry, see D.M. BOYD AND N.B. ELLISON, 'Social Network Sites: Definition, History, and Scholarship', *Journal of Computer-Mediated Communication* 2008, vol. 13, no. 1, (210), pp. 214-219 and J. HEIDEMANN, M. KLIER AND F. PROBST, 'Online Social Networks: A Survey of a Global Phenomenon', *Computer Networks* 2012, vol. 56, no. 18, (3866), pp. 3869-3871.

27. See G. PALLIS, D. ZEINALIPOUR-YAZTI AND M.D. DIKAIAKOS, 'Online Social Networks: Status and Trends' in A. VAKALI AND L.C. JAIN (eds), *New Directions in Web Data Management 1. Studies in Computational Intelligence*, Berlin Heidelberg, Springer, 2011, (213), p. 220.

28. Alternative social networks that do not rely on advertising include Ello, MeWe and diaspora*. Ello and MeWe both rely on a freemium business model whereby users pay for additional services and features (see https://ello.co/wtf/about/ello-manifesto/ and https://mewe.com/faq). The free social network diaspora* relies on voluntary donations and has not been very

enable them to integrate applications in its platform,[29] but every time a user makes a purchase through the payment platform that Facebook provides it receives a fee from the application developer at issue.[30] These purchases mainly originate from games. Nevertheless, advertising still constitutes the key revenue source of Facebook. In the last quarter of 2015, 96% of Facebook's revenue was reported to originate from advertising.[31] Advertising also accounts for the largest part of Twitter's income. Twitter's other revenue source is the licensing of data.[32] Until August 2015, Twitter worked with a number of certified data resellers including DataSift and NTT Data which bought a licence from Twitter to access, search and analyse the full stream of tweets. Companies that needed Twitter data for example for providing social analytics services to clients thus had to contact one of these resellers. As of August 2015, Twitter established direct relationships with companies using Twitter data for commercial use.[33]

Social network providers are able to improve the quality of their service to users by increasing the relevance of social interactions and suggested contacts that are displayed to a particular user. An algorithm is used to select which pieces of information are most relevant for a specific user. For example, the stories that are displayed in a user's News Feed on Facebook are influenced by the connections and activity of that user on the platform. The stories from friends with whom a particular user interacts the most will appear highest in his or her News Feed.[34] Facebook's algorithm responds to signals of users including: how often a particular user interacts with a specific friend, page or public figure who posted a story; the number of likes, shares and comments a post receives in general and from the friends of the user at issue; how much the user has interacted with this type of post in the past; whether or not the user and others are hiding or reporting a given post.[35] By monitoring and

---

successful. In August 2012, its founders handed the project over to the users who have continued developing the social network on a voluntary basis while depending on donations (see https://joindiaspora.com/).

29. While Facebook is currently free for developers, Facebook notes in its Platform Policy for developers that it cannot guarantee that the platform will always be free. See Facebook, 'Platform Policy. 6. Things you should know', available at https://developers.facebook.com/policy.

30. 'Facebook will earn a 30% service fee, plus any applicable sales tax or VAT, in connection with each Facebook Payments transaction on our platform'. See Facebook, 'Payments Terms', 1 January 2015, available at https://developers.facebook.com/policy/payments_terms/.

31. In the fourth quarter of 2015, USD 5.63 billion of Facebook's total revenue of USD 5.841 billion came from advertising, thus amounting to 96% of its total revenue. See J. Constine, 'Facebook Climbs To 1.59 Billion Users And Crushes Q4 Estimates With $5.8B Revenue', *TechCrunch*, 27 January 2016, available at http://techcrunch.com/2016/01/27/facebook-earnings-q4-2015/.

32. In the fourth quarter of 2013, Twitter's revenue from data licensing accounted for 23 million dollar while the company raised 220 million dollar by way of selling advertisements. See S. Hargreaves, 'Twitter Forecasts Slowing Sales and User Growth', *CNN Money*, 6 February 2014, available at http://money.cnn.com/2014/02/05/technology/social/twitter-earnings/.

33. Z. Hofer-Shall, 'Working Directly with the Twitter Data Ecosystem', *Gnip Company Blog*, 10 April 2015, available at https://blog.gnip.com/twitter-data-ecosystem/.

34. Facebook, 'How News Feed Works', available at https://en-gb.facebook.com/help/327131014036297/.

35. Facebook for Business, 'News Feed FYI: A Window into News Feed', available at https://www.facebook.com/business/news/News-Feed-FYI-A-Window-Into-News-Feed.

collecting information about the behaviour of users on their platform, social network providers are thus able to improve the relevance of their social network features.

As a result of the content that users upload and the profile that they have constructed, social network providers can gather information about their users that is utilised to sell targeted advertising. Facebook enables advertisers to target users on the basis of location, demographics (including age, gender and education), interests (based on Facebook pages that a user 'liked' and hobbies and interests it mentioned in its profile), behaviours (such as purchase behaviour and device usage), connections (to reach users who are connected to the advertiser's page, event or application as well as their friends), custom audiences (to create audiences based on the advertiser's own customer data, including emails, phone numbers or user IDs) and lookalike audiences (to create audiences based on insights the advertiser gained from Facebook marketing to find more people who like its products and services).[36] Advertising on Twitter takes place in the form of so-called promoted tweets, promoted accounts and promoted trends. Promoted tweets are purchased by advertisers and appear in a user's timeline if the tweet is likely to be interesting and relevant to that user. The relevance of a promoted tweet for a particular user is assessed on the basis of several aspects such as what or who a user chooses to follow, how a user interacts with a tweet and what or who a user retweets.[37] When an advertiser promotes its Twitter-account, it is displayed to relevant users on the basis of the public list of whom they follow.[38] Third, promoted trends appear at the topic of the trending topics list on Twitter and are time-, context-, and event-sensitive trends promoted by advertisers. Users are able to click on a promoted trend to view all the related tweets including a promoted tweet from the advertiser at the top. Users are also able to tweet about the promoted trend by including the trending hashtag or the trend terms.[39]

The main distinction with advertising on search engines is that social network providers are able to sell advertisements containing social context. For example, Facebook enables the display of stories about social actions a user's friends have taken, such as 'liking' a page or checking in to a restaurant, as advertisements.[40] In Google+ itself no advertisements are shown. However, Google displays so-called shared endorsements as advertisements in its other services. If a user takes an action on Google+, including '+1'ing', commenting and following, his or her profile name and photo can be displayed across all Google services to other people that he or she has

---

36. Facebook for Business, 'Reach All the Right People', available at https://www.facebook.com/business/products/ads/ad-targeting/.
37. Twitter, 'What are Promoted Tweets?', available at http://support.twitter.com/articles/142101-what-are-promoted-tweets.
38. 'When an advertiser promotes an account, Twitter's algorithm looks at that account's followers and determines other accounts that those users tend to follow. If a user follows some of those accounts, but not the advertiser's account, then Twitter may recommend the advertiser's Promoted Account to that user'. See Twitter, 'Promoted Promotions', available at https://blog.twitter.com/2010/promoted-promotions.
39. Twitter, 'What are Promoted Trends?', available at https://support.twitter.com/articles/282142.
40. Facebook, 'An Update to Facebook Ads', 9 January 2014, available at https://www.facebook.com/notes/facebook-and-privacy/an-update-to-facebook-ads/643198592396693/.

chosen to share that content with, unless this function is manually turned off in the privacy settings.[41] In addition, Google enables AdWords advertisers to turn Google + posts into display ads that run across the web.[42]

Although search engines and social networks have different functionalities, both services are converging due to the cooperation between companies in both segments. Bing integrates data from several social networks, including Facebook, Twitter and Foursquare, a location-based social network site for mobile devices, in its search results. Next to the web search results, Bing displays a so-called social sidebar that contains posts or comments from friends and experts on these social networks that are relevant to the search query and that may help the user to find the best answer to his or her request.[43] In turn, Facebook introduced the search functionality 'Social Graph' in January 2013 that enables users to find content shared by their friends on Facebook. Google provides both a search engine and a social network. When a user is signed in to its Google Account, Google combines the information that users provided on its other services or that it collected about users on these other services including its social network Google + for displaying relevant search results.[44]

2.2.3 E-commerce Platforms

In the context of the rising popularity of the internet in the 1990s, companies started to look at the online environment as a new sales channel. The prevailing e-commerce platforms Amazon and eBay both started their business in the mid-1990s. Amazon established itself as an online retailer for books but rapidly expanded its product range. In addition to its own retailing activities, Amazon launched the Amazon Marketplace

---

41. 'For example, your friends might see that you rated an album 4 stars on the band's Google Play page. And the + 1 you gave your favorite local bakery could be included in an ad that the bakery runs through Google'. See Google, 'Terms of Service', 11 November 2013, available at http://www.google.com/intl/en/policies/terms/changes/.
42. Google Inside AdWords, ' + Post ads now available to all advertisers and support Hangouts on Air', 16 April 2014, available at http://adwords.blogspot.nl/2014/04/post-ads-now-available-to-all.html.
43. An example provided by Bing is: 'Imagine you're planning a trip to New York. When using Bing, you not only will find great search results about the city, but you'll also find information from your friends who live or have visited in the sidebar. Now you know which of your friends might have the inside scoop on what to do, or better yet might want to join you'. See Bing, 'Bing Social Updates Arrive Today: For Every Search, There is Someone Who Can Help', Bing Blogs, 17 January 2013, available at http://www.bing.com/blogs/site_blogs/b/search/archive/2013/01/17/bing-social-updates-arrive-today-for-every-search-there-is-someone-who-can-help.aspx.
From May 2013 onwards it is possible to react to the posts of friends on Facebook displayed in Bing's social sidebar directly without having to leave Bing. See Bing, 'Comment and Like Stuff on Facebook Directly from Bing', Bing Blogs, 10 May 2013, available at http://www.bing.com/blogs/site_blogs/b/search/archive/2013/05/10/comment-and-like-stuff-on-facebook-directly-from-bing.aspx.
44. 'Our search box now gives you great answers not just from the web, but your personal stuff too. So if I search for restaurants in Munich, I might see Google + posts or photos that people have shared with me, or that are in my albums'. See A. WHITTEN, 'Updating Our Privacy Policies and Terms of Service', Google Official Blog, 24 January 2012, available at http://googleblog.blogspot.be/2012/01/updating-our-privacy-policies-and-terms.html.

in November 2000.[45] On this platform Amazon acts as an intermediary enabling sellers to offer their goods at a fixed price to potential buyers. eBay similarly provides a platform for sellers and buyers to come together. eBay started as an online auction platform where buyers can enter bids in order to acquire a product and has been expanded to offer sellers the option to supply their goods at a fixed price.

Most e-commerce platforms such as Amazon and eBay provide buyers free access to their platform and charge sellers different types of fees for putting their goods for sale on their website. These fees include charges for monthly subscriptions and individual transactions.[46] Advertising services form an additional revenue source for both Amazon and eBay. In addition to the fees Amazon receives from sellers and advertisers, it generates revenue by acting as a retailer and selling products on its own behalf.

The recommendation or recommender system is central to the working of e-commerce platforms. Since transaction fees form part of the revenue of these platforms, it is vital that relevant purchase suggestions are made to users so that they engage in as many transactions as possible. The availability of information about the purchasing behaviour of users, their virtual shopping cart and the items they have viewed, liked or rated creates advantages for incumbent providers that have been able to improve their recommendation system with every interaction made in the past. The collection and analysis of data on the behaviour and preferences of users permits the platform to better predict in what products users are interested based on their similarity with other users. Think of, for example, the products that Amazon features under 'Customers Who Viewed This Item Also Viewed' or 'Customers Who Bought This Item Also Bought'. In order to return the most relevant purchase suggestions to users, recommendation systems typically use an algorithm based on so-called collaborative filtering. This is a method of making automatic predictions about the interests of users by collecting preferences from many users. In addition to matching users with similar interests and making recommendations on this basis, e-commerce platforms create profiles of returning users leading to personalised recommendations which are made in accordance with, among others, the individual purchase history of users and the items they have rated and liked in the past.[47]

Advertisements on Amazon are displayed to users in several places such as in the search results and on product pages. Advertisers can add keywords to their product ads which enables Amazon to show them to potentially interested customers conducting a search on its website. Advertisements are also displayed on existing product pages targeting users who are looking for the same or similar products that are already offered for sale on Amazon. On the basis of the product category and the description provided

---

45. Amazon Press Releases, 'Amazon Marketplace a Winner for Customers, Sellers and Industry; New Service Grows over 200 Percent in First Four Months', 19 March 2001, available at http://phx.corporate-ir.net/phoenix.zhtml?c = 176060&p = irol-newsArticle&ID = 502691&highlight = .
46. See eBay, 'Standard selling fees', available at http://pages.ebay.com/help/sell/fees.html and Amazon, 'Sell on Amazon', available at http://www.amazon.com/gp/seller-account/mm-product-page.html?topic = 200274770.
47. See also J.P. Mangalindan, 'Amazon's Recommendation Secret', *Fortune*, 30 July 2012, available at http://fortune.com/2012/07/30/amazons-recommendation-secret/.

by the advertiser Amazon determines where advertisements appear in accordance with what is most relevant to users.[48] eBay provides several targeting possibilities on the basis of demographic, geographic, contextual and behavioural factors.[49] Both Amazon and eBay also engage in personalised advertising based on personal information provided by users and previous purchases and products viewed on their platforms.[50]

2.3   MULTI-SIDED BUSINESSES

By creating interactions between users and advertisers, online platforms act as multi-sided businesses. Before describing the multi-sided nature of search engines, social networks and e-commerce platforms, attention will be paid to the developing economic theory on multi-sided platforms.

2.3.1   Multi-sidedness in General

While multi-sided businesses have existed for a much longer time, only around 2002 they were discovered as constituting a particular type of industry that deserves special attention from competition authorities and courts. Several scholars contributed to the development of the concept, but the term 'two-sided market' seems to have been introduced by Rochet and Tirole.[51] Armstrong uses the same term,[52] whereas Caillaud and Jullien[53] and Parker and Van Alstyne[54] refer to respectively 'indirect network effects' and 'two-sided network effects'. Evans speaks of 'multi-sided platforms' in order to distinguish the businesses that serve several customer groups from the markets in which they compete.[55]

---

48. Amazon, 'Amazon Product Ads. Frequently Asked Questions', available at http://services. amazon.com/product-ads-on-amazon/faq.htm?ld = NSGoogleAS.
49. eBay, 'Data that delivers', available at http://advertising.ebay.nl/home.
50. Amazon, 'Amazon Advertising Preferences', available at http://www.amazon.com/gp/dra/ info; eBay, 'Privacy Policy', 11 September 2013, available at http://pages.ebay.com/help/poli ciesfs-policy.html.
51. J.-C. ROCHET AND J. TIROLE, 'Cooperation among Competitors: Some Economics of PaymentCcard Associations', *RAND Journal of Economics* 2002, vol. 33, no. 4, (549); J.-C. ROCHET AND J. TIROLE, 'Platform Competition in Two-Sided Markets', *Journal of the European Economic Association* 2003, vol. 1, no. 4, (990); J.-C. ROCHET AND J. TIROLE, 'Two-Sided Markets: A Progress Report', *RAND Journal of Economics* 2006, vol. 37, no. 3, (645).
52. M. ARMSTRONG, 'Competition in Two-Sided Markets', *RAND Journal of Economics* 2006, vol. 37, no. 3, (668).
53. B. CAILLAUD AND B. JULLIEN, 'Competing Cybermediaries', *European Economic Review* 2001, vol. 45, no. 4-6, (797); B. CAILLAUD AND B. JULLIEN, 'Chicken & Egg: Competition among Intermediation Service Providers', *RAND Journal of Economics* 2003, vol. 34, no. 2, (309).
54. G.G. PARKER AND M.W. VAN ALSTYNE, 'Two-Sided Network Effects: A Theory of Information Product Design', *Management Science* 2005, vol. 51, no. 10, (1494).
55. D.S. EVANS AND R. SCHMALENSEE, 'The Industrial Organization of Markets with Two-Sided Platforms', *Competition Policy International* 2007, vol. 3, no. 1, (151), pp. 152-153; D.S. EVANS, 'Competition and Regulatory Policy for Multi-Sided Platforms with Applications to the Web Economy', *SSRN Working Paper* March 2008, available at http://papers.ssrn.com/sol3/papers. cfm?abstract_id = 1090368.

The concept of multi-sidedness relies on the theories of network externalities and multi-product pricing.[56] At the core of the network externalities literature lies the finding that end-users do not take into account or, in other words, do not internalise the impact of their purchase on others. However, the theory of network externalities in itself cannot sufficiently analyse behaviour of multi-sided businesses, since it does not take multi-sidedness into account. While the multi-product pricing literature describes the interdependency of pricing decisions, it does not allow for externalities in the consumption of different products. A buyer of a razor will usually also take into account the price of razorblades in his purchase decision and will thus internalise the impact of his purchase on the demand and surplus of other products. However, an end-user in a multi-sided market does not consider the effect of his purchase on the other side of the market. The theory of multi-sidedness therefore combines elements from both the theory of network externalities and multi-product pricing. From the economic literature on network externalities, it derives the notion that there are non-internalised externalities among end-users. From the multi-product pricing theory, it borrows the focus on price structure.[57]

In this book, the term 'multi-sided market' is not used because of its inherent assumption that multi-sided businesses cannot compete with one-sided businesses in a relevant market defined for competition law purposes, while there is no reason to exclude this possibility from the outset. To avoid a biased approach towards market definition in competition law, reference is only made to 'multi-sided businesses' or 'multi-sided platforms' here. In the economic literature, however, the concept of multi-sidedness has been developed and described as a form of market structure. Several definitions of 'multi-sided markets' have been put forward by scholars in this regard.[58]

According to Rochet and Tirole, '*a market with network externalities is a two-sided market if platforms can effectively cross-subsidize between different categories of end users that are parties to a transaction*'. They claim that most markets with network externalities are multi-sided markets.[59] Later on, Rochet and Tirole proposed a different definition: '*a market is two-sided if the platform can affect the volume of*

56. J.-C. ROCHET AND J. TIROLE, 'Platform Competition in Two-Sided Markets', *Journal of the European Economic Association* 2003, vol. 1, no. 4, (990), pp. 993-994 and J.-C. ROCHET AND J. TIROLE, 'Two-Sided Markets: A Progress Report', *RAND Journal of Economics* 2006, vol. 37, no. 3, (645), p. 646. On the link with the theory on network effects, see M. RYSMAN, 'The Economics of Two-Sided Markets', *Journal of Economic Perspectives* 2009, vol. 23, no. 3, (125), p. 127. On the link with the multi-product pricing literature, see G.G. PARKER AND M.W. VAN ALSTYNE, 'Two-Sided Network Effects: A Theory of Information Product Design', *Management Science* 2005, vol. 51, no. 10, (1494), pp. 1496-1497.
57. J.-C. ROCHET AND J. TIROLE, 'Platform Competition in Two-Sided Markets', *Journal of the European Economic Association* 2003, vol. 1, no. 4, (990), pp. 993-994 and J.-C. ROCHET AND J. TIROLE, 'Two-Sided Markets: A Progress Report', *RAND Journal of Economics* 2006, vol. 37, no. 3, (645), p. 646.
58. See J. LI, 'Is Online Media a Two-Sided Market?', *Computer Law and Security Review* 2015, vol. 31, no. 1, (99), pp. 101-102 who distinguishes between three schools of thought regarding the definition of multi-sided platforms.
59. J.-C. ROCHET AND J. TIROLE, 'Platform Competition in Two-Sided Markets', *Journal of the European Economic Association* 2003, vol. 1, no. 4, (990), pp. 1017-1018.

transactions by charging more to one side of the market and reducing the price paid by the other side by an equal amount; in other words, the price structure matters, and platforms must design it so as to bring both sides on board'.[60] Armstrong defines multi-sided markets as markets involving *'two groups of agents who interact via "platforms," where one group's benefit from joining a platform depends on the size of the other group that joins the platform'*.[61]

In the view of Evans, three conditions have to be met for a market to be multi-sided. First, there must be two or more distinct groups of customers. For example, shopping malls have to attract retailers and visitors. Second, externalities have to be associated with the two groups of customers becoming connected or coordinated in some way. Shoppers benefit when their favourite shop is located in a mall nearby, while a retailer benefits from being in a location that attracts interested shoppers. Third, an intermediary is required that internalises the externalities created by one group for the other group. The shopping mall brings customers and retailers together and enables both groups to generate value from their interaction that they would not, or at least not to that extent, have obtained without it.[62]

A phrase that is often used to characterise multi-sidedness is the need of a firm 'to get both sides on board'.[63] In the example of the shopping mall, enough retailers have to be present in the mall in order to attract shoppers and enough customers must visit the mall in order to encourage retailers to open a shop. This leads to the 'chicken-and-egg' problem.[64] Retailers will only join the mall when there is a prospect that a sufficient number of shoppers will visit the mall. Shoppers, in turn, will only be inclined to come to the mall when there are enough appealing shops. Thus, the mall has to find the right price structure to make sure that both groups will be present in good proportions, while at the same time making money.[65] In practice, most malls do not charge customers for a visit, while retailers have to pay to open a shop.[66]

---

60. J.-C. Rochet and J. Tirole, 'Two-Sided Markets: A Progress Report', *RAND Journal of Economics* 2006, vol. 37, no. 3, (645), pp. 664-665.
61. M. Armstrong, 'Competition in Two-Sided Markets', *RAND Journal of Economics* 2006, vol. 37, no. 3, (668), p. 668.
62. D.S. Evans, 'The Antitrust Economics of Multi-Sided Platform Markets', *Yale Journal on Regulation* 2003, vol. 20, no. 2, (325), pp. 331-333.
63. J.-C. Rochet and J. Tirole, 'Platform Competition in Two-Sided Markets', *Journal of the European Economic Association* 2003, vol. 1, no. 4, (990), p. 990; J.-C. Rochet and J. Tirole, 'Two-Sided Markets: A Progress Report', *RAND Journal of Economics* 2006, vol. 37, no. 3, (645), pp. 645-646; D.S. Evans, 'The Antitrust Economics of Multi-Sided Platform Markets', *Yale Journal on Regulation* 2003, vol. 20, no. 2, (325), p. 328; L. Filistrucchi, D. Geradin and E. Van Damme, 'Identifying Two-Sided Markets', *World Competition* 2013, vol. 36, no. 1, (33), p. 34.
64. See B. Caillaud and B. Jullien, 'Chicken & Egg: Competition among Intermediation Service Providers', *RAND Journal of Economics* 2003, vol. 34, no. 2, (309).
65. D.S. Evans, 'The Antitrust Economics of Multi-Sided Platform Markets', *Yale Journal on Regulation* 2003, vol. 20, no. 2, (325), p. 331.
66. For an analysis of externalities in shopping malls, see E.D. Gould, B.P. Pashigian and C.J. Prendergast, 'Contracts, Externalities, and Incentives in Shopping Malls', *Review of Economics and Statistics* 2005, vol. 87, no. 3, (411).

While Rochet & Tirole at first relied on the existence of indirect network effects to identify multi-sided platforms,[67] in later work they refer to the under inclusiveness of such a definition and propose to look at whether the price structure of the platform affects the economic outcome.[68] A reference can also be made here to Hagiu & Wright who argue that the critical feature of multi-sided platforms is their capacity to enable direct interactions between distinct types of affiliated customer groups. In their view, indirect network effects are neither necessary nor sufficient for a business to constitute a multi-sided platform.[69] However, most scholars agree that the essential feature of a multi-sided business is the existence of indirect network effects.[70]

In the economic literature on network effects that was initiated by respectively Katz and Shapiro[71] and Farrell and Saloner,[72] a distinction is made between direct and indirect network effects. Both network effects arise when the utility that a single consumer derives from consumption of a good increases with the number of other consumers purchasing the good. In case of a direct network effect, an increase in the number of purchasers directly raises the overall quality of the product. A commonly used example of a good having direct network effects is the telephone network. The utility that a consumer derives from purchasing a telephone is a function of the number of others that have already joined the telephone network. An indirect network effect exists when an increase in the number of consumers of a good leads to a higher demand for compatible products that make the good more valuable in an indirect way. An example of this is the hardware-software paradigm. Depending on the number of other purchasers of a hardware good, its value rises for a single consumer because the amount and variety of compatible software will increase with the quantity of hardware units that have been sold.[73]

---

67. J.-C. ROCHET AND J. TIROLE, 'Platform Competition in Two-Sided Markets', *Journal of the European Economic Association* 2003, vol. 1, no. 4, (990), pp. 1017-1018.
68. J.-C. ROCHET AND J. TIROLE, 'Two-Sided Markets: A Progress Report', *RAND Journal of Economics* 2006, vol. 37, no. 3, (645), p. 657.
69. A. HAGIU AND J. WRIGHT, 'Multi-Sided Platforms', *International Journal of Industrial Organization* November 2015, vol. 43, (162), pp. 163-164. In order for a direct interaction to be present, Hagiu & Wright argue that the distinct customer groups have to '*retain control over the key terms of the interaction, as opposed to the intermediary taking control of those terms*'. With regard to the requirement of the customer groups to be affiliated with the platform, users on each side have to '*consciously make platform-specific investments that are necessary in order for them to be able to directly interact with each other*' in the view of Hagiu & Wright.
70. See in particular D.S. EVANS, 'The Antitrust Economics of Multi-Sided Platform Markets', *Yale Journal on Regulation* 2003, vol. 20, no. 2, (325), pp. 331-333 and L. FILISTRUCCHI, D. GERADIN AND E. VAN DAMME, 'Identifying Two-Sided Markets', *World Competition* 2013, vol. 36, no. 1, (33), pp. 37-39.
71. M.L. KATZ AND C. SHAPIRO, 'Network Externalities, Competition, and Compatibility', *American Economic Review* 1985, vol. 75, no. 3, (424); M.L. KATZ AND C. SHAPIRO, 'Technology Adoption in the Presence of Network Externalities', *Journal of Political Economy* 1986, vol. 94, no. 4, (822).
72. J. FARRELL AND G. SALONER, 'Standardization, Compatibility, and Innovation', *RAND Journal of Economics* 1985, vol. 16, no. 1, (70); J. FARRELL AND G. SALONER, 'Installed Base and Compatibility: Innovation, Product Preannouncements, and Predation', *American Economic Review* 1986, vol. 76, no. 5, (940).
73. M.L. KATZ AND C. SHAPIRO, 'Network Externalities, Competition, and Compatibility', *American Economic Review* 1985, vol. 75, no. 3, (424), p. 424.

In the case of multi-sidedness, the 'indirectness' of the network effect does not relate to the complementarity of products but to the connection between the different sides of a platform. Parker and Van Alstyne referred to 'two-sided network effects' to clarify that the network effects must cross customer groups and differ from the 'ordinary' type of indirect network effects.[74] If users on one side of the platform buy a good that affects another side's choice of a different good, this special type of indirect network effect is present that may point to the multi-sidedness of a market. Put simply, the more users join one side of the platform, the more valuable the platform becomes for customers on the other side. As new users join Facebook, for example, more advertisers will be inclined to buy (additional) advertising space on Facebook, since they will reach a larger number of potential buyers. The term 'cross-side' network effect is also used to denote that the strength of one side of the platform has an impact on the growth of another side.[75]

To prevent that terms are mixed up, a clear distinction has to be made between the 'ordinary' type of indirect network effect that occurs in one-sided markets and the 'peculiar' type of network effect that is often also simply referred to as indirect network effect but which points to the multi-sidedness of a business.[76] Therefore, the term 'multi-sided network effect' is used in this book to refer to a network effect that crosses customer groups in multi-sided platforms.[77] When reference is made to 'indirect network effects', this only concerns the type of network effects that signify the complementarity of products in one-sided markets.

It is vital that the customer groups are not able to internalise the multi-sided network effects on their own. In that case, the platform would not be needed as an intermediary between the different sides.[78] Multi-sided network efforts that are not appropriated by the customer groups are referred to as externalities,[79] since they are

---

74. G.G. Parker and M.W. Van Alstyne, 'Two-Sided Network Effects: A Theory of Information Product Design', *Management Science* 2005, vol. 51, no. 10, (1494), p. 1496.

75. E.G. Weyl, 'A Price Theory of Multi-Sided Platforms', *American Economic Review* 2010, vol. 100, no. 4, (1642), p. 1644. Weyl uses the notion 'same-side network effect' to refer to direct network effects in one-sided markets which entail that the value of a particular side of a platform increases with the number of users on that side.

76. On this distinction in the context of Google's search engine, see also S. Van Loon, *The Power of Google: First Mover Advantage or Abuse of a Dominant Position?* in A. Lopez-Tarruella (ed.) *Information Technology and Law Series*, Google and the Law. Empirical Approaches to Legal Aspects of Knowledge-Economy Business Models, T.M.C. Asser Press, 2012, p. 27.

77. Devine uses this term in the same context. See K.L. Devine, 'Preserving Competition in Multi-Sided Innovative Markets: How Do You Solve a Problem Like Google?', *North Carolina Journal of Law & Technology* 2008, vol. 10, no. 1, (59), p. 82.

78. In the context of search engines, Manne & Wright argue that advertisers fully internalise the multi-sided network effects by paying the search engine provider a price every time a user clicks on their advertisement. See G.A. Manne and J.D. Wright, 'Google and the Limits of Antitrust: The Case Against the Case Against Google', *Harvard Journal of Law & Public Policy* 2010, vol. 34, no. 1, (171), p. 209. However, as explained below, the fact that advertisers pay the search engine provider instead of paying the users directly, proves that the presence of the search engine is necessary as an intermediary to internalise the network effects that the two groups cannot internalise on their own.

79. While the terms 'network effects' and 'network externalities' are used interchangeably in academic literature, formally the concept of network effects is different than that of network externalities: '*Network effects should not properly be called network externalities unless the*

external to or not accounted for in the individual decisions of the customers.[80] For example, shoppers do not take into account that by visiting a shopping mall they make it more attractive for retailers to open a shop there. Because of information and transaction costs, it is difficult for members of distinct customer groups to internalise the externalities themselves.[81] As long as the intermediary can coordinate the interaction more efficiently than the two customer groups are able to do themselves in a bilateral relationship, the platform is multi-sided. In theory, retailers could pay customers directly, instead of paying the shopping mall, to visit their stores but this does not happen in practice. The mall thus facilitates the interaction between the two groups.[82]

One way in which the customer groups can internalise the multi-sided network effects is by passing through the difference in cost of interacting to the other side.[83] Filistrucchi et al. mention the example of an already established couple that goes to a nightclub. If the man would be charged more than his girlfriend for entering the club, the couple could decide to split the total costs in equal amounts. In this situation, only the price level and not the price structure matters. Since the focus on price structure is a necessary element of a multi-sided platform, the business turns into a one-sided firm that sells complementary goods.[84] In more economic terms, if the so-called Coase theorem does not apply to the interaction between the two customer sides, the platform is multi-sided.[85] Under the Coase theorem, bargaining will lead to an efficient outcome irrespective of the initial allocation of property provided that transaction costs are

---

participants in the market fail to internalize these effects'. See S.J. LIEBOWITZ and S.E. MARGOLIS, 'Network Externalities (Effects)', *The New Palgraves Dictionary of Economics and the Law*, Palgrave Macmillan, 1998, available at http://wwwpub.utdallas.edu/~liebowit/palgrave/network.html.

80. L. FILISTRUCCHI, D. GERADIN AND E. VAN DAMME, 'Identifying Two-Sided Markets', *World Competition* 2013, vol. 36, no. 1, (33), p. 38.

81. D.S. EVANS, 'The Antitrust Economics of Multi-Sided Platform Markets', *Yale Journal on Regulation* 2003, vol. 20, no. 2, (325), pp. 332-333.

82. While it is common for retailers to attract customers to their shops by giving discounts, this does not enable both groups to internalise the externalities that are derived from their interaction in a shopping mall. A discount only becomes reality when a shopper buys a product. For appropriating the externalities, it would be required for the retailer to pay customers as soon as they enter the shop irrespective of whether they make a purchase. See also the example of dating clubs given by Evans where it is common that men are charged a higher price than women for a visit. With regard to the possibility of internalising the benefits of getting together, Evans argues: *'Men could in theory go around a singles bar and pay women to consider them as romantic prospects, but it tends not to happen'*. See D.S. EVANS, 'The Antitrust Economics of Multi-Sided Platform Markets', *Yale Journal on Regulation* 2003, vol. 20, no. 2, (325), p. 333.

83. J.-C. ROCHET AND J. TIROLE, 'Platform Competition in Two-Sided Markets', *Journal of the European Economic Association* 2003, vol. 1, no. 4, (990), p. 1018; J.-C. ROCHET AND J. TIROLE, 'Two-Sided Markets: A Progress Report', *RAND Journal of Economics* 2006, vol. 37, no. 3, (645), p. 649.

84. L. FILISTRUCCHI, D. GERADIN AND E. VAN DAMME, 'Identifying Two-Sided Markets', *World Competition* 2013, vol. 36, no. 1, (33), pp. 41-42 and footnote 44.

85. For an analysis of the condition that Coasian bargaining has to be unavailable in order for a business to be regarded as multi-sided, see D. AUER AND N. PETIT, 'Two-Sided Markets and the Challenge of Turning Economic Theory into Antitrust Policy', *The Antitrust Bulletin* 2015, vol. 60, no. 4, (426), pp. 431-439.

sufficiently low. However, according to Coase, transaction costs are in practice rarely low enough to enable parties to discuss and negotiate among themselves.[86]

Whether a particular intermediary constitutes a one-sided or a two-sided business often is a firm's choice rather than a fixed outcome derived from the structure of the market. Therefore, Rysman proposes to speak of 'two-sided strategies' instead of 'two-sided markets'.[87] Indeed, Armstrong shows that a supermarket can also be regarded as a two-sided platform. In his model, the supermarket fixes the price per consumer and pays the supplier based on how many consumers visit the supermarket.[88] This contradicts the usual characterisation of a supermarket as a one-sided reseller in which a supplier sells its products to the supermarket which takes possession of the products and resells them to consumers, without the supplier being dependent on the actual behaviour of consumers.

Hagiu argues that the one-sided merchant or reseller and the two-sided platform or marketplace should be seen as the two extreme cases. Several businesses exist that have features of both. In Hagiu's view, *'there is a continuum of forms of intermediation'*.[89] Although the iTunes store, for example, exhibits multi-sided network effects by bringing publishers and consumers together, the extent of Apple's control over the pricing and distribution of songs and videos makes the platform more similar to a reseller which takes possession of the songs and videos it distributes.[90] Therefore, multi-sidedness seems to be a matter of degree.[91] Furthermore, the multi-sided nature of a business may not always be decisive for the analysis. According to Rysman, *'the interesting question is often not whether a market can be defined as two-sided - virtually all markets might be two-sided to some extent - but how important two-sided issues are in determining outcomes of interest'*.[92] In the view of Evans, the strength of the multi-sided network effects will determine whether the multi-sidedness *'matters enough to have a substantive effect on the results of economic analysis'*.[93] Filistrucchi et al. conclude that, although there is still controversy about the exact definition of

---

86. R.H. COASE, 'The Problem of Social Cost', *The Journal of Law & Economics* October 1960, vol. 3, (1). The work of Coase was formalised by Stigler as the 'Coase theorem' in 1966. See G.J. STIGLER, *The Theory of Price*, New York, Macmillan 1966.

87. M. RYSMAN, 'The Economics of Two-Sided Markets', *Journal of Economic Perspectives* 2009, vol. 23, no. 3, (125), p. 126.

88. M. ARMSTRONG, 'Competition in Two-Sided Markets', *RAND Journal of Economics* 2006, vol. 37, no. 3, (668), pp. 684-686.

89. A. HAGIU, 'Merchant or Two-Sided Platform?', *Review of Network Economics* 2007, vol. 6, no. 2, (115), p. 118.

90. A. HAGIU, 'Merchant or Two-Sided Platform?', *Review of Network Economics* 2007, vol. 6, no. 2, (115), pp. 116 and 128-129. See also the more recent work in A. HAGIU AND J. WRIGHT, 'Marketplace or Reseller?', *Management Science* January 2015, vol. 61, no. 1, (184) in which the decision of intermediaries to function as a market place or as a reseller is modelled.

91. D.S. EVANS AND R. SCHMALENSEE, 'The Industrial Organization of Markets with Two-Sided Platforms', *Competition Policy International* 2007, vol. 3, no. 1, (151), p. 173.

92. M. RYSMAN, 'The Economics of Two-Sided Markets', *Journal of Economic Perspectives* 2009, vol. 23, no. 3, (125), p. 127.

93. D.S. EVANS, 'Competition and Regulatory Policy for Multi-Sided Platforms with Applications to the Web Economy', *SSRN Working Paper* March 2008, p. 5-6, available at http://papers.ssrn.com/sol3/papers.cfm?abstract_id = 1090368.

multi-sided platforms, the different definitions proposed are consistent enough to allow the identification of those markets where multi-sidedness might matter.[94]

2.3.2 Establishing a Multi-sided Business

Because of the multi-sided network effects, multi-sided businesses have to attract several customer groups at the same time. To ensure that all sides of the platform will be present, the provider has to make commitments to customers on side A that customers on side B will be there once they join the platform and vice versa.[95] For some multi-sided businesses such as payment card systems, yellow pages and transaction platforms, these commitments must take place almost simultaneously. For example, consumers will only acquire a payment card when they know they can use it at stores and vice versa, merchants will only participate in new payment systems when they know that enough customers will make use of it. In other multi-sided platforms, the commitments take place sequentially.[96] Operating system providers usually start attracting developers for writing applications well before the system is launched to users. This is to prevent that users will not be interested in purchasing a licence once the operating system is launched, due to the lack of sufficient applications that run on the operating system.[97]

Next to making reliable commitments, the chicken-and-egg problem can be solved by setting a price structure. By determining the price for a particular side of the platform, the business should take into account to what extent the presence of that side attracts customers on the other side. For example, in advertising-based online platforms, advertisers usually benefit more from the presence of users than users value the advertiser side. In order to convince users to join the platform, the business could decide to let users join the platform for free or even pay them to join.[98] This is especially likely in the introductory period of a platform to attract users and make the platform valuable for the other side.[99] The business will then cross-subsidise the loss on the user

---

94. L. Filistrucchi, D. Geradin and E. Van Damme, 'Identifying Two-Sided Markets', *World Competition* 2013, vol. 36, no. 1, (33), p. 43.
95. D.S. Evans, 'Competition and Regulatory Policy for Multi-Sided Platforms with Applications to the Web Economy', *SSRN Working Paper* March 2008, p. 6, available at http://papers.ssrn. com/sol3/papers.cfm?abstract_id = 1090368.
96. D.S. Evans, 'Two-Sided Markets', in *Market Definition in Antitrust. Theory and Case Studies*, ABA Section of Antitrust Law 2012, Chapter XII, p. 6, available at http://papers.ssrn.com/ sol3/papers.cfm?abstract_id = 1396751&download = yes.
97. See A. Hagiu, 'Pricing and Commitment by Two-Sided Platforms', *RAND Journal of Economics* 2006, vol. 37, no. 3, (720).
98. An example of a situation (outside the scope of online platforms) in which a customer group is paid to interact with the other side is the discounts and rewards that credit card providers offer to cardholders when they use their credit card to pay merchants. See M. Rysman, 'The Economics of Two-Sided Markets', *Journal of Economic Perspectives* 2009, vol. 23, no. 3, (125), p. 129.
99. D.S. Evans, 'The Antitrust Economics of Multi-Sided Platform Markets', *Yale Journal on Regulation* 2003, vol. 20, no. 2, (325), p. 352.

side by charging advertisers more than the marginal costs of the advertiser side.[100] Unlike pricing in one-sided markets, the optimal price on a particular side of a multi-sided platform does not follow marginal cost on that side.[101] In accordance with the Ramsey pricing rule,[102] the best strategy is to charge a higher price to the customer group which has more inelastic demand and is thus less sensitive to price than the customers on the other side of the platform. Since users are more responsive to price and their participation attracts a large number of advertisers on the other side who are relatively price inelastic, the user side will be subsidised.[103] The use of skewed pricing by multi-sided platforms also reflects the fact that one customer group is easier to get on board than the other.

In addition, the price structure of a platform is influenced by the presence of 'marquee' and 'captive' customers. Marquee customers make the multi-sided business more valuable to customers on the other side of the platform. As a result, the platform can raise the price for participation to customers on the other side. At the same time, the price to the marquee customer side will be lowered. For example, the American Express business clientele was appreciated so much by merchants that American Express was able to charge a relatively high price to merchants in comparison to other payment card providers.[104] Captive customers are extremely loyal to the platform irrespective of the price that is charged, for example because of long-term contracts. This allows the platform to increase its price to these captive customers and reduce the price to the other side.[105]

Platforms may also attract customers by investing in one side of the market in order to lower the costs of participation for customers on that side. For example, by offering developer support, operating system providers can make it easier and less costly for developers to write applications for their operating system. This may discourage developers from writing applications for competing operating systems.[106]

---

100. Caillaud and Jullien refer to the 'divide-and-conquer' nature of pricing strategies which consists of: '*subsidizing the participation of one side (divide) and recovering the loss on the other side (conquer)*'. See B. CAILLAUD AND B. JULLIEN, 'Chicken & Egg: Competition among Intermediation Service Providers', *RAND Journal of Economics* 2003, vol. 34, no. 2, (309), p. 310.

101. D.S. EVANS, 'The Antitrust Economics of Multi-Sided Platform Markets', *Yale Journal on Regulation* 2003, vol. 20, no. 2, (325), p. 328.

102. Ramsey pricing has been described for the first time in the context of taxation by F.P. RAMSEY, 'A Contribution to the Theory of Taxation', *Economic Journal* 1927, vol. 37, no. 145, (47).

103. M. RYSMAN, 'The Economics of Two-Sided Markets', *Journal of Economic Perspectives* 2009, vol. 23, no. 3, (125), p. 130. See also the overview of several multi-sided business models in J.-C. ROCHET AND J. TIROLE, 'Platform Competition in Two-Sided Markets', *Journal of the European Economic Association* 2003, vol. 1, no. 4, (990), p. 992.

104. D.S. EVANS, 'The Antitrust Economics of Multi-Sided Platform Markets', *Yale Journal on Regulation* 2003, vol. 20, no. 2, (325), p. 353.

105. J.-C. ROCHET AND J. TIROLE, 'Platform Competition in Two-Sided Markets', *Journal of the European Economic Association* 2003, vol. 1, no. 4, (990), pp. 1007-1008.

106. D.S. EVANS, 'Antitrust Issues Raised by the Emerging Global Internet Economy', *Northwestern University Law Review Colloquy* 2008, vol. 102, (285), p. 354; J.-C. ROCHET AND J. TIROLE, 'Platform Competition in Two-Sided Markets', *Journal of the European Economic Association* 2003, vol. 1, no. 4, (990), p. 1017.

According to Rysman, potential platforms may also overcome the chicken-and-egg problem by starting as a one-sided firm and switching to a multi-sided business model as they become more established. An example is Amazon that started as a one-sided merchant for the sale of books and now also provides a platform where sellers and buyers meet.[107] In the early days, Google acted as a one-sided firm too providing search services to users and trying to gain revenue from licensing its search engine to other firms. Two years after Google was launched, it started to sell advertising slots and turned into a multi-sided platform.[108]

To be successful, the platform has to achieve a critical mass of both customer groups. The platform has to attract enough customers at all sides to ensure that it creates sufficient value for everyone. Furthermore, it is vital that the sides of the platform grow in a stable and balanced way. For example, online platforms that attract users by giving them access to content, either created by other users (e.g., online social networks) or by the platform provider itself (e.g., newspaper websites) have to make sure that there is a good balance between content and advertising. If the amount of advertising would overtake the availability of content, users could be driven away from the platform. By getting as much customers as possible on board, the platform can also prevent rival businesses from establishing themselves. A platform that has more customers on both sides on board is more valuable than its competitors and will therefore likely attract even more customers.[109]

2.3.3 Multi-sided Nature of Online Platforms

Although the advertising-based media industry is generally accepted to be multi-sided,[110] it can be seen as a peculiar form of a multi-sided business. Unlike multi-sided platforms such as shopping malls and payment card systems where both customer groups value the other side, advertising may not always positively affect the demand of

---

107. M. RYSMAN, 'The Economics of Two-Sided Markets', *Journal of Economic Perspectives* 2009, vol. 23, no. 3, (125), p. 132.

108. In a paper, Google's founders have even noted that '[t]he goals of the advertising business model do not always correspond to providing quality search to users' and that 'advertising funded search engines will be inherently biased towards the advertisers and away from the needs of the consumers'. See S. BRIN & L. PAGE, 'The Anatomy of a Large-Scale Hypertextual Web Search Engine', 8 Appendix A, available at http://infolab.stanford.edu/pub/papers/google.pdf. See also K.L. DEVINE, 'Preserving Competition in Multi-Sided Innovative Markets: How Do You Solve a Problem Like Google?', North Carolina Journal of Law & Technology 2008, vol. 10, no. 1, (59), pp. 72-73.

109. D.S. EVANS, 'Competition and Regulatory Policy for Multi-Sided Platforms with Applications to the Web Economy', *SSRN Working Paper* March 2008, pp. 9-10, available at http://papers.ssrn.com/sol3/papers.cfm?abstract_id = 1090368.

110. See L. FILISTRUCCHI, D. GERADIN AND E. VAN DAMME, 'Identifying Two-Sided Markets', *World Competition* 2013, vol. 36, no. 1, (33), p. 36; M. RYSMAN, 'The Economics of Two-Sided Markets', *Journal of Economic Perspectives* 2009, vol. 23, no. 3, (125), p. 125; D.S. EVANS, 'The Antitrust Economics of Multi-Sided Platform Markets', *Yale Journal on Regulation* 2003, vol. 20, no. 2, (325), p. 335.

'consumers' of media content.[111] Empirical research shows that, although advertisers value a television channel more if it has more viewers, viewers tend to be averse to advertising.[112] If advertising drives customers on the other side of the market away, a negative multi-sided network effect is present. Since research has shown that the value of a TV channel diminishes for viewers as advertising increases, the TV market can be characterised as having one negative multi-sided network effect. In order to establish a multi-sided platform, at least one customer group must be found that is interested in interacting with the other side. This implies that at a minimum one positive multi-sided network effect has to be present.[113] Because advertisers value a platform more when the number of users that it attracts increases, the advertising-based media industry, including the TV market, is commonly acknowledged to be multi-sided.[114]

Although it is not entirely clear what the attitude of users towards advertisements on online platforms is, these businesses are widely regarded as multi-sided plat-forms.[115] As advertisers positively value the user side, online intermediaries qualify as multi-sided platforms under the principle that only one positive multi-sided network effect has to be present for rendering a business multi-sided.[116] In certain

---

111. Yellow pages are an exception to this, since readers are likely to value the advertisements as they form part of the content. See D.S. EVANS, 'The Antitrust Economics of Multi-Sided Platform Markets', *Yale Journal on Regulation* 2003, vol. 20, no. 2, (325), p. 335.
112. K.C. WILBUR, 'A Two-Sided, Empirical Model of Television Advertising and Viewing Markets', *Marketing Science* 2008, vol. 27, no. 3, (356).
113. L. FILISTRUCCHI, D. GERADIN AND E. VAN DAMME, 'Identifying Two-Sided Markets', *World Competition* 2013, vol. 36, no. 1, (33), pp. 37-38.
114. However, G. LUCHETTA, 'Is the Google Platform a Two-Sided Market?', *Journal of Competition Law and Economics* 2014, vol. 10, no. 1, (185) and J. LI, 'Is Online Media a Two-Sided Market?', *Computer Law and Security Review* 2015, vol. 31, no. 1, (99) challenge the mainstream approach by arguing that advertising-supported media should not be regarded as multi-sided because no transaction occurs between advertisers and consumers of media products, and because the indirect network effects between these customer groups are not necessarily reciprocal. Luchetta's and Li's definition of multi-sided platforms seems to be too limited, since it only includes platforms that are necessarily two-sided because of their structure. Further-more, the value that advertisers attach to interaction with consumers of media are not taken into account under their approach.
115. See, for example, D.S. EVANS, 'Competition and Regulatory Policy for Multi-Sided Platforms with Applications to the Web Economy', *SSRN Working Paper* March 2008, pp. 26-31, available at http://papers.ssrn.com/sol3/papers.cfm?abstract_id = 1090368; M. RYSMAN, 'The Econom-ics of Two-Sided Markets', *Journal of Economic Perspectives* 2009, vol. 23, no. 3, (125), p. 125; L. FILISTRUCCHI, D. GERADIN AND E. VAN DAMME, 'Identifying Two-Sided Markets', *World Competition* 2013, vol. 36, no. 1, (33), p. 36; F. THÉPOT, 'Market Power in Online Search and Social Networking: A Matter of Two-Sided Markets', *World Competition* 2013, vol. 36, no. 2, (195), pp. 198-199. However, Luchetta argues that search engines like Google should not be framed as a two-sided platform but as retailers of personal information that buy users' personal data in the upstream market in exchange for search services and sell the information to advertisers in the downstream market. See G. LUCHETTA, 'Is the Google Platform a Two-Sided Market?', *Journal of Competition Law and Economics* 2014, vol. 10, no. 1, (185).
116. Manne & Wright specify that the strength of this network effect should be determined on the basis of the quality and not the quantity of users. In their view, advertisers on search engines may not value an increase in users that only look for information and do not buy the products or services they advertise. For this reason, advertisers would only care about the other side of the platform to the extent that its size corresponds with increased sales. See G.A. MANNE AND J.D. WRIGHT, 'Google and the Limits of Antitrust: The Case Against the Case Against Google', *Harvard Journal of Law & Public Policy* 2010, vol. 34, no. 1, (171), pp. 208-209. However, as

circumstances, the advertiser side may exert a positive multi-sided network externality on users. Users that are looking for a purchase through a search engine will positively value the display of advertisements in their search results. However, it is not clear whether searchers that are not interested in making a purchase enjoy positive or negative externalities from advertising or whether they are indifferent. Next to transactional queries that look for websites to perform a purchase, informational queries that are meant to obtain data or information and navigational queries that look for a specific URL on the internet can be distinguished.[117] As it is estimated that only 10% of all search queries aim at making a purchase, it remains uncertain how the majority of searchers that look for information or specific URLs value advertising.[118]

On e-commerce platforms buyers and sellers exert positive network externalities on each other. Both groups attach value to each other's presence, since the likelihood of a transaction increases as the number of members on the other side of the platform grows. With regard to the advertising services provided by e-commerce platforms, the interaction between buyers and advertisers is relevant. Since sellers are not interested in making a purchase but rather want to vend their own products and services, they do not fall within the audience of advertisers and may even be seen as competitors. However, users on e-commerce platforms often change sides: a customer may be a seller in one transaction and a buyer in another.[119] When reference is made here to 'users' of e-commerce platforms in relation to advertisers, customers qualifying as buyers in a certain transaction are targeted. With regard to the link between users and advertisers on e-commerce platforms the same applies as explained above in the context of advertising on search engines. While it is clear that advertisers benefit from the presence of users, the multi-sided network effects may not be reciprocal and even be negative. Nevertheless, since the majority of users on e-commerce platforms are looking for a purchase, users will more likely positively value the display of advertisements that highlight products similar to the one they are seeking. The multi-sided network effect that the advertiser side exerts on users could thus be positive.

For online social networks, advertising that includes social context might be positively valued by users. Sponsored stories on Facebook are an example of such a type of advertising. Sponsored stories were provided by Facebook until April 2014[120] and offered businesses the possibility to display their brand or product as a message coming from users. When a user engaged with a page, app or event that a business had

stated by D.S. Evans, 'The Online Advertising Industry: Economics, Evolution, and Privacy', *Journal of Economic Perspectives* 2009, vol. 23, no. 3, (37), p. 51: '*Unless behavioral targeting is sufficiently precise, advertisers may prefer to reach a larger group of individuals*'.

117. A. Broder, 'A Taxonomy of Web Search', *Special Interest Group on Information Retrieval (SIGIR) Forum* 2002, vol. 36, no. 2, (3).

118. A study has estimated that 80% of the queries are informational, while navigational and transactional search queries both account for 10% of total search queries. See B.J. Jansen, D.L. Booth and A. Spink, 'Determining the Informational, Navigational, and Transactional Intent of Web Queries', *Information Processing and Management* 2008, vol. 44, (1251).

119. D.S. Evans, 'The Antitrust Economics of Multi-Sided Platform Markets', *Yale Journal on Regulation* 2003, vol. 20, no. 2, (325), pp. 331-332.

120. Facebook discontinued sponsored stories as from 9 April 2014. See Facebook, 'An Update to Facebook Ads', 9 January 2014, available at https://www.facebook.com/notes/facebook-and -privacy/an-update-to-facebook-ads/643198592396693/.

paid to highlight, a message or story was displayed on the user's page to all of his or her contacts containing the action of the user in relation to the business, as well as the logo and the link to the business page.[121] One could argue that users value this type of advertising positively because it forms part of the user content and provides details of the interests and activities of contacts.[122] However, users often like a page because they will get a discount or another type of advantage as a result of which the interaction with a certain business does not necessarily say something about the interests of users. Furthermore, sponsored stories were one of the most controversial types of advertising on Facebook that even led to the filing of a class action lawsuit in the United States regarding privacy violations which Facebook settled in August 2013.[123]

While users on search engines and social networks may not be interested in the advertisements that are displayed, one can argue that advertisers still exert a positive multi-sided network externality on users by way of financing the platform. Prevailing search engines such as Google and social network sites like Facebook rely to a large extent on advertising revenues.[124] Advertising allows these providers to continue to offer their platform to users without having to charge them a monetary fee and to invest in the development of the platform. The more advertisers join the platform, the more funding is available to keep the platform free and attractive for users. Although advertisers thus do seem to impose a positive network externality on users,[125] this externality is smaller than the network effect that the user side exerts on advertisers. The difference in the size of the two multi-sided network effects explains why online platforms are usually offered to users free of charge while advertisers have to pay to interact with users.

Whereas users and advertisers are the two predominant customer groups on search engines and social networks, in both platforms a third group of customers can be identified. Website owners or content providers form the third side in search engine platforms. The search engine connects users with website owners on the basis of their search query. Unlike advertisers, website owners do not pay the search engine for

---

121. For example, when a user 'likes' a certain page on Facebook a message is displayed ('John likes Starbucks') containing the logo of the business and the link to the relevant page on the user's Facebook profile. See Facebook, 'Sponsored Stories for Marketplace', 20 October 2011, available at http://www.facebook.com/ads/stories/SponsoredStoriesGuide_Oct2011.pdf.

122. F. Thépot, 'Market Power in Online Search and Social Networking: A Matter of Two-Sided Markets', *World Competition* 2013, vol. 36, no. 2, (195), p. 204.

123. *Angel Fraley et al. v. Facebook, Inc.*, No. 11-CV-01726 RS (N.D. Cal. August 26, 2013), available at http://blogs.reuters.com/alison-frankel/files/2013/08/facebookfraley-approval.pdf.

124. This is not the case for e-commerce platforms that mainly rely on revenue from subscription and transaction fees paid by sellers.

125. K.L. Devine, 'Preserving Competition in Multi-Sided Innovative Markets: How Do You Solve a Problem Like Google?', *North Carolina Journal of Law & Technology* 2008, vol. 10, no. 1, (59), pp. 82-83. This statement is subject to the caveat that an increasing amount of advertising on the platform may drive users away at a certain point. In that situation, a negative indirect network effect is present. However, the fact that advertisements are present on the platform indicates that the positive indirect network effect exerted by users on advertisers outweighs the negative indirect network effect from advertisers to users. Otherwise, it would not make sense for the platform to include the advertiser side.

being included in the search results.[126] Their websites are displayed in the non-sponsored or organic search results in the order of relevance as determined by the search algorithm. Instead of qualifying a search engine as a three-sided platform bringing users, advertisers and website owners together, one could also argue that a search engine consists of two two-sided platforms bundled into one: one platform that brings website owners and users together and another platform that connects advertisers with users. In social networks, applications providers constitute the third group of customers on the platform. Application developers on Facebook have free access to the platform for integrating their services such as games.[127] Social networks could also be framed as comprising two interconnected two-sided platforms: one platform that matches application developers with users and vice versa, and another platform that lets advertisers interact with users. The advertiser side forms the only revenue source in the currently predominant search engine and social networking platforms.

The question can be raised whether and to what extent revenue streams other than advertising are available to fund search engine and social networking platforms. While social network providers could start charging developers for integrating applications into their platform, it is questionable whether they will be able to extract enough revenues from developers to maintain the same level of quality and investment in new features.[128] A decrease in revenue may lead to a lower quality of the platform and require the social network provider to charge users. In theory, search engine providers could start charging website owners for being included in the organic search results. However, this would restrict the number of web pages that the search engine can display to match the user's search query and lead to a decrease in relevance of search results. Since the quality of the search results is vital for keeping users on the platform, it is unlikely that search engine providers will start to require website owners to pay for having their website indexed. Instead, the search engine provider will probably start charging searchers a monetary fee for using the search engine. Even though other revenue streams are potentially available, the reliance on an advertising-based business model enables the currently predominant platform providers to offer their services to users for free while maintaining the quality of the platform and ensuring investment in new functionalities. The third customer groups in search engines and social networks are not considered here further, as their role on the

---

126. Some website owners may pay companies like Google and Microsoft for selling advertising space on their websites to advertisers. However, in this context Google and Microsoft do not act in their capacity as search engine providers, but as advertising intermediaries that connect website owners wishing to make money by selling advertising space on their websites with advertisers interested in displaying their campaigns on third party websites to potential buyers. Both companies have set up separate services for this, AdSense and pubCenter respectively.

127. While Facebook is currently free for developers, Facebook notes in its Platform Policy for developers that it cannot guarantee that the platform will always be free. See Facebook, 'Platform Policy. 6. Things you should know', available at https://developers.facebook.com/policy.

128. Social networks that do not rely on advertising include Ello, MeWe and diaspora*. However, so far they have been not been able to compete effectively with the prevailing social networks such as Facebook and Google + which could be partly due to the inviability of their respective business models. While diaspora* relies on voluntary donations, Ello and MeWe employ a freemium business model whereby users pay for additional services.

respective platforms as website owners and application developers is subordinate to the interaction between users and advertisers.

Bork & Sidak state that the indirect network effect that advertisers would exert on users does not raise barriers to entry, because advertising revenues are not the only source of funding for investing in product improvements.[129] In addition, Manne & Wright argue that the argument does not turn on network effects but merely points to supply-side economies of scale and only concerns the question of how to finance a platform. They explain that providers of online platforms can also choose to use other revenue sources to fund the platform. For example, Microsoft could rely on its revenues from the sale of operating systems to improve its search engine Bing.[130] However, although providers indeed may rely on revenue sources that do not come from the platform itself, the viability of such a business model can be questioned. The fact that the provision and development of the platform is dependent on income from external origins makes its continuous operation vulnerable. As discussed above, in the absence of advertising revenues, the provider will likely start to charge users a monetary fee. Furthermore, the decision of the provider to rely on advertising reinforces the multi-sided nature of a platform, because two-sidedness often is a choice of a firm rather than a fixed structure of a market.[131]

2.4 NETWORK ECONOMY CHARACTERISTICS OF ONLINE PLATFORMS

Online platforms form part of the so-called network economy which consists of firms that rely on interconnection for the transmission of their goods or services. Whereas old network industries such as electricity, gas and railways depend on physical infrastructures and tangible assets, new network industries including online intermediaries such as search engines, social networks and e-commerce platforms are characterised by the predominance of virtual networks and technology. Unlike old economy businesses, new economy industries are subject to rapid technological change and innovation. Since both types of industries form part of the network economy, they possess similar features such as economies of scale, network effects and switching costs.

2.4.1 Economies of Scale

Firms active in the network economy have to make substantial investments in order to enter the market. Once the initial investment is made, the incremental costs of creating additional units decreases and may even be negligible. As a result, supply-side

---

129. R.H. BORK AND J.G. SIDAK, 'What Does the Chicago School Teach About Internet Search and the Antitrust Treatment of Google?', *Journal of Competition Law and Economics* 2012, vol. 8, no. 4, (663), p. 692.
130. G.A. MANNE AND J.D. WRIGHT, 'Google and the Limits of Antitrust: The Case Against the Case Against Google', *Harvard Journal of Law & Public Policy* 2010, vol. 34, no. 1, (171), pp. 210-211.
131. See M. RYSMAN, 'The Economics of Two-Sided Markets', *Journal of Economic Perspectives* 2009, vol. 23, no. 3, (125), p. 126.

economies of scale are present according to which the average costs of providing products and services decline as the scale of production increases. In economic terms, network economy industries are characterised by relatively high fixed costs and low marginal costs.[132] This is also the case for search engines, social networks and e-commerce platforms.

The creation of these online platforms require substantial investments in server infrastructure to ensure that the traffic can be handled effectively. In addition, investments in research and development (R&D) are necessary to develop advertising tools as well as, respectively, a search algorithm for search engines, social networking features for social networks and a recommendation system for e-commerce platforms.[133] The setting-up of these platforms therefore involves relatively high fixed costs.[134] Although constant investments are necessary to maintain and improve the quality of the respective platforms, the extra costs of displaying an additional advertisement, answering an additional search query, facilitating an additional interaction among users and making an additional purchase suggestion are very limited. Online platforms therefore exhibit increasing returns giving rise to supply-side economies of scale.[135]

2.4.2 Network Effects[136]

Network effects or network externalities are a source of scale economies in consumption rather than production and are therefore also referred to as demand-side economies of scale. Many network industries are characterised by network effects which

---

132. C. SHAPIRO AND H.R. VARIAN, *Information Rules. A Strategic Guide to the Network Economy*, Harvard Business School Press, 1999, p. 3.

133. In *Microsoft/Yahoo*, the European Commission referred to '*hardware, cost of indexing the web, human capital, cost of developing and updating the algorithm and IP patents*' as investments that have to be made in order to enter the market for online search (Case No COMP/M.5727 – *Microsoft/Yahoo! Search Business*, 18 February 2010, par. 111). In its Special report on digital markets, the Monopolkommission, an independent expert committee advising the German government and legislature in the area of competition policy, argued that the high fixed costs for setting up a search engine '*constitute a considerable market entry barrier on the search engine market*' (MONOPOLKOMMISSION, 'Competition policy: The challenge of digital markets', Special report No. 68, July 2015, par. 200, available at http://www.monopolkommission.de/images/PDF/SG/s68_fulltext_eng.pdf).

134. In Microsoft/Yahoo, the European Commission noted the following with regard to the search engine market: 'Microsoft estimates that the capital expenditure required to enter the market is approximately USD 1 000 million in hardware and USD 1 000 million in human capital. On top of that, Microsoft estimates that a new entrant would have to spend several billions of dollars to develop and update the algorithm. Finally, Microsoft explains that there are very significant costs that a new entrant would have to bear related to the necessity to have a large database' (Case No COMP/M.5727 – Microsoft/Yahoo! Search Business, 18 February 2010, par. 111).

135. See also O. BRACHA AND F. PASQUALE, 'Federal Search Commission? Access, Fairness, and Accountability in the Law of Search', *Cornell Law Review* 2008, vol. 93, no. 6, (1149), p. 1181.

136. Only 'one-sided' network effects will be considered here. Network effects that point to the multi-sidedness of an online platform and cross customer groups fall outside the scope of this subsection. See above at section 2.3.1, where a distinction has been made between 'ordinary' one-sided indirect network effects and multi-sided network effects that are often also simply referred to as indirect network effects.

occur when the utility that a consumer derives from consumption of a good increases with the number of others purchasing the good. A network effect is either direct when a product or service becomes more valuable as the number of users grows, or indirect when the increasing number of users of a good leads to more complementary products or services which raise the value of the network.[137] While network effects are beneficial to consumers in the short term by increasing consumption utility, they also make it easier for undertakings to achieve a dominant position and to reinforce barriers to entry which may have negative effects on competition and innovation in the long run.[138] In the context of the review of Facebook's acquisition of WhatsApp, the European Commission stated in this regard that '*the existence of network effects as such does not a priori indicate a competition problem*' but that such effects may '*raise competition concerns in particular if they allow the merged entity to foreclose competitors and make more difficult for competing providers to expand their customer base*'.[139]

The advertiser side of online platforms is not characterised by the presence of positive network effects. Advertisers do not benefit when more advertisers join a platform. To the contrary, the display of additional advertisements may impose a cost on the advertisers that have already advertised on the platform. In these circumstances, a 'congestion effect' or negative network effect may arise according to which the value of the platform for advertisers decreases as more advertisers join. This can be explained by the fact that advertisers have to compete for the attention of the user. Furthermore, the platform may be able to impose higher prices on advertisers when the demand for displaying advertisements rises.[140]

In online social networks, both direct and indirect network effects are present on the user side of the platform. The value that a user derives from a social network directly increases in accordance with the number of other users that are on the network since more people can be reached through the same system. As more users join the social network and the variety of available personal information grows, the number of compatible applications that are offered on the platform such as games will also increase. This indirectly raises the value of the network for its users.[141] In accordance with the multi-sided nature of social networks, network effects only start to create value once a critical mass of users, advertisers and application developers is achieved

---

137. M.L. KATZ AND C. SHAPIRO, 'Network Externalities, Competition, and Compatibility', *American Economic Review* 1985, vol. 75, no. 3, (424), pp. 424-425.
138. See also P.J. HARBOUR AND T.I. KOSLOV, 'Section 2 In A Web 2.0 World: An Expanded Vision of Relevant Product Markets', *Antitrust Law Journal* 2010, vol. 76, no. 3, (769), p. 778 who use the *Microsoft* case as an illustration.
139. Case No COMP/M.7217 – *Facebook/WhatsApp*, 3 October 2014, par. 130.
140. A.V. LERNER, 'The Role of "Big Data" in Online Platform Competition', *SSRN Working Paper* August 2014, p. 59, available at http://papers.ssrn.com/sol3/papers.cfm?abstract_id = 2482 780. In the context of search engines, see G.A. MANNE AND J.D. WRIGHT, 'Google and the Limits of Antitrust: The Case Against the Case Against Google', *Harvard Journal of Law & Public Policy* 2010, vol. 34, no. 1, (171), pp. 212-213. See also J. FARRELL AND P. KLEMPERER, 'Coordination and Lock-In: Competition with Switching Costs and Network Effects' in M. ARMSTRONG AND R. PORTER (eds.), *Handbook of Industrial Organization, Volume 3*, Elsevier, 2007, (1967), p. 2018.
141. S.W. WALLER, 'Antitrust and Social Networking', *North Carolina Law Review* 2012, vol. 90, no. 5, (1771), pp. 1787-1788.

at which point the social network will become self-sustaining.[142] First mover advantages therefore only seem to occur after a critical mass has been reached.[143] For attaining a critical mass of users, not only the total number of users is important but also the amount of interactions among users. Features that facilitate user interactions thus help the social network to gain a critical mass by increasing the degree of connectedness among its users.[144]

Nevertheless, a particular user may not attach value to having additional users on the social network with whom he or she does not share common interests or a common language. The heterogeneity of user preferences in the form of the identity of the people with whom a specific user would like to interact through the social network may thus offset the network effects to a certain extent.[145] In the context of consumer communications apps, the European Commission indeed noted that the relevance of the user base appears to be more important than its overall size. However, the Commission also made clear that the size of the network can have a value for users in two ways: (1) a larger network implies that it is more likely that existing contacts will already be using a communications app; and (2) a larger network will afford greater opportunities for contact acquisition and discovery.[146] Respondents to the market investigation conducted in the context of the acquisition of WhatsApp by Facebook had indicated that the size of the user base and the number of a user's friends or relatives on the same communications app are parameters which raise the utility of the service for a user since they increase the number of people he or she can reach. For that reason, the Commission considered that network effects did exist in the market for consumer communications apps.[147]

Direct network effects do not play a role on the user side of search engines and e-commerce platforms, because unlike in communication services users do not directly benefit if others employ the same search engine or e-commerce platform. The benefit that a user gets from having more users on the same platform is indirect.[148] The search results that a search engine produces, the interactions and contacts that a social network suggests, and the purchase recommendations that an e-commerce platform makes become more relevant in accordance with the number of exchanges completed.

With regard to the performance of search engines it has been reported that next to a well-functioning search algorithm, the availability of data on previous search

---

142. In this context, a social network is considered to be self-sustaining when it keeps expanding without any intervention from the provider.
143. See S.W. WALLER, 'Antitrust and Social Networking', *North Carolina Law Review* 2012, vol. 90, no. 5, (1771), p. 1788.
144. J.C. WESTLAND, 'Critical Mass and Willingness to Pay for Social Networks', *Electronic Commerce Research and Applications* 2010, vol. 9, no. 1, (6), pp. 16-18 and B. WANG, 'Survival and Competition among Social Networking Websites. A Research Commentary on "Critical Mass and Willingness to Pay for Social Networks" by J. CHRISTOPHER WESTLAND', *Electronic Commerce Research and Applications* 2010, vol. 9, no. 1, (20), pp. 20-21.
145. C.S. YOO, 'When Antitrust Met Facebook', *George Mason Law Review* 2012, vol. 19, no. 5, (1147), pp. 1151-1152.
146. Case No COMP/M.7217 – *Facebook/WhatsApp*, 3 October 2014, par. 88.
147. Case No COMP/M.7217 – *Facebook/WhatsApp*, 3 October 2014, par. 129.
148. G.A. MANNE AND J.D. WRIGHT, 'Google and the Limits of Antitrust: The Case Against the Case Against Google', *Harvard Journal of Law & Public Policy* 2010, vol. 34, no. 1, (171), p. 211.

queries is crucial. This data includes the search queries entered into the search engine and the links subsequently clicked on by users. The personal information such as age, gender and occupation that a search engine has collected about users also gives rise to a network effect, because it improves the ability of the search engine to offer better results to users that have the same age, gender and occupation. The more search data the search engine can access, the more relevant the search results that it returns will be.[149] As relevance is also critical to, respectively, recommendation systems and social network features, the same applies to the role of data in e-commerce platforms and social networks. In particular, information about the purchasing behaviour of users is employed by providers of e-commerce platforms to give users more relevant suggestions for future purchases. By observing the behaviour of users on their platform, providers learn about the preferences of users and are better able to predict in what products users are interested on the basis of their similarity with other users. Social network providers, in their turn, gather data about the activity and connections of users on their platform and use this information to select the most relevant social interactions to be displayed to users.

It is important to note that a provider will also become better at targeting advertisements as the amount and variety of data that it has gathered about users increases. The more detailed information is available about the profile, interests and behaviour of users, the more precise possibilities a provider can offer advertisers to select the category of users to which an ad should be displayed. Better targeted advertising services will give the provider the opportunity to increase its revenue. This is especially the case for online platforms employing a pay-per-click advertising model which entails that an advertiser only pays when a user clicks on its advertisement. To gain revenue, the platform thus has to ensure that the advertisements displayed to a specific user are so relevant that he or she clicks on them. Furthermore, more advertisers will be attracted to a particular platform as the targeting possibilities improve because of the higher probability that a user buys the advertised product or service. As a consequence of the rise in demand for advertising, the advertising revenues of the provider will also increase. This phenomenon can be referred to as economies of scale in terms of the monetisation of user data by providing targeted advertising services.[150]

With regard to the role of data in search engines, it has been argued that the value of having additional information declines as the amount of data rises. The strength of the network effect thus depends on the volume at which the returns from additional information start to diminish. The lower the amount at which the benefits from

---

149. D.S. EVANS, 'The Economics of the Online Advertising Industry', *Review of Network Economics* September 2008, vol. 7, no. 3, (359), p. 373; J. GRIMMELMANN, 'The Structure of Search Engine Law', *Iowa Law Review* 2007, vol. 93, no. 1, (1), pp. 10-11; C. ARGENTON AND J. PRÜFER, 'Search Engine Competition with Network Externalities', *Journal of Competition Law and Economics* 2012, vol. 8, no. 1, (73), p. 76; G. LUCHETTA, 'Is the Google Platform a Two-Sided Market?', *Journal of Competition Law and Economics* 2014, vol. 10, no. 1, (185), p. 196.

150. See the discussion in A.V. LERNER, 'The Role of "Big Data" in Online Platform Competition', *SSRN Working Paper* August 2014, pp. 41-44, available at http://papers.ssrn.com/sol3/papers.cfm?abstract_id=2482780. See also section 7.2 below.

supplementary data begin to decrease, the weaker the network effect related to search data is and the more likely it is that multiple providers can obtain the necessary information.[151] In this light, Manne & Wright argue that above a certain minimum scale that is necessary to develop an effective search algorithm, additional searches and users only provide a limited advantage.[152] Similarly, Bork & Sidak state that only a low number of searches have to be conducted in order for a new search engine to initiate the process of learning by doing and to start competing with the incumbent provider.[153] According to Lerner, there are many inputs other than search data to provide high quality search results such as engineering resources and web crawling and indexing technologies.[154]

In the *Microsoft/Yahoo* merger decision, the European Commission found no conclusive evidence that the scale of data collection leads to more relevant search results. Google argued that the importance of scale has been largely overstated, because the value of incremental data declines as the amount of data increases. Nevertheless, the respondents to the market investigation almost unanimously indicated that a large volume of search queries is an important aspect of a successful search engine. Scale seems particularly important for being able to improve the relevance of less frequent search queries (so-called tail queries). For the most frequent queries, the relevance gap between Google and, respectively, Microsoft and Yahoo identified in the market investigation was only very small.[155] The Commission concluded that '*it is plausible that the merged entity through innovation and through its access to a larger index will be able to provide personalised search results better aligned to users' preferences*'.[156]

Microsoft/Yahoo merger decision

Microsoft and Yahoo entered into several partnership agreements in 2009 that were approved under the EU Merger Regulation by the European Commission in February 2010. Under the agreements, Microsoft acquired an exclusive license to Yahoo's search technologies and the right to integrate Yahoo's search technologies into its existing search services. Microsoft became the exclusive internet search and search advertising provider used by Yahoo. In exchange, Microsoft paid a certain percentage of the search revenues generated on Yahoo's and its partners' websites to Yahoo.

---

151. H.A. SHELANSKI, 'Information, Innovation, and Competition Policy for the Internet', *University of Pennsylvania Law Review* 2013, vol. 161, no. 6, (1663), p. 1681.
152. G.A. MANNE AND J.D. WRIGHT, 'Google and the Limits of Antitrust: The Case Against the Case Against Google', *Harvard Journal of Law & Public Policy* 2010, vol. 34, no. 1, (171), p. 212.
153. R.H. BORK AND J.G. SIDAK, 'What Does the Chicago School Teach About Internet Search and the Antitrust Treatment of Google?', *Journal of Competition Law and Economics* 2012, vol. 8, no. 4, (663), pp. 688-691.
154. A.V. LERNER, 'The Role of "Big Data" in Online Platform Competition', *SSRN Working Paper* August 2014, pp. 30-32, available at http://papers.ssrn.com/sol3/papers.cfm?abstract_id=24 82780.
155. Case No COMP/M.5727 – *Microsoft/Yahoo! Search Business*, 18 February 2010, paras 160-174.
156. Case No COMP/M.5727 – *Microsoft/Yahoo! Search Business*, 18 February 2010, par. 225.

> The Commission concluded that Microsoft's and Yahoo's activities in internet search and online search advertising in the EEA were limited with combined market shares generally below 10% while Google was found to enjoy market shares of above 90% at the time of the merger. Microsoft argued that it would become a more credible alternative to Google and provide greater value to advertisers by acquiring Yahoo due to the increase of scale in search advertising. The investigation of the Commission had indicated that scale is indeed an important element to be an effective competitor in search advertising. With regard to the potential effects of the merger on the different market players, namely advertisers, users, online publishers and distributors of search technology, the Commission's investigation had shown that market participants did not expect the transaction to have negative effects on competition or on their business. They even expected it to increase competition in internet search and search advertising by allowing Microsoft to become a stronger competitor to Google.
>
> Case No COMP/M.5727 – *Microsoft/Yahoo! Search Business*, 18 February 2010, paragraphs 4-6, 152-153, 112, 121-122, 200, 226, 237-238, 246.

Lerner argues that tail queries are also subject to diminishing returns to scale, because the provision of relevant search results in response to these queries involves clever engineering and good web crawling technologies rather than the use of search data.[157] However, the probability that a search engine provider can match the tail query with a similar query that it has already seen before is likely to increase in accordance with the amount of search data that is available. Even though the perfect search result for a new unique query can probably not be provided, the most relevant search results may be displayed by relating new unique queries to existing queries that the search engine handled in the past. While the added value of a frequently made search query thus seems limited, less frequent search queries may make a significant contribution towards improving search results. Such infrequent search queries include in particular queries consisting of several terms (so-called long-tail queries) and queries relating to current events for which no information is yet available on users' conduct.[158]

The ability of an online platform or another type of computer program to make and improve predictions on the basis of an algorithm that learns from data is called 'machine learning'. In the context of the *Microsoft/Yahoo* merger decision, Microsoft argued that with larger scale a search engine can run tests on how to improve the

---

157. A.V. Lerner, 'The Role of "Big Data" in Online Platform Competition', *SSRN Working Paper* August 2014, p. 38, available at http://papers.ssrn.com/sol3/papers.cfm?abstract_id = 2482 780.
158. Monopolkommission, 'Competition policy: The challenge of digital markets', Special report No. 68, July 2015, par. 202.

algorithm and that it is possible to experiment more and faster as traffic volume increases because experimental traffic will take up a smaller proportion of overall traffic.[159]

If the intent of users making search queries changes due to a recent event, it is vital for a search engine to learn quickly and adapt to the new demands as soon as possible. When a celebrity dies, for example, search engines want to stop sending users to general pages about the performer and instead refer them to the latest news. How well a search engine is able to do this depends on how quickly it can get the required data. For an incumbent search engine provider it is easier to collect up-to-date information, because it has already established a large base of returning users which enables it to quickly adapt to new preferences of users. Google will thus adapt faster than Bing, because more people come to Google first.[160] The partnership that Google concluded with Twitter in February 2015 giving Google complete access to the full stream of tweets passing through Twitter on a second-by-second basis also has to be put against this background. Because information shared on Twitter is very timely, tweets are very useful for a search engine provider to have indexed in order to enable users to find up-to-date information quickly.[161]

Controversy exists about the nature of the indirect benefit to users. Argenton & Prüfer refer to this benefit as an indirect network externality on the ground that users do not take into account that they enable a search engine to improve the relevance and quality of its search results by inserting additional search queries and clicking on particular search results.[162] Other scholars argue that this type of indirect benefit cannot be seen as a network effect, but should be referred to as a learning economy.[163]

According to Katz & Shapiro, a network effect arises if the attractiveness of a good today depends on its sale history and if consumers today also care about the future success of the good. When only the first type of increasing return to scale occurs, in their view demand-side economies of scale other than network effects are present, such as learning economies.[164] In other words, if there is no link between the value that

---

159. Case No COMP/M.5727 – *Microsoft/Yahoo! Search Business*, 18 February 2010, paras 162 and 223.
160. K. O'TOOLE, 'Susan Athey: How Big Data Changes Business Management. The Stanford Economist Explains How Troves of Digital Data Will Reshape Competition', *Insights by Stanford Business*, 20 September 2013, available at http://www.gsb.stanford.edu/insights/susan-athey-how-big-data-changes-business-management.
161. See S. FRIER, 'Twitter Reaches Deal to Show Tweets in Google Search Results', *Bloomberg*, 5 February 2015, available at http://www.bloomberg.com/news/articles/2015-02-05/twitter-said-to-reach-deal-for-tweets-in-google-search-results.
162. C. ARGENTON AND J. PRÜFER, 'Search Engine Competition with Network Externalities', *Journal of Competition Law and Economics* 2012, vol. 8, no. 1, (73), p. 79.
163. R.H. BORK AND J.G. SIDAK, 'What Does the Chicago School Teach About Internet Search and the Antitrust Treatment of Google?', *Journal of Competition Law and Economics* 2012, vol. 8, no. 4, (663), pp. 688-691; G. LUCHETTA, 'Is the Google Platform a Two-Sided Market?', *Journal of Competition Law and Economics* 2014, vol. 10, no. 1, (185), p. 196.
164. M.L. KATZ AND C. SHAPIRO, 'Technology Adoption in the Presence of Network Externalities', *Journal of Political Economy* 1986, vol. 94, no. 4, (822), p. 824. Similarly, Economides argues that a network effect is present when '*the value of a unit of the good increases with the expected number of units to be sold*'. See N. ECONOMIDES, 'The Economics of Networks', *International Journal of Industrial Organization* 1996, vol. 14, no. 6, (673), p. 678.

users attach to the good and the future number of users, the good may be subject to learning economies instead of network externalities. Since the relevance of the search results that the search engine produces depends on the number of past users and search queries, one could argue that a user of a search engine is not concerned with the future success of the search engine when he or she enters a new search query.[165] As a result, no network effects would be present on the user side of a search engine.

Although Argenton & Prüfer refer to the indirect benefit that users enjoy on search engines as a network externality, they state that the phenomenon they have identified as an indirect network effect can also be regarded as a special form of learning by doing. Unlike the common type of learning effects that relate to the intangible production process in sectors like the aircraft industry, the learning economies in search engines concern data about previous searches that can be shared among firms.[166] The exact nature of the indirect benefit that users enjoy of the number of past searches on search engines is thus not clear. In a speech, the former Commissioner for Competition referred to '*strong economies of scale in user information that allow search engines to improve the service they bring to their users*' without specifying whether these scale economies have to be regarded as network effects.[167]

2.4.3   Switching Costs and Lock-In

Another common characteristic of network industries is the existence of switching costs that consumers incur when changing suppliers. As soon as a consumer makes an investment specific to his or her current provider that must be duplicated for any new supplier, switching costs are created.[168] Due to switching costs, consumers can become locked-in to a given technology or platform. In this situation, the costs of changing to a new product or service are so high that consumers will stay with their current provider even if they prefer the products or services of a different supplier. The degree of lock-in is determined by the level of the switching costs.[169]

A distinction can be made between inherent switching costs that are intrinsic to the nature of a product or service and strategic switching costs that reflect explicit choices made by firms in order to create switching costs. If a dominant undertaking acts to increase switching costs above their inherent level, this may be an indication of the

165. G. Luchetta, 'Is the Google Platform a Two-Sided Market?', *Journal of Competition Law and Economics* 2014, vol. 10, no. 1, (185), p. 196.
166. C. Argenton and J. Prüfer, 'Search Engine Competition with Network Externalities', *Journal of Competition Law and Economics* 2012, vol. 8, no. 1, (73), pp. 80-81.
167. Speech former Competition Commissioner Almunia, 'Competition in the online world', LSE Public Lecture London, 11 November 2013, SPEECH/13/905, available at http://europa.eu/rapid/press-release_SPEECH-13-905_en.htm.
168. J. Farrell and P. Klemperer, 'Coordination and Lock-In: Competition with Switching Costs and Network Effects' in M. Armstrong and R. Porter (eds.), *Handbook of Industrial Organization, Volume 3*, Elsevier, 2007, (1967), pp. 1971-1972 and 1977.
169. C. Shapiro and H.R. Varian, *Information Rules. A Strategic Guide to the Network Economy*, Harvard Business School Press, 1999, p. 104.

abusive nature of the behaviour.[170] Although switching costs always seem to be related to either financial expenses or the time and effort of consumers, several types can be distinguished such as contractual, compatibility, learning and search costs.[171]

In online platforms, switching costs can be present on both the user and advertiser side. Potential switching costs do not seem to prevent advertisers from using several differentiated advertising platforms, since multi-homing[172] is common in the online advertising industry.[173] Nevertheless, advertisers may experience switching costs when they want to change providers or use their advertisements on several platforms and cannot move their existing advertising campaigns to another platform. By restricting the possibilities of advertisers to transfer their advertising campaigns to competing services, providers of advertising platform create switching costs. Ultimately, this may lead to a situation of lock-in when advertisers find it too burdensome to manually re-enter all the details of their advertising campaign in the new platform and for that reason decide to stay with the platform they joined first even if better or cheaper options are available.

In the *Google* case, which was opened in November 2010 after complaints from competitors about Google's search activities,[174] the European Commission expressed the concern that Google was creating switching costs for advertisers by limiting the portability of advertising campaigns on Google's AdWords advertising platform. In particular, the Commission is worried that Google puts '*contractual restrictions on software developers which prevent them from offering tools that allow the seamless transfer of search advertising campaigns across AdWords and other platforms for search*

---

170. A.S. Edlin and R.G. Harris, 'The Role of Switching Costs in Antitrust Analysis: A Comparison of Microsoft and Google', *Yale Journal of Law and Technology* 2013, vol. 15, (169), p. 176.
171. For different categorisations of switching costs, see J. Farrell and P. Klemperer, 'Coordination and Lock-In: Competition with Switching Costs and Network Effects' in M. Armstrong and R. Porter (eds.), *Handbook of Industrial Organization, Volume 3*, Elsevier, 2007, (1967), p. 1977; C. Shapiro and H.R. Varian, *Information Rules. A Strategic Guide to the Network Economy*, Harvard Business School Press, 1999, p. 117; O. Shy, *The Economics of Network Industries*, Cambridge, Cambridge University Press, 2001, pp. 4-5 and A.S. Edlin and R.G. Harris, 'The Role of Switching Costs in Antitrust Analysis: A Comparison of Microsoft and Google', *Yale Journal of Law and Technology* 2013, vol. 15, (169), pp. 178-184.
172. Multi-homing occurs if a customer relies on more than one platform for the same service, while single-homing refers to the situation where a customer uses only one platform for a specific service. See J.-C. Rochet and J. Tirole, 'Platform Competition in Two-Sided Markets', *Journal of the European Economic Association* 2003, vol. 1, no. 4, (990), pp. 992-993; D.S. Evans, 'Competition and Regulatory Policy for Multi-Sided Platforms with Applications to the Web Economy', *SSRN Working Paper* March 2008, pp. 10-11, available at http://papers.ssrn.com/sol3/papers.cfm?abstract_id=1090368.
173. For switching behaviour of advertisers in the search engine industry, see Case No COMP/M.4731 –*Google/ DoubleClick*, 11 March 2008, par. 335 and footnote 172. Although Google showed that the majority of advertisers were multi-homing, the European Commission concluded that Google had a sufficient degree of market power to be able to foreclose rivals in the search advertising market because of the high level of ad targeting that competitors could not achieve.
174. Press Release European Commission, 'Antitrust: Commission probes allegations of antitrust violations by Google', 30 November 2010, IP/10/1624, available at http://europa.eu/rapid/press-release_IP-10-1624_en.htm.

advertising'.[175] In the negotiations about a potential settlement, Google made commitments to stop imposing obligations that prevent advertisers from porting and managing advertising campaigns across competing services.[176] If the commitments become final, Google will no longer be able to prevent developers from offering functionality that copies online advertising campaigns between advertising services. Such a tool will enable advertisers to transfer their campaigns across different platforms and eliminate switching costs in the market.[177]

Users of search engines do not seem to experience high switching costs.[178] While a personal computer (PC) or a mobile device usually runs a single operating system that is only able to support a limited number of compatible applications, a user has unlimited access to every search engine that is available on the internet regardless of which operating system or web browser is installed. Because of the openness of the internet and the absence of compatibility costs, users can easily switch to another search engine and use several search engines at the same time.[179] In this context, Google often states that *'competition is only one click away'*. Nevertheless, a user may be reluctant to leave a search engine that has accumulated information about its preferences and is therefore better able to adapt the search results to its expectations. The trend towards personalisation of search results may therefore raise switching costs and start to lock-in users if they cannot take their search history with them when changing search engines. In addition, this form of lock-in encourages user inertia. Even though better alternatives are available, users may tend to stay with the search engine they are most familiar with.[180]

On e-commerce platforms both buyers and sellers may experience switching costs. Because of the personalisation of recommendation suggestions, a buyer may

---

175. Speech former Competition Commissioner Almunia, 'Statement of Commissioner Almunia on the Google antitrust investigation', Press room Brussels, 21 May 2012, SPEECH/12/372, available at http://europa.eu/rapid/press-release_SPEECH-12-372_en.htm.

176. Commitments of Google in Case COMP/C-3/39.740 *Foundem and others*, 3 April 2013, paras 27-31, available at http://ec.europa.eu/competition/antitrust/cases/dec_docs/39740/39740_8608_5.pdf. In October 2013, Google offered improved commitments to the Commission which included a new proposal providing stronger guarantees against circumvention of the earlier commitments regarding portability of advertising campaigns. See speech former Competition Commissioner Almunia, 'The Google antitrust case: what is at stake?', 1 October 2013, SPEECH/13/786, available at http://europa.eu/rapid/press-release_SPEECH-13-768_en.htm.

177. A similar commitment was adopted in the US by way of a consent decree that put an end to the Google investigation, see http://ftc.gov/opa/2013/01/google.shtm.

178. K.L. DEVINE, 'Preserving Competition in Multi-Sided Innovative Markets: How Do You Solve a Problem Like Google?', *North Carolina Journal of Law & Technology* 2008, vol. 10, no. 1, (59), p. 86; R.H. BORK AND J.G. SIDAK, 'What Does the Chicago School Teach About Internet Search and the Antitrust Treatment of Google?', *Journal of Competition Law and Economics* 2012, vol. 8, no. 4, (663), pp. 671-672.

179. A.S. EDLIN AND R.G. HARRIS, 'The Role of Switching Costs in Antitrust Analysis: A Comparison of Microsoft and Google', *Yale Journal of Law and Technology* 2013, vol. 15, (169), pp. 193-194.

180. N. ZINGALES, 'Product Market Definition in Online Search and Advertising', *The Competition Law Review* March 2013, vol. 9, no. 1, (29), p. 44; K.L. DEVINE, 'Preserving Competition in Multi-Sided Innovative Markets: How Do You Solve a Problem Like Google?', *North Carolina Journal of Law & Technology* 2008, vol. 10, no. 1, (59), p. 87. See also O. BRACHA AND F. PASQUALE, 'Federal Search Commission? Access, Fairness, and Accountability in the Law of Search', *Cornell Law Review* 2008, vol. 93, no. 6, (1149), p. 1182 and footnote 183 who refers to some empirical studies on switching costs in search engines.

stick with the platform that has collected information about its purchasing behaviour and is able to make more relevant suggestions for future purchases on the basis of previous preferences. This issue is similar to that of personalisation of search results. With regard to the position of sellers, the reputation that they have built up on a particular platform forms a source of switching costs. E-commerce platform providers add ratings to the seller's profile on the basis of the number of positive or negative scores the seller has received.[181] This enables sellers to gain reputation and attract buyers. When a seller cannot transfer its reputation developed on one platform to another, it may be discouraged from using a competing platform on which it does not benefit from the feedback scores collected previously. Buyers may be reluctant to enter into transactions with a seller that does not yet have any ratings. By limiting the portability of the sellers' reputations, e-commerce platform providers can thus try to lock-in sellers to their system.[182]

Since the central feature of social networks is the provision of personal information by users, social network providers can create switching costs by limiting the possibility for users to transfer their profile and other uploaded content such as videos, photos and status updates to a competing service.[183] Although social network providers do allow users to export their data,[184] transferring a profile to a competing service requires a lot of time and effort, in particular because the data is not extracted in a format that can be easily imported into another social network. As a result, in practice users have to manually re-enter their profile information, photos, videos and other information in the new platform if they want to switch from one social network to another. By restricting the portability of this data, social network providers try to lock-in users to their service. Because of the switching costs, users may find it too cumbersome to change to another service and stay with the online social network of their first choice, even if better or more privacy-friendly services become available.[185]

In its *Facebook/WhatsApp* merger decision, the European Commission made clear that it had not found any evidence suggesting that data portability issues would constitute a significant barrier to consumers' switching in the case of consumer communications apps. According to the Commission, communication via apps tends to consist to a significant extent of short and spontaneous chats which do not necessarily

---

181. eBay and Amazon are examples of e-commerce platforms that add feedback scores and ratings to the profiles of sellers, see respectively http://pages.ebay.com/help/feedback/scores-reputation.html and http://www.amazon.com/gp/help/customer/display.html?nodeId = 537806.
182. R.C. PICKER, 'Competition and Privacy in Web 2.0 and the Cloud', *Northwestern University Law Review Colloquy* 2008, vol. 103, (1), pp. 6-7. See also the reference made there to the case that the United States Federal Trade Commission started against ReverseAuction.com for sending unsolicited commercial email to eBay users after gathering their personal information including feedback ratings by registering as an eBay user and agreeing to the eBay User Agreement.
183. P. SWIRE AND Y. LAGOS, 'Why the Right to Data Portability Likely Reduces Consumer Welfare: Antitrust and Privacy Critique', *Maryland Law Review* 2013, vol. 72, no. 2, (335), p. 338.
184. Facebook offers the 'Download Your Info' feature (https://www.facebook.com/help/131112897028467) and Google has the 'Google Takeout' service (https://support.google.com/takeout/answer/2508459?hl = en&ref_topic = 2508503).
185. G. ZANFIR, 'The Right to Data Portability in the Context of the EU Data Protection Reform', *International Data Privacy Law* 2012, vol. 2, no. 3, (149), p. 152.

carry long-term value for consumers. The Commission also considered that the messaging history remains accessible on a user's smartphone even if the user starts using a different communications app. Finally, the Commission took into account that the contact list can be easily ported since a competing app, after obtaining consent of the user, would get access to his or her phone book on the basis of which existing contacts can be identified.[186] The question is whether the Commission will come to the same conclusion with regard to the transfer of profile information and other personal content in social networking services. Social networks offer users more than a basic communications service and instead focus on enabling users to create a personal profile which may include interests, activities, photo albums and comments of other users. The abandonment of such a carefully constructed digital identity in a particular social network is more likely to raise switching costs than is the case for communications apps.

In the context of the introduction of the right to data portability in the General Data Protection Regulation,[187] the Commission argued with regard to the use of online services that *'the loss of contact information, calendar history, interpersonal communications exchanges and other kinds of personally or socially relevant data which is very difficult to recreate or restore [...] effectively creates a lock-in with the specific service for the user and makes it effectively very costly or even impossible to change provider and benefit from better services available on the market'.*[188] In a more general perspective, the former Commissioner for Competition stated in a speech that retention of data should not serve as barriers to switching in markets that build on users uploading their personal data. In addition, he argued that *'[c]ustomers should not be locked in to a particular company just because they once trusted them with their content'.* In his view, competition concerns may arise *'if customers were prevented from switching from a company to another because they cannot carry their data along'.*[189]

The extent of multi-homing may reduce the switching costs in the market. However, while many users have profiles on several social networks at the same time, this type of multi-homing often concerns social networks serving a different purpose.[190] For example, an individual may have a profile on Facebook to interact with his or her friends as well as a profile on LinkedIn in order to maintain his or her business

---

186. Case No COMP/M.7217 – *Facebook/WhatsApp*, 3 October 2014, paras 113-115 and 134.
187. Article 20 of Regulation (EU) No 2016/679 of the European Parliament and of the Council of 27 April 2016 on the protection of natural persons with regard to the processing of personal data and on the free movement of such data, and repealing Directive 95/46/EC (General Data Protection Regulation) [2016] OJ L 119/1.
188. Commission Staff Working Paper — Impact Assessment accompanying the General Data Protection Regulation and the Directive on the protection of individuals with regard to the processing of personal data by competent authorities for the purposes of prevention, investigation, detection or prosecution of criminal offences or the execution of criminal penalties, and the free movement of such data (Impact Assessment report), SEC(2012) 72 final, p. 28.
189. Speech former Competition Commissioner Almunia, 'Competition and personal data protection', Privacy Platform event: Competition and Privacy in Markets of Data Brussels, 26 November 2012, SPEECH/12/860, available at http://europa.eu/rapid/press-release_SPEECH -12-860_en.htm.
190. F. THÉPOT, 'Market Power in Online Search and Social Networking: A Matter of Two-Sided Markets', *World Competition* 2013, vol. 36, no. 2, (195), p. 219.

network. The degree of user lock-in in social networks can be illustrated by the fact that the numerous changes made to the privacy policies of social networks like Facebook have not led to a direct decline in activity in spite of the fierce opposition that these changes have sometimes caused on the part of the users.[191]

Apart from the switching costs that originate from the practical inability of users to move their data to a different social network, users may also become locked-in to a particular social network for social reasons.[192] The currently predominant social networks are not interoperable in the sense that users of social network A cannot directly interact with users of social network B unless they have also created a profile on social network B. For this reason, users are required to join the social network on which their contacts are present or, more generally, the social network that has the most users. The user's decision to join a particular social network is therefore often not based on the quality of the platform but merely depends on its user base. As a result, users may not be able to join the social network that has their preference in terms of functionality and privacy-friendliness.

In the context of internet consumer communications services, the General Court in *Cisco* followed the reasoning of the European Commission outlined in its *Microsoft/Skype* merger decision that it is not difficult for users to switch to competing services considering that users typically communicate with only a small group of family and friends which would make it easy for them to coordinate a move to another service.[193] However, it has to be recognised that users do not interact in closed groups of only a few contacts in the sense that every individual in the group will usually communicate with users forming part of different groups which leads to a much more complex level of interconnection than that presented by the Commission and the General Court.[194]

---

191. S.W. WALLER, 'Antitrust and Social Networking', *North Carolina Law Review* 2012, vol. 90, no. 5, (1771), pp. 1791-1792. Although a direct effect after the implementation of new privacy policies is not visible, studies indicate that the growth of Facebook has been gradually declining and may decrease further in the next years (see P. CAUWELS AND D. SORNETTE, 'Quis Pendit Ipsa Pretia: Facebook Valuation and Diagnostic of a Bubble Based on Nonlinear Demographic Dynamics', *The Journal of Portfolio Management* 2012, vol. 38, no. 2, (56) and J. CANNARELLA AND J.A. SPECHLER, 'Epidemiological Modeling of Online Social Network Dynamics', *ArXiv* 2013, (1)). The type of switching costs referred to here is not only present in social networks, but also occurs in other forms of cloud computing and online services. See R.C. PICKER, 'Competition and Privacy in Web 2.0 and the Cloud', *Nothwestern University Law Review Colloquy* 2008, vol. 103, (1), pp. 6-7 describing switching costs in auction platforms like eBay.
192. S.W. WALLER, 'Antitrust and Social Networking', *North Carolina Law Review* 2012, vol. 90, no. 5, (1771), p. 1789.
193. Case No COMP/M.6281 – *Microsoft/Skype*, 7 October 2011, paras 92 and 130; Judgment in *Cisco Systems Inc. and Messagenet SpA v. Commission*, T-79/12, ECLI:EU:T:2013:635, paras 52 and 80. See also C.S. YOO, 'When Antitrust Met Facebook', *George Mason Law Review* 2012, vol. 19, no. 5, (1147), p. 1152 who makes the same argument for social networks.
194. A. LAMADRID DE PABLO, 'A comment on Case T-79/12 Cisco Systems and Messagenet v European Commission (Microsoft/Skype)', *Chillin'Competition*, 12 May 2014, available at http://chilling competition.com/2014/05/12/a-comment-on-case-t-7912-cisco-systems-and-messagenet-v-eu ropean-commission-microsoftskype/ stating that '*groups of people are interconnected and do not communicate in movable autarkic nodules*'.

Therefore, the fact that social network users engage in a regular two-way interaction with only a few people[195] may not necessarily dilute the switching costs or lock-in that they experience.

Microsoft/Skype merger decision and Cisco judgment

In October 2011, the European Commission approved the acquisition of Skype by Microsoft. At the time of the merger, Microsoft and Skype both provided internet-based communications software enabling users to communicate over the internet by way of instant messaging, voice calls and video communications.

The Commission identified internet consumer and enterprise communications services as the markets affected by the proposed concentration. The Commission left the exact market definition of consumer communications services open and argued that the concentration did not give rise to competition concerns even though the new entity would become the market leader for video calls on Windows-based PCs, having a market share of between 80% and 90%. The Commission considered that market shares only provided a limited indication of competitive strength in the consumer communications services market which was a nascent and dynamic sector in which market shares can change quickly within a short period of time and in which products are offered free of charge. With regard to the market for enterprise communications, the investigation of the Commission confirmed that Skype had a limited market presence for these products and did not compete directly with Microsoft's enterprise communication product Lync.

Since Microsoft and Skype were active in neighbouring markets, the Commission also investigated possible conglomerate effects. As regards consumer communications services, the Commission found that the new entity had the ability but not the incentive to distort competition in favour of Microsoft's and Skype's products by degrading the interoperability of those products with competing products or by entering into bundling or tying practices. Furthermore, even if such a strategy would be employed, the anticompetitive effects would be non-existent or at most limited in the Commission's view. As regards enterprise communications services, the Commission argued that Skype was at the time of the merger not an enterprise product, therefore its interoperability could not be considered decisive for competitors and a bundle or a tie between Skype and Microsoft's products would not be a must have product for enterprises. Furthermore, Lync was found to face competition from other strong players in enterprise communications such as Cisco.

In December 2013, the General Court dismissed the appeal brought by Cisco and Messagenet against the Commission decision. The General Court confirmed that

---

195. In *Microsoft/Skype*, the Commission states that '*According to Facebook data, users engage in regular two-way interaction with four to six people*'. See Case No COMP/M.6281 – Microsoft/Skype, 7 October 2011, par. 92 and the reference included in footnote 51.

the Commission was correct in finding that even on the narrow market for video calls on Windows-based PCs the combined market share of 80% to 90% was not indicative of market power given the particular characteristics of the market in question which is marked by short innovation cycles and products which are free. The General Court also held that the Commission's assessment of possible conglomerate effects was correct. In particular, the General Court rejected the argument of Cisco and Messagenet that Microsoft would be able to reserve to Lync preferential interoperability with Skype and with Skype's large user base to the detriment of competitors.

Case No COMP/M.6281 - *Microsoft/Skype*, 7 October 2011.

Judgment in *Cisco Systems Inc. and Messagenet SpA v. Commission*, T-79/12, ECLI:EU:T:2013:635.

2.4.4 Barriers to Entry

The presence of network economy features discussed above may lead to entry barriers that protect the position of incumbents and make it difficult for new entrants to gain a foothold on the market. Different definitions of barriers to entry have been put forward in the economic literature. The two definitions that have gained most attention are the ones of respectively Bain and Stigler. According to Bain, an entry barrier is any advantage that allows an incumbent to earn above-normal profits without the threat of entry.[196] Stigler defined entry barriers as sunk costs that must be borne by a firm seeking to enter an industry but that are not borne by firms already in the industry.[197] While economies of scale would qualify as entry barriers under Bain's definition, Stigler's notion rules out scale economies as barriers to entry.[198]

In the Guidance Paper on exclusionary conduct under Article 102 TFEU, the European Commission made clear that it regards economies of scale and scope as entry barriers. In the Commission's view, entry barriers may also take the form of '*privileged access to essential inputs or natural resources, important technologies or an established distribution and sales network*'. Furthermore, barriers to entry may include '*costs and other impediments, for instance resulting from network effects, faced by customers in switching to a new supplier*'. More controversially, the Commission states that a dominant undertaking's own conduct may create entry barriers, '*for example where it has made significant investments which entrants or competitors would have to match, or where it has concluded long-term contracts with its customers that have appreciable*

---

196. J.S. BAIN, Barriers to New Competition: Their Character and Consequences in Manufacturing Industries, Harvard University Press, 1956, p. 3.
197. G.J. STIGLER, *The Organization of Industry*, Richard D. Irwin, 1968, p. 67.
198. R. SCHMALENSEE, 'Sunk Costs and Antitrust Barriers to Entry', *American Economic Review* May 2004, vol. 94, no. 2, (471), p. 471.

foreclosing effects'.[199] This broad approach may have as a result that all network economy markets are found to be characterised by entry barriers, since network effects and switching costs are to some extent inherent to the network economy. Although network effects and switching costs tend to reinforce the position of the market leader and may lead to highly concentrated markets,[200] these economic features do not by definition prevent new firms from displacing the incumbent.[201]

Barriers to entry played an important role in two different *Microsoft* decisions of the European Commission. In both the 2004 Commission decision,[202] upheld by the General Court in 2007,[203] in which Microsoft was held liable for refusing to licence interoperability information and for tying the Windows PC operating system to Windows Media Player, as well as the 2009 commitment decision[204] involving the tying of Internet Explorer to Windows, indirect network effects were identified in the PC operating system market that was dominated by Microsoft. In the Commission's view, the indirect network effects raised a so-called applications barrier to entry as a result of which potential competing operating systems could only be successfully launched if a critical mass of compatible applications was already available for them.[205] However, the Commission has not always regarded network effects as a source of barriers to entry.

In the *Cisco* judgment, the General Court agreed with the Commission's conclusion in its *Microsoft/Skype* merger decision that the direct network effects present in the internet consumer communications services market did not give rise to entry barriers because users multi-homed and were able to switch providers easily.[206] Similarly, the Commission argued in *Facebook/WhatsApp* that the network effects in the market for consumer communications apps were unlikely to shield the merged entity from

---

199. Communication from the Commission — Guidance on the Commission's enforcement priorities in applying Article 82 of the EC Treaty to abusive exclusionary conduct by dominant undertakings (Guidance Paper) [2009] OJ C 45/7, par. 17.
200. See speech former Competition Commissioner Almunia, 'Abuse of dominance: a view from the EU', Fordham's Competition Law Institute Annual Conference New York, 27 September 2013, SPEECH/13/758, available at http://europa.eu/rapid/press-release_SPEECH-13-758_en.htm.
201. S.J. LIEBOWITZ AND S.E. MARGOLIS, 'Are Network Externalities a New Source of Market Failure?', *Research in Law and Economics* 1995, vol. 17, (1); D.F. SPULBER, 'Unlocking Technology: Antitrust and Innovation', *Journal of Competition Law and Economics* 2008, vol. 4, no. 4, (915); D.S. EVANS AND R. SCHMALENSEE, 'Some Economic Aspects of Antitrust Analysis in Dynamically Competitive Industries' in A.B. JAFFE, J. LERNER AND S. STERN (eds.), *Innovation Policy and the Economy, Volume 2*, MIT Press, 2002, (1), pp. 9-10.
202. Case COMP/C-3/37.792 – *Microsoft*, 24 March 2004.
203. Judgment in *Microsoft v. Commission*, T-201/04, ECLI:EU:T:2007:289.
204. Case COMP/C-3/39.530 – *Microsoft (tying)*, 16 December 2009.
205. Judgment in *Microsoft v. Commission*, T-201/04, ECLI:EU:T:2007:289, par. 1088 and Case COMP/C-3/39.530 – *Microsoft (tying)*, 16 December 2009, paras 25-28.
206. Judgment in *Cisco Systems Inc. and Messagenet SpA v. Commission*, T-79/12, ECLI:EU:T:2013:635, par. 81. Although the reasoning on the ease with which users can switch due to the small groups in which they communicate may not be convincing as explained above, the Commission relied on an empirical study that confirmed the fact that users employed different internet communication services at the same time which reduces the potential for entry barriers to arise. For a further discussion of this issue, see I. GRAEF, 'Sneak preview of the future application of European competition law on the Internet?: Cisco and Messagenet', *Common Market Law Review* 2014, vol. 51, no. 4, (1263), pp. 1275-1276.

competition from new and existing communications apps.[207] The Commission argued that the network effects were mitigated because of the fast-moving nature of the sector as a result of which any leading market position even if assisted by network effects is unlikely to be incontestable.[208] In addition, the Commission had found no significant costs preventing consumers from switching considering that communications apps are offered free of charge or at a very low price, customers of communications apps normally multi-home and neither Facebook Messenger nor WhatsApp were pre-installed on a large basis of handsets.[209]

As to the assessment of switching costs and network effects, the General Court in *Cisco* seems to contradict earlier statements made by the Commission in the context of Microsoft's behaviour in the market for PC operating systems. In its commitment decision involving the tying of Internet Explorer to Windows, the Commission argued that although web browsers are downloadable for free, users are prevented from switching to competing browsers *'due to the barriers associated with such a switch, such as searching, choosing and installing such a competing web browser, which can stem from a lack of technical skills, or be related to the user's inertia'*.[210] In *Cisco*, the General Court maintained that the *Microsoft/Skype* case had to be distinguished from the situations that formed the basis of the Commission's earlier decisions involving Microsoft, because contrary to the latter situations *'there are no technical or economic constraints which prevent users from downloading several communications applications on their operating device, especially as the software concerned is free, easy to download and takes up little space on their hard drives'*.[211]

In fact, the General Court thus did not distinguish the *Microsoft/Skype* merger from previous cases but countered earlier findings of the Commission that switching does not occur even if the software is available by way of a free download.[212] Nevertheless, a market study referred to by the Commission in its *Microsoft/Skype* decision confirmed that consumers use different communications services at the same time, while the majority of both consumers and enterprises using Internet Explorer did not download other web browsers at the time of adoption of the commitment decision in 2009.[213] Instead of pretending that the factual scenarios in the markets for client PC operating systems and consumer communications services were different, the General Court could have argued that the studies showed that the situation has altered and users have apparently become better informed and more experienced in downloading and installing software. This would have made the General Court's analysis more credible.[214]

---

207. Case No COMP/M.7217 – *Facebook/WhatsApp*, 3 October 2014, par. 135.
208. Case No COMP/M.7217 – *Facebook/WhatsApp*, 3 October 2014, par. 132.
209. Case No COMP/M.7217 – *Facebook/WhatsApp*, 3 October 2014, paras 109-111.
210. Case COMP/C-3/39.530 – *Microsoft (tying)*, 16 December 2009, par. 48.
211. Judgment in *Microsoft v. Commission*, T-201/04, ECLI:EU:T:2007:289, par. 79.
212. Case No COMP/M.6281 – *Microsoft/Skype*, 7 October 2011, par. 92 and footnote 52.
213. Case COMP/C-3/39.530 – *Microsoft (tying)*, 16 December 2009, paras 50-53.
214. See also I. Graef, 'Sneak Preview of the Future Application of European Competition Law on the Internet?: Cisco and Messagenet', *Common Market Law Review* 2014, vol. 51, no. 4, (1263), pp. 1275-1276.

In *Facebook/WhatsApp*, the Commission seems to distinguish the factual situations in the markets for client PC operating systems in 2009 and consumer communications apps in 2014 by noting that neither Facebook Messenger nor WhatsApp are pre-installed on a large basis of handsets while Microsoft tied Internet Explorer to its PC operating system. By referring to its 2009 *Microsoft* commitment decision targeting the latter practice, the Commission claimed that: *'[s]oftware pre-installation can make switching more difficult, in view of users' inertia which leads to the so-called "status quo bias"'*. Because users have to actively download both Facebook Messenger and WhatsApp, the Commission considered that they are more likely to actively download a competing consumer communications app.[215] While the stance towards switching costs and network effects thus seems to have changed in the *Microsoft/Skype* and *Facebook/WhatsApp* cases, Commission officials still refer to network economy characteristics in speeches for their potential to protect the position of incumbents and to raise barriers to entry.

To counter claims that there is no need for antitrust intervention in high-tech markets on the ground that the rapid pace of technological innovation would make entrenched positions of market power impossible to maintain, former Director-General for Competition Italianer stated: *'In reality, these markets may often have characteristics which actually increase the likelihood of entrenched market power over time. These could for instance be network effects, sunk costs, tipping, lock-in and so on'*. In particular, he argued that network effects may act as barriers to entry and can also lead to the tipping of the market in favour of one player or technology which has reached a critical mass.[216] The former Commissioner for Competition noted in a similar fashion that features such as economies of scale and network effects *'make it easier for companies to become gatekeepers in their respective markets than it is in the brick-and-mortar economy - and by "gatekeeper" I mean a specific type of dominant firm which holds a strategic position along the value chain'*.[217]

The fact that contradicting outcomes are often reached with regard to the issue of whether the existence of network economy characteristics in a market give rise to entry barriers may be caused by the context in which these features are analysed. In this regard, it seems particularly relevant whether a case is examined under the merger review procedure or under the prohibition of abuse of dominance. Mergers are assessed ex ante as a result of which the existence of network effects and switching costs may be considered less problematic because of the unknown pace of an innovation cycle. Abuse of dominance cases, to the contrary, require the Commission to analyse markets in a backward-looking manner. Previous findings about network

---

215. Case No COMP/M.7217 – *Facebook/WhatsApp*, 3 October 2014, par. 111.
216. Speech former Director-General for Competition Italianer, 'Prepared remarks on: Level-playing field and innovation in technology markets', Conference on Antitrust in Technology, Palo Alto (US), 28 January 2013, pp. 3-4, available at http://ec.europa.eu/competition/speeches/text/sp2013_01_en.pdf.
217. Speech former Competition Commissioner Almunia, 'Competition in the online world', LSE Public Lecture London, 11 November 2013, SPEECH/13/905, available at http://europa.eu/rapid/press-release_SPEECH-13-905_en.htm.

effects or switching costs as a source of entry barriers in the context of merger cases may therefore not be automatically transposed to abuse of dominance proceedings involving the same market.[218]

The entry barriers that may be found in social networks, search engines and e-commerce platforms have a different nature than those playing a role in earlier competition cases. Whereas the barriers to entry in the abovementioned 2004 and 2009 *Microsoft* decisions resulted from technological blocking and tying, the entry barriers in online platforms have an informational character.[219] By accumulating information about the behaviour and interests of users, online platform providers are able to improve their services to users in the form of more relevant search results, social interactions and purchase recommendations as well as to advertisers in the form of better targeted ads. The amount and variety of user data to which incumbent social networks, search engines and e-commerce platforms have access may constitute a barrier to entry for potential competitors.[220] However, due to diminishing returns to scale, the value of having additional user data may decline at a certain point. The strength of the entry barrier would then depend on the volume of information at which the benefits of additional data begin to decline. If the benefits of extra information start to diminish only at a very high amount of data, large volumes of information can give a competitive advantage to a leading platform. In such circumstances, control of the largest share of user data may contribute to dominance.[221]

Whether the volume of data to which an incumbent has access gives rise to an entry barrier is subject to controversy. Opponents claim that new entrants do not need to have access to a large quantity of data in order to compete effectively, because data is widely available, has a non-rivalrous nature (which means that collecting data from some users does not prevent other companies from collecting identical data from the same users; also as a result of user multi-homing), the cost of data collection and analysis is very low and the competitive success of online platforms is driven by more

---

218. A.D. CHIRITA, 'Google's Anti-Competitive and Unfair Practices in Digital Leisure Markets', *The Competition Law Review* 2015, vol. 11, no. 1, (109), pp. 125-126.
219. C. BUTTS, 'The Microsoft Case 10 Years Later: Antitrust and New Leading "New Economy" Firms', *Northwestern Journal of Technology and Intellectual Property* Spring 2010, vol. 8, no. 2, (275), pp. 290-291. See also speech former Competition Commissioner Almunia, 'Looking back at five years of competition enforcement in the EU', Global Antitrust Enforcement Symposium (Georgetown) Washington, 10 September 2014, SPEECH/14/588, available at http://europa.eu/rapid/press-release_SPEECH-14-588_en.htm?locale = en: '*In the digital sectors, network effects can be closely linked with big data – the access to big data is becoming a major barrier to entry*'.
220. Bork & Sidak state that scale cannot be a barrier to entry for search engines since Google started operating four years after Yahoo and still managed to become the market leader. Bork & Sidak also argue that learning by doing cannot be considered as an entry barrier in search engines, because it is a cost that the incumbent provider also has to bear. However, the restrictive definition of barriers to entry of Stigler that they follow is not used by the European Commission (R.H. BORK AND J.G. SIDAK, 'What Does the Chicago School Teach About Internet Search and the Antitrust Treatment of Google?', *Journal of Competition Law and Economics* 2012, vol. 8, no. 4, (663), pp. 690-691).
221. H.A. SHELANSKI, 'Information, Innovation, and Competition Policy for the Internet', *University of Pennsylvania Law Review* 2013, vol. 161, no. 6, (1663), p. 1681. See also section 2.4.2 above.

than the amount of user data collected.[222] Nevertheless, if the information necessary to compete on equal footing is not readily available to new entrants, the amount of user data collected by incumbent online platforms may constitute an entry barrier.[223] Whether data gives rise to a barrier to entry thus depends on the circumstances of the case which means that it cannot be excluded at the outset that user data constitutes an entry barrier.

The different character of the entry barriers can also be seen from the policy that social network providers such as Facebook pursue. Contrary to Microsoft which was fined by the Commission in 2004 for not giving competitors access to its technology necessary to develop complementary applications, Facebook gives developers free and open access to its application programming interfaces. With regard to the ability of third parties to get access to user data, Facebook's policy is more restrictive as its general conditions prohibit other websites from acquiring users' content and information on its platform.[224]

In addition to the aggregation of user data, the lack of data and advertising portability may lead to obstacles to market entry for new firms.[225] If users and advertisers cannot bring their data or advertising campaigns with them when moving to another provider, they may find it too cumbersome to switch and become locked-in to the provider that they decided to join first. As evidenced by the statements in the *Microsoft/Skype* and *Facebook/WhatsApp* merger cases, the potential entry barriers in markets for online services are considered to be of a less durable character than the technological barriers identified in the market for PC operating systems. The significance of barriers to entry in the market for social networks, search engines and

---

222. See A.V. LERNER, 'The Role of "Big Data" in Online Platform Competition', *SSRN Working Paper* August 2014, pp. 20-34, available at http://papers.ssrn.com/sol3/papers.cfm?abstract_id = 24 82780 and D.S. TUCKER AND H.B. WELLFORD, 'Big Mistakes Regarding Big Data', *The Antitrust Source* 2014, vol. 14, no. 2, (1), pp. 3, 4, 6 and 7.

223. For proponents of the view that data may constitute entry barriers, see Autorité de la concurrence and Bundeskartellamt, 'Competition Law and Data', 10 May 2016, pp. 25-27, available at http://www.autoritedelaconcurrence.fr/doc/reportcompetitionlawanddatafinal. pdf; PRELIMINARY OPINION OF THE EUROPEAN DATA PROTECTION SUPERVISOR, 'Privacy and competitiveness in the age of big data: The interplay between data protection, competition law and consumer protection in the Digital Economy', March 2014, paras 66-68; H.A. SHELANSKI, 'Information, Innovation, and Competition Policy for the Internet', *University of Pennsylvania Law Review* 2013, vol. 161, no. 6, (1663), p. 1679; N. NEWMAN, 'Search, Antitrust, and the Economics of the Control of User Data', *Yale Journal on Regulation* 2014, vol. 31, no. 2, (401), p. 401; D. GERADIN AND M. KUSCHEWSKY, 'Competition Law and Personal Data: Preliminary Thoughts on a Complex Issue', *SSRN Working Paper* February 2013, p. 2, availabe at http://papers.ssrn.com/sol3/papers.cfm?abstract_id = 2216088; L. KIMMEL AND J. KESTENBAUM, 'What's Up with WhatsApp? A Transatlantic View on Privacy and Merger Enforcement in Digital Markets', *Antitrust Magazine* 2014, vol. 29, no. 1, (48), p. 52; A.P. GRUNES AND M.E. STUCKE, 'No Mistake About It: The Important Role of Antitrust in the Era of Big Data', *The Antitrust Source* 2015, vol. 14, no. 4, (1), pp. 7-8.

224. Under Facebook's Terms of Services on Safety, Facebook prohibits automatic collection of user content: 'You will not collect users' content or information, or otherwise access Facebook, using automated means (such as harvesting bots, robots, spiders, or scrapers) without our prior permission', available at https://www.facebook.com/legal/terms.

225. C.S. YOO, 'When Antitrust Met Facebook', *George Mason Law Review* 2012, vol. 19, no. 5, (1147), pp. 1154-1155.

e-commerce platforms is therefore dependent on whether they present a lasting competitive advantage for the incumbent providers.

Irrespective of the existence of inherent barriers to entry that are intrinsic to the nature of the market in which providers of online platforms operate, firms may deliberately raise entry barriers by creating switching costs for users and advertisers, or by preventing competitors from gathering user data through exclusivity contracts with users and advertisers. According to the competition concerns identified by the European Commission in its *Google* investigation, Google allegedly engaged in both types of behaviour vis-à-vis advertisers by restricting the portability of advertising campaigns and by de facto obliging third-party websites to obtain all or most of their online search advertisements from Google.[226]

2.5 CONCLUSION

Search engines and social networks employ a similar business model. Providers of both types of online platforms offer users access to their services free of charge and fund their platforms by way of advertising. E-commerce platforms still mainly rely on revenues from transaction fees although advertising is becoming an increasing source of income. While the three types of platforms have different functionalities, there is a trend towards convergence. For example, Bing has integrated social networking features in its search results and Facebook has introduced a search functionality in its social network. Furthermore, e-commerce platforms may also be considered vertical search engines on the ground that buyers use services like Amazon Marketplace and eBay as places to look for products they are interested in purchasing.

As intermediaries between users and advertisers, online platforms can be regarded as multi-sided platforms. However, the advertising-based media industry is a peculiar type of multi-sided business considering that users may not always positively value the presence of advertisers on the other side of the market. Nevertheless, under prevailing economic theory advertising-based media qualify as multi-sided businesses because advertisers benefit from the interaction with users. On e-commerce platforms, users are more likely to appreciate advertising as they are looking to purchase relevant products and services. While users on search engines and social networks may not be interested in the display of advertisements, the fact that advertisers finance the respective platforms may give rise to a positive multi-sided network effect exerted by advertisers on users.

With regard to the network economy characteristics of online platforms, there is discussion about the extent to which one-sided network effects and switching costs are present in search engines, social networks and e-commerce platforms. The issue that is of importance is whether these features give rise to entry barriers in the specific

---

226. Speech former Competition Commissioner Almunia, 'Statement of Commissioner Almunia on the Google antitrust investigation', Press room Brussels, 21 May 2012, SPEECH/12/372, available at http://europa.eu/rapid/press-release_SPEECH-12-372_en.htm.

circumstances of a case. The informational nature distinguishes the potential entry barriers in online platforms from the ones found in previous competition cases which had a technological character.

The multi-sided nature and the presence of network economy features may affect the way competition assessments have to be conducted on online platforms. By forming part of a rapidly changing environment, innovation also plays an important role in the markets in which search engines, social networks and e-commerce platforms operate. This raises questions about the relationship between competition and innovation in dynamic markets including the internet.

CHAPTER 3

Evaluating the Link Between Competition and Innovation

3.1 INTRODUCTION

While price is still the predominant parameter for competition, in rapidly developing sectors such as the online intermediary industry competition is typically taking place on the basis of the level of innovation. Because users get access to most internet services including search engines, social networks and e-commerce platforms free of charge, they choose their provider based on aspects other than price such as quality and innovation.[227] For these reasons, it is particularly important in this sector to consider to what extent competition law interventions affect the level of innovation by changing market conditions.

Although it is widely accepted that competition creates incentives for undertakings to continue to attract customers by keeping prices low, the relationship between competition and innovation is not that uncontroversial. In the twentieth century, two divergent views emerged in the economic literature on the impact of market structure on innovation incentives. While Schumpeter argued that monopolies favour innovation, Arrow expressed the opposing view that competition is good for innovation. More recently, Aghion established a non-linear model for measuring innovation incentives according to which an increase in the level of competition at a certain level starts to diminish innovation.

---

227. Case No COMP/M.6281 – *Microsoft/Skype*, 7 October 2011, paras 81-84. This was also considered by the Commission in its decision concerning the acquisition of Yahoo's search business by Microsoft. See Case No COMP/M.5727 – *Microsoft/Yahoo! Search Business*, 18 February 2010, par. 119.

Undertakings in the online intermediary sector often do not compete by lowering their prices but by introducing products and services that create a new market. In this context, two types of innovation and competition are distinguished in economic and business literature.

Section 3.2 discusses how the level of competition and innovation can be measured and how accurate currently used indicators of these phenomena are. This is followed by an analysis of economic theory and empirical studies on the causal relationship between market structure and innovation in section 3.3. In section 3.4, different forms of innovation and competition are described as well as their significance in dynamic sectors including the online intermediary industry.

3.2 MEASURING COMPETITION AND INNOVATION

Before the relationship between competition and innovation can be discussed, attention has to be paid to the way both concepts are measured. In economic and empirical research, proxies are used to quantify competition and innovation. The existence of a strong and reliable link between the proxy and the concept that is measured is vital.[228]

3.2.1 Indicators of Competition

Several proxies can be used to measure the level of competition in a market. Indicators that are often relied upon include market shares, firm size, market concentration and the price-cost margin. Market concentration is measured by the so-called Herfindahl-Hirschman Index which is calculated by squaring the market share of each firm in the market and then summing the resulting numbers. The outcome of the calculation ranges from 0 to 1 (or from 0 to 10,000 if whole percentages are used), moving from a large number of equally sized firms to a monopolist. The Herfindahl-Hirschman Index increases both as the number of undertakings in the market drops and as the difference in size between those firms grows.[229]

Price-cost margin is also referred to as the Lerner Index and is typically used as an indicator of market power. The price-cost margin is the difference between price and marginal cost as a function of price ($[P-MC]/P$) and ranges from 0 to 1 with higher numbers implying greater market power. The larger the difference between price and marginal cost, the greater the degree of market power. Under the Lerner Index, the price in a perfectly competitive market equals marginal cost resulting in no market power and a price-cost margin of 0.[230] As opposed to the price-cost margin, market shares and market concentration rely more directly on a particular definition of the

---

228. J.B. Baker, 'Beyond Schumpeter vs. Arrow: How Antitrust Fosters Innovation', *Antitrust Law Journal* 2007, vol. 74, no. 3, (575), pp. 583-584.
229. See Guidelines on the assessment of horizontal mergers under the Council Regulation on the control of concentrations between undertakings (EU Horizontal Merger Guidelines) [2004] OJ C31/5, paras 16 and 19-21 for the application of the Herfindahl-Hirschman Index in merger review.
230. A.P. Lerner, 'The Concept of Monopoly and the Measurement of Monopoly Power', *Review of Economic Studies* June 1934, vol. 1, no. 3, (157).

geographic and product market.[231] The main problem with the application of the price-cost margin is that it may be hard to find information about the costs of firms in the market. In addition, the theoretical foundations of the price-cost margin as a competition measure are not robust in the sense that models can be identified where more intense competition leads to a higher instead of a lower price-cost margin.[232]

The Boone indicator aims to address this issue by establishing a relationship between relative profit differences and efficiency. The idea underlying the Boone indicator is that competition enhances the performance of efficient firms and impairs the performance of inefficient firms which is reflected in their respective profits. In other words, more intense competition leads to a reallocation of output to more efficient firms which changes the relationships between the profitability of market players.[233]

The discussed proxies may give an indication of the level of competition in the market. Nevertheless, it has to be noted that markets in which only a couple of firms are active can be highly competitive whereas competition can be weak in markets with a lot of players.[234]

3.2.2 Indicators of Innovation

R&D investment and patent activity are most commonly used as indicators of innovation. It is difficult to design a single indicator capturing all the different aspects that have an impact on innovation. Patent activity signals technological progress, but not all patents are brought to the market and lead to new products. Similarly, the amount of R&D investment may indicate the importance that market players attach to innovation, but it does not capture the effects or the success rate of the innovation activities in the economy.[235] R&D expenditure is an input to innovation that does not directly lead to innovative output. In other words, higher investment in R&D does not automatically

---

231. See P. AGHION, N. BLOOM, R. BLUNDELL, ET AL., 'Competition and Innovation: An Inverted-U Relationship', *Quarterly Journal of Economics* 2005, vol. 120, no. 2, (701), pp. 704-705.

232. J. BOONE, 'A New Way to Measure Competition', *The Economic Journal* 2008, vol. 118, no. 531, (1245), p. 1245.

233. J. BOONE, 'A New Way to Measure Competition', *The Economic Journal* 2008, vol. 118, no. 531, (1245).

234. In addition, these proxies assume the existence of a market with homogenous products. In order to take product differentiation into account, Farrell & Shapiro developed a tool referred to as 'upward pricing pressure' (UPP) to assess concerns in merger cases about unilateral price effects in markets for differentiated products (J. FARRELL AND C. SHAPIRO, 'Antitrust Evaluation of Horizontal Mergers: An Economic Alternative to Market Definition', *The B.E. Journal of Theoretical Economics: Policies and Perspectives* 2010, vol. 10, no. 1, (1)). Under their leadership, UPP was incorporated into the 2010 Horizontal Merger Guidelines (United States Department of Justice and Federal Trade Commission, 'Horizontal Merger Guidelines', 19 August 2010, par. 6.1).

235. R.J. GILBERT, 'Competition and Innovation' in W.D. COLLINS (ed.), *Issues in Competition Law and Policy*, Volume I, Chapter 24, American Bar Association Antitrust Section, 2008, (577), p. 17, available at http://eml.berkeley.edu/ ~ gilbert/wp/competition_and_innovation.pdf.

translate into more innovation output.[236] Often, a combination of several proxies is used in economic studies to make the analysis more accurate. In their model that is discussed below, Aghion et al. measured innovation by looking at the average number of patents acquired by firms in the industry weighed by the number of times each patent has been cited by another patent.[237] Nevertheless, the fact remains that such indicators rather point to inventive activity which may or may not translate into innovation.

The European Commission measures the innovation performance of the different Member States of the European Union in order to assess the strength and weaknesses of each country's research and innovation system.[238] The method that the Commission uses in its yearly Innovation Union Scoreboard shows the complexity of measuring innovation. The measurement framework, referred to as the Summary Innovation Index, consists of three types of main indicators which are each composed of several so-called innovation dimensions which in their turn include a total of twenty-five different factors. For the main indicators a distinction is made between 'enablers' that constitute the basic building blocks for innovation to take place (including human resources, open, excellent and attractive research systems as well as finance and support), 'firm activities' which capture the innovation efforts at the level of the firm (including firm investments, linkages and entrepreneurship as well as intellectual assets) and 'outputs' which cover the effects of the innovation activities of firms on the economy as a whole (including innovators and economic effects such as employment).[239]

In September 2013, the Commission introduced a new indicator that focuses solely on innovation output and that complements the Innovation Union Scoreboard and the Summary Innovation Index. This new indicator consists of four components that are chosen for their policy relevance. The first component is technological innovation as measured by patents. Patents are a crucial form of output of R&D investment and therefore show the ability of an economy to transfer knowledge into technology. Secondly, regard is had to the employment in knowledge-intensive activities as a percentage of total employment. This component captures the structural orientation of a country towards knowledge-intensive activities. The third component is the competitiveness of knowledge-intensive goods and services and is measured by aggregating '*in equal weights the contribution of the trade balance of high-tech and*

---

236. R. GILBERT, 'Looking for Mr. Schumpeter. Where Are We in the Competition-Innovation Debate?' in A.B. JAFFE, J. LERNER AND S. STERN (eds.), *Innovation Policy and the Economy*, The MIT Press, 2006, (159), p. 191.
237. P. AGHION, N. BLOOM, R. BLUNDELL, ET AL., 'Competition and Innovation: An Inverted-U Relationship', *Quarterly Journal of Economics* 2005, vol. 120, no. 2, (701), pp. 703-704.
238. Such activities can be traced back to the work of Freeman and Lundvall relating to what later has been referred to as 'National Innovation Systems'. See C. FREEMAN, *Technology and Economic Performance: Lessons from Japan*, London, Pinter, 1987; B.-Å. LUNDVALL (ed.), *National Innovation Systems: Towards a Theory of Innovation and Interactive Learning*, London, Pinter, 1992; and C. FREEMAN, 'The "National System of Innovation" in Historical Perspective', *Cambridge Journal of Economics 1995, 19, 5-24* 1995, vol. 19, no. 1, (5).
239. See EUROPEAN COMMISSION, 'Innovation Union Scoreboard 2015', pp. 7-8, available at http://ec .europa.eu/growth/industry/innovation/facts-figures/scoreboards/files/ius-2015_en.pdf.

medium-tech products to the total trade balance, and knowledge-intensive services as a share of the total services exports'. This factor reflects the ability of the economy to export innovative products and to participate in global trade. The last component is formed by the employment in fast-growing firms of innovative sectors. According to studies, growth depends to a large extent upon fast-growing firms that generate a disproportionally share of jobs and contribute to increased innovation investments during economic recessions.[240] The new indicator thus combines several proxies that relate to the output of innovation activities.

3.2.3 Reliability of the Indicators

Although there seems to be a relatively well-developed method for calculating the total rate of innovation in a country, it continues to be very hard to find reliable proxies for measuring the level of innovation in a particular industry or market. According to Gilbert, a complete analysis of the factors that influence innovation activity requires *'estimates of the expected values of discoveries and data on the R&D activities of all potential innovators'*. Since innovations often originate from unexpected sources such as firms in unrelated industries and even from individual inventions, it is very hard to detect all the potential sources of innovation.[241]

With regard to indicators for competition, Gilbert argues that *'competition depends on the levels and industry distribution of firm costs, qualities, and brand recognition, on barriers to entry, on characteristics of demand, and on whatever animal spirits might motivate managers'*.[242] Proxies such as market shares, market concentration and price-cost margin may therefore not be able to capture all the different factors that influence the level of competition in a market. While economic scholarship is still in search for appropriate indicators that unambiguously quantify the rate of competition and innovation in an industry, a combination of several proxies for the measurement of each phenomenon seems to be the best approach for now.

3.3 ECONOMIC THEORY AND EMPIRICAL EVIDENCE ON THE RELATIONSHIP BETWEEN COMPETITION AND INNOVATION

Underlying the discussion in economics about the significance of market structure for innovation is the presumption that more innovation is beneficial for society. In the European Union, the alleged importance of innovation for economic growth is apparent from the role that innovation plays in the Europe 2020 strategy *'for smart,*

---

240. Communication from the Commission to the European Parliament, the Council, the European Economic and Social Committee and the Committee of the Regions. Measuring innovation output in Europe: towards a new indicator, COM(2013) 624 final, 13 September 2013, pp. 3-4.
241. R. GILBERT, 'Looking for Mr. Schumpeter. Where Are We in the Competition-Innovation Debate?' in A.B. JAFFE, J. LERNER AND S. STERN (eds.), *Innovation Policy and the Economy*, The MIT Press, 2006, (159), p. 191.
242. R. GILBERT, 'Looking for Mr. Schumpeter. Where Are We in the Competition-Innovation Debate?' in A.B. JAFFE, J. LERNER AND S. STERN (eds.), *Innovation Policy and the Economy*, The MIT Press, 2006, (159), p. 192.

sustainable and inclusive growth.[243] One of the flagship initiatives of this strategy is the so-called Innovation Union which aims at improving *'framework conditions and access to finance for research and innovation so as to ensure that innovative ideas can be turned into products and services that create growth and jobs'*.[244] Innovation is seen as one of the main drivers of economic growth in the European Union. Economic research confirms that R&D investment leads to productivity growth. Studies also show that the benefits of innovation to society are higher than the benefits to the firms that invest in R&D.[245] Innovation concerns are high on the agenda of competition authorities,[246] although the relationship between competition and innovation is not clear-cut.

3.3.1 Schumpeter

The debate in the economic literature about the relationship between market structure and innovation dates back to the view attributed to Joseph Schumpeter that monopolies benefit innovation and that perfect competition is not necessarily the best market structure for stimulating R&D investment.[247] Schumpeter argued that monopolistic prices are not always higher and monopoly outputs smaller than competitive prices and outputs, because certain advantages only occur on the monopoly level. In his opinion, superior methods are available to the monopolist *'because monopolization may increase the sphere of influence of the better, and decrease the sphere of influence of the inferior, brains, or because the monopoly enjoys a disproportionately higher financial standing'*.[248] In other words, monopolies have more funding for R&D investment and have greater incentives to innovate, since they have a better prospect of reaping the benefits from inventions. In case several competitors implement a new

---

243. Communication from the Commission. EUROPE 2020. A strategy for smart, sustainable and inclusive growth, COM(2010) 2020, 3 March 2010.

244. Communication from the Commission to the European Parliament, the Council, the European Economic and Social Committee and the Committee of the Regions. Europe 2020 Flagship Initiative. Innovation Union, COM(2010) 546 final, 6 October 2010, p. 6.

245. See Z. GRILICHES, 'The Search for R&D Spillovers', *Scandinavian Journal of Economics* 1992, vol. 94 Supplement, (S29); T.F. BRESNAHAN, 'The Mechanisms of Information Technology's Contribution to Economic Growth' in J.-P. TOUFFUT (ed.), *Institutions, Innovation and Growth. Selected Economic Papers*, Edward Elgar Publishing, 2003, (116).

246. See for instance, speech former Competition Commissioner Almunia, 'Intellectual property and competition policy', IP Summit 2013 Paris, 9 December 2013, SPEECH/13/1042, available at http://europa.eu/rapid/press-release_SPEECH-13-1042_en.htm: *'both competition policy and the intellectual-property protection system do contribute to create the right framework for innovators'*; and speech former Competition Commissioner Almunia, 'Competition, innovation and growth: an EU perspective on the challenges ahead', Third BRICS International Competition Conference New Delhi, 21 November 2013, SPEECH/13/958, available at http://europa. eu/rapid/press-release_SPEECH-13-958_en.htm: *'we want to protect competition on the merits, foster innovation, and keep markets open and fair'*.

247. A distinction is made between Mark I and Mark II when referring to the work of Schumpeter. The early view of innovation that Schumpeter advanced in 1911 in *The Theory of Economic Development* is referred to as 'Schumpeter Mark I' and the later view proposed by Schumpeter in 1942 in *Capitalism, Socialism and Democracy* that is discussed here is referred to as 'Schumpeter Mark II'.

248. J.A. SCHUMPETER, *Capitalism, Socialism and Democracy*, Routledge, 1942 (version published in 2003), pp. 100-101.

technology, the benefits resulting from the invention have to be shared which may reduce each firm's future incentives to innovate.

In addition, Schumpeter stated that a monopoly can only be retained '*by alertness and energy*' because of the pressure of potential entry of competitors introducing improved products in the market. Due to this pressure, the monopolist would continue to innovate and the price would move towards or even beyond the competitive price.[249] Schumpeter used the Aluminum Company of America as an example of a monopoly that kept innovating to retain its position. From 1890 to 1929, the price of its product, corrected for inflation, fell to 8.8%, while its output increased from 30 metric tons to 103,400. In Schumpeter's view, competing firms would have been about equally successful.[250]

Schumpeter is also well known for characterising capitalism as an evolutionary process or a '*perennial gale of creative destruction*' in which old technologies are replaced by new ones. He derived the term creative destruction from the work of Karl Marx and presented it as an economic theory on innovation. In Schumpeter's view, creative destruction is a process that '*incessantly revolutionizes the economic structure from within, incessantly destroying the old one, incessantly creating a new one*'.[251] Schumpeter did not regard perfect competition, under which firms produce homogeneous goods and do not have any influence on the price, as the most important type of competition. He argued that what counts is '*competition from the new commodity, the new technology, the new source of supply, the new type of organization*'. This type of competition leading to creative destruction '*commands a decisive cost or quality advantage and [...] strikes not at the margins of the profits and the outputs of the existing firms but at their foundations and at their very lives*'. It forms an ever-present threat that '*disciplines before it attacks*' and that is as effective '*as a bombardment in comparison with forcing a door*'.[252]

3.3.2 Arrow

In 1962, Kenneth Arrow put forward a different vision entailing that competition rather than monopoly promotes innovation. He explained that the incentive to innovate has to be assessed by comparing the potential profits from an invention with the costs. The economic model that Arrow established showed that incentives to innovate are less in monopolistic than in competitive markets, because the monopolist already benefits from profits without investing in R&D. Unlike an innovating competitor, a monopolist that innovates bears the cost of foregoing the monopoly profits it can continue to earn when it decides not to invest in R&D. According to Arrow, a firm in a competitive

---

249. J.A. SCHUMPETER, *Capitalism, Socialism and Democracy*, Routledge, 1942 (version published in 2003), pp. 101-102.
250. J.A. SCHUMPETER, *Capitalism, Socialism and Democracy*, Routledge, 1942 (version published in 2003), footnote 20 on pp. 101-102.
251. J.A. SCHUMPETER, *Capitalism, Socialism and Democracy*, Routledge, 1942 (version published in 2003), pp. 82-83.
252. J.A. SCHUMPETER, *Capitalism, Socialism and Democracy*, Routledge, 1942 (version published in 2003), pp. 84-85.

market has more incentives to innovate, because it has more to gain from innovation. Instead, the monopolist jeopardises its established profit flow by innovating. As Steve Jobs, co-founder and former CEO of Apple, once said in an interview: *'what's the point of focusing on making the product even better when the only company you can take business away from is yourself?'*[253]

In Arrow's view, the only valid ground for arguing that a monopolistic market structure creates superior incentives to innovate is that a monopolist may be better able to capture the benefits of innovation due to its stable position on the market. However, the incentives to innovate resulting from the better appropriability opportunities have to be offset against the monopolist's disincentive to innovate resulting from giving up the monopoly profits that it can continue to earn without innovating. Arrow argued that on balance, the competitive incentive to innovate always exceeds the monopolist's incentive.[254] The limitation on the monopolist's incentive to innovate is also referred to as the 'replacement effect', since the monopolist accelerates its own replacement instead of developing a new business by innovating.[255] The replacement effect will be strongest when the new technology completely substitutes the old one and when the monopolist does not expect a new entrant coming to the market.[256]

Arrow's replacement effect may be outweighed by the incentive of a monopolist to invest in R&D in order to pre-empt the entry of potential competitors. The incentive of the monopolist to pre-empt is the profit that it would lose if a rival successfully enters the market.[257] If the incentive of the monopolist to pre-empt is stronger than the replacement effect, Arrow's vision that competition leads to more innovation than monopoly does not hold.[258] However, uncertainty about the probability of success of rivals to enter the market may undermine the pre-emption incentive of a monopolist.[259] The monopolist has no incentive to pre-empt if there is a large probability that competitors will not be able to gain any market share.[260]

---

253. As quoted by R. GILBERT, 'Looking for Mr. Schumpeter. Where Are We in the Competition-Innovation Debate?' in A.B. JAFFE, J. LERNER AND S. STERN (eds.), *Innovation Policy and the Economy*, The MIT Press, 2006, (159), p. 179 and footnote 19.
254. K.J. ARROW, 'Economic Welfare and the Allocation of Resources for Invention' in H.M. GROVES (ed.), *The Rate and Direction of Inventive Activity: Economic and Social Factors*, National Bureau of Economic Research, 1962, (609), pp. 619-622.
255. J. TIROLE, *The Theory of Industrial Organization*, MIT Press, 1988, p. 392.
256. J.B. BAKER, 'Beyond Schumpeter vs. Arrow: How Antitrust Fosters Innovation', *Antitrust Law Journal* 2007, vol. 74, no. 3, (575), p. 579.
257. R.J. GILBERT, 'Competition and Innovation' in W.D. COLLINS (ed.), *Issues in Competition Law and Policy*, Volume I, Chapter 24, American Bar Association Antitrust Section, 2008, (577), p. 14, available at http://eml.berkeley.edu/~gilbert/wp/competition_and_innovation.pdf.
258. See R.J. GILBERT AND D.M.G. NEWBERY, 'Preemptive Patenting and the Persistence of Monopoly', *American Economic Review* June 1982, vol. 72, no. 3, (514).
259. See J.F. REINGANUM, 'Uncertain Innovation and the Persistence of Monopoly', *American Economic Review* September 1983, vol. 73, no. 4, (741).
260. R.J. GILBERT, 'Competition and Innovation' in W.D. COLLINS (ed.), *Issues in Competition Law and Policy*, Volume I, Chapter 24, American Bar Association Antitrust Section, 2008, (577), p. 15, available at http://eml.berkeley.edu/~gilbert/wp/competition_and_innovation.pdf.

3.3.3   Aghion

Both Schumpeter and Arrow assumed that there is a linear relationship between market structure and innovation implying that the two variables increase or decrease proportionally to each other. When this linear relationship is plotted in a graph, a straight line is visible. Following Scherer[261] and Levin et al.[262] who allowed nonlinearities in the relationship between competition and innovation and discovered the existence of an inverted-U shape, Aghion et al. developed an inverted-U model. According to this model, more competition initially leads to an increase in the level of innovation until the optimal point is reached beyond which additional competition has a chilling effect on innovation. Evidence for this theoretical model was found in empirical data. The data also provided support for the statement that the inverted-U relationship between competition and innovation becomes steeper, the smaller the technological distance between competitors in an industry.[263] Contrary to Schumpeter's model which assumes that innovation overturns existing market structures, Aghion et al. adopt a form of step-by-step innovation in which a technological laggard cannot leapfrog the existing leader in the industry, but must first catch up with the current leader before it can try to take technological leadership itself. In addition, Aghion et al. assume that each industry is characterised by duopoly instead of monopolistic competition.[264]

Aghion et al. draw attention to the 'escape-competition effect' that in their view occurs in 'neck-and-neck sectors' where firms operating at similar technological levels are encouraged to innovate in order to acquire a lead over their rival. In these industries, more competition may reduce the profits of a firm in case it decides not to innovate (pre-innovation rents) by more than it reduces the profits if the firm decides to invest in innovation (post-innovation rents). In sectors where innovations are introduced by laggard firms which are always one step behind the leader in an industry, the rate of innovation will decrease as more competition evolves in the view of Aghion et al. Additional competition in these sectors will mainly affect the post-innovation rents of the laggard firm which first has to catch up with the leader in its sector and go through the less profitable neck-and-neck stage before it can become a leader itself. Aghion et al. refer to this phenomenon as the 'Schumpeterian effect'.[265]

In a later article, Aghion et al. have specifically examined the effect of the threat of entry on the innovation incentives of an incumbent firm. In their empirical model,

261. F.M. SCHERER, 'Market Structure and the Employment of Scientists and Engineers', *The American Economic Review* June 1967, vol. 57, no. 3, (524).
262. R.C. LEVIN, W.M. COHEN AND D.C. MOWERY, 'R&D Appropriability, Opportunity, and Market Structure: New Evidence on Some Schumpeterian Hypotheses', *The American Economic Review* May 1985, vol. 75, no. 2, (20).
263. P. AGHION, N. BLOOM, R. BLUNDELL, ET AL., 'Competition and Innovation: An Inverted-U Relationship', *Quarterly Journal of Economics* 2005, vol. 120, no. 2, (701), pp. 701-728.
264. P. AGHION, C. HARRIS, P. HOWITT, ET AL., 'Competition, Imitation and Growth with Step-by-Step Innovation', *Review of Economic Studies* 2001, vol. 68, no. 3, (467), pp. 468-469.
265. P. AGHION, N. BLOOM, R. BLUNDELL, ET AL., 'Competition and Innovation: An Inverted-U Relationship', *Quarterly Journal of Economics* 2005, vol. 120, no. 2, (701), pp. 701-728.

they found that depending on the distance from the 'technological frontier', the threat of entry either spurs or discourages innovation. In sectors close to the frontier, the threat of entry encourages innovation because the incumbents know *'that they can escape and survive entry by innovating successfully, and so they react with more intensive innovation activities aimed at escaping the threat'*. In so-called laggard industries that are further behind the technological frontier, the threat of entry discourages innovation since *'incumbents have no hope to win against an entrant'*.[266] This would suggest that dynamic markets, which are usually close to the technological frontier, are likely to experience an increase in the level of innovation as a result of a threat of entry.[267]

3.3.4 Appraisal

Although the economic literature discussed above has led to opposing views which makes it difficult to reach strong conclusions on the relationship between market structure and innovation, it is possible to make some general remarks. Gilbert identifies a few conditions under which the economic theory discussed above supports the proposition that competition, instead of monopoly, is more likely to benefit innovation. First, if intense competition in the old product exists, the pre-innovation profit of a firm will be lower which in turn increases its incentive to innovate, since it does not have a high and stable profit flow that it will forego by innovating (the escape-competition effect). Secondly, if the innovation makes the old technology obsolete, the monopolist's gain from innovation does not exceed the gain to a new competitor.[268] The innovation is such a major improvement that a new market is established on which the innovator will be a monopolist as the only provider of the new technology.[269] The third factor that is of importance in Gilbert's view is the extent to which the monopolist can price discriminate among consumers after innovating. It is more attractive for a monopolist to work on a new technology if it will be able to price discriminate by offering both its old and new product. However, if price discrimination is not likely, Arrow's replacement effect suggests that a competitive market structure rather than a monopoly benefits innovation. Lastly, if market conditions make pre-emption unlikely

---

266. P. Aghion, R. Blundell, R. Griffith, et al., 'The Effects of Entry on Incumbent Innovation and Productivity', *The Review of Economics and Statistics* February 2009, vol. 91, no. 1, (20), p. 20.
267. J. Galloway, 'Driving Innovation: A Case for Targeted Competition Policy in Dynamic Markets', *World Competition* 2011, vol. 34, no. 1, (73), p. 79.
268. This is presupposing that the monopolist cannot innovate at a lower cost than the new competitor.
269. R. Gilbert, 'Looking for Mr. Schumpeter. Where Are We in the Competition-Innovation Debate?' in A.B. Jaffe, J. Lerner and S. Stern (eds.), *Innovation Policy and the Economy*, The MIT Press, 2006, (159), pp. 168-169 and R.J. Gilbert, 'Competition and Innovation' in W.D. Collins (ed.), *Issues in Competition Law and Policy*, Volume I, Chapter 24, American Bar Association Antitrust Section, 2008, (577), pp. 22-23, available at http://eml.berkeley.edu/ ~gilbert/wp/competition_and_innovation.pdf.

for example due to the existence of alternative R&D paths that the incumbent cannot foreclose, a monopolist will not have an incentive to innovate in order to pre-empt the market entry of rivals.[270]

Similarly, Baker has formulated four principles that relate the level of innovation in an industry to the extent to which competition takes place in the market. The first principle states that competition in innovation that is defined as '*competition among firms seeking to develop the same new product or process*' encourages innovation. According to this principle, firms in a race to innovate try harder to win. The second principle entails that '*competition among rivals producing an existing product encourages those firms to find ways to lower costs, improve quality, or develop better products*'. This is a translation of the finding of Aghion et al. that investment in innovation may allow firms to escape competition. However, if firms do not expect to escape competition by innovating but rather believe to be subject to more competition, they have less incentive to innovate. This forms the third principle. The fourth principle involves the incentive of a firm to pre-empt the entry of rivals. According to this principle, '*a firm will have an extra incentive to innovate if in doing so it can discourage potential rivals from investing in R&D*'. In this situation, the firm not only benefits from its investments by introducing new or better products, but also by discouraging potential rivals from innovating.[271]

The existence of incentives to innovate at the side of market players is vital for innovation to take place. An innovation incentive can be defined as '*the difference in profit that a firm can earn if it invests in R&D compared to what it would earn if it did not invest*'.[272] Since the scope of an innovation incentive depends on many factors that sometimes have opposing effects, it is hard to predict how an incentive will be affected by a certain development or intervention, for example on the basis of competition law, in the market. Against the background of the economic theory, Gilbert has identified four factors that influence the existence of innovation incentives: (1) the profit that can be gained from innovation in the form of selling a new product; (2) the existing profit that is eliminated by innovating (Arrow's replacement effect); (3) the reduction of competition that occurs when a firm is able to differentiate its products or lower its production costs by innovating (Aghion's escape-the-competition effect); and (4) the possibility to pre-empt competition by deterring rivals from entering the market. As the incentive to pre-empt can offset Arrow's replacement effect, the second and the fourth factors point in opposite directions. The exact scope of the innovation incentive depends on the extent to which each of the four factors are present in the specific

---

270. R.J. GILBERT, 'Competition and Innovation' in W.D. COLLINS (ed.), *Issues in Competition Law and Policy*, Volume I, Chapter 24, American Bar Association Antitrust Section, 2008, (577), p. 23, available at http://eml.berkeley.edu/~gilbert/wp/competition_and_innovation.pdf.
271. J.B. BAKER, 'Beyond Schumpeter vs. Arrow: How Antitrust Fosters Innovation', *Antitrust Law Journal* 2007, vol. 74, no. 3, (575), pp. 579-581.
272. R. GILBERT, 'Looking for Mr. Schumpeter. Where Are We in the Competition-Innovation Debate?' in A.B. JAFFE, J. LERNER AND S. STERN (eds.), *Innovation Policy and the Economy*, The MIT Press, 2006, (159), p. 162.

technological and market conditions.[273] For instance, robust intellectual property protection may increase the strength of the first factor, since an innovator will be better able to capture the benefits from introducing new products.[274]

The economic theories put forward by Schumpeter, Arrow and others have been tested in numerous empirical studies.[275] Although early studies confirmed the Schumpeterian hypothesis that the level of innovation tends to be larger in concentrated industries, in later and more refined statistical analyses this observation did not hold true.[276] Several problems can be identified from which the early empirical studies suffered such as failure to control for other factors that may influence innovation incentives and failure to take into account the differences in technological opportunities and appropriability across industries.[277] For reaching a reliable conclusion on the link between competition and innovation, the effect of competition has to be isolated. In some industries, technological possibilities may be greater or firms may have better guarantees that they are protected from competition after innovating because of, for example, broad and strong intellectual property rights.[278] Although later studies including the inverted-U model of Aghion et al. have tried to address these problems, it remains difficult to control for differences in industry characteristics and for factors other than competition that may affect innovation.[279] According to Gilbert, an ideal way to test the effect of competition on innovation *would be a natural experiment in which external and unforeseen events cause a discrete change in the extent of competition in an industry with no other consequences for other determinants of innovation, such as technological opportunity or appropriability*.[280] However, in his view none of the available studies in the literature entirely isolate the influence of factors other than

---

273. R.J. GILBERT, 'Competition and Innovation' in W.D. COLLINS (ed.), *Issues in Competition Law and Policy*, Volume I, Chapter 24, American Bar Association Antitrust Section, 2008, (577), pp. 8-9, available at http://eml.berkeley.edu/~gilbert/wp/competition_and_innovation.pdf.

274. Gilbert also discusses the significance of distinctions between product and process innovations for the relationship between competition and innovation. See R. GILBERT, 'Looking for Mr. Schumpeter. Where Are We in the Competition-Innovation Debate?' in A.B. JAFFE, J. LERNER AND S. STERN (eds.), *Innovation Policy and the Economy*, The MIT Press, 2006, (159), pp. 159-215.

275. An overview of the empirical studies that test the relationship between competition and innovation can be found in R. GILBERT, 'Looking for Mr. Schumpeter. Where Are We in the Competition-Innovation Debate?' in A.B. JAFFE, J. LERNER AND S. STERN (eds.), *Innovation Policy and the Economy*, The MIT Press, 2006, (159), pp. 188-189.

276. R. GILBERT, 'Looking for Mr. Schumpeter. Where Are We in the Competition-Innovation Debate?' in A.B. JAFFE, J. LERNER AND S. STERN (eds.), *Innovation Policy and the Economy*, The MIT Press, 2006, (159), p. 190.

277. See R. GILBERT, 'Looking for Mr. Schumpeter. Where Are We in the Competition-Innovation Debate?' in A.B. JAFFE, J. LERNER AND S. STERN (eds.), *Innovation Policy and the Economy*, The MIT Press, 2006, (159), pp. 191-200.

278. J.B. BAKER, 'Beyond Schumpeter vs. Arrow: How Antitrust Fosters Innovation', *Antitrust Law Journal* 2007, vol. 74, no. 3, (575), p. 584.

279. See J.B. BAKER, 'Beyond Schumpeter vs. Arrow: How Antitrust Fosters Innovation', *Antitrust Law Journal* 2007, vol. 74, no. 3, (575), pp. 584-585.

280. R. GILBERT, 'Looking for Mr. Schumpeter. Where Are We in the Competition-Innovation Debate?' in A.B. JAFFE, J. LERNER AND S. STERN (eds.), *Innovation Policy and the Economy*, The MIT Press, 2006, (159), pp. 197-199.

changes in competition.[281] The empirical literature remains ambiguous and therefore it is difficult to make strong conclusions about the effect of competition on innovation.[282]

Even though the economic and empirical literature on the link between market structure and innovation is not conclusive, there have been attempts to find a middle ground between Schumpeter and Arrow as the two main schools of thought. Motta argued in this regard that an environment *'where there exists some competition but also high enough market power coming from the innovative activities, might be the most conducive to R&D output'*.[283]

Another attempt to reconcile the divergent views in economic theory has been made by Shapiro who maintained that the perspectives of Schumpeter and Arrow are *'fully compatible and mutually reinforcing'*.[284] In particular, he argued that there is no need for a universal theory of the relationship between competition and innovation as far as competition policy is concerned. To this end, he offered three principles on which Schumpeter and Arrow converge in his view: (1) the contestability principle according to which the prospect of gaining or protecting profitable sales by providing greater value to customers spurs innovation; (2) the appropriability principle which states that increased appropriability spurs innovation; and (3) the synergies principle according to which combining complementary assets enhances innovation capabilities and thus spurs innovation.[285] Following Shapiro, the views of Schumpeter and Arrow could be brought together by making a distinction between an ex post and ex ante perspective on innovation incentives. While Schumpeter focuses on the ex post perspective by arguing that firms will only invest if they can expect to appropriate the benefits resulting from their innovations, Arrow focuses on the ex ante perspective by asking himself what the best environment to promote innovation is and suggests that it is in a competitive environment that firms innovate more. Against this background, Director-General for Competition Laitenberger argued that *'as long as competition policy does not negatively affect equitable appropriability – for instance, as long as it respects IPRs – it will be compatible with both Arrow and Schumpeter'*.[286]

---

281. See for a discussion of several studies in this regard, R. GILBERT, 'Looking for Mr. Schumpeter. Where Are We in the Competition-Innovation Debate?' in A.B. JAFFE, J. LERNER AND S. STERN (eds.), *Innovation Policy and the Economy*, The MIT Press, 2006, (159), pp. 197-199 and R.J. GILBERT, 'Competition and Innovation' in W.D. COLLINS (ed.), *Issues in Competition Law and Policy*, Volume I, Chapter 24, American Bar Association Antitrust Section, 2008, (577), pp. 18-19, available at http://eml.berkeley.edu/ ~ gilbert/wp/competition_and_innovation.pdf.
282. R. GILBERT, 'Looking for Mr. Schumpeter. Where Are We in the Competition-Innovation Debate?' in A.B. JAFFE, J. LERNER AND S. STERN (eds.), *Innovation Policy and the Economy*, The MIT Press, 2006, (159), pp. 205-206.
283. M. MOTTA, *Competition Policy. Theory and Practice*, Cambridge University Press, 2004, p. 57.
284. C. SHAPIRO, 'Competition and Innovation: Did Arrow Hit the Bull's Eye?' in J. LERNER AND S. STERN (eds.), *The Rate and Direction of Inventive Activity Revisited*, NBER, 2012, (361), p. 363.
285. C. SHAPIRO, 'Competition and Innovation: Did Arrow Hit the Bull's Eye?' in J. LERNER AND S. STERN (eds.), *The Rate and Direction of Inventive Activity Revisited*, NBER, 2012, (361), pp. 364-365.
286. Speech Director-General for Competition Laitenberger, 'Competition and Innovation', CRA Annual Conference Brussels, 9 December 2015, p. 8, available at http://ec.europa.eu/competition/speeches/text/sp2015_04_en.pdf.

What can be concluded from the review of the economic theory and empirical research on the interaction between competition and innovation is that there is no universal theory of the relationship between competition and innovation and, consequently, no optimal market structure for stimulating innovation across the economy or even within a specific industry sector.[287] The economic and empirical literature does not provide support for a conclusion that monopoly is beneficial for innovation as Schumpeter put forward. At the same time, there is no support for the finding of Arrow that a competitive market structure favours innovation. Although a plea for a case-by-case assessment may not come as a surprise, it is still worth emphasising that no general conclusion can be made on the appropriate way to relate innovation to market structure.[288] The only general assumption that can be made for a sector is that there is room for competition enforcement in limited circumstances. Because of the absence of a clear link between market structure and innovation, the establishment of a competitive market in itself may not necessarily benefit the level of innovation in an industry. Nevertheless, it should also be accepted that competition policy can be essential for fostering innovation in certain circumstances.[289]

3.4 DIFFERENT TYPES OF INNOVATION

In new economy markets, innovation should not only be considered for assessing the effects of competition enforcement on society but also for determining the extent to and how market participants compete. In rapidly developing industries, which include online platforms, innovation has become the main parameter of competition. It is in these sectors that firms compete by creating products that overthrow or disrupt established market structures.

3.4.1 Disruptive versus Sustaining Innovation

The concept of disruptive innovation has been introduced in the business literature by Bower & Christensen who used it to explain why leading companies often fail to stay at the top of their industry when technologies or markets change.[290] They make a distinction between two types of technological innovations: sustaining and disruptive technologies.

---

287. Sidak & Teece even argue that the relationship between market structure and innovation is not a useful framing of the issue, since market structure does not seem to be a major determinant of innovation. J.G. SIDAK AND D.J. TEECE, 'Dynamic Competition in Antitrust Law', *Journal of Competition Law and Economics* 2009, vol. 5, no. 4, (581), p. 588.
288. See also M.L. KATZ AND H.A. SHELANSKI, '"Schumpeterian" Competition and Antitrust Policy in High-Tech Markets', *Competition* 2005, vol. 14, (47), pp. 18-20.
289. J. GALLOWAY, 'Driving Innovation: A Case for Targeted Competition Policy in Dynamic Markets', *World Competition* 2011, vol. 34, no. 1, (73), p. 80.
290. The findings put forward in J.L. BOWER AND C.M. CHRISTENSEN, 'Disruptive Technologies: Catching the Wave', *Harvard Business Review* 1995, vol. 73, no. 1 (January-February), (43) have been further developed by Christensen in C.M. CHRISTENSEN, *The Innovator's Dilemma. When New Technologies Cause Great Firms to Fail*, Harvard Business School Press, 1997.

Sustaining technologies present some level of improvement of an existing product but retain the aspects of the product that customers value. For example, in the disk-drive industry sustaining technologies concerned technical measures that increased the storage capacity of hard disks.[291] Sustaining technologies can be either of an incremental nature or have a breakthrough or radical character. Both types concern improvements of established products that do not affect existing markets. An incremental innovation is an improvement of a product in ways that customers expect, while a discontinuous or radical innovation is unexpected but nevertheless does not affect established markets.[292]

Disruptive technologies have features that differ from the ones that mainstream customers value and often perform worse in at least one dimension that is particularly important for these customers. An example that Bower & Christensen mention is the introduction of the transistor radio that had inferior sound quality but offered new features such as small size, light weight and portability that eventually led to the establishment of a new market for small and portable radios.[293] An important characteristic of a disruptive technology is that the aspects of the new product that customers do value improve at such a rapid rate that the new technology permeates established markets. Products based on disruptive technologies have features that initially only a few customers value. Often, they are cheaper, simpler and more convenient to use.[294] For example, the reason why PCs have replaced mainframe computers is not because of their superior technical performance but because PCs started to meet the needs of most customers. The same has happened with the introduction of tablets and smartphones relying on internet services and mobile applications that are gradually overtaking the market for PC hardware and software.

It is important to stress that the term 'sustaining technology' as used by Christensen does not merely refer to the concept of incremental innovation. Similarly, Christensen's notion of 'disruptive technology' cannot be equated with breakthrough or radical innovation. Both incremental and breakthrough or radical innovation fall within the category of sustaining technology as described by Christensen. The disruptiveness that Christensen refers to concerns a specific form of disruption that affects established markets. While the concepts of incremental and breakthrough or radical innovation refer to technological progress and qualify the innovation with respect to the prior state of the art (an improvement of a product versus an unexpected and significant technological change), the notions of sustaining and disruptive technologies rather refer to the relationship between the innovation and the value network around

291. J.L. Bower and C.M. Christensen, 'Disruptive Technologies: Catching the Wave', *Harvard Business Review* 1995, vol. 73, no. 1 (January-February), (43), p. 45.
292. C.M. Christensen, *The Innovator's Dilemma. When New Technologies Cause Great Firms to Fail*, Harvard Business School Press, 1997, p. 11. See C.M. Christensen and M.E. Raynor, *The Innovator's Solution: Creating and Sustaining Successful Growth*, Harvard Business School Press, 2003, footnote 3 on p. 34.
293. J.L. Bower and C.M. Christensen, 'Disruptive Technologies: Catching the Wave', *Harvard Business Review* 1995, vol. 73, no. 1 (January-February), (43), p. 45.
294. C.M. Christensen, *The Innovator's Dilemma. When New Technologies Cause Great Firms to Fail*, Harvard Business School Press, 1997, pp. 149-151.

it. In this perspective, a sustaining technology develops within the value network, whereas a disruptive technology comes from outside the value network and displaces it.[295]

Bower & Christensen show that established companies do invest in the development of new technologies, but only as long as they address the needs of their existing customers. Since disruptive technologies initially do not meet the demands of mainstream customers, leading companies do not invest in the development of these technologies. At the time of their introduction, disruptive technologies only appeal to small or emerging markets and therefore look financially unattractive for established companies due to the low profit margins that are not sufficient to compensate their high cost structures. Because established companies are inclined to stay close to their existing customers, they do not sufficiently track the emergence of disruptive technologies that may attack their position in the market in the future.

Furthermore, leading companies tend to innovate faster than the needs of their customers evolve so that many undertakings eventually provide products or services that are too sophisticated or expensive for most of their customers. By introducing sustaining technologies in the higher tiers of their markets, leading companies create space for disruptive technologies to emerge at the bottom of the market. At the point mainstream customers become interested in the disruptive technology, it is often already too late for the established companies to catch up. The new entrants will overtake the existing market and dominate the new market for the disruptive technology.[296]

In his later book that he co-authored with Raynor, Christensen changed the term 'disruptive technology' to 'disruptive innovation' arguing that it was not the technology itself that was disruptive but rather the use that companies made of it, or in other words the innovation that companies pursued by incorporating the new technology.[297] Christensen and Raynor also specified that there are actually two different types of disruption: low-end and new-market disruption.

Low-end disruption attacks customers that do not need the high level of performance offered by established firms in the market. New-market disruption does not target existing customers, but competes against non-consumption and has to attract new customers that have not owned or used the prior generation of products or services. An example of new-market disruption is the introduction of the PC that enabled individuals to operate a computer system themselves, rather than relying on

---

295. A. DE STREEL AND P. LAROUCHE, 'Disruptive Innovation and Competition Policy Enforcement', *Note for OECD Global Forum on Competition*, DAF/COMP/GF(2015)7, 20 October 2015, p. 2, available at http://www.oecd.org/officialdocuments/publicdisplaydocumentpdf/?cote = DAF /COMP/GF(2015)7&docLanguage = En.

296. J.L. BOWER AND C.M. CHRISTENSEN, 'Disruptive Technologies: Catching the Wave', *Harvard Business Review* 1995, vol. 73, no. 1 (January-February), (43), p. 47.

297. C.M. CHRISTENSEN AND M.E. RAYNOR, *The Innovator's Solution: Creating and Sustaining Successful Growth*, Harvard Business School Press, 2003, pp. 32-34 and footnote 3.

mainframe-systems that could only be used by skilled people. As the performance of the new-market disruption improves, at a certain point in time it will become good enough to attract customers.[298]

3.4.2   Appraisal

According to the business literature discussed above, every market cycle ends with the introduction of a disruptive innovation leading to the creation of a new market that renders the existing market obsolete. In the new market, sustaining innovations will be introduced in the higher ends of the market until a new disruptive innovation comes up at the bottom of the market that will once again overturn the existing market. Even though the process described by Christensen is more complicated than the linear process that Schumpeter had in mind, it has some similarities with the latter's notion of creative destruction according to which old technologies are constantly displaced by new ones that change the entire market structure. In new economy markets, competition often takes place by way of creative destruction. Previous champions in the ICT sector have been driven out of the market by new firms that introduced disruptive innovations. IBM's leading position in the market for mainframe computers has been overturned by Intel's hardware and Microsoft's operating systems which started to dominate the market for PCs. In turn, their positions are being attacked by providers of tablets and smartphones and by internet companies who introduce disruptive innovations in the form of online platforms and applications in mobile operating systems.

The introduction of new technologies that displace existing markets is commonly referred to as 'competition *for* the market' and contrasted with 'competition *in* the market' which is the conventional type of competition that takes place in established markets.[299] Competition *in* the market comprises competition on the basis of price and output as well as sustaining innovation which both take place in established markets, whereas competition *for* the market involves disruptive innovation which attacks existing market structures and leads to the development of new markets. The latter type of competition typically results into a monopoly position that is likely to persist for some time, until a new monopolist comes up that overturns the position of the previous incumbent. Although this type of competition is not yet well-developed in the literature, it seems that in sectors characterised by strong competition *for* the market, competitive pressure primarily comes from subsequent rather than concurrent competitors. The expectation of getting substantial market power encourages new entrants to introduce disruptive innovations that may enable them to overtake the position of

---

298. C.M. CHRISTENSEN AND M.E. RAYNOR, *The Innovator's Solution: Creating and Sustaining Successful Growth*, Harvard Business School Press, 2003, pp. 43-49.

299. D.S. EVANS AND R. SCHMALENSEE, 'Some Economic Aspects of Antitrust Analysis in Dynamically Competitive Industries' in A.B. JAFFE, J. LERNER AND S. STERN (eds.), *Innovation Policy and the Economy, Volume 2*, MIT Press, 2002, (1), p. 1. It is also possible to distinguish between competition ex ante (for the market) and competition ex post (in the market). See M.L. KATZ AND C. SHAPIRO, 'Antitrust in Software Markets' in J.A. EISENACH AND T.M. LENARD (eds.), *Competition, Innovation and the Microsoft Monopoly: Antitrust in the Digital Marketplace*, Kluwer Academic Publishers, 1999, p. 57.

the incumbent. However, if competition *for* the market is strong, market participants may have less incentive to compete within the market which could negatively affect product variety and prices.[300]

As shown in the business literature, competition *in* the market tends to come from the leading firms in the market, whereas new entrants typically compete *for* the market. Christensen refers to 'asymmetric motivation' as a cause for the fact that leading companies usually only introduce sustaining innovations that better serve their current customers and thus only compete within the market, while disruptive innovation comes from new entrants that compete for the market.[301] However, the economic and empirical literature on the relationship between competition and innovation discussed in the previous section can also explain this phenomenon. Because of the replacement effect, leading firms may have less incentive than new entrants to engage in disruptive innovation that overturns existing markets and leads established companies to forego existing profit flows.[302]

Although Schumpeter regards competition *for* the market in the form of creative destruction as the most important driver for innovation, competition *in* the market is vital for follow-on innovation. Follow-on innovation or cumulative innovation consists of improvements to existing products and would be referred to as sustaining innovation in the business literature. A trade-off has to be struck between encouraging competition *in* and *for* the market which stimulate different types of innovation.[303] Competition *for* the market can be seen as a form of horizontal competition which involves the development of competing products that are mutually substitutable. This type of competition therefore typically results in disruptive innovation and the dominance of subsequent successful firms. Instead, competition *in* the market is a form of vertical competition that mainly stimulates follow-on innovation and leads to product improvements or complementary products.

The two types of competition and innovation contribute to societal welfare in a different way. The preference of one model over the other therefore amounts to a policy choice. Although subsequent periods of dominance may incentivise new innovators to become the new market leader, it is important for the price level and product variety that a certain degree of competition *in* the market is also present. This will stimulate the

---

300. A. VAN ROOIJEN, *The Software Interface Between Copyright and Competition Law. A Legal Analysis of Interoperability in Computer Programs* in P.B. HUGENHOLTZ (ed.) *Information Law Series*, Kluwer Law International 2010, pp. 34-36.

301. C.M. CHRISTENSEN AND M.E. RAYNOR, *The Innovator's Solution: Creating and Sustaining Successful Growth*, Harvard Business School Press, 2003, p. 35.

302. R. GILBERT, 'Looking for Mr. Schumpeter. Where Are We in the Competition-Innovation Debate?' in A.B. JAFFE, J. LERNER AND S. STERN (eds.), *Innovation Policy and the Economy*, The MIT Press, 2006, (159), p. 183; R.J. GILBERT, 'Competition and Innovation' in W.D. COLLINS (ed.), *Issues in Competition Law and Policy*, Volume I, Chapter 24, American Bar Association Antitrust Section, 2008, (577), p. 14, available at http://eml.berkeley.edu/~gilbert/wp/competition_and_innovation.pdf.

303. P. LAROUCHE, 'The European Microsoft Case at the Crossroads of Competition Policy and Innovation', *Antitrust Law Journal* 2008, vol. 75, no. 3, (601), pp. 610-611.

incumbent to continue to innovate in order to keep its leading position. Therefore, a careful balance has to be found between the two models.[304]

In periods in between races of competition *for* the market the incumbent should be under sufficient competitive pressure from new entrants to prevent it from prolonging its dominant position and delaying the entry of subsequent competitors contrary to consumer demands. Opponents of competition enforcement in dynamic industries claim that competition authorities should not interfere in new economy markets because of the temporary character of market power and the risk of deterring innovation in rapidly developing sectors.[305] They argue that the costs from over-enforcement are significantly higher than the costs from under-enforcement because the latter costs are mitigated by the self-correcting nature of the market which will bring a new wave of creative destruction keeping the market sufficiently competitive.[306] However, if the incumbent enters into exclusionary strategies that postpone or even prevent the next wave of creative destruction from ever occurring, competition authorities should intervene.

While temporary market power itself may not be harmful, practices that enable the incumbent to abuse its position and to create a durable form of market power should be avoided.[307] In order to keep markets dynamic, competitive pressure from subsequent monopolists has to be maintained. In other words, it is necessary to keep markets contestable in the sense that entry and exit barriers have to be low.[308] In this respect, impediments to innovation resulting from undertakings strategically raising

---

304. In the context of a duty to disclose interoperability information, see I. GRAEF, 'How Can Software Interoperability Be Achieved under European Competition Law and Related Regimes?', *Journal of European Competition Law & Practice* 2014, vol. 5, no. 1, (6), p. 19 arguing that '*In early phases of market development, a duty to disclose interoperability information should only be mandated in very limited circumstances, since in this period competition between systems could be particularly beneficial for innovation.*

   In later stages of market development, the need for mandated interoperability increases as the prevailing system continues to dominate the market'.

305. H.A. SHELANSKI, 'Information, Innovation, and Competition Policy for the Internet', *University of Pennsylvania Law Review* 2013, vol. 161, no. 6, (1663), pp. 1670-1671; D.F. SPULBER, 'Unlocking Technology: Antitrust and Innovation', *Journal of Competition Law and Economics* 2008, vol. 4, no. 4, (915), pp. 962-965.

306. See G.A. MANNE AND J.D. WRIGHT, 'Google and the Limits of Antitrust: The Case Against the Case Against Google', *Harvard Journal of Law & Public Policy* 2010, vol. 34, no. 1, (171), p. 186 and G.A. MANNE AND J.D. WRIGHT, 'Innovation and the Limits of Antitrust', *Journal of Competition Law and Economics* 2010, vol. 6, no. 1, (153), p. 167. This claim originates from the error-cost framework put forward in F. EASTERBROOK, 'The Limits of Antitrust', *Texas Law Review* 1984, vol. 63, no. 1, p. 15.

307. S.W. WALLER, 'Antitrust and Social Networking', *North Carolina Law Review* 2012, vol. 90, no. 5, (1771), pp. 1802-1803.

308. Baumol, who is primarily associated with the theory of contestability, relies on Stigler's definition of entry barriers (see section 2.4.4) meaning that market entry is considered free when '*the entrant suffers no disadvantage in terms of production technique or perceived product quality relative to the incumbent*'. Exit is considered costless when '*any firm can leave without impediment, and in the process of departure can recoup any costs incurred in the entry process*'. Contestable markets are conducive to 'hit-and-run entry' which is the process whereby new firms enter the market to benefit from the above-average price level set by the incumbent until the incumbent responds to the new competitive pressure of the entrants by lowering the price to a normal level as a result of which the new entrants will leave the market (W.J. BAUMOL, 'Contestable Markets: An Uprising in the Theory of Industry Structure', *American Economic*

entry barriers can have as detrimental effects for society as an intervention by competition authorities.[309] Therefore, new economy sectors such as the online intermediary industry should not be immune from competition law intervention.[310] Instead, competition authorities should handle these markets with care and put effort into analysing how conduct of undertakings may affect innovation.[311] In a similar fashion, former Director-General for Competition Italianer expressed his scepticism about claims that competition concerns may simply disappear in the online world by arguing that *'We enforce competition law in the present, not in the future'* and *'Nobody will know what the situation will be ten, or even five, years from now. This means that any of these companies is until further notice a potential client for us – and some already are'*.[312]

While competition *for* and *in* the market constitute the two prevailing types of competition, firms do not necessarily compete either within existing markets or for future markets. In this regard, Petit coined the term 'moligopolists' for firms that have a monopoly for a certain service but that at the same time compete in oligopoly for other services. As examples, he refers to Microsoft as a monopolist in PC operating systems and an oligopolist in internet browsers and internet search, to Google as a monopolist in internet search and an oligopolist in self-driving cars and wearable computers in the form of glasses, and to Apple as a monopolist in handsets and an oligopolist in online social networks.[313] These firms have overlapping activities even though they do not operate in the exact same relevant markets as defined under competition law. It is therefore unclear how the competitive pressure that these firms exert on each other can be analysed in competition cases.

3.5   CONCLUSION

Existing indicators of competition and innovation may not reliably reflect the presence of these two phenomena. As it is difficult if not impossible to bring all the different factors that influence competition and innovation together in proxies, it has to be recognised that the models or assumptions employed in economic theories and

---

Review 1982, vol. 72, no. 1, (1), pp. 3-4). See also W.J. BAUMOL, J.C. PANZAR AND R.D. WILLIG, *Contestable Markets and the Theory of Industry Structure*, Harcourt Brace Jovanovich, 1982.

309. The European Commission even argued in its *Microsoft* decision that the specific characteristics of the new economy *'would rather suggest that there is an increased likelihood of positions of entrenched market power, compared to certain "traditional industries"'* (Case COMP/C-3/ 37.792 – *Microsoft*, 24 March 2004, par. 470).

310. In the context of the software market, see M.L. KATZ AND C. SHAPIRO, 'Antitrust in Software Markets' in J.A. EISENACH AND T.M. LENARD (eds.), *Competition, Innovation and the Microsoft Monopoly: Antitrust in the Digital Marketplace*, Kluwer Academic Publishers, 1999, pp. 37-38.

311. H.A. SHELANSKI, 'Information, Innovation, and Competition Policy for the Internet', *University of Pennsylvania Law Review* 2013, vol. 161, no. 6, (1663), pp. 1692-1693.

312. Speech former Director-General for Competition Italianer, 'Competition Policy in the Digital Age', 47th Innsbruck Symposium – 'Real sector economy and the internet – digital interconnection as an issue for competition policy', 7 March 2014, pp. 3-4, available at http://ec.europa .eu/competition/speeches/text/sp2014_01_en.pdf.

313. N. PETIT, 'Antitrust and The Challenge of Policing "Moligopolists"', Keynote at Ninth CLEEN Workshop, 28-29 May 2015, Tilburg, available at http://orbi.ulg.ac.be//handle/2268/182226.

empirical studies are always a simplification of reality and may thus not reliably predict the level of competition or innovation in an actual market. Nevertheless, in the absence of more accurate indicators, currently used proxies such as market concentration and the level of R&D investment may be relied upon with a degree of caution.

Economic theory and empirical studies have reached different conclusions on the issue of how market structure and innovation relate to each other. A general causal relationship between the two therefore does not seem to exist. Because of the many factors that influence the effect of competition on innovation, it is not possible to identify an optimal market structure for stimulating innovation in a specific sector. Competition authorities should thus rely on a case-by-case assessment.

Two types of innovation and competition are distinguished in economic and business literature. Competition *for* the market typically provides stronger incentives for disruptive innovation which is likely to result into products or technologies that overtake the existing market and will dominate the new market. Competition *in* the market, on the other hand, puts market players under pressure to operate as efficiently as possible within the existing market and generally stimulates follow-on innovation in the form of product improvements or complementary products. Both types of competition and innovation bring value to society albeit in a different way. The choice to favour one over the other involves a trade-off between diverse interests. Although competition in dynamic sectors such as the online intermediary industry typically takes place for the market, the importance of the other type of competition should not be undervalued. In particular when the market finds itself in a period waiting for the next wave of creative destruction to occur, the need for competition *in* the market grows to ensure that the leading undertaking is under pressure to keep the quality and price of products at a competitive level.

CHAPTER 4

Market Definition and Dominance on Online Platforms

4.1 INTRODUCTION

As discussed in the previous chapters, online platforms are characterised by their multi-sided nature, their network economy features and the predominance of disruptive innovation and competition *for* the market. Because of these characteristics, the standard approach towards market definition and the assessment of dominance may have to be adapted to reliably assess competition issues on search engines, social networks and e-commerce platforms.

When evaluating alleged abusive behaviour and proposed concentrations, competition authorities and courts start their analysis by defining the relevant product and geographic market. The relevant product market includes all products or services which are regarded as substitutes by consumers on the basis of their characteristics, prices and intended use.[314] The relevant geographic market comprises the area in which the conditions of competition are sufficiently homogeneous and which can be distinguished from neighbouring areas because the conditions of competition are appreciably different in those areas.[315] Although it has been put forward that market definition is not useful anymore in the context of the more economic approach towards competition enforcement and considering that the combination of market power and consumer harm should be sufficient for finding anticompetitive harm regardless of any market definition,[316] it is still an important step conducted by competition authorities and courts in competition cases.

---

314. Commission Notice on the definition of relevant market for the purposes of Community competition law [1997] OJ C 372/5, par. 7.
315. Commission Notice on the definition of relevant market for the purposes of Community competition law [1997] OJ C 372/5, par. 8.
316. See notably, L. KAPLOW, 'Why Ever Define Markets?', *Harvard Law Review* December 2010, vol. 124, no. 2, (437) and L. KAPLOW, 'Market Definition: Impossible and Counterproductive',

At the same time, market definition should not be seen as a goal in itself but as a means to identify the market position of undertakings and to assess whether their behaviour has a competitive impact on the market. A clear definition of the relevant market is not necessary in every competition case.[317] As seen below, the European Commission regularly decides to leave the exact scope of the relevant market open in merger cases on the ground that the concentration at issue would not give rise to competition concerns under any alternative market definition. Although some indications may be derived from such merger decisions, no strong conclusions can be drawn about the appropriate market definition in the industry under investigation.

In section 4.2, attention is paid to how relevant markets should be delineated for multi-sided platforms. This is followed by a discussion of market definition in new economy industries where disruptive innovation typically predominates in section 4.3. Section 4.4 focuses on the assessment of dominance on online platforms. While the chapter focuses on EU competition law, relevant cases in other jurisdictions will also be considered because of the limited number of precedents in the online intermediary sector.

4.2 MARKET DEFINITION OF MULTI-SIDED BUSINESSES

Several approaches have been put forward for defining markets in which multi-sided platforms operate. An issue that has to be considered before determining the relevant market and assessing dominance is whether the multi-sidedness of a platform is critical to the competition analysis. Multi-sidedness should be seen as a matter of degree.[318] If the multi-sided nature of a business is merely an aspect of the industry that is not determinative for a particular competition issue involving a multi-sided platform, it may not be sufficiently pronounced so as to affect the behaviour of the firm and the way competition takes place. Ultimately, it is an empirical question whether and in which circumstances multi-sided aspects are sufficiently substantial to have an influence on the application of competition law.[319]

Antitrust Law Journal 2013, vol. 79, no. 1, (361). For a reply to Kaplow, see G.J. WERDEN, 'The Relevant Market: Possible and Productive', *Antitrust Law Journal Online* April 2014, (1).

317. In the context of the private competition dispute between internet companies Qihoo and Tencent in China, the Chinese Supreme Court argued: '*Even without a clear definition of the relevant market, a judgment of a company's market position and its eventual impact of competition on a market can be carried out by excluding direct evidence against the defendant about its monopoly behavior. An explicit and clear definition of the relevant market is not necessary in every case of abuse of a dominant market position*'. See Chinese Supreme Court in (2013) C3FJ4, *Qihoo/Tencent*, 16 October 2014, (A)(1), English translation available via https://www.competitionpolicyinternational.com/assets/DecisionTranslation.pdf?utm_source = TencentWebinar&utm_campaign = April + 30 % 2C + 2013&utm_medium = email.

318. See section 2.3.1.

319. D.S. EVANS AND M. NOEL, 'Defining Antitrust Markets When Firms Operate Two-Sided Platforms', *Columbia Business Law Review* 2005, vol. 2005, (101), p. 128.

4.2.1 An Approach for Market Definition of Multi-sided Platforms

Because of the link between the two customer groups on online platforms, it is not correct to define and analyse the relevant market for each side in isolation. If the provider does not behave like a one-sided firm but takes the interdependence of the two sides of the platform into account in its pricing and production decisions, the application of a one-sided logic may lead to an erroneous assessment of the competitive strength of the multi-sided business.[320] If the product or service is given away at one side of the platform, there is a particular risk that the free side will be overlooked in the market definition.[321] The *KinderStart v. Google* case in the United States illustrates this. In this case, the Court for the Northern District of California declined to apply antitrust law to internet search on the ground that the claimants had not cited any authority indicating that antitrust law is concerned with competition in the provision of free services. Although the District Court was aware that the provision of search functionality may lead to revenue from other sources, it argued that the search market could not be regarded as a relevant market for antitrust purposes on the ground that KinderStart had not alleged that anyone pays Google to search.[322]

Instead of basing the market definition for an online platform on the services that are offered, the relevant market could be defined in accordance with the way the provider monetises its business. For online intermediaries this would mean that the relevant market consists of a market for personal information monetised through advertising.[323] Such an approach is consistent with the nature of these platforms which do not gain revenue by selling their technology to consumers like 'traditional' ICT companies such as Microsoft and Intel, but rely on deriving benefits from valuable information they collect about their users.[324]

---

320. See D.S. Evans, 'The Antitrust Economics of Multi-Sided Platform Markets', *Yale Journal on Regulation* 2003, vol. 20, no. 2, (325), pp. 356-358. For a description of some other basic fallacies that can arise from applying a one-sided economic logic to multi-sided businesses, see J. Wright, 'One-Sided Logic in Two-Sided Markets', *Review of Network Economics* 2004, vol. 3, no. 1, (44).

321. D.S. Evans, 'The Antitrust Economics of Multi-Sided Platform Markets', *Yale Journal on Regulation* 2003, vol. 20, no. 2, (325), p. 358; L. Filistrucchi, D. Geradin, E. van Damme, et al., 'Market Definition in Two-Sided Markets: Theory and Practice', *Journal of Competition Law and Economics* 2014, vol. 10, no. 2, (293), p. 321; J. Wright, 'One-sided Logic in Two-Sided Markets', *Review of Network Economics* 2004, vol. 3, no. 1, (44), p. 62.

322. *KinderStart.com, LLC v. Google, Inc.*, No. C 06-2057 JF (RS), 2007 WL 831806 (N.D. Cal. 16 March 2007), par. 5.

323. In her dissenting statement as a Federal Trade Commissioner in the *Google/DoubleClick* merger, Pamela Jones Harbour suggested to define a market for data, separate and apart from the markets for the services offered by the merging parties. See Dissenting Statement of Commissioner Pamela Jones Harbour, *Google/DoubleClick*, FTC File No. 071-0170, 20 December 2007, p. 9, available at http://www.ftc.gov/sites/default/files/documents/public_statements/statement-matter-google/doubleclick/071220harbour_0.pdf and P.J. Harbour and T.I. Koslov, 'Section 2 In A Web 2.0 World: An Expanded Vision of Relevant Product Markets', *Antitrust Law Journal* 2010, vol. 76, no. 3, (769), pp. 783-787 for a further development of the concept of data markets.

324. C. Butts, 'The Microsoft Case 10 Years Later: Antitrust and New Leading "New Economy" Firms', *Northwestern Journal of Technology and Intellectual Property* Spring 2010, vol. 8, no. 2, (275), p. 290. See also S.W. Waller, 'Antitrust and Social Networking', *North Carolina Law*

However, a correct market definition under current competition law standards requires the existence of supply and demand for the product or service.[325] One can doubt whether the collection of personal data from users by providers of online platforms constitutes an economic exchange. Although one may argue that users are increasingly aware that they give access to their personal information by utilising the features of online platforms,[326] the provision of data does not seem to constitute a genuine supply of a product by users in exchange for being able to employ search or social networking functionalities. Contrary to usual economic transactions, users as suppliers of data cannot determine the amount and type of information they want to supply and do not have influence on what they will get in return. Instead, the providers of the online services unilaterally decide what type and which amount of data will be extracted and impose their practices on users as a take-it-or-leave-it offer. This interaction between users and providers therefore seems to constitute a form of one-sided retrieval of information rather than an economic transaction.

Facebook/WhatsApp merger decision

The *Facebook/WhatsApp* investigation of the European Commission covered three areas: consumer communications services, social networking services and online advertising services. With regard to the relevant market for consumer communications services, the Commission found that Facebook Messenger and WhatsApp were not close competitors and that consumers would continue to have a wide choice of alternative communications apps after the transaction. The Commission did not take a final view on the existence and the still evolving boundaries of a potential market for social networking services and concluded that, irrespective of the exact market borders, Facebook and WhatsApp were only distant competitors given the differences between the functionalities and focus of their services. In the area of online advertising services, the Commission argued that the merger would not raise competition concerns even if Facebook would introduce targeted advertising on WhatsApp or start collecting data from WhatsApp users with a view to improving the accuracy of the targeted ads served on Facebook's social networking platform. In the Commission's view, there would continue to be a sufficient number of alternative providers to Facebook for the supply of targeted advertising after the merger, and a large amount of internet user data that are valuable for advertising purposes were not within Facebook's exclusive control.

Review 2012, vol. 90, no. 5, (1771), pp. 1784-1785 and F. Thépot, 'Market Power in Online Search and Social Networking: A Matter of Two-Sided Markets', *World Competition* 2013, vol. 36, no. 2, (195), pp. 217-218.

325. See Commission Notice on the definition of relevant market for the purposes of Community competition law [1997] OJ C 372/5, paras 13-23.

326. See R. Casadesus-Masanell and A. Hervas-Drane, 'Competing with Privacy', *Harvard Business School Working Paper 13-085* October 2013, p. 4, available at http://www.hbs.edu/faculty/ Publication%20Files/13-085_95c71478-a439-4c00-b1dd-f9d963b99c34.pdf who *'expect consumers to become increasingly familiar with privacy tradeoffs in the marketplace'*.

> Case No COMP/M.7217 – *Facebook/WhatsApp*, 3 October 2014, paragraphs
> 101-115, 146-158, 172-179 and 184-189.

Current competition law standards only allow for the definition of a market for data in case the information is actually traded. Examples are the data licensing activities of Twitter and the sale of collected personal information about consumers by data brokers to other businesses. Under prevailing competition law principles, the relevant market for online services such as search engines, social networks and e-commerce platforms thus cannot take data as object as long as there is no economic transaction between the respective providers and users for data, and the providers of these online platforms do not sell or trade data to third parties.[327] So far, the European Commission has not yet had to define a market for personal data or for any of its particular usages.[328]

In its *Facebook/WhatsApp* merger decision, the Commission expressly stated that it had not investigated any possible market definition with respect to the provision of data or data analytics services, since neither of the parties involved was active in any such potential markets. At the time of the merger, Facebook only used the information about its users for the provision of targeted advertising services and did not sell user data to third parties or offer any data analytics services. WhatsApp did not collect personal data that would be valuable for advertising purposes and messages sent through WhatsApp by users were not stored in WhatsApp's service but only on the users' mobile devices or elected cloud. As a result, the Commission did not see a reason to consider the existence of a potential market for personal data.[329] In such circumstances, current competition law principles only allow for a market definition based on the services that online platforms offer. Even if it is considered that users pay for the free services with their personal data, the focus of market definition under existing standards is on the type of product or service offered instead of on the means of payment.[330]

The crucial issue with respect to market definition of multi-sided businesses is whether one market for the platforms as a whole should be defined or whether separate markets should be distinguished for each of the sides of the platform. The European Commission explicitly considered this question in the context of payment cards. In its *MasterCard* decision of December 2007, the Commission did not define one but several relevant markets for payment card systems. MasterCard argued that one relevant

---

327. See also the discussion in I. GRAEF, 'Market Definition and Market Power in Data: The Case of Online Platforms', *World Competition* 2015, vol. 38, no. 4, (473), p. 490.
328. Speech former Competition Commissioner Almunia, 'Competition and personal data protection', Privacy Platform event: Competition and Privacy in Markets of Data Brussels, 26 November 2012, SPEECH/12/860.
329. Case No COMP/M.7217 – *Facebook/WhatsApp*, 3 October 2014, paras 70-72.
330. See section 4.3.2 below where it is argued that, despite the limitations of current competition law standards, a potential market for data may be defined in addition to the markets for the services provided to users and advertisers. This in order to take better account of potential competition and to make competition analysis more conducive towards innovation. See also section 5.2 below for a further analysis of the role of data as a currency for digital services offered to users without any monetary charges.

market existed in which different payment card systems' services compete with each other and with all other forms of payment including cash and cheques.[331] The Commission did not accept this market definition proposed by MasterCard and stated that *'Two-sided demand does not imply the existence of one single "joint product" supplied by a "joint venture"'*.[332] Instead, the Commission identified an upstream or network market in which card scheme owners compete to persuade financial institutions to join their schemes and a downstream market in which competition between financial institutions for card-related activities takes place. Within this downstream market, the Commission distinguished between a relevant market for acquiring and a relevant market for issuing services.[333] In its decision, the Commission relied on the restrictive effects of the alleged practices in the acquiring market. The General Court upheld the market definition relied upon by the Commission.[334] Before the Court of Justice, the General Court's assessment of the market definition was not challenged as a result of which the Court of Justice dismissed the ground of appeal relating to market definition.[335]

MasterCard case

In its 2007 decision, the Commission concluded that MasterCard's multilateral interchange fees (MIFs) for cross-border payment card transactions with MasterCard and Maestro consumer debit and credit cards in the European Economic Area (EEA) violated Article 101(1) TFEU. MIFs are fees charged by a cardholder's bank (the issuing bank) to a merchant's bank (the acquiring bank) for each payment made at a merchant's outlet with a payment card. The Commission concluded that MasterCard's MIFs restricted competition between acquiring banks and inflated the cost of card acceptance by retailers without leading to proven efficiencies under Article 101(3) TFEU.

MasterCard was given six months to conform to the Commission's order to set its MIFs in compliance with the EU competition rules. MasterCard appealed the Commission decision before the General Court and pending the judgment, in April 2009, unilaterally undertook to reduce its cross-border MIFs to 0.30% of the transaction value for consumer credit cards and 0.20% of the transaction value for consumer debit cards and to amend other rules and practices. The judgment of the General Court which upheld the decision of the Commission was issued on 24 May 2012.

---

331. Cases COMP/34.579 - *MasterCard*, COMP/36.518 - *EuroCommerce* and COMP/38.580 - *Commercial Cards*, 19 December 2007, paras 250-255.
332. Cases COMP/34.579 - *MasterCard*, COMP/36.518 - *EuroCommerce* and COMP/38.580 - *Commercial Cards*, 19 December 2007, par. 257.
333. Cases COMP/34.579 - *MasterCard*, COMP/36.518 - *EuroCommerce* and COMP/38.580 - *Commercial Cards*, 19 December 2007, paras 278-282.
334. Judgment in *MasterCard*, T-111/08, ECLI:EU:T:2012:260, paras 172-175.
335. Judgment in *MasterCard*, C-382/12 P, ECLI:EU:C:2014:2201, par. 159.

On 11 September 2014, the Court of Justice confirmed that MasterCard's MIFs for cross-border payment transactions in the EEA restrict competition in breach of Article 101 TFEU.

In July 2015, the Commission issued a new Statement of Objections to Master-Card on cross-border rules and MIFs relating to payments made by cardholders from non-EEA countries.

Cases COMP/34.579 - *MasterCard*, COMP/36.518 - *EuroCommerce* and COMP/ 38.580 - *Commercial Cards*, 19 December 2007.

Press Release European Commission, 'Antitrust: Commissioner Kroes takes note of MasterCard's decision to cut cross-border Multilateral Interchange Fees (MIFs) and to repeal recent scheme fee increases', 1 April 2009, IP/09/515, available at http://europa.eu/rapid/press-release_IP-09-515_en.htm?locale = en.

Judgment in *MasterCard*, T-111/08, ECLI:EU:T:2012:260.

Judgment in *MasterCard*, C-382/12 P, ECLI:EU:C:2014:2201.

Press Release European Commission, 'Antitrust: Commission sends Statement of Objections to MasterCard on cross-border rules and inter-regional interchange fees', 9 July 2015, IP/15/5323, available at http://europa.eu/rapid/press-release_IP-15-5323_en.htm.

In the literature, opposing views are present. In the context of search engines for instance, some authors claim that a different relevant market for each side of the platform must be delineated while others seem to allude to the definition of one market for the search engine as a whole.[336] Arguably the most comprehensive contribution to the academic debate is the framework developed by Filistrucchi et al. which distinguishes between multi-sided transaction markets ('payment card type') and multi-sided non-transaction markets ('media type') in order to identify the appropriate approach towards market definition of multi-sided platforms.[337]

Depending on the qualification of the platform, Filistrucchi et al. argue that one relevant market for the whole platform or several interrelated relevant markets for each side have to be defined.[338] In transaction markets, as the name suggests, a visible

---

336. See T. Hoppner, 'Defining Markets for Multi-Sided Platforms: The Case of Search Engines', *World Competition* 2015, vol. 38, no. 3, (349), pp. 352-356 (arguing that separate relevant markets have to be defined for each of the sides of a search engine) and J.D. Ratliff and D.L. Rubinfeld, 'Is There a Market for Organic Search Engine Results and Can Their Manipulation Give Rise to Antitrust Liability?', *Journal of Competition Law and Economics* 2014, vol. 10, no. 3, (517), pp. 534-538 (arguing that the relevant market should be broad enough to encompass both search advertising and organic search).
337. L. Filistrucchi, D. Geradin and E. Van Damme, 'Identifying Two-Sided Markets', *World Competition* 2013, vol. 36, no. 1, (33), pp. 40-41.
338. Wright suggested that the necessity to define separate relevant markets on each side of a multi-sided platform depends on whether it charges membership fees or transaction fees. In his view, one relevant market for the whole platform has to be defined if a transaction fee is charged. In this situation, it would not make sense to define separate markets, since the

transaction takes place between the different customer groups which makes it impossible for a business in the market to target only one customer group. Undertakings present in these markets are therefore by definition multi-sided platforms.[339] An example is the payment card industry where a payment card provider has to be active on the buyer as well as on the merchant side of the platform in order to do business. Because a single and observable transaction takes place, it is impossible to use platform A on the buyer side and platform B on the merchant side. Either the buyer and the merchant both use platform A or the transaction does not take place through platform A.[340] Since a firm is either on both sides of the platform or on none, one relevant market should be defined for platforms in multi-sided transaction markets in the view of Filistrucchi et al.[341] This also applies to the interaction between buyers and sellers on e-commerce platforms. Since a transaction takes place between the two customer groups, it is impossible for an e-commerce platform to be active on only one side. However, between users and advertisers on e-commerce platforms no observable transaction occurs. The working of e-commerce platforms is similar to that of search engines, social networks and other media businesses as far as the relationship between users and advertisers is concerned.

Media markets can be considered as multi-sided non-transaction markets. In these markets, the situation is different. Because no observable transaction takes place,[342] it is possible for a competing undertaking to be active on only one side of the platform. In other words, platforms in multi-sided non-transaction markets may also

---

platform collects revenues from all sides of the platform at the same time. See J. WRIGHT, 'One-Sided Logic in Two-Sided Markets', *Review of Network Economics* 2004, vol. 3, no. 1, (44), p. 62. However, the framework proposed by Filistrucchi et al. in which the presence of an observable transaction is determinative for the question whether one or separate relevant markets on each side of a platform should be defined, seems more accurate. Even if the platform charges a membership fee, a transaction between the sides may take place that would justify the definition of only one relevant market for the entire platform. See L. FILISTRUCCHI, D. GERADIN, E. VAN DAMME, ET AL., 'Market Definition in Two-Sided Markets: Theory and Practice', *Journal of Competition Law and Economics* 2014, vol. 10, no. 2, (293), p. 302.

339. However, this does not mean that only multi-sided platforms are included in the relevant market. Direct transactions between both sides that do not require intermediation from a third party could form a substitute for multi-sided platforms facilitating an interaction. For instance, multi-sided payment card providers may experience competitive pressure from direct cash payments. See L. FILISTRUCCHI, D. GERADIN, E. VAN DAMME, ET AL., 'Market Definition in Two-Sided Markets: Theory and Practice', *Journal of Competition Law and Economics* 2014, vol. 10, no. 2, (293), p. 303.

340. Other examples of multi-sided transaction markets are auction houses and operating systems. See L. FILISTRUCCHI, D. GERADIN AND E. VAN DAMME, 'Identifying Two-Sided Markets', *World Competition* 2013, vol. 36, no. 1, (33), p. 41.

341. L. FILISTRUCCHI, D. GERADIN, E. VAN DAMME, ET AL., 'Market Definition in Two-Sided Markets: Theory and Practice', *Journal of Competition Law and Economics* 2014, vol. 10, no. 2, (293), pp. 301-302.

342. Filistrucchi et al. argue that although a user may decide to buy a product after seeing an advertisement, such a delayed transaction is usually not identifiable in the sense that it is impossible to say whether a user has purchased a product because he or she has seen a particular ad in a newspaper or on a search engine. The platform is thus unable to charge a per-transaction fee in multi-sided non-transaction markets. See L. FILISTRUCCHI, D. GERADIN, E. VAN DAMME, ET AL., 'Market Definition in Two-Sided Markets: Theory and Practice', *Journal of Competition Law and Economics* 2014, vol. 10, no. 2, (293), p. 298 and footnote 11.

face competition from one-sided undertakings. For instance, an online search engine may experience competitive pressure from single-sided libraries on the user side. In addition, multi-sided businesses having only one overlapping customer side may compete with each another. An online search engine may theoretically, for example, compete with online social networks on the advertiser side, while its users will not regard the social network features substitutable to the search services that the search engine offers. If only one relevant market encompassing the two sides of the online search engine would be defined, the competitive pressure from single-sided firms and multi-sided businesses that overlap with the relevant platform on only one side would by definition be overlooked. It is therefore submitted that the variety of entities from which multi-sided online platforms experience competitive pressure is better reflected by a market definition which takes the services offered by their providers as object.[343] This is also reason why, according to Filistrucchi et al., the most viable option would be to define a separate relevant market for each side of the online platform while taking into account the other sides as well.

Only in case the multi-sided network effects on the platform are not reciprocal, market definition on the side of the platform that does not exert an externality on the other can take place without considering the other side in the view of Filistrucchi et al.[344] In this context, the Autorité de la concurrence (the French competition authority) argued in its sector inquiry into the online advertising industry that it is sufficient to confine the competition analysis of search engines to the advertising side, because it would not '*markedly modify the approach*' if the user side is also taken into account. In the view of the Autorité de la concurrence: '*a moderate reduction in the number of commercial links is unlikely to prompt a web user to change search engines if the relevance of the organic results remains unchanged*'.[345]

In the *Microsoft/Yahoo* merger case, the Commission had to apply competition law to internet search for the first time. With regard to market definition, the Commission did not take a position on whether web search should be regarded as a relevant market of its own. Instead, it only assessed the legality of the transaction with regard to the market for online advertising.[346] However, the Commission did consider the link between the user and advertiser side by examining potential anticompetitive

---

343. See also A. Gebicka and A. Heinemann, 'Social Media & Competition Law', *World Competition* 2014, vol. 37, no. 2, (149), p. 156 who argue against the notion of a market for user data in a similar fashion by stating: '*Competitive pressure – or its absence – could not adequately be taken into consideration if the kind of services offered to the consumer is modified or disappears entirely behind the general commercial interest underlying any business activity*'.
344. L. Filistrucchi, D. Geradin, E. van Damme, et al., 'Market Definition in Two-Sided Markets: Theory and Practice', *Journal of Competition Law and Economics* 2014, vol. 10, no. 2, (293), pp. 321-322.
345. Autorité de la Concurrence, Avis n° 10-A-29 du 14 décembre 2010 sur le fonctionnement concurrentiel de la publicité en ligne, par. 180, English version available at http://www. autoritedelaconcurrence.fr/doc/10a29_en.pdf. Argenton and Prüfer also argue that the multi-sidedness may not be pronounced in search engines so as to require an analysis of both the user and advertiser side in the competition assessment. See C. Argenton and J. Prüfer, 'Search Engine Competition with Network Externalities', *Journal of Competition Law and Economics* 2012, vol. 8, no. 1, (73), p. 83.
346. Case No COMP/M.5727 – *Microsoft/Yahoo! Search Business*, 18 February 2010, paras 85-87.

effects of the transaction on innovation, relevance and variety of internet search to users.[347] The Commission thus seems to have considered both sides together by way of a 'business ecosystem', as proposed by Evans, in which one cannot look at one side of the market in isolation of the other.[348] In its abuse of dominance investigation against Google, the Commission appears to distinguish two interrelated markets with regard to Google's search engine: web search and online search advertising. In a press release, the Commission stated that it *'has concerns that Google may be abusing its dominant position in the markets for web search, online search advertising and online search advertising intermediation in the European Economic Area (EEA)'.*[349]

In the context of its approval of Facebook's acquisition of WhatsApp, the Commission similarly identified separate relevant markets for the services provided to users on the one hand and the services offered to advertisers on the other hand. With regard to market definition on the user side, the Commission investigated the possibility of defining a relevant market for consumer communications services and social networking services. On the advertiser side, the Commission considered the existence of further subsegmentations of the online advertising market.[350] Instead of relying on a single relevant market for the platform or confining the analysis to the advertiser side, like the Autorité de la concurrence proposed in its sector inquiry, the Commission thus appears to follow the approach described by Filistrucchi et al. applicable to non-transaction markets as regards market definition of multi-sided online platforms. According to this approach, separate relevant markets have to be defined for the user and advertiser side of search engines, e-commerce platforms and social networks.

For search engines and social networks a third relevant market can be distinguished consisting of, respectively, content providers and application developers.[351] These customer groups are not analysed here further, since their role on the platform is subordinate to the interaction between users and advertisers. With regard to content providers on search engines, the interaction seems to be rather one-sided as search

---

347. Case No COMP/M.5727 – *Microsoft/Yahoo! Search Business*, 18 February 2010, paras 202-226.
348. D.S. EVANS, 'The Antitrust Economics of Free', *Competition Policy International* 20 May 2011, vol. 7, pp. 21-22, available at http://papers.ssrn.com/sol3/papers.cfm?abstract_id = 1813193. Alternative approaches that Evans puts forward include the possibility to define the market around one product and consider the role of the complementary product in the analysis of market power and the approach whereby separate markets are defined for each side of the platform while interdependencies are taken into account in the analysis of market power. On the former approach, see also N. ZINGALES, 'Product Market Definition in Online Search and Advertising', *The Competition Law Review* March 2013, vol. 9, no. 1, (29), pp. 35-36.
349. Press Release European Commission, 'Antitrust: Commission seeks feedback on commitments offered by Google to address competition concerns', 25 April 2013, IP/13/371, available at http://europa.eu/rapid/press-release_IP-13-371_en.htm. The market for online search advertising intermediation is not relevant here, since it does not involve advertising on Google's search engine pages. Instead, it relates to Google's AdSense service which enables third parties to gain revenue by selling advertising space on their own websites to Google which looks for interested advertisers to fill these spots.
350. Case No COMP/M.7217 – *Facebook/WhatsApp*, 3 October 2014, section 4 on relevant markets.
351. See T. HOPPNER, 'Defining Markets for Multi-Sided Platforms: The Case of Search Engines', *World Competition* 2015, vol. 38, no. 3, (349), pp. 364-366 who distinguishes a third relevant market with regard to search engines for indexing web content between search engine providers and website owners.

engine providers are free to crawl the internet and index content in order to provide relevant results to search queries of users. One can therefore question whether the interaction between these website owners and the search platform provider amounts to an economic exchange, which constitutes a necessary precondition for being able to define a relevant market for competition purposes.[352]

4.2.2 Relevant Product Market for the User Side

On the user side, it has to be assessed which products or services are substitutable for online search engines, e-commerce platforms and social networks from the perspective of consumers. In its decision concerning the acquisition of Yahoo's search business by Microsoft, the European Commission made some remarks about the general characteristics of an online search engine. The Commission distinguished general or horizontal internet search from vertical internet search, which targets a specific type of service, and site search, covering only the content of a particular website.[353] Ultimately, the Commission left open whether internet search constitutes a separate relevant market. It also did not answer the question whether horizontal and vertical search engines fall within the same relevant market and whether offline search facilities can be seen as substitutes for online search engines, such as travel agencies for looking for holidays and libraries for looking for information.[354] However, statements made in the *Google Shopping* case indicate that the Commission regards horizontal internet search as a separate relevant product market. In a statement, the Commissioner for Competition argued: '*Google has had market shares of more than 90% in general internet search in most EU Member States for many years*'.[355]

Google investigation

In November 2010, the European Commission opened an investigation against Google after having received complaints from competitors. Through former Competition Commissioner Almunia, the Commission expressed four concerns

---

352. See G. Luchetta, 'Is the Google Platform a Two-Sided Market?', *Journal of Competition Law and Economics* 2014, vol. 10, no. 1, (185), p. 194 and in particular footnote 29. According to T. Hoppner, 'Defining Markets for Multi-Sided Platforms: The Case of Search Engines', *World Competition* 2015, vol. 38, no. 3, (349), p. 365, the interaction between search engine providers and website operators amounts to an economic exchange because a website owners has either actively permitted indexing by registering its URL for inclusion in a search engine's index or by including certain meta tags in its web page, or, in the alternative, the failure of a website operator to use any technical tools to block the inclusion of its URL in a search engine's index can be considered as implied consent to the indexing of its web page. However, as Luchetta makes clear, the interaction between search engine providers and website operators rather seems to constitute a mere one-sided retrieval of information comparable to the non-economic interaction between map providers and owners of land properties, or between restaurant guides and restaurant owners.
353. Case No COMP/M.5727 – *Microsoft/Yahoo! Search Business*, 18 February 2010, paras 31-32.
354. Case No COMP/M.5727 – *Microsoft/Yahoo! Search Business*, 18 February 2010, par. 86.
355. Speech Competition Commissioner Vestager, 'Statement by Commissioner Vestager on antitrust decisions concerning Google', STATEMENT/15/4785, 15 April 2015, available at http://europa.eu/rapid/press-release_STATEMENT-15-4785_en.htm?locale = en.

relating to Google's search activities and gave Google the opportunity to propose commitments to prevent the finding of a violation of Article 102 TFEU and the imposition of a fine. The four concerns of the Commission included: (1) the fact that Google displays links to its own specialised search services (such as Google Shopping, Google Flights and Google Maps) more favourably than links of competing services; (2) the way Google copies content from competing vertical search services and uses it in its own offerings without obtaining prior authorisation; (3) the exclusivity agreements of Google which require third parties to obtain all or most of their requirements of search advertisements from Google; and (4) the contractual restrictions that Google puts to the portability of online search advertising campaigns from its platform AdWords to the platforms of competitors. To address the concerns of the Commission, Google offered three consecutive sets of commitments (namely in April 2013, October 2013 and February 2014). With regard to the first and most controversial concern of the Commission, Google committed to label and separate promoted links to its own specialised search services so that users can distinguish them from organic search results and to display links to three rival specialised search services in a place clearly visible to users.

While the former Competition Commissioner Almunia initially seemed to be of the view that the commitments from Google were adequate to address the concerns, he decided to reject the latest version of the commitments before the end of his mandate in November 2014 and asked Google to improve its offer.

In April 2015, the current Competition Commissioner Vestager decided to refrain from concluding a settlement with Google. Instead, the Commission sent Google a Statement of Objections alleging that it has abused its dominant position in the market for general internet search services in the EEA by systematically favouring its own comparison shopping product, Google Shopping, in its general search results pages. In addition, the Commission continues its investigation of other aspects of Google's search activities including the favourable treatment by Google in its general search results of other specialised search services (such as Google Maps) and concerns relating to the copying of rivals' web content, advertising exclusivity and restrictions on advertising portability. In parallel, the Commission opened a separate formal investigation into Google's Android mobile operating system in April 2015 for which it sent a Statement of Objections to Google in April 2016.

Press Release European Commission, 'Antitrust: Commission probes allegations of antitrust violations by Google', IP/10/1624, 30 November 2010.

Speech former Competition Commissioner Almunia, 'Statement of Commissioner Almunia on the Google antitrust investigation', Press room Brussels, 21 May 2012, SPEECH/12/372.

Press Release European Commission, 'Antitrust: Commission seeks feedback on commitments offered by Google to address competition concerns', 25 April 2013, IP/13/371.

> Speech former Competition Commissioner Almunia, 'The Google antitrust case: what is at stake?', 1 October 2013, SPEECH/13/786.
>
> Press Release European Commission, 'Antitrust: Commission obtains from Google comparable display of specialised search rivals', 5 February 2014, IP/14/116, available at http://europa.eu/rapid/press-release_IP-14-116_en.htm.
>
> Speech former Competition Commissioner Almunia, 'Presenting the Annual Competition Report', SPEECH/14/615, 23 September 2014, available at http://europa.eu/rapid/press-release_SPEECH-14-615_en.htm.
>
> Press Release European Commission, 'Antitrust: Commission sends Statement of Objections to Google on comparison shopping service; opens separate formal investigation on Android', 15 April 2015, IP/15/4780.
>
> Press Release European Commission, 'Antitrust: Commission sends Statement of Objections to Google on Android operating system and applications – Factsheet', MEMO/16/1484, 20 April 2016, available at http://europa.eu/rapid/press-release_MEMO-16-1484_en.htm.

So far, the European Commission has not yet made any specific statements about market definition of e-commerce platforms. Since these businesses enable users to search for products they would like to purchase, the user side of e-commerce platforms can be regarded as a vertical or specialised search engine focused on shopping. The fact that the Commission seems to rely on a relevant market for horizontal internet search in the *Google Shopping* case, may indicate that the Commission does not consider vertical search engines as substitutes for a general web search service like the one offered by Google. At the same time, vertical search services are increasingly putting horizontal search engines under pressure. Although platforms such as Facebook and Amazon do not possess an index of the entire web and may therefore not be regarded as complete substitutes to Google's horizontal search service, they are likely to create considerable competitive pressure for specific search queries whereby users are looking to purchase a certain product or service.[356] Nevertheless, considering the statements of the Commission in the *Google Shopping* case, it is likely that vertical search will also be regarded as a relevant market of its own. Depending on whether vertical search engines targeting a service different than shopping are found to exert competitive pressure on e-commerce platforms, a separate relevant product market may be defined for vertical search solely encompassing shopping or a broader market including vertical search engines for other online content.

In the context of the *Facebook/WhatsApp* merger, the European Commission had to consider a potential relevant market for social networking services for the first time.

---

356. MONOPOLKOMMISSION, 'Competition policy: The challenge of digital markets', Special report No. 68, July 2015, par. 218. See also S. BROOS AND J. MARCOS RAMOS, 'Google, Google Shopping and Amazon: The Importance of Competing Business Models and Two-Sided Intermediaries in Defining Relevant Markets', SSRN *Working Paper* November 2015, pp. 13-14, available at http://papers.ssrn.com/sol3/papers.cfm?abstract_id=2696045who even argue that Google and Amazon should be considered as operating in the same relevant market.

While the Commission left the exact boundaries of such a market open, it made a number of statements with regard to the relationship between mobile consumer communications apps and social networks. The Commission concluded that although communications apps like Facebook Messenger and WhatsApp offer certain elements which are typical of a social networking service, in particular sharing of messages and photos, there are important differences between these two types of services.[357]

In the Commission's view, social networking services tend to offer a richer social experience than communications apps. Whereas users of social networks are able to indicate their interests, activities or life events, and express opinions on other users' postings, the functionalities of communications apps are more limited and focus on enabling basic communication between users. According to the Commission, there are also differences in usage in the sense that communications apps facilitate instant real-time communication, while messages in social networks are not normally expected to be responded to in real time. As a last difference, the Commission noted that social networking services tend to enable communication and information sharing with a wider audience than communications apps. Whereas postings on a social network are generally shared with all contacts of a user, communication on communication apps is more personal and mainly occurs on a one-to-one basis or within small groups of a limited number of users.[358]

Ultimately, the Commission decided to leave open whether communications apps such as Facebook Messenger and WhatsApp fall within the scope of a potential market for social networking services, because the acquisition of WhatsApp by Facebook would not give rise to serious doubts as to its compatibility with the internal market under any alternative market definition.[359] Therefore, no strong conclusions can be drawn from the *Facebook/WhatsApp* merger decision about the view of the Commission to the market definition of social networking services.

In *Microsoft/Skype*, the Commission did take into account the competitive pressure coming from Facebook and Google in its analysis of the market for internet consumer communications services consisting of instant messaging, voice and video calls.[360] The Commission even argued that these players have a competitive advantage towards Microsoft because they offer communications services as part of a broader user experience through Facebook's social network and Google +.[361] The General Court confirmed that Facebook and Google would exert competitive pressure on the merged entity.[362] However, the fact that social networking providers such as Facebook and Google are considered to impose competitive constraints on providers of internet consumer communications services like Skype, does not mean that the latter services, in turn, have to be included in the competition analysis of a potential market for social

357. Case No COMP/M.7217 – *Facebook/WhatsApp*, 3 October 2014, par. 61.
358. Case No COMP/M.7217 – *Facebook/WhatsApp*, 3 October 2014, paras 54-56.
359. Case No COMP/M.7217 – *Facebook/WhatsApp*, 3 October 2014, par. 62.
360. Case No COMP/M.6281 – *Microsoft/Skype*, 7 October 2011, paras 18, 25, 105, 108, 109, 112 and 124.
361. Case No COMP/M.6281 – *Microsoft/Skype*, 7 October 2011, par. 127.
362. Judgment in *Cisco Systems Inc. and Messagenet SpA v. Commission*, T-79/12, ECLI:EU:T:2013:635, paras 70, 72, and 81.

networking services considering the richer user experience offered by social network providers. If communications apps were to be regarded as substitutes for social networks, the number of alternative providers in the relevant market would expand substantially, making it less likely that any of the market players has a dominant position.

Apart from communications apps, online services that enable interaction and exchange of content between users, such as YouTube, may also be considered as substitutes for social networks.[363] In the context of the *Facebook/WhatsApp* merger, the Commission noted that users employ online services, including communications apps and social networking services, in a complementary manner. Indeed, evidence was found that users of communications apps extensively multi-home. The existence of a considerable overlap between the user bases of WhatsApp and Facebook further confirmed this.[364]

Besides the relationship between social networking services and communications apps, the Commission assessed possible subsegmentations of a potential market for social networks in its *Facebook/WhatsApp* merger decision. The Commission argued that social networking services should not be further segmented according to the platform (PC, smartphone and tablet) or the operating system (such as Windows, Mac, Android and iOS) on which they are available, because the time and resources needed for developing a social network for a particular platform or operating system did not appear to be significant enough to support the existence of separate markets.[365]

With regard to a possible differentiation depending on the intended use of social networking services, respondents to the market investigation considered that a distinction could be drawn between social networks promoting interpersonal contact for private and entertainment purposes (such as Facebook or Google+) and services which are used for professional purposes (such as LinkedIn or Xing) even though the respondents acknowledged that there are overlaps between the purposes of intended use. Since no competition concerns would arise under any alternative market definition, the Commission decided to leave open whether social networking services should be segmented according to the intended use.[366]

In other jurisdictions, statements have also been made about the market definition of social networking services. In the private competition case *Qihoo/Tencent*, the Chinese Supreme Court ruled in October 2014 that instant messaging services constitute a separate relevant market of which microblogging services, such as Twitter, and social networks do not form part. The Court considered in this perspective, as did the European Commission in *Facebook/WhatsApp*,[367] that communication via social networking and microblogging platforms is aimed at an open group of a larger number of

---

363. Case No COMP/M.7217 – *Facebook/WhatsApp*, 3 October 2014, par. 150.
364. The Commission noted that 70-90% of WhatsApp active users are also Facebook users. See Case No COMP/M.7217 – *Facebook/WhatsApp*, 3 October 2014, par. 151 and footnote 85.
365. Case No COMP/M.7217 – *Facebook/WhatsApp*, 3 October 2014, paras 57-59.
366. Case No COMP/M.7217 – *Facebook/WhatsApp*, 3 October 2014, paras 59-60.
367. See Case No COMP/M.7217 – *Facebook/WhatsApp*, 3 October 2014, par. 56.

users, while instant messaging mainly consists of mutual private communications or internal communications within small groups.[368]

In a 2007 private competition dispute involving Myspace, the Court for the Central District of California defined a narrow relevant market for 'Internet-based social networking'. Internet connectivity services are not regarded as substitutes, because their main purpose is to give users access to the Internet. Online dating sites also fell outside the relevant market, since social networks have more functions than dating sites such as getting in touch with old contacts and keeping current friends informed about life.[369] The District Court did not consider potential offline substitutes in the form of so-called brick-and-mortar undertakings that provide people a physical location to meet and exchange views.

It can indeed be doubted whether equivalents exist in the offline world for the possibilities that online search engines, social networks and e-commerce platforms offer their users. The strength of these online platforms lies in the fact that they can be accessed everywhere as long as the user is connected to the internet. Contrary to for example libraries, meeting places and street markets, users of online search engines, social networks and e-commerce platforms do not have to go to a specific geographic location to be able to use the functionalities of these platforms. Furthermore, the amount of information and communication possibilities to which online platforms give users access cannot be compared with brick and mortar facilities that always have spatial limitations.[370]

With regard to the availability of online substitutes for search engines, social networks and e-commerce platforms, the growing convergence between the different functionalities provided by online platforms has to be taken into account. An example of convergence among internet services is the introduction by Facebook of a search functionality in its social network which enables users to search through posts, photos, videos and links shared on its platform.[371] Although the Commission left the market definition for internet search open in its *Microsoft/Yahoo* merger decision, it explicitly distinguished Facebook's social search functionality from internet search by arguing that this type of site search is limited to content from Facebook.[372] This indicates that Facebook's social network will not be included in a potential relevant market for horizontal internet search.[373]

---

368. Chinese Supreme Court in (2013) C3FJ4, *Qihoo/Tencent*, 16 October 2014, (E)(1).
369. *LiveUniverse, Inc. v. MySpace, Inc.*, No. CV 06-6994 AHM (RZx), 2007 WL 6865852 (C.D. Cal. June 4, 2007), par. 6. The Ninth Circuit confirmed the ruling of the District Court. See *LiveUniverse, Inc. v. MySpace, Inc.*, 304 Fed. Appx. 554 (9th Circ. 22 December 2008).
370. See also J. KAGAN, 'Bricks, Mortar, and Google: Defining the Relevant Antitrust Market for Internet-Based Companies', *New York Law School Law Review* 2010/11, vol. 55, no. 1, (271), pp. 290-291.
371. See http://search.fb.com/.
372. Case No COMP/M.5727 – *Microsoft/Yahoo! Search Business*, 18 February 2010, par. 32.
373. T. HOPPNER, 'Defining Markets for Multi-Sided Platforms: The Case of Search Engines', *World Competition* 2015, vol. 38, no. 3, (349), p. 363 argues that social search functionalities embedded in social networks have to be regarded as a separate relevant market next to markets for horizontal search, vertical search and semantic search (consisting of services directly providing answers to user queries like as Ask.com).

E-commerce platforms can be seen as vertical search engines on which users look for products they are interested in purchasing. The Commission seems to regard horizontal search as a separate market in the *Google* case as a result of which companies like Amazon and eBay are not included in the competition analysis. Nevertheless, it is increasingly being put forward that internet services are converging and can therefore be seen as substitutes although their functionality may differ to a certain extent.[374] The view has even been expressed that all internet services are in competition with each other for the attention of the user.[375] This would imply that there is a very broad market making it almost impossible for any undertaking to attain a dominant position.

The *Microsoft/Skype* and *Facebook/WhatsApp* merger decisions provide evidence for the statement that the functionalities of online platforms are still likely to be decisive for the definition of the relevant product market. By defining the relevant market as the market for internet consumer communications in *Microsoft/Skype* and by considering a potential market for social networks in *Facebook/WhatsApp*, the Commission confirmed that the differences in purpose of online services justify the definition of separate relevant markets. In the Commission's view, several relevant markets can thus be identified on the internet. With regard to the existence of an internet-wide relevant market for the attention of the user, the Chinese Supreme Court explicitly stated in *Qihoo/Tencent* that '*there exist obvious differences in properties, characteristics, functions and purpose of key products or services, provided on various Internet application platforms*' as a result of which '*it is difficult to say that products or services on different platforms that provide different applications and functions can effectively substitute each other*'.[376]

4.2.3 Relevant Product Market for the Advertiser Side

On the advertiser side, it is important to know whether a separate market has to be defined for, respectively, online and offline advertising and if so, whether a further distinction must be made between, for example search and non-search advertising. The European Commission has consistently held that online and offline advertising do not fall within the same relevant market.[377]

---

374. See N. Zingales, 'Product Market Definition in Online Search and Advertising', *The Competition Law Review* March 2013, vol. 9, no. 1, (29), pp. 43-46 and F. Thépot, 'Market Power in Online Search and Social Networking: A Matter of Two-Sided Markets', *World Competition* 2013, vol. 36, no. 2, (195), pp. 217-218.
375. See D.S. Evans, 'Attention Rivalry Among Online Platforms', *Journal of Competition Law and Economics* 2013, vol. 9, no. 2, (313). See also section 4.3.2 below where it is argued that a broad market for the attention of the internet user may be defined in order to make competition analysis more conducive towards innovation.
376. Chinese Supreme Court in (2013) C3FJ4, *Qihoo/Tencent*, 16 October 2014, (G)(2).
377. See Case IV/JV.1 – *Telia/Telenor/Schibstedt*, 27 May 1998; Case IV/M.1439 – *Telia/Telenor*, 13 October 1999; Case COMP/JV.48 – *Vodafone/Vivendi/Canal Plus*, 20 July 2000; Case No COMP/M.4731 – *Google/ DoubleClick*, 11 March 2008; Case No COMP/M.5727 – *Microsoft/ Yahoo! Search Business*, 18 February 2010 and Case No COMP/M.7217 – *Facebook/WhatsApp*, 3 October 2014, par. 79.

In its *Google/DoubleClick* merger decision, the Commission explained that online advertising has several characteristics that distinguish it from offline advertising. First, online advertising is capable of reaching a more targeted audience in a more effective way. On the internet, an advertiser can choose to display an advertisement to a particular group of users. In offline advertising, advertisers cannot target their audience as precisely as in online advertising by combining information available about the user's interests and preferences. Second, the measurement of the effectiveness of online advertisements is more precise compared with the systems available in offline advertising. In online advertising, advertisers can check how many users have viewed or clicked on their ads which enables them to retarget advertisements if necessary. The third distinguishing factor is the pricing mechanism applied to online advertising. Whereas offline pricing is estimated on the basis of general criteria, online advertising is paid on the basis of the exact number of users that viewed or clicked on the ad. The traditional offline media do not allow for such a precise connection between the reach and cost of the ad.[378]

Google/DoubleClick merger decision

At the time of the proposed concentration, the two parties were engaged in the following relevant activities. Google operated an internet search engine, offered online advertising space on its own websites and provided intermediation services to publishers and advertisers for the sale of online advertising space on partner websites through its AdSense network. DoubleClick was mainly active in the sale of ad serving, management and reporting technology worldwide to website publishers, advertisers and advertising agencies.

The Commission's market investigation pointed out that Google and DoubleClick were not exerting a significant competitive constraint on each other's activities. Therefore, the merger did not seem to significantly impede effective competition with regard to the elimination of actual competition. While it could not be excluded that DoubleClick would, absent the merger, have developed into an effective competitor of Google in the market for online ad intermediation, it was rather likely in the Commission's view that a sufficient number of other competitors would be left in the market. As a result, sufficient competitive pressure would remain after the merger. On this basis, the Commission concluded that the elimination of DoubleClick as a potential competitor would not have an adverse impact on competition in that market.

The Commission also analysed the potential effects of non-horizontal relationships between Google and DoubleClick. Concerns expressed by third parties involved foreclosure scenarios based on DoubleClick's market position in ad serving, foreclosure scenarios based on Google's market position in search advertising and online ad intermediation services, and foreclosure scenarios based on the combination of DoubleClick's and Google's databases on customer

---

378. Case No COMP/M.4731 – *Google/ DoubleClick*, 11 March 2008, paras 45-46.

online behaviour. The Commission found that such types of foreclosure would be unlikely to occur. Even if such scenarios did occur, they would not result in a significant impediment to effective competition according to the Commission. With regard to the possible combination of data of Google and DoubleClick after the merger, the Commission stated that this would be very unlikely to bring more traffic to AdSense so as to squeeze out competitors and ultimately enable the merged entity to charge higher prices for its intermediation services.

Case No COMP/M.4731 – *Google/ DoubleClick*, 11 March 2008, paragraphs 4-5, 192, 221-222, 278, 286-289, 329-332, 356-366.

In the merger cases *Google/DoubleClick*, *Microsoft/Yahoo* and *Facebook/WhatsApp*, the Commission discussed whether potential submarkets could be delineated within the broader online advertising market. A market for intermediation in online advertising was defined in *Google/DoubleClick* which separates 'direct sales' from 'intermediated sales' by publishers of web space to advertisers.[379] In the context of direct sales, advertisers and publishers negotiate the sale of online advertising space directly. Intermediated sales, on the other hand, are sales which require the involvement of an advertising platform which acts as intermediary matching advertisers and publishers by acquiring a publisher's web space through syndication agreements and filling this space by searching for interested advertisers. In *Microsoft/Yahoo*, the Commission left the exact product market definition with regard to intermediation open as the transaction would not raise any serious doubts under any alternative market definition.[380] Since online advertising intermediation results in the display of advertisements on third-party web pages instead of in the search results of the search engine platform, it will not be considered here further.[381]

Within the market of online advertising, a distinction can be made according to the way advertisements are selected to appear on a user's screen (search or non-search ads) and their visual appearance (text or display ads).[382] Both correspond to some extent in the sense that search ads tend to be almost exclusively text ads, whereas non-search ads can be either text or display ads.[383] In *Google/DoubleClick*, *Microsoft/Yahoo* and *Facebook/WhatsApp*, the Commission did not have to decide whether separate relevant markets existed for respectively search and non-search advertising, since the transactions reviewed in the three cases would not raise serious doubts as to the compatibility with the internal market under any of these market segmentations.[384]

---

379. Case No COMP/M.4731 – *Google/ DoubleClick*, 11 March 2008, par. 68.
380. Case No COMP/M.5727 – *Microsoft/Yahoo! Search Business*, 18 February 2010, par. 83.
381. Only if direct and intermediated sales of online advertisements impose competitive pressure on each other should intermediation be taken into account in the competition analysis of search engines. See also footnote 349.
382. Case No COMP/M.4731 – *Google/ DoubleClick*, 11 March 2008, par. 48.
383. Case No COMP/M.4731 – *Google/ DoubleClick*, 11 March 2008, par. 14.
384. Case No COMP/M.4731 – *Google/ DoubleClick*, 11 March 2008, par. 56 and Case No COMP/ M.5727 – *Microsoft/Yahoo! Search Business*, 18 February 2010, par. 75. With regard to the online advertising intermediation market defined in *Google/DoubleClick*, the Commission also

In *Google/DoubleClick*, the Commission found that search and non-search advertising may exert some degree of constraint on each other from the perspective of the advertiser. The essential difference between the two types of advertising for advertisers is the way of targeting. While for search ads the targeting is based on the exact intent of the user that it revealed by entering the search query, for non-search ads the targeting is based on more general criteria such as the context of the visited web page and the geographical location of the user. Although search and non-search ads thus have different appearance and targeting properties, the Commission argued that from the advertiser's point of view they can be considered substitutable to a certain extent on the ground that the differences of technical nature and aims are diminishing. In particular, the ability of non-search ads to target relevant users is improving and the use of search ads for building brand awareness is increasing.[385] However, from the publisher's point of view the distinction between the two types of online advertising is more clear. When a publisher decides to allocate space on a web page to a non-search ad, it cannot replace this space by selling search ads, since the latter only appear on a new web page generated by the search query which does not form part of the publisher's content inventory. For this reason, the Commission concluded that search and non-search ads have to be considered as complementary in the perspective of the publisher.[386] Although the Commission considered that search and non-search ads are substitutable on the demand side, supply side interchangeability thus seems more questionable.

In *Microsoft/Yahoo*, Microsoft argued that search advertising is a separate product market, because the format and pricing of search ads is different, it is purchased by advertisers for different purposes than non-search advertising and search advertising is sold through an auction system which is not the case for other types of online advertising. The results from the market investigation were mixed in the sense that not all respondents confirmed the arguments submitted by Microsoft as reasons for making a distinction between search and non-search ads. A number of responses even highlighted a degree of convergence between the two types of online advertising.[387] Since the transactions in both *Google/DoubleClick* and *Microsoft/Yahoo* would not raise serious doubts as to the compatibility with the internal market under any further market segmentation, the Commission could leave the exact product market definition open.

The Commission left the scope of the relevant market open for the same reason in its *Facebook/WhatsApp* decision. However, the Commission did make clear that the market investigation supported to a large extent the existence of a subsegmentation of the online advertising market between search and non-search advertising. The majority of the advertisers who took part in the market investigation considered that search and non-search advertisements are not substitutable because they serve different

---

    left open whether this market could be subdivided according to whether the intermediation concerns search or non-search advertisements (Case No COMP/M.4731 – *Google/ DoubleClick*, 11 March 2008, paras 70-73).

385. Case No COMP/M.4731 – *Google/ DoubleClick*, 11 March 2008, paras 50-53.
386. Case No COMP/M.4731 – *Google/ DoubleClick*, 11 March 2008, paras 54-55.
387. Case No COMP/M.5727 – *Microsoft/Yahoo! Search Business*, 18 February 2010, paras 63-74.

purposes. While search ads mainly serve to generate direct user traffic to a merchant's website, non-search ads are primarily used to build brand awareness.[388]

Since the Commission left open whether a further subsegmentation between online search and online non-search advertising was appropriate in the *Google/DoubleClick*, *Microsoft/Yahoo* and *Facebook/WhatsApp* mergers, future cases have to point out whether separate markets are to be defined for search and non-search advertising. If it is found that both types of online advertising fall within the same relevant market, Google and to a lesser extent Amazon, as providers of search advertising space (in this context Amazon's e-commerce platform can be regarded as a vertical search engine competing with Google for attracting advertisers interested in displaying ads in or alongside search results), and Facebook, as provider of non-search related advertising space, would be competing with each other which would reduce each of their market power.[389]

From the public statements made in press releases in the context of the *Google* case, it seems that the Commission is taking the view that online search advertising constitutes a relevant market of its own. For example, in a 2013 press release the Commission stated: *'Google also has a very strong position in the market for online search advertising'*.[390] The definition of separate relevant markets for search and non-search online advertisements is in line with the approach taken by competition authorities in other jurisdictions.[391]

In its sector inquiry into the online advertising industry in 2010, the Autorité de la concurrence concluded that search advertising constitutes a separate relevant market on which it found Google to be dominant. The substitutability between search and non-search ads was considered to be relatively limited mainly because of the more precise targeting possibilities of search advertising.[392] In the *Navx* case, the Autorité de la concurrence had already stated that online search-based advertising is likely to constitute a separate relevant market within the broader sector of online advertising.[393] Both in the *Navx* case and in the sector inquiry, the Autorité de la concurrence refers to the US *Google/DoubleClick* merger decision in which the Federal Trade Commission defined separate relevant markets for search and non-search advertising by arguing that *'advertising space sold by search engines is not a substitute for space sold directly*

---

388. Case No COMP/M.7217 – *Facebook/WhatsApp*, 3 October 2014, par. 76.
389. F. Thépot, 'Market Power in Online Search and Social Networking: A Matter of Two-Sided Markets', *World Competition* 2013, vol. 36, no. 2, (195), p. 214.
390. Press Release European Commission, 'Antitrust: Commission seeks feedback on commitments offered by Google to address competition concerns', 25 April 2013, IP/13/371, available at http://europa.eu/rapid/press-release_IP-13-371_en.htm.
391. T. Hoppner, 'Defining Markets for Multi-Sided Platforms: The Case of Search Engines', *World Competition* 2015, vol. 38, no. 3, (349), p. 361 even argues that a potential market for online search advertising should be divided further in a relevant market for horizontal and a relevant market for vertical search advertising.
392. Autorité de la Concurrence, Avis n° 10-A-29 du 14 décembre 2010 sur le fonctionnement concurrentiel de la publicité en ligne, par. 137-194 (with regard to market definition) and 224-269 (with regard to Google's dominance).
393. Autorité de la Concurrence, Décision n° 10-MC-01 du 30 juin 2010 relative à la demande de mesures conservatoires présentée par la société Navx, paras 124-130, French version available at http://www.autoritedelaconcurrence.fr/pdf/avis/10mc01.pdf.

or indirectly by publishers of vice versa' because *'the evidence shows that the sale of search advertising does not operate as a significant constraint on the prices or quality of other online advertising'.*[394] In the view of the Autorité de la concurrence, Facebook may improve its ability to target advertisements by relying on user profile data in the future, but at the time of the sector inquiry the targeting of profiles of social network users could not be regarded as an alternative to search-based ads. The reason given for this was that advertisements on Facebook do not satisfy active queries of users but are rather used for branding campaigns based on 'likes' by users.[395]

Although leaving open whether potential subsegmentations of the relevant market for online advertising can constitute relevant markets in their own right, the Commission examined in *Facebook/WhatsApp* whether a separate relevant product market should be defined for the provision of online non-search advertising services on social networking sites. This would mean that within a potential relevant market for online non-search advertising a further segmentation is made between online non-search advertising on social networking sites and online non-search advertising on other websites or platforms. The results of the market investigation were mixed in this regard. While a number of respondents considered that other forms of non-search advertising are not as effective as advertising on social networking websites, other respondents took the view that many other advertising platforms offering non-search ads are equally well-placed to serve non-search needs.[396] In a US private competition case against Myspace, the plaintiff alleged a relevant market for 'advertising on Internet-based social networking sites' arguing that there are no good substitutes because: *'Such sites offer advertisers the unique ability to tap into user-generated content and to establish "buzz" about their products through word of mouth as users comment upon and share the advertising with others, essentially integrating an advertiser's message into the rumor mill'.*[397] Since the Court for the Central District of California considered that there was no anticompetitive conduct and causal antitrust injury, it could leave open whether this market definition was adequate.

While leaving open whether the market for online advertising should be segmented between mobile and PC-based advertising, such a potential subsegmentation has been considered by the Commission in a number of merger cases. In *Microsoft/ Yahoo*, the Commission examined whether mobile search advertising should be distinguished from PC-based search advertising. In that regard, the market investigation had revealed that a majority of the respondents did not consider mobile search advertising as a separate relevant market even though it presents some distinguishing

---

394. Statement of the Federal Trade Commission, *Google/DoubleClick*, FTC File No. 071-0170, 20 December 2007, p. 3, available at http://www.ftc.gov/system/files/documents/public_statements/418081/071220googledc-commstmt.pdf as referred to in Autorité de la Concurrence, Décision n° 10-MC-01 du 30 juin 2010 relative à la demande de mesures conservatoires présentée par la société Navx, par. 130 and Autorité de la Concurrence, Avis n° 10-A-29 du 14 décembre 2010 sur le fonctionnement concurrentiel de la publicité en ligne, par. 109.

395. Autorité de la Concurrence, Avis n° 10-A-29 du 14 décembre 2010 sur le fonctionnement concurrentiel de la publicité en ligne, paras 167-170.

396. Case No COMP/M.7217 – *Facebook/WhatsApp*, 3 October 2014, par. 77.

397. *LiveUniverse, Inc. v. MySpace, Inc.*, No. CV 06-6994 AHM (RZx), 2007 WL 6865852 (C.D. Cal. 4 June 2007), par. 17.

technical and commercial features in terms of the size of the ads and the appropriateness of location-based advertising.[398] In the context of the setting up of a joint venture in the United Kingdom involving Telefónica, Vodafone and Everything Everywhere, the Commission assessed whether mobile online (search or non-search) advertising accessed on a mobile handset such as a smartphone and a tablet constitutes a product market separate from static online (search or non-search) advertising accessed through desktop or laptop computers. The Commission argued that these two types of online advertising currently present significant differences, which may diminish at some point in the future, but left open whether a distinction should be made.[399] In *Facebook/WhatsApp*, the Commission noted that the results of the market investigation as regards a possible segmentation between online advertising on PCs and mobile devices were mixed. While some respondents highlighted the differences between advertising on different platforms in terms of technical characteristics, user experience and ad profitability, other respondents submitted that they are essentially substitutable.[400]

4.2.4 Relevant Geographic Market for Online Platforms

With regard to the geographic market definition for online advertising and its possible subsegments, the Commission concluded in a number of merger decisions that the relevant geographic market should be defined as national in scope or alongside linguistic borders within the EEA. Factors pointing to such a market definition included, in the Commission's view, customers' purchasing preferences and languages, and the presence of support and sales networks located at national level.[401]

While leaving the exact geographic market definition for internet search open in its *Microsoft/Yahoo* merger decision, the Commission argued that the geographic scope of such a potential market could be wider than national or linguistic markets because search engines like Google and Yahoo operate on a global basis and strive to index the whole internet. In addition, the Commission considered that fluency in English, the language of most of the websites, is increasingly extended across the world. From a demand side perspective, the Commission acknowledged, however, that many users require access to a search engine and to search results in their own language.[402] Continuing in the latter vein, the Commission referred to the EEA as the appropriate geographic scope of a potential market for web search in the context of the *Google Shopping* case.[403] Considering that e-commerce platforms can be regarded as vertical

---

398. Case No COMP/M.5727 – *Microsoft/Yahoo! Search Business*, 18 February 2010, paras 77-81.
399. Case No COMP/M.6314 – *Telefónica UK/Vodafone UK/Everything Everywhere/JV*, 4 September 2012, paras 153-159.
400. Case No COMP/M.7217 – *Facebook/WhatsApp*, 3 October 2014, par. 78.
401. Case No COMP/M.5727 – *Microsoft/Yahoo! Search Business*, 18 February 2010, paras 91-93; Case No COMP/M.4731 – *Google/ DoubleClick*, 11 March 2008, par. 82-84; Case No COMP/M.7217 – *Facebook/WhatsApp*, 3 October 2014, paras 81-83.
402. Case No COMP/M.5727 – *Microsoft/Yahoo! Search Business*, 18 February 2010, paras 96-98.
403. Press Release European Commission, 'Antitrust: Commission sends Statement of Objections to Google on comparison shopping service; opens separate formal investigation on Android', 15 April 2015, IP/15/4780, available at http://europa.eu/rapid/press-release_IP-15-4780_en.htm.

search engines, it is likely that the Commission will apply a similar reasoning about the geographic market definition of these services.

In *Facebook/WhatsApp*, the Commission concluded that the geographic market for online social networking services includes at least the EEA. While there were indications that the geographic scope of the market could be worldwide given the global scope of the internet, the Commission considered that the relevant geographic market for the assessment of the case was EEA-wide in line with a more conservative approach. In this perspective, the Commission explained that although respondents to the market investigation stated that there are generally no differences in a social networking service offered in different geographic regions in terms of price, functionalities, platforms and operating systems served, limited geographic adjustments appear to be present relating to language and minor functionalities. Other possible geographic differences mentioned by the Commission include marketing costs, legal/regulatory requirements and customers' preferences.[404]

4.2.5 Economic Tools for Market Definition on Multi-sided Platforms

The economic tools that are used to define relevant markets may have to be adapted to the specific features of multi-sided platforms. The so-called SSNIP test, which stands for Small but Significant and Non-transitory Increase in Price, is commonly used for market definition in one-sided markets. This test seeks to identify the market as the smallest set of substitutable products or services within which a hypothetical monopolist can profitably impose a significant (5% to 10%) and non-transitory (one year) increase in price. If such a price increase would lead a significant number of customers to switch to another product, the latter product can be seen as a substitute and should thus be included in the relevant market. The elasticity of demand is central to the application of the SSNIP test. In case the demand elasticity cannot be estimated, the SSNIP test is usually performed by way of an analysis of the 'critical loss'. The critical loss is the maximum loss of sales that can be sustained by a hypothetical monopolist as a result of a price increase without rendering the price increase unprofitable. If the actual loss following the particular price increase is less than the critical loss, the price increase is profitable. The relevant market is defined as soon as the profit gains from the price increase are equal to the loss of profits from the decrease in sales for the given set of products in the market.[405]

To account for the multi-sided network effects, the changes in demand and profit as a result of a price increase on one side should be considered simultaneously on all sides of the platform. Unlike in one-sided markets where the demand of only one customer group has to be taken into account, in two-sided markets it must be recognised that the demand on one side of the platform is linked with the demand on another side. The SSNIP test should therefore not be applied to the different sides of the platform in isolation. If it is not acknowledged that a reduction of the number of

---

404. Case No COMP/M.7217 – *Facebook/WhatsApp*, 3 October 2014, paras 64-68.
405. See Commission Notice on the definition of relevant market for the purposes of Community competition law [1997] OJ C 372/5, paras 17-18.

customers on side A will likely lead to a drop in the number of customers on side B too, the competitive constraints between the different customer groups are overlooked.[406]

The SSNIP test will be difficult to apply to online platforms, since users of these services are typically given access free of charge. In that situation, it is impossible to determine from which benchmark the price rise of 5% to 10% should be calculated. A price increase of a product with zero price would still be zero.[407] Because users expect online services to be offered free of charge, the fact that a fee is charged, even if it is only a symbolic fee of for example EUR 1 cent per search, may drive a significant number of users to other platforms that continue to give users access to their functionality free of charge.[408] Price is therefore not a reliable indicator to measure the substitutability of services in the online environment where providers compete on the basis of non-price dimensions such as quality and innovation. With regard to markets characterised by competition *for* the market where innovation rather than price is the relevant parameter, it has been suggested to apply a 5% to 10% reduction in R&D expenditures instead of an increase in price.[409]

However, it is also important to recognise the multi-sided nature of online platforms according to which the free user side is financed by advertisers who do pay a price for interacting with users. As regards the assessment of substitutability on the advertiser side of online platforms, it has been proposed to rely on surveys and interviews in order to assess whether advertisers would still employ the advertising services of a particular platform if the number of users on the other side dropped with 5% to 10% while advertising prices remained the same.[410] In the context of the Chinese *Qihoo/Tencent* private competition dispute, the Guangdong Court in its 2013 judgment explicitly ignored the advertiser side of an instant messaging service by rejecting the approach put forward by the economic expert in the case to conduct a SSNIP test by engaging in a reduction in quality or an increase in the display of advertisements to users. Instead, the Court focused on evidence related to price even though the service was provided to users free of charge. It argued that although quality and advertising are relevant, '*a more important factor to be considered is whether a lot of demand*

---

406. Several scholars have made specific suggestions on how to modify the SSNIP test for application to multi-sided platforms: D.S. EVANS AND M.D. NOEL, 'The Analysis of Mergers that involve Multisided Platform Businesses', *Journal of Competition Law and Economics* 2008, vol. 4, no. 3, (663); A. ALEXANDROV, G. DELTAS AND D.F. SPULBER, 'Antitrust And Competition In Two-Sided Markets', *Journal of Competition Law and Economics* 2011, vol. 7, no. 4, (775) and L. FILISTRUCCHI, D. GERADIN, E. VAN DAMME, ET AL., 'Market Definition in Two-Sided Markets: Theory and Practice', *Journal of Competition Law and Economics* 2014, vol. 10, no. 2, (293), pp. 329-333.
407. D.S. EVANS, 'The Antitrust Economics of Free', *Competition Policy International* 20 May 2011, vol. 7, pp. 22-23, available at http://papers.ssrn.com/sol3/papers.cfm?abstract_id=1813193; N. ZINGALES, 'Product Market Definition in Online Search and Advertising', *The Competition Law Review* March 2013, vol. 9, no. 1, (29), pp. 33-34.
408. D. AUER AND N. PETIT, 'Two-Sided Markets and the Challenge of Turning Economic Theory into Antitrust Policy', *The Antitrust Bulletin* 2015, vol. 60, no. 4, (426), p. 443.
409. P.A. GEROSKI, 'Competition in Markets and Competition for Markets', *Journal of Industry, Competition and Trade* 2003, vol. 3, no. 3, (151), pp. 159-160 and in particular footnote 13.
410. J. VERHAERT, 'The Challenges Involved with the Application of Article 102 TFEU to the New Economy: A Case Study of Google', *European Competition Law Review* 2014, vol. 35, no. 6, (265), pp. 269-270.

substitution will be generated if a hypothetical monopolist charges the service at a small scale continuously.[411] On appeal, the Chinese Supreme Court dismissed the approach of the Guangdong Court and stated that the application of the SSNIP test in the case at hand was improper because instant messaging services were offered free of charge to users and providers instead competed on quality.[412] In the view of the Chinese Supreme Court, a price rise from zero to any amount, however small, would imply a major change in the product characteristics or business model and would result in a too broad relevant market including many products in the same market that are not substitutes.[413]

An approach that has been put forward to measure the substitutability of the functionality offered to users by online social networks is to apply a Small but Significant Non-transitory Decrease in Quality ('SSNDQ') by enabling a provider to limit its maintenance expenses which would result in users having log in problems, website shut-downs, crashes due to user overload or users becoming victims of spam or hacking.[414] In *Qihoo/Tencent*, the Chinese Supreme Court referred to the SSNDQ test as a possible instrument for measuring the substitutability of free services. However, the Supreme Court also recognised the difficulty in assessing a quality decline and in obtaining relevant data. For this reason, the Supreme Court argued that an SSNDQ test is useful for quantitative rather than qualitative analysis.[415] In particular, it would be challenging to simulate a decrease in quality that is equivalent to a price increase of 5% to 10% and to quantify the effects of quality degradation on the revenues of the market players in order to determine to profitableness of such a degradation. Furthermore, one can doubt whether all users experience a decrease in quality of an online service in the same way. Quality is not as objective as price as an indicator.[416]

The same can be said of a rise in the display of ads on online platforms. The attitude of users towards advertising may differ which makes the number of displayed ads an unreliable indicator of the utility experienced by users.[417] The amount of

411. D.S. EVANS AND V. YANHUA ZHANG, 'The Qihoo v. Tencent Landmark Decision', *Competition Policy International* 9 April 2013, p. 3. See also T. JIANG, 'The Qihoo/Tencent Dispute in the Instant Messaging Market: The First Milestone in the Chinese Competition Law Enforcement?', *World Competition* 2014, vol. 37, no. 3, (369), pp. 376-377 and 384 who contends that the Guangdong Court merely borrowed the concept of SSNIP without properly conducting the underlying economic test.
412. Chinese Supreme Court in (2013) C3FJ4, *Qihoo/Tencent*, 16 October 2014, (B)(3).
413. D. STALLIBRASS AND S. PANG, 'Clash of Titans: How China Disciplines Internet Markets', *Journal of European Competition Law & Practice* 2015, vol. 6, no. 6, (418), p. 419.
414. A. GEBICKA AND A. HEINEMANN, 'Social Media & Competition Law', *World Competition* 2014, vol. 37, no. 2, (149), pp. 157-159.
415. Chinese Supreme Court in (2013) C3FJ4, *Qihoo/Tencent*, 16 October 2014, (B)(3).
416. See the 2013 OECD report on quality in competition analysis in which it is concluded that although quality is regarded as an important non-price parameter for competition, competition authorities have not yet succeeded in incorporating systematically the assessment of quality within competition analysis (OECD POLICY ROUNDTABLES, 'The Role and Measurement of Quality in Competition Analysis', 28 October 2013, available at http://www.oecd.org/competition/Quality-in-competition-analysis-2013.pdf).
417. See J.M. NEWMAN, 'Antitrust in Zero-Price Markets: Foundations', *SSRN Working Paper* July 2014, pp. 33-34, available at http://papers.ssrn.com/sol3/papers.cfm?abstract_id=2474874& download=yes who proposes to transform the SSNIP test into a so-called SSNIC (Small but

personal data extracted by a provider of an online service also does not seem to be a good proxy for assessing substitutability because users may not notice an increase in the quantity of data collected especially due to the fact that the privacy policies of online services often lack in transparency and accessibility.[418]

As regards search engines, social networks and e-commerce platforms, a decrease in the relevance of, respectively, search results, social interactions and purchase suggestions may enable competition authorities to measure the degree of substitutability of the services provided to users.[419] The difficulty with this approach is that users do not know what the most relevant search results, social interactions or purchase suggestions in a particular situation are and therefore cannot assess the level of relevance of the results, interactions and suggestions returned by the service. In this perspective, search engines, social networks and recommendation systems of e-commerce platforms can be seen as credence goods. It therefore seems hard if not impossible to simulate how users perceive a small reduction in relevance. In addition, such an approach merely takes the user side of the platform into account and disregards the link with advertisers which may lead to an erroneous assessment of the competitive dynamics in the market.[420] In conclusion: whereas economists agree that the multi-sided nature of the market has to be taken into account when applying the SSNIP test, there is no consensus on how the SSNIP test can be modified in order to adequately measure the substitutability of online services offered in a multi-sided environment.

4.3 MARKET DEFINITION IN NEW ECONOMY INDUSTRIES

As discussed in section 4.2.2, the statements made by the European Commission in the context of the *Google* case and its merger decisions in *Microsoft/Yahoo*, *Microsoft/Skype* and *Facebook/WhatsApp* indicate that relevant product markets are still defined on the basis of the functionality offered to users. As a result, numerous relatively narrow relevant markets can be distinguished on the internet such as a market for horizontal search, a market for consumer communications services and a market for social networking.

By defining relevant markets narrowly on the basis of the features made available to users, the Commission implicitly chooses to focus on preserving sustaining innovation within existing markets rather than encouraging disruptive innovation in new markets. If the relevant market is defined around the specific functionality offered,

---

Significant and Non-transitory Increase in Costs (to consumers)) test which relies on increases in attention costs (more advertisements) or information costs (more personal data extracted) to test the substitutability of online platforms.

418. In the context of social networks, see for instance E. WAUTERS, V. DONOSO AND E. LIEVENS, 'Optimizing Transparency for Users of Social Networking Sites', *info* 2014, vol. 16, no. 6, (8).

419. D. AUER AND N. PETIT, 'Two-Sided Markets and the Challenge of Turning Economic Theory into Antitrust Policy', *The Antitrust Bulletin* 2015, vol. 60, no. 4, (426), p. 443.

420. See also J. VERHAERT, 'The Challenges Involved with the Application of Article 102 TFEU to the New Eeconomy: A Case Study of Google', *European Competition Law Review* 2014, vol. 35, no. 6, (265), p. 270.

potential competitive constraints from related or future services are not taken into account.[421] This is all the more relevant in the new economy where market players typically compete by introducing new services instead of by substituting or improving existing services. Since the preference for one type of competition or innovation can be regarded as a policy choice,[422] it is a valid decision of the Commission to favour competition *in* the market and sustaining innovation over competition *for* the market and disruptive innovation. Nevertheless, it is worth considering how traditional competition analysis in general and market definition specifically could be adapted to better take account of the predominance of innovation over price as a parameter of competition in new economy industries.

4.3.1 US Initiative Towards a Framework for Innovation in Competition Analysis

Traditional competition law analysis relies on an assessment of a certain type of behaviour in existing markets. Incentives for disruptive innovation may be hard to accommodate, since this type of innovation takes place before a market for the new development exists. A starting point for developing a framework for taking into account disruptive innovation would be to define markets more loosely and impose less strict market boundaries. The current approach towards market definition according to which a product either falls within or outside the relevant market may be too mechanical and lead to the situation that products which are not perfect substitutes but which still impose some degree of competitive pressure, are excluded from the assessment.[423] For new economy industries, this may result in the definition of very narrow relevant markets and unjustified findings of dominance.[424]

The United States pioneered in giving innovation a more prominent place in competition analysis. While holding leadership positions at the Antitrust Division of the United States Department of Justice (DoJ), Gilbert and Sunshine[425] initiated a debate about the role of innovation in merger analysis in the 1990s. In a scholarly article, they introduced the concept of 'innovation markets' which would enable competition authorities to measure the impact of a merger in downstream product markets as well as in upstream innovation markets. In their view, the latter approach is necessary to assess the effects of a proposed transaction on innovation in markets where the merging parties are not actual or even potential competitors prior to the

421. C. AHLBORN, D.S. EVANS AND A.J. PADILLA, 'Competition Policy in the New Economy: Is European Competition Law Up to the Challenge?', *European Competition Law Review* 2001, vol. 22, no. 5, (156), p. 162.
422. See section 3.4.2 above.
423. D.S. EVANS AND M. NOEL, 'Defining Antitrust Markets When Firms Operate Two-Sided Platforms', *Columbia Business Law Review* 2005, vol. 2005, (101), pp. 130-131.
424. C. AHLBORN, D.S. EVANS AND A.J. PADILLA, 'Competition Policy in the New Economy: Is European Competition Law Up to the Challenge?', *European Competition Law Review* 2001, vol. 22, no. 5, (156), pp. 161-162.
425. Both Richard J. Gilbert and Steven C. Sunshine were formerly Deputy Assistant Attorneys General in the Antitrust Division of the United States Department of Justice.

merger.[426] If competition authorities limit their analysis to current product markets, competition enforcement may be either too restrictive or too permissive. Firms outside the product market that put competitive pressure on the incumbent with regard to innovation would be disregarded if the competition authority only looks at existing markets. Alternatively, competition concerns may be overlooked in case undertakings are not active on the same product market while competing fiercely with respect to innovation.[427]

In order to address these issues, Gilbert and Sunshine proposed to drop the focus on product markets and to assess the anticompetitive effects of a merger by way of the following five steps: (1) identify the overlapping R&D activities of the merging firms; (2) identify alternative sources of R&D that are reasonable substitutes for the activities of the merging firms; (3) evaluate actual and potential competition from downstream products which would render a reduction in R&D unprofitable; (4) assess the increase in concentration in R&D that would occur as a result of the merger; and (5) assess whether the merger would lead to R&D efficiencies offsetting a potential reduction in R&D investments.[428]

Although Gilbert and Sunshine described the innovation market methodology in the context of merger review, they made clear that it could also be applied to evaluate other arrangements such as R&D agreements.[429] The innovation market concept was adopted in the latter field in the 1995 Antitrust Guidelines for the Licensing of Intellectual Property. The Guidelines specify that in addition to product markets and technology markets, innovation markets can be used as a framework for assessing the effect of a licensing agreement on competition in developing new or improved goods or processes. An innovation market was defined as consisting of:

> the research and development directed to particular new or improved goods or processes, and the close substitutes for that research and development. The close substitutes are research and development efforts, technologies, and goods[430] that significantly constrain the exercise of market power with respect to the relevant research and development, for example by limiting the ability and incentive of a hypothetical monopolist to retard the pace of research and development. The Agencies will delineate an innovation market only when the capabilities to engage in the relevant research and development can be associated with specialized assets or characteristics of specific firms.[431]

---

426. R.J. GILBERT AND S.C. SUNSHINE, 'Incorporating Dynamic Efficiency Concerns in Merger Analysis: The Use of Innovation Markets', *Antitrust Law Journal* 1995, vol. 63, no. 2, (569), p. 570.
427. B.R. KERN, 'Innovation Markets, Future Markets, or Potential Competition: How Should Competition Authorities Account for Innovation Competition in Merger Reviews?', *World Competition* 2014, vol. 37, no. 2, (173), p. 174.
428. R.J. GILBERT AND S.C. SUNSHINE, 'Incorporating Dynamic Efficiency Concerns in Merger Analysis: The Use of Innovation Markets', *Antitrust Law Journal* 1995, vol. 63, no. 2, (569), pp. 595-597.
429. R.J. GILBERT AND S.C. SUNSHINE, 'Incorporating Dynamic Efficiency Concerns in Merger Analysis: The Use of Innovation Markets', *Antitrust Law Journal* 1995, vol. 63, no. 2, (569), p. 594.
430. The Guidelines contain the following footnote: 'For example, the licensor of research and development may be constrained in its conduct not only by competing research and development efforts but also by other existing goods that would compete with the goods under development'.
431. United States Department of Justice and Federal Trade Commission, 'Antitrust Guidelines for the Licensing of Intellectual Property', 6 April 1995, par. 3.2.3. The introduction of the

In the 2010 US Horizontal Merger Guidelines, the reliance on markets was dropped and instead the concept of 'innovation competition' was introduced. The relevant question is whether a merger is likely to diminish innovation competition by encouraging the merged firm to curtail its innovative efforts below the level that would prevail in the absence of the merger. According to the 2010 US Horizontal Merger Guidelines, the curtailment of innovation can '*take the form of reduced incentive to continue with an existing product-development effort or reduced incentive to initiate development of new products*'.[432] An example of a US merger case in which the notion 'innovation competition' has been applied is the acquisition of General Motor's Allison Transmission Division by ZF Friedrichshafen. In addition to the two product markets identified in the complaint (the market for automatic transmissions for transit buses and the market for automatic transmissions for heavy refuse route trucks), the DoJ also expressed concerns regarding a third market that was defined as the market for '*technological innovation in the design, development and production of heavy automatic transmissions*'. The definition of this market enabled the DoJ to assess the effect of the proposed transaction on the development of future technologies.[433]

4.3.2 EU Approach Towards Innovation in Competition Enforcement

A notion similar to innovation competition has been adopted in the EU under the name 'competition in innovation' in the 2011 Guidelines on the Applicability of Article 101 TFEU to Horizontal Co-operation Agreements (EU Horizontal Guidelines). The European Commission acknowledges that competition in innovation in the context of R&D cooperation in some cases cannot be sufficiently assessed by analysing actual or potential competition in existing product or technology markets.[434] However, in

---

innovation market in the Intellectual Property Guidelines led to criticism from scholars, in particular G.A. HAY, 'Innovations in Antitrust Enforcement', *Antitrust Law Journal* 1995, vol. 64, no. 1, (7); R.J. HOERNER, 'Innovation Markets: New Wine in Old Bottles?', *Antitrust Law Journal* 1995, vol. 64, no. 1, (49); and R.T. RAPP, 'The Misapplication of the Innovation Market Approach to Merger Analysis', *Antitrust Law Journal* 1995, vol. 64, no. 1, (19). For a description of the criticism that they expressed, see J. DREXL, 'Anticompetitive Stumbling Stones on the Way to a Cleaner World: Protecting Competition in Innovation Without a Market', *Journal of Competition Law and Economics* 2012, vol. 8, no. 3, (507), pp. 517-518.

432. United States Department of Justice and Federal Trade Commission, 'Horizontal Merger Guidelines', 19 August 2010, par. 6.4.

433. *United States v. General Motors Corp.*, Civ. No. 93-530 (D.Del. filed Nov. 16, 1993). For a more elaborate description of this case and other US cases that dealt with innovation competition, see B.R. KERN, 'Innovation Markets, Future Markets, or Potential Competition: How Should Competition Authorities Account for Innovation Competition in Merger Reviews?', *World Competition* 2014, vol. 37, no. 2, (173), pp. 184-190.

434. Communication from the Commission - Guidelines on the applicability of Article 101 of the TFEU to horizontal co-operation agreements (EU Horizontal Guidelines) [2011] OJ C11/1, par. 119. In the previous version of the EU Horizontal Guidelines, reference was made to 'innovation markets' instead of 'competition in innovation'. However, the Commission did not define the term innovation market. See Commission Notice - Guidelines on the applicability of Article 81 of the EC Treaty to horizontal cooperation agreements [2001] OJ C3/02, par. 60.

industries in which the innovation process is not clearly structured so as to allow the identification of R&D poles, the Commission sees no other option than to rely on these existing markets.[435]

In industries in which the innovative efforts are structured in such a way that it is possible to identify competing R&D poles at an early stage, such as the pharmaceutical sector where new products have to go through regulatory approval procedures, the Commission suggests to analyse whether a sufficient number of R&D poles will remain after the agreement takes effect. The following approach is proposed by the Commission:

> The starting point of the analysis is the R&D of the parties. Then credible competing R&D poles have to be identified. In order to assess the credibility of competing poles, the following aspects have to be taken into account: the nature, scope and size of any other R&D efforts, their access to financial and human resources, know-how/patents, or other specialised assets as well as their timing and their capability to exploit possible results. An R&D pole is not a credible competitor if it cannot be regarded as a close substitute for the parties' R&D effort from the viewpoint of, for instance, access to resources or timing.[436]

The framework enables competition authorities to take into account incentives for disruptive innovation, since it does not merely rely on competition in existing markets.[437]

Following the approach introduced in the area of Article 101 TFEU in the EU Horizontal Guidelines, the European Commission could look at R&D investments in the other branches of competition law to assess competition in innovation beyond existing relevant product markets. In situations in which it is possible to identify competing R&D poles that are aimed at developing substitutable products or technology, the Commission suggests in the Guidelines on Horizontal Co-operation Agreements to analyse whether after the relevant cooperation agreement there will be a sufficient number of remaining R&D poles.[438] A similar approach could be applied to market definition in merger and abuse of dominance cases in the online environment where market players do not merely compete by lowering prices and improving products in existing markets but also by introducing new products which shift demand and create a new market of their own. In this context, R&D investment can be seen as input to new products and technologies. Instead of relying on a pure product market definition,

---

435. Communication from the Commission - Guidelines on the applicability of Article 101 of the TFEU to horizontal co-operation agreements (EU Horizontal Guidelines) [2011] OJ C11/1, par. 122.
436. Communication from the Commission - Guidelines on the applicability of Article 101 of the TFEU to horizontal co-operation agreements (EU Horizontal Guidelines) [2011] OJ C11/1, par. 120.
437. See also J. DREXL, 'Anticompetitive Stumbling Stones on the Way to a Cleaner World: Protecting Competition in Innovation Without a Market', Journal of Competition Law and Economics 2012, vol. 8, no. 3, (507), pp. 520-522.
438. Communication from the Commission - Guidelines on the applicability of Article 101 of the TFEU to horizontal co-operation agreements (EU Horizontal Guidelines) [2011] OJ C11/1, paras 119-120.

upstream markets for R&D expenditure could be defined.[439] However, as the Commission argues in the EU Horizontal Guidelines this method only works if it is possible to identify R&D efforts at an early stage. In the ICT sector, companies often do not disclose this type of information as a result of which it becomes hard to apply this approach. In addition, it is impossible to know which R&D investments will effectively lead to new products in future markets.[440]

Nevertheless, even in case the precise R&D efforts are unobservable it could still be possible to identify the assets to which potential competitors need access in order to compete with the incumbent. The US 1995 Antitrust Guidelines for the Licensing of Intellectual Property already referred to such resources as 'specialised assets'.[441] The notion was also incorporated in the EU Horizontal Guidelines which mentions know-how and patents as examples.[442] The application of the notion of specialised assets would make the definition of the relevant market dependent on the capabilities and resources that are necessary for a firm to have in order to innovate. The proposed acquisition of Northrop Grumman by Lockheed Martin in 1998 in the US illustrates this. In the case, the DoJ defined a market for the '*development, production and sale of high performance fixed-wing military aircraft for the U.S. military*' while it could not observe on what particular innovations the companies were working. In this context, the DoJ stated: '*Northrop, Lockheed, and Boeing do all pursue new ideas and designs for future high performance fixed-wing military aircraft to meet specific combat needs, and these firms are the only companies that have the capabilities to compete for combined electronics system integration and military airframe upgrades*'.[443]

Although R&D investments and specialised assets such as patents and know-how may be imperfect proxies of the level of innovation in an industry,[444] the type of R&D and assets in which investments are made can give an indication of the direction in which innovation will develop and could form a starting point for defining a relevant market that is more favourable to innovation as compared to a strict product market definition. As more hints become available on what will constitute the technology of the future, it will be easier to identify the required inputs and thus the relevant market for innovation. In order to make market definition more conducive to disruptive innovation, a very wide relevant market should be defined as long as it is not clear which products or technologies will dominate in the future.

---

439. See also M.L. Katz and H.A. Shelanski, '"Schumpeterian" Competition and Antitrust Policy in High-Tech Markets', *Competition* 2005, vol. 14, (47), p. 50.
440. J.G. Sidak and D.J. Teece, 'Dynamic Competition in Antitrust Law', *Journal of Competition Law and Economics* 2009, vol. 5, no. 4, (581), pp. 612-614.
441. US Department of Justice and Federal Trade Commission, 'Antitrust Guidelines for the Licensing of Intellectual Property', 6 April 1995, par. 3.2.3.
442. Communication from the Commission - Guidelines on the applicability of Article 101 of the TFEU to horizontal co-operation agreements (EU Horizontal Guidelines) [2011] OJ C11/1, par. 120.
443. *United States v. Lockheed Martin Corp.*, Civ. No. 98-00731 (D.D.C. filed 23 March 1998). See further, B.R. Kern, 'Innovation Markets, Future Markets, or Potential Competition: How Should Competition Authorities Account for Innovation Competition in Merger Reviews?', *World Competition* 2014, vol. 37, no. 2, (173), pp. 185-186.
444. See section 3.2.

An example of such a broad relevant market for internet services would be a market for attention. This market definition is favourable to disruptive innovation, since it does not rely on the specific service that is offered to internet users. Instead, a market for attention implies that all businesses that attract consumers to their websites or mobile applications compete for the limited time that users spend online irrespective of the specific functionalities of the products and services that are offered.[445] An alternative market definition for online platforms that does not take the specific service or functionality offered to users and advertisers as object but is based on the input needed to deliver those services would be a market for the data used to tailor the services to the specific needs of users and advertisers. As discussed above,[446] such a relevant market for user data cannot be defined under current standards for market definition unless the data is sold as a separate product to third parties. However, most players like Google and Facebook do not trade user data to third parties but use the collected information as an input for the provision of relevant functionalities to users and targeted advertising services to advertisers.

It is submitted that the definition of an additional relevant market for user data is still appropriate in such circumstances even though, strictly speaking, there is no supply and demand for data. By regarding data as a specialised asset in analogy to the EU Horizontal Guidelines, a hypothetical or potential market for data can be defined in addition to the actual relevant markets for the services provided to users and advertisers. This will enable competition authorities and courts to take a form of potential competition into consideration whereby online platform providers do not only compete in the product markets for the specific services offered to users and advertisers but also in a broader market for data that can be deployed for improving the quality and relevance of these services.[447] In addition, a more forward-looking stance towards market definition can be taken in this way which goes beyond analysing current usages of data in narrowly-drawn relevant markets for products and services.[448]

Critics may argue that the number of markets to be examined would be endless if relevant markets were to be defined around internally generated and used inputs to other products, as is the case with the data-dependent services provided to users and advertisers by online platforms.[449] One should note, however, that data is more than just a form of input for the services delivered to users and advertisers on online

---

445. D.S. Evans, 'Attention Rivalry Among Online Platforms', *Journal of Competition Law and Economics* 2013, vol. 9, no. 2, (313).
446. See section 4.2.1 above.
447. In a similar vein, P.J. Harbour and T.I. Koslov, 'Section 2 In A Web 2.0 World: An Expanded Vision of Relevant Product Markets', *Antitrust Law Journal* 2010, vol. 76, no. 3, (769), p. 773 argue that a data market definition would better reflect reality in which internet companies often derive value from data far beyond the initial purposes for which the data has been collected in the first place.
448. P.J. Harbour and T.I. Koslov, 'Section 2 In A Web 2.0 World: An Expanded Vision of Relevant Product Markets', *Antitrust Law Journal* 2010, vol. 76, no. 3, (769), p. 784.
449. D.S. Tucker and H.B. Wellford, 'Big Mistakes Regarding Big Data', *The Antitrust Source* 2014, vol. 14, no. 2, (1), pp. 4-5 arguing that personal data cannot constitute a relevant product market unless it is sold to customers.

platforms. By collecting data and monitoring the behaviour of users, internet players can also detect changes in interests which enable them to adapt to consumer preferences by introducing new services following potential trends.[450] The latter role of data collection and analysis in the development of new services is not considered when only relying on relevant markets for current products or services. It is argued that this peculiarity of data justifies and even demands a deviation from existing competition law standards. By defining and investigating a potential market for data in addition to the relevant markets for the services currently offered by a particular provider, competition analysis will better reflect the competitive reality of the environment in which online platforms operate.[451] In addition, it also becomes possible to analyse the competitive constraints applicable to the asset to which potential competitors of incumbent providers need access in order to compete in future product markets.[452]

However, the Commission notice on market definition seems to stand in the way of applying an approach that would take account of the role potential competition in online markets. Although the EU Horizontal Guidelines recognise that in some cases the level of competition cannot be sufficiently assessed by relying on existing markets, the Commission notice on market definition states that competitive constraints arising from potential competition should not be taken into account in the market definition on the ground that such constraints are generally less immediate. According to the Commission notice, these constraints can only be assessed in later stages of the competition assessment.[453] By focusing on business models instead of end products and services as a starting point for the competition analysis, it could be assessed how a company makes profits and which other market players are able to put pressure on that profit stream. In this way, market definition would be better able to capture the dynamic nature of fast-moving industries.[454] Even though such a more forward-looking approach to market definition would be desirable to make competition enforcement more conducive to disruptive innovation, it thus remains to be seen whether competition authorities and courts are willing to move away from strict product market definitions as required by the Commission notice in merger and abuse of dominance cases.

In competition cases in the ICT sector, the European Commission still focuses on preserving sustaining innovation within existing markets. At the same time, disruptive innovation seems to have played a very important role in solving the competition

---

450. Monopolkommission, 'Competition policy: The challenge of digital markets', Special report No. 68, July 2015, paras 78 and 110.
451. For an analysis of the added value of the definition of an additional relevant market for data in merger cases, see section 10.4.1 below.
452. See also the analysis in I. Graef, 'Market Definition and Market Power in Data: The Case of Online Platforms', World Competition 2015, vol. 38, no. 4, (473), pp. 494-495.
453. Commission Notice on the definition of relevant market for the purposes of Community competition law [1997] OJ C 372/5, paras 14 and 24. See also C. Ahlborn, D.S. Evans and A.J. Padilla, 'Competition Policy in the New Economy: Is European Competition Law Up to the Challenge?', European Competition Law Review 2001, vol. 22, no. 5, (156), pp. 161-162.
454. Study for the ECON Committee of the European Parliament, 'Challenges for Competition Policy in a Digitalised Economy', July 2015, pp. 51 and 70-71, available at http://www.europarl.europa.eu/RegData/etudes/STUD/2015/542235/IPOL_STU(2015)542235_EN.pdf.

concerns. In *Microsoft*,[455] the European Commission intervened in the market for PC operating systems. Although the Commission tried to preserve sustaining innovation in this market by forcing Microsoft to give competitors access to its technology, it seems that the competition concerns were rather solved by disruptive innovation coming from Google and others who brought the internet to the forefront diminishing the significance of Microsoft's dominant position in the market for PC operating systems. In the *Google* investigation, the Commission still appears to concentrate on preserving sustaining innovation in the market for search engines,[456] while disruptive innovation coming from other internet platforms such as social networks and mobile applications may reduce the relevance of Google's position in this market. As a result, even though the existing competition tools can be adapted to make market definition more conducive to disruptive innovation, it is questionable that the Commission will take a different approach in the future.

4.4 ASSESSING DOMINANCE ON ONLINE PLATFORMS

The multi-sidedness and rapidly changing nature of online platforms also raises questions about the appropriate assessment of dominance of providers of search engines, social networks and e-commerce platforms. Dominance is defined in case law of the Court of Justice as '*a position of economic strength enjoyed by an undertaking which enables it to prevent effective competition being maintained on the relevant market by giving it the power to behave to an appreciable extent independently of its competitors, customers and ultimately of its consumers*'.[457]

4.4.1 Room for Competition in Markets in Which Multi-sided Businesses Operate

The multi-sidedness of a business also has consequences for the assessment of market power. The interdependencies between the customer groups affect the ability of the platform to behave independently of competitors. Noel and Evans explain that in principle the link between the different customer groups in a multi-sided platform limits the extent to which a price increase on any side of the platform is profitable. All else equal, market power would decrease. To illustrate: a price increase on side A reduces the number of customers on that side and makes the platform less attractive for customers on side B that are interested in interacting with the other group of customers. Therefore, an increase in price on side A will lead to a decrease in the number of

---

455. Case COMP/C-3/37.792 - *Microsoft*, 24 March 2004 and Judgment in *Microsoft v. Commission*, T-201/04, ECLI:EU:T:2007:289.
456. In the statement announcing the sending of a Statement of Objections to Google, the Commissioner for Competition argued: '*Google has had market shares of more than 90% in general internet search in most EU Member States for many years*' which suggests that the Commission aims to preserve competition in the search market. See Statement Competition Commissioner Vestager, 'Statement by Commissioner Vestager on antitrust decisions concerning Google', STATEMENT/15/4785, 15 April 2015.
457. Judgment in *United Brands v. Commission*, Case 27/76, ECLI:EU:C:1978:22, par. 65.

customers on side B as well as in the price they are willing to pay.[458] However, the multi-sided network effects between the different sides of the platform may also give rise to barriers to entry. As each side of the platform and the corresponding multi-sided network effect grows, it becomes more difficult for new entrants to gain market share.[459]

Before a new entrant is able to successfully enter a multi-sided market, it needs to acquire a critical mass of customers on all sides of the platform. Without a user base, an online platform will not attract advertisers on whom it relies to make the platform profitable. Advertisers will likely join the platform that has the most solid user base, since they have an interest in displaying their products or services to as many users as possible.[460] Once one platform has achieved a critical mass, it may be hard for a competitor to gain a foothold on the market. It needs a strong user base itself before advertisers will be interested in joining, as they can already reach users through the platform that has established itself first. However, Lerner argues that multi-sided network effects in online platforms are not significant. As users' demand for a platform is not driven by the availability of advertisements, multi-sided network effects do, in his view, not prevent users from switching once a smaller rival or new entrant offers a better service.[461]

Nevertheless, markets in which multi-sided businesses compete are typically quite concentrated. Because of the multi-sided network effects, these markets are generally characterised by the presence of a few firms that have a large market share. Therefore, they can be seen as 'winner-take-most' or 'few-winners-take-all' businesses.[462] Multi-sided platforms are usually not 'winner-take-all' businesses, since they evolve relatively slowly as they have to find the right price structure and attract

---

458. D.S. EVANS AND M. NOEL, 'Defining Antitrust Markets When Firms Operate Two-Sided Platforms', *Columbia Business Law Review* 2005, vol. 2005, (101), p. 129.

459. K.L. DEVINE, 'Preserving Competition in Multi-Sided Innovative Markets: How Do You Solve a Problem Like Google?', *North Carolina Journal of Law & Technology* 2008, vol. 10, no. 1, (59), p. 88.

460. However, Lerner argues that advertisers paying on a cost-per-click basis do not necessarily derive more value from advertising on a platform with more users because the advertising on such a platform entails proportionately higher costs as compared to a platform with fewer users due to the fact that an ad may obtain more user clicks on a larger platform. See A.V. LERNER, 'The Role of "Big Data" in Online Platform Competition', *SSRN Working Paper* August 2014, p. 58, available at http://papers.ssrn.com/sol3/papers.cfm?abstract_id = 2482780. Nevertheless, what is most relevant for advertisers is the likelihood that the display of an ad amounts to a purchase. Therefore, the cost of advertising in itself does not give a complete picture of the value that an advertiser derives from advertising on a particular platform. In general, the number of purchases of an advertised product or service may increase with the number of users that are on the platform. If the number of purchases is indeed relatively higher on a larger platform, the higher sales may outweigh the higher costs of advertising resulting from the higher number of clicks by users. See also footnote 116.

461. A.V. LERNER, 'The Role of "Big Data" in Online Platform Competition', *SSRN Working Paper* August 2014, pp. 60-61, available at http://papers.ssrn.com/sol3/papers.cfm?abstract_id = 2482780.

462. D.S. EVANS, 'Competition and Regulatory Policy for Multi-Sided Platforms with Applications to the Web Economy', *SSRN Working Paper* March 2008, p. 13, available at http://papers.ssrn.com/sol3/papers.cfm?abstract_id = 1090368.

customers on all sides of the platform. Because of product differentiation and the existence of heterogeneous customers, several platforms are able to coexist to a certain extent.[463]

According to Evans & Noel, five factors determine the relative size of multi-sided platforms and their competitors. Multi-sided network effects and scale economies promote larger platforms with fewer competitors, while congestion, multi-homing and platform differentiation limit the size of these platforms and give more room for competition.[464] The extent of multi-homing also affects the pricing strategy of the platform. Multi-homing will intensify price competition leading to lower prices on the side on which multi-homing is least prevalent. By lowering the prices, customers are discouraged from switching to other platforms that may also give them access to the same customers on the other side. When buyers, for example, multi-home on e-commerce platforms, sellers have several options for reaching them. By charging lower prices to a seller for joining a platform, the seller may be tempted to abandon other online e-commerce platforms if most buyers can be reached through the platform with the lowest price. Lower prices are thus used in an attempt to 'steer' sellers toward an exclusive relationship. The mere possibility of multi-homing may also encourage platform providers to lower their prices in order to dissuade customers from joining other platforms.[465]

If both sides of a platform single-home it will be relatively hard for new entrants to attract customers, since the incumbent platform offers exclusive access to both customer groups. Because of first mover advantages, the platform that will get the most customers on board first will likely have a strong position on the market. In case of single-homing the following applies: the more successful a platform is at attracting customers, the less successful rivals will be.[466] By requiring exclusivity from customers, a platform can prevent customers from multi-homing and tie them to its business.[467] However, such exclusivity agreements may raise competition issues. One of the concerns that the European Commission has expressed in the *Google* case relates to the agreements that Google concludes with websites on which it delivers search advertisements that are displayed alongside the search results following a search query of a user in a website's search box. In the Commission's view, these agreements result

---

463. D.S. Evans, 'The Antitrust Economics of Multi-Sided Platform Markets', *Yale Journal on Regulation* 2003, vol. 20, no. 2, (325), p. 350; D.S. Evans, 'Competition and Regulatory Policy for Multi-Sided Platforms with Applications to the Web Economy', *SSRN Working Paper* March 2008, p. 17, available at http://papers.ssrn.com/sol3/papers.cfm?abstract_id=1090368.
464. See D.S. Evans and M. Noel, 'Defining Antitrust Markets When Firms Operate Two-Sided Platforms', *Columbia Business Law Review* 2005, vol. 2005, (101), pp. 120-124.
465. J.-C. Rochet and J. Tirole, 'Platform Competition in Two-Sided Markets', *Journal of the European Economic Association* 2003, vol. 1, no. 4, (990), p. 993 and D.S. Evans, 'The Antitrust Economics of Multi-Sided Platform Markets', *Yale Journal on Regulation* 2003, vol. 20, no. 2, (325), pp. 346-347.
466. D.S. Evans, 'Competition and Regulatory Policy for Multi-Sided Platforms with Applications to the Web Economy', *SSRN Working Paper* 2008, pp. 10 and 17, available at http://papers.ssrn.com/sol3/papers.cfm?abstract_id=1090368.
467. See R.S. Lee, 'Vertical Integration and Exclusivity in Platform and Two-Sided Markets', *American Economic Review* 2013, vol. 103, no. 7, (2960).

in de facto exclusivity requiring websites to obtain all or most of their search advertisements from Google and shutting out competing providers of search advertising intermediation services.[468]

The markets for search engines, social networks and e-commerce platforms are quite concentrated with a single player maintaining the leading position, respectively Google, Facebook and Amazon. Despite the market leadership of these undertakings, several smaller competitors are able to successfully operate their business. This scenario is in line with the framework established by Evans and Noel as regards the relative size of multi-sided platforms and their competitors. Economies of scale and multi-sided network effects are inherent to search engines, social networks and e-commerce platforms as a result of which the markets in which their providers operate are characterised by a certain level of concentration. Nevertheless, because of platform differentiation and multi-homing by users and advertisers, competitors are able to attract customers to their platform and impose competitive pressure on the market leaders.

4.4.2   Establishing Dominance of Online Platform Providers

Because of the link between the user and advertiser side of an online platform, it is important to consider both sides in conjunction with each other when assessing dominance. In two cases involving payment cards, the Court of Justice made clear that the interaction between the different sides of a multi-sided platform has to be taken into account when analysing whether a measure violates Article 101 TFEU. In the context of an assessment of whether certain price measures adopted by an economic interest grouping within a French payment card system were by nature harmful to the proper functioning of normal competition under Article 101(1) TFEU, the Court of Justice argued in *Cartes Bancaires* that it is necessary '*to take into consideration all relevant aspects [...] of the economic or legal context in which that coordination takes place, it being immaterial whether or not such an aspect relates to the relevant market*'. According to the Court of Justice, that must particularly be the case when '*there are interactions between the two facets of a two-sided system*' such as those between the activities of the issuing of bank cards to consumers and the acquisition of merchants for their acceptance in the case at hand.[469]

***Cartes Bancaires* case**
In October 2007, the European Commission adopted a decision in which it concluded that Groupement des Cartes Bancaires, an economic interest grouping which managed a French payment card system, infringed Article 101(1) TFEU. The decision targeted the price measures implemented by the Groupement which

---

468. Speech former Competition Commissioner Almunia, 'Statement of Commissioner Almunia on the Google antitrust investigation', Press room Brussels, 21 May 2012, SPEECH/12/372, available at http://europa.eu/rapid/press-release_SPEECH-12-372_en.htm.
469. Judgment in *Cartes Bancaires*, C-67/13 P, ECLI:EU:C:2014:2204, paras 78-79.

were found to hinder the issuing of cards in France at competitive rates by new entrants. Although the tariffs were in principle applicable to all members of the Groupement, they were found to have been applied in such a way as to hinder the issuing of cards by smaller banks who were prepared to offer cards at a price lower than that of the large banks. The Commission concluded that the measures were anticompetitive by object and by effect.

The General Court upheld the Commission decision in its judgment of November 2012. In September 2014, the Court of Justice ruled on the appeal and set aside the ruling of the General Court in so far as the latter had held that the tariffs had as their object the restriction of competition. The Court of Justice argued that, although the General Court had set out the reasons why the measures at issue were capable of restricting competition, it in no way had explained in what respect that restriction of competition revealed a sufficient degree of harm in order to be characterised as a restriction by object. For that reason, the Court of Justice referred the case back to the General Court in order to examine whether the price measures had the effect of restricting competition.

In June 2016, the General Court upheld the Commission decision and argued that the tariffs had the effect of restricting competition. The General Court annulled the decision only insofar as it prohibited Groupement des Cartes Bancaires to carry out activities with a similar 'object' in the future.

Case COMP/D1/38606 – *Goupement des Cartes Bancaires "CB"*, 17 October 2007.

Judgment in *Cartes Bancaires*, T-491/07, ECLI:EU:T:2012:633.

Judgment in *Cartes Bancaires*, C-67/13 P, ECLI:EU:C:2014:2204.

Judgment in *Cartes Bancaires*, T-491/07, ECLI:EU:T:2016:379.

In *MasterCard*, the Court of Justice similarly stated that for assessing whether a measure, in case the setting of multilateral interchange fees in the MasterCard payment system, which in principle infringes the prohibition of Article 101(1) TFEU can be justified under Article 101(3) TFEU:

> it is necessary to take into account the system of which that measure forms part, including, where appropriate, all the objective advantages flowing from that measure not only on the market in respect of which the restriction has been established, but also on the market which includes the other group of consumers associated with that system, in particular where, as in this instance, it is undisputed that there is interaction between the two sides of the system in question.[470]

The Court of Justice dismissed the argument that the General Court had wrongly ignored the multi-sided nature of the MasterCard system. In the view of the Court of Justice, the General Court had specifically recognised that there was interaction

---

470. Judgment in *MasterCard*, C-382/12 P, ECLI:EU:C:2014:2201, par. 237.

between the two sides of the payment system, since it had examined the role of the multilateral interchange fees in balancing the issuing and acquiring side.[471]

Although these cases did not touch upon the assessment of dominance of multi-sided businesses, the statements of the Court of Justice that all relevant aspects of the economic or legal context of a two-sided system, and in particular the interaction between the two customer sides, have to be taken into account in the context of Article 101 TFEU may have relevance for competition analysis in general. When transposing the spirit of the rulings to the fields of merger review and Article 102 TFEU, the reasoning of the Court of Justice may be interpreted as indicating that the link between the different sides of a multi-sided platform also has to be considered when analysing whether an undertaking possesses a dominant position in the relevant market.

However, multi-sidedness does not always have to be determinative for the assessment of dominance. As explained earlier, it is an empirical question whether the multi-sidedness of a business is sufficiently pronounced so as to affect the competition analysis in a particular case.[472] In its 2004 *Microsoft* decision, the European Commission did not explicitly consider the multi-sided nature of the market for client PC operating systems but based its analysis on the indirect network effects that were identified in the market. The fact that the Commission did not apply the theory of multi-sidedness to the case is not surprising considering that economic research about the issue was still in its early stages at the time of the adoption of the *Microsoft* decision.[473] In fact, indirect network effects can be considered as the notion closest to multi-sidedness at that time.

A PC operating system is to be regarded as a multi-sided platform because it brings users and application developers together. The two groups of customers are connected through reciprocal multi-sided network effects since both groups attach value to the size of the other group. On the one hand, the utility that a user derives from a PC operating system depends on the applications that are and will be available for it. On the other hand, application developers are interested in writing applications for the PC operating systems that are most popular among users. The Commission summarised the phenomenon as follows: '*the more popular an operating system is, the more applications will be written to it and the more applications are written to an operating system, the more popular it will be among users*'.[474] The Commission formalised this mechanism in terms of indirect network effects giving rise to an applications barrier to entry according to which potential competing operating systems can only be successfully launched if a critical mass of compatible applications was already available for them.[475] By taking into account the indirect network effects in its assessment of Microsoft's dominance, the Commission seems to have succeeded in understanding

---

471. Judgment in *MasterCard*, C382/12 P, ECLI:EU:C:2014:2201, par. 238.
472. See section 4.2 above.
473. The Commission decision was adopted only one year after the publication of the seminal paper of Rochet and Tirole that is considered to have initiated the increased attention for multi-sided businesses in economic research. See J.-C. ROCHET AND J. TIROLE, 'Platform Competition in Two-Sided Markets', *Journal of the European Economic Association* 2003, vol. 1, no. 4, (990).
474. Case COMP/C-3/37.792 – *Microsoft*, 24 March 2004, paras 449-450.
475. Case COMP/C-3/37.792 – *Microsoft*, 24 March 2004, paras 453 and 459.

the competitive dynamics of the market for client PC operating systems and in analysing the impact of Microsoft's behaviour. The application of the theory of multi-sidedness in the decision would therefore probably not have led to a different outcome.[476]

Dominance on each side of a multi-sided platform depends on the degree of competition on the different sides. In the online intermediary industry, the market position of a provider is dependent on its success with users as well as advertisers. Since the competitive dynamics in a multi-sided market are best reflected when two different relevant markets are defined instead of one relevant market for the platform as a whole,[477] the market power of, for example, a search engine provider, cannot be reliably determined by solely considering market shares on either the user or advertiser side of the market. In order to fully take into account the link between the user and advertiser side, dominance has to be assessed for the platform in its entirety and not for each side in isolation. The identification of different sets of market shares for each relevant market does not seem to capture the interaction between the user and advertiser side of a multi-sided platform. As a consequence, the question arises whether market shares are an adequate proxy for assessing whether a businesses that competes in a multi-sided market has a dominant position.[478]

4.4.3   From Market Shares to Potential Competition?

Market shares have always played an important role in the assessment of the competitive strength of undertakings in competition enforcement. It follows from case law of the Court of Justice that very large market shares are in themselves, and save in exceptional circumstances, evidence of the existence of a dominant position.[479] While not touching upon whether market shares constitute a reliable indicator of dominance of multi-sided businesses, the European Commission argued in its *Microsoft/Skype* merger decision that market shares only provide a limited indication of competitive strength in the context of the market for (single-sided) internet consumer communications services because of the nascent and dynamic nature of the sector as a result of which market shares can change quickly within a short period of time.[480] In its *Cisco* judgment, the General Court confirmed this finding of the Commission and argued that *'the consumer communications sector is a recent and fast-growing sector which is characterized by short innovation cycles in which large market shares may turn out to be*

---

476. See also D. Auer and N. Petit, 'Two-Sided Markets and the Challenge of Turning Economic Theory into Antitrust Policy', *The Antitrust Bulletin* 2015, vol. 60, no. 4, (426), p. 454 who reach the same conclusion.
477. See section 4.2.1 above.
478. See D.S. Evans, 'The Antitrust Economics of Multi-Sided Platform Markets', *Yale Journal on Regulation* 2003, vol. 20, no. 2, (325), p. 359.
479. Judgment in *Hoffman-La Roche v. Commission*, Case 85/76, ECLI:EU:C:1979:36, par. 41 and Judgment in *Akzo Chemie v. Commission*, C-62/86, ECLI:EU:C:1991:286, par. 60.
480. Case No COMP/M.6281 – *Microsoft/Skype*, 7 October 2011, par. 78.

ephemeral'. In such a dynamic context, *'high market shares are not necessarily indicative of market power and, therefore, of lasting damage to competition'* in the view of the General Court.[481]

The fact that the services are offered free of charge was also a relevant factor in assessing market power according to the General Court. Since users expect to receive consumer communications services free of charge, the potential for providers to set their pricing policy freely is significantly restricted. Any attempt to make users pay would run the risk of reducing the attractiveness of the services and of encouraging users to switch to other providers continuing to offer their services for free. Given the level of innovation on the market, undertakings would also run the risk of reducing the attractiveness of their communications services if they decided to stop innovating.[482] Even though Microsoft would post-merger have a market share of 80% to 90% on the narrowest possible relevant market for video calls delivered on Windows-based PCs, the Commission and the General Court concluded that the concentration would not give rise to competition concerns because of the dynamic character of the sector and the existence of sufficient alternative providers to which consumers could easily switch.[483]

In *Facebook/WhatsApp*, the Commission referred to and relied upon the statement of the General Court that high market shares are not necessarily indicative of market power in the market for consumer communications services. In line with the formulation of the General Court in *Cisco*, the Commission noted that *'the consumer communications sector is a recent and fast-growing sector which is characterized by frequent market entry and short innovation cycles in which large market shares may turn out to be ephemeral'*.[484] In its analysis of the possible consequences of the concentration in the market for social networking services the Commission did not pay attention to the level of market shares and the extent to which they are determinative for the existence of dominance.[485] Both the Commission and the General Court in the context of the *Microsoft/Skype* merger as well as the Commission in *Facebook/WhatsApp* confined the statement that the value of market shares is limited for measuring the competitive strength of undertakings to the consumer communications market and did not consider the validity of this statement to other dynamic markets as well. A similar reasoning could be applied to social networks, search engines and e-commerce platforms that all form part of a dynamic sector. Nevertheless, in earlier merger decisions involving internet services, in particular the acquisition of Yahoo's

---

481. Judgment in *Cisco Systems Inc. and Messagenet SpA v. Commission*, T-79/12, ECLI:EU:T:2013:635, par. 69. A similar reasoning has been applied by the Guangdong Court in the *Qihoo/Tencent* case with a reference to the Commission decision in *Microsoft/Skype*, see T. JIANG, 'The Qihoo/Tencent Dispute in the Instant Messaging Market: The First Milestone in the Chinese Competition Law Enforcement?', *World Competition* 2014, vol. 37, no. 3, (369), p. 380.
482. Judgment in *Cisco Systems Inc. and Messagenet SpA v. Commission*, T-79/12, ECLI:EU:T:2013:635, par. 73.
483. Case No COMP/M.6281 – *Microsoft/Skype*, 7 October 2011, paras 120-132 and Judgment in *Cisco Systems Inc. and Messagenet SpA v. Commission*, T-79/12, ECLI:EU:T:2013:635, paras 68-95.
484. Case No COMP/M.7217 – *Facebook/WhatsApp*, 3 October 2014, par. 99.
485. See Case No COMP/M.7217 – *Facebook/WhatsApp*, 3 October 2014, paras 143-163.

search business by Microsoft and the acquisition of DoubleClick by Google, the Commission still used market shares to measure the competitive strength of undertakings in the markets for internet search and online advertising.[486] In addition, in the *Google* investigation the Commission referred to the market share of Google as an indication that it has a dominant position.[487]

One could argue that market shares are still a good proxy for assessing market power in established dynamic markets in which market shares have been relatively stable for a longer period of time. In *Akzo*, the Court of Justice referred to a three year period as basis for a stable market share.[488] While social media, online search and e-commerce can also be regarded as dynamic sectors that are still evolving, the positions of, respectively, Facebook, Google and Amazon, are more stable than that of Skype in the nascent market for communications services at the time of the acquisition by Microsoft. According to the Commission in *Microsoft/Skype*, the latter market was anticipated to grow immensely with the number of users of instant messaging expected to triple from 2010 to 2016 and the number of video calls expected to increase from 3.2 billion in 2011 to 29.6 billion in 2015.[489]

If it is considered that market shares have to be taken into account for determining the competitive strength of undertakings on the user side of online platforms such as social networks, search engines and e-commerce platforms, it is important to find an accurate methodology for calculating market shares. The Commission argued in *Microsoft/Skype* that market shares based on volume in terms of unique users constitute better indicators for the market power of undertakings in the market for consumer communications services than market shares in value as these services are provided free of charge. In the Commission decision, a unique user was defined as an individual that has actively used a given service for a period of one month.[490] According to the Commission in *Facebook/WhatsApp*, the user engagement with a communications service is best examined by considering whether the service is actually used every month and day or by looking at the number of messages exchanged between users. The Commission did not consider monthly minutes of use as a reliable metric because the length of communications could also depend on exogenous factors such as the relationship between the users of the service. For the calculation of market shares in the market for communications services in the context of *Facebook/WhatsApp*, no relevant datasets were available to determine the actual use of these services according to the methodology that the Commission considered to be the most

---

486. Case No COMP/M.5727 – *Microsoft/Yahoo! Search Business*, 18 February 2010, paras 112-130 and Case No COMP/M.4731 – *Google/ DoubleClick*, 11 March 2008, paras 96-118.
487. In the statement announcing the sending of a Statement of Objections to Google, the Commissioner for Competition argued: '*Google has had market shares of more than 90% in general internet search in most EU Member States for many years*'. See Statement Competition Commissioner Vestager, 'Statement by Commissioner Vestager on antitrust decisions concerning Google', STATEMENT/15/4785, 15 April 2015.
488. Judgment in *Akzo Chemie v. Commission*, C-62/86, ECLI:EU:C:1991:286, par. 59.
489. Case No COMP/M.6281 – *Microsoft/Skype*, 7 October 2011, paras 70-72.
490. Case No COMP/M.6281 – *Microsoft/Skype*, 7 October 2011, paras 79-80.

reliable.[491] If market shares are deemed important for assessing the competitiveness of markets on the user side of online platforms, the question is thus whether relevant information is available on the basis of which the different market positions can be determined in an accurate and reliable way.

Instead of solely relying on market shares, it is submitted that competition authorities and courts should look at the strength of potential competition in order to assess whether a particular undertaking is able to behave independently from its competitors, customers and consumers. Unlike in traditional industries where competition takes place in the market on the basis of price and output, in new economy industries competition tends to come from subsequent competitors that compete for the market and overturn the existing market structure. Although an undertaking may have a high market share, it can nevertheless be under significant competitive pressure if new firms are able to take over its leading position. As long as entry barriers are low, the market is contestable and new entrants may challenge the incumbent's market power. As discussed in section 2.4 above, the network economy characteristics of online platforms may give rise to entry barriers protecting the position of incumbents and reducing the possibility for potential competition to flourish. If entry barriers can be identified, the crucial question to be answered is whether they give incumbents a lasting competitive advantage in the factual circumstances of the case.

In line with the proposal made in section 4.3 to use R&D investments as a basis for market definition, attention could also be paid to R&D investments in the assessment of the competitive strength of an undertaking.[492] If several undertakings in the market invest heavily in R&D, competition may be substantial despite the existence of high market shares. If the precise R&D efforts of a firm cannot be identified, regard could be had to the extent to which it has access to specialised assets. For instance, the concentration of relevant know-how or user data at one online platform could be an indication for dominance. As an alternative to R&D investments and specialised assets, the recent entry of new market participants may be an indication that the market is sufficiently competitive.[493]

4.5 CONCLUSION

In several perspectives, online platforms raise new challenges for competition enforcement. Because of their multi-sided nature and the predominance of innovation as a

---

491. Case No COMP/M.7217 – *Facebook/WhatsApp*, 3 October 2014, paras 96-98 and footnotes 44-45.
492. See M.L. Katz and H.A. Shelanski, '"Schumpeterian" Competition and Antitrust Policy in High-Tech Markets', *Competition* 2005, vol. 14, (47), p. 47; J.G. Sidak and D.J. Teece, 'Dynamic Competition in Antitrust Law', *Journal of Competition Law and Economics* 2009, vol. 5, no. 4, (581), pp. 614-616.
493. See also C. Ahlborn, D.S. Evans and A.J. Padilla, 'Competition Policy in the New Economy: Is European Competition Law Up to the Cchallenge?', *European Competition Law Review* 2001, vol. 22, no. 5, (156), p. 162 who propose to rely on contestability in the form of potential entry as a test of market power.

parameter of competition, traditional competition analysis may not be sufficiently able to reflect how competition takes place on search engines, social networks and e-commerce platforms. Although online platforms have some specific characteristics that have to be taken into account in competition law analysis, the tools that are used to define relevant markets and to assess dominance are flexible enough to be adapted to these services. While economists agree that competition authorities and courts have to consider the multi-sided nature of a market when applying the competition rules, there is little consensus on how, for example, the SSNIP test has to be modified in order to adequately capture the competitive dynamics in online markets where services are provided free of charge on one side of the platform.

A critical issue for market definition of multi-sided businesses is whether one market for the platform as a whole or several markets corresponding with each of the sides of the platform have to be delineated. In previous cases involving search engines and social networks, the European Commission defined separate relevant markets for the user and the advertiser side of these platforms. Such an approach is submitted to be preferable because it enables competition authorities and courts to consider the variety of entities from which multi-sided online platforms may experience competitive pressure. In order to enable competition authorities and courts to take a more forward-looking approach to competition analysis in merger and abuse of dominance cases, it is proposed to rely on the notion of competition in innovation and regard user data as a specialised asset in analogy to the EU Horizontal Guidelines. Even if user data is not traded to third parties and no supply and demand for data can be identified, it is still desirable to define a potential market for data in addition to the relevant markets for the services provided to users and advertisers. In this way, the significance of data for the development of new products and services can be taken into account.

Because of the multi-sided network effects present in online platforms, there is a tendency towards 'winner-take-most' or 'few-winners-take-all' markets. As competition in new economy markets typically leads to the development of new markets, it is argued that benchmarks or proxies other than price and market shares have to be used to reliably conduct market definition and assess dominance. Because of the fast-moving nature of the sector, market boundaries are fluctuating and online platform providers may impose competitive pressure on each other despite offering different functionalities to users. In this regard, the current approach towards market definition could be adapted in the sense that relevant markets would have to be defined more loosely in order to reflect the dynamic process of competition in new economy industries. However, the European Commission still relies on narrowly defined and functionality-based relevant product markets. With regard to the assessment of dominance, the statements of the European Commission and the General Court in the *Microsoft/Skype* merger, which the Commission referred to and relied upon in *Facebook/WhatsApp*, reveal that both institutions regard potential competition as a more relevant indicator than market shares in the dynamic market of internet consumer communications services. In order to operationalise potential competition,

competition authorities could examine the extent of recent entry in the market and measure the R&D investments of the different market participants. By relying on potential competition as an alternative to market shares in dynamic industries such as the online intermediary sector, competition analysis can be made more conducive towards innovation.

PART II

Data as Essential Facility

In the online environment, personal information has become a raw material or necessary input for companies that are employing business models dependent on the acquisition and monetisation of data. Online search engines, social networks and e-commerce platforms rely on data as an input to provide targeted advertising possibilities and to deliver services to users that are of the relevance and quality they expect. By keeping the vast quantities of collected data to themselves, incumbent providers like Google, Facebook and Amazon are able to foreclose competition from new entrants and companies that would like to develop complementary services but do not have access to the required information. Against this background, the question can be posed how competition law tools can be applied to effectively tackle competitiveness issues involving data on online platforms.

While several potential competition problems with regard to access to data can be distinguished, the focus of the second part of the book lies on refusals to give access to data on online platforms. To that end, the application of the so-called essential facilities doctrine is analysed in the US and EU decision-making practice and case law to identify the current legal standards applicable to refusals to deal. In addition, a more coherent framework for the future application of the essential facilities doctrine is set out taking into account the underlying economic interests in refusal to deal cases. Afterwards, possible scenarios relating to refusals to give access on online platforms are discussed and it is analysed how a relevant market for data can be defined, how market power with regard to data can be established and how the abusive nature of refusals to deal involving data can be assessed.

CHAPTER 5
Setting the Scene

5.1 INTRODUCTION

The competitive strength of online platforms is increasingly being determined by the amount and the quality of the data they hold. Both on the user and the advertiser side of online platforms the use of data forms an important means to attract customers. Advertisers benefit from better targeted advertising services which increase the probability that an advertised product or service is actually purchased by the users to which the ad is displayed. The more detailed the profile is that a provider has about its users, the more precise possibilities it can offer its advertisers for selecting their intended audience. On the user side of online platforms, the relevance of services to users is a key competitive differentiator on the internet. By using data to increase the relevance of search results, suggested social network interactions and recommendations for future purchases, providers of search engines, social networks and e-commerce platforms are able to improve the quality of their services and attract users to their platforms. Against this background, this chapter looks at several aspects of data in order to set the scene for the analysis in the next chapters.

In section 5.2, the importance of data in the digital economy is discussed as well as how information about users is collected and used by providers of search engines, social networks and e-commerce platforms. Afterwards, section 5.3 pays attention to the way in which the interest of, respectively, users and online platform providers is protected under EU law. Given the fundamental role of data for competition on the internet, the scope for competition issues in this environment is also growing. In this perspective, limitations on data portability, a lack of interoperability of online platforms and potential refusals to give access to user data are identified in section 5.4 as possible areas of concern which may attract scrutiny of competition authorities. The last issue is at the heart of the second part of the book and is analysed in detail in Chapter 6.

5.2 ROLE OF DATA IN THE DIGITAL ECONOMY

Data is playing an increasingly important role in the digital economy. The World Economic Forum has considered personal data to constitute a new economic asset class.[494] Data is also referred to as '*the new oil*' or '*the new currency*' of the twenty-first century.[495] The phenomenon of data becoming a type of currency can be illustrated by the fact that companies have started to offer consumers the possibility to replace part of the monetary payment for a product or service by giving permission to collect their data. For instance, American telecommunications company AT&T gives consumers who agree to be tracked online a discount of 29 dollar per month on their broadband subscription and Amazon sells Kindle tablets and e-readers at a discounted price to consumers who are willing to accept targeted advertisements to be displayed on the device.[496]

The use of data as a currency is also reflected in the proposal for a Digital Content Directive that the European Commission introduced in December 2015. Article 3(1) of the proposal makes clear that the Digital Content Directive would apply to any contract where digital content, such as music or digital games, is supplied to a consumer and, in exchange, '*a price is to be paid or the consumer actively provides counter-performance other than money in the form of personal data or any other data*'.[497] For the purposes of the proposal for a Digital Content Directive, '*a service allowing sharing of and any other interaction with data in digital form provided by other users of the service*' is also regarded as 'digital content'.[498] A social network or a communications app would thus fall within the scope of application of the Digital Content Directive. The proposal aims at giving consumers the same rights when they enter into a contract for the supply of digital content whether they pay with money or with data. In this context, one of the recitals to the proposal states that the introduction of a '*differentiation depending on the nature of the counter-performance would discriminate between business models*' and '*would provide an unjustified incentive for businesses to move towards offering*

---

494. World Economic Forum, 'Personal Data: The Emergence of a New Asset Class', January 2011, available at http://www3.weforum.org/docs/WEF_ITTC_PersonalDataNewAsset_Report_201 1.pdf.

495. See the speech of former Consumer Commissioner Kuneva at the Roundtable on Online Data Collection, Targeting and Profiling, 31 March 2009, SPEECH/09/156, available at http://europa.eu/rapid/press-release_SPEECH-09-156_en.htm: '*Personal data is the new oil of the internet and the new currency of the digital world*'; and the speech of Competition Commissioner Vestager, 'Competition in a big data world', DLD 16 Munich, 17 January 2016, available at https://ec.europa.eu/commission/2014-2019/vestager/announcements/competition-big-data-world_en: '*These incredibly powerful tools, like search engines and social media, are available for free. In many cases, that's because we as consumers have a new currency that we can use to pay for them – our data*'.

496. M. Bergen, 'AT&T Gives Discount to Internet Customers Who Agree To Be Tracked. Customers Must Pay $29 More to Avoid Targeted Ads', *Ad Age*, 18 February 2015, available at http://adage.com/article/digital/t-u-verse-ad-tracking-discount-subscribers/297208/.

497. Article 3(1) of the proposal for a Directive of the European Parliament and of the Council on certain aspects concerning contracts for the supply of digital content (proposal for a Digital Content Directive), 9 December 2015, COM(2015) 634 final.

498. Article 2(1)(c) of the proposal for a Digital Content Directive.

digital content against data'.[499] By introducing a proposal for a Directive in this field, the Commission thus explicitly recognises that data constitutes a form of payment for digital services and should give rise to the same legal protection for consumers.

Technological advances enabling the collection, analysis and storage of growing amounts of information have strengthened the ability and the incentive of companies to gather and use personal data.[500] Brick-and-mortar companies such as shops, supermarkets, banks, insurance, energy and telecommunications companies collect information about their customers in the form of, respectively, transactional data, information about calls made by consumers and data relating to their financial position or energy consumption. Customer information is valuable for any business, but this is even more so for online businesses that have developed business models depending on the acquisition and monetisation of personal data.[501] While it is not new for companies to gather information about their customers, the scope of the gathered data, the precision with which a company can link an action to a specific customer and the sheer quantity of information collected on the internet cannot be compared to the brick-and-mortar world. For example, prior to the advent of online shopping, stores did not have access to abandoned shopping carts and complete lists of past purchases enabling them to tailor products automatically to the needs and interests of consumers.[502]

The term 'big data' is often used to describe the exponential growth in the availability and use of data resulting in massive datasets that traditional database systems cannot effectively manage and process.[503] According to a widely adopted definition provided by information technology research and advisory company Gartner, big data is *'high-volume, high-velocity and high-variety information assets that demand cost-effective, innovative forms of information processing for enhanced insight*

---

499. Recital 13 of the proposal for a Digital Content Directive.
500. Speech former Competition Commissioner Almunia, 'Competition and personal data protection', Privacy Platform event: Competition and Privacy in Markets of Data Brussels, 26 November 2012, SPEECH/12/860.
501. H.A. SHELANSKI, 'Information, Innovation, and Competition Policy for the Internet', *University of Pennsylvania Law Review* 2013, vol. 161, no. 6, (1663), p. 1678.
502. A. GOLDFARB AND C. TUCKER, 'Privacy and Innovation' in J. LERNER AND S. STERN (eds.), *Innovation Policy and the Economy*, University of Chicago Press, 2012, (65), p. 71.
503. Definitions that have been put forward include: V. MAYER-SCHÖNBERGER AND K. CUKIER, *Big Data: A Revolution That Will Transform How We Live, Work and Think*, John Murray, 2013, p. 6: 'big data refers to things one can do at a large scale that cannot be done at a smaller one, to extract new insights or create new forms of value, in ways that change markets, organizations, the relationship between citizens and governments, and more'; ARTICLE 29 WORKING PARTY, 'Opinion 03/2013 on purpose limitation', WP 203, 2 April 2013, p. 35: 'Big data refers to the exponential growth both in the availability and in the automated use of information: it refers to gigantic digital datasets held by corporations, governments and other large organisations, which are then extensively analysed [...] using computer algorithms'; and EUROPEAN DATA PROTECTION SUPERVISOR, Opinion 7/2015 Meeting the challenges of big data. A call for transparency, user control, data protection by design and accountability, 19 November 2015, p. 7: big data *'refers to the practice of combining huge volumes of diversely sourced information and analysing them, using more sophisticated algorithms to inform decisions. Big data relies not only on the increasing ability of technology to support the collection and storage of large amounts of data, but also on its ability to analyse, understand and take advantage of the full value of data (in particular using analytics applications)'*.

and decision making.[504] Big data is thus not only characterised by its volume, but also by its complexity in terms of the different types of structured or unstructured data and the need for the data to be collected and analysed quickly. Two 'V's may be added to this '3V' big data definition. One for veracity which is an indicator of the quality and trustworthiness of the data.[505] And another for value which relates to the increasing economic and social value to be obtained from the use of data.[506]

It is important to note that big data is not necessarily personal data. The current Data Protection Directive and the future General Data Protection Regulation define 'personal data' as *'any information relating to an identified or identifiable natural person'*. Under the Data Protection Directive, an identifiable person is defined as *'one who can be identified, directly or indirectly, in particular by reference to an identification number or to one or more factors specific to his physical, physiological, mental, economic, cultural or social identity'*. The General Data Protection Regulation specifies that *'an identifiable person is one who can be identified, directly or indirectly, in particular by reference to an identifier such as a name, an identification number, location data, online identifier or to one or more factors specific to the physical, physiological, genetic, mental, economic, cultural or social identity of that natural person'*.[507]

Although not all big data can be traced back to individuals, most of the information collected about users by online platforms qualifies as personal data. For example, the Article 29 Working Party[508] concluded that the search history of an individual is personal data if the individual to which it relates is identifiable.[509] In return for free access to their functionalities, providers of online services including search engines, social networks and e-commerce platforms gather data about the profile of users, their interests and online behaviour. The collection of personal data consequently operates as an indispensable currency used to compensate the providers

---

504. Gartner IT Glossary, 'Big data', available at http://www.gartner.com/it-glossary/big-data/.
505. See for instance IBM Big Data & Analytics Hub, 'The Four V's of Big Data', available at http://www.ibmbigdatahub.com/infographic/four-vs-big-data.
506. ORGANISATION FOR ECONOMIC CO-OPERATION AND DEVELOPMENT (OECD), *Supporting Investment in Knowledge Capital, Growth and Innovation*, OECD Publishing, 2013, p. 325.
507. Article 2(a) Directive 95/46/EC of the European Parliament and of the Council of 24 October 1995 on the protection of individuals with regard to the processing of personal data and on the free movement of such data (Data Protection Directive) [1995] OJ L 281/31 and Article 4(1) of Regulation (EU) No 2016/679 of the European Parliament and of the Council of 27 April 2016 on the protection of natural persons with regard to the processing of personal data and on the free movement of such data, and repealing Directive 95/46/EC (General Data Protection Regulation) [2016] OJ L 119/1. For a further analysis of the concept of personal data, see ARTICLE 29 WORKING PARTY, 'Opinion 4/2007 on the concept of personal data', WP 136, 20 June 2007.
508. The Article 29 Working Party was set up under Article 29 of the Data Protection Directive and is composed of a representative from the national data protection authority of each EU Member State, a representative of the European Data Protection Supervisor (the independent supervisory authority that is responsible for ensuring that all EU institutions and bodies respect people's right to personal data protection and privacy when processing their personal data) and a representative of the European Commission.
509. ARTICLE 29 WORKING PARTY, 'Opinion 1/2008 on data protection issues related to search engines', WP 148, 4 April 2008, p. 8.

for the delivery of their services to users.[510] One may also regard the provision of personal data by users or their exposure to targeted advertisements as costs they have to incur in order to be able to use the online functionalities without having to pay a monetary fee.[511]

The user data held by online platforms encompasses several types of information. On the one hand, users provide data themselves in the form of, for example, profile information, photos and lists of friends or contacts on social networks and search queries inserted in the search box of search engines and e-commerce platforms. On the other hand, providers of online platforms obtain or create data by means of analysing the behaviour and habits of users. The use of 'cookies' typically plays an important role in the collection of this type of behavioural data. Information about the user's interests and preferences is stored by the web browser in a text file that is sent back to the server every time the user accesses a server's page using the same web browser.[512]

Next to cookies, other tracking methods exist such as fingerprinting and social plugins. Fingerprinting enables unique identification of a device or application without the use of cookies. The most well-known forms of fingerprinting are 'device finger-printing' and 'browser fingerprinting'. Fingerprints are generated by combining a set of information elements that can be used to single out, link or infer a user or device over time.[513] Social plugins are website components, such as Facebook's 'Like' button and Google + 's ' + 1', that are integrated into many websites outside a social network. They facilitate the sharing of third-party content within social networks, but also enable social network providers to track users outside the social network and to collect additional information about their preferences.[514]

---

510. Preliminary Opinion of the European Data Protection Supervisor, 'Privacy and competitiveness in the age of big data: The interplay between data protection, competition law and consumer protection in the Digital Economy', March 2014, par. 1. See section 4.2.1 above, for an analysis of the role of data as a currency under current market definition standards.
511. Newman refers to these costs as, respectively, information and attention costs. See J.M. Newman, 'Antitrust in Zero-Price Markets: Foundations', SSRN Working Paper July 2014, pp. 32-33, available at http://papers.ssrn.com/sol3/papers.cfm?abstract_id = 2474874& download = yes.
512. For the installation of and access to cookies, consent of the user is required. See Article 5(3) of the ePrivacy Directive (Directive 2002/58/EC of the European Parliament and of the Council of 12 July 2002 concerning the processing of personal data and the protection of privacy in the electronic communications sector (ePrivacy Directive) [2002] OJ L 201/37) as amended by the Citizens' Rights Directive (Directive 2009/136/EC of the European Parliament and of the Council of 25 November 2009 [2009] OJ L 337/11). For a discussion on the introduction of the requirement for consent and its practical implementation, see E. Kosta, 'Peeking into the Cookie Jar: The European Approach towards the Regulation of Cookies', International Journal of Law and Information Technology 2013, vol. 21, no. 4, (380).
513. Article 29 Working Party, 'Opinion 9/2014 on the application of Directive 2002/58/EC to device fingerprinting', 25 November 2014, WP 224, p. 4. In this Opinion, the Article 29 Working Party made clear that the consent rules for cookies in the ePrivacy Directive also apply to device fingerprinting.
514. See also Monopolkommission, 'Competition policy: The challenge of digital markets', Special report No. 68, July 2015, par. 75. For an analysis of the use of these technologies in Facebook's social network, see B. Van Alsenoy, V. Verdoodt, R. Heyman, et al., 'From Social Media Service to Advertising Network. A Critical Analysis of Facebook's Revised Policies and Terms', report

In addition to, what it refers to as, 'volunteered data' explicitly shared by users and 'observed data' obtained by recording the actions of users online, the World Economic Forum distinguishes a third type of data: so-called inferred data which can be derived from the analysis of volunteered or observed information.[515] The last category may also be regarded as 'metadata' which is data that describes other data or, in other words, data about data.

Online intermediaries can employ the collected user data as an input of production to improve their services by offering better targeted advertising services and by increasing the relevance and quality of the functionalities provided to users. User data may also form an additional revenue stream for online platforms if they sell it as a commodity or a raw material to third parties.[516] For example, Twitter licenses data to companies using Twitter data to build products, to analyse internally or to serve other commercial purposes.[517] Amazon, Facebook and Google all clarify in their privacy policies that they do not sell personal data to third parties.[518] They do not share data with advertisers and only use the information that they have collected about their users in order to provide advertisers the possibility to target their ads to particular categories of users.

At the same time, social network providers are increasingly teaming up with third parties in order to be able to offer better targeted advertising services. For example, Facebook entered into two new partnerships in 2015. In March 2015, Facebook announced its collaboration with DataSift, a leading social data platform that provides real-time, human-generated data enabling companies to aggregate, filter and extract insights from data on social networks, blogs and news websites. With the help of DataSift, Facebook introduced so-called topic data which shows marketers what audiences are saying on Facebook about events, brands, subjects and activities enabling them to make better decisions about how they market on Facebook.[519]

---

commissioned by the Belgian Privacy Commission, 25 August 2015, pp. 89-102, available at http://www.law.kuleuven.be/citip/en/news/item/facebooks-revised-policies-and-terms-v1-3.pdf.

515. WORLD ECONOMIC FORUM, 'Personal Data: The Emergence of a New Asset Class', January 2011, p. 7.

516. H.A. SHELANSKI, 'Information, Innovation, and Competition Policy for the Internet', *University of Pennsylvania Law Review* 2013, vol. 161, no. 6, (1663), pp. 1680 and 1682.

517. For the Twitter Official Partner Program, see https://partners.twitter.com/about.

518. See respectively: Amazon.com Privacy Notice, 'Does Amazon.com Share the Information It Receives?', available at https://www.amazon.com/gp/help/customer/display.html?nodeId=468496#GUID-A2C397AB-68FE-4592-B4A2-7550D73EEFD2__SECTION_3DF674DAB5B7439FB2A9B4465BC3E0AC; Facebook Help Centre, 'Does Facebook sell my information?', available at https://www.facebook.com/help/152637448140583; Google Privacy, 'Is Google using my data? What for?', available at https://support.google.com/googleforwork/answer/6056650?hl=en.

519. Examples of the use of topic data that Facebook gives include:

- *A business selling a hair de-frizzing product can see demographics on the people talking about humidity's effects on their hair to better understand their target audience.*
- *A fashion retailer can see the clothing items its target audience is talking about to decide which products to stock.*
- *A brand can see how people are talking about their brand or industry to measure brand sentiment.*

Facebook relies on DataSift's technology to aggregate and deliver summary results from topic data. All the information used for topic data is anonymised and aggregated. Topic data only provides guidance for marketers and cannot be used to targets ads directly. In addition, marketers do not get the actual topic data from DataSift but only the analyses and interpretations of the information.[520] In May 2015, Facebook entered into a partnership with IBM with the goal of integrating Facebook's targeted advertising technology into IBM's own marketing services for retailers enabling them to combine data they have about their customers with Facebook data. IBM has access to Facebook's anonymised and aggregate audience insights in order to give marketers a better picture of their target audiences.[521] IBM had already established a similar partnership with Twitter in October 2014.[522]

Apart from partnerships with specific third parties and Twitter's data licensing activities, the prevailing online platform providers do not sell or actively disclose data. The so-called data brokers do sell data to third parties and are thus active on a market for data. Data brokers collect information from publicly available websites such as social networks single-handedly and combine this with data from public records in order to create profiles of consumers that they can resell to companies who in their turn may use it for various purposes such as identity verification, fraud prevention or marketing.[523] Facebook has, without sharing any personal data, partnered with data brokers including Acxiom, Datalogix and Epsilon enabling advertisers to target their advertisements to Facebook users not only on the basis of their expressed interests on the social network but also based on the products and brands they buy across both desktop and mobile as revealed by the data held by these third parties.[524]

Even though these partnerships do not give the third parties involved access to the personal data on Facebook's social network, they come very close to the situation in which Facebook discloses or shares data to or with third parties. In such a case, one could argue that Facebook, or other providers that have similar partnerships, is active

---

See Facebook for Business, 'Topic Data: Learn What Matters to Your Audience', available at https://www.facebook.com/business/news/topic-data.

520. See also, J. Constine, 'Facebook Finally Lets Its Firehose Be Tapped for Marketing Insights Thanks to DataSift', *TechCrunch*, 10 March 2015, available at http://techcrunch.com/2015/0 3/10/facebook-topic-data/#.lvtbsd:KVhL: '*Brands issue the forward-looking queries through a third-party analytics provider that submits them to DataSift, which can run them against Facebook's data. DataSift hands the analytics tool back anonymized statistical data about posts that match the query since it was issued that can be formed into charts and insights, or bundled with social analytics from other networks*'.

521. Press Release IBM, 'IBM and Facebook Team Up to Deliver Personalized Brand Experiences Through People-Based Marketing', 6 May 2015, available at http://www-03.ibm.com/press/us/en/pressrelease/46760.wss.

522. Press Release IBM, 'Twitter and IBM Form Global Partnership to Transform Enterprise Decisions', 29 October 2014, available at http://www-03.ibm.com/press/us/en/pressrelease/45265.wss.

523. See, for example, FTC Report, 'Protecting Consumer Privacy in an Era of Rapid Change. Recommendations for Business and Policymakers', March 2012, p. 68, available at https://www.ftc.gov/sites/default/files/documents/reports/federal-trade-commission-report-protecting-consumer-privacy-era-rapid-change-recommendations/120326privacyreport.pdf.

524. Facebook, 'What are partner categories and how are they different from Facebook categories?', available at https://en-gb.facebook.com/business/help/298717656925097.

on a market for data. As proposed in section 4.3.2 above, competition authorities and courts could define a potential market for data in addition to the relevant markets for the existing services offered on the platform. This would make competition analysis more forward-looking and better reflect the competitive constraints under which providers of online platforms are currently operating. In particular, mergers and conduct of incumbent providers in the online environment may have as objective the accumulation of additional data to be used to improve existing services or to develop new ones.[525] The partnerships that providers increasingly enter into with third parties provide support for the existence of a (potential) market for data.

The fact that data operates as a type of currency for 'free' digital services, as recognised by the European Commission in its proposal for a Digital Content Directive, forms another argument in favour of the definition of such a potential market. Even though the focus of market definition under existing competition law standards is on the type of product or service instead of on the means of payment,[526] an additional analysis of the competitive constraints relating to data would be desirable in order to complete the interaction of a provider with consumers on the user side of its platform. At the same time, one should note that the role of data in online platforms goes beyond constituting a currency used by consumers to pay for otherwise free services. Even if Google, for example, would starting charging users for making a search, it would still need to collect information on the queries that users have looked for and the links that are subsequently clicked on in order to be able to continue to deliver relevant search results to users. While the provision of data by users may not qualify as an economic exchange under existing decision-making practice, its significance as an input to improve the relevance of existing services and to monitor possible trends which could result into successful new products would justify a deviation from current competition law standards.[527]

5.3 PROTECTION OF USER DATA UNDER DATA PROTECTION AND INTELLECTUAL PROPERTY REGIMES

With regard to the protection of data, a distinction can be made between users, who have a personal interest in the protection of the information they have provided to online platforms, and providers, who have an interest in user data for commercial reasons because they rely on data for the delivery of good quality services to users and advertisers. While the interests of users are protected in particular under the European data protection regime, online platform providers may invoke copyright, sui generis database protection and trade secret laws to protect the datasets they have built around user data.

---

525. A.P. GRUNES AND M.E. STUCKE, 'No Mistake About It: The Important Role of Antitrust in the Era of Big Data', *The Antitrust Source* 2015, vol. 14, no. 4, (1), p. 3.
526. See also the discussion in section 4.2.1 above.
527. See also the analysis in section 4.3.2 above.

5.3.1 Protection of Personal Data under the European Data Protection Regime

Throughout the years, a number of scholars have been calling for the introduction of property rights in personal information with the goal of achieving a better protection of personal data.[528] Ownership of personal information is argued to enable individuals to negotiate with firms about an adequate compensation and the uses to which they are willing to have their data put. However, scholars have also identified difficulties with granting property rights in personal data and have raised doubts about whether such a bargaining process would indeed lead to a higher level of protection.[529] Instead of vesting property rights in personal data and enabling individuals to bargain for their interests by way of a market-oriented mechanism, the EU legislature decided to take a human rights-based approach and to provide for a minimum level of data protection in legislation.[530]

In 1995, the Data Protection Directive was adopted in order to harmonise the existing national data protection laws of the EU Member States. The Data Protection Directive aims to ensure that personal data is processed fairly, lawfully and in accordance with a specified purpose.[531] In January 2012, the European Commission introduced a proposal for a General Data Protection Regulation that will replace the Data Protection Directive which was said to be in need for an update in order to be able to adequately deal with technological developments that have brought new challenges for the protection of personal data.[532] The General Data Protection Regulation is based on Article 16 TFEU, which establishes the principle that everyone has the right to the protection of personal data concerning them and was introduced as the new legal basis for the adoption of data protection rules by the Lisbon Treaty. Following its final adoption in April 2016, the General Data Protection Regulation will enter into force on 25 May 2018 after which the Data Protection Directive will be repealed and cease to have legal effect.[533] In the area of electronic communications, the ePrivacy Directive

---

528. See, for example, R.S. MURPHY, 'Property Rights in Personal Information: An Economic Defense of Privacy', *Georgetown Law Journal* 1996, vol. 84, no. 7, (2381); L. LESSIG, 'The Architecture of Privacy', *Vanderbilt Journal of Entertainment Law & Practice* 1999, vol. 1, no. 1, (56), pp. 63-64; P.M. SCHWARTZ, 'Property, Privacy, and Personal Data', *Harvard Law Review* 2004, vol. 117, no. 7, (2056); J. LUND, 'Property Rights to Information', *Northwestern Journal of Technology and Intellectual Property* 2011, vol. 10, no. 1, (1); C. REES, 'Tomorrow's Privacy: Personal Information as Property', *International Data Privacy Law* 2013, vol. 3, no. 4, (220).

529. See in particular, P. SAMUELSON, 'Privacy As Intellectual Property?', *Stanford Law Review* 2000, vol. 52, no. 5, (1125), pp. 1136-1146; and M.A. LEMLEY, 'Private Property', *Stanford Law Review* 2000, vol. 52, no. 5, (1545).

530. For a detailed analysis of the European perspective on the propertisation of personal data, see N. PURTOVA, *Property Rights in Personal Data. A European Perspective* in P.B. HUGENHOLTZ (ed.) *Information Law Series*, Alphen aan den Rijn, Kluwer Law International, 2011.

531. See Article 6(1) of the Data Protection Directive.

532. Proposal for a Regulation of the European Parliament and of the Council on the protection of individuals with regard to the processing of personal data and on the free movement of such data ('proposal for a General Data Protection Regulation'), 25.1.2012, COM(2012) 11 final.

533. Articles 94(1) and 99(2) of Regulation (EU) No 2016/679 of the European Parliament and of the Council of 27 April 2016 on the protection of natural persons with regard to the processing of personal data and on the free movement of such data, and repealing Directive 95/46/EC (General Data Protection Regulation) [2016] OJ L 119/1.

complements the current Data Protection Directive and the future General Data Protection Regulation. The ePrivacy Directive is specifically applicable to the processing of personal data as well as the protection of privacy in the electronic communications sector.[534]

In addition to these instruments of secondary EU law, personal data is protected in the framework of the Council of Europe under Article 8 of the European Convention on Human Rights[535] which guarantees the right to respect for private and family life of which the right to protection of personal data is considered to form part.[536] Furthermore, the European Union proclaimed the Charter of Fundamental Rights of the European Union[537] in 2000 which became legally binding as a source of primary EU law in December 2009 with the entry into force of the Lisbon Treaty.[538] The Charter of Fundamental Rights does not only comprise a right to respect for private and family life in Article 7, but also establishes a right to data protection in Article 8 giving data protection, already enshrined in Article 16 TFEU, the status of a fundamental right in EU law.[539]

5.3.2 Copyright and Sui Generis Database Protection for User Data

Although no specific property rights have been created for personal data as such, this type of information may in some circumstances fall under the scope of protection of any of the existing intellectual property rights. Copyright and sui generis database protection are of relevance in this respect. Copyright law protects the expression of an original idea by granting the authors temporary exclusive rights, including the right of reproduction and the right of communication to the public.[540] Ideas, facts or data in itself do not qualify for copyright protection. Personal data such as name, age and occupation is factual information and therefore not copyrightable. However, users may hold copyright over posts, photos and videos that they have uploaded on online social networks if such content meets the originality requirement.

---

534. In its Digital Single Market strategy launched in May 2015, the European Commission announced a review of the ePrivacy Directive. See Communication from the Commission to the European Parliament, the Council, the European Economic and Social Committee and the Committee of the Regions. A Digital Single Market Strategy for Europe, COM(2015) 192 final, 6 May 2015, p. 13.
535. Council of Europe, European Convention for the Protection of Human Rights and Fundamental Freedoms, as amended, 4 November 1950.
536. See, for example, ECHR 16 February 2000, *Amann v. Switzerland*, No. 27798/95, ECLI:CE:ECHR:2000:0216JUD002779895, par. 65 and ECHR 4 May 2000, *Rotaru v. Romania*, No. 28341/95, ECLI:CE:ECHR:2000:0504JUD002834195, par. 43.
537. Charter of Fundamental Rights of the European Union [2012] OJ C 326/391.
538. See Article 6(1) of the Consolidated version of the Treaty on European Union [2012] OJ C 326/13.
539. For a more in-depth discussion of the relationship between the right to respect for private and family life (i.e., the right to privacy) and the right to data protection, see section 8.2 below.
540. Articles 2 and 3 of Directive 2001/29/EC of the European Parliament and of the Council of 22 May 2001 on the harmonisation of certain aspects of copyright and related rights in the information society (Information Society Directive) [2001] OJ L 167/10.

It is important to note that most social networks have a provision in their general conditions by which users agree to grant the provider a licence to use any intellectual property protected content uploaded on the platform. In Facebook's Statement of Rights and Responsibilities, for example, it is stated that: *'For content that is covered by intellectual property rights, like photos and videos (IP content), [...] you grant us a non-exclusive, transferable, sub-licensable, royalty-free, worldwide license to use any IP content that you post on or in connection with Facebook (IP License). This IP License ends when you delete your IP content or your account unless your content has been shared with others, and they have not deleted it'.*[541] This implies that users give Facebook a right to use any intellectual property protected material posted on the social network in either non-commercial or commercial way. Irrespective of whether such a wide-ranging clause is legally valid, users retain the right to continue to use and exploit their copyrighted content themselves because the licence granted to Facebook is non-exclusive.[542]

While users hold copyright over original posts, photos and videos, providers of online platforms may be able to claim copyright protection over the databases they have created on the basis of the data collected about users. Under the Database Directive, a database is defined as *'a collection of independent works, data or other materials arranged in a systematic or methodical way and individually accessible by electronic or other means'.*[543] The Database Directive provides for a dual regime of protection of databases by granting copyright protection to the structure of original databases and by establishing a newly created sui generis right protecting the content of databases in general.

Under Article 3(1) of the Directive, *'databases which, by reason of the selection or arrangement of their contents, constitute the author's own intellectual creation'* are protected by copyright. The copyright protection of a database only covers the structure of the data and does not extend to its content.[544] In *Football Dataco*, a preliminary reference case involving football league fixture lists in the United Kingdom, the Court of Justice clarified that the notion of the author's own intellectual creation refers to the criterion of originality. In the view of the Court, a database meets the requirement of originality *'when, through the selection or arrangement of the data which it contains, its author expresses his creative ability in an original manner by making free and creative choices and thus stamps his "personal touch"'.*[545] The Court also made clear that the originality requirement is not satisfied *'when the setting up of*

---

541. Facebook, 'Statement of Rights and Responsibilities. Sharing Your Content and Information', available via https://en-gb.facebook.com/legal/terms.
542. For an analysis of the validity of this clause in Facebook's Statement of Rights and Responsibilities under copyright and contract law, see B. VAN ALSENOY, V. VERDOODT, R. HEYMAN, ET AL., 'From Social Media Service to Advertising Network. A Critical Analysis of Facebook's Revised Policies and Terms', report commissioned by the Belgian Privacy Commission, 25 August 2015, pp. 76-81.
543. Article 1(2) of Directive 96/9/EC of the European Parliament and of the Council of 11 March 1996 on the legal protection of databases (Database Directive) [1996] OJ L 77/20.
544. Article 3(2) of the Database Directive.
545. Judgment in *Football Dataco Ltd and Others v. Yahoo! UK Ltd and Others*, C-604/10, ECLI:EU:C:2012:115, par. 38.

the database is dictated by technical considerations, rules or constraints which leave no room for creative freedom'.[546] Furthermore, the intellectual effort and skill of creating data is irrelevant as well as whether the selection or arrangement of the data includes the addition of important significance to that data.[547] Lastly, the Court argued that the significant labour and skill required for setting up a database does not as such justify copyright protection if that labour and that skill do not express any originality in the selection or arrangement of the data which that database contains.[548]

Irrespective of the eligibility of a database for copyright protection with regard to the selection or arrangement of the data, a database as a whole may qualify for protection under the sui generis database right created by Article 7(1) of the Database Directive[549] if *'there has been qualitatively and/or quantitatively a substantial investment in either the obtaining, verification or presentation of the contents'.* Both copyright and sui generis protection under the Database Directive are without prejudice to any rights subsisting in the underlying elements or data that make up the database such as copyright but also data protection and privacy.[550] Whereas copyright requires an original expression of the creative freedom of the author, investment is the relevant criterion for sui generis database protection. A database that does not meet the originality requirement of copyright may therefore still benefit from protection under the sui generis right as long as considerable human, technical or financial resources are invested in its creation.[551]

In four related preliminary rulings delivered in November 2004, the Court of Justice made clear that the substantial investment required for a database to be protected under the sui generis right must relate to the creation of a database as such and that investment in creating the materials which make up the contents of the database cannot be taken into account. The Court justified the exclusion of the mere creation of materials from sui generis protection by arguing that the latter's purpose is *'to promote the establishment of storage and processing systems for existing information and not the creation of materials capable of being collected subsequently in a database'.*[552] Only investment in the obtaining, verification or presentation of pre-existing contents may be considered. In the Court's view, investment in obtaining the contents of a database must be understood *'to refer to the resources used to seek out existing independent materials and collect them in the database'* and investment in the verification of the contents of a database concerns *'the resources used, with a view to*

---

546. Judgment in *Football Dataco Ltd and Others v. Yahoo! UK Ltd and Others*, C-604/10, ECLI:EU:C:2012:115, par. 39.
547. Judgment in *Football Dataco Ltd and Others v. Yahoo! UK Ltd and Others*, C-604/10, ECLI:EU:C:2012:115, paras 33 and 41.
548. Judgment in *Football Dataco Ltd and Others v. Yahoo! UK Ltd and Others*, C-604/10, ECLI:EU:C:2012:115, par. 42.
549. See Article 7(4) of the Database Directive.
550. See respectively, Articles 3(2) and 7(4) of the Database Directive.
551. Recital 7 of Directive 96/9/EC of the Database Directive.
552. Judgment in *Fixtures Marketing Ltd v. Oy Veikkaus Ab*, C-46/02, ECLI:EU:C:2004:694, par. 34; Judgment in *The British Horseracing Board Ltd and Others v. William Hill Organization Ltd*, C-203/02, ECLI:EU:C:2004:695, par. 31; Judgment in *Fixtures Marketing Ltd v. Svenska Spel AB*, C-338/02, ECLI:EU:C:2004:696, par. 24; Judgment in *Fixtures Marketing Ltd v. Organismos prognostikon agonon podosfairou AE (OPAP)*, C-444/02, ECLI:EU:C:2004:697, par. 40.

ensuring the reliability of the information contained in that database, to monitor the accuracy of the materials collected when the database was created and during its operation'. For its part, investment in the presentation of the contents of the database must be understood to refer to *'the resources used for the purpose of giving the database its function of processing information, that is to say those used for the systematic or methodical arrangement of the materials contained in that database and the organisation of their individual accessibility'.*[553] With regard to the distinction between creating and obtaining data, the Court of Justice argued that activities which are *'indivisibly linked'* to the creation of data cannot be taken into account for the purposes of assessing substantial investment in the obtaining of the contents of the database.[554]

While the term of protection for copyright is seventy years after the death of the author,[555] the sui generis database right is only valid for fifteen years from the first of January of the year following the date of completion of the making of the database.[556] However, any substantial change to the contents of the database which would result in the database being considered to be a substantial new investment will lead to the start of a new term of protection of the renewed database.[557] The author of a database protected under the sui generis right is entitled *'to prevent extraction and/or re-utilization of the whole or of a substantial part, evaluated qualitatively and/or quantitatively, of the contents of that database'.*[558] In addition, the sui generis database right protects against the *'repeated and systematic extraction and/or re-utilization of insubstantial parts of the contents of the database implying acts which conflict with a normal exploitation of that database or which unreasonably prejudice the legitimate interests of the maker of the database'.*[559] The rights to prevent extraction and re-utilisation correspond with the rights of reproduction and communication to the public as granted to authors of copyright protectable databases.[560] Extraction is defined as the transfer of all or a substantial part of the contents of a database to another medium and re-utilisation means the making available to the public of all or a substantial part of the contents of a database by the distribution of copies, by renting, by online or other forms of transmission.[561]

---

553. Judgment in *Fixtures Marketing Ltd v. Oy Veikkaus Ab*, C-46/02, ECLI:EU:C:2004:694, paras 34 and 37; Judgment in *The British Horseracing Board Ltd and Others v. William Hill Organization Ltd*, C-203/02, ECLI:EU:C:2004:695, paras 31 and 34; Judgment in *Fixtures Marketing Ltd v. Svenska Spel AB*, C-338/02, ECLI:EU:C:2004:696, paras 24 and 27; Judgment in *Fixtures Marketing Ltd v. Organismos prognostikon agonon podosfairou AE (OPAP)*, C-444/02, ECLI:EU:C:2004:697, paras 40 and 43.

554. Judgment in *Fixtures Marketing Ltd v. Organismos prognostikon agonon podosfairou AE (OPAP)*, C-444/02, ECLI:EU:C:2004:697, par. 49. See also M.J. DAVISON AND P.B. HUGENHOLTZ, 'Football Fixtures, Horseraces and Spin Offs: The ECJ Domesticates the Database Right', *European Intellectual Property Review* 2005, vol. 27, no. 3, (113), pp. 113-114.

555. Article 1 of Directive 2006/116/EC of the European Parliament and of the Council of 12 December 2006 on the term of protection of copyright and certain related rights [2006] OJ L 372/12.

556. Article 10(1) and (2) of the Database Directive.

557. Article 10(3) of the Database Directive.

558. Article 7(1) of the Database Directive.

559. Article 7(5) of the Database Directive.

560. Article 5 of the Database Directive.

561. Article 7(2)(a) and (b) of the Database Directive.

In *The British Horseracing Board* case, the Court of Justice argued that, in the light of the objective of the sui generis right to protect the maker of the database against acts by the user which go beyond the legitimate rights and thereby harm the investment of the maker,[562] those terms have to be interpreted '*as referring to any act of appropriating and making available to the public, without the consent of the maker of the database, the results of his investment, thus depriving him of revenue which should have enabled him to redeem the cost of the investment*'.[563] It is irrelevant whether the act of extraction or re-utilisation is for the purpose of creating a competing database or not, for a commercial or non-commercial purpose, or forms part of an activity other than the creation of a database.[564] In addition, the concepts of extraction and re-utilisation do not imply direct access to a database in the sense that acts carried out from a source other than the database concerned are liable just as much as acts carried out directly from that database.[565] However, the protection does not cover mere consultation of a database.[566]

In the same judgment, the Court of Justice also clarified the term 'substantial part' of the contents of the database concerned that has to be affected by the extraction and re-utilisation in order to be prohibited under Article 7(1) of the Database Directive. Whereas the substantial part evaluated quantitatively refers to the volume of the data extracted or re-utilised and has to be assessed in relation to the volume of the contents of the database as a whole, the substantial part evaluated qualitatively concerns the scale of the investment in the obtaining, verification or presentation of the contents of the subject of the act of extraction or re-utilisation, regardless of whether that subject represents a quantitatively substantial part of the general contents of the protected database. Furthermore, the intrinsic value of the materials affected by the act of extraction or re-utilisation does not constitute a relevant criterion for the assessment of whether the part at issue is substantial in the Court's view.[567]

In order for providers of online platforms such as Google, Facebook and Amazon to be able to rely on database protection, it first has to be determined whether their respective datasets can be regarded as '*a collection of independent works, data or other materials arranged in a systematic or methodical way and individually accessible by electronic or other means*' which is the definition given to a database by Article 1(2) of the Database Directive. As made clear by the Court of Justice, the reference to the independence of the materials making up the collection has to be understood in such a way as to require the materials to be '*separable from one another without their*

---

562. Judgment in *The British Horseracing Board Ltd and Others v. William Hill Organization Ltd*, C-203/02, ECLI:EU:C:2004:695, par. 45 and recital 42 of the Database Directive.
563. Judgment in *The British Horseracing Board Ltd and Others v. William Hill Organization Ltd*, C-203/02, ECLI:EU:C:2004:695, par. 51.
564. Judgment in *The British Horseracing Board Ltd and Others v. William Hill Organization Ltd*, C-203/02, ECLI:EU:C:2004:695, paras 47-48.
565. Judgment in *The British Horseracing Board Ltd and Others v. William Hill Organization Ltd*, C-203/02, ECLI:EU:C:2004:695, par. 53.
566. Judgment in *The British Horseracing Board Ltd and Others v. William Hill Organization Ltd*, C-203/02, ECLI:EU:C:2004:695, par. 54.
567. Judgment in *The British Horseracing Board Ltd and Others v. William Hill Organization Ltd*, C-203/02, ECLI:EU:C:2004:695, paras 70-72.

informative, literary, artistic, musical or other value being affected.[568] In line with recital 17 of the Database Directive, a recording of an audiovisual, cinematographic, literary or musical work as such therefore does not fall within the scope of the Directive. With respect to the datasets of providers of online platforms, the question rises whether individual pieces of information about users have value of their own. While the dataset of a provider of an online platform becomes more useful as the amount of information that it contains increases, separate parts of information, such as the age, occupation, location etc. of a particular user, can still be considered to carry value in their own right. Unlike the recording of a musical or literary composition which only has value as a complete work, a dataset of an online platform provider can be divided in separate items which each have individual value.

Once the existence of a collection of independent materials has been established, classification of a collection as a database also requires that the independent materials making up that collection be systematically or methodically arranged and individually accessible in one way or another. According to the Court of Justice, this implies that the collection has to be contained in a fixed base of some sort and must include means such as an index, table of contents or particular plan or method of classification to allow the retrieval of any independent material contained within it.[569] Search engine, social network and e-commerce platform providers are likely to use a particular method for classifying data and to be able to retrieve individual pieces of information about a particular user as a result of which their datasets also meet this part of the definition of databases as contained in Article 1(2) of the Database Directive. The next question is whether their databases qualify for copyright and/or sui generis protection.

Under Article 3(1) of the Database Directive, the structure of a database can be protected under copyright if the selection or arrangement of its contents constitutes the author's own intellectual creation. As made clear by the Court of Justice in *Football Dataco*, this has to be understood as requiring that the database be original in the sense that '*through the selection or arrangement of the data which it contains, its author expresses his creative ability in an original manner by making free and creative choices and thus stamps his "personal touch"*'.[570] The setting up of datasets by providers of search engines, social networks and e-commerce platforms is not solely dictated by rules or technical considerations in the sense that there is room for their providers to make free and creative choices with regard to the selection or arrangement of the data. Therefore, the datasets of online platform providers are capable to qualify for copyright protection under the Database Directive.[571]

Irrespective of whether the structure of their datasets can be copyright protected, the providers may rely on the sui generis database right to protect their datasets as a

---

568. Judgment in *Fixtures Marketing Ltd v. Organismos prognostikon agonon podosfairou AE (OPAP)*, C-444/02, ECLI:EU:C:2004:697, par. 29.
569. Judgment in *Fixtures Marketing Ltd v. Organismos prognostikon agonon podosfairou AE (OPAP)*, C-444/02, ECLI:EU:C:2004:697, paras 30-31.
570. Judgment in *Football Dataco Ltd and Others v. Yahoo! UK Ltd and Others*, C-604/10, ECLI:EU:C:2012:115, par. 38.
571. See also I. GRAEF, 'Market Definition and Market Power in Data: The Case of Online Platforms', *World Competition* 2015, vol. 38, no. 4, (473), pp. 480-481.

whole if there has been a substantial investment in either the obtaining, verification or presentation of the contents of the database. The Court of Justice argued that investment in data-generating activities has to be disregarded when assessing whether the dataset qualifies for sui generis protection.[572] The fact that a database producer creates data itself, as is the case for online platform providers that create so-called inferred data by analysing the information collected about users, does not, in the Court's view, in itself preclude the producer from claiming protection under the sui generis right as long as it can establish that the obtaining, presentation or verification of the data required substantial investment *'which was independent of the resources used to create those materials'*.[573]

By making this statement the Court of Justice also seems to have rejected the approach originating in the Netherlands where courts had in some instances denied sui generis protection on the sole ground that the databases were mere by-products of a main activity without checking whether, nevertheless, a substantial investment had been made in the obtaining, presentation or verification of the contents of the database.[574] This implies that the mere fact that the datasets built by search engine, social network and e-commerce platform providers form a 'spin-off' of their main activity, namely the delivery of services to users and advertisers, does not prevent them from benefiting from sui generis database protection insofar as they can establish that a substantial investment has been made in the obtaining, presentation or verification of data that is not indivisibly linked to its creation. This is likely to be the case since significant resources are required to set up a tool for collecting pre-existing information about the profile and interests of users that is not generated by online platform providers as such.[575]

Investment in the obtaining of user data in terms of the resources employed to seek out independent items of information about users and collect them in a database would thus be most relevant for assessing whether a dataset of a provider of a search engine, social network or e-commerce platform qualifies for protection under the sui generis right. In this light, the European Commission noted in its *Microsoft/Yahoo* merger decision that Microsoft had explained that *'there are very significant costs that*

---

572. Judgment in *Fixtures Marketing Ltd v. Oy Veikkaus Ab*, C-46/02, ECLI:EU:C:2004:694, par. 34; Judgment in *The British Horseracing Board Ltd and Others v. William Hill Organization Ltd*, C-203/02, ECLI:EU:C:2004:695, par. 31; Judgment in *Fixtures Marketing Ltd v. Svenska Spel AB*, C-338/02, ECLI:EU:C:2004:696, par. 24; Judgment in *Fixtures Marketing Ltd v. Organismos prognostikon agonon podosfairou AE (OPAP)*, C-444/02, ECLI:EU:C:2004:697, par. 40.

573. See the statements of the Court of Justice in Judgment in *Fixtures Marketing Ltd v. Oy Veikkaus Ab*, C-46/02, ECLI:EU:C:2004:694, paras 39-40; Judgment in *The British Horseracing Board Ltd and Others v. William Hill Organization Ltd*, C-203/02, ECLI:EU:C:2004:695, paras 35-36; Judgment in *Fixtures Marketing Ltd v. Svenska Spel AB*, C-338/02, ECLI:EU:C:2004:696, paras 29-30; Judgment in *Fixtures Marketing Ltd v. Organismos prognostikon agonon podosfairou AE (OPAP)*, C-444/02, ECLI:EU:C:2004:697, paras 45-46.

574. E. DERCLAYE, 'The Court of Justice Interprets the Database Sui Generis Right for the First Time', *European Law Review* 2005, vol. 30, no. 3, (420), p. 428. For a discussion of relevant Dutch cases, see E. DERCLAYE, 'Databases Sui Generis Right: Should We Adopt the Spin-Off Theory?', *European Intellectual Property Review* 2004, vol. 26, no. 9, (402), pp. 403-404.

575. See also I. GRAEF, 'Market Definition and Market Power in Data: The Case of Online Platforms', *World Competition* 2015, vol. 38, no. 4, (473), p. 481.

a new entrant would have to bear related to the necessity to have a large database'.[576] Online platform providers would thus be able to rely on sui generis protection for their datasets provided that they can show that substantial investments are required to obtain, verify or present user data.

5.3.3 Trade Secret Protection for Datasets

Providers of search engine, social network and e-commerce platforms may also benefit from trade secret protection for their datasets. Contrary to the situation of copyright and sui generis protection, there is not yet a harmonised system for the protection of trade secrets in the European Union.[577] In November 2013, the Commission adopted a proposal for a Directive on the protection of undisclosed know-how and business information with the objective of aligning the laws dealing with trade secrecy in the EU Member States though the introduction of common definitions, procedures and sanctions.[578] The Trade Secrets Directive entered into force in July 2016, following its adoption by the Council at the end of May 2016 and its publication in the Official Journal of the European Union in June 2016.[579] Member States have until 9 June 2018 to implement the provisions of the Trade Secrets Directive into national law.[580] At the national level, more far-reaching protection may be offered against the unlawful acquisition, use or disclosure of trade secrets than that required in the Trade Secrets Directive provided that compliance with certain articles is ensured.[581]

With regard to the scope of protection of trade secrets, the Directive follows the three requirements set out in Article 39(2) of the TRIPS Agreement:[582] (1) the information is secret in the sense that it is not, as a body or in the precise configuration and assembly of its components, generally known among or readily accessible to persons within the circles that normally deal with the kind of information in question; (2) the information has commercial value because it is secret; and (3) the information has been subject to reasonable steps under the circumstances, by the person lawfully in control of the information, to keep it secret.[583] Unlike copyright and sui generis database protection which grant right holders an exclusive right to prevent third parties from using the subject matter of protection, a trade secret is only protected against

---

576. Case No COMP/M.5727 – *Microsoft/Yahoo! Search Business*, 18 February 2010, par. 111.
577. For an analysis of the differences in trade secret protection between EU Member States, see Study on Trade Secrets and Confidential Business Information in the Internal Market, prepared for the European Commission, April 2013, available at http://ec.europa.eu/internal_market/iprenforcement/docs/trade-secrets/130711_final-study_en.pdf.
578. Proposal for a Directive of the European Parliament and of the Council on the protection of undisclosed know-how and business information (trade secrets) against their unlawful acquisition, use and disclosure, COM(2013) 813 final.
579. Article 20 of Directive 2016/943 of the European Parliament and of the Council of 8 June 2016 on the protection of undisclosed know-how and business information (trade secrets) against their unlawful acquisition, use and disclosure (Trade Secrets Directive) [2016] OJ L 157/1.
580. Article 19(1) of the Trade Secrets Directive.
581. Article 1(1) of the Trade Secrets Directive.
582. Agreement on Trade-Related Aspects of Intellectual Property Rights (TRIPS Agreement), Annex 1C to the Agreement Establishing the World Trade Organization of 1994.
583. Article 2(1) of the Trade Secrets Directive.

unlawful acquisition, use and disclosure.[584] Trade secret protection cannot be invoked against the use of information obtained through legitimate means such as independent discovery or creation.[585] Commercially valuable business information or know-how may thus be protected as long as it is kept secret by the holder by way of, for example, non-disclosure or confidentiality agreements.

By keeping their datasets secret, providers of online platforms may be able to protect the information that they have collected about users under trade secret laws.[586] The recitals of the Directive on trade secrets and the accompanying impact assessment, respectively, state that undisclosed know-how and business information as protected under the Directive may cover '*a diverse range of information that extends beyond technological knowledge to commercial data such as information on customers and suppliers*'[587] and that '*[i]nformation kept as trade secrets (such as list of clients/ customers; internal datasets containing research data or other) may include personal data*'[588] thereby confirming that user data falls within the ambit of trade secret protection. Since the success of an online platform is largely determined by its control over user data and other data that is relevant for improving the quality of its services, this information has considerable commercial value when it is shielded from competitors.[589] While factual data about users such as their age, gender and occupation can hardly qualify as secret information, data relating to the interests they have expressed on a particular online platform, information about their online behaviour or the online purchasing history of users may not be generally known and thus qualify for trade secret protection.[590]

As they are dependent on their user base, providers of online platforms are typically not willing to give competitors access to the information they have gathered about users. For example, Facebook's general conditions prohibit third-party websites from acquiring content and information of users on its platform without its prior permission.[591] Furthermore, Facebook has already invoked trade secret protection as a

---

584. Subsections 2-5 of Article 4 of the Trade Secrets Directive specify the circumstances in which the acquisition, use and disclosure of a trade secret is considered unlawful.
585. In Article 3 of the Trade Secrets Directive, situations are mentioned in which the acquisition, use and disclosure of a trade secret is considered lawful.
586. In addition, their algorithms may be the subject of trade secret protection.
587. Recital 2 of the Trade Secrets Directive.
588. Annex 21 of the Commission Staff Working Document. Impact Assessment. Accompanying the document. proposal for a Directive of the European Parliament and of the Council on the protection of undisclosed know-how and business information (trade secrets) against their unlawful acquisition, use and disclosure, 28 November 2013, SWD(2013) 471 final, p. 254.
589. See J. DREXL, 'Droit de la concurrence et propriété intellectuelle à l'ère du numérique', *A quoi sert la concurrence?* September 2014, available at http://aquoisertlaconcurrence.org/articles/ droit-de-la-concurrence-et-propriete-intellectuelle-a-lere-du-numerique/ who argues that in the online environment competition policy will interact with personal data and trade secret protection.
590. See also I. GRAEF, 'Market Definition and Market Power in Data: The Case of Online Platforms', *World Competition* 2015, vol. 38, no. 4, (473), p. 482.
591. Under Facebook's Terms of Services on Safety, Facebook prohibits automatic collection of user content: '*You will not collect users' content or information, or otherwise access Facebook, using automated means (such as harvesting bots, robots, spiders, or scrapers) without our prior permission*', available at https://www.facebook.com/legal/terms.

justification for not disclosing all personal data in response to an access request of an individual user. The social network provider claimed that one of the sections of the Irish Data Protection Acts, to which Facebook is subject because its international headquarters are located in Ireland, *'carves out an exception to subject access requests where the disclosures in response would adversely affect trade secrets or intellectual property'*.[592] In its opinion on the proposal for a Directive on trade secrets, the European Data Protection Supervisor (EDPS)[593] referred to this claim of Facebook as an illustration of the fact that trade secret protection may interfere with the rights of data subjects in the field of data protection.

Next to the right of data subjects to have access to personal data under Article 12 of the Data Protection Directive, the right to data portability as introduced in Article 20 of the General Data Protection Regulation[594] may also be affected in case personal data forms part of a trade secret. The EDPS therefore recommended to acknowledge the relevance of personal data to the concept of trade secrets more explicitly in the proposal for a Directive on trade secrets by including a clarification that the proposed Directive will in no way restrict the rights of the data subject under the Data Protection Directive. In addition, the EDPS suggested to provide for an adjudication process in the event of a conflict between the protection of trade secrets and the right to access to personal data involving the relevant supervisory authorities including the national data protection authority.[595] As a result, in addition to copyright and the sui generis database right, trade secret laws are of relevance with respect to the protection of the datasets of online platform providers.

5.4 POTENTIAL COMPETITION PROBLEMS INVOLVING ACCESS TO DATA AND ONLINE PLATFORMS

Against the background of the fundamental role of data in the digital economy, access to data as collected by providers of online services is mentioned by scholars as one of the issues likely to attract scrutiny of competition authorities and courts worldwide.[596]

---

592. Email from Facebook to Max Schrems, 28 September 2011, available at http://www.europe-v -facebook.org/FB_E-Mails_28_9_11.pdf. See also G. MOODY, 'Facebook Says Some of Your Personal Data Is Its "Trade Secrets or Intellectual Property"', *Techdirt*, 12 October 2011, available at https://www.techdirt.com/articles/20111011/12190216306/facebook-says-some-your-personal-data-is-its-trade-secrets-intellectual-property.shtml.

593. The EDPS is the independent supervisory authority which oversees the data-processing activities of the EU institutions and provides the EU institutions with advice on data protection issues.

594. See section 5.4.1 below.

595. European Data Protection Supervisor, 'Opinion on the proposal for a directive of the European Parliament and of the Council on the protection of undisclosed know-how and business information (trade secrets) against their unlawful acquisition, use and disclosure', 12 March 2014, paras 14 and 19-22.

596. D.S. EVANS, "Antitrust Issues Raised by the Emerging Global Internet Economy", *Northwestern University Law Review Colloquy* 2008, vol. 102, (285), p. 304; C.S. Yoo, "When Antitrust Met Facebook", *George Mason Law Review* 2012, vol. 19, no. 5, (1147), pp. 1154-1158; S.W. WALLER, "Antitrust and Social Networking", *North Carolina Law Review* 2012, vol. 90, no. 5, (1771), pp. 1799-1800.

Providers of online platforms have an interest in keeping their systems closed because they depend on their user base for monetising their business. In this perspective, three specific competition concerns can be identified relating to possible limitations on data portability (section 5.4.1), a lack of interoperability of online platforms (section 5.4.2) and potential refusals to give access to user data (section 5.4.3).

5.4.1 Data Portability

Restrictions on portability of data are one of the issues with regard to access to online platforms that may give rise to competition problems. One of the concerns that the European Commission expressed in the *Google* case concerns the limitations that the search engine provider allegedly imposed on the portability of advertising campaigns on its AdWords advertising platform. The Commission entered into negotiations with Google about commitments to end the imposition of obligations on advertisers preventing them from moving their advertising campaigns to competing platforms.[597] In the US, the Federal Trade Commission closed its investigation when Google offered voluntary concessions to remove restrictions on AdWords that make it difficult for advertisers to manage advertising campaigns across multiple platforms.[598] By restricting the possibility of advertisers to move their campaigns to another advertising platform, providers create switching costs that may let advertisers decide to stay with their current provider for the sole reason that they find it too cumbersome to manually re-insert their advertising campaign in a new platform.[599] The fact that the European Commission as well as the US Federal Trade Commission took action to redress the switching costs of advertisers in a competition investigation demonstrates that portability can form a competition issue.

Users may also experience switching costs if their provider does not enable them to move their personal information, for example a social network profile, to a competing service. With the increasing use of a particular online service, the amount of personal data collected in this service becomes an obstacle for moving to another provider, even if better or more privacy-friendly alternatives are available.[600] Against

---

597. Commitments of Google in Case COMP/C-3/39.740 *Foundem and others*, 3 April 2013, paras 27-31, available at http://ec.europa.eu/competition/antitrust/cases/dec_docs/39740/39740_8608_5.pdf. In October 2013, Google offered improved commitments to the Commission which included a new proposal providing stronger guarantees against circumvention of the earlier commitments regarding portability of advertising campaigns. See speech former Competition Commissioner Almunia, 'The Google antitrust case: what is at stake?', 1 October 2013, SPEECH/13/768, available at http://europa.eu/rapid/press-release_SPEECH-13-768_en.htm.
598. Press Release US Federal Trade Commission, 'Google Agrees to Change Its Business Practices to Resolve FTC Competition Concerns In the Markets for Devices Like Smart Phones, Games and Tablets, and in Online Search', 3 January 2013, available at http://www.ftc.gov/news-events/press-releases/2013/01/google-agrees-change-its-business-practices-resolve-ftc.
599. See also section 2.4.3 above.
600. Commission Staff Working Paper — Impact Assessment accompanying the General Data Protection Regulation and the Directive on the protection of individuals with regard to the processing of personal data by competent authorities for the purposes of prevention, investigation, detection or prosecution of criminal offences or the execution of criminal penalties, and the free movement of such data (Impact Assessment report), SEC(2012) 72 final, p. 28.

this background, Article 20 of the General Data Protection Regulation introduces the so-called right to data portability which gives a data subject[601] the right to receive his or her personal data that he or she has provided to a controller[602] in a structured, commonly used and machine-readable format and to transmit this data to another controller. Where technically feasible, the data subject also has the right to have the data transmitted directly from one controller to another.[603]

Looking at the Impact Assessment report as drawn up by the Commission, it seems that the right to data portability is mainly targeted at social networks. In the Impact Assessment report, the personal data that may be transferred under the right to data portability is described as *'photos or a list of friends'* and *'contact information, calendar history, interpersonal communications exchanges and other kinds of personally or socially relevant data'*.[604] When the General Data Protection Regulation enters into force, the right to data portability will thus enable users of social networks to transfer their profile, contacts, photos and videos to another social networking platform. A Facebook user will, for instance, be entitled to receive her personal data which she has provided to Facebook in a reusable format and to transmit this data to Google +. If technically feasible, she will also have the right to obtain that this data is transmitted directly to Google +, instead of receiving the data from Facebook and transmitting it herself to Google +.[605]

The scope of application of the right to data portability is not limited to social networks. According to Article 20(1) of the General Data Protection Regulation, the new right will apply to any type of processing of personal data carried out by automated means and based on consent or on a contract. It will therefore address other forms of cloud computing and web services as well.[606] The question rises whether the right to data portability will also apply to search engines and e-commerce platforms enabling users to take their search history and purchasing history with them when switching to a new platform. Because of the personalisation of search results on search engines and purchase suggestions on e-commerce platforms, users may feel bound to stay with their current platform that has collected data about their interests and search or purchasing behaviour and is consequently able to return more relevant search results

---

601. Article 4(1) of the General Data Protection Regulation defines a data subject as *'an identified or identifiable natural person'* and specifies that *'an identifiable person is one who can be identified, directly or indirectly, in particular by reference to an identifier such as a name, an identification number, location data, online identifier or to one or more factors specific to the physical, physiological, genetic, mental, economic, cultural or social identity of that natural person'*.
602. The term 'controller' is defined under Article 4(7) of the General Data Protection Regulation as *'the natural or legal person, public authority, agency or any other body which, alone or jointly with others, determines the purposes and means of the processing of personal data'*.
603. Article 20(2) of the General Data Protection Regulation.
604. Impact Assessment report, p. 28.
605. For an analysis of the application of the right to data portability in the social networking environment and a comparison with the obligation of number portability in the telecommunications sector, see I. GRAEF, 'Mandating portability and interoperability in online social networks: Regulatory and competition law issues in the European Union', *Telecommunications Policy* 2015, vol. 39, no. 6, (502), pp. 505-509.
606. P. SWIRE AND Y. LAGOS, 'Why the Right to Data Portability Likely Reduces Consumer Welfare: Antitrust and Privacy Critique', *Maryland Law Review* 2013, vol. 72, no. 2, (335), pp. 337-338.

or purchase suggestions. The wording of Article 20(1) makes clear that the right to data portability only covers personal data that the data subject has provided to a controller. But providers do not only possess information that has been provided by users themselves. They also obtain information about the behaviour of users on their platform (observed data) and create data for analytical purposes (inferred data). The latter type of data will most likely fall outside the scope of the right to data portability, but the situation with regard to observed data is less clear.

Since the search or purchasing history of a user consists of information provided by the user as well as data generated by the provider, this type of data lies between the two extremes. While the user enters search queries into a search engine and provides transaction or payment information to an e-commerce platform, the respective providers create a profile on the basis of the actions that a particular user undertakes on their platform. The General Data Protection Regulation does not clarify the status of this type of profiles which consist of a combination of data provided by the user and data created by the provider. A similar situation can be observed with regard to the profile of sellers on e-commerce platforms. Whereas the contact information and the advertisements are provided by the seller him- or herself, the provider adds feedback scores to the seller's profile on the basis of the number of positive or negative ratings the seller has received. It is not clear whether the part of the seller's profile that involves the reputation that a seller has built on a particular e-commerce platform will also be portable under the right to data portability, since strictly interpreted it is not provided by the data subject.[607] A clarification of the exact scope of application of the right to data portability in these cases is therefore welcome.

The right to data portability will not only enable data subjects to switch between providers offering similar services but, as made clear by the EDPS, will also allow them to take advantage of additional value-added services developed by third parties. Upon the request and based on the consent of data subjects, these third parties will be able to get access the necessary data for providing their own services. For example, if applied to smart metering, the right to data portability will enable data subjects to transmit data on their energy usage to a third party who can advise them whether an alternative supplier could offer a better price, based on their patterns of electricity consumption.[608] Such an application of the right to data portability may help data subjects to exercise their other data protection rights, such as the right to rectify personal data, and may lower entry barriers to markets that require access to personal data.[609]

---

607. P. SWIRE AND Y. LAGOS, 'Why the Right to Data Portability Likely Reduces Consumer Welfare: Antitrust and Privacy Critique', *Maryland Law Review* 2013, vol. 72, no. 2, (335), pp. 347-349.
608. PRELIMINARY OPINION OF THE EUROPEAN DATA PROTECTION SUPERVISOR, 'Privacy and competitiveness in the age of big data: The interplay between data protection, competition law and consumer protection in the Digital Economy', March 2014, par. 26.
609. EUROPEAN DATA PROTECTION SUPERVISOR, Opinion 7/2015 Meeting the challenges of big data. A call for transparency, user control, data protection by design and accountability, 19 November 2015, p. 13.

While its main policy objective is to ensure that individuals are in control of their personal data and trust the online environment,[610] the right to data portability may also reduce lock-in by enabling users to switch easily between services. In this light, the previous Competition Commissioner argued in a speech that the proposed right to data portability *'goes to the heart of competition policy'* and that *'portability of data is important for those markets where effective competition requires that customers can switch by taking their own data with them'*. By stating *'[w]hether this is a matter for regulation or competition policy, only time will tell'*, he acknowledged the right to data portability as a new tool under data protection law but at the same time did not eliminate competition law intervention for facilitating data portability. In this regard, the previous Competition Commissioner also explicitly noted that *'[i]n time, personal data may well become a competition issue; for instance, if customers were prevented from switching from a company to another because they cannot carry their data along'*.[611]

It therefore cannot be excluded that the European Commission will also intervene on the basis of competition law if a dominant firm does not allow users to take their data with them when switching services.[612] In this regard, the *Facebook/WhatsApp* merger decision in which the European Commission assessed whether data portability issues constituted a barrier to consumers' switching in the context of consumer communications apps is instructive. Even though the European Commission did not find any evidence that this was indeed the case,[613] the fact that these issues were investigated under merger review indicates the potential of competition law to address data portability. In particular, a refusal of a dominant firm to facilitate data portability may constitute a form of abuse by exploiting consumers or excluding competitors. In the latter fashion, a lack of data portability may lead to entry barriers for competitors and violate Article 102(b) TFEU by limiting markets and technical development to the prejudice of consumers.[614]

Finally, it is instructive to note that the proposal for a Digital Content Directive includes a provision enabling a form of data portability. Article 13(2)(c) of the proposal requires a supplier to provide a consumer who terminates a contract for the supply of digital content *'with technical means to retrieve all content provided by the consumer*

---

610. Impact Assessment report, p. 43.
611. Speech former Competition Commissioner Almunia, 'Competition and personal data protection', Privacy Platform event: Competition and Privacy in Markets of Data Brussels, 26 November 2012, SPEECH/12/860.
612. D. MEYER, 'Facebook Beware? EU Antitrust Chief Warns over Data Portability', 27 November 2012, available at http://www.zdnet.com/facebook-beware-eu-antitrust-chief-warns-over-data-portability-7000007950/. See also, D. GERADIN AND M. KUSCHEWSKY, 'Competition Law and Personal Data: Preliminary Thoughts on a Complex Issue', SSRN *Working Paper* February 2013, p. 11, availabe at http://papers.ssrn.com/sol3/papers.cfm?abstract_id = 2216088.
613. Case No COMP/M.7217 – *Facebook/WhatsApp*, 3 October 2014, paras 113-115 and 134. For a more detailed analysis, see section 2.4.3 above.
614. C.S. YOO, 'When Antitrust Met Facebook', *George Mason Law Review* 2012, vol. 19, no. 5, (1147), pp. 1154-1155 and D. GERADIN AND M. KUSCHEWSKY, 'Competition Law and Personal Data: Preliminary Thoughts on a Complex Issue', SSRN *Working Paper* February 2013, p. 11, availabe at http://papers.ssrn.com/sol3/papers.cfm?abstract_id = 2216088.

and any other data produced or generated through the consumer's use of the digital content to the extent that data has been retained by the supplier'. The provision goes on to state that the consumer is *'entitled to retrieve the content free of charge, without significant inconvenience, in reasonable time and in a commonly used data format'*.[615] Considering that, as explained in section 5.2 above, a social network or a communications app would also fall within the scope of application of the proposed Directive, this provision provides additional protection to consumers going beyond the right to data portability as contained in the General Data Protection Regulation. Unlike the latter right which only covers personal data provided by the data subject, Article 13(2)(c) of the proposal for a Digital Content Directive also enables a consumer to retrieve any other data, to the extent that it has been retained by the supplier, generated through the use of the digital content which is not as such provided by the consumer. In addition, the latter provision makes explicit that consumers are entitled to retrieve the content free of charge and in a reasonable time whereas no such specific requirements apply under the right to data portability.

On the other hand, it should be kept in mind that the proposal for a Digital Content Directive does not entitle consumers to have their digital content directly transmitted to a new provider. This while Article 20 of the General Data Protection Regulation provides data subjects with a right to ask for a direct transfer of provided personal data where this is technically feasible. These differences in scope can be explained by the distinct underlying objectives of the two instruments. While the right to data portability aims to give data subjects more control over their personal data, the relevant provision in the proposal for a Digital Content Directive aims to ensure that consumers benefit from effective protection in relation to the right to terminate the contract.[616]

5.4.2 Interoperability of Online Platforms

The lack of interoperability of online platforms may also become an area of interest for competition authorities. Interoperability can be defined as *'the ability to transfer and render useful data and other information across systems, applications or components'*.[617] Under the Computer Programs Directive, interoperability is regarded as a form of functional interconnection or interaction and described as *'the ability to exchange information and mutually to use the information which has been exchanged'*.[618] It is important to note that interoperability has to be seen as a matter of

---

615. Article 16(4)(b) of the proposal for a Digital Content Directive provides for a similar obligation for suppliers with regard to long-term contracts for the supply of digital content.
616. Recital 39 of the proposal for a Digital Content Directive.
617. J. PALFREY AND U. GASSER, *Interop: The Promise and Perils of Highly Interconnected Systems*, New York, Basic Books, 2012, p. 5.
618. Recital 10 of Directive 2009/24/EC of the European Parliament and of the Council of 23 April 2009 on the legal protection of computer programs [2009] OJ L 111/16.

degree.[619] The enforcement of data portability would already require a certain level of interoperability between online services.[620]

In order to establish an effective form of data portability, there should be a technical measure that makes it possible to seamlessly transfer user data from one online service, for example a social network, to another. This implies that the 'receiving' social network is able to process the data extracted from another platform in an efficient manner. To some extent, this would require a standard format for data storage to enable providers to exchange user data and mutually use the information exchanged. Considering the differences as to how content and messages are displayed on the personal page of users in different social networks, this might require some platforms to change part of their design.[621] As a result, the implementation of the right to data portability may have an impact on innovation by requiring some form of standardisation between different market players.

Since communication and interaction among users is at the core of the functionality that social networks offer to users, interoperability is particularly relevant for these online services that currently still operate as closed systems. Interoperability of online social networks would enable users to connect with each other regardless of their social network provider. Full social network interoperability therefore goes further than enabling data portability between social networks. Data portability permits users to move their profile to another social network and requires a certain level of interoperability in order to facilitate the transmission of user data between platforms, but does not allow users to reach someone that is not on the same social network. While Facebook, for instance, enables users to send messages to 'traditional' email systems such as Hotmail, Yahoo! or Gmail and vice versa, it is not possible to post materials on someone's Facebook page without having a Facebook profile. Full social network interoperability would thus, for example, enable a Google+ user to upload pictures or post messages on someone's Facebook page directly without having to create a profile on Facebook. In a report of a workshop organised by the EDPS in the European Parliament in June 2014, it was questioned in this regard whether data portability could be effective without dominant networks being compelled to interconnect.[622]

The imposition of interoperability requirements on social network providers under competition law would redress the direct network effects that are present in the

---

619. J. PALFREY AND U. GASSER, *Interop: The Promise and Perils of Highly Interconnected Systems*, New York, Basic Books, 2012, p. 8.
620. See S.Y. WAHYUNINGTYAS, 'Interoperability for Data Portability between Social Networking Sites (SNS): The Interplay between EC Software Copyright and Competition Law', *Queen Mary Journal of Intellectual Property* 2015, vol. 5, no. 1, (46).
621. C.S. YOO, 'When Antitrust Met Facebook', *George Mason Law Review* 2012, vol. 19, no. 5, (1147), p. 1155.
622. EUROPEAN DATA PROTECTION SUPERVISOR, 'Report of workshop on Privacy, Consumers, Competition and Big Data', 2 June 2014, p. 4, available at https://secure.edps.europa.eu/EDPSWEB/webdav/site/mySite/shared/Documents/Consultation/Big%20data/14-07-11_EDPS_Report_Workshop_Big_data_EN.pdf.

market.[623] If social networks would be interoperable, the direct network effects would not be limited to a specific social network anymore in the sense that the users of the social networks at issue benefit from the combined user base. Enabling interoperability of social networks could therefore be a way to remedy the direct network effects and to stimulate competition *in* the market. In addition, switching costs and the degree of user lock-in would be reduced. In particular, the social lock-in of users would be addressed, since the number of people that a user can reach is not limited anymore to the number of users on the social network that the user decided to join. Social network interoperability enables users to switch services without losing their social network connection with the users of the platform they joined first. In the presence of interconnection between social networks, users that switched to another platform are still able to contact their friends who decided to stay with the former service. For example, when a user would leave Facebook for a smaller and less well-known social network he or she can still remain in touch with his or her Facebook friends through the new platform. As a result, it would not be necessary for users anymore to join the social network of their friends or more generally, the social network that has the most users once social networks are interoperable. Instead, users would be able to join the social network of their preference.[624]

The *Microsoft* case illustrates that a lack of interoperability can constitute a competition problem. In its 2004 decision,[625] which was confirmed by the General Court in 2007,[626] the European Commission found that Microsoft abused its dominant position on the market for client PC operating systems by denying to share interoperability information with competitors in the derivative market for work group server operating systems.[627] With regard to the social networking environment, scholars have already called upon the European Commission to impose interconnection requirements on social network providers.[628] However, competition authorities can only intervene on an ex post basis (with the exception of merger review). Before the European Commission, or a national competition authority, would be entitled to impose interoperability remedies on the basis of EU competition rules, it would need to establish that the social network provider at issue is abusing its dominant position on a given market by denying interoperability with other social networks.

Irrespective of whether incumbent social network providers like Facebook can be found dominant and abuse their market power by denying interoperability with competing platforms, one can doubt whether competition law is the most suitable

---

623. For a discussion of the extent to which direct network effects are present on social networks, see section 2.4.2 above.
624. S.W. Waller, 'Antitrust and Social Networking', *North Carolina Law Review* 2012, vol. 90, no. 5, (1771), p. 1789.
625. Case COMP/C-3/37.792 - *Microsoft*, 24 March 2004.
626. Judgment in *Microsoft v. Commission*, T-201/04, ECLI:EU:T:2007:289.
627. In addition to the refusal to license interoperability information, the *Microsoft* case involved the tying of Microsoft's Windows Media Player to its dominant client PC operating system Windows. For a more elaborate analysis of the interoperability issue in the *Microsoft* case, see section 6.2.2 below.
628. I. Brown and C.T. Marsden, *Regulating Code: Good Governance and Better Regulation in the Information Age*, MIT Press, 2013, pp. 190-191.

instrument to ensure interoperability of social networks. Article 102 TFEU only empowers competition authorities to intervene in situations of abuse of dominance as a result of which interconnection requirements may only be imposed on the dominant social network provider to remedy abusive behaviour. For enabling effective interaction between social networking sites, interconnection requirements should be imposed in general on all social networks and in all situations. If interconnection obligations are applied to the dominant social network provider exclusively, interoperability would only be available between the leading social network and the other networking sites in the market. No interconnection would exist among the non-dominant social networks. Therefore, 'real' interoperability can only be established when all social network providers are obliged to participate in the process.

In this regard, a comparison can be made with the telecommunications sector where interoperability was imposed on all providers by way of regulation on EU level. In the 1997 Open Network Provision Directive, which formed part of the regulatory framework on the basis of which the telecommunications market in the European Union was liberalised in January 1998, a provision was included that obliged operators of public electronic communications networks to ensure interconnection of their networks in order to enable users on different networks to communicate with each other. The regulatory framework for interoperability in telecommunications is based on the principle that undertakings receiving requests for interconnection to their network should negotiate and conclude agreements on a commercial basis for the purpose of ensuring the provision of communication services throughout the European Union. Operators of public electronic communications networks have a right, and when requested by other undertakings, an obligation to negotiate interconnection with each other.[629]

In the Digital Single Market Strategy for Europe that the European Commission adopted in May 2015, reference is made to the lack of data portability between services and the lack of open and interoperable systems in general as representing a barrier for the cross-border flow of data and the development of new services. The Commission indicated that it is planning to propose a European 'Free flow of data' initiative in 2016 which may also address these issues.[630] When considering the desirability of imposing interconnection requirements similar to the ones adopted in the telecommunications

---

629. Article 4(1) of Directive 97/33/EC of the European Parliament and of the Council of 30 June 1997 on interconnection in Telecommunications with regard to ensuring universal service and interoperability through application of the principles of Open Network Provision (ONP) [1997] OJ L 199/32. The current version of this provision is Article 4(1) of Directive 2002/19/EC of the European Parliament and of the Council of 7 March 2002 on access to, and interconnection of, electronic communications networks and associated facilities (Access Directive) [2002] OJ L 108/7 as amended by Directive 2009/140 of the European Parliament and of the Council of 25 November 2009 [2009] OJ L 337/37.
630. Communication from the Commission to the European Parliament, the Council, the European Economic and Social Committee and the Committee of the Regions. A Digital Single Market Strategy for Europe, COM(2015) 192 final, 6 May 2015, pp. 14-15.

sector on social networks or other services, one should look at the public interest underlying this part of the telecommunications regulation and compare the respective market situations. In this regard, the need for interoperability of social networks seems to be less compelling than interconnection between public electronic communications networks.

One of the recitals to the 1997 Open Network Provision Directive states that '*it is necessary to ensure adequate interconnection within the Community of certain networks and interoperability of services essential for the social and economic well-being of Community users*'.[631] Considering the numerous alternatives that people these days have at their disposal to communicate with each other, interoperability of social networks does not seem to be necessary for ensuring the social and economic well-being of users in the European Union. Instead, interconnection between social networks may serve a different goal namely the advancement of effective competition in the online social networking environment.[632] This was also one of the objectives of the obligation to interconnect public electronic communications networks. Recital 2 of the 1997 Open Network Provision Directive notes in this regard that '*fair, proportionate and non-discriminatory conditions for interconnection and interoperability are key factors in fostering the development of open and competitive markets*'. When interconnection between public electronic communications networks was mandated, no alternative means were available on the market for enabling end-users to interact with each other at a distance.

The need for interoperability between social networks with the aim of stimulating effective competition does therefore not seem to be equally compelling when comparing the current market situation with the electronic communications sector in the 1990s. In the light of the current dynamic nature of the social network environment, it can thus be doubted whether it would be desirable for the Commission to introduce regulation to ensure interoperability of social networks. In addition, considering the possible innovation implications of such an interventionist approach, the imposition of interconnection requirements in the social network sector does not seem proportionate at this point in time.

5.4.3 Refusals to Give Competitors Access to User Data

The potential competition issue to which the remainder of this part of the book is devoted concerns the situation whereby competitors or new entrants become dependent on the user data gathered by incumbent online platforms for developing their own products or services. Given the importance of data in the digital economy, the

---

631. Recital 5 of Directive 97/33/EC of the European Parliament and of the Council of 30 June 1997 on interconnection in Telecommunications with regard to ensuring universal service and interoperability through application of the principles of Open Network Provision (ONP) [1997] OJ L 199/32.
632. For a more in-depth comparison of interoperability between public electronic communications networks and online social networks, see I. GRAEF, 'Mandating Portability and Interoperability in Online Social Networks: Regulatory and Competition Law Issues in the European Union', *Telecommunications Policy* 2015, vol. 39, no. 6, (502), pp. 510-512.

information that providers of search engines, social networks and e-commerce platforms collect about their users may form a necessary input of production for other market participants. It is instructive in this regard how an ecosystem has started to develop around the personal data that online platforms collect. For example, Twitter has established certified data resellers that sell access to its tweets to companies that analyse Twitter data for providing social analytics services to clients.[633] In these circumstances, potential competitors may request incumbent providers access to the data accumulated on their platforms in order to introduce competing or complementary services.

While the right to data portability as put forward in the General Data Protection Regulation will give users in certain circumstances the possibility to transfer their data between online platforms, it does not entitle the providers to claim access to this data. The new right thus only affects the relationship between users and their provider, and does not change the situation between providers themselves.[634] Similarly, providers do not get access to the information about users collected on a rival platform if interoperability of social networks would be established. Although the level of competition in the market would increase if data portability and interoperability are to be enforced, competitors and new entrants will still have to rely on competition law in order to get access to user data as an input for developing their own products or services.

By refusing rivals access to their datasets, dominant providers may foreclose competition and engage in abusive behaviour under Article 102 TFEU. In this context, the question rises whether the denial of a dominant platform provider to grant competitors access to user data could constitute a refusal to deal and lead to liability under the so-called essential facilities doctrine.[635] This doctrine attacks a particular form of exclusionary anticompetitive conduct by which a dominant undertaking refuses to give access to a type of infrastructure or other form of facility to which rivals need access in order to be able to compete. As will be discussed in more detail in the next chapter, the essential facilities doctrine has already been applied to physical infrastructures including ports and tunnels but also to intangible assets protected by intellectual property rights.

---

633. For the Twitter Official Partner Program, see https://partners.twitter.com/about.
634. See also D. GERADIN AND M. KUSCHEWSKY, 'Competition Law and Personal Data: Preliminary Thoughts on a Complex Issue', *SSRN Working Paper* February 2013, p. 10, availabe at http://papers.ssrn.com/sol3/papers.cfm?abstract_id = 2216088.
635. See D. GERADIN AND M. KUSCHEWSKY, 'Competition Law and Personal Data: Preliminary Thoughts on a Complex Issue', *SSRN Working Paper* February 2013, pp. 13-15, availabe at http://papers.ssrn.com/sol3/papers.cfm?abstract_id = 2216088; PRELIMINARY OPINION OF THE EUROPEAN DATA PROTECTION SUPERVISOR, 'Privacy and competitiveness in the age of big data: The interplay between data protection, competition law and consumer protection in the Digital Economy', March 2014, paras 40 and 66-68; and Autorité de la concurrence and Bundeskartellamt, 'Competition Law and Data', 10 May 2016, pp. 17-18, available at http://www.autoritedelaconcurrence.fr/doc/reportcompetitionlawanddatafinal.pdf who have pointed to the possibility that data collected by online platform providers may constitute an essential facility under EU competition law.

5.5 CONCLUSION

Providers of search engines, social networks and e-commerce platforms are increasingly dependent on access to data for the provision of services to users and advertisers that are of the quality these customers expect. By being active on online platforms, users enable providers to gather data about their profile, interests and online behaviour. A distinction can be made between data voluntarily shared by users, data obtained by observing the actions of users and data derived from the analysis of this volunteered or observed information.

In order to prevent third parties from using the collections of data on which they have based their business model, providers of online platforms can in certain circumstances rely on copyright, sui generis database and trade secret protection. The personal interest of users in their information is protected under Article 16 TFEU and EU secondary data protection legislation. In addition, data protection has the status of a human right under the European Convention on Human Rights and of a fundamental right in EU law under the Charter of Fundamental Rights of the European Union.

Since the success of their business largely relies on the acquisition and monetisation of user data, online platform providers have an incentive to keep their systems closed. This may lead to foreclosure of competitors and give rise to competition problems. Restrictions on the portability of online advertising campaigns have already attracted the attention of the European Commission in the *Google* case. In the area of data protection, the General Data Protection Regulation will introduce a new right to data portability giving individuals more control over their personal data. Once entered into force, the right to data portability will not only serve a data protection purpose but will also address competition-related access issues by diminishing switching costs and lock-in of users. At the same time, as evidenced by the statements of the previous Competition Commissioner, the implementation of the right to data portability will not exclude interventions for facilitating data portability on competition law grounds.

Secondly, interoperability concerns may be identified, in particular on social networks which currently still operate as closed platforms. However, considering the many possibilities that users currently have to interact, it does not seem to be necessary or desirable to mandate interconnection between social networks by way of regulation as has happened in the telecommunications sector.

The third competition concern relates to potential refusals of dominant providers to give competitors and new entrants access to the user data they have gathered on their platforms. This issue forms the focus of the second part of the book. Before analysing possible scenarios relating to data access refusals on online platforms, the current legal standards of the essential facilities doctrine in the European Union and the United States are discussed and a possible framework for its future application is set out taking into account the underlying economic interests in refusal to deal cases.

CHAPTER 6

Normative Analysis of the Essential Facilities Doctrine

6.1 INTRODUCTION

The essential facilities doctrine can be considered to form an important part of current EU and US competition or antitrust law. However, as will become clear in this chapter, the United States Supreme Court and the EU Courts have never formally recognised the existence of the doctrine. The US Supreme Court explicitly referred to the essential facilities doctrine in its *Trinko*[636] judgment but neither approved nor refuted the doctrine. In the EU, the General Court and the Court of Justice have never even mentioned the term 'essential facilities doctrine' in their judgments. The European Commission only expressly used the word 'essential facility' in four decisions involving access to port and railway infrastructures in the 1990s.[637]

Lower US courts appear to have developed an essential facilities doctrine, dealing with situations in which existing as well as new customers can claim access to an input that is necessary for competition, separate from or in addition to the concept of refusal to deal according to which only the disruption of supply to existing customers (irrespective of the indispensability of the input) may violate Section 2 of the Sherman Act. Such a differentiation is, however, currently not apparent in the EU. In European competition law, the difference between the two notions merely seems to be a matter

---

636. *Verizon Communications v. Law Offices of Curtis V. Trinko, LLP,* 540 U.S. 398 (2004).
637. Case IV/34.174 - *B&I Line PLC v. Sealink Harbours Ltd. & Sealink Stena Ltd.* [1992] 5 CMLR 255, par. 41; Case IV/34.689 - *Sea Containers v. Stena Sealink* [1994] OJ L 15/8, par. 66; Commission Decision 94/119/EC - *Port of Rødby* [1994] OJ L 55/52, par. 12; Commission Decision 94/894/EC - *Eurotunnel* [1994] OJ L 354/66, par. 56.

of semantics.[638] Although in the early cases of *Commercial Solvents*[639] and *United Brands*[640] which involved terminations of existing levels of supply less strict standards have been used to establish a duty to deal than in later cases dealing with access requests from new customers, the General Court assessed the disruption of supply that was in stake in *Microsoft*,[641] the latest essential facilities case on the EU level,[642] under the stringent exceptional circumstances test set out in *Magill*[643] and *IMS Health*.[644] This implies that a refusal to deal can only be held abusive under the current standards of Article 102 TFEU if it relates to an indispensable or essential input. The concepts of refusal to deal or supply on the one hand and essential facilities on the other hand therefore both require 'essentiality'. For this reason, the two terms are used interchangeably in this book in the context of EU competition law. Where specific reference is made to instances in which a dominant undertaking discontinues existing levels of supply, the term 'disruption of supply' is used.

In section 6.2, the current legal standards applicable to refusals to deal in the US and EU are analysed. Afterwards, the difference in approach on both sides of the Atlantic is explained by discussing the schools of economic thought that have influenced the development of the essential facilities doctrine in the US and EU in section 6.3. Before setting out a proposed framework for the application of the essential facilities doctrine in future cases in section 6.8, attention is paid, respectively, to the economic trade-off to be made in refusal to deal cases in section 6.4, to the need for a more coherent framework in section 6.5, to the principles underlying the proposed framework in section 6.6, and to the role of intellectual property rights in essential facilities cases in section 6.7.

6.2 UNRAVELLING THE LEGAL STANDARDS FOR REFUSALS TO DEAL IN THE UNITED STATES AND THE EUROPEAN UNION

In order to fully understand the current legal standards for refusals to deal, it is necessary to look at the evolution of the essential facilities doctrine. The doctrine originated in the United States but is also applied in the European Union where it has developed along a different line. While the US Supreme Court made clear in its *Trinko*

---

638. See also D. GERADIN, 'Limiting the Scope of Article 82 EC: What Can the EU Learn from the U.S. Supreme Court's Judgment in *Trinko* in the Wake of *Microsoft*, *IMS*, and *Deutsche Telekom?*', *Common Market Law Review* 2004, vol. 41, no. 6, (1519), pp. 1525-1526.
639. Judgment in *Istituto Chemioterapico Italiano and Commercial Solvents v. Commission*, Joined cases 6 and 7/73, ECLI:EU:C:1974:18.
640. Judgment in *United Brands v. Commission*, Case 27/76, ECLI:EU:C:1978:22.
641. Judgment in *Microsoft v. Commission*, T-201/04, ECLI:EU:T:2007:289.
642. In 2008, the Court of Justice did deliver a judgment in a preliminary reference case which may be interpreted in such a way as to set a different standard for disruptions of supply (Judgment in *Sot. Lélos kai Sia EE and Others v. GlaxoSmithKline AEVE Farmakeftikon Proïonton*, Joined Cases C-468/06 to C-478/06, ECLI:EU:C:2008:504, par. 34). See section 6.8.3 below for a discussion of this issue.
643. Judgment in *Telefis Eireann and Independent Television Publications Ltd v. Commission of the European Communities (Magill)*, Joined cases C-241/91 and C-242/91, ECLI:EU:C:1995:98.
644. Judgment in *IMS Health GmbH & Co. OHG v. NDC Health GmbH & Co. KG*, C-418/01, ECLI:EU:C:2004:257.

judgment[645] that antitrust liability for refusals to deal should remain very limited, the European Commission and the Court of Justice seem to favour a more extensive interpretation of the essential facilities doctrine.

The analysis below consists of a discussion of the most relevant US and EU refusal to deal cases. It should be noted that this section does not intend to give a complete overview of these cases. Since it is the aim of this section to discuss the evolution of the essential facilities doctrine in the US and the EU, only the most influential cases are analysed that have impacted on the development of the current legal standards for refusals to deal in US antitrust and EU competition law.

6.2.1 Development of the Essential Facilities Doctrine in the United States

The essential facilities doctrine emerged in the United States under Section 2 of the Sherman Act which deals with monopolisation and is the US equivalent of Article 102 TFEU.[646] The doctrine is said to have originated in the judgment of the US Supreme Court in *Terminal Railroad* in 1912. The case concerned an association of railroad companies which had acquired all existing railroad bridges and terminal facilities over the Mississippi River into and out of Saint Louis. The Supreme Court found that the conditions of the arrangement between the members of the association were so as to prohibit any other reasonable means of entering the city and therefore amounted to a violation of both Sections 1 (corresponding to Article 101 TFEU) and 2 of the Sherman Act. Instead of ordering a dissolution of the association as the government had requested, the Supreme Court imposed a duty on the members of the association to provide any competitor with joint ownership and control of the terminal properties or, in case a competing railroad company chose not to become a joint owner, give access to the infrastructure under reasonable terms.[647] Although the case may not have clearly set out a rule that a denial of access is anticompetitive once it involves a facility that is not duplicable and to which a firm needs access in order to enter the market, the Supreme Court did hold that the association of railroad companies possessed a facility essential for competition in the railroad industry in Saint Louis. In addition, it adopted a remedy that forced the members of the association to deal with their competitors.[648]

---

645. *Verizon Communications v. Law Offices of Curtis V. Trinko, LLP* (*Trinko*), 540 U.S. 398 (2004).
646. While Section 2 of the Sherman Act is concerned with monopolisation or attempted monopolisation, Article 102 TFEU prohibits abuses of a dominant position. As a result, achieving a dominant position may lead to liability under Section 2 of the Sherman Act but is not in itself problematic under Article 102 TFEU which focuses instead on the behaviour of a dominant firm.
647. *United States v. Terminal Railroad Association of St. Louis*, 224 U.S. 383 (1912), at 409-411.
648. For a discussion of the *Terminal Railroad* case and the origin of the essential facilities doctrine (in the early days also known as the 'bottleneck theory') in the United States, see D.E. TROY, 'Unclogging the Bottleneck: A New Essential Facility Doctrine', *Columbia Law Review* 1983, vol. 83, no. 2, (441), pp. 447-452; T.G. KRATTENMAKER AND S.C. SALOP, 'Anticompetitive Exclusion: Raising Rivals' Costs to Achieve Power over Price', *Yale Law Journal* 1986, vol. 96, no. 2, (209), pp. 234-236; G.J. WERDEN, 'The Law and Economics of the Essential Facility Doctrine', *Saint Louis University Law Journal* 1987, vol. 32, no. 2, (433), pp. 435-437 and 441-447; J.R. RATNER, 'Should There Be an Essential Facility Doctrine?', *University of California, Davis Law Review* 1988, vol. 21, no. 2, (327), pp. 335-338; D.J. GERBER, 'Rethinking the

Later cases decided by the US Supreme Court that are associated with the essential facilities doctrine include: *Associated Press*[649] in which the bylaws of the news agency limiting membership and access to news for competitors were found to violate the Sherman Act; *Lorain Journal*[650] concerning a local newspaper which was found to have engaged in anticompetitive behaviour by refusing to publish announcements from businesses who advertised through the local radio station; *Otter Tail*[651] involving a vertically integrated power company which was found to have breached the Sherman Act by refusing to supply electricity on the wholesale level to municipalities wishing to resell the energy to consumers and to compete with Otter Tail on the retail market; *Aspen Skiing*[652] in which antitrust liability was established for the unilateral termination of a joint ticket giving access to all four ski facilities in Aspen three of which were operated by Aspen Skiing; and *Kodak*[653] in which a manufacturer of copying and micrographic equipment who started to refuse to sell replacement parts to companies servicing Kodak equipment was denied its motion for having the case decided on the basis of summary judgment (without a full trial). While the Supreme Court never mentioned or recognised the essential facilities doctrine in these cases,[654] lower courts applied the concept in their judgments.[655]

In *Hecht*,[656] the term 'essential facilities' was used for the first time in the context of a dispute concerning a restrictive covenant in the stadium lease contract of the Washington Redskins. A potential franchisee of the American Football League challenged the covenant that prohibited leasing the stadium to any other professional football team. The Court of Appeals of the District of Columbia Circuit explicitly stated that the essential facilities doctrine was applicable to the case and quoted the classification given by Neale who is the first commentator articulating the doctrine:[657] *'where facilities cannot practically be duplicated by would-be competitors, those in possession of them must allow them to be shared on fair terms. It is illegal restraint of trade to foreclose the scarce facility'.*[658] According to the Court: *'[t]o be "essential" a facility need not be indispensable; it is sufficient if duplication of the facility would be economically infeasible and if denial of its use inflicts a severe handicap on potential*

Monopolist's Duty to Deal: A Legal and Economic Critique of the Doctrine of "Essential Facilities"', *Virginia Law Review* 1988, vol. 74, no. 6, (1069).

649. *Associated Press v. United States*, 326 U.S. 1 (1945).
650. *Lorain Journal Co. v. United States*, 342 U.S. 143 (1951).
651. *Otter Tail Power Co. v. United States*, 410 U.S. 366 (1973).
652. *Aspen Skiing Co. v. Aspen Highlands Skiing Corp.*, 472 U.S. 585 (1985).
653. *Eastman Kodak Co. v. Image Technical Services, Inc.*, 504 U.S. 451 (1992).
654. With the exception of *Aspen* where the Supreme Court stated in a footnote: *'we find it unnecessary to consider the possible relevance of the "essential facilities" doctrine'*. See *Aspen Skiing Co. v. Aspen Highlands Skiing Corp.*, 472 U.S. 585 (1985), at footnote 44.
655. For a list of US Court of Appeals judgments from 1980 until 2003 in which the essential facilities doctrine has been applied, see E. ELHAUGE, 'Defining Better Monopolization Standards', *Stanford Law Review* 2003, vol. 56, no. 2, (253), footnote 20 on pp. 261-262.
656. *Hecht v. Pro-Football, Inc.*, 570 F.2d 982 (D.C. Cir. 1977), *cert. denied*, 436 U.S. 956 (1978).
657. D.E. TROY, 'Unclogging the Bottleneck: A New Essential Facility Doctrine', *Columbia Law Review* 1983, vol. 83, no. 2, (441), p. 448 who notes that Neale referred to the essential facilities doctrine with the term 'bottleneck monopolies'.
658. A.D. NEALE, *The Antitrust Laws of the United States*, 2nd edition, 1970, at 67 as quoted in *Hecht v. Pro-Football, Inc.*, 570 F.2d 982 (D.C. Cir. 1977), at 992.

market entrants'. However, *'the antitrust laws do not require that an essential facility be shared if such sharing would be impractical or would inhibit the defendant's ability to serve its customers adequately'*.[659]

In the later *MCI* case[660] concerning AT&T's refusal to let MCI interconnect with its local distribution network preventing MCI to compete with AT&T in the long-distance telephone market, the Seventh Circuit Court established that a firm with monopoly power is liable under the essential facilities doctrine when: (1) the monopolist controls an essential facility; (2) a competitor cannot practically or reasonably duplicate the facility; (3) the monopolist denies the use of the facility to a competitor; and (4) it was feasible to provide (access to) the facility.[661] This test has been widely applied by lower courts in the United States until the Supreme Court delivered its judgment in *Trinko*.[662]

While the Supreme Court has not yet had the opportunity to rule on the scope of antitrust liability for refusals to license intellectual property rights, the US Courts of Appeals of different circuits have been confronted with the issue. Three cases are of particular importance, because they set out the main approaches used by lower courts.

Data General concerned a refusal of a computer manufacturer to continue to license its copyrighted diagnostic software to third-party maintainers with whom it competed in the aftermarket for maintenance and repair of its computers. The Court of Appeals for the First Circuit stated that *'in passing the Copyright Act, Congress itself made an empirical assumption that allowing copyright holders to collect license fees and exclude others from using their works creates a system of incentives that promotes consumer welfare in the long term'* as a result of which antitrust defendants cannot be required *'to prove and reprove the merits of this legislative assumption in every case where a refusal to license a copyrighted work comes under attack'*. Nevertheless, the First Circuit also recognised that the Copyright Act did not explicitly aim to limit the scope of the Sherman Act.[663] In an attempt to harmonise the two legislative acts, the Court argued that while exclusionary conduct may include a monopolist's refusal to license a copyright, the *'author's desire to exclude others from use of its copyrighted work is a presumptively valid business justification for any immediate harm to consumers'*. In the Court's view, this presumption could only be rebutted in *'rare cases in which imposing antitrust liability is unlikely to frustrate the objectives of the Copyright Act'*.[664] This would particularly be the case if there was evidence that the copyright was acquired in an unlawful manner. However, in the factual circumstances

---

659. *Hecht v. Pro-Football, Inc.*, 570 F.2d 982 (D.C. Cir. 1977), at 992-993.
660. *MCI Communications v. American Telephone & Telegraph Co.*, 708 F.2d 1081 (7th Cir. 1983), cert. denied, 464 U.S. 891 (1983).
661. *MCI Communications v. American Telephone & Telegraph Co.*, 708 F.2d 1081 (7th Cir. 1983), at 1132-1133.
662. S.W. WALLER AND W. TASCH, 'Harmonizing Essential Facilities', *Antitrust Law Journal* 2010, vol. 76, no. 3, (741), p. 743.
663. *Data General Corp. v. Grumman Systems Support Corp.*, 36 F.3d 1147 (1st Cir. 1994), at 1886-1887.
664. *Data General Corp. v. Grumman Systems Support Corp.*, 36 F.3d 1147 (1st Cir. 1994), at 1887 and footnote 64.

at issue the Court found that there was insufficient proof to rebut the presumption of legality of the refusal to license copyrighted software.[665]

In *Kodak*, the case mentioned above that the Supreme Court sent for a full trial,[666] the Court of Appeals for the Ninth Circuit applied the presumption of legality established in *Data General* also to patents and extended the possible means of rebutting the presumption to include evidence of anticompetitive intent on the part of the right holder in refusing to license. The Ninth Circuit held that the presumption of legality of Kodak's refusal to continue to sell replacement parts, some of which were patented and copyrighted, to companies competing with Kodak in the service market for its copying and micrographic equipment, could be rebutted by evidence of pretext which masked Kodak's anticompetitive conduct and enabled the Court to establish a violation of Section 2 of the Sherman Act.[667] The reliance of the Ninth Circuit in *Kodak* on evidence of pretext as a means to rebut the presumption of legality of a refusal to license was not followed by the Court of Appeals for the Federal Circuit in *Xerox*.

The latter case involved a refusal of Xerox, a leading manufacturer of copiers and printers, to continue to license patented equipment parts and copyrighted manuals and diagnostic software to independent service organisations competing with Xerox in the service market. The Federal Circuit held that inventions protected by patent law were free from liability under US antitrust laws as long as there was no indication of illegal tying, fraud and sham litigation.[668] The Federal Circuit also explicitly declined to take into account evidence of pretext in assessing a potential rebuttal of the presumption of legality of a refusal to license copyrighted material. Since there was no evidence in the case that the patents and copyrights at issue were obtained by unlawful means or were used to gain monopoly power beyond the statutory patent and copyright grants, the Court concluded that Xerox's refusal to license did not constitute a violation of the US antitrust laws.[669]

In *Trinko*, the US Supreme Court also applied a restrictive approach to refusals to deal in general (the case did not involve intellectual property rights). The Supreme Court referred to the essential facilities doctrine in its judgment as a concept having been '*crafted by some lower courts*'.[670] Without taking a position on whether the doctrine should be considered as established law, the Court made clear that it refused to extend antitrust liability for refusals to deal beyond the circumstances present in *Aspen Skiing*[671] which is the leading Supreme Court case in which an antitrust violation

---

665. *Data General Corp. v. Grumman Systems Support Corp.*, 36 F.3d 1147 (1st Cir. 1994), at 1188.
666. See *Eastman Kodak Co. v. Image Technical Services, Inc.*, 504 U.S. 451 (1992).
667. *Image Technical Services Inc. v. Eastman Kodak Co.*, 125 F.3d 1195 (9th Cir. 1997), at 1219-1220.
668. *In re Independent Service Organizations Antitrust Litigation (Xerox)*, 203 F.3d 1322 (Fed. Cir. 2000), at 1327.
669. *In re Independent Service Organizations Antitrust Litigation (Xerox)*, 203 F.3d 1322 (Fed. Cir. 2000), at 1328-1329.
670. *Verizon Communications v. Law Offices of Curtis V. Trinko, LLP (Trinko)*, 540 U.S. 398 (2004), at 410.
671. *Aspen Skiing Co. v. Aspen Highlands Skiing Corp.*, 472 U.S. 585 (1985).

was established for this type of behaviour.[672] In its *Trinko* judgment, the Supreme Court stated that *Aspen Skiing* is '*at or near the outer boundary*' of liability under Section 2 of the Sherman Act and constitutes a limited exception upon which can only be relied in situations where a monopolist terminates a voluntary and profitable prior course of dealing.[673] In *Aspen Skiing*, the monopolist was unwilling to renew the joint ski ticket that it had offered together with its competitor for many years and decided to forego short-term profits by refusing to deal which formed an indication of the anticompetitive character of its behaviour.[674] The facts in *Trinko* were different in several ways.

The 1996 Telecommunications Act imposed a duty upon Verizon as the incumbent local exchange carrier in New York to share its telephone network with competitors. Part of the statutory obligation involved the provision of access to operations support systems without which a rival cannot fill its customers' orders. Some of Verizon's competitors in the local telecommunications market dependent on access to these systems claimed that Verizon was not fulfilling its obligation and that it had filled rivals' orders on a discriminatory basis as part of an anticompetitive scheme to discourage customers from becoming or remaining customers of Verizon's competitors in violation of Section 2 of the Sherman Act.[675] Since Verizon did not voluntarily engage in a course of dealing with its rivals and it was not clear that it would have ever done so absent the duty contained in the Telecommunications Act, the Supreme Court considered that in this situation Verizon's prior conduct could shed no light upon whether the refusal to deal was '*prompted not by competitive zeal but by anticompetitive malice*'.[676]

There was also a difference in pricing behaviour between the two cases. While in *Aspen Skiing* the monopolist refused to sell at its own retail price suggesting a calculation that its future monopoly retail price would be higher, no such conclusion could be drawn from Verizon's reluctance to interconnect at the cost-based rate of compensation available under the Telecommunications Act.

Furthermore, whereas in *Aspen Skiing* the monopolist refused to provide its competitor with a product it already sold at the retail level, the systems to which Verizon had to offer its rivals access were not available to the public.[677] On the basis of these arguments, the Supreme Court decided that the *Trinko* case did not fit with the limited exception of *Aspen Skiing* to the principle established in *Colgate* that the Sherman Act as a general matter '*does not restrict the long recognized right of [a] trader*

---

672. *Verizon Communications v. Law Offices of Curtis V. Trinko, LLP* (*Trinko*), 540 U.S. 398 (2004), at 410-411.
673. *Verizon Communications v. Law Offices of Curtis V. Trinko, LLP* (*Trinko*), 540 U.S. 398 (2004), at 409.
674. *Verizon Communications v. Law Offices of Curtis V. Trinko, LLP* (*Trinko*), 540 U.S. 398 (2004), at 408-409.
675. *Verizon Communications v. Law Offices of Curtis V. Trinko, LLP* (*Trinko*), 540 U.S. 398 (2004), at 402-404.
676. *Verizon Communications v. Law Offices of Curtis V. Trinko, LLP* (*Trinko*), 540 U.S. 398 (2004), at 409.
677. *Verizon Communications v. Law Offices of Curtis V. Trinko, LLP* (*Trinko*), 540 U.S. 398 (2004), at 409-410.

or manufacturer engaged in an entirely private business, freely to exercise his own independent discretion as to parties with whom he will deal'.[678]

By qualifying the essential facilities doctrine as a concept crafted by lower courts and by referring to Areeda's seminal article criticising the doctrine,[679] the Supreme Court seems to have aimed to restrain further expansion of the circumstances in which US antitrust law accepts liability for refusals to deal. Nevertheless, the Supreme Court also stated that it finds *'no need either to recognize [...] or to repudiate'* the essential facilities doctrine.[680] After the *Trinko* case, a duty to deal can still be imposed in the United States in case the following two cumulative conditions are met: (1) the monopolist entered into a pre-existing voluntary course of dealing; and (2) the monopolist is willing to sacrifice short-term profits in order to achieve an anticompetitive end.[681]

By stating that *'traditional antitrust principles [do not] justify adding [Trinko] to the few existing exceptions from the proposition that there is no duty to aid competitors',*[682] the Supreme Court did not exclude the possibility that liability for a refusal to deal under US antitrust law could be accepted in situations other than *Aspen*. It merely noted that the facts of *Trinko* did not justify the establishment of a new exception to the principle that undertakings are free to choose their own trading partners. However, the scope for such a new exception seems limited considering that the Supreme Court affirmed its *Trinko* reasoning in its 2009 judgment in *linkLine*.

The *linkLine* case involved an action brought by Internet Service Providers (ISPs) alleging that incumbent telephone companies that owned infrastructure and facilities necessary to provide digital subscriber line (DSL) service monopolised the regional DSL market by squeezing the ISP's profits by charging them a high wholesale price for DSL transport and charging consumers a low retail price for DSL service. The Supreme Court argued that for such a price squeeze to violate Section 2 of the Sherman Act there must be proof that the monopolist either refused to deal under circumstances that created an antitrust duty to deal or engaged in predatory pricing under the standards established in relevant precedents.[683] In the view of the Supreme Court, it was clear from *Trinko* that *'if a firm has no antitrust duty to deal with its competitors at wholesale, it certainly has no duty to deal under terms and conditions that the rivals find commercially advantageous'.*[684] In its discussion of the *'limited circumstances in which a firm's unilateral refusal to deal with its rivals can give rise to antitrust liability',* the

---

678. *United States v. Colgate & Co.*, 250 U.S. 300 (1919), at 307.
679. P. AREEDA, 'Essential Facilities: An Epithet in Need of Limiting Principles', *Antitrust Law Journal* 1989, vol. 58, no. 3, (841) referred to in *Verizon Communications v. Law Offices of Curtis V. Trinko, LLP (Trinko)*, 540 U.S. 398 (2004), at 411.
680. *Verizon Communications v. Law Offices of Curtis V. Trinko, LLP (Trinko)*, 540 U.S. 398 (2004), at 411.
681. See, for example, *Novell, Inc. v. Microsoft Corp.*, 731 F.3d 1064 (10th Cir. 2013), at 1074-1075, *cert. denied*, 134 S. Ct. 1947 (2014).
682. *Verizon Communications v. Law Offices of Curtis V. Trinko, LLP (Trinko)*, 540 U.S. 398 (2004), at 411.
683. *Pacific Bell Telephone Co. v. linkLine Communications, Inc. (linkLine)*, 555 U.S. 438 (2009), at 448.
684. *Pacific Bell Telephone Co. v. linkLine Communications, Inc. (linkLine)*, 555 U.S. 438 (2009), at 450.

Supreme Court kept to the exception of *Aspen* and did not refer to the broader essential facilities doctrine as applied by lower courts before *Trinko*.[685]

The restrictive approach towards US antitrust liability for refusals to deal that the Supreme Court set out in *Trinko* has thus been confirmed in *linkLine*. With regard to the factual scenario of the case, the Supreme Court argued that in *linkLine*, as in *Trinko*, there was no antitrust duty to deal considering that the duty of the incumbent telephone companies to lease wholesale DSL transport service to the ISPs arose from regulations of the Federal Communications Commission and not from the Sherman Act.[686] The Supreme Court concluded that the price squeeze in *linkLine* did not amount to a violation of Section 2 of the Sherman Act on the ground that the ISPs had neither established a duty-to-deal claim nor a predatory pricing claim.[687]

6.2.2 Development of the Essential Facilities Doctrine in the European Union[688]

The essential facilities doctrine is also applied in competition cases in the European Union. *Commercial Solvents* is the first European case in which a refusal to deal was at stake.

Commercial Solvents decision
Commercial Solvents was the manufacturer of aminobutanol, a raw material necessary for the production of ethambutol which is used in the treatment of tuberculosis. Commercial Solvents stopped to supply the raw material to Zoja, its regular customer and competitor on the derivative market for the pharmaceutical substance ethambutol. Zoja was dependent on the supply of aminobutanol and

---

685. *Pacific Bell Telephone Co. v. linkLine Communications, Inc. (linkLine)*, 555 U.S. 438 (2009), at 448-449.
686. *Pacific Bell Telephone Co. v. linkLine Communications, Inc. (linkLine)*, 555 U.S. 438 (2009), at 450.
687. *Pacific Bell Telephone Co. v. linkLine Communications, Inc. (linkLine)*, 555 U.S. 438 (2009), at 457.
688. As already explained above, section 6.2 does not give a complete overview of the essential facilities cases decided in the US and EU. With regard to the EU, a number of Commission decisions and subsequent judgments of the General Court relating to the air transport sector, and access to port and rail infrastructures delivered in the period from 1988 until 1998 are not discussed (in particular: Commission Decision 88/589/EEC - *London European v. Sabena* [1988] OJ L 317/47; Commission Decision 92/213/EEC - *British Midland v. Aer Lingus* [1992] OJ L 96/34; Case IV/34.174 - *B&I Line PLC v. Sealink Harbours Ltd. & Sealink Stena Ltd.* [1992] 5 CMLR 255; Commission Decision 94/19/EC - *Sea Containers v. Stena Sealink* [1994] OJ L 15/8; Commission Decision 94/119/EC - *Port of Rødby* [1994] OJ L 55/52; Commission Decision 94/210/EC - *HOV SVZ v. MCN* [1994] OJ L 104/34 (upheld by Judgment in *Deutsche Bahn v. Commission*, T-229/94, ECLI:EU:T:1997:155); Commission Decision 94/594/EC - *ACI* [1994] OJ L 224/28; Commission Decision 94/663/EC - *European Night Services* [1994] OJ L 259/20 (annulled by Judgment in *European Night Services*, Joined Cases T-374/94, T-375/94, T-384/94 and T-388/94, ECLI:EU:T:1998:198); Commission Decision 94/894/EC - *Eurotunnel* [1994] OJ L 354/66 (annulled by Judgment in *Eurotunnel*, Joined cases T-79/95 and T-80/95, ECLI:EU:T:1996:155)). For a detailed analysis of these cases, see P. Larouche, *Competition Law and Regulation in European Telecommunications*, Hart Publishing, 2000, pp. 180-193.

complained to the European Commission that Commercial Solvents was abusing its dominant position as world leader in the production of the raw material to eliminate Zoja from the market place in Europe as a producer of ethambutol. As there was no valid reason why Zoja could not be supplied anymore, the Commission imposed a fine on Commercial Solvents and ordered it to resume the supplies to Zoja.

Case IV/26.911 - *Zoja/C.S.C. - I.C.I.* [1972] OJ L 299/51.

The Court of Justice agreed with the Commission that the conduct of Commercial Solvents constituted an abuse of a dominant position and upheld the imposition of a fine. The Court argued that a dominant supplier abuses its dominant position when it refuses to supply to a customer which is at the same time a competitor in the derivative market '*with the object of reserving such raw material for manufacturing its own derivatives*' and '*therefore risks eliminating all competition on the part of this customer*'.[689]

Subsequently, two cases followed in which the refusal to supply, unlike the factual situation in *Commercial Solvents*, was not targeted at a competitor but at a customer of the dominant undertaking. *United Brands* concerned a refusal of UBC, a dominant banana wholesaler, to continue to supply Olesen, one of its distributors in Denmark, with its 'Chiquita' bananas because Olesen had participated in an advertising campaign for the competing 'Dole' bananas. The Court of Justice endorsed the conclusion of the Commission and found that the interference in the management of Olesen's business which was designed to dissuade UBC's distributors from advertising or selling bananas bearing competing brand names amounted to abuse of dominance. In the Court's view, an undertaking in a dominant position '*cannot stop supplying a long standing customer who abides by regular commercial practice, if the orders placed by that customer are in no way out of the ordinary*'[690] on the ground that such conduct is inconsistent with Article 102 TFEU (at that time Article 86 of the Treaty establishing the European Economic Community (TEEC)) '*since the refusal to sell would limit markets to the prejudice of consumers and would amount to discrimination which might in the end eliminate a trading party from the relevant market*'.[691] Although the Court held that a dominant undertaking should in principle be entitled to protect its own commercial interests if they are attacked, a refusal to deal cannot be tolerated if its purpose is to strengthen and abuse a dominant position.[692] With regard to the facts in the case, the Court argued that UBC's conduct amounted to a serious interference with the independence of small and medium-sized firms which implies the right to give preference to competitors' goods and was '*designed to have a serious adverse effect on*

---

689. Judgment in *Istituto Chemioterapico Italiano and Commercial Solvents v. Commission*, Joined cases 6 and 7/73, ECLI:EU:C:1974:18, par. 25.
690. Judgment in *United Brands v. Commission*, Case 27/76, ECLI:EU:C:1978:22, par. 182.
691. Judgment in *United Brands v. Commission*, Case 27/76, ECLI:EU:C:1978:22, par. 183.
692. Judgment in *United Brands v. Commission*, Case 27/76, ECLI:EU:C:1978:22, par. 189.

competition on the relevant banana market by only allowing firms dependent on the dominant undertaking to stay in business'.[693]

A few months after the delivery of its *United Brands* judgment, the Court of Justice had to decide in the *BP* case whether the decision of BP, a dominant supplier of petroleum products in the Netherlands, to reduce the delivery to one of its occasional customers, namely ABG, in the period of shortage during the oil crisis in the 1970s with a rate different from that applied to its long-term contractual customers qualified as an abuse of a dominant position. Unlike the Commission which had held that a dominant undertaking *'must distribute "fairly" the quantities available amongst all its customers'*,[694] the Court found that BP could not be accused of having applied a less favourable treatment to an occasional customer than that which it reserved for its traditional customers during the oil crisis.[695] One of the factors that the Court took into account for reaching its conclusion that BP did not abuse its dominant position was the fact that ABG found supplies other than those coming from BP and was able to stay in the market during the crisis.[696] While the essentiality of the requested input was not considered in *Commercial Solvents* and *United Brands*,[697] the relevance that was attached to the availability of alternative means of supply in *BP* may be seen as preceding the introduction of the indispensability requirement in *Télémarketing*.

The Court of Justice developed its reasoning set out in *Commercial Solvents* in the *Télémarketing* case in the context of a refusal to deal with a competitor active in a different market.

***Télémarketing* case**
The case involved a preliminary reference of a Belgian court with regard to the refusal of RTL, at that time a statutory monopolist in the Belgian television advertising market, to continue to permit a third party to provide telemarketing services (i.e., advertisements carrying a telephone number which invite consumers to make a phone call to obtain information on the product offered) on its television channel unless it would display the telephone number of RTL's exclusive agent for television advertising.

Judgment in *CBEM v. CLT & IPB (Télémarketing)*, Case 311/84, ECLI:EU:C:1985:394.

The Court held that the *Commercial Solvents* ruling also applied to the case of an undertaking with a dominant position on the market in a service which is indispensable

---

693. Judgment in *United Brands v. Commission*, Case 27/76, ECLI:EU:C:1978:22, paras 193-194.
694. Judgment in *Benzine en Petroleum Handelsmaatschappij BV and others v. Commission*, Case 77/77, ECLI:EU:C:1978:141, par. 21.
695. Judgment in *Benzine en Petroleum Handelsmaatschappij BV and others v. Commission*, Case 77/77, ECLI:EU:C:1978:141, par. 32.
696. Judgment in *Benzine en Petroleum Handelsmaatschappij BV and others v. Commission*, Case 77/77, ECLI:EU:C:1978:141, par. 42.
697. For a further discussion of this issue, see section 6.8.3 below.

for the activities of another undertaking on a different market. In the Court's view, RTL's behaviour amounted in practice to a refusal to supply the services of its television station to any other telemarketing undertaking. The Court argued that such conduct has to be considered as abuse of dominance if the *'refusal is not justified by technical or commercial requirements relating to the nature of the television, but is intended to reserve to the agent any telemarketing operation broadcast by the said station, with the possibility of eliminating all competition from another undertaking'*.[698]

In two other preliminary ruling cases, the Court of Justice started to apply the essential facilities doctrine to intellectual property. In *Renault*[699] and *Volvo*,[700] the two respective car manufacturers refused independent repairers a licence to use the protected design of their cars to make spare parts. As the very subject matter of the right of the holder of a protected design is to prevent third parties from using its design, the Court of Justice held that a refusal to grant a licence cannot in itself constitute an abuse. However, the Court made clear that the exercise of an exclusive right by its holder may be prohibited by Article 102 TFEU (at that time Article 86 TEEC) if it involves *'certain abusive conduct such as the arbitrary refusal to supply spare parts to independent repairers'*.[701] The distinction that the Court made in these two cases between the existence and exercise of intellectual property rights has been followed in later intellectual property licensing cases. Whereas the existence of intellectual property rights validly granted under the law of the EU Member States including the right to exclude others from using the protected subject matter is not subject to EU competition rules, their exercise may in certain circumstances violate Article 102 TFEU.[702]

The Court of Justice relied on its *Volvo* and *Renault* judgments in *Magill*[703] where it upheld the judgment of the General Court and the decision of the European Commission ordering three Irish broadcasting companies to provide the publishing company Magill with a copyright licence for the weekly listings of their television programmes.

Magill case

Each station published its own weekly television guide and granted a license to newspapers to publish daily listings one or two days in advance. Magill

---

698. Judgment in *CBEM v. CLT & IPB (Télémarketing)*, Case 311/84, ECLI:EU:C:1985:394, par. 26.
699. Judgment in *Renault v. Maxicar*, Case 53/87, ECLI:EU:C:1988:472.
700. Judgment in *Volvo v. Eric Veng*, Case 238/87, ECLI:EU:C:1988:477.
701. Judgment in *Volvo v. Eric Veng*, Case 238/87, ECLI:EU:C:1988:477, paras 15-16.
702. The legal basis for the fact that the existence of intellectual property rights granted under national law is not affected by EU law can be found in Article 345 TFEU which states that the EU treaties will not prejudice the rules governing the system of property ownership in the Member States. For a discussion on the origin of the existence/exercise paradigm in free movement cases and its subsequent development under Articles 101 and 102 TFEU, see J. KALLAUGHER, 'Existence, Exercise, and Exceptional Circumstances: The Limited Scope for a More Economic Approach to IP Issues under Article 102 TFEU' in S. ANDERMAN AND A. EZRACHI (eds.), *Intellectual Property and Competition Law. New Frontiers*, Oxford University Press, 2011, (113), pp. 120-126.
703. Judgment in *Telefis Eireann and Independent Television Publications Ltd v. Commission of the European Communities (Magill)*, Joined cases C-241/91 and C-242/91, ECLI:EU:C:1995:98.

attempted to introduce a comprehensive television guide consisting of the weekly programme listings of all three channels which was a product not available on the market in Ireland at that time. By claiming copyright protection for their own weekly programme listings, the three broadcasting stations prevented Magill from introducing such a comprehensive television guide.

Judgment in *Telefis Eireann and Independent Television Publications Ltd v. Commission of the European Communities (Magill)*, Joined cases C-241/91 and C-242/91, ECLI:EU:C:1995:98, paragraphs 7-10.

The Court of Justice followed its statement in *Volvo* that in exceptional circumstances the exercise of an exclusive right may involve abusive behaviour.[704] The Court then listed three circumstances which led to the conclusion that the conduct of the broadcasting companies amounted to abuse of dominance. First, considering that the broadcasting companies were the only sources of the basic information on programme listings which is the indispensable raw material for compiling a comprehensive weekly television guide, they were able to prevent the appearance of a new product for which potential consumer demand existed. Second, there was no justification for the refusal to license either in the activity of television broadcasting or in that of publishing television magazines. Third, the broadcasting companies reserved to themselves the secondary market of weekly television guides by excluding all competition on that market through their denial of access to the basic information indispensable for the compilation of such guides.[705] The *Magill* case left unanswered whether the prevention of the appearance of a new product as mentioned under the first circumstance forms a necessary condition for the imposition of a duty of deal or whether it is sufficient that the input to which access has been requested is indispensable for the provision of the product or service of the access seeker.

In *Tiercé Ladbroke*, the General Court considered that the television broadcasting of horse races, although constituting an additional and suitable service for bettors, was not in itself indispensable for the provision of the main activity of bookmakers.[706] On this ground the Court held that the refusal of a transmission licence for sound and pictures of French horse races to a Belgian company providing betting services on the Belgian market could not be regarded as abusive conduct. In this context, the General Court stated that a refusal to license could fall within the prohibition of Article 102 TFEU if it *'concerned a product or service which was either essential for the exercise of the activity in question, in that there was no real or potential substitute, or was a new product whose introduction might be prevented, despite specific, constant and regular*

---

704. Judgment in *Telefis Eireann and Independent Television Publications Ltd v. Commission of the European Communities (Magill)*, Joined cases C-241/91 and C-242/91, ECLI:EU:C:1995:98, par. 50.
705. Judgment in *Telefis Eireann and Independent Television Publications Ltd v. Commission of the European Communities (Magill)*, Joined cases C-241/91 and C-242/91, ECLI:EU:C:1995:98, paras 52-56.
706. Judgment in *Tiercé Ladbroke v. Commission*, T-504/93, ECLI:EU:T:1997:84, par. 132.

potential demand on the part of consumers'.[707] This statement from the General Court suggesting that the new product condition as introduced in *Magill* is alternative to the indispensability test has not been followed by the Court of Justice in *IMS Health*.

The latter case involved the refusal of IMS, a company active in providing data on regional sales of pharmaceutical products in Germany, to grant a licence to its competitor NDC for the use of the copyrighted brick structure that IMS had developed consisting of 1860 bricks, each corresponding with a certain geographical area.

IMS Health case

On application of IMS, a German court had imposed an interlocutory order on NDC prohibiting it from using the 1860 brick structure on the basis of the finding that the structure was a database protected under German copyright law. Since the 1860 brick structure had become a de facto industry standard, the interlocutory order had the effect of preventing NDC from competing on the German market for the provision of regional sales data of pharmaceutical products.

Judgment in *IMS Health GmbH & Co. OHG v. NDC Health GmbH & Co. KG*, C-418/01, ECLI:EU:C:2004:257, paragraphs 4-17.

In the proceedings on the merits, the German court decided to stay proceedings and to refer preliminary questions to the Court of Justice on whether the refusal to license of IMS constituted abusive behaviour.[708] In its answer, the Court referred to the *Volvo* and *Magill* judgments in its statement that *'exercise of an exclusive right by the owner may, in exceptional circumstances, involve abusive conduct'.*[709] On the legal test to be applied, the Court argued:

> *[i]t is clear from that case-law that, in order for the refusal by an undertaking which owns a copyright to give access to a product or service indispensable for carrying on*

---

707. Judgment in *Tiercé Ladbroke v. Commission*, T-504/93, ECLI:EU:T:1997:84, par. 131.
708. In parallel to the preliminary reference procedure, the European Commission imposed interim measures ordering IMS to license its brick structure to NDC (Case COMP D3/38.044 – *NDC Health/IMS Health: Interim measures*, Commission decision 2002/165/EC, 3 July 2001). IMS appealed the Commission decision, but in the end there was no need for the General Court to render a judgment since the Commission had withdrawn its decision ordering interim measures in August 2003 on the ground of a material change in circumstances that resulted from a judgment of a German court and an improvement in the market position of NDC (Case COMP D3/38.044 – *NDC Health/IMS Health: Interim measures*, Commission decision 2003/741/EC, 13 August 2003 and Judgment in *IMS Health, Inc. v. Commission*, T-184/01, ECLI:EU:T:2005:95). In the period before the withdrawal of the Commission decision, the President of the General Court had suspended execution of the interim measures until the General Court would had given judgment in the main action (Judgment in *IMS Health Inc. v. Commission*, T-184/01 R, ECLI:EU:T:2001:200 (order of 10 August 2001) and [2001] ECR II-03193 (order of 26 October 2001)). An appeal of NDC against the latter order of the President of the General Court was dismissed by the President of the Court of Justice (Judgment in *NDC Health GmbH & Co. KG and NDC Health Corporation v. Commission and IMS Health Inc.*, C-481/01 P(R), ECLI:EU:C:2002:223).
709. Judgment in *IMS Health GmbH & Co. OHG v. NDC Health GmbH & Co. KG*, C-418/01, ECLI:EU:C:2004:257, par. 35.

a particular business to be treated as abusive, it is sufficient that three cumulative conditions be satisfied, namely, that that refusal is preventing the emergence of a new product for which there is a potential consumer demand, that it is unjustified and such as to exclude any competition on a secondary market.[710]

The Court of Justice thus made clear that the requirements of indispensability, which is mentioned in the introductory part of the sentence, and prevention of the emergence of a new product are cumulative. In the context of the last condition calling for the exclusion of any competition on a secondary market, the Court stated that for the determination of the primary market *'it is sufficient that a potential market or even hypothetical market can be identified'* and that *'it is determinative that two different stages of production may be identified and that they are interconnected, inasmuch as the upstream product is indispensable for the supply of the downstream product'.*[711] With regard to the interpretation of the indispensability requirement, the *Bronner*[712] case is instructive.

Bronner concerned a preliminary reference from an Austrian court and preceded the judgment of the Court of Justice in *IMS Health*. *Bronner* did not deal with a refusal to license an intellectual property right but involved a denial of access to a newspaper home-delivery scheme.

Bronner case

Mediaprint and Oscar Bronner were both newspaper publishers in Austria. Only Mediaprint had a nationwide home-delivery scheme for newspapers in which it did not want to include the newspaper published by Oscar Bronner.

Judgment in *Oscar Bronner GmbH & Co. KG v. Mediaprint Zeitungs*, C-7/97, ECLI:EU:C:1998:569, paragraphs 4-8.

The Court of Justice concluded that this behaviour of Mediaprint did not amount to abuse of dominance. In the Court's view, in order to establish a violation of Article 102 TFEU it is necessary *'not only that the refusal of the service comprised in home delivery be likely to eliminate all competition in the daily newspaper market on the part of the person requesting the service and that such refusal be incapable of being objectively justified, but also that the service in itself be indispensable to carrying on that person's business, inasmuch as there is no actual or potential substitute in existence for that home-delivery scheme'.*[713] The Court indicated that although it had qualified the refusal to deal in *Commercial Solvents* as abuse of dominance, it did so to the extent that the

---

710. Judgment in *IMS Health GmbH & Co. OHG v. NDC Health GmbH & Co. KG*, C-418/01, ECLI:EU:C:2004:257, par. 38.
711. Judgment in *IMS Health GmbH & Co. OHG v. NDC Health GmbH & Co. KG*, C-418/01, ECLI:EU:C:2004:257, paras 44-45.
712. Judgment in *Oscar Bronner GmbH & Co. KG v. Mediaprint Zeitungs*, C-7/97, ECLI:EU:C:1998:569.
713. Judgment in *Oscar Bronner GmbH & Co. KG v. Mediaprint Zeitungs*, C-7/97, ECLI:EU:C:1998:569, par. 41.

refusal was likely to eliminate all competition on the part of the undertaking dependent on access to the requested input.[714] This was not the case in *Bronner*. According to the Court, several alternatives were available for the distribution of Oscar Bronner's daily newspaper, such as delivery by post and sales in shops and at kiosks, even though they might be less advantageous. Furthermore, the Court noted that it was not enough for Oscar Bronner to argue that it is not economically viable to set up its own system due to the small circulation of its own newspaper. For such access to be capable of being regarded as indispensable, it would be necessary, in the Court's view, to establish at the very least that it is not economically viable to create a second home-delivery scheme with a circulation comparable to that of the newspapers distributed by the existing scheme.[715] Although the Court of Justice relied on its *Magill* judgment, the new product condition introduced there was not applied in *Bronner*. An explanation for this could be that the Court is of the opinion that this requirement only has to be met in cases involving intellectual property rights. The General Court in *Microsoft* also noted that the new product condition is found only in the case law on the exercise of an intellectual property right.[716]

Microsoft involved two separate types of abusive behaviour. In addition to a refusal to license interoperability information necessary for non-Microsoft work group server operating systems to communicate with Microsoft's dominant client PC operating system Windows, the case involved the integration of Microsoft's Windows Media Player to its client PC operating system. Both types of conduct were deemed abusive by the European Commission in its 2004 decision[717] which was made public a week before the Court of Justice delivered its judgment in *IMS Health*. Whereas the Court in the latter judgment interpreted the circumstances identified with regard to the refusal to license in *Magill* as exhaustive, the European Commission took a different approach in its *Microsoft* decision.

On the basis of its own assessment of the previous case law, the Commission concluded that there was no '*exhaustive checklist of exceptional circumstances [which] would have the Commission disregard a limine other circumstances of exceptional character that may deserve to be taken into account when assessing a refusal to supply*'.[718] Instead of confining itself to the exceptional circumstances present in *Magill*, the Commission stated that it had analysed '*the entirety of the circumstances surrounding*' Microsoft's refusal to license.[719] An additional circumstance considered by the Commission was that Microsoft's conduct involved a disruption of previous

---

714. Judgment in *Oscar Bronner GmbH & Co. KG v. Mediaprint Zeitungs*, C-7/97, ECLI:EU:C:1998:569, par. 38.
715. Judgment in *Oscar Bronner GmbH & Co. KG v. Mediaprint Zeitungs*, C-7/97, ECLI:EU:C:1998:569, paras 43-46.
716. Judgment in *Microsoft v. Commission*, T-201/04, ECLI:EU:T:2007:289, par. 334.
717. Case COMP/C-3/37.792 - *Microsoft*, 24 March 2004.
718. Case COMP/C-3/37.792 - *Microsoft*, 24 March 2004, par. 555.
719. Case COMP/C-3/37.792 - *Microsoft*, 24 March 2004, par. 558.

levels of supply. With the development of Windows 2000, Microsoft lessened the level of disclosures of interoperability information to Sun, the competitor in the market for work group server operating systems that filed a complaint to the Commission about Microsoft's behaviour. The Commission found that many of the already limited disclosures undertaken by Microsoft with respect to Windows NT had been discontinued after the introduction of Windows 2000.[720] In the Commission's view, Microsoft's disruption of previous levels of supply was part of a strategy. Until Microsoft did not have a credible alternative for the work group server operating systems developed by its competitors, it had incentives to have its client PC operating system interoperate with non-Microsoft work group server operating systems. While entering the work group server operating market, it was important for Microsoft to pledge support for already existing technologies in order to gain market share and confidence of customers. Once its own work group server operating system became accepted in the market, Microsoft's incentives changed and holding back access to the interface information started to be the right strategy.[721]

While the Commission made clear in its decision that it did not consider the criteria developed in previous case law as exhaustive, the General Court kept to the exceptional circumstances as established in *IMS Health* in its judgment. The Court argued that it would only assess the additional circumstances invoked by the Commission if one of the four conditions set out in that case were not present.[722] Since the Court came to the conclusion that Microsoft's refusal to license met the exceptional circumstances test, there was no need to proceed to the assessment of the circumstances identified by the Commission. The General Court thereby left open the issue of whether other exceptional circumstances can also be relevant in essential facilities cases. Although the Court relied on the same exceptional circumstances as taken into account in earlier cases,[723] it followed the Commission in applying lower standards for the fulfilment of the conditions. With regard to the indispensability requirement, the Court explained that in order to compete viably on the market it is necessary for competitors to be able to interoperate with Windows on an equal footing whereas the Court of Justice made clear in *Bronner* that access is not indispensable if alternatives are available even though they are less advantageous.[724] The Court also stated that it is not required for the Commission to demonstrate that all competition on the market is eliminated as a result of a refusal to license. What matters, in the view of the Court, is that the refusal is liable or likely to eliminate all effective competition.[725]

Concerning the new product condition, the General Court confirmed the finding of the Commission that the prevention of the appearance of a new product cannot be the only parameter for determining whether a refusal to license is capable of causing

---

720. Case COMP/C-3/37.792 - *Microsoft*, 24 March 2004, paras 578-584.
721. Case COMP/C-3/37.792 - *Microsoft*, 24 March 2004, paras 587-588.
722. Judgment in *Microsoft v. Commission*, T-201/04, ECLI:EU:T:2007:289, par. 336.
723. Judgment in *Microsoft v. Commission*, T-201/04, ECLI:EU:T:2007:289, paras 331-333.
724. Judgment in *Microsoft v. Commission*, T-201/04, ECLI:EU:T:2007:289, par. 421.
725. Judgment in *Microsoft v. Commission*, T-201/04, ECLI:EU:T:2007:289, par. 563. The General Court relied upon this statement in *Clearstream* (Judgment in *Clearstream Banking AG and Clearstream International SA v. Commission*, T-301/04, ECLI:EU:T:2009:317, par. 148).

prejudice to consumers in the context of Article 102(b) TFEU. The fact that the Commission did not apply the new product condition as such can be explained by considering that at the time of the adoption of the *Microsoft* decision the *IMS Health* judgment, which clarified the status of this requirement, was not yet delivered.[726] The General Court thus had to decide in *Microsoft* whether the Commission's approach that relied on the text of Article 102(b) TFEU instead of on a strict new product condition was in line with the statement of the Court of Justice in *IMS Health* that the prevention of the appearance of a new product is a necessary requirement for the imposition of a duty to license. The Court decided to follow the Commission in adopting a flexible stance on what can constitute a new product and argued that prejudice to consumers under Article 102(b) TFEU may occur '*where there is a limitation not only of production or markets, but also of technical development*'.[727] This is a considerably broader standard than the one applied by the Court of Justice in *IMS Health* where it was held that a refusal to license '*may be regarded as abusive only where the undertaking which requested the license does not intend to limit itself essentially to duplicating the goods or services already offered on the secondary market by the owner of the intellectual property right, but intends to produce new goods or services not offered by the owner of the right and for which there is a potential consumer demand*'.[728] Despite the fact that Sun could not identify a new product that it would offer once given access to the interoperability information, the new product circumstance was considered present on the ground that the refusal of Microsoft restricted technical development.[729]

As an objective justification for its refusal to license, Microsoft argued that the provision of interoperability information would have a negative effect on its incentives to innovate. However, the General Court concluded that the Commission had correctly dismissed this justification considering that Microsoft had not sufficiently established the negative impact on its innovation incentives but merely put forward vague, general and theoretical arguments without specifying the technologies or products in which its future incentives to invest would be eliminated.[730]

Since Microsoft decided not to appeal the judgment, the Court of Justice did not get the chance to express its view on the case and on whether it endorses the application of the lower standards for the establishment of abuse for a refusal to license. For this reason, it remains uncertain if the *Microsoft* judgment sets out a new and more expansionist approach to refusals to deal or whether the reasoning of the European Commission and the General Court cannot be transposed to other cases considering the super dominant position of Microsoft in the market for client PC

---

726. See section 6.8.3 below for an alternative explanation which rests upon the fact that *Microsoft* involved a disruption of supply. Since Microsoft's competitors were already active on the market for work group server operating systems, they were not able to identify a new product because they merely wanted to continue to compete on that market by offering the work group server operating systems that they had already developed to consumers.
727. Judgment in *Microsoft v. Commission*, T-201/04, ECLI:EU:T:2007:289, par. 647.
728. Judgment in *IMS Health GmbH & Co. OHG v. NDC Health GmbH & Co. KG*, C-418/01, ECLI:EU:C:2004:257, par. 49.
729. Judgment in *Microsoft v. Commission*, T-201/04, ECLI:EU:T:2007:289, par. 665.
730. Judgment in *Microsoft v. Commission*, T-201/04, ECLI:EU:T:2007:289, paras 697-698.

operating systems which may have led the two institutions to adapt the legal require-ments to the peculiar factual circumstances of the *Microsoft* case.

6.2.3 Comparison Between the US and EU Standards Applicable to Refusals to Deal

What is clear from this overview of cases that have been most influential in the development of the current legal standards for refusals to deal in the United States and the European Union is that the scope of application of the essential facilities doctrine on the two sides of the Atlantic differs considerably. Whereas the room for antitrust liability for refusals to deal in the United States remains very limited after the judgment of the Supreme Court in *Trinko*, the European Commission and the General Court have expanded the reach of the essential facilities doctrine in *Microsoft* as compared to previous EU refusal to deal cases.

The most apparent difference is the fact that absolute refusals to deal, where no prior course of dealing for the requested input exists, cannot give rise to a violation of Section 2 of the Sherman Act while the disruption of previous levels of supply is not a necessary requirement of the essential facilities doctrine in the European Union. In other words, cases involving a termination of supply may lead to liability under both United States and European Union competition rules whereas only European compe-tition authorities can intervene in situations involving absolute refusals to deal provided that the four exceptional circumstances of the essential facilities doctrine are present. Even though the approach towards the essential facilities doctrine differs substantially across the Atlantic, the principle on which EU and US competition authorities as well as courts agree is that a duty to deal imposed on the basis of competition law should be the exception to the rule. However, there is no agreement on the appropriate scope of such an exception under which intervention of a competition authority or court is appropriate.

Different interests are at stake in essential facilities cases. The imposition of a duty to deal with the objective of promoting free competition affects the interests of the dominant firm consisting of the generally recognised principles of freedom to con-tract,[731] including the right to choose one's trading partners,[732] and freedom to dispose

---

731. In *Bayer*, the General Court explicitly acknowledged the freedom to do business in the context of the assessment of refusals to deal under Article 102 TFEU (at that time Article 86 TEEC): '*The case-law of the Court of Justice indirectly recognises the importance of safeguarding free enterprise when applying the competition rules of the Treaty where it expressly acknowledges that even an undertaking in a dominant position may, in certain cases, refuse to sell or change its supply or delivery policy without falling under the prohibition laid down in Article 86*' (Judgment in *Bayer v. Commission*, T-41/96, ECLI:EU:T:2000:242, par. 180).

732. The fact that the Sherman Act generally does not restrict the right of a firm to freely choose its trading partners was explicitly acknowledged by the US Supreme Court in *United States v. Colgate & Co.*, 250 U.S. 300 (1919), at 307. However, in *Kodak* the Supreme Court made clear that the right to refuse to deal with competitors is not absolute but exists only if there are legitimate competitive reasons for the refusal (*Eastman Kodak Co. v. Image Technical Services, Inc.*, 504 U.S. 451 (1992), at 483).

of one's property.[733] The decision of a competition authority or court to interfere with the interests of a dominant undertaking for the purpose of protecting effective competition therefore requires a careful balancing exercise.[734] However, this weighing of interests is not as straightforward as it may seem.

Contrary to what the balancing test between the two sets of interests suggests, a duty to deal may not always be beneficial to competition. As Advocate General Jacobs made clear in *Bronner*, a duty to deal will increase competition in the short term but may put incentives for competitors to develop competing facilities in the long term at risk. In addition, the incentives of dominant undertakings to invest in new facilities may be reduced if competitors are given access too easily. On the long run, it therefore seems procompetitive to allow a dominant undertaking to keep facilities developed for its own business to itself.[735] Similarly, the US Supreme Court argued in *Trinko* that compulsory sharing conflicts with the underlying purpose of antitrust law, since it may lessen incentives for the monopolist, the rival, or both to invest in economically beneficial facilities.[736] As a result, the protection of free competition as such involves conflicting considerations.

6.3 INFLUENCE OF AMERICAN AND EUROPEAN SCHOOLS OF ECONOMIC THOUGHT ON THE DEVELOPMENT OF THE ESSENTIAL FACILITIES DOCTRINE

The development of the essential facilities doctrine in the United States and the European Union can be seen against the background of different schools of economic thought that have informed competition policy over the last decades. While EU competition policy and case law has been predominantly influenced by the ordoliberal school of thought that emerged in Germany, the pre-Chicago (also referred to as the Harvard school), Chicago and post-Chicago schools having their origin in the United States inspired the application of competition principles at that side of the Atlantic.[737]

---

733. Opinion of Advocate General Jacobs in *Oscar Bronner GmbH & Co. KG v. Mediaprint Zeitungs*, C-7/97, ECLI:EU:C:1998:264, par. 56.
734. See Opinion of Advocate General Jacobs in *Oscar Bronner GmbH & Co. KG v. Mediaprint Zeitungs*, C-7/97, ECLI:EU:C:1998:264, par. 57; Opinion of Advocate General Tizzano in *IMS Health GmbH & Co. OHG v. NDC Health GmbH & Co. KG*, C-418/01, ECLI:EU:C:2003:537, par. 62 as quoted in Judgment in *IMS Health GmbH & Co. OHG v. NDC Health GmbH & Co. KG*, C-418/01, ECLI:EU:C:2004:257, par. 48.
735. Opinion of Advocate General Jacobs in *Oscar Bronner GmbH & Co. KG v. Mediaprint Zeitungs*, C-7/97, ECLI:EU:C:1998:264, par. 57.
736. *Verizon Communications v. Law Offices of Curtis V. Trinko, LLP (Trinko)*, 540 U.S. 398 (2004), at 407-408.
737. See, for example, E. ROUSSEVA, *Rethinking Exclusionary Abuses in EU Competition Law*, Hart Publishing, 2010, p. 26 and more specifically for a comparison between Article 102 TFEU and Section 2 of the Sherman Act, P. LAROUCHE AND M.P. SCHINKEL, 'Continental Drift in the Treatment of Dominant Firms: Article 102 TFEU in Contrast to Section 2 Sherman Act' in R.D. BLAIR AND D.D. SOKOL (eds.), *The Oxford Handbook of International Antitrust Economics. Volume 2*, Oxford University Press, 2015, (153). Although the different US Chicago schools have also influenced the development of EU competition law, this effect is more remote and will therefore not be considered here.

The traditional pre-Chicago concern in essential facilities cases revolves around the vertical leveraging of market power. In the view of the pre-Chicago school, a vertically integrated undertaking refusing to supply an input, which is the classic scenario of an essential facilities case, restricts competition in the downstream market by extending its market power in the upstream market for the input to the downstream market for the complementary product or service. By denying non-integrated competitors and new entrants access to the necessary input, the monopolist is able to drive them off or keep them out of the downstream market.[738]

Chicago school economists denounced this reasoning by arguing that a firm with a monopoly in an upstream market cannot gain additional power by becoming the sole player in the downstream market. According to the Chicago school, there is only one monopoly profit to be reaped. Under the single monopoly profit theory, a monopolist can extract the entire monopoly profit in the upstream market by charging the monopoly price for the input and therefore does not have any anticompetitive incentives to engage in leveraging.[739] Chicago school economists concluded that, as a consequence, the decision of a monopolist to integrate into a downstream market must necessarily have procompetitive effects.[740]

Economists of the subsequent post-Chicago school began to question the single monopoly profit theory and identified situations in which leveraging of market power is anticompetitive.[741] In particular, the post-Chicago economic analysis suggests that the assumptions required for the single monopoly profit theory to apply do not hold in regulated industries in which the monopolist cannot freely set its price and may refuse competitors access to unregulated downstream markets in order to raise its downstream prices and avoid the price regulation in the upstream market,[742] in markets

---

738. T. KÄSEBERG, *Intellectual Property, Antitrust and Cumulative Innovation in the EU and the US*, Hart Publishing, 2012, p. 98.
739. See notably, R.H. BORK, *The Antitrust Paradox. A Policy at War with Itself*, The Free Press, 1993, p. 229. Microsoft relied on the single monopoly profit theory to support its claim before the European Commission that its refusal to license interoperability information was objectively justified (Case COMP/C-3/37.792 - *Microsoft*, 24 March 2004, par. 765).
740. See D.J. GERBER, 'Rethinking the Monopolist's Duty to Deal: A Legal and Economic Critique of the Doctrine of "Essential Facilities"', *Virginia Law Review* 1988, vol. 74, no. 6, (1069), pp. 1083-1086; J.R. RATNER, 'Should There Be an Essential Facility Doctrine?', *University of California, Davis Law Review* 1988, vol. 21, no. 2, (327), p. 361.
741. For an economic analysis of potential anticompetitive effects of leveraging in the context of tying (but also applicable to refusal to deal scenarios), see M.D. WHINSTON, 'Tying, Foreclosure, and Exclusion', *American Economic Review* 1990, vol. 80, no. 4, (837).
742. D.J. GERBER, 'Rethinking the Monopolist's Duty to Deal: A Legal and Economic Critique of the Doctrine of "Essential Facilities"', *Virginia Law Review* 1988, vol. 74, no. 6, (1069), pp. 1087-1088. This scenario has also been included by the European Commission in its Guidance Paper on exclusionary conduct under Article 102 TFEU as an example of a situation in which a refusal to deal leads to consumer harm (Communication from the Commission — Guidance on the Commission's enforcement priorities in applying Article 82 of the EC Treaty to abusive exclusionary conduct by dominant undertakings (Guidance Paper) [2009] OJ C 45/7, par. 88).

having multiple types of buyers,[743] and if the monopolist can raise entry barriers in the upstream market by way of leveraging its market power to a downstream market.[744,745]

Early US cases associated with the essential facilities doctrine such as *Terminal Railroad* and *Otter Tail*, in which the Supreme Court held the vertically integrated monopolists in the two cases liable for refusing to deal, seem to be influenced by the pre-Chicago leveraging theory according to which monopolists have an incentive to extend their market power in the upstream market to a market for a complementary product.[746] The *Trinko* judgment in which the Supreme Court made clear that the scope of antitrust liability for refusals to deal should be limited, seems to be informed by Chicago school economics which strives for per se legality of monopoly leveraging.[747] Traces of the post-Chicago school are said to have appeared in *Kodak* in which the Supreme Court held that the right to refuse to deal is not absolute but exists only in case of legitimate business justifications.[748]

The development of European competition law has been influenced by the ordoliberal school of thought that originated in Germany at the University of Freiburg. At the heart of ordoliberalism lies the belief that the *'treatment of all practical politico-legal and politico-economic questions must be keyed to the idea of the economic constitution'*.[749] Under the ordoliberal school of thought, there is a need for the state to prevent and constrain the concentration of private power which could endanger the competitive process. The aim of competition policy, in the view of the ordoliberalists, is to spur market participation by defending the economic freedom of individual market actors and to protect competition as an institution.[750]

The emphasis on the need for the protection of the competitive process in itself is apparent in the early EU essential facilities cases *Commercial Solvents, United Brands*,

---

743. T.G. Krattenmaker and S.C. Salop, 'Anticompetitive Exclusion: Raising Rivals' Costs to Achieve Power over Price', *Yale Law Journal* 1986, vol. 96, no. 2, (209), p. 224.

744. This was one of the grounds on the basis of which the European Commission denied Microsoft's claim that its refusal to license interoperability information could be objectively justified under the single monopoly profit theory (Case COMP/C-3/37.792 - *Microsoft*, 24 March 2004, paras 768-769).

745. For an overview of other situations in which the single monopoly profit theory does not hold, see S.C. Salop, 'Avoiding Error in the Antitrust Analysis of Unilateral Refusals to Deal', *Statement to the Antitrust Modernization Commission* 21 September 2005, p. 3.

746. D.S. Evans and A.J. Padilla, 'Designing Antitrust Rules for Assessing Unilateral Practices: A Neo-Chicago Approach', *The University of Chicago Law Review* 2005, vol. 72, no. 1, (73), p. 76.

747. J. Drexl, 'IMS Health and Trinko - Antitrust Placebo for Consumers Instead of Sound Economics in Refusal-to-Deal Cases', *International Review of Intellectual Property and Competition Law* 2004, vol. 35, no. 7, (788), pp. 795-797; E. Rousseva, *Rethinking Exclusionary Abuses in EU Competition Law*, Hart Publishing, 2010, p. 112. See also M. Lao, 'Aspen Skiing and Trinko: Antitrust Intent and "Sacrifice"', *Antitrust Law Journal* 2005, vol. 73, no. 1, (171), pp. 172-173 and 208.

748. D.S. Evans and A.J. Padilla, 'Designing Antitrust Rules for Assessing Unilateral Practices: A Neo-Chicago Approach', *The University of Chicago Law Review* 2005, vol. 72, no. 1, (73), pp. 78-79.

749. F. Böhm, W. Eucken and H. Grossmann-Doerth, 'The Ordo Manifesto of 1936' in A. Peacock and H. Willgerodt (eds.), *Germany's Social Market Economy: Origins and Evolution*, London, MacMillan, 1989, (15), p. 23.

750. For a detailed description of the foundations of ordoliberalism and its influence on the development of competition law, see D.J. Gerber, *Law and Competition in Twentieth Century Europe: Protecting Prometheus*, Clarendon Press, 1998, pp. 232-265.

Télémarketing and even in *Bronner*. In these cases, the Court of Justice seems to have protected the economic freedom of individual downstream competitors of the dominant undertakings by concluding that the elimination of a single competitor amounts to abuse of dominance.[751] In *Commercial Solvents*, the Court of Justice argued that the refusal to supply the competitor in the derivative market *'risks eliminating all competition on the part of this customer'*.[752] The Court similarly stated in *United Brands* that *'the refusal to sell would limit markets to the prejudice of consumers and would amount to discrimination which might in the end eliminate a trading party from the relevant market'*.[753] Although the Court of Justice added the indispensability of the requested input to the requirements that have to be met for the imposition of a duty to deal in *Télémarketing*, the Court still argued that a refusal to supply *'with the possibility of eliminating all competition from another undertaking'* amounts to abuse.[754]

In later refusal to deal cases, the focus seems to have shifted from the protection of the economic freedom of individual market actors to the protection of competition on the market in general.[755] In his Opinion in *Bronner*, Advocate General Jacobs stated that in this regard that when assessing refusals to deal *'it is important not to lose sight of the fact that the primary purpose of Article [102 TFEU] is to prevent distortion of competition - and in particular to safeguard the interests of consumers - rather than to protect the position of particular competitors'*.[756] Nevertheless, the Court of Justice still noted that in order to find an abuse in the *Bronner* case it would be necessary for the refusal to *'be likely to eliminate all competition in the daily newspaper market on the part of the person requesting the service'*.[757] In *Magill* and *IMS Health*, the Court of Justice referred to the exclusion of all or any competition on the market instead of the elimination of a single competitor as the relevant standard for assessing the abusive nature of a refusal to deal.[758] In *Microsoft*, the General Court has lowered this standard by accepting that it is not necessary to demonstrate that all competition on the market would be eliminated as long as the refusal at issue is liable or likely to eliminate all

751. E. ROUSSEVA, *Rethinking Exclusionary Abuses in EU Competition Law*, Hart Publishing, 2010, pp. 83-88.
752. Judgment in *Istituto Chemioterapico Italiano and Commercial Solvents v. Commission*, Joined cases 6 and 7/73, ECLI:EU:C:1974:18, par. 25.
753. Judgment in *United Brands v. Commission*, Case 27/76, ECLI:EU:C:1978:22, par. 183.
754. Judgment in *CBEM v. CLT & IPB (Télémarketing)*, Case 311/84, ECLI:EU:C:1985:394, par. 26.
755. E. ROUSSEVA, *Rethinking Exclusionary Abuses in EU Competition Law*, Hart Publishing, 2010, pp. 89-92 and 111-112.
756. Opinion of Advocate General Jacobs in *Oscar Bronner GmbH & Co. KG v. Mediaprint Zeitungs*, C-7/97, ECLI:EU:C:1998:264, par. 58.
757. Judgment in *Oscar Bronner GmbH & Co. KG v. Mediaprint Zeitungs*, C-7/97, ECLI:EU:C:1998:569, par. 41.
758. Judgment in *Telefis Eireann and Independent Television Publications Ltd v. Commission of the European Communities (Magill)*, Joined cases C-241/91 and C-242/91, ECLI:EU:C:1995:98, par. 56 where the Court of Justice held that the Irish broadcasting companies *'reserved to themselves the secondary market of weekly television guides by excluding all competition on that market'*; Judgment in *IMS Health GmbH & Co. OHG v. NDC Health GmbH & Co. KG*, C-418/01, ECLI:EU:C:2004:257, par. 38 where the Court of Justice referred to the requirement that the refusal must be *'such as to exclude any competition on a secondary market'*.

effective competition on the market.[759] Nevertheless, the emphasis still lies on the elimination of competition on the entire market and not of an individual competitor.

Although the most recent European Union case law on refusals to deal has left the ordoliberal tradition behind and the European Commission has started to implement a less formalistic and more economic, effects-based approach to the application of the European competition rules,[760] EU competition policy in general still seems to be characterised by its emphasis on the importance of keeping markets open.[761] In the context of the Europe 2020 strategy, the European Commission argued in this connection: *'given that undistorted competition and well-functioning competitive markets are key for innovation, a strict enforcement of competition rules that ensure market access and opportunities for new entrants is a necessary condition'*.[762] Furthermore, the effects-based approach introduced by the Commission in the Guidance Paper on exclusionary conduct does not seem to gain traction at the EU Courts, in particular when it comes to the assessment of loyalty or exclusivity rebates under Article 102 TFEU.

In 2012, the Court of Justice held on appeal in *Tomra* with regard to exclusivity rebates that, for the purposes of proving abuse of dominance, it is sufficient to show that the abusive conduct of the dominant firm tends to restrict competition or that the conduct is capable of having that effect.[763] In other words, the Court of Justice did not require proof of actual anticompetitive effects of Tomra's rebates on competition.[764] In its 2014 *Intel* judgment, the General Court even held that exclusivity rebates have to be regarded as quasi-per se illegal under Article 102 TFEU. In particular, the General Court argued that it was not necessary to engage in an economic analysis of the capability of the rebates to foreclose a hypothetical competitor as efficient as Intel (the 'as efficient competitor test') as required under the Guidance Paper[765] introduced by

---

759. Judgment in *Microsoft v. Commission*, T-201/04, ECLI:EU:T:2007:289, par. 563.
760. See Communication from the Commission — Guidance on the Commission's enforcement priorities in applying Article 82 of the EC Treaty to abusive exclusionary conduct by dominant undertakings (Guidance Paper) [2009] OJ C 45/7.
761. See, for example, in the context of competition enforcement in the new economy, speech former Director-General for Competition Italianer, 'Innovation and competition policy in the IT sector: the European perspective', Conference on Innovation, Competition Policy and Online Service Providers in Beijing, 26 June 2012, p. 2, available at http://ec.europa.eu/competition/speeches/text/sp2012_04_en.pdf: '*Markets are most conducive to innovation when they are open and accessible to all. But in digital industries, network effects and lock-in might create entrenched market positions which can be used to exclude new entrants or which can be otherwise exploited. It is therefore important to safeguard a level-playing field and access to markets, platforms and data that can be useful in developing new and innovative digital products and services*'.
762. Communication from the Commission to the European Parliament, the Council, the European Economic and Social Committee and the Committee of the Regions. Europe 2020 Flagship Initiative. Innovation Union, COM(2010) 546 final, 6 October 2010, p. 8.
763. Judgment in *Tomra*, C-549/10 P, ECLI:EU:C:2012:221, paras 68-70.
764. Judgment in *Tomra*, C-549/10 P, ECLI:EU:C:2012:221, par. 79.
765. Communication from the Commission — Guidance on the Commission's enforcement priorities in applying Article 82 of the EC Treaty to abusive exclusionary conduct by dominant undertakings (Guidance Paper) [2009] OJ C 45/7, paras 23-27 and 37-45.

the Commission.[766] The *Intel* judgment spurred intense debates in scholarship about the goals of Article 102 TFEU and about the future of the effects-based approach.[767] The judgment from the Court of Justice on appeal is eagerly awaited and hoped to provide more clarity in this regard.

In the United States, competition authorities and courts tend to be less interventionist than their European counterparts and rely on the strength of the self-correcting mechanism of the market.[768] This difference in belief, despite an overall agreement on the insights from economics, may explain the divergent approaches that are currently applied to refusals to deal on the two sides of the Atlantic.[769] In addition, unlike the role of the antitrust rules in the US, EU competition policy is seen as one of the means for achieving the integration of the EU internal market.[770] In this regard, former Director-General for Competition Italianer stated: *'What we aspire to in Europe – a true single market – already exists in the US, with all the benefits it entails. Competition forces in the US may therefore be better able to rectify competition problems that occur, whereas in the EU the self-healing force of competition may not yet be as fully developed'.*[771]

6.4 ECONOMIC TRADE-OFF IN ESSENTIAL FACILITIES CASES

Although the evolution of different schools of economic thought can explain the development of the essential facilities doctrine in the US and EU, the question remains

---

766. Judgment in *Intel Corp. v. European Commission*, T-286/09, ECLI:EU:T:2014:547, paras 80-93 and 142-153.
767. See, among others, J.S. VENIT, 'Case T-286/09 Intel v Commission—The Judgment of the General Court: All Steps Backward and No Steps Forward', *European Competition Journal* 2014, vol. 10, no. 2, (203); P. NIHOUL, 'The Ruling of the General Court in Intel: Towards the End of an Effect-based Approach in European Competition Law?', *Journal of European Competition Law & Practice* 2014, vol. 5, no. 8, (521); P. IBÁÑEZ COLOMO, 'Intel and Article 102 TFEU Case Law: Making Sense of a Perpetual Controversy', *LSE Legal Studies Working Paper No. 29/2014* November 2014, available at http://papers.ssrn.com/sol3/papers.cfm?abstract_id = 2530878& rec = 1&srcabs = 2567628&alg = 1&pos = 3; W. WILS, 'The Judgment of the EU General Court in Intel and the So-Called More Economic Approach to Abuse of Dominance', *World Competition* 2014, vol. 37, no. 4, (405); P. REY AND J.S. VENIT, 'An Effects-Based Approach to Article 102: A Response to Wouter Wils', *World Competition* 2015, vol. 38, no. 1, (3); R. WHISH, 'Intel v Commission: Keep Calm and Carry on!', *Journal of European Competition Law & Practice* 2015, vol. 6, no. 1, (1); N. PETIT, 'Intel, Leveraging Rebates and the Goals of Article 102 TFEU', *European Competition Journal* 2015, vol. 11, no. 1, (26); and D. GERADIN, 'Loyalty Rebates after Intel: Time for the European Court of Justice to Overrule Hoffman-La Roche', *Journal of Competition Law and Economics* 2015, vol. 11, no. 3, (579).
768. See E.M. FOX, 'Monopolization, Abuse of Dominance, and the Indeterminacy of Economics: The U.S./E.U. Divide', *Utah Law Review* 2006, vol. 2006, no. 3, (725), p. 728.
769. T. KÄSEBERG, *Intellectual Property, Antitrust and Cumulative Innovation in the EU and the US*, Hart Publishing, 2012, p. 253.
770. EUROPEAN COMMISSION, XXVth Report on Competition Policy 1995, COM(96)126 final, p. 15: 'competition policy is an important tool for achieving the goal of, and maintaining, an internal market, in particular via the enforcement of rules ensuring that the regulatory barriers to trade which have been removed are not replaced by private or other public restrictions having the same effect'.
771. Speech former Director-General for Competition Italianer, 'Prepared remarks on: Level-playing field and innovation in technology markets', Conference on Antitrust in Technology, Palo Alto (US), 28 January 2013, p. 7, available at http://ec.europa.eu/competition/speeches/text/sp2013_01_en.pdf.

how economic considerations should be adequately transformed into a legal frame-work for assessing essential facilities cases. The trade-off that has to be made in these cases is often referred to as one between ex post static and ex ante dynamic efficiency or as a balancing exercise between short- and long-term interests.[772] In the short run, obliging a dominant firm to share its facility with competitors will stimulate competi-tion on the basis of price and output (static competition) in downstream markets. In the long run, however, the imposition of a duty to deal may reduce the incentives of the dominant firm, its competitors and market participants in general to invest in innova-tion (dynamic competition).[773] As a result, there is a need to balance the short term benefits from static competition with the long-term gains from dynamic competition.[774]

While the balancing exercise is often phrased in this way, it is submitted that it is more precise to speak of a trade-off between competition *in* the market and competi-tion *for* the market. Indeed, the imposition of a duty to deal does not only stimulate static competition on the basis of price and output but also enables competitors of the dominant firm to introduce complementary products or follow-on innovation. The term competition *in* the market encompasses static competition as well as the introduction of sustaining innovations and therefore better captures the different interests that are at stake in this context. Although innovation is a complex process that may have unpredictable outcomes, competition *in* and *for* the market each typically lead to a different type of innovation.

On the basis of the review of the economic and business literature conducted in part I,[775] it is assumed for the purposes of the further analysis of the essential facilities doctrine that competition *for* the market generally provides stronger incentives for disruptive innovation whereas competition *in* the market primarily stimulates sustain-ing innovation. Since one type of competition typically takes precedence over the other, a market is characterised by either competition *for* or *in* the market at a certain point in time. Considering that both types of competition and innovation bring value to

---

772. D. GERADIN, 'Limiting the Scope of Article 82 EC: What Can the EU Learn from the U.S. Supreme Court's judgment in *Trinko* in the wake of *Microsoft*, *IMS*, and *Deutsche Telekom*?', *Common Market Law Review* 2004, vol. 41, no. 6, (1519), p. 1539 (phrasing the trade-off as one between ex post allocative efficiency and ex ante dynamic efficiency) and A. ANDREANGELI, 'Interoper-ability as an "essential facility" in the Microsoft case - encouraging competition or stifling innovation?', *European Law Review* 2009, vol. 34, no. 4, (584), pp. 597 and 602-603 (distin-guishing between short and long term effects in the context of the duty to license imposed in *Microsoft*).
773. Static competition leads to static efficiency which comprises both allocative and productive efficiency. Whereas productive efficiency is concerned with the production of goods at minimum cost, allocative efficiency involves the ability to allocate scarce resources in such a way as to generate highest utility for society. Dynamic competition results in dynamic efficiency which refers to the extent to which new products or services are introduced. For a more economic description of these concepts in relation to market power, see M. MOTTA, *Competition Policy. Theory and Practice*, Cambridge University Press, 2004, pp. 40-64.
774. A similar analysis has to be made when comparing the potential effects of open versus closed systems. See in this regard the report of the AUTORITÉ DE LA CONCURRENCE AND THE COMPETITION & MARKETS AUTHORITY, 'The economics of open and closed systems', 16 December 2014, pp. 15-30, available at http://www.autoritedelaconcurrence.fr/doc/economics_open_closed_ systems.pdf.
775. See section 3.4.1 above.

society, the decision to give preference to one over the other amounts to a policy choice. When determining whether or not to intervene in a market, competition authorities often have to make a choice between encouraging competition *in* or *for* the market. Such a trade-off is present in essential facilities cases too, although it remains implicit in most instances.

The *Microsoft* case can be used to illustrate the balancing exercise in essential facilities cases. By way of a refusal to license interoperability information, Microsoft prevented its competitors in the market for work group server operating systems from developing their own products which would be able to run on the dominant Windows client PC operating system. By finding that Microsoft's refusal to deal amounted to abuse of dominance, the Commission forced Microsoft to provide its competitors in the market for work group server operating systems with the necessary interoperability information. In so doing, the Commission chose to favour competition *in* the market over competition *for* the market. Indeed, by entitling competitors in the market for work group server operating systems access to Microsoft's technology, the Commission stimulated competition on the basis of price and output but also created room for follow-on innovation to flourish.

If the Commission alternatively had declined to intervene in the market and had decided that Microsoft's behaviour was not abusive, competitors would not have been able to compete on static parameters or to introduce sustaining innovations in the form of complementary or substitutable products for Windows. Rather, the incentives to invest in innovation of Microsoft's competitors would be directed at developing a new technology disrupting the market for client PC operating systems. By keeping the market for work group server operating systems open, the Commission thus decided to give priority to static competition and sustaining innovation in existing markets over disruptive innovation in new products or services having the potential to make current market structures obsolete and in particular Microsoft's dominance in client PC operating systems. Nevertheless, neither the Commission nor the General Court explained why static competition and sustaining innovation should prevail over disruptive innovation in this case.[776]

In conclusion, the trade-off to be made by competition authorities and courts in essential facilities cases amounts to a choice between giving competitors access to the required input which would enable them to create products complementary to that of the dominant firm or denying access as a result of which competitors would be incentivised to develop substitutes competing with the product of the dominant firm. While the first scenario provides stronger incentives for competition *in* the market and sustaining innovation, the second scenario will primarily stimulate competition *for* the market and disruptive innovation.

---

776. See P. LAROUCHE, 'The European Microsoft Case at the Crossroads of Competition Policy and Innovation', *Antitrust Law Journal* 2008, vol. 75, no. 3, (601), pp. 610-611 and 613.

Figure 6.1   Trade-Off to Be Made in Essential Facilities Cases

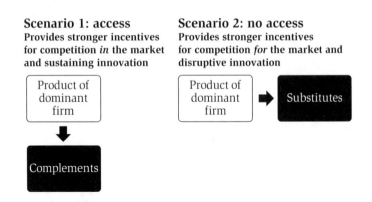

6.5   NEED FOR A MORE COHERENT APPLICATION OF THE ESSENTIAL FACILITIES DOCTRINE

As can be concluded from Part I, current competition policy, in particular market definition and the assessment of dominance, is equipped to deal with short-term concerns. Incentives for competition *for* the market are hard to accommodate in competition analysis, because they involve long-term considerations about market developments that are by their nature difficult to predict. Since both competition *in* and *for* the market contribute, albeit in a different manner, to societal welfare, the decision which type of competition should receive preference amounts to a policy issue.[777] It is therefore a valid policy option for competition authorities and courts to favour competition *in* the market which is easier to anticipate and leads to observable results on the short run in the form of increased competition in downstream markets, lower prices and more product variety.[778] Nevertheless, this does not mean that incentives for competition *for* the market should be disregarded. In order to make the trade-off transparent, it is submitted that incentives for competition *for* the market should be explicitly considered in essential facilities cases even if preference is given to competition *in* the market.

The application of the essential facilities doctrine in Commission decisions and judgments of the EU courts is focused on stimulating competition *in* the market considering that incentives for competition *for* the market are not openly analysed. The only explicit reference to the trade-off between the two types of competition is made by Advocate General Jacobs in his Opinion in *Bronner* where he argued that:

---

777. See section 3.4.2.
778. See D. GERADIN, 'Limiting the Scope of Article 82 EC: What Can the EU Learn from the U.S. Supreme Court's judgment in *Trinko* in the wake of *Microsoft*, *IMS*, and *Deutsche Telekom*?', *Common Market Law Review* 2004, vol. 41, no. 6, (1519), p. 1540.

In the long term it is generally pro-competitive and in the interest of consumers to allow a company to retain for its own use facilities which it has developed for the purpose of its business. For example, if access to a production, purchasing or distribution facility were allowed too easily there would be no incentive for a competitor to develop competing facilities. Thus while competition was increased in the short term it would be reduced in the long term. Moreover, the incentive for a dominant undertaking to invest in efficient facilities would be reduced if its competitors were, upon request, able to share the benefits.[779]

The lack of analysis of the effect of a duty to deal on incentives for competition *for* the market is most apparent in the *Microsoft* case where the European Commission and the General Court assessed the impact of a compulsory licence on the innovation incentives of Microsoft and the industry in general.

Microsoft tried to objectively justify its refusal to license by arguing that an obligation to disclose the interoperability information would have a significant negative impact on its incentives to innovate. With respect to this claim, the Commission concluded that a detailed examination of the scope of the duty to license at stake indicated that '*on balance, the possible negative impact of an order to supply on Microsoft's incentives to innovate is outweighed by its positive impact on the level of innovation of the whole industry (including Microsoft)*'.[780] Because the Commission found that Microsoft's innovation incentives would not be negatively affected as a result of the duty to license, there was no need to assess the positive impact on the entire industry and to engage in a balancing exercise.[781] In the Commission's view, Microsoft's incentives to innovate were dependent on the competitive pressure that it experienced in the market for work group server operating systems. The Commission argued that Microsoft's innovation incentives would not diminish but rather increase once being required to share the interoperability information with competitors on the ground that its work group server operating system products would be subject to more competition from rivals.[782]

The General Court endorsed the Commission's conclusion and considered that '*Microsoft merely put forward vague, general and theoretical arguments [...] without specifying the technologies or products*' in which its incentives to innovate would be significantly reduced.[783] As regards Microsoft's argument that its incentives to invest in client PC and work group server operating systems in general would decline, the Court noted that the Commission rightly refuted this claim by showing that a duty to license would not enable competitors to clone Microsoft's products.[784] The assessment conducted by the Commission and the Court thus only takes account of potential

---

779. Opinion of Advocate General Jacobs in *Oscar Bronner GmbH & Co. KG v. Mediaprint Zeitungs*, C-7/97, ECLI:EU:C:1998:264, par. 57.
780. Case COMP/C-3/37.792 - *Microsoft*, 24 March 2004, par. 783.
781. See also S. Vezzoso, 'The Incentives Balance Test in the EU Microsoft Case: A Pro-innovation "Economics-Based" Approach?', *European Competition Law Review* 2006, vol. 27, no. 7, (382), p. 385 and F. Lévêque, 'Innovation, Leveraging and Essential Facilities: Interoperability Licensing in the EU Microsoft Case', *World Competition* 2005, vol. 28, no. 1, (71), pp. 78-79.
782. Case COMP/C-3/37.792 - *Microsoft*, 24 March 2004, par. 725.
783. Judgment in *Microsoft v. Commission*, T-201/04, ECLI:EU:T:2007:289, par. 698.
784. Judgment in *Microsoft v. Commission*, T-201/04, ECLI:EU:T:2007:289, paras 699-700.

changes in incentives to invest in client PC and work group server operating system products. By merely devoting attention to how the situation in the existing markets would change once Microsoft would be required to give access to its interoperability information, the two institutions disregarded the effect that a duty to license may have on long-term incentives to invest in new products and technology overthrowing the dominance of Microsoft.[785]

As evidenced by the description of the development of the essential facilities doctrine in the European Union in section 6.2.2 above, the application of the doctrine in the decision-making practice of the European Commission and case law of the EU courts has not been coherent. While new Commission decisions and court judgments have always referred to and relied upon the reasoning applied in earlier essential facilities cases, every case gave rise to new issues and the exceptional circumstances test was adapted accordingly.

In its Guidance Paper on exclusionary conduct, the Commission indicated that it regards refusal to deal practices as an enforcement priority if: (1) the refusal relates to a product or service that is objectively necessary to be able to compete effectively on a downstream market; (2) the refusal is likely to lead to elimination of effective competition on the downstream market; and (3) the refusal is likely to lead to consumer harm.[786] However, the Guidance Paper is a soft law instrument and does not impose binding standards on the Commission, let alone the EU courts. In addition, the document only aims to set out the enforcement priorities of the Commission and is not intended to constitute a statement of the law with regard to exclusionary conduct.[787] For that reason, it cannot be assumed that the Commission will apply the same conditions for examining the abusive nature of a refusal to deal once it has decided to launch a formal investigation into a certain case.

The establishment of a more coherent framework for the application of the essential facilities doctrine would enable competition authorities and courts to assess new cases more consistently and predictably. It is submitted that, for transparency reasons, explicit account should be taken of the trade-off between competition *in* and *for* the market in order to better align the application of the essential facilities doctrine with the underlying economic interests in refusal to deal scenarios.

6.6 PRINCIPLES UNDERLYING THE PROPOSED FRAMEWORK

Instead of phrasing essential facilities cases in terms of a balancing exercise between the interests of individual undertakings and the interest in the protection of free

---

785. G. SURBLYTE, 'The Refusal to Disclose Trade Secrets as an Abuse of Market Dominance - Microsoft and Beyond' in J. DREXL (ed.) *Munich Series on European and International Competition Law*, 28, Berne Stämpfli Publishers Ltd., 2011, pp. 137-138.
786. Communication from the Commission — Guidance on the Commission's enforcement priorities in applying Article 82 of the EC Treaty to abusive exclusionary conduct by dominant undertakings (Guidance Paper) [2009] OJ C 45/7, par. 81.
787. Communication from the Commission — Guidance on the Commission's enforcement priorities in applying Article 82 of the EC Treaty to abusive exclusionary conduct by dominant undertakings (Guidance Paper) [2009] OJ C 45/7, paras 2-3.

competition, refusals to deal can also be considered from an economic perspective as the analysis of the policy choice between protecting competition *in* and *for* the market in section 6.4 indicates. An economic approach to refusal to deal cases would allow for the translation of such considerations into an appropriate legal test. To that end, several insights can be drawn from the economic trade-off between competition *in* and *for* the market which form the principles on which the proposed framework for essential facilities cases is built.

6.6.1 Balance Between Competition in and for the Market Is Established over Time

Incentives to invest in disruptive innovation can be negatively affected due to a too interventionist policy of competition enforcement. The prospect of a dominant position may be necessary for incentivising investment in new types of disruptive innovation. The imposition of far-reaching competition remedies could curb those incentives. Nevertheless, in order to keep the price level and the product variety at a competitive level, competition authorities should intervene when necessary to ensure a certain degree of competition *in* the market. This will also put the incumbent under pressure to fight for maintaining its leading position in line with its incentive to pre-empt the entry of potential competitors.[788] In the words of former Director-General for Competition Italianer: *'history tells us that competition for the market, as exemplified by disruptive innovations which introduce totally new business models in high tech markets, may happen slower than predicted. Take mainframes or PC operating systems as examples: they have had stable market presence for decades. There is therefore a need to foster competition not only for the market but also in such markets'.*[789]

In sum, the presence of competition *in* and *for* the market has to be in balance in order to have a healthy competitive environment. Since the two types of competition cannot be equally present in a market at the same point in time, the balance should rather be seen as one that is established over time.

---

788. See section 3.3.2 above.
789. Speech former Director-General for Competition Italianer, 'Prepared remarks on: Level-playing field and innovation in technology markets', Conference on Antitrust in Technology, Palo Alto (US), 28 January 2013, p. 4.

Figure 6.2   A Market Where Competition for and in the Market Are in Perfect Balance

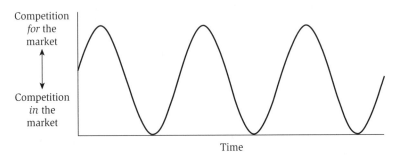

Whereas in sectors predominantly characterised by competition *for* the market a temporary form of market power is inevitable, the market can still be considered competitive as long as new entrants are able to attack the dominant position of the incumbent. However, the winner of a race *for* the market should be prevented from extending its gained dominance and from delaying the start of a new round of competition *for* the market. Competitive pressure can be considered vital in this perspective.[790] When market dynamics have failed to exert sufficient competitive pressure, competition authorities should intervene in order to restore the level of competition *in* the market.

Figure 6.3   A Market Where New Processes of Competition for the Market Are Delayed

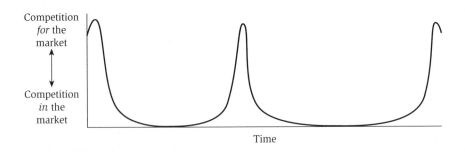

6.6.2   Competition Enforcement Can Only Restore the Process of Competition in the Market

Competition *for* the market, in principle, cannot be revitalised by way of an intervention of a competition authority. This is because this type of competition and the

---

790. See also R. PARDOLESI AND A. RENDA, 'The European Commission's Case Against Microsoft: Kill Bill?', *World Competition* 2004, vol. 27, no. 4, (513), pp. 528-535.

disruptive innovation that it generates is by nature hard to foresee. The business literature discussed in Part I[791] indicates that new products or services that render existing market structures obsolete are typically developed by new entrants instead of by current market players which are more inclined to stay close to their existing customers. Indeed, many of the disruptive inventions present in the technology industry today come from small start-ups which were initially run by only a few people. Examples include companies such as Skype and WhatsApp (now acquired by respectively Microsoft and Facebook) which started to attack the business model of telecommunications operators by enabling users to make free calls and send free messages over the internet without having to rely on the telephone network of their telecom provider.

In order to preserve incentives for competition *for* the market and disruptive innovation, the best approach for competition authorities is to refrain from intervening in order to ensure that the prospect of dominance for new entrants is maintained. The only type of innovation that a competition law intervention can directly stimulate is sustaining innovation which results from competition *in* the market. The imposition of a duty to deal in essential facilities cases enables competitors to introduce complementary products and follow-on innovation, whereas in the absence of a competition law intervention no sustaining innovation can occur and competitors will instead invest in disruptive innovation. Nevertheless, the creation of competition *in* the market by way of competition enforcement may indirectly create room for the disruptive inventions of competitors to gradually take over the leading position of the incumbent by making its dominance in the existing market less significant.[792] The effects of the enforcement actions of the United States Department of Justice and the European Commission against the integration of Microsoft's web browser Internet Explorer in its client PC operating system may serve as an example.

Both institutions entered into a settlement with Microsoft in order to bring the tying of Internet Explorer to Windows to an end. In the US settlement concluded in 2002, Microsoft committed that it would not retaliate against original equipment manufacturers (OEMs) distributing non-Microsoft middleware including Internet Explorer.[793] The commitment decision adopted by the European Commission in 2009 did not only require Microsoft to let OEMs free in deciding which web browser to pre-install on PCs they shipped but also obliged the company to display a so-called

---

791. See section 3.4.1 above.
792. G. SURBLYTE, 'The Refusal to Disclose Trade Secrets as an Abuse of Market Dominance - Microsoft and Beyond' in J. DREXL (ed.) *Munich Series on European and International Competition Law*, 28, Berne Stämpfli Publishers Ltd., 2011, p. 131.
793. Other Microsoft middleware to which the settlement applied was Microsoft's Java Virtual Machine, Windows Media Player, Windows Messenger and Outlook Express. The settlement also obliged Microsoft to disclose all interfaces used by Microsoft middleware to interoperate with Windows and any communication protocol installed on a Windows operating system which is used to interoperate with a Microsoft server operating system product. This interoperability-related duty was, however, less far-reaching as that imposed by the European Commission in its 2004 decision upheld by the General Court in 2007 (see section 6.2.2). See *United States v. Microsoft Corp.*, 231 F.Supp.2d 144 (D.D.C. 2002), p. 11 (for the remedy related to the tying issue), p. 13 (for the definition of the term 'Microsoft middleware'), pp. 26-32 (for the remedy related to the interoperability issue).

browser choice screen to users. By way of a Windows software update, users who had Internet Explorer set as their default web browser were provided with the opportunity to choose to install a competing browser.[794] The US and EU competition law interventions targeted the market for web browsers (although the US settlement had a broader scope and did not merely focus on the market for web browsers). While the actions had as their objective to restore competition *in* the market for web browsers, the commitments arguably also had as their effect that scope was created for competition *for* the market in the form of a market shift to Google and other internet players which has made the dominance of Microsoft in the market for client PC operating systems less important.

One can only speculate about what would have happened absent the EU and US interventions. If the two jurisdictions would have allowed Microsoft to integrate its web browser into the Windows operating system, Microsoft might also have set Bing as the default search engine in Internet Explorer thereby using its dominance in the market for client PC operating systems to prevent or delay the rise of Google and other internet companies which have moved consumer demand in client PC hardware and software to mobile devices and online platforms.[795] By opening up the market for web browsers, the US DOJ and the European Commission imposed competitive pressure on Microsoft which possibly distracted the company and enabled the start of a new race of competition *for* the market.

In the context of Microsoft's refusal to license interoperability information in the European Union, it has been argued that the duty imposed by the European Commission in its 2004 decision and upheld by the General Court in 2007 did not only stimulate competition *in* the market for work group server operating systems but also *for* the client PC operating system market.[796] This is because of the peculiar nature of interoperability information. Unlike in earlier European essential facilities cases where two markets in a vertical relationship were at stake, *Microsoft* involved two neighbouring markets. The interoperability information that Microsoft was obliged to supply did not only assist undertakings in the derivative market in introducing competing work group server operating systems that were compatible with the Windows client PC operating system but also enabled firms to attack Microsoft's dominance in the latter market by developing their own client PC operating systems which were interoperable with Microsoft's dominant work group server operating system and as a result directly competed with Windows in the main market.[797]

---

794. Commitments annexed to Case COMP/C-3/39.530 – *Microsoft (tying)*, 16 December 2009, paras 1-17. In March 2013, the Commission imposed a fine on Microsoft for not displaying the browser choice screen in the period 17 May 2011 until 16 July 2012 to 15.3 million users who had bought PCs with Windows 7 Service Pack 1 pre-installed and Internet Explorer set as the default web browser (Case AT.39530 – *Microsoft (Tying)*, 6 March 2013, paras 38-46).
795. M. YGLESIAS, 'The Justice Department Was Absolutely Right to Go After Microsoft in the 1990s', *Slate*, 26 August 2013, available at http://www.slate.com/blogs/moneybox/2013/08/26/microsoft_antitrust_suit_the_vindication_of_the_justice_department.html.
796. G. SURBLYTE, 'The Refusal to Disclose Trade Secrets as an Abuse of Market Dominance - Microsoft and Beyond' in J. DREXL (ed.) *Munich Series on European and International Competition Law*, 28, Berne Stämpfli Publishers Ltd., 2011, pp. 121-122.
797. Case COMP/C-3/37.792 - *Microsoft*, 24 March 2004, par. 769.

The duty to license in the *Microsoft* case thus affected both markets, since the interoperability information could be implemented in non-Microsoft work group server operating systems in the derivative market as well as in non-Microsoft client PC operating systems in the main market.[798] In previous essential facilities cases, only the derivative market was targeted by the competition law intervention. For example, in *IMS Health* the effect of a potential duty to license would only be felt in the derivative market for the provision of data on the sale of pharmaceutical products in Germany and did not permit competitors to introduce a competing brick structure in the main market. The same goes for *Magill* where the publishing company was able to enter the derivative market for weekly television guides whereas the main market for programme listings remained unaffected as a result of the duty to deal.

Microsoft should thus be seen as an exception where the duty to license had an impact on both the main and derivative market because of the special character of interoperability information which connects systems in different levels of the value chain and thus also different markets. Nevertheless, if firms would have started to develop their own client PC operating systems implementing the interoperability information in the main market, this form of competition would still have qualified as competition *in* the market considering that the new client PC operating systems would have been substitutable to Microsoft's Windows operating system. Non-Microsoft client PC operating systems should therefore be considered as sustaining innovations. As noted above, the disruptive innovation that has overthrown Microsoft's dominance in client PC operating systems is the advancement of the internet in the form of the rise of internet players like Google and Facebook. Therefore, the direct competition that was made possible in the main market for client PC operating systems as a result of the imposition of the duty to license in the *Microsoft* case cannot be regarded as a form of competition *for* the market.

With regard to the possible effect of the duty to license on competition *for* the market, the Commission stated in its decision that it found evidence that Microsoft's leveraging of dominance from the client PC operating system market to the market for work group server operating systems was not a goal in itself. In the Commission's view, internal communication between executives indicated that Microsoft aimed to capture the work group server operating system market so that it could take the leveraging strategy from there to the internet where players such as Sun, Oracle and Netscape were launching new services which Microsoft feared might strip its dominance in client PC operating systems of its competitive importance in the long term.[799] However, even if the imposition of the duty to license prevented Microsoft from launching a similar

---

798. This was also one of the main points that Microsoft made in a reaction to the Commission decision arguing that the decision goes well beyond previously established standards: '*The broadest practical impact of the Microsoft decision concerns the mandatory licensing of the technologies in the Windows server operating system so they can be incorporated into directly competing server operating systems in the same primary market*'. See Microsoft Corporation, 'The European Commission's Decision in the Microsoft Case and its Implications for Other Companies and Industries', April 2004, available at http://www.microsoft.com/presspass/download/legal/EuropeanCommission/CommentonECMicrosoftDecision.pdf.
799. Case COMP/C-3/37.792 - *Microsoft*, 24 March 2004, paras 770-777.

leveraging strategy onto the internet, a possible effect on the process of competition *for* the market could only occur indirectly through the renewed competitive pressure on the market for work group server operating systems. In this context, one of Microsoft's executives at the time stated: '*What we are trying to do is use our server control to do new protocols and lock out Sun and Oracle specifically [...]. Now, I don't know if we'll get to that or not, but that's what we are trying to do*'.[800]

Competition law interventions can only have an indirect impact on competition *for* the market as the effects of the US and EU enforcement actions against Microsoft's tying of Internet Explorer to Windows have illustrated. It is impossible for a competition authority or court to directly re-establish the process of competition *for* the market. This is because this type of competition and the disruptive innovation that it generates is by nature difficult or even impossible to predict. The best approach for competition authorities to incentivise competition *for* the market may be to abstain from acting so that the prospect of dominance for new entrants is preserved.

In *Trinko*, the US Supreme Court stated that the possession of monopoly and the charging of monopoly prices is an important element of the free-market system: '*The opportunity to charge monopoly prices-at least for a short period-is what attracts "business acumen" in the first place; it induces risk taking that produces innovation and economic growth*'.[801] A competition law intervention may thus lower incentives for competition *for* the market. In order to determine whether market forces have failed to keep an appropriate balance between competition *in* and *for* the market over time, competition authorities can take into account the stage of development and the specific characteristics of the market in order to assess whether a competition law intervention with the aim of restoring competition *in* the market is appropriate.

6.6.3 Market Specifics Are Instrumental in Determining Whether a Competition Law Intervention Is Appropriate

At the beginning of a market cycle, a competition law intervention is only appropriate in very limited circumstances considering that the market is still developing and market dynamics are likely to be vigilant. Once an incumbent establishes itself and continues to dominate the market, the need for competition enforcement increases. Competition authorities may therefore intervene on a more general basis in later stages of market development.[802] The stability of market shares or the absence of recent entry of new firms can form indications that the market is in a mature stage of development.[803]

---

800. Case COMP/C-3/37.792 - *Microsoft*, 24 March 2004, par. 778.
801. Verizon Communications v. Law Offices of Curtis V. Trinko, LLP (Trinko), 540 U.S. 398 (2004), at 407.
802. In the context of a duty to disclose interoperability information, see I. GRAEF, 'How Can Software Interoperability Be Achieved under European Competition Law and Related Regimes?', *Journal of European Competition Law & Practice* 2014, vol. 5, no. 1, (6), p. 19.
803. It may be noted that such a determination of the scope for competition enforcement on the basis of the stage of development of the market resembles the requirement of dominance. Nevertheless, in cases where dominance is found despite the fact that the market has not yet

With regard to the specific market characteristics to be taken into account, an issue that can play a crucial role is whether external market failures materialise. In the presence of external market failures, the fact that the incumbent remains dominant may not result from its competitive success but merely be a consequence of the market situation grown around the incumbent's dominance. The scope for competition enforcement is wider in those cases because a competition law intervention may re-establish the level of competition *in* the market which market forces itself are unable to achieve. In such situations, it may be reasonable for competition authorities and courts to continue to guarantee competition *in* the market and protect consumers against abuse of dominance as long as a new wave of competition *for* the market does not arise.

Competition enforcement in markets not characterised by external market failures, on the other hand, should be subject to stricter conditions considering that the self-correcting mechanism of the market to adequately address possible competition problems of itself is stronger in the absence of such market failures. In these circumstances, a competition law intervention to stimulate competition *in* the market may not be needed and carries a higher risk of unnecessarily reducing incentives for competition *for* the market by taking away the prospect of dominance for new entrants.

Although the presence of strong network effects, switching costs and entry barriers may form an indication that external market failures are present, these economic characteristics do not necessarily result into market failures. The critical issue is whether market characteristics enable an incumbent to artificially extend its dominance in time. External market failures can particularly occur in the context of standardisation or in cases where network effects and lock-in prevent competitors from entering the market and from introducing their own products or services due to the fact that consumers are not interested in switching to a new system.[804] In such circumstances, a competition law intervention is desirable in order to correct the market situation grown around the dominant position of the incumbent.[805]

In the *Microsoft* case, indirect network effects were identified which gave rise to an applications barrier to entry due to which a competitor could only launch a new operating system if a sufficient number of compatible applications was already available.[806] In addition, because of the lack of interoperability between non-Microsoft

---

matured, it is useful to take into account the stage of development of the market in assessing whether competition enforcement is appropriate.

804. J. DREXL, 'Abuse of Dominance in Licensing and Refusal to License: A "More Economic Approach" to Competition by Imitation and to Competition by Substitution' in C.D. EHLERMANN AND I. ATANASIU (eds.), *European Competition Law Annual 2005: The Interaction between Competition Law and Intellectual Property Law*, Hart Publishing, 2007, (647), pp. 651-653.
805. In the context of refusals to license intellectual property rights, see G. GHIDINI AND E. AREZZO, 'On the Intersection of IPRs and Competition Law With Regard to Information Technology Markets' in C.D. EHLERMANN AND I. ATANASIU (eds.), *European Competition Law Annual 2005: The Interaction between Competition Law and Intellectual Property Law*, Hart Publishing, 2007, (105), pp. 114-115 and J. DREXL, 'IMS Health and Trinko - Antitrust Placebo for Consumers Instead of Sound Economics in Refusal-to-Deal Cases', *International Review of Intellectual Property and Competition Law* 2004, vol. 35, no. 7, (788), pp. 792-793.
806. Case COMP/C-3/37.792 – *Microsoft*, 24 March 2004, paras 458-459 and Judgment in *Microsoft v. Commission*, T-201/04, ECLI:EU:T:2007:289, par. 1088.

work group server operating systems and the Windows client PC operating system, users were locked-in to Microsoft's work group server operating systems. They could not benefit from competing work group server operating systems which differed from those of Microsoft on important parameters such as security, reliability, processing speed and the innovative nature of certain functionalities.[807] The network effects and user lock-in made Microsoft's position in the market for client PC operating systems sustainable and turned Windows in a de facto industry standard.

In such circumstances, the imposition of a duty to deal seems appropriate in order to open up the market and put the incumbent under pressure to continue to compete on price and product variety. The latter played a role in *Microsoft* since the results from a survey had indicated that competing work group server operating systems functioned better than those of Microsoft with respect to a number of features that were valued by consumers such as reliability, availability and security.[808] As a result, the lead of Microsoft in the market for work group server operating systems had '*to be explained not so much by the merits of its products as by its interoperability advantage*'.[809] The market situation grown around the interoperability information thus protected Microsoft from being attacked by competitors in the work group server operating system market which had introduced products that were considered of better quality than those of Microsoft. By way of ordering Microsoft to give these competitors access to the interoperability information, the market situation could be corrected and competition *in* the market was restored.

Although the decision to intervene in a market amounts to a policy choice, the specific characteristics and stage of development of the market may inform competition authorities about the appropriate approach in a particular situation. When the market is locked-in due to switching costs and network effects, and the incumbent has had a stable dominant position for some time, it seems justified for a competition authority to intervene on the basis of looser conditions in order to open up the process of competition *in* the market through the imposition of a duty to deal.

By lowering the standards for holding a refusal to license abusive under Article 102 TFEU in *Microsoft*, the European Commission and the General Court may have deliberately tailored the application of the essential facilities doctrine to the particular market situation in the case. In that light, one could argue that the higher standards established in *Magill* and *IMS Health* are still valid for cases in which no external market failures are present.[810] In markets not characterised by the existence of external market failures, a duty to deal should indeed be imposed on the basis of stricter conditions because of the stronger self-correcting mechanism of the market and to ensure that incentives for competition *for* the market are not put at risk.

---

807. Case COMP/C-3/37.792 – *Microsoft*, 24 March 2004, par. 694 and Judgment in *Microsoft v. Commission*, T-201/04, ECLI:EU:T:2007:289, paras 240 and 650-653.
808. Case COMP/C-3/37.792 – *Microsoft*, 24 March 2004, par. 699 and Judgment in *Microsoft v. Commission*, T-201/04, ECLI:EU:T:2007:289, paras 407-412 and 652.
809. Judgment in *Microsoft v. Commission*, T-201/04, ECLI:EU:T:2007:289, par. 407.
810. I. GRAEF, 'Tailoring the Essential Facilities Doctrine to the IT Sector: Compulsory Licensing of Intellectual Property Rights after *Microsoft*', *Cambridge Student Law Review* 2011, vol. 7, no. 1, (1), p. 18.

6.7 ROLE OF INTELLECTUAL PROPERTY AND TRADE SECRET LAW

Under Article 102 TFEU, a different legal standard applies to refusals to license intellectual property rights as compared to refusals to deal in general. In addition to the requirements of indispensability, exclusion of competition on a secondary market and the absence of an objective justification, the new product condition has to be met in order to hold a refusal to license abusive under EU competition law. However, as is discussed below, the new product condition does not seem capable of addressing all situations in which a competition law intervention is necessary in order to restore competition in markets where intellectual property rights are present. Furthermore, there is no clear economic rationale for treating intellectual property rights differently than other types of assets under the essential facilities doctrine. Some forms of protection may even pose competition problems of themselves in case information is shielded that competitors need in order to enter a market.

6.7.1 Analysing Refusals to License in the Light of the Interface Between Competition and Intellectual Property Law

The application of the essential facilities doctrine to intellectual property rights is controversial because it lies at the heart of the interface between competition and intellectual property law. The modern view of the relationship between the two areas of law is that they are not in conflict but rather share the same objective of promoting innovation and enhancing consumer welfare.[811] While competition law tries to protect consumer welfare by putting pressure on firms to compete and innovate, intellectual property law aims to encourage creativity and inventiveness by granting protection in the form of exclusive rights.[812] Through exclusivity the right holder is given an opportunity to reap the rewards of his or her creation on the market. It is therefore not the grant of the intellectual property right in itself which gives rise to incentives for innovation, but the competitive process which determines the value of the subject matter underlying the exclusive right and the reward for its creation in accordance with market demand. In the words of Ullrich: *'competition is a prerequisite to the well functioning of the intellectual property system'* and *'intellectual property, indeed, represents nothing else than a means of competition, an opportunity to act in*

---

811. Both in the EU and the US, it is recognised that competition and intellectual property law share a common goal. See Communication from the Commission. Guidelines on the application of Article 101 of the Treaty on the Functioning of the European Union to technology transfer agreements [2014] OJ C89/3, par. 7: *'Indeed, both bodies of law share the same basic objective of promoting consumer welfare and an efficient allocation of resources'*. See US Department of Justice and Federal Trade Commission, Antitrust Guidelines for the Licensing of Intellectual Property, 6 April 1995, par. 1.0: *'The intellectual property laws and the antitrust laws share the common purpose of promoting innovation and enhancing consumer welfare'*.
812. Drexl refers to the identical goals of competition and intellectual property law as the theory of complementarity. See J. DREXL, 'IMS Health and Trinko - Antitrust Placebo for Consumers Instead of Sound Economics in Refusal-to-Deal Cases', *International Review of Intellectual Property and Competition Law* 2004, vol. 35, no. 7, (788), pp. 792-793.

competition according to the market rules of profit maximization.[813] As a result, both intellectual property rights and competition are necessary in order to promote innovation.

By establishing a duty to deal in the form of a compulsory licence, competition enforcement limits the scope of protection that is offered to right holders by intellectual property law. In particular, the imposition of a compulsory licence on the basis of competition law takes away the right to exclude third parties from using the subject matter underlying the intellectual property right.[814] Nevertheless, in the light of the complementary goals of competition law and intellectual property law it is appropriate for competition authorities to intervene in certain circumstances to promote innovation when the intellectual property system is unable to do so.

To identify these situations, Drexl relies on the difference between competition by substitution and competition by imitation as an analytical tool.[815] Intellectual property rights restrict static competition, which amounts to competition on the basis of price and output, in order to encourage dynamic competition or, in a simpler term, innovation.[816] By granting exclusive rights to inventors and creators, intellectual property law prevents third parties from copying the protected subject matter by competing on static parameters (competition by imitation). But intellectual property protection does not exclude third parties from the process of dynamic competition which concerns the development of a different or superior product that would compete with the product of the right holder in the same market (competition by substitution). Intellectual property law thus relies on the exclusion of competition by imitation to encourage competition by substitution.[817]

Drexl identifies two situations in which competition authorities should intervene by imposing a compulsory licence on the ground that the assumption that an intellectual property right contributes to dynamic competition does not hold in those

---

813. H. ULLRICH, 'Intellectual Property, Access to Information, and Antitrust: Harmony, Disharmony, and International Harmonization' in R.C. DREYFUSS, D.L. ZIMMERMAN AND H. FIRST (eds.), *Expanding the Boundaries of Intellectual Property. Innovation Policy for the Knowledge Society*, Oxford University Press, 2001, (365), p. 373. See also M.-O. MACKENRODT, 'Assessing the Effects of Intellectual Property Rights in Network Standards' in J. DREXL (ed.), *Research Handbook on Intellectual Property and Competition Law*, Edward Elgar, 2008, (80), pp. 84-85 and C. RITTER, 'Refusal to Deal and "Essential Facilities": Does Intellectual Property Require Special Deference Compared to Tangible Property?', *World Competition* 2005, no. 28, (281), pp. 293-294.

814. A.B. LIPSKY AND J.G. SIDAK, 'Essential Facilities', *Stanford Law Review* 1999, vol. 51, no. 5, (1187), pp. 1219-1220 arguing that the essential facilities doctrine should not be applied to intellectual property rights because compulsory dealings are inconsistent with the exclusivity that is necessary to preserve incentives to create under intellectual property protection.

815. This is most explicitly put forward in J. DREXL, 'Abuse of Dominance in Licensing and Refusal to License: A "More Economic Approach" to Competition by Imitation and to Competition by Substitution' in C.D. EHLERMANN AND I. ATANASIU (eds.), *European Competition Law Annual 2005: The Interaction between Competition Law and Intellectual Property Law*, Hart Publishing, 2007, (647), pp. 651-653.

816. See M.-O. MACKENRODT, 'Assessing the Effects of Intellectual Property Rights in Network Standards' in J. DREXL (ed.), *Research Handbook on Intellectual Property and Competition Law*, Edward Elgar, 2008, (80), pp. 81-82.

817. J. DREXL, 'IMS Health and Trinko - Antitrust Placebo for Consumers Instead of Sound Economics in Refusal-to-Deal Cases', *International Review of Intellectual Property and Competition Law* 2004, vol. 35, no. 7, (788), p. 805.

circumstances. The first scenario relates to situations in which the intellectual property system provides such a broad scope of protection that the intellectual property right not only excludes competition by imitation but also competition by substitution. An example of such a situation can be found in the *Magill* case where it was argued by commentators that the programme listings were not worthy of copyright protection.[818] As a result of the fact that the Irish broadcasting stations were granted copyright over basic information not available from another source, the protection automatically excluded dynamic competition in the market for weekly television guides. Whereas these kind of problems may be best solved within the intellectual property system itself, the second situation identified by Drexl can only be addressed by way of competition enforcement.

The presence of external market failures constitutes the second scenario in which intellectual property law may not reach its objective of encouraging innovation. An intellectual property right that usually would not affect competition by substitution may do so due to specific market circumstances lying outside the intellectual property system. *IMS Health* and *Microsoft* form illustrations of this. In *IMS Health*, the pharmaceutical companies were locked-in to the 1860 brick structure of IMS which had become a de facto standard. Since they had been involved in the development of the brick structure by making suggestions for optimising the segmentation in geographical areas, the pharmaceutical companies were accustomed to the system of IMS and did not want to work with different brick structures. PII, a competitor of IMS, tried to market structures consisting of 2201 bricks but this was met with reticence on the part of potential clients.[819] As a result, competition by substitution could not occur in *IMS Health* due to the market characteristics grown around the copyright protection of the 1860 brick structure.[820]

A similar situation was at stake in *Microsoft*. Due to network effects and user lock-in, Microsoft's PC operating system Windows had become a de facto industry standard. Due to these external market failures, undertakings could only compete *in* the market for work group server operating systems by making their products interoperable with Windows. Because Microsoft refused to disclose the interoperability

---

818. See, among others, R. Greaves, 'Magill Est Arrivé...RTE and ITP v Commission of the European Communities', *European Competition Law Review* 1995, vol. 16, no. 4, (244), p. 246; Opinion of Advocate General Jacobs in *Oscar Bronner GmbH & Co. KG v. Mediaprint Zeitungs*, C-7/97, ECLI:EU:C:1998:264, par. 63; B. Doherty, 'Just What Are Essential Facilities', *Common Market Law Review* 2001, vol. 38, no. 2, (397), p. 429; M. Motta, *Competition Policy. Theory and Practice*, Cambridge University Press, 2004, p. 68.

819. Judgment in *IMS Health GmbH & Co. OHG v. NDC Health GmbH & Co. KG*, C-418/01, ECLI:EU:C:2004:257, paras 5-7.

820. J. Drexl, 'IMS Health and Trinko - Antitrust Placebo for Consumers Instead of Sound Economics in Refusal-to-Deal Cases', *International Review of Intellectual Property and Competition Law* 2004, vol. 35, no. 7, (788), p. 805. Others have argued that *IMS Health* can be explained in the same way as *Magill* in the sense that the brick structure developed by IMS did not justify copyright protection. See C. Ritter, 'Refusal to Deal and "Essential Facilities": Does Intellectual Property Require Special Deference Compared to Tangible Property?', *World Competition* 2005, no. 28, (281), pp. 285-286 and M. Motta, *Competition Policy. Theory and Practice*, Cambridge University Press, 2004, p. 68.

information, which was assumed to be protected by intellectual property rights,[821] competitors were prevented from doing so.

6.7.2   Limits of the New Product Condition

In the United States, Courts of Appeals have expressed conflicting views on the appropriate treatment of refusals to license intellectual property rights under antitrust law. Whereas the Ninth Circuit Court argued in *Kodak* that proof of anticompetitive intent on the part of right holder could be invoked to rebut the presumption of legality of a refusal to license, the Federal Circuit held in *Xerox* that inventions protected by patent law were immune from antitrust liability except in the case of illegal tying, fraud and sham litigation.[822] The US Supreme Court has not yet rendered judgment on the legal test that should be applied to refusals to license. The *Kodak* and *Xerox* cases preceded the judgment of the Supreme Court in *Trinko*, but since the latter case did not concern intellectual property rights it is unclear to what extent the reasoning in *Trinko* is also valid for refusals to license.[823]

Unlike in the United States where it remains ambiguous whether and in which circumstances a refusal to license an intellectual property right may violate antitrust law, it is clear that intellectual property rights are not immune from competition law intervention in the European Union.[824] Under the essential facilities doctrine in Europe, a different standard applies to refusals to deal involving intellectual property rights as compared to refusals to deal in general. As the General Court observed in *Microsoft*, the new product condition is only apparent in the case law on the exercise of an intellectual property right.[825] As a consequence, in order to hold a refusal to license abusive under Article 102 TFEU the new product requirement has to be met in addition to the conditions of indispensability, exclusion of competition on a secondary market and the absence of an objective justification which constitute the three relevant criteria to assess refusals to deal involving non-intellectual property protected assets.

According to the Court of Justice in *IMS Health*, the requirement of the prevention of the emergence of a new product is applied to determine whether the refusal to license at issue '*prevents the development of the secondary market to the detriment of*

---

821. Microsoft claimed that its interoperability information was protected by patent, copyright as well as trade secret law. The European Commission concluded that it could not be excluded that ordering Microsoft to disclose its communication protocols and to allow use of them by third parties would restrict the exercise of Microsoft's intellectual property rights. The General Court followed the approach of the Commission. See Case COMP/C-3/37.792 – *Microsoft*, 24 March 2004, par. 190, 546 and footnote 249 and Judgment in *Microsoft v. Commission*, T-201/04, ECLI:EU:T:2007:289, paras 270-273 and 289.
822. See section 6.2.1 above.
823. See also M.A. CARRIER, 'Refusals to License Intellectual Property after *Trinko*', *DePaul Law Review* 2006, vol. 55, no. 4, (1191).
824. In the context of Article 101 TFEU, see Communication from the Commission. Guidelines on the application of Article 101 of the Treaty on the Functioning of the European Union to technology transfer agreements [2014] OJ C89/3, par. 7: '*The fact that intellectual property laws grant exclusive rights of exploitation does not imply that intellectual property rights are immune from competition law intervention*'.
825. See Judgment in *Microsoft v. Commission*, T-201/04, ECLI:EU:T:2007:289, par. 334.

consumers'.[826] It is only in that case that the interest in protection of free competition can prevail over the interest in protection of the intellectual property right and the economic freedom of its owner in the view of the Court. The new production condition reflects how intellectual property law aims to stimulate innovation: by excluding third parties from copying protected subject matter, the development of different or improved products is encouraged. The logic behind the introduction of the requirement may lie in the fact that an intellectual property right does not fulfil its function of promoting innovation when it is used to prevent the emergence of a new product. Such an exceptional circumstance may for that reason be considered relevant for assessing whether a refusal to license is abusive under competition law.

In accordance with the scope of protection offered by an intellectual property right, a competitor who would like to have a license in order to duplicate the product of the right holder cannot successfully rely on Article 102 TFEU whereas a competitor who aims to introduce a new product can expect to get a licence on the basis of the essential facilities doctrine (provided that the other three exceptional circumstances are also present). This would mean that a competition law intervention for a refusal to license is only justified if competition by substitution is constrained.[827] However, as argued by Drexl, the imposition of a compulsory licence on the basis of competition law may also be appropriate to restore competition by imitation when competition by substitution cannot occur due to external market failures. These situations are not captured by the new product condition.

If the new product condition is applied as a necessary requirement for the imposition of a compulsory licence, only cases in which the intellectual property system itself fails by providing such an extensive scope of protection that competition by substitution is automatically excluded (first scenario identified by Drexl) can be held abusive under EU competition law. Cases involving refusals to license in which the intellectual property right at issue does not promote innovation due to external market failures (second scenario identified by Drexl) escape liability under Article 102 TFEU.[828] Under the new product requirement, the access seeker has to show that it will not merely imitate the product of the right holder.

In *Magill*, which forms an example of the first scenario, the copyright was so broad as to cover the basic information that Magill needed to introduce the new product, namely the comprehensive weekly television guide. In this case, the new product requirement could be adequately applied to restore competition by substitution through obliging IMS to grant Magill a copyright licence. However, in situations where market characteristics such as network effects and lock-in are present,

---

826. Judgment in *IMS Health GmbH & Co. OHG v. NDC Health GmbH & Co. KG*, C-418/01, ECLI:EU:C:2004:257, par. 48.
827. J. DREXL, 'Abuse of Dominance in Licensing and Refusal to License: A "More Economic Approach" to Competition by Imitation and to Competition by Substitution' in C.D. EHLERMANN AND I. ATANASIU (eds.), *European Competition Law Annual 2005: The Interaction between Competition Law and Intellectual Property Law*, Hart Publishing, 2007, (647), pp. 653-654.
828. J. DREXL, 'Abuse of Dominance in Licensing and Refusal to License: A 'More Economic Approach' to Competition by Imitation and to Competition by Substitution' in C.D. EHLERMANN AND I. ATANASIU (eds.), *European Competition Law Annual 2005: The Interaction between Competition Law and Intellectual Property Law*, Hart Publishing, 2007, (647), p. 654.

competitors cannot compete by substitution because their customers are not interested in a new product. In *IMS Health*, the pharmaceutical companies did not have an interest in the availability of a different brick structure on the market because they had become locked-in to the system of IMS. The switch to a new brick structure was therefore considered too costly.

In contrast to the situation in *Magill*, the pharmaceutical companies in *IMS Health* did not benefit from the judgment because they were not interested in having a new brick structure. Unlike the television viewers in *Magill* who were willing to buy a comprehensive television guide, the competitors of IMS would not have been able to convince the pharmaceutical companies to switch to their system even if they were in a position to introduce a new brick structure. Instead, the pharmaceutical companies would have benefited from having a brick structure similar to that of IMS on the market so that there would at least be competition on the basis of price or variety.[829]

Similarly, in *Microsoft* Windows had become the de facto industry standard as a result of which consumers were only interested in using work group server operating systems that were compatible with the Windows client PC operating system. In order to viably remain on the market for work group server operating systems, competitors thus had to ensure that their own work group server operating systems were interoperable with Windows. The General Court held in its *Microsoft* judgment that a restriction of technical development was sufficient for fulfilling the new product requirement. Indeed, due to the external market failures present in the case a mere technical development of Microsoft's product would arguably have been more beneficial to consumers who were locked-in to Windows and as a result preferred competition on the basis of price or variety over having an entirely new work group server operating system in the market that was incompatible with Windows.

While the new product condition introduced in *Magill* was adequate to solve the competition problem in that case and to restore competition by substitution, the market characteristics in *IMS Health* and *Microsoft* made it commercially unviable for the competitors of, respectively, IMS and Microsoft to introduce a new product. The new product requirement is therefore not suitable to address cases where external market failures exclude competition by substitution. It does not make sense to require access seekers to intend to offer a new product when the market will not accept such a form of innovation due to the existence of external market failures. The consequence of allowing competitors to imitate the creation or invention of the right holder is that the core of the intellectual property right which restricts third parties from engaging in

---

829. J. DREXL, 'IMS Health and Trinko - Antitrust Placebo for Consumers Instead of Sound Economics in Refusal-to-Deal Cases', *International Review of Intellectual Property and Competition Law* 2004, vol. 35, no. 7, (788), pp. 802-803: '*Price competition, at least in this case, turns out to be much more vital than innovation*'. See also D. RIDYARD, 'Compulsory Access under EC Competition Law - A New Doctrine of "Convenient Facilities" and the Case for Price Regulation', *European Competition Law Review* 2004, vol. 25, no. 11, (669), p. 670: '*If it was established that foreclosing competition allowed IMS to sustain an inefficient and abusive outcome on the market for pharmaceutical market research products, then the public policy case for allowing NDC to enter the market through compulsory licensing of the brick structure is valid even if the only "innovation" provided is a competitive price*'.

copying activities is affected. However, one should recognise that the promotion of innovation is not the only way in which consumer welfare can be protected under competition and intellectual property law.

Considering that both legal fields aim to enhance consumer welfare, a competition law intervention that affects the exclusivity of an intellectual property right should be accepted in situations where a duty to deal cannot restore dynamic competition in the form of innovation. By doing so, consumers can at least benefit from static competition on the basis of price and output in these cases. Even though the intellectual property right itself is not the cause of the dominant position, its exercise enables the right holder to continue to exploit its dominance in a way which is not in line with the rationale behind intellectual property law to encourage dynamic competition through the restriction of static competition. By limiting the exercise of the intellectual property right on the basis of competition law, it can be prevented that the right holder is overcompensated for its investments which would not have met with a similar degree of success in the absence of the external market failures. At the same time, no adverse incentives to invest in innovation should be created by allowing imitation to take place on a too general basis and without providing an adequate reward to the right holder. As made clear by Drexl, a balance could be found by applying Article 102 TFEU to limit the exercise of the intellectual property right but also to entitle the right holder to ask licensees for a reasonable royalty rate allowing for the recovery of its investments.[830]

Although the imposition of a compulsory licence in order to enable imitation puts more far-reaching limits on the exercise of an intellectual property right than in case the access seeker is required to introduce a new product, the existence of the exclusive right in itself remains untouched. The distinction between the existence of intellectual property rights, which should not be subject to EU competition rules, and their exercise, which may violate Article 102 TFEU, as introduced by the Court of Justice in the early cases of *Volvo* and *Renault* is thus upheld. Since the new product condition, as currently interpreted and applied by the Commission and the EU Courts, is incapable of enhancing consumer welfare in cases where market circumstances prevent competitors from competing by introducing novel products, it is inconsistent with the complementary nature of intellectual property and competition law.

The adequacy of the new product requirement has also been questioned on other grounds. It has been noted that, contrary to what the new product condition implies, consumer demand does not depend on the product itself but on its characteristics and its performance on each characteristic. As a result, it would be more accurate from an economic perspective to look at the individual characteristics of a product instead of at the product as a whole. In addition, the new product condition only requires the intent to introduce a new product and therefore does not assess whether actual consumer

---

830. J. Drexl, 'IMS Health and Trinko - Antitrust Placebo for Consumers Instead of Sound Economics in Refusal-to-Deal Cases', *International Review of Intellectual Property and Competition Law* 2004, vol. 35, no. 7, (788), pp. 804-806 and J. Drexl, 'Abuse of Dominance in Licensing and Refusal to License: A "More Economic Approach" to Competition by Imitation and to Competition by Substitution' in C.D. Ehlermann and I. Atanasiu (eds.), *European Competition Law Annual 2005: The Interaction between Competition Law and Intellectual Property Law*, Hart Publishing, 2007, (647), pp. 655 and 663.

demand will exist for the product once it has been brought to the market. In that context, it is claimed that the new product condition is unable to serve as a proxy for what is most relevant to test: the loss for consumers if the improvement of the product is blocked due to the refusal to license.[831]

Commentators have also argued that the concept of 'novelty' is difficult to apply because it is not a well-established and clearly definable notion.[832] It is still uncertain how different a product should be in comparison with existing ones and to what extent it should already be clearly identifiable in order to be considered 'new' under the legal standards of the essential facilities doctrine. Whereas the Court of Justice held in *IMS Health* that a refusal to license '*may be regarded as abusive only where the undertaking which requested the license does not intend to limit itself essentially to duplicating the goods or services already offered on the secondary market by the owner of the intellectual property right, but intends to produce new goods or services not offered by the owner of the right and for which there is a potential consumer demand*',[833] the General Court in *Microsoft* followed the approach of the European Commission that prejudice to consumers under Article 102(b) TFEU may occur '*where there is a limitation not only of production or markets, but also of technical development*'.[834] Under the latter standard, the burden of proof is much lower and it merely suffices for competitors to argue that the refusal to license prevents them from introducing a product differentiation without the need to specify a concrete form of innovation that they will generate. In other words, anything other than mere imitation is sufficient to constitute a new product. It remains to be seen if this definition of the new product condition will be upheld in future cases.

Although the degree of novelty required in the *IMS Health* and *Microsoft* cases differs considerably, the two cases reach the same conclusion on the fact that the new product or technical development which the access seeker intends to introduce has to compete with that of the right holder in the derivative market. In that sense, the new product or technical development has to be substitutable to that of the right holder and fall within the same relevant market.[835] In both *IMS Health* and *Microsoft*, it was made clear that the prevention of the emergence of a new product should have occurred on the secondary market in which the dominant undertaking was present and in which it tried to foreclose competition by refusing to license (in *IMS Health* the German market for the provision of regional sales data of pharmaceutical products and in *Microsoft* the market for work group server operating systems).

---

831. F. Lévêque, 'Innovation, Leveraging and Essential Facilities: Interoperability Licensing in the EU Microsoft Case', *World Competition* 2005, vol. 28, no. 1, (71), pp. 75-76.
832. D. Geradin, 'Limiting the Scope of Article 82 EC: What Can the EU Learn from the U.S. Supreme Court's judgment in *Trinko* in the Wake of *Microsoft*, *IMS*, and *Deutsche Telekom*?', *Common Market Law Review* 2004, vol. 41, no. 6, (1519), p. 1531.
833. Judgment in *IMS Health GmbH & Co. OHG v. NDC Health GmbH & Co. KG*, C-418/01, ECLI:EU:C:2004:257, par. 49.
834. Judgment in *Microsoft v. Commission*, T-201/04, ECLI:EU:T:2007:289, par. 647.
835. On the notion of substitution in the context of the new product condition, see D. Geradin, 'Limiting the Scope of Article 82 EC: What Can the EU Learn from the U.S. Supreme Court's judgment in *Trinko* in the Wake of *Microsoft*, *IMS*, and *Deutsche Telekom*?', *Common Market Law Review* 2004, vol. 41, no. 6, (1519), pp. 1531-1532.

A different interpretation of the new product requirement would be incompatible with the condition relating to the exclusion of competition on a secondary market which requires that the dominant undertaking reserves the derivative market to itself by denying a competitor access to an essential facility. It would not make sense to hold the new product requirement applicable to situations where access seekers aim to launch a new product on a market on which the dominant undertaking is not active, because in such cases there is no leveraging of market power while this is necessary for a refusal to licence to be considered abusive under current standards. As a result, the essential facilities doctrine currently does not support competitors who would like to introduce a new product on a new market different from that on which the dominant undertaking is present.[836]

6.7.3 Do Intellectual Property Rights and Trade Secrets Require a Different Treatment under the Essential Facilities Doctrine?

The various limits of the new product condition raise doubts about its reliability to distinguish situations in which the imposition of a compulsory licence is appropriate from those in which a competition authority should not intervene. As a consequence, the question rises whether a different legal standard should at all apply to intellectual property rights or whether they should be treated in the same way as other forms of property in refusal to deal cases. The need for a more demanding test to hold refusals to license abusive under Article 102 TFEU seems to be based on the premise that there is an inherent conflict between intellectual property and competition law. However, as recognised by the European Commission,[837] the two fields of law share the objective of encouraging innovation and enhancing consumer welfare. It therefore seems inconsistent with the modern view of the complementary relationship between intellectual property and competition law to apply a higher legal threshold to refusals to license intellectual property rights as compared to refusals involving non-intellectual property protected goods and services.

Indeed, proponents of a distinct approach to intellectual property in the context of the essential facilities doctrine do not provide reasons for why intellectual property rights should be treated with special care other than the claim that competition law interventions will impede on the exclusivity of the right and will negatively affect future investment in intellectual property.[838] A restriction on the exclusivity of an

---

836. E. ROUSSEVA, *Rethinking Exclusionary Abuses in EU Competition Law*, Hart Publishing, 2010, pp. 124-125 and D. GERADIN, 'Limiting the Scope of Article 82 EC: What Can the EU Learn from the U.S. Supreme Court's Judgment in *Trinko* in the Wake of *Microsoft*, *IMS*, and *Deutsche Telekom*?', *Common Market Law Review* 2004, vol. 41, no. 6, (1519), p. 1531. For a critical analysis of the current interpretation of the essential facilities doctrine in this regard, see section 6.8.2.2 below where it is submitted that it should be possible to impose a duty to deal in case effective competition is excluded on a downstream market on which the dominant undertaking is not (yet) present.

837. See the statement of the European Commission in the current Technology Transfer Guidelines as quoted in footnote 811.

838. See, for example, A.B. LIPSKY AND J.G. SIDAK, 'Essential Facilities', *Stanford Law Review* 1999, vol. 51, no. 5, (1187), pp. 1219-1220: '*a legal rule of mandatory sharing and compulsory*

intellectual property right is not problematic if one regards the fields of competition and intellectual property law as complementary instruments that are working towards the same goal of protecting consumer welfare. According to the modern view of the relationship between the two areas of law, it would be appropriate for competition authorities to step in and preserve consumer welfare by encouraging competition on static parameters when an intellectual property right does not achieve its objective of promoting innovation.[839]

With regard to the effect of a duty to license on innovation incentives, Advocate General Jacobs stated in *Bronner*: '*particular care is required where the goods or services or facilities to which access is demanded represent the fruit of substantial investment. That may be true in particular in relation to refusal to license intellectual property rights. Where such exclusive rights are granted for a limited period, that in itself involves a balancing of the interest in free competition with that of providing an incentive for research and development and for creativity*'.[840] It is claimed that intellectual property rights require special protection because they are more vulnerable to free-riding and duplication than other types of property.[841] However, in practice a lot of time and effort may be needed to gather the know-how necessary for copying, for instance, a patented invention.[842] Furthermore, intellectual property rights are not the only type of asset whose development requires significant investment. Similar levels of investments may be necessary for the construction of tunnels, ports, telephone networks and other physical infrastructures.[843]

It should also be noted that not all investment in intellectual property necessarily promotes innovation or consumer welfare. Many patents are not practiced or enforced and may even be used to block competition instead of to protect returns to innovation.

---

dealings [...] *is inconsistent with the exclusivity that is necessary to preserve incentives to create, the core operative device of intellectual property law in a market economy*' and '*the essential facilities doctrine cannot be applied to intellectual property. To do so would threaten the basic objective of the legal systems that create incentives for the production of information, and would thus threaten technical progress*'; D.W. CARLTON, 'A General Analysis of Exclusionary Conduct and Refusal to Deal - Why *Aspen* and *Kodak* are Misguided', *Antitrust Law Journal* 2001, vol. 68, no. 3, (659), p. 674: '*antitrust should be especially wary when its action reduces the return to innovators of intellectual property because we know that there already is too little incentive to create such intellectual property*' and E. DERCLAYE, 'Abuses of Dominant Position and Intellectual Property Rights: A Suggestion to Reconcile the Community Courts Case Law', *World Competition* 2003, vol. 26, no. 4, (685), p. 701: '*there are reasons to be more prudent when imposing compulsory licences on copyright holders rather than on owners of other types of property. A difference in treatment, most probably in the direction of a lower incursion of competition law into copyright's scope than into the scope of other forms of property, is therefore justified*'.

839. See section 6.7.2 above.
840. Opinion of Advocate General Jacobs in *Oscar Bronner GmbH & Co. KG v. Mediaprint Zeitungs*, C-7/97, ECLI:EU:C:1998:264, par. 62.
841. See J. LANGENFELD, 'Intellectual Property and Antitrust: Steps Toward Striking a Balance', *Case Western Reserve Law Review* 2001, vol. 52, no. 1, (91), p. 93.
842. C. RITTER, 'Refusal to Deal and "Essential Facilities": Does Intellectual Property Require Special Deference Compared to Tangible Property?', *World Competition* 2005, no. 28, (281), p. 290.
843. B. DOHERTY, 'Just What are Essential Facilities', *Common Market Law Review* 2001, vol. 38, no. 2, (397), p. 429 and F. LÉVÊQUE, 'Innovation, Leveraging and Essential Facilities: Interoperability Licensing in the EU Microsoft Case', *World Competition* 2005, vol. 28, no. 1, (71), p. 80.

It therefore does not seem correct to assume that the innovations which are most valuable to society are protected by some form of intellectual property. A more lenient approach towards refusals to license is thus hard to justify on the ground that investment in intellectual property needs more protection than investment in other assets.[844]

There does not seem to be a solid economic rationale for applying a different legal test to refusals to license than to refusals to deal involving non-intellectual property protected assets. Nevertheless, this does not mean that all forms of intellectual property protection or protected information are similar and should be treated in the same way. The *Microsoft* case raised the issue of whether trade secret protection should be equated with intellectual property rights such as patents and copyrights. Microsoft had argued before the European Commission that its interoperability information was protected by patent, copyright and trade secret law.[845] The Commission did not assess whether Microsoft was indeed able to invoke any of these forms of protection but merely stated that it could not be excluded that ordering Microsoft to disclose its protocols and to allow use of them by third parties would restrict the exercise of Microsoft's intellectual property rights.[846]

It is not clear from its decision whether the Commission regarded trade secret protection as equivalent to intellectual property. The Commission simply noted: '*It is possible that such a use* [referring to the implementation of the interoperability information in third-party products] *could be prevented by Microsoft relying on intellectual property rights. Furthermore, the specifications at issue may constitute innovations that are currently not disclosed and are protected by trade secrecy*' and '*Microsoft in fact invokes such intellectual property rights over the relevant information to resist disclosure and the subsequent use that could be made of it*'.[847] Whereas the Commission mentioned trade secret protection in addition to intellectual property in the first quote, it referred to a general form of intellectual property protection against disclosure in the latter sentence.[848]

The General Court pointed out that it was not necessary to analyse Microsoft's claim that its interoperability information was protected by intellectual property law, because the Commission had based its decision on the assumption that the conduct at issue was not a mere refusal to supply a product or service but a refusal to license intellectual property rights. In so doing, the Commission, in the words of the Court, '*chose the strictest legal test and therefore the one most favourable to Microsoft*'. On this ground, the General Court stated that the arguments of Microsoft derived from the

---

844. H.A. SHELANSKI, 'Unilateral Refusals to Deal in Intellectual and Other Property', *Antitrust Law Journal* 2009, vol. 76, no. 2, (369), pp. 385-386.
845. As quoted in Case COMP/C-3/37.792 - Microsoft, 24 March 2004, footnote 249: 'The interoperability information requested by Sun constitutes valuable intellectual property protected by copyright, trade secret laws and patents'.
846. Case COMP/C-3/37.792 - *Microsoft*, 24 March 2004, paras 190 and 546.
847. Case COMP/C-3/37.792 - *Microsoft*, 24 March 2004, par. 190.
848. J. DREXL, 'Refusal to Grant Access to Trade Secrets as an Abuse of Market Dominance' in S. ANDERMAN AND A. EZRACHI (eds.), *Intellectual Property and Competition Law. New Frontiers*, Oxford University Press, 2011, (165), p. 171.

alleged intellectual property rights could not affect the lawfulness of the Commission decision.[849] The General Court made a more clear statement than the Commission on the relationship between trade secret protection and intellectual property by noting that it would proceed on the presumption that Microsoft's interoperability information was '*covered by intellectual property rights or constitute trade secrets and that those secrets must be treated as equivalent to intellectual property rights*'.[850]

It is not clear from the outset that trade secrets can be equated with intellectual property rights. In fact, trade secret protection has several characteristics that distinguish it from intellectual property law. First, trade secret protection is not yet harmonised in the European Union unlike many other forms of intellectual property protection. As discussed in section 5.3.3 above, the entry into force of the national provisions to be adopted in implementation of the Trade Secrets Directive will change this situation.

Second, the secret character of a trade secret stands in contrast to the disclosure of the invention that is required for obtaining patent protection. Since trade secret laws only protect information from being acquired by, disclosed to or used by others in an unlawful manner,[851] the protection cannot be invoked against the use of information or know-how obtained through legitimate means such as independent discovery or creation.[852] Unlike intellectual property rights which grant right holders an absolute exclusive right to prevent any third party from using the subject matter of protection without authorisation, trade secrets are only protected against unfair conduct.[853] The trade secret is not owned by its holder but merely offers a form of protection against conduct that affects its secrecy in an unlawful manner. For this reason, trade secrecy is regulated under unfair competition law in most countries and does not belong to the field of exclusive protection of intangible property.[854]

An additional difference between trade secret and intellectual property protection is that trade secrets do not necessarily involve innovation. As opposed to, for example, patent and copyright law which require, respectively, an inventive step and originality for an invention or creation to be protected, trade secret law does not guarantee that the underlying information is innovative. The main condition for trade secret protection is that the information is kept secret. As a result, the economic value of a trade secret does

---

849. Judgment in *Microsoft v. Commission*, T-201/04, ECLI:EU:T:2007:289, paras 283-284.
850. Judgment in *Microsoft v. Commission*, T-201/04, ECLI:EU:T:2007:289, par. 289.
851. Subsections 2-5 of Article 4 of the Trade Secrets Directive specify the circumstances in which the acquisition, use and disclosure of a trade secret is considered unlawful.
852. In Article 3 of the Trade Secrets Directive, situations are mentioned in which the acquisition, use and disclosure of a trade secret is considered lawful.
853. J. DREXL, 'Refusal to Grant Access to Trade Secrets as an Abuse of Market Dominance' in S. ANDERMAN AND A. EZRACHI (eds.), *Intellectual Property and Competition Law. New Frontiers*, Oxford University Press, 2011, (165), p. 178.
854. For an analysis of the nature of trade secret protection in the United States and several EU Member States, see G. SURBLYTE, *The Refusal to Disclose Trade Secrets as an Abuse of Market Dominance - Microsoft and Beyond* in J. DREXL (ed.) *Munich Series on European and International Competition Law*, 28, Berne Stämpfli Publishers Ltd., 2011, pp. 19-88.

not necessarily lie in the technological superiority of the underlying information but may also relate to the monopoly position that can be created and secured by keeping the information secret.[855]

The latter scenario seems to have occurred in the *Microsoft* case. Although Microsoft invoked patent and copyright protection for its interoperability information, those claims can be considered as doubtful. Microsoft identified at least one patent that its competitors would be infringing when implementing the interoperability information.[856] However, the fact that the relevant protocols remained unavailable to Microsoft's competitors in the work group server operating system market excludes the possibility that all the interfaces were covered by the patent. If the interoperability information was protected by the patent, it would have been publicly accessible considering that the patent process requires disclosure of the underlying invention.[857]

Copyright protection for software only extends to the expression of a computer program and does not cover the underlying ideas and principles, including those underlying its interfaces.[858] Beyond the unprotected ideas and principles, interoperability information is copyrightable as long as it can be regarded as original in the sense that it is the author's own intellectual creation.[859] Even if Microsoft's interfaces could be protected by copyright, it is unclear whether the introduction of non-Microsoft work group server operating systems compatible with Windows involved a reproduction of Microsoft's interoperability information. In the absence of such a reproduction, a copyright infringement cannot be established. In this regard, the Commission argued: '[n]ot only is it [...] possible to provide interface specifications without giving access to all implementation details, but it has been outlined above that it is common practice in the industry to do so'[860] and 'the specifications should [...] not be reproduced, adapted, arranged or altered, but should be used by third parties to write their own specification-compliant interfaces'.[861]

---

855. J. DREXL, 'Refusal to Grant Access to Trade Secrets as an Abuse of Market Dominance' in S. ANDERMAN AND A. EZRACHI (eds.), *Intellectual Property and Competition Law. New Frontiers*, Oxford University Press, 2011, (165), pp. 182-183.
856. Case COMP/C-3/37.792 - *Microsoft*, 24 March 2004, footnote 249 and Judgment in *Microsoft v. Commission*, T-201/04, ECLI:EU:T:2007:289, paras 270 and 278.
857. Microsoft itself made the statement that '[the] patented inventions are of course publicly disclosed as part of the patent process, but the protocols themselves remain highly proprietary and confidential' (Case COMP/C-3/37.792 - Microsoft, 24 March 2004, footnote 249).
858. Article 1(2) of Directive 2009/24/EC of the European Parliament and of the Council of 23 April 2009 on the legal protection of computer programs [2009] OJ L 111/16. With regard to the copyrightability of interoperability information, a distinction is made between interface implementations, which constitute a protectable expression as long as they meet the originality requirement, and interface specifications, which can be regarded as the rules and methods underlying an interface and therefore fall outside the scope of copyright protection. See P. SAMUELSON, T. VINJE AND W. CORNISH, 'Does Copyright Protection under the EU Software Directive Extend to Computer Program Behaviour, Languages and Interfaces?', *European Intellectual Property Review* 2012, vol. 34, no. 3, (158), p. 164 and Case COMP/C-3/37.792 - Microsoft, 24 March 2004, paras 24 and 570.
859. Article 1(3) of Directive 2009/24/EC of the European Parliament and of the Council of 23 April 2009 on the legal protection of computer programs [2009] OJ L 111/16.
860. Case COMP/C-3/37.792 - *Microsoft*, 24 March 2004, par. 571.
861. Case COMP/C-3/37.792 - *Microsoft*, 24 March 2004, par. 1004.

The General Court shared the Commission's view on the questionability of Microsoft's copyright claim.[862] Microsoft's own conduct of withholding the interoperability information from competitors indicates that its key intention was to secure the secrecy of the interfaces rather than to prevent or redress an infringement of patent and copyright law.[863] In that context, Microsoft contested the argument of the Commission that *'an undertaking suffers less damage when it discloses a business secret than when it is required to allow infringement of its patents or copyright'*.[864]

It also has to be noted that interoperability information does not necessarily involve innovation. Interfaces may even be seen as a mere by-product of computer programming. As such, the trade secret protection at issue in the *Microsoft* case did not seem to promote innovation but rather gave Microsoft the opportunity to build a dominant position in the market for work group server operating systems by keeping its protocols to itself once it had gained a stable position in that market.[865]

Intellectual property rights such as a patent or copyright encourage innovation by preventing third parties from copying the underlying subject matter. While the exclusivity of these intellectual property rights stimulates competitors to invent around the right holder's invention or creation, trade secret protection may rather encourage imitation because it allows third parties to copy the underlying subject matter in case they have unravelled the secret by way of, for example, independent discovery or reverse engineering.[866] Since trade secret protection does not depend on the fulfilment of qualitative requirements concerning the subject matter of protection but only requires that commercially valuable information is kept secret, it may more easily lead to competition problems. In this sense, a trade secret holder can rely on trade secrecy to protect its dominance in a market by refusing to share or disclose know-how with competitors. If independent discovery or reverse engineering is not successful, this may lead to non-innovative information being protected under trade secret law and shielded from competition for an infinite period of time. In these circumstances, there seems to be more room for competition law intervention.

In its Discussion Paper on the application of Article 102 TFEU to exclusionary abuses, the Commission indeed argued that it may not be appropriate to apply to

---

862. Judgment in *Microsoft v. Commission*, T-201/04, ECLI:EU:T:2007:289, par. 286.
863. See J. DREXL, 'Refusal to Grant Access to Trade Secrets as an Abuse of Market Dominance' in S. ANDERMAN AND A. EZRACHI (eds.), *Intellectual Property and Competition Law. New Frontiers*, Oxford University Press, 2011, (165), pp. 168-169 and G. SURBLYTE, 'The Refusal to Disclose Trade Secrets as an Abuse of Market Dominance - Microsoft and Beyond' in J. DREXL (ed.) *Munich Series on European and International Competition Law*, 28, Berne Stämpfli Publishers Ltd., 2011, p. 15. With regard to the validity of Microsoft's patent claim, it is notable that the General Court stated that it was only a few weeks before the adoption of the Commission decision and at the Commission's insistence that Microsoft identified a patent (Judgment in *Microsoft v. Commission*, T-201/04, ECLI:EU:T:2007:289, par. 278).
864. Judgment in *Microsoft v. Commission*, T-201/04, ECLI:EU:T:2007:289, par. 273.
865. G. SURBLYTE, 'The Refusal to Disclose Trade Secrets as an Abuse of Market Dominance - Microsoft and Beyond' in J. DREXL (ed.) *Munich Series on European and International Competition Law*, 28, Berne Stämpfli Publishers Ltd., 2011, p. 7.
866. G. SURBLYTE, 'The Refusal to Disclose Trade Secrets as an Abuse of Market Dominance - Microsoft and Beyond' in J. DREXL (ed.) *Munich Series on European and International Competition Law*, 28, Berne Stämpfli Publishers Ltd., 2011, p. 179.

refusals to give access to trade secrets the same high standards for intervention as those which are developed for refusals to license intellectual property rights.[867] In the appeal procedure before the General Court, the Commission also stated that Microsoft may not be correct to equate trade secrets with intellectual property rights considering that '*the protection that such secrets enjoy under national law is normally more limited than that given to copyright or patents*'. With regard to the factual scenario of *Microsoft*, the Commission pointed out that '*the value of the "secret" concerned lies not in the fact that it involves innovation but in the fact that it belongs to a dominant undertaking*'.[868] Despite these statements of the Commission, the General Court treated trade secrets as equivalent to intellectual property rights.

In the Guidance Paper on exclusionary conduct under Article 102 TFEU that was adopted after the public consultation following the issuance of the Discussion paper and after the General Court delivered its judgment in *Microsoft*, the Commission did not separately mention trade secrets anymore and merely referred to refusals to give access to interoperability information as a subcategory of refusals to license intellectual property rights.[869] Although there does not seem to be a need for a different or lower standard of intervention for refusals to give access to trade secrets, the characteristics of trade secret protection should be taken into account when applying the conditions of the essential facilities doctrine to a refusal to disclose a trade secret. In particular, it must be kept in mind that the information underlying a trade secret does not necessarily involve innovation and that trade secret protection may lead to the control of information on which competitors are dependent for being able to enter a market.[870] While the European Commission and the General Court have not explicitly taken into account the effects of trade secret protection in the *Microsoft* case, an adequate outcome was reached by recognising the importance of interoperability information for competition *in* the market for work group server operating systems.

Another form of protection which does not in itself promote innovation is the sui generis database right introduced by the Database Directive. As discussed in section 5.3.2 above, the Directive has created an exclusive right for producers of databases, valid for fifteen years, to protect their investment in terms of time, effort, energy and financial resources irrespective of whether the database is innovative in character. These so-called non-original databases benefit from sui generis protection as long as the database maker can show that '*there has been qualitatively and/or quantitatively a substantial investment in either the obtaining, verification or presentation of the*

---

867. DG Competition discussion paper on the application of Article 82 of the Treaty to exclusionary abuses, December 2005, par. 242. See also the discussion in T. KÄSEBERG, *Intellectual Property, Antitrust and Cumulative Innovation in the EU and the US*, Hart Publishing, 2012, pp. 125-126.
868. Judgment in *Microsoft v. Commission*, T-201/04, ECLI:EU:T:2007:289, par. 280.
869. Communication from the Commission — Guidance on the Commission's enforcement priorities in applying Article 82 of the EC Treaty to abusive exclusionary conduct by dominant undertakings (Guidance Paper) [2009] OJ C 45/7, par. 78. See also the discussion in T. KÄSEBERG, *Intellectual Property, Antitrust and Cumulative Innovation in the EU and the US*, Hart Publishing, 2012, pp. 125-126.
870. J. DREXL, 'Refusal to Grant Access to Trade Secrets as an Abuse of Market Dominance' in S. ANDERMAN AND A. EZRACHI (eds.), *Intellectual Property and Competition Law. New Frontiers*, Oxford University Press, 2011, (165), p. 183.

contents'.[871] Unlike patents and copyrights which protect inventiveness and creativeness by requiring, respectively, an inventive step or originality to qualify for protection, the sui generis database right does not provide incentives for innovation but rather protects the investments of database producers against free-riding by third parties. To that end, the Database Directive provides for a right for the maker of the database *'to prevent extraction and/or re-utilization of the whole or of a substantial part, evaluated qualitatively and/or quantitatively, of the contents of that database'.*[872]

By excluding third parties from extracting and re-utilising data, the sui generis database right may give rise to competition problems in cases where a database is the only possible source of the information contained therein. Whereas copyright protects the original expression of an idea and leaves untreated facts and ideas in the public domain, the sui generis database right entitles a database maker to exclude others from re-utilising mere factual information and data.[873] To mitigate this risk, recital 47 of the Database Directive makes clear that *'protection by the sui generis right must not be afforded in such a way as to facilitate abuses of a dominant position'* and that *'the provisions of this Directive are without prejudice to the application of Community or national competition rules'.*[874] In addition, the Court of Justice interpreted the sui generis right restrictively by excluding investment in the creation of data from the scope of protection.[875] The Court argued that only investment in the obtaining, verification or presentation of pre-existing contents can be taken into account when assessing whether the required substantial investment has been made.

By ruling that the creation of data cannot count towards substantial investment, the Court reduced the likelihood that so-called single-source databases where the data is created by the same entity as the entity that establishes the database attract sui generis protection.[876] Because of the restrictive interpretation that the Court has given to the scope of the sui generis database right, potential competition problems relating to situations where a database maker can prevent others from re-utilising

---

871. Article 7(1) of the Database Directive. According to Article 3(1), original databases which *'by reason of the selection or arrangement of their contents, constitute the author's own intellectual creation'* are protected by copyright.
872. Article 7(1) of the Database Directive.
873. P.B. HUGENHOLTZ, 'Abuse of Database Right: Sole-Source Information Banks under the EU Database Directive' in F. LÉVÊQUE AND H.A. SHELANSKI (eds.), *Antitrust, Patents and Copyright: EU and US Perspectives*, Edward Elgar, 2005, (203), p. 203.
874. See I. LIANOS, 'Competition Law and Intellectual Property Rights: Is the Property Rights' Approach Right?' in J. BELL AND C. KILPATRICK (eds.), *The Cambridge Yearbook of European Legal Studies. Volume 8*, 2005-2006, (153), pp. 174-175 who discusses the restrictive interpretation that the Court of Justice has given to the scope of protection of the sui generis database right in order to prevent anticompetitive effects from occurring. See also section 5.3.2 above.
875. Judgment in Fixtures Marketing Ltd v. Oy Veikkaus Ab, C-46/02, ECLI:EU:C:2004:694, par. 34; Judgment in The British Horseracing Board Ltd and Others v. William Hill Organization Ltd, C-203/02, ECLI:EU:C:2004:695, par. 31; Judgment in Fixtures Marketing Ltd v. Svenska Spel AB, C-338/02, ECLI:EU:C:2004:696, par. 24; Judgment in Fixtures Marketing Ltd v. Organismos prognostikon agonon podosfairou AE (OPAP), C-444/02, ECLI:EU:C:2004:697, par. 40.
876. EUROPEAN COMMISSION, 'DG Internal Market and Services Working Paper. First evaluation of Directive 96/9/EC on the legal protection of databases', 12 December 2005, pp. 14-15, available at http://ec.europa.eu/internal_market/copyright/docs/databases/evaluation_report_en.pdf.

self-generated information contained in a database have also been mitigated.[877] Nevertheless, a database consisting of self-created data can still obtain protection under the sui generis database right if a substantial investment has been made in either the verification or the presentation of its content. A database maker creating its own data may get around the restrictive interpretation of the scope of protection of the sui generis database right by the Court of Justice by clearly differentiating investment in creating data from subsequent investment in the verification or presentation of the data through the introduction of separate procedural systems.[878] Therefore, competition issues are not completely excluded. The fact that the sui generis database right protects investment and not innovation should be taken into account when assessing refusals to license such rights as well as the higher probability of anticompetitive effects as compared to intellectual property rights that promote innovation.

As a conclusion of this section, it is submitted that there is no convincing economic basis for treating refusals to license intellectual property rights or trade secrets differently than refusals to deal in general. Nevertheless, one should take into account the peculiarities of the respective form of protection in a specific case, in particular when trade secret or sui generis database protection are involved considering that both do not necessarily encourage innovation and may in some circumstances even give rise to competition problems of themselves.

6.8 A PROPOSED FRAMEWORK FOR THE APPLICATION OF THE ESSENTIAL FACILITIES DOCTRINE

After devoting attention to market definition and assessment of dominance, the framework set out below distinguishes between three different scenarios as regards essential facilities cases: absolute refusals to deal involving inputs which the dominant undertaking has not previously supplied to others (section 6.8.2), disruptions of existing levels of supply (section 6.8.3) and discriminatory conditions of supply (section 6.8.4).[879]

In addition to this three-part typology, two other differentiations can be made with respect to refusals to deal. While most essential facilities cases involve unilateral decisions of dominant undertakings to refuse to deal, it is also possible that two or more firms team up together and engage in a concerted action not to do business with a certain party. The latter is referred to as a 'collective' refusal to deal and may also give rise to coordination concerns under Article 101 TFEU. Such concerns are not addressed in this book. Next to outright refusals to deal whereby the dominant undertaking does

---

877. E. DERCLAYE, 'The Court of Justice Interprets the Database Sui Generis Right for the First Time', *European Law Review* 2005, vol. 30, no. 3, (420), p. 428.
878. M.J. DAVISON AND P.B. HUGENHOLTZ, 'Football Fixtures, Horseraces and Spin Offs: The ECJ Domesticates the Database Right', *European Intellectual Property Review* 2005, vol. 27, no. 3, (113), p. 116.
879. The same categorisation of refusals to deal has been made by the European Commission in its 1998 Access Notice applicable to the telecommunications sector (see Notice on the application of the competition rules to access agreements in the telecommunications sector - framework, relevant markets and principles [1998] OJ C 265/2, par. 84).

not supply at all or even refuses to negotiate about supply, constructive or indirect refusals to deal can be distinguished which, in the words of the European Commission, may *'take the form of unduly delaying or otherwise degrading the supply of the product or involve the imposition of unreasonable conditions in return for the supply'*.[880]

Since the analysis of potential anticompetitive exclusionary effects of collective and unilateral refusals to supply is similar, no further attention will be paid to this distinction. Discriminatory refusals to deal and margin squeezes can be regarded as constructive refusals to deal and are discussed in section 6.8.4. If a constructive refusal to deal forms part of a wider tying or bundling strategy which aims to exclude rivals from the market, the anticompetitive nature of the behaviour may rather be found in those latter practices than in the indispensability of the input that is withheld. Application of the essential facilities doctrine may for that reason not lead to the identification of abusive conduct in those cases.[881]

6.8.1 Market Definition and Dominance in Essential Facilities Cases

Market definition is different for the application of the essential facilities doctrine than for the assessment of other types of abusive conduct or for the review of mergers. The conduct that the essential facilities doctrine aims to redress under the current legal standards in the European Union is the leveraging of market power from the main market in which the holder of the essential facility is dominant to a derivative market in which it tries to strengthen its current market position by refusing to (continue to) supply a competitor (that wants to become) active in that market. As a result, in essential facilities cases two related relevant markets have to be defined. The approach of the European Commission and the EU courts towards market definition in essential facilities cases has been consistent up to the *Microsoft* case.

Before *Microsoft*, the upstream or primary market had been defined in such a way as to contain the product or service to which access was requested. The downstream or secondary market in its turn comprised the derivative product or service that would be offered by the access seeker once it was given access to the necessary input.[882] As an illustration, the primary market in *Magill* comprised the listings of television programmes to which Magill asked access in order to be able to publish a weekly television guide, the secondary market. Similarly, in *IMS Health* the copyrighted brick structure developed by IMS which divided Germany in 1860 districts constituted the primary market, while the service of providing pharmaceutical companies with data on the sale of pharmaceutical products formed the secondary market in which NDC wanted to

---

880. Communication from the Commission — Guidance on the Commission's enforcement priorities in applying Article 82 of the EC Treaty to abusive exclusionary conduct by dominant undertakings (Guidance Paper) [2009] OJ C 45/7, par. 79.
881. For a further description of these additional distinctions with regard to refusals to deal, see T. Käseberg, *Intellectual Property, Antitrust and Cumulative Innovation in the EU and the US*, Hart Publishing, 2012, pp. 102, 103 and 106.
882. L. Hou, 'The Essential Facilities Doctrine – What Was Wrong in Microsoft?', *International Review of Intellectual Property and Competition Law* 2012, vol. 43, no. 4, (451), pp. 463-464.

compete with IMS. Since the brick structure of IMS had become the industry standard, NDC argued that access to the system was indispensable to be able to compete with IMS in the downstream market.

The scenario at issue in *IMS Health* differs in one aspect from the facts of the *Magill* case. The Irish broadcasting stations in the *Magill* case had already provided their programme listings to newspapers prior to Magill's request for a copyright licence as a result of which it was clear that the broadcasting stations were able and willing to offer the television listings to third parties as a separate product. It was therefore logical to define an upstream market for television listings even though the newspapers were provided with a copyright licence free of charge and a market for the programme listings in the strict sense of the word did not yet exist. In *IMS Health*, the definition of an upstream market for the 1860 brick structure was more controversial because IMS had not provided any third party access to its system before NDC requested a licence. IMS only relied upon the brick structure in supplying regional sales data to pharmaceutical companies.[883]

In its *IMS Health* judgment, the Court of Justice made clear that the fact that the requested input has never been marketed separately does not preclude the possibility of identifying a separate relevant market for the input or of applying the essential facilities doctrine altogether. To this end, the Court referred to the *Bronner* judgment in which an upstream relevant market for home delivery of daily newspapers was defined even though Mediaprint had not marketed its home-delivery scheme as a separate product.[884] In the Court's view, it therefore appeared that, for the purposes of the application of the earlier case law, the identification of a potential or even a hypothetical market is sufficient which is the case *'where the products or services are indispensable in order to carry on a particular business and where there is an actual demand for them on the part of undertakings which seek to carry on the business for which they are indispensable'*.[885] The Court went on to explain that *'it is determinative that two different stages of production may be identified and that they are interconnected, inasmuch as the upstream product is indispensable for the supply of the downstream product'*.[886] In other words, an upstream market for the input can be defined as long as the access seeker is able to show that it needs the input in order to compete on a related downstream market.

As a consequence, it is possible for a competition authority or court to oblige a dominant undertaking under the essential facilities doctrine in the European Union to provide third parties access to a necessary input which merely constitutes an

---

883. See also the opinion of Advocate General Tizzano in *IMS Health* who argued that it was already clear from the *Magill* and *Bronner* judgments that in order to identify an upstream market, the Court of Justice does not deem it necessary that the requested input be autonomously marketed by the dominant undertaking (Opinion of Advocate General Tizzano in *IMS Health GmbH & Co. OHG v. NDC Health GmbH & Co. KG*, C-418/01, ECLI:EU:C:2003:537, par. 56).

884. Judgment in *IMS Health GmbH & Co. OHG v. NDC Health GmbH & Co. KG*, C-418/01, ECLI:EU:C:2004:257, paras 42-43.

885. Judgment in *IMS Health GmbH & Co. OHG v. NDC Health GmbH & Co. KG*, C-418/01, ECLI:EU:C:2004:257, par. 44.

886. Judgment in *IMS Health GmbH & Co. OHG v. NDC Health GmbH & Co. KG*, C-418/01, ECLI:EU:C:2004:257, par. 45.

intermediary product and has never been marketed independently. In its Guidance Paper on exclusionary conduct under Article 102 TFEU, the European Commission relied on the *IMS Health* judgment when making clear that it does not regard it as necessary for the refused product to have been already traded. According to the Commission, '*it is sufficient that there is demand from potential purchasers and that a potential market for the input at stake can be identified*'.[887] The US Supreme Court, to the contrary, does not seem to be willing to hold monopolists liable for refusing to supply a product which has not been marketed before. One of the grounds on the basis of which the Supreme Court denied antitrust liability in *Trinko* was that the systems to which Verizon had to offer its rivals access were not otherwise marketed or available to the public but existed '*only deep within the bowels of Verizon*'.[888]

Criticism has been expressed by commentators that the concept of potential or hypothetical markets is so broad as to open the door to access requests which will change existing market structures and undermine investments in cases where the requested input has not been marketed independently before.[889] With regard to intellectual property rights, it is argued that although a licence can always be 'hypothetically' marketed independently from the product or service in which it is incorporated, this does not imply that an upstream licensing market actually exists.[890] In addition, it has been pointed out that such an interpretation would lead to situations in which a right holder can be forced to license the intellectual property right as a separate product even though it may not be rational to do so and that this may discourage dominant firms from investing in new production processes.[891]

While it is a far-reaching interference in the business model of an undertaking to require it to start marketing an input as a stand-alone product, such interventions should be possible because otherwise perverse incentives are created for dominant firms to prevent an enforcement action by deciding not to market an input that is indispensable for competitors as a separate product. To ensure as much as possible that the benefits of the imposition of such a duty to deal outweigh the negative effects, competition authorities and courts should not force dominant undertakings to market a necessary input independently when this is not technically or commercially viable. Examples of such situations may involve cases where it would be very costly for the dominant undertaking to 'unbundle' the input from the final product or where congestion may occur once the facility is shared with third parties.

---

887. Communication from the Commission — Guidance on the Commission's enforcement priorities in applying Article 82 of the EC Treaty to abusive exclusionary conduct by dominant undertakings (Guidance Paper) [2009] OJ C 45/7, par. 79.
888. Verizon Communications v. Law Offices of Curtis V. Trinko, LLP (Trinko), 540 U.S. 398 (2004), at 410. See also T. KÄSEBERG, Intellectual Property, Antitrust and Cumulative Innovation in the EU and the US, Hart Publishing, 2012, p. 186.
889. L. HOU, 'The Essential Facilities Doctrine – What Was Wrong in Microsoft?', *International Review of Intellectual Property and Competition Law* 2012, vol. 43, no. 4, (451), p. 456.
890. B. CONDE GALLEGO, 'Unilateral Refusal to License Indispensable Intellectual Property Rights – US and EU Approaches' in J. DREXL (ed.), *Research Handbook on Intellectual Property and Competition Law*, Edward Elgar Publishing, 2008, (215), pp. 226-228.
891. D. GERADIN, 'Limiting the Scope of Article 82 EC: What Can the EU Learn from the U.S. Supreme Court's Judgment in *Trinko* in the Wake of *Microsoft*, *IMS*, and *Deutsche Telekom*?', *Common Market Law Review* 2004, vol. 41, no. 6, (1519), p. 1530.

It is important to note that the concept of hypothetical or potential markets makes it possible for access seekers to compete with the dominant undertaking in a horizontal way. If an input is regarded as constituting the upstream market even though it is not marketed independently, a successful access seeker will be able to compete with the dominant undertaking on the only 'real' market at issue. In the *IMS Health* case, where the 1860 brick structure of IMS was held to form the upstream market, such a scenario occurred. IMS had not traded or granted third parties access to the system prior to NDC's request for a licence and only used the brick structure as a way to supply the pharmaceutical companies with relevant sales data. The imposition of a duty to license would therefore have had the effect of enabling NDC to compete directly with IMS in the provision of data on the sale of pharmaceutical products.[892] Whereas the essential facilities doctrine could formerly only be applied to launch vertical and indirect competition, the introduction of the concept of hypothetical or potential markets in *IMS Health* makes it possible for a duty to deal to give rise to horizontal or direct competition.

The *Microsoft* case revolved around the refusal of Microsoft to give competitors access to interoperability information which would allow them to introduce non-Microsoft work group server operating systems for Microsoft's client PC operating system Windows. Unlike in earlier cases where the definition of the upstream market was based on the input being requested, the European Commission did not define a market for interoperability information or, more broadly, for interoperability with Windows. Instead, the Commission relied upon client PC operating systems as the main market.[893] It is unclear why the Commission deviated from the earlier practice of taking the requested input as a starting point for the definition of the main market. In its decision, the Commission merely stated that, with regard to the refusal to license, the following two markets were relevant: the market for client PC operating systems which forms the main market and the market for work group server operating systems which constitutes the derivative market.[894]

Since Microsoft had previously provided third parties access to its interoperability information, it would have been possible for the Commission to define a market for interoperability considering that supply and demand for the information existed. The problem may have laid with the fact that interoperability is a matter of degree rather than a black-and-white concept which makes the process of market definition more complex.[895] In particular, the definition of a relevant market for interoperability with

---

892. See A. VAN ROOIJEN, 'The Software Interface between Copyright and Competition Law. A Legal Analysis of Interoperability in Computer Programs' in P.B. HUGENHOLTZ (ed.) *Information Law Series*, Kluwer Law International 2010, p. 130.

893. Since the *Microsoft* case did not concern two markets in a vertical relationship but two neighbouring markets, the terms 'main' and 'derivative' market are used instead of 'upstream' and 'downstream' market or 'primary' and 'secondary' market.

894. Case COMP/C-3/37.792 - *Microsoft*, 24 March 2004, par. 323. The third market defined in the decision, the market for streaming media players, was only relevant for assessing the behaviour of Microsoft consisting of the tying of Windows Media Player to Windows.

895. See L. HOU, 'The Essential Facilities Doctrine – What Was Wrong in Microsoft?', *International Review of Intellectual Property and Competition Law* 2012, vol. 43, no. 4, (451), p. 464 who argues that the fact that the Commission did not define the main market on the basis of the

Windows would have required the Commission to decide which levels of interoperability should be regarded as substitutable to one another.[896]

An alternative explanation for why the Commission chose not to base the relevant market on the interoperability information might be found in the peculiar nature of interoperability which connects markets in a 'two-way' manner. Unlike the usual scenario in which the requested input can only be used to create competing products at one level in the value chain, the sharing of interoperability information with third parties may affect two levels of business activity. In this sense, the interoperability information to be licensed by Microsoft could not only be used by competitors to launch non-Microsoft work group server operating systems but also, even though it was not at issue in the case, non-Microsoft client PC operating systems.[897]

In addition, the Commission may have chosen to focus on client PC operating systems as the main market and on work group server operating systems as the derivative market due to the strong links between these two products.[898] Nevertheless, an upstream market definition that is based on the input to which access is being requested should remain the rule in essential facilities cases because such an approach forces competition authorities and courts to assess at the outset of a case whether the facility deemed essential by the access seeker is capable of being sold as an independent product on a given market.

For determining the scope of the two relevant markets in essential facilities cases, the approach generally employed for market definition in competition cases can be applied. For defining the boundaries of the upstream market, it has to be assessed which products or services, if any, are substitutable to the input requested by the access seeker. Market definition of the downstream market involves an analysis of whether the product or service that the access seeker would like to offer once given access to the requested input has any substitutes. One should note, however, that market definition in the context of the application of the essential facilities doctrine often amounts to an artificial exercise. This is because the definition of an upstream market for a product that has not yet been traded before can only be based on

interoperability information being requested resulted in the broadening of the conditions of indispensability and elimination of competition on a secondary market.

896. The European Commission and the General Court did consider the required degree of interoperability when assessing the indispensability of the interoperability information (Case COMP/C-3/37.792 - *Microsoft*, 24 March 2004, paras 33, 666-692 and 743-763; and Judgment in *Microsoft v. Commission*, T-201/04, ECLI:EU:T:2007:289, par. 207-245). For an analysis, see P. LAROUCHE, 'The European Microsoft Case at the Crossroads of Competition Policy and Innovation', *Antitrust Law Journal* 2008, vol. 75, no. 3, (601), pp. 609-610.

897. See section 6.6.2 above.

898. Case COMP/C-3/37.792 - Microsoft, 24 March 2004, par. 526: the client PC and work group server operating system markets 'are closely associated through commercial and technical links. Therefore, an isolated analysis of the competitive conditions on the market for work group server operating systems - ignoring Microsoft's overwhelming dominance in the neighbouring client PC operating system market - fails to deliver an accurate picture of Microsoft's true market power. Indeed, Microsoft's dominance over the client PC operating system market has a significant impact on the adjacent market for operating systems for work group servers'.

assumptions on how the market could be structured instead of on concrete market evidence relating to supply and demand as in usual circumstances.[899]

In accordance with the Commission notice on market definition, firms are subject to three types of competitive constraints which should be taken into account when defining a relevant market. Whereas demand-side substitutability is the most relevant indicator of market definition, constraints arising from supply-side substitutability and potential competition can also play a role when the analysis of demand-side substitution is inconclusive. For examining demand-side substitutability, the question is whether the access seeker and other potential customers of the requested input can switch to readily available substitutes. Supply-side substitutability involves an assessment of whether the essential facility holder and other potential suppliers are able to easily switch production to other products and market them in the relevant market. Constraints arising from potential competition are only scrutinised in exceptional circumstances and after the relevant market has already been ascertained.[900]

The definition of the upstream market is key to the assessment of dominance of the essential facility holder. The likelihood of finding dominance increases the narrower the market is defined. When no dominance is found on the upstream market, the refusal to deal cannot be held abusive. The boundaries of the downstream market have to be set in order to be able to assess the abusive nature of the refusal to deal, because one of the exceptional circumstances that have to be present for establishing a violation of Article 102 TFEU is the exclusion of all effective competition on the downstream market.

The relevant market on which the essential facility holder has to be found dominant is the upstream market. If there is no existing substitute for the requested input and if it is unlikely that a substitute will become available in the near future, the dominance of the owner of the essential facility is established as such. When substitutes to the requested input are offered on the relevant market, the market power of the holder of the essential facility has to be measured by analysing the actual and potential competition from third parties.

As discussed in Part I, instead of solely relying on market shares as an indicator of dominance in dynamic markets the European Commission is also increasingly taking into account potential competition and recent entry when assessing whether an undertaking holds a dominant position on a given market.[901] An assessment of potential competition may be particularly relevant in cases where the requested input has not yet been provided as an independent product and a market for the input does not yet exist. In the absence of potential competition, dominance will in such situations usually be given with the fact that the requested input is considered to form a relevant market of its own because no other firm has already traded the input on a market.

---

899. P. LAROUCHE, *Competition Law and Regulation in European Telecommunications*, Hart Publishing, 2000, pp. 207 and 212.
900. Commission Notice on the definition of relevant market for the purposes of Community competition law [1997] OJ C 372/5, paras 13-24.
901. See section 4.4.2 above.

With regard to inputs protected by intellectual property law, it is important to note that the grant of an intellectual property right does not in itself lead to dominance.[902] While an intellectual property right gives rise to exclusivity, this does not equal with a dominant position on a given market because consumers may regard other products in which the intellectual property right at stake is not incorporated as substitutes.

6.8.2 Absolute Refusals to Supply

Absolute refusals to supply are understood in this book as refusals whereby the essential facility holder has not given any other undertaking access to the requested input. The proposed framework for assessing absolute refusals to deal starts from the current four-prong exceptional circumstances test set out in European Union case law: (1) the refusal relates to a product or service indispensable to the exercise of a particular activity on a downstream market; (2) the refusal is of such a kind as to exclude any effective competition on that downstream market; (3) the refusal prevents the appearance of a new product for which there is potential consumer demand; and (4) there is no objective justification for the refusal.[903]

6.8.2.1 Indispensability

The requirement of indispensability of the requested input can be considered as consisting of two different elements: (1) the objective necessity of the input for being able to compete on the downstream market; and (2) the absence of economically viable substitutes for the input.

The purpose of the first element of the indispensability test is to examine the relationship between the input and the product or service that the requesting undertaking would like to introduce on the downstream market once given access to the input. Whether access to a certain input is objectively necessary can normally be easily established by applying common knowledge of the sector concerned.[904] For example, in *Tiercé Ladbroke* it was quite uncontroversial for the General Court to point out that the television broadcasting of horse races is not indispensable for the taking of bets on horse races. In particular, the Court stated: *'transmission is not indispensable, since it takes place after bets are placed, with the result that its absence does not in itself affect the choices made by bettors and, accordingly, cannot prevent bookmakers from pursuing*

---

902. The Court of Justice explicitly stated in Magill: 'So far as dominant position is concerned, it is to be remembered at the outset that mere ownership of an intellectual property right cannot confer such a position' (Judgment in Telefis Eireann and Independent Television Publications Ltd v. Commission of the European Communities (Magill), Joined cases C-241/91 and C-242/91, ECLI:EU:C:1995:98, par. 46).
903. These are the four exceptional circumstances as reproduced by the General Court in Judgment in *Microsoft v. Commission*, T-201/04, ECLI:EU:T:2007:289, paras 332-333.
904. L. Hou, 'The Essential Facilities Doctrine – What Was Wrong in Microsoft?', *International Review of Intellectual Property and Competition Law* 2012, vol. 43, no. 4, (451), p. 458.

their business'.[905] The refusal of a transmission licence to a Belgian bookmaking company for broadcasting French horse races did for that reason not constitute abuse of dominance in the Court's view.

The second element of indispensability seeks to examine whether actual or potential substitutes for the input exist. The analysis to be conducted in this regard has similarities to market definition in the sense that both types of assessments involve an evaluation of the substitutability of the input with alternative products or services. The statements that the Court of Justice made in *Bronner* illustrate the overlap between the market definition exercise and the indispensability test. With regard to the definition of the relevant market, the Court made clear that it was for the national court to determine *'whether home-delivery schemes constitute a separate market, or whether other methods of distributing daily newspapers, such as sale in shops or at kiosks or delivery by post, are sufficiently interchangeable with them to have to be taken into account also'*.[906] In the subsequent analysis of whether access to Mediaprint's home-delivery scheme was indispensable, the Court argued that one of the factors to be considered is the availability of these other methods of distributing daily newspapers: *'it is undisputed that other methods of distributing daily newspapers, such as by post and through sale in shops and at kiosks, even though they may be less advantageous for the distribution of certain newspapers, exist and are used by the publishers of those daily newspapers'*.[907]

The question is whether there is a difference in the degree of substitutability required for defining the relevant market on the one hand, and for establishing the indispensability of the input on the other hand. The fact that the Court considered the distribution of newspapers by post and through sale in shops and at kiosks as sufficiently substitutable in the context of the indispensability test *'even though they are less advantageous for the distribution of certain newspapers'* indicates that a lesser degree of substitutability may be required in assessing the indispensability of an input as compared to the degree of substitutability needed for including products or services in the same relevant market.[908]

Further evidence for the close connection between the market definition exercise and the indispensability test can be found in *IMS Health* in which the Court of Justice seems to regard the indispensability of the requested input as an aspect to be taken into account in the definition of the upstream relevant market. The Court held that it is sufficient that a potential or hypothetical upstream market can be identified which is the case *'where the products or services are indispensable in order to carry on a particular business'* and that *'it is determinative that two different stages of production may be identified and that they are interconnected, inasmuch as the upstream product*

---

905. Judgment in *Tiercé Ladbroke v. Commission*, T-504/93, ECLI:EU:T:1997:84, par. 132.
906. Judgment in *Oscar Bronner GmbH & Co. KG v. Mediaprint Zeitungs*, C-7/97, ECLI:EU:C:1998:569, par. 34.
907. Judgment in *Oscar Bronner GmbH & Co. KG v. Mediaprint Zeitungs*, C-7/97, ECLI:EU:C:1998:569, par. 43.
908. E. ROUSSEVA, *Rethinking Exclusionary Abuses in EU Competition Law*, Hart Publishing, 2010, pp. 115-117.

is indispensable for the supply of the downstream product'.[909] When defining potential or hypothetical upstream markets, the indispensability of the requested input may thus determine the scope of the upstream relevant market.[910]

The Court of Justice made clear in *Bronner* that, in addition to the absence of readily available substitutes, it has to be established that *'there are no technical, legal or even economic obstacles capable of making it impossible, or even unreasonably difficult'*, for the requesting undertaking to produce a substitute, either alone or in cooperation with others.[911] While it is not sufficient that duplication would be difficult or expensive, absolute impossibility is not required.[912] The economic viability of duplication is the main factor to be considered in determining whether the creation of a substitute is a realistic potential alternative to granting access to the requested input.

It is important to note that the Court of Justice in *Bronner* referred not to the feasibility of setting up a second home-delivery scheme with a small circulation of daily newspapers to be distributed but to the creation of a scheme for the distribution of newspapers with a circulation comparable to that of Mediaprint.[913] As a result, in order to accept the existence of economic obstacles it must be established that duplication of the requested input *'is not economically viable for production on a scale comparable to that of the undertaking which controls the existing product or service'*.[914] In this regard, the European Commission stated in its Guidance Paper on exclusionary conduct under Article 102 TFEU that it *'will normally make an assessment of whether competitors could effectively duplicate the input produced by the dominant undertaking in the foreseeable future'* and that *'an input is likely to be impossible to replicate when it involves a natural monopoly due to scale or scope economies, where there are strong network effects or when it concerns so-called "single source" information'*.[915]

The presence of switching costs may also be of relevance as evidenced by *IMS Health*. The Court of Justice argued that the degree of participation by users in the development of the copyrighted 1860 brick structure of IMS and the outlay, particularly in terms of costs, on the part of potential users in order to work with an alternative structure were factors to be taken into account by the national court in determining whether access to the brick structure of IMS was indispensable. The Court stated that the high level of participation by the pharmaceutical companies in the improvement of

---

909. Judgment in *IMS Health GmbH & Co. OHG v. NDC Health GmbH & Co. KG*, C-418/01, ECLI:EU:C:2004:257, paras 44-45.
910. E. Rousseva, Rethinking Exclusionary Abuses in EU Competition Law, Hart Publishing, 2010, p. 119.
911. Judgment in *Oscar Bronner GmbH & Co. KG v. Mediaprint Zeitungs*, C-7/97, ECLI:EU:C:1998:569, par. 44.
912. See also Communication from the Commission — Guidance on the Commission's enforcement priorities in applying Article 82 of the EC Treaty to abusive exclusionary conduct by dominant undertakings (Guidance Paper) [2009] OJ C 45/7, par. 83.
913. Judgment in *Oscar Bronner GmbH & Co. KG v. Mediaprint Zeitungs*, C-7/97, ECLI:EU:C:1998:569, paras 45-46.
914. Judgment in *IMS Health GmbH & Co. OHG v. NDC Health GmbH & Co. KG*, C-418/01, ECLI:EU:C:2004:257, par. 28.
915. Communication from the Commission — Guidance on the Commission's enforcement priorities in applying Article 82 of the EC Treaty to abusive exclusionary conduct by dominant undertakings (Guidance Paper) [2009] OJ C 45/7, par. 83 and footnote 3.

the brick structure of IMS had created a dependency in regard to that structure as a consequence of which those companies would have to make significant efforts in order to be able to use a different brick structure. In that light, the Court argued that *'[t]he supplier of that alternative structure might therefore be obliged to offer terms which are such as to rule out any economic viability of business on a scale comparable to that of the undertaking which controls the protected structure'*.[916]

Although there is a degree of overlap between the market definition exercise and the requirement of indispensability of the requested input, there is sufficient reason to retain the latter as an independent condition under the essential facilities doctrine. It can be noted in this perspective that the objective necessity of the input, which constitutes the first element of indispensability, does not play a role in the determination of relevant markets. This component of indispensability aims to establish whether access to the input is needed for being able to compete on the downstream market. The fact that a company is found to hold a dominant position on the upstream relevant market for the input does not necessarily entail that access to the input is required for developing the product or service that the requesting undertaking would like to introduce on the downstream market. The *Tiercé Ladbroke* case in which broadcasting of horse races was not considered to be indispensable for a bookmaking company to be able to take bets on horse races serves as an illustration.

With respect to the second element of indispensability, the degree of substitutability to be applied seems higher in the context of the indispensability test as compared to the market definition exercise as a result of which the overlap between the two types of assessments is not complete. Even if the holder of the input is considered to hold a dominant position on the upstream relevant market, the input may nevertheless not meet the indispensability test in case duplication of the input is economically viable or an alternative to the input held by the dominant firm is anticipated to become available in the foreseeable future. In the latter situation, the upstream relevant market is currently not sufficiently competitive to prevent a finding of dominance but is expected to tend towards competition in the medium term so that the requested input cannot be considered indispensable. Such a requirement of indispensability that takes the dynamic nature of the industry into account reduces the risk that an obligation to give access to the requested input undermines the incentives of competitors to invest in developing alternatives to be introduced in the upstream relevant market.[917]

---

916. Judgment in *IMS Health GmbH & Co. OHG v. NDC Health GmbH & Co. KG*, C-418/01, ECLI:EU:C:2004:257, paras 29-30.
917. See T. Käseberg, *Intellectual Property, Antitrust and Cumulative Innovation in the EU and the US*, Hart Publishing, 2012, pp. 157-158 who suggests to rely on a period of two years for assessing the indispensability of an input in order to align the essential facilities doctrine with merger review and with the three-criteria test in sector-specific electronic communications regulation where the same time horizon is applied.

6.8.2.2 Exclusion of All Effective Competition on the Downstream Market

The second condition of the essential facilities doctrine requires that the refusal to supply excludes all effective competition on the downstream market. The way in which this requirement has been applied in previous essential facilities cases on EU level indicates that the relevant issue is whether the essential facility holder reserves the downstream market to itself by denying a competitor access to the requested input. In the context of the application of the condition of exclusion of effective competition in *Magill*, the Court of Justice explicitly stated that the Irish broadcasting stations '*reserved to themselves the secondary market of weekly television guides by excluding all competition on that market*'.[918] Similarly, in *IMS Health*, the Court of Justice argued that the refusal was '*such as to reserve to the owner of the intellectual property right the market for the supply of data on sales of pharmaceutical products in the Member State concerned by eliminating all competition on that market*'.[919]

It can be concluded from these statements that the requirement of exclusion of effective competition aims to target the situation in which an essential facility holder is already active on the downstream market and tries to reserve that market to itself by refusing to deal. The other EU essential facilities cases also involved dominant undertakings trying to prevent third parties from becoming their competitors in the downstream market. For instance, by refusing to give access to its interoperability information, Microsoft aimed to keep Sun out of the downstream market for work group server operating systems in which Microsoft itself wanted to strengthen its position.

Under this interpretation, the condition of exclusion of effective competition does not capture the scenario in which a requesting undertaking needs access to the essential facility in order to enter a market on which the holder of the facility is not (yet) active, because the essential facility holder does not reserve the downstream market to itself by refusing to deal in that situation. In this factual scenario, the downstream market to be entered by the requesting undertaking will typically be a new market.[920] An existing market implies that others have been able to become active on the market without having access to the input held by the dominant undertaking in the upstream market. In that case, the input to which access is sought does not seem to be indispensable for competition on the downstream market and the access request will likely be rejected for not meeting the first requirement of the essential facilities doctrine.

In *Tiercé Ladbroke*, the General Court was confronted with a scenario in which the essential facility holder was not present on the downstream market. Ladbroke, a company providing betting services on the Belgian market, was refused a transmission

---

918. Judgment in Telefis Eireann and Independent Television Publications Ltd v. Commission of the European Communities (Magill), Joined cases C-241/91 and C-242/91, ECLI:EU:C:1995:98, par. 56.
919. Judgment in *IMS Health GmbH & Co. OHG v. NDC Health GmbH & Co. KG*, C-418/01, ECLI:EU:C:2004:257, par. 52.
920. See also E. Rousseva, *Rethinking Exclusionary Abuses in EU Competition Law*, Hart Publishing, 2010, p. 125.

licence for sound and pictures of French horse races. One of the reasons why the General Court held that the refusal did not amount to abuse under Article 102 TFEU was that the organisers of the French horse races were not competitors of Ladbroke on the relevant market for the provision of betting services in Belgium and could therefore not be seeking to reserve that downstream market for themselves.[921] The condition of exclusion of effective competition was thus interpreted restrictively in this case. Nevertheless, it is important to note that the refusal to license in *Tiercé Ladbroke* did not prevent Ladbroke from being active in the downstream market for betting services in Belgium. In fact, Ladbroke was already present in and even had the largest share of that market.[922] As a result, the General Court argued that the indispensability requirement was also not met, because television broadcasting of horse races could not be considered indispensable for the taking of bets.[923]

The question is whether the European Commission and the EU courts will hold on to the current interpretation of the requirement of exclusion of effective competition once they have to decide on a case involving a refusal to deal that prevents the requesting undertaking from opening up a new market. One could argue that it is not likely that such a case will occur because a dominant undertaking does not have an incentive to refuse access in such a situation. Since the essential facility holder is not active on the downstream market that the requesting undertaking would like to enter, it does not have to protect its position on that market and will only gain revenue from selling access to the requested input. The owner of the essential facility may nevertheless be incentivised to refuse access to the requested input if it is planning to become active on the new market itself in the near future. To be effective in such a situation, the requirement of exclusion of effective competition should not entail that the access seeker has to compete with the essential facility holder in the downstream market upon having access to the necessary input.

The second condition of the essential facilities doctrine should also be considered met in case effective competition is excluded on a downstream market on which the dominant undertaking is not present. In the latter situation, the essential facilities doctrine would apply to behaviour that does not consist in the leveraging of market power from the upstream market in which the essential facility holder possesses a dominant position into the downstream market in which it wants to strengthen its market position by precluding the entry of competitors. One could argue that the other scenario is more damaging to innovation and consumer welfare than leveraging, because it implies that the owner of the essential facility is capable of preventing the development of a new market by refusing to deal.[924]

The requirement of exclusion of effective competition is usually considered in close connection with the indispensability test. For instance, in *Magill* the Court of Justice noted that by reserving the downstream market of weekly television guides to

---

921. Judgment in *Tiercé Ladbroke v. Commission*, T-504/93, ECLI:EU:T:1997:84, par. 133.
922. Judgment in *Tiercé Ladbroke v. Commission*, T-504/93, ECLI:EU:T:1997:84, par. 130.
923. Judgment in *Tiercé Ladbroke v. Commission*, T-504/93, ECLI:EU:T:1997:84, par. 132.
924. E. ROUSSEVA, Rethinking Exclusionary Abuses in EU Competition Law, Hart Publishing, 2010, p. 125.

themselves, the Irish broadcasting companies were *'excluding all competition on that market since they denied access to the basic information which is the raw material indispensable for the compilation of such a guide'*.[925] In the Guidance Paper on exclusionary conduct under Article 102 TFEU, the European Commission made clear that once the requirement of indispensability is met, it *'considers that a dominant undertaking's refusal to supply is generally liable to eliminate, immediately or over time, effective competition in the downstream market'*.[926] As such, the exclusion of effective competition on the downstream market can be seen as a consequence of the indispensability of the requested input.[927]

Nevertheless, it is important to preserve the requirement of exclusion of effective competition as a separate condition of the essential facilities doctrine because it determines what degree of foreclosure of competition brings about liability for a refusal to deal and, as a result, what degree of competition is protected under the essential facilities doctrine.[928] To this end, the General Court made clear in *Microsoft* that it is not necessary for the Commission to demonstrate that all competition on the market would be eliminated. What matters, in the Court's view, is that the refusal is liable or likely to eliminate all effective competition on the market. The Court particularly noted that *'the fact that the competitors of the dominant undertaking retain a marginal presence in certain niches on the market cannot suffice to substantiate the existence of such competition'*.[929] In this perspective, the Court also explicitly stated that Article 102 TFEU does not apply only from the time when there is no more competition on the market:

> *If the Commission were required to wait until competitors were eliminated from the market, or until their elimination was sufficiently imminent, before being able to take action under Article 82 EC, that would clearly run counter to the objective of that provision, which is to maintain undistorted competition in the common market and, in particular, to safeguard the competition that still exists on the relevant market.*[930]

Since the requirement of exclusion of effective competition overlaps with the indispensability test, the fulfilment of one condition may influence the application of the other. In this sense, the degree of indispensability of the requested input that is required for meeting the indispensability test may be assessed in accordance with the degree of competition that is necessary for effective competition in the downstream market as determined under the condition of exclusion of effective competition. As

925. Judgment in Telefis Eireann and Independent Television Publications Ltd v. Commission of the European Communities (Magill), Joined cases C-241/91 and C-242/91, ECLI:EU:C:1995:98, par. 56.
926. Communication from the Commission — Guidance on the Commission's enforcement priorities in applying Article 82 of the EC Treaty to abusive exclusionary conduct by dominant undertakings (Guidance Paper) [2009] OJ C 45/7, par. 85.
927. N. LE, 'What Does "Capable of Eliminating All Competition" Mean?', *European Competition Law Review* 2005, vol. 26, no. 1, (6), pp. 6-10.
928. See also T. KÄSEBERG, Intellectual Property, Antitrust and Cumulative Innovation in the EU and the US, Hart Publishing, 2012, pp. 158-159 and 226-228.
929. Judgment in *Microsoft v. Commission*, T-201/04, ECLI:EU:T:2007:289, par. 563.
930. Judgment in *Microsoft v. Commission*, T-201/04, ECLI:EU:T:2007:289, par. 561.

made clear by the General Court, the European Commission adopted such an approach in *Microsoft* for determining whether the interoperability information at issue was indispensable: the Commission, first of all, *'considered what degree of interoperability with the Windows domain architecture non-Microsoft work group server operating systems must achieve in order for its competitors to be able to remain viably on the market and, second, it appraised whether the interoperability that Microsoft refused to disclose was indispensable to the attainment of that degree of interoperability'*.[931] Although a certain level of interoperability was already possible with Microsoft's client PC operating system Windows, the General Court followed the finding of the European Commission that access to Microsoft's interoperability information was indispensable. This because non-Microsoft work group server operating systems had to be capable of interoperating with Windows on an equal footing with Windows work group server operating systems if they were to be marketed viably on the market.[932]

The two-stage approach implemented by the Commission in *Microsoft* seems a sensible way to test the first two conditions of the essential facilities doctrine. According to this approach, in a first step, the degree of competition is defined that is necessary for enabling effective competition in the downstream market which determines, in a second step, the degree of indispensability that the requested input has to meet in order to be considered indispensable under the first requirement of the essential facilities doctrine.

6.8.2.3 Prevention of the Introduction of a New Product

The third condition of the essential facilities doctrine that has been developed in the *Magill* and *IMS Health* case law of the Court of Justice requires that the refusal to deal prevents the introduction of a new product. The new product requirement is only applied in cases concerning refusals to license intellectual property rights.[933] However, as argued earlier,[934] there does not seem to be a solid economic basis for applying a different legal test to refusals to license than to refusals to deal involving non-intellectual property protected assets. For this reason, no separate standard for intervention or additional condition is put forward under this framework for holding a refusal to license an intellectual property right abusive. Both types of refusals to deal are thus assessed in the same way under the proposed framework.

As made clear by the Court of Justice, the new product condition aims to determine whether a refusal to license *'prevents the development of the secondary market to the detriment of consumers'*.[935] Such damage to consumer welfare may occur as well due to a refusal to deal involving an asset not protected by an intellectual property right. Whether essential facility holders are trying to prevent new market

---

931. Judgment in *Microsoft v. Commission*, T-201/04, ECLI:EU:T:2007:289, par. 369.
932. Judgment in *Microsoft v. Commission*, T-201/04, ECLI:EU:T:2007:289, paras 371-436.
933. See Judgment in *Microsoft v. Commission*, T-201/04, ECLI:EU:T:2007:289, par. 334.
934. See section 6.7.3 above.
935. Judgment in *IMS Health GmbH & Co. OHG v. NDC Health GmbH & Co. KG*, C-418/01, ECLI:EU:C:2004:257, par. 48.

developments from occurring is an issue which in principle deserves to be considered for absolute refusals to deal in general and not merely for absolute refusals to license. However, as shown above,[936] the new product condition in its current form has some shortcomings. It is therefore meaningful to consider the appropriateness of other conditions or tests put forward in the literature.

In order to operationalise the new product condition and to ensure that its application leads to consistent results, a test has been suggested for identifying whether a product is new under the exceptional circumstances test of *Magill* and *IMS Health*. According to this test developed by Ahlborn, Evans & Padilla, a product can be considered new if it *'satisfies potential demand by meeting the needs of consumers in ways that existing products do not'* in the sense that the product brings in *'at current prices consumers who were not satisfied before'* thereby expanding the market *'by a significant amount'*.[937] In other words, the relevant question is whether the introduction of the product would add a new class of consumers to the market whose preferences were such that they preferred not to buy anything prior to the launch of the 'new' product.

Although this test gives a clearer and more objective definition to novelty, it has been criticised because it does not regard products as 'new' that better satisfy existing consumer preferences but do not expand the market. This while it is clear that consumers may also benefit from better quality products which do not necessarily lead to new demand.[938] As such, the test does not solve the problem that the new product requirement is unable of protecting the interests of consumers in cases where specific market characteristics prevent competitors from successfully introducing novel products.

As argued by Drexl, the imposition of a duty to deal is appropriate to restore competition by imitation when external market failures are present so that consumers can at least benefit from static competition on the basis of price and output in situations where dynamic competition on the basis of innovation is not possible.[939] In this context, it is worthwhile to reflect on whether the distinction between competition by substitution and competition by imitation, as relied upon by Drexl, can be used as an analytical tool alternative to the new product condition.[940] The adoption of that distinction for the purpose of applying the essential facilities doctrine would entail that in cases where no external market failures are present, access seekers are required to indicate a specific product they would like to introduce that is not merely a duplication

---

936. See section 6.7.2 above.
937. C. AHLBORN, D.S. EVANS AND A.J. PADILLA, 'The Logic & Limits of the "Exceptional Circumstances Test" in *Magill* and *IMS Health'*, *Fordham International Law Journal* 2004-2005, vol. 28, no. 4, (1109), pp. 1147-1148.
938. See I. LIANOS, 'Competition Law and Intellectual Property Rights: Is the Property Rights' Approach Right?' in J. BELL AND C. KILPATRICK (eds.), *The Cambridge Yearbook of European Legal Studies. Volume 8*, 2005-2006, (153), p. 163 and T. KÄSEBERG, *Intellectual Property, Antitrust and Cumulative Innovation in the EU and the US*, Hart Publishing, 2012, p. 159.
939. For a more elaborate analysis of these issues, see section 6.7.2 above.
940. See also B. CONDE GALLEGO, 'Unilateral Refusal to License Indispensable Intellectual Property Rights – US and EU Approaches' in J. DREXL (ed.), *Research Handbook on Intellectual Property and Competition Law*, Cheltenham, Edward Elgar Publishing, 2008, (215), pp. 235-238.

of the product offered by the essential facility holder. In turn, if such a form of competition by substitution is not possible due to the characteristics of the market at issue, access seekers should be allowed to compete by imitation and to introduce a product similar to that of the essential facility holder.

One should note, however, that the product to be launched by the access seeker in both situations will compete with the product of the essential facility holder in the same relevant product market. The difference of competition by substitution and competition by imitation thus merely relates to competition *in* existing markets and does not consider incentives for competition *for* new markets.[941] As an analytical tool to be used for the application of the essential facilities doctrine, the distinction relied upon by Drexl gives an incomplete picture of the different interests that are at stake in refusal to deal scenarios, considering that it does not account for the trade-off between, on the one hand, competition *for* the market and disruptive innovation and, on the other hand, competition *in* the market and sustaining innovation.

Taking this economic trade-off fully into account would require a tool that differentiates on the basis of the type of competition or innovation that is at risk in a particular market situation. The new product requirement is by its very nature capable of implementing such an exercise under the essential facilities doctrine because it determines what level of innovativeness the product or service to be introduced by the access seeker has to bring about. In this context, an adapted version of the new product condition can be proposed that accounts for these differences in market characteristics.

Even though the distinction between competition by imitation and competition by substitution does not appropriately reflect the economic trade-off to be made in essential facilities cases, its underlying logic according to which the scope for competition law liability for refusals to deal is wider in situations where external market failures are present can be retained in order to make the policy choice between competition *for* and *in* the market more objective. External market failures such as the presence of network effects and switching costs may make it commercially unviable for competitors to introduce a new product. If, for instance, consumers are locked-in to a particular standard, a requirement that access seekers have to introduce a new product is of no relevance because consumers are not willing to switch to a different system. Instead of making the applicability of the new product dependent on whether the asset to which access is requested is protected by intellectual property law, the new product condition could differentiate based on whether external market failures occur in the market. Indeed, external market failures may enable the incumbent to extend its dominance in time irrespective of whether the asset to which access is requested is protected by an intellectual property right or not.

---

941. See the definition that Drexl gives to competition by substitution: 'Intellectual property protection reacts to this phenomenon by excluding the freedom to compete by imitation, but **does not exclude the possibility to develop a superior intangible good that**, qualifying for IP protection or not, **would compete with the prior intangible good in the same market (competition by substitution)**' [emphasis added] (J. Drexl, 'IMS Health and Trinko - antitrust placebo for consumers instead of sound economics in refusal-to-deal cases', International Review of Intellectual Property and Competition Law 2004, vol. 35, no. 7, (788), p. 805).

Considering that there is no convincing economic rationale for treating intellectual property rights differently than other types of assets under the essential facilities doctrine,[942] it is proposed to focus instead on the presence of external market failures as a way to determine whether the new product condition should be met in order to hold a refusal to deal abusive under Article 102 TFEU. It is submitted that the essential facilities doctrine will be better able to adequately address all scenarios in which refusals to deal require competition law intervention by adapting the new product requirement in this way.

With regard to situations where external market failures are present, the new product condition should be dropped to ensure that access seekers who intend to introduce sustaining innovations or products similar to that of the dominant undertaking are able to gain access to the necessary input. This way, the process of competition *in* the market can be (re-)launched. As explained above,[943] the potential competition problems in markets that are characterised by external market failures relate to the fact that an incumbent may try to prolong its dominance by preventing competitors from entering the market and competing on price or through offering better quality products. The imposition of a duty to deal in such markets will open up the process of competition *in* the market and ensure that price levels and product variety are kept at a competitive level.

Therefore, if the market is locked-in due to the presence of network effects or switching costs and the essential facility holder has had a stable dominant position for some time, competition authorities should be able to impose a duty to deal even if the access seeker is not able to indicate a new product that it would like to introduce once given access to the requested input (provided that the other conditions of the essential facilities doctrine are met). As outlined in section 6.7.2 above, *IMS Health* and *Microsoft* form examples of such situations where external market failures prevented potential competitors from entering the market by introducing their own products due to the fact that consumers were not interested in switching to a new type of brick structure or client PC operating system.

In situations not characterised by external market failures, however, the new product condition should be applied strictly to encourage investments in innovation. As described earlier,[944] the process of competition *for* the market cannot, in principle, be launched by way of a competition law intervention and incentives for this type of competition are best preserved by avoiding government interference in the market and thereby maintaining the prospect of dominance for new entrants. Competition enforcement in markets where external market failures are absent should be subject to stricter conditions, considering that the self-correcting nature of the market is stronger in these circumstances as a result of which a competition law intervention to encourage competition *in* the market risks unnecessarily lowering incentives for competition *for*

---

942. See section 6.7.3 above.
943. See section 6.6.3 above.
944. See section 6.6.3 above.

the market. By strictly applying the new product condition, possible negative effects on incentives to invest in competition *for* the market and disruptive innovation are counteracted as much as possible.

Table 6.1   Existence of External Market Failures as a Determining Factor for whether the New Product Condition Should Be Met

External Market Failures	No External Market Failures
- Main risk is that dominant firm is able to extend its dominance in time - not because of its competitive success but due to the external market conditions	- Because of the stronger self-correcting nature of the market, a competition law intervention to stimulate the process of competition *in* the market is less pressing
- While a competition law intervention will reduce incentives for competition *for* the market and disruptive innovation, such an effect may be outweighed by the increased level of competition *in* the market that would not have occurred but for the intervention	- Due to the absence of external market failures, there is more room for other market players to attack the dominance of the incumbent by competing on price, quality or output or by introducing sustaining innovations *in* the market
- By intervening, a competition authority can prevent that the dominant firm is overcompensated for its investments and will stop to invest in quality or sustaining innovations because of the limited level of competition *in* the market	- A competition law intervention in markets not characterised by external market failures therefore carries a higher risk of reducing incentives for competition *for* the market and disruptive innovation
- Overcompensation contradicts the goal of competition law to guarantee effective competition and, with regard to inputs protected by intellectual property law, is not in line with the rationale of the intellectual property system either	

Since the interpretations given to the new product condition by the EU courts are ambivalent[945] and may consequently give rise to unpredictable outcomes, there is a need for more clarity on how the requirement has to be applied. The Guidance Paper on exclusionary conduct under Article 102 TFEU issued by the European Commission also does not shed a clear light on this issue and merely echoes the differing standards

---

945. While the Court of Justice made clear in *Magill* and *IMS Health* that the new product must be clearly identifiable and not offered by the essential facility holder, the General Court argued in *Microsoft* that a mere limitation of technical development is sufficient for meeting the new product requirement. See section 6.2.2 above.

put forward in case law on the EU level. One of the factors that the Commission deems relevant for prioritising refusal to deal cases is the likelihood of consumer harm. In this regard, the Commission stated that such consumer harm may particularly occur: '*if the undertaking which requests supply does not intend to limit itself essentially to duplicating the goods or services already offered by the dominant undertaking on the downstream market, but intends to produce new or improved goods or services for which there is a potential consumer demand or is likely to contribute to technical development*'.[946] The Commission thus endorses the fact that different thresholds currently exist for meeting the new product requirement but does not clarify which threshold should apply in which situation.

By relying on the concept of substitutability as an indicator of the 'newness' of a product, the standard to be used for the application of the new product requirement becomes more clearly defined and easier to employ.[947] In order to be considered new, the product to be introduced by the access seeker should either have no or a relatively low degree of substitutability to the product of the essential facility holder. In case the product is non-substitutable to the existing product, its introduction creates a new market in which the owner of the essential facility is not active.[948] In this situation, the second condition of exclusion of effective competition should, as explained in the previous subsection, not be understood as meaning that the owner of the essential facility must exclude competition on a downstream market in which it competes with the access seeker upon the imposition of the duty to deal. Such a reading would prevent competition authorities from intervening in cases where access seekers are planning to use the requested input as a way to open up a new market.

A low degree of substitutability implies that the product that the access seeker intends to launch is of such better quality or has such additional features that it becomes incomparable to the existing product of the essential facility holder. Whereas mere product differentiation is insufficient to meet this standard, the establishment of a new market is not required. The lower the degree of substitutability to the existing product, the more will consumers benefit from the introduction of the product of the access seeker because it constitutes a new or hugely improved product or leads to significant follow-on innovation.[949]

Under the proposed framework, the fulfilment of the new product condition in markets not characterised by external market failures would require that the potential

---

946. Communication from the Commission — Guidance on the Commission's enforcement priorities in applying Article 82 of the EC Treaty to abusive exclusionary conduct by dominant undertakings (Guidance Paper) [2009] OJ C 45/7, par. 87.

947. D. GERADIN, 'Limiting the scope of Article 82 EC: What can the EU learn from the U.S. Supreme Court's judgment in *Trinko* in the wake of *Microsoft*, *IMS*, and *Deutsche Telekom*?', *Common Market Law Review* 2004, vol. 41, no. 6, (1519), pp. 1531-1532.

948. As explained in the context of the condition of exclusion of effective competition in section 6.8.2.2, it is assumed in this scenario that the imposition of a duty to deal leads to the establishment of a new market and does not merely enable an access seeker to enter an existing market on which the essential facility holder is not present. In the latter case, it is doubtful that the first condition of the essential facilities doctrine, requiring indispensability of the requested input, is fulfilled.

949. T. KÄSEBERG, Intellectual Property, Antitrust and Cumulative Innovation in the EU and the US, Hart Publishing, 2012, p. 160.

new product adds substantial utility to consumers thereby incentivising market players to invest in innovation. No or a relatively low degree of substitutability can be used as a proxy for such significant value to consumers. Substitutability may be easier for competition authorities to examine than the more abstract notion of novelty currently relied upon by the European Commission and the EU courts. The adoption of the concept of substitutability under the new product requirement would imply that the product to be launched by the access seeker already has to be concretely defined. Otherwise, it would be impossible to assess the degree of substitutability to the existing product of the essential facility holder.

As a result, the fact that a refusal to deal limits technical development, which the General Court accepted as amounting to the prevention of the launch of a new product in *Microsoft*, would not suffice under the new product requirement proposed here. Such an interpretation of the new product requirement rests on a mere presumption that consumers will benefit from the general development of the industry which competitors of the essential facility holder will bring about upon having access to the requested input, without the need to define a concrete product or service that such development may create. In addition, under this reading the new product requirement would add no extra legal hurdle to the first two conditions of the essential facilities doctrine in the sense that a limitation of technical development can be seen as an inevitable consequence of the indispensability of the requested input and of the exclusion of all effective competition on the downstream market. If access to the input of the essential facility holder is necessary for downstream competition, it is logical that the general development of the industry is restricted due to the refusal to deal.[950]

6.8.2.4 Absence of an Objective Justification

After the presence of the aforementioned exceptional circumstances is identified, the essential facility holder can still try to invoke an objective justification for its refusal to deal to prevent the establishment of an abuse under Article 102 TFEU. In order to be successful, the justification has to prevail over the exceptional circumstances of indispensability, exclusion of effective competition and prevention of the emergence of a new product. While the burden of proof of the existence of these three conditions is borne by the competition authority or court, it is for the owner of the essential facility to put forward an objective justification.[951] Previous cases indicate that it is very difficult for a dominant undertaking to succeed in justifying its refusal to deal once the other requirements of the essential facilities doctrine have been met.

In the early refusal to supply case law, the Court of Justice hinted at possible justifications.[952] In *Commercial Solvents* and *BP*, the Court suggested that capacity constraints in supply may constitute a valid reason for an essential facility holder to

---

950. E. Rousseva, *Rethinking Exclusionary Abuses in EU Competition Law*, Hart Publishing, 2010, pp. 123-124.
951. Judgment in *Microsoft v. Commission*, T-201/04, ECLI:EU:T:2007:289, par. 688.
952. See L. Hou, 'The Essential Facilities Doctrine – What Was Wrong in Microsoft?', *International Review of Intellectual Property and Competition Law* 2012, vol. 43, no. 4, (451), p. 462.

refuse to deal. The Court of Justice argued in *Commercial Solvents* that the statements of Commercial Solvents concerning capacity limits could not be taken into account in the case because, even though the production possibilities of the raw material to which Zoja sought access were not unlimited, it was clear that Commercial Solvents was able to satisfy Zoja's needs in view of its production capacity and Zoja's very small percentage of Commercial Solvents' production.[953] One may conclude from this analysis of the Court that capacity constraints can constitute an objective justification for a refusal to deal provided that the dominant undertaking succeeds in proving that it is not able to meet the demand of the access seeker.

In *BP*, the Court of Justice held that it was not abusive for a dominant supplier of petroleum products to reduce the delivery to one of its non-regulator customers in the period of shortage during the oil crisis with more than the rate that it applied to its regular customers.[954] As a result, a lack of supply due to a crisis affecting an entire industry may form a valid reason for disrupting existing levels of supply to an occasional customer.[955]

As evidenced by *Télémarketing*, a second type of objective justification for a refusal to deal includes technical or commercial requirements. The Court of Justice made clear that one of the factors that the national court should take into account in assessing whether the refusal of RTL to continue to permit a third party to provide telemarketing services on its television channel amounted to abuse was whether the refusal could be *'justified by technical or commercial requirements relating to the nature of the television'*.[956]

Lastly, in *United Brands* the Court stated that a dominant undertaking *'cannot stop supplying a long standing customer who abides by regular commercial practice, if the orders placed by that customer are in no way out of the ordinary'*.[957] In *Sot. Lélos v. GlaxoSmithKline*, the Court of Justice relied on its statement in *United Brands* and argued that *'in order to appraise whether the refusal by a pharmaceuticals company to supply wholesalers involved in parallel exports constitutes a reasonable and proportionate measure in relation to the threat that those exports represent to its legitimate commercial interests, it must be ascertained whether the orders of the wholesalers are out of the ordinary'*.[958] The Court clarified that an order may be out of the ordinary in terms of quantity and that *'a producer of pharmaceutical products must be in a position to protect its own commercial interests if it is confronted with [such] orders'*.[959] The

953. Judgment in *Istituto Chemioterapico Italiano and Commercial Solvents v. Commission*, Joined cases 6 and 7/73, ECLI:EU:C:1974:18, paras 27-28.
954. Judgment in Benzine en Petroleum Handelsmaatschappij BV and others v. Commission, Case 77/77, ECLI:EU:C:1978:141, par. 32.
955. E. ROUSSEVA, 'The Concept of "Objective Justification" of an Abuse of a Dominant Position: Can It Help to Modernise the Analysis under Article 82 EC?', *The Competition Law Review* 2006, vol. 2, no. 2, (27), pp. 38-39.
956. Judgment in *CBEM v. CLT & IPB (Télémarketing)*, Case 311/84, ECLI:EU:C:1985:394, par. 26.
957. Judgment in *United Brands v. Commission*, Case 27/76, ECLI:EU:C:1978:22, par. 182.
958. Judgment in *Sot. Lélos kai Sia EE and Others v. GlaxoSmithKline AEVE Farmakeftikon Proïonton*, Joined Cases C-468/06 to C-478/06, ECLI:EU:C:2008:504, par. 70.
959. Judgment in *Sot. Lélos kai Sia EE and Others v. GlaxoSmithKline AEVE Farmakeftikon Proïonton*, Joined Cases C-468/06 to C-478/06, ECLI:EU:C:2008:504, par. 76. For a discussion

Court of Justice thus made clear that a dominant undertaking cannot be held liable for a refusal to supply if the access request constitutes improper commercial behaviour of which an order that is out of the ordinary in terms of quantity forms an example.

Microsoft is the first case in which the notion of objective justification has been analysed in detail in a refusal to deal context. In order to justify its refusal to give access to interoperability information, Microsoft did not rely on any of the abovementioned objective justifications but tried to justify its behaviour by invoking three different arguments. In the first place, Microsoft claimed that its refusal to supply was objectively justified by the intellectual property rights which it argued to hold over the interoperability information.[960] The General Court rejected this argument by considering that the mere fact of holding intellectual property rights cannot in itself constitute justification for a refusal to grant a licence. As made clear by the Court, a refusal to license an intellectual property right could otherwise never be considered an infringement of Article 102 TFEU, while the Court of Justice specifically stated the contrary in *Magill* and *IMS Health*.[961]

Second, Microsoft relied on the fact that the technology which it was required to disclose to its competitors was secret, that it was of great value for licensees and that it contained significant innovation.[962] This reasoning of Microsoft did not succeed either. The General Court noted that the secret nature of the technology at issue was the consequence of a unilateral business decision of Microsoft and that there is no reason why secret technology should enjoy a higher level of protection than technology which has necessarily been disclosed to the public by its inventor in a patent-application procedure. The Court also made clear that once the indispensability requirement is met the interoperability information is necessarily of great value to the competitors who wish to have access to it and that it is inherent in the fact that the undertaking concerned holds an intellectual property right that the subject matter of that right is innovative or original.[963]

Finally, Microsoft tried to justify its refusal to give access to the interoperability information by arguing that forced disclosure of the necessary protocols would adversely affect its incentives to innovate.[964] In this respect, the General Court endorsed the findings of the European Commission and argued that Microsoft did not sufficiently establish the significant negative impact that a duty to disclose the interoperability information would have on its incentives to innovate. In the Court's view, Microsoft merely put forward vague, general and theoretical arguments on this point and did not specify the technologies or products that would be affected by reduced incentives to invest.[965] The Court also argued that the imposition of a duty to deal did not allow Microsoft's competitors to copy its products, that it was normal

---

of the factors that the Court of Justice deemed relevant in considering whether an order is out of the ordinary in terms of quantity, see section 6.8.3 below.
960. Judgment in *Microsoft v. Commission*, T-201/04, ECLI:EU:T:2007:289, par. 666.
961. Judgment in *Microsoft v. Commission*, T-201/04, ECLI:EU:T:2007:289, par. 690.
962. Judgment in *Microsoft v. Commission*, T-201/04, ECLI:EU:T:2007:289, par. 667.
963. Judgment in *Microsoft v. Commission*, T-201/04, ECLI:EU:T:2007:289, paras 692-695.
964. Judgment in *Microsoft v. Commission*, T-201/04, ECLI:EU:T:2007:289, par. 668.
965. Judgment in *Microsoft v. Commission*, T-201/04, ECLI:EU:T:2007:289, paras 697-699.

practice in the industry to make interoperability information public as evidenced by Microsoft's own disclosure policy on earlier versions of Windows and that a similar disclosure made under the United States settlement had no negative impact on Microsoft's incentives to innovate.[966]

Microsoft also asserted before the General Court that the Commission had applied a new evaluation test when rejecting its objective justification '*which is legally defective and marks a radical departure from the tests defined in the case-law*'.[967] Microsoft referred to the paragraph in the *Microsoft* decision of the Commission where the latter noted that '*a detailed examination of the scope of the disclosure at stake leads to the conclusion that, on balance, the possible negative impact of an order to supply on Microsoft's incentives to innovate is outweighed by its positive impact on the level of innovation of the whole industry (including Microsoft)*'.[968] The General Court argued that Microsoft's claim that the Commission used a new test was based on a misreading of the decision and that the paragraph in question merely contained the findings of the Commission's analysis.[969] According to the Court, the Commission came to its conclusion '*not by balancing the negative impact which the imposition of a requirement to supply the information at issue might have on Microsoft's incentives to innovate against the positive impact of that obligation on innovation in the industry as a whole, but after refuting Microsoft's arguments*' including those relating to the fear that its products might be cloned and to the fact that disclosure of interoperability was widespread in the industry concerned.[970]

Although the General Court neither endorsed nor rejected a test balancing the positive and negative effects of a duty to deal, the analysis by the European Commission and the General Court of Microsoft's argument about the impact of forced disclosure of interoperability information on its incentives to innovate has led scholars to comment on the introduction of a so-called incentives balance test under the essential facilities doctrine.[971] The adoption of such a test for assessing whether a refusal to deal is objectively justified would imply that, after it has been established that the requirements of indispensability, exclusion of effective competition and new product are met, a justification can only be accepted if the dominant undertaking is able to show that the negative impact of a duty to deal on its own incentives to innovate outweighs the positive impact of a duty to deal on the level of innovation in the whole industry.[972]

In *Microsoft*, the Commission expressed the view that Microsoft's innovation incentives would not be negatively affected due to the imposition of a duty to deal. For

---

966. Judgment in *Microsoft v. Commission*, T-201/04, ECLI:EU:T:2007:289, paras 700-703.
967. Judgment in *Microsoft v. Commission*, T-201/04, ECLI:EU:T:2007:289, para. 669.
968. Case COMP/C-3/37.792 - *Microsoft*, 24 March 2004, par. 783.
969. Judgment in *Microsoft v. Commission*, T-201/04, ECLI:EU:T:2007:289, paras 704-709.
970. Judgment in *Microsoft v. Commission*, T-201/04, ECLI:EU:T:2007:289, par. 710.
971. See S. VEZZOSO, 'The Incentives Balance Test in the EU Microsoft Case: A Pro-innovation "Economics-Based" Approach?', *European Competition Law Review* 2006, vol. 27, no. 7, (382) and C. SCHMIDT AND W. KERBER, 'Microsoft, Refusal to License Intellectual Property Rights, and the Incentives Balance Test of the EU Commission', *SSRN Working Paper* November 2008, available at http://papers.ssrn.com/sol3/papers.cfm?abstract_id=1297939.
972. See Judgment in *Microsoft v. Commission*, T-201/04, ECLI:EU:T:2007:289, par. 669.

the assessment of the objective justification raised by Microsoft, it was thus not necessary to evaluate the positive impact on the entire industry and to conduct a balancing exercise.[973] Whereas such a balancing of innovation incentives has not yet been undertaken by the European Commission or the EU courts, scholars have assessed the pros and cons of the implementation of a balancing test in future competition cases. While the incentives balance test in general is considered to constitute an interesting approach from an economic perspective,[974] the test is said to be difficult to apply because of the uncertainties surrounding the working of innovation processes.[975] In addition, it is argued that a balancing test will reduce legal certainty because it is almost impossible for any company to apply such a test ex ante.[976]

As such, the balancing exercise to be undertaken in this context has similarities to the analysis that is conducted under the new product requirement. By determining what level of innovativeness the access seeker has to pursue in order to get access to the requested input, the new product condition already balances the interest of the dominant undertaking with the interest in free competition or, in other words, the interest of the entire industry.[977] The analysis to be carried out under the two requirements would thus overlap if a balancing exercise similar to the one undertaken under the new product condition takes place under the condition of objective justification.[978]

In this regard, it seems an insurmountable task for a dominant undertaking to objectively justify its refusal to deal by proving that the balance tilts in its favour when the competition authority has already established that the interest in free competition should prevail over the interest of the dominant undertaking under the new product requirement. Furthermore, a possible negative effect on the innovation incentives of the dominant undertaking is not merely a defence for its own refusal to deal but also a concern about the long-term effects of a competition law intervention on competition

---

973. Case COMP/C-3/37.792 - *Microsoft*, 24 March 2004, par. 725. See also section 6.5 above. For a critical analysis of the European Commission's application of the incentives balance test to the facts of the *Microsoft* case, see F. LÉVÊQUE, 'Innovation, Leveraging and Essential Facilities: Interoperability Licensing in the EU Microsoft Case', *World Competition* 2005, vol. 28, no. 1, (71), pp. 78-79.

974. C. SCHMIDT AND W. KERBER, 'Microsoft, Refusal to License Intellectual Property Rights, and the Incentives Balance Test of the EU Commission', *SSRN Working Paper* November 2008, pp. 15-20, available at http://papers.ssrn.com/sol3/papers.cfm?abstract_id=1297939.

975. S. VEZZOSO, 'The Incentives Balance Test in the EU Microsoft Case: A Pro-innovation "Economics-Based" Approach?', *European Competition Law Review* 2006, vol. 27, no. 7, (382), pp. 386-388.

976. J. KILLICK, '*IMS* and *Microsoft* Judged in the Cold Light of *IMS*', *The Competition Law Review* 2004, vol. 1, no. 2, (23), p. 44.

977. See the statement of the Court of Justice in the context of a refusal to license an intellectual property right: the new product condition '*relates to the consideration that, in the balancing of the interest in protection of the intellectual property right and the economic freedom of its owner against the interest in protection of free competition, the latter can prevail only where refusal to grant a licence prevents the development of the secondary market to the detriment of consumers*' (Judgment in *IMS Health GmbH & Co. OHG v. NDC Health GmbH & Co. KG*, C-418/01, ECLI:EU:C:2004:257, par. 48).

978. See also E. ROUSSEVA, *Rethinking Exclusionary Abuses in EU Competition Law*, Hart Publishing, 2010, p. 131.

and innovation in the sector in general.[979] It would therefore be more appropriate to deal with such a concern under the assessment of abuse rather than as an objective justification at the end of the analysis under the essential facilities doctrine. This would also put the burden of proof on the competition authority instead of on the dominant undertaking.

All in all, a balancing of innovation incentives as proposed by the Commission in *Microsoft* should not be regarded as a desirable test or tool considering the inherent difficulties relating to its practical application and its unpredictability.[980] Instead of such an open-ended balancing exercise, the adapted version of the new product condition as proposed in the previous subsection may be used as a way to determine in which circumstances the interest of the industry as a whole should prevail over the interest of the dominant undertaking.

As suggested earlier,[981] in markets characterised by external market failures the new product condition may be dropped to make sure that access seekers wishing to introduce sustaining innovations can also get access to the necessary input. In this situation, it is thus assumed that the interest of the industry as a whole in getting access to the requested input outweighs the interest of the dominant undertaking to refuse to deal once the requirements of indispensability and exclusion of effective competition have been met. In markets where no external market failures occur, it is proposed to apply the new product requirement strictly. In such cases, the competition authority has to assess whether the product that the access seeker wants to introduce meets the level of innovativeness required for the balance to shift to the interest in free competition. The balancing of the interest of the dominant undertaking with the interest in free competition would thus not take place when considering an objective justification, but form part of the assessment of the abusive nature of the refusal to deal.

Appropriate defences that a dominant undertaking may put forward to justify its refusal to deal include the objective justifications suggested in the early refusal to deal case law such as capacity restraints in supply (*Commercial Solvents* and *BP*), technical or commercial requirements (*Télémarketing*) and improper commercial behaviour of the access seeker (*United Brands*). In addition, a dominant undertaking may try to justify its refusal to deal by showing that it would not have invested in the creation of the requested input in the first place if it had known beforehand that it would have to share it with competitors (ex ante efficiency defence) or that the duty to deal will disrupt its business operations by posing unreasonable costs (ex post efficiency defence).

The dominant undertaking may succeed in relying on the first type of defence by proving that it would not be able to recoup its investment as well as a reasonable profit

---

979. P. LAROUCHE, 'The European Microsoft Case at the Crossroads of Competition Policy and Innovation', *Antitrust Law Journal* 2008, vol. 75, no. 3, (601), p. 615.
980. See D. GERADIN, 'Limiting the Scope of Article 82 EC: What Can the EU Learn from the U.S. Supreme Court's Judgment in *Trinko* in the Wake of *Microsoft*, *IMS*, and *Deutsche Telekom*?', *Common Market Law Review* 2004, vol. 41, no. 6, (1519), pp. 1542-1543 and footnote 76 who also argues that a balancing test may introduce a bias in favour of access seekers.
981. See section 6.8.2.3 above.

if it had to supply access seekers at their maximum ability to pay. Examples of the second type of justification would include situations where congestion occurs due to the duty to supply or where extra capacity has to be installed in order to successfully accommodate access requests.[982] Such justifications are more workable than requiring a dominant undertaking to conduct a balancing of innovation incentives and should therefore be preferred over a type of incentives balance test as suggested by the European Commission in its *Microsoft* decision.

6.8.3 Disruptions of Supply

The second type of scenario that can be distinguished with regard to refusals to deal is that of a disruption of existing levels of supply. Disruptions of supply have a behavioural element that is absent in absolute refusals to deal where the ground for competition law intervention is more structural and does not lie in the conduct of the dominant firm but in the fact that it holds an input which is essential for competition on a downstream market.[983] Whereas absolute refusals to deal are remedied by way of the imposition of a positive duty on dominant undertakings to actively promote competition by providing competitors access to a particular facility, disruptions of existing levels of supply instead give rise to a mere negative duty to refrain from certain anticompetitive action.[984] Yet, the same legal standards apply to absolute refusals to deal and disruptions of supply in current EU competition law. This is evidenced by the *Microsoft* case which involved a termination of supply of previous levels of interoperability information to Microsoft's competitors in the market for work group server operating systems but was nevertheless assessed by the General Court under the strict exceptional circumstances test set out in the cases of *Magill* and *IMS Health* which dealt with absolute refusals to deal.

While the European Commission in 2005 still expressed the view that different legal conditions should be applicable to a termination of an existing supply relationship in its Discussion Paper,[985] it made clear in its Guidance Paper on exclusionary conduct under Article 102 TFEU of 2009 that it would use the same criteria for determining enforcement priorities, which are based on the conditions of the exceptional circumstances test,[986] for cases of disruption of existing levels of supply and refusals to supply a good or service which the dominant undertaking has not previously supplied to

---

982. These two types of defences are put forward in T. Käseberg, *Intellectual Property, Antitrust and Cumulative Innovation in the EU and the US*, Hart Publishing, 2012, pp. 162-163.

983. P. Larouche, Competition Law and Regulation in European Telecommunications, Hart Publishing, 2000, p. 209.

984. See also Opinion of Advocate General Jacobs in *Oscar Bronner GmbH & Co. KG v. Mediaprint Zeitungs*, C-7/97, ECLI:EU:C:1998:264, par. 34.

985. DG Competition discussion paper on the application of Article 82 of the Treaty to exclusionary abuses, December 2005, paras 217-236.

986. According to the Guidance Paper on exclusionary conduct under Article 102 TFEU, the Commission will consider a refusal to deal as an enforcement priority if: (1) it relates to a product or service that is objectively necessary to be able to compete effectively on a downstream market; (2) it is likely to lead to elimination of effective competition on the downstream market; and (3) it is likely to lead to consumer harm (Communication from the

others. At the same time, the Commission acknowledged in the Guidance Paper that it is more plausible that a termination of an existing supply arrangement meets the criteria than an absolute refusal to deal. First, the Commission may be more likely to regard the input in question as indispensable when *'the requesting undertaking had made relationship-specific investments in order to use the subsequently refused input'*. Second, *'the fact that the owner of the essential input in the past has found it in its interest to supply is an indication that supplying the input does not imply any risk that the owner receives inadequate compensation for the original investment'*.[987] Nevertheless, since the conditions of the exceptional circumstances test are also used for assessing disruptions of supply, it seems that the less strict standards applied to terminations of existing supply relationships in the early case law of *Commercial Solvents* are not valid anymore.

A difference between the two types of tests is that the *Commercial Solvents* reasoning, unlike the exceptional circumstances test of *Magill* and *IMS Health*, does not require essentiality or indispensability of the requested input. In its *Commercial Solvents* judgment, the Court of Justice even made clear that arguments relating to whether Zoja was able to adapt its installations and its manufacturing processes in order to continue its production of ethambutol based on other raw materials were irrelevant to the dispute.[988] Similarly, in *United Brands* the Court of Justice merely based its conclusion on the fact that United Brands stopped the supply to a long-standing customer acting in accordance with usual commercial practice and did not discuss whether the banana deliveries from United Brands were essential for Olesen or whether alternative means of supply were available.[989] It was only until the *Télémarketing* case that the requirement of indispensability was explicitly mentioned by the Court of Justice.[990]

The fact that disruptions of supply are currently assessed under the exceptional circumstances test of *Magill* and *IMS Health* may lead to undesirable outcomes. This can be best illustrated by analysing the application of the new product condition, which is another requirement that was absent in the *Commercial Solvents* reasoning, to the facts of the *Microsoft* case. As discussed earlier,[991] the European Commission and the General Court have lowered the standard for the fulfilment of the new product requirement in *Microsoft*. A possible explanation for this may be found in the fact that Microsoft's competitors were not able to identify a new product that they would like to

---

Commission — Guidance on the Commission's enforcement priorities in applying Article 82 of the EC Treaty to abusive exclusionary conduct by dominant undertakings (Guidance Paper) [2009] OJ C 45/7, par. 81).

987. Communication from the Commission — Guidance on the Commission's enforcement priorities in applying Article 82 of the EC Treaty to abusive exclusionary conduct by dominant undertakings (Guidance Paper) [2009] OJ C 45/7, par. 84.

988. Judgment in *Istituto Chemioterapico Italiano and Commercial Solvents v. Commission*, Joined cases 6 and 7/73, ECLI:EU:C:1974:18, par. 15.

989. Judgment in *United Brands v. Commission*, Case 27/76, ECLI:EU:C:1978:22, par. 182. See also P. Larouche, *Competition Law and Regulation in European Telecommunications*, Oxford, Hart Publishing, 2000, p. 168.

990. Judgment in *CBEM v. CLT & IPB (Télémarketing)*, Case 311/84, ECLI:EU:C:1985:394, par. 26.
991. See section 6.2.2 above.

introduce upon having access to Microsoft's interoperability information, because they were already active on the market for work group server operating systems and merely wanted to keep competing on that market by continuing to offer their work group server operating systems to consumers. While the European Commission stated in its *Microsoft* decision that the disruption of previous levels of supply '*is of interest when assessing instances of refusal to supply*',[992] the European Commission and the General Court still applied the four-prong exceptional circumstances test to the facts of the case. Both institutions solved the problem with regard to the new product condition by arguing that a mere limitation of technical development suffices to meet this requirement.

The application of the new product requirement to disruptions of supply has the consequence that downstream competitors who were already active on the market and have likely made commercial decisions on the basis of the supply have to identify a new product that they would like to introduce in the market in order to continue to have access to the input of the dominant firm. If downstream competitors cannot point to such a new product (or, if the *Microsoft* standard is used and upheld in future cases: a new technical development) that they would like to develop on the basis of the requested input, they have no cause of action under Article 102 TFEU towards a dominant undertaking that decides to enter the downstream market itself and withdraws previous levels of supply in order to become the sole supplier of the downstream product.[993]

To prevent these situations, disruptions of supply should be assessed under different legal standards than absolute refusals to deal. As demonstrated by the *Microsoft* case in which Microsoft was found to have engaged in a strategy to exclude competitors from the downstream market for work group server operating systems, a disruption of supply may be used to drive downstream competitors off the market. It is therefore worth considering if a separate cause of action for disruptions of supply under Article 102 TFEU can be based on the predatory nature of such behaviour.

In this regard, a comparison can be made with the US where two cumulative conditions have to be met in order for a refusal to deal to amount to a violation of Section 2 of the Sherman Act: (1) the monopolist entered into a pre-existing voluntary course of dealing; and (2) the monopolist is willing to forsake short-term profits in order to achieve an anticompetitive end.[994] The willingness of a dominant undertaking to sacrifice short-term profits by unilaterally terminating a voluntary and thus presumably profitable course of dealing reveals the predatory character of a refusal to deal and forms a reliable proxy for assessing the abusive nature of a disruption of supply. A proposed legal test in EU competition law specifically applicable to disruptions of supply may therefore be based on the US framework.

---

992. Case COMP/C-3/37.792 - *Microsoft*, 24 March 2004, par. 556.
993. D. GERADIN, 'Limiting the Scope of Article 82 EC: What Can the EU Learn from the U.S. Supreme Court's Judgment in *Trinko* in the Wake of *Microsoft, IMS*, and *Deutsche Telekom*?', *Common Market Law Review* 2004, vol. 41, no. 6, (1519), p. 1538 who refers to this as '*the absurdity of the "new product" test*'.
994. See Verizon Communications v. Law Offices of Curtis V. Trinko, LLP (Trinko), 540 U.S. 398 (2004), at 409.

A first step may in that light involve establishing a voluntary prior course of dealing for an indispensable input between the dominant undertaking and the existing customer. A pre-existing business relationship based on a regulatory duty, such as the statutory access obligation that the US Telecommunications Act imposed on Verizon in *Trinko*, does not qualify as a voluntary course of dealing. If the dominant undertaking has not engaged in a prior course of dealing on a voluntary basis, the predatory nature of the disruption of supply cannot be established because there is no presumption that the dominant undertaking profited from the course of dealing and decided to forego these profits by terminating the business relationship.[995]

The input which forms the object of the dispute has to be indispensable in terms of its objective necessity for competition in the downstream market and the absence of economically viable substitutes.[996] If the input is not indispensable, the existing customer will not be driven off the market once the dominant undertaking starts to deny access to the requested input. Either the input is not objectively necessary for competition on the downstream market which means that the existing customer does not need access to the input in order to be active on that market. Or there are actual or potential substitutes for the input as a result of which the existing customer can avoid being excluded from the downstream market by relying on one of these alternative sources of supply. Because no anticompetitive effects arise if the indispensability requirement is not met, it is submitted that a disruption of supply involving a non-essential input should not be regarded as abusive under Article 102 TFEU.[997]

A second step for determining whether a disruption of supply amounts to a violation of the EU prohibition on abuse of dominance (outside the conditions of the exceptional circumstances test of *Magill* and *IMS Health*) would involve establishing the anticompetitive nature of the termination of the prior course of dealing. In devising a legal test for the assessment of whether a termination of an existing business relationship is anticompetitive, the case law of the EU courts on predatory pricing may serve as a source of inspiration. In the *Akzo* case, the Court of Justice put forward a two-tier approach for assessing predatory pricing conduct under Article 102 TFEU. According to the Court, pricing below average variable cost is presumed to be abusive because a '*dominant undertaking has no interest in applying such prices except that of eliminating competitors so as to enable it subsequently to raise its prices by taking advantage of its monopolistic position*',[998] while pricing below average total cost but

---

995. In Trinko, the US Supreme Court argued that in the absence of a voluntary course of dealing 'the defendant's prior conduct sheds no light upon the motivation of its refusal to deal-upon whether its regulatory lapses were prompted not by competitive zeal but by anticompetitive malice' (Verizon Communications v. Law Offices of Curtis V. Trinko, LLP (Trinko), 540 U.S. 398 (2004), at 409).
996. See section 6.8.2.1 above for a more elaborate discussion of the indispensability condition.
997. R. Subiotto and R. O'Donoghue, 'Defining the Scope of the Duty of Dominant Firms to Deal with Existing Customers under Article 82 EC', *European Competition Law Review* 2003, vol. 24, no. 12, (683), p. 687.
998. Judgment in *Akzo Chemie v. Commission*, C-62/86, ECLI:EU:C:1991:286, par. 71.

above average variable cost is only regarded as abusive if proof of '*a plan for eliminating a competitor*'[999] or, in other words, of '*intention to eliminate competition*'[1000] can be established.

These insights from the EU case law on predatory pricing can be transposed to the area of disruptions to supply in the following way. The sacrifice of short-term profits that results from a dominant undertaking's decision to disrupt existing levels of supply gives rise to a presumption of a plan or intent to eliminate competition considering that the dominant firm has no interest in terminating the existing business relationship except that of eliminating competitors from the downstream market so as to enable it subsequently to raise its prices to consumers. The abusive nature of the disruption to supply is then in principle established, unless the dominant undertaking is able to successfully invoke an objective justification.

If the willingness of the dominant undertaking to forsake short-term profits cannot be established, proof of a plan or intent to eliminate competition would be necessary in order to hold a disruption of supply abusive under Article 102 TFEU. In line with the *Post Danmark I* judgment, in which the Court of Justice seems to have accepted proof of anticompetitive effects as a substitute for proof of a plan or intent to eliminate competition,[1001] competition authorities and courts may also rely on anticompetitive effects in order to prove the predatory nature of a disruption of supply. One way to establish such anticompetitive effects may be to demonstrate that the termination leads to the exclusion of all effective competition on the downstream market.[1002] In such a case, the assessment of a disruption of supply would overlap to a large extent with the exceptional circumstances test applicable to absolute refusals to deal because both the indispensability of the input and the exclusion of all effective competition are considered. Nevertheless, if the dominant undertaking is foregoing short-term profits by disrupting previous levels of supply, no proof of anticompetitive effects is necessary and a violation of Article 102 TFEU can be established without having to consider whether all effective competition is excluded on the downstream market.

---

999. Judgment in *Akzo Chemie v. Commission*, C-62/86, ECLI:EU:C:1991:286, par. 72.
1000. Judgment in *Tetra Pak International SA v. Commission (Tetra Pak II)*, T-83/91, ECLI:EU:T:1994:246, par. 151 and Judgment in *France Télécom SA v. Commission*, T-340/03, ECLI:EU:T:2007:22, par. 197.
1001. Judgment in *Post Danmark A/S v. Konkurrencerådet (Post Danmark I)*, C-209/10, ECLI:EU:C:2012:172, paras 29 and 40. See E. ROUSSEVA AND M. MARQUIS, 'Hell Freezes Over: A Climate Change for Assessing Exclusionary Conduct under Article 102 TFEU', *Journal of European Competition Law & Practice* 2013, vol. 4, no. 1, (32), p. 36. In the Guidance Paper on exclusionary conduct under Article 102 TFEU, the European Commission also considered evidence of foreclosure effects as a way to establish the predatory nature of conduct (Communication from the Commission — Guidance on the Commission's enforcement priorities in applying Article 82 of the EC Treaty to abusive exclusionary conduct by dominant undertakings (Guidance Paper) [2009] OJ C 45/7, paras 67-73).
1002. For a discussion of this requirement in the context of absolute refusals to deal, see section 6.8.2.2 above.

Figure 6.4   Proposed Three-Step Framework for Assessing the Abusive Nature of Disruptions of Supply under Article 102 TFEU

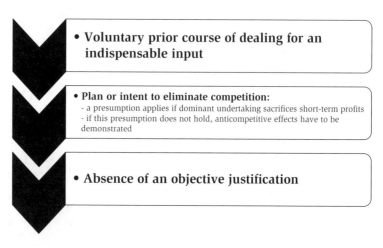

- **Voluntary prior course of dealing for an indispensable input**

- **Plan or intent to eliminate competition:**
  - a presumption applies if dominant undertaking sacrifices short-term profits
  - if this presumption does not hold, anticompetitive effects have to be demonstrated

- **Absence of an objective justification**

Once a voluntary prior course of dealing for an indispensable input has been identified and the anticompetitive nature of the disruption of supply has been established, the dominant undertaking must, in a third step, be given the chance to objectively justify the unilateral termination of its business relationship with the existing customer. Since the dominant undertaking voluntarily decided to deal in the past, it will be hard to proof that a disruption of supply is justified. Nevertheless, two defences may be particularly relevant.

If the dominant undertaking notices that the existing customer starts having trouble paying for access to the requested input, it may invoke the inability to pay of that customer as a justification for the disruption of supply. In addition, as made clear by the Court of Justice in *Sot. Lélos v. GlaxoSmithKline* a dominant undertaking may protect its own commercial interests if it is confronted with orders from existing customers that are out of the ordinary. The Court explained that an order could be out of the ordinary if it consists of *'quantities which are out of all proportion to those previously sold by the same wholesalers to meet the needs of the market'*.[1003] In order to ascertain whether the orders are ordinary, *'the previous business relations'* between the parties as well as *'the size of those orders in relation to the requirements of the market'* were thus relevant in the Court's view.[1004] These statements of the Court of Justice may imply that no violation of Article 102 TFEU can be established if a dominant undertaking refuses to supply an existing customer with quantities in excess of those ordinarily ordered by that customer.

1003. Judgment in *Sot. Lélos kai Sia EE and Others v. GlaxoSmithKline AEVE Farmakeftikon Proïonton*, Joined Cases C-468/06 to C-478/06, ECLI:EU:C:2008:504, par. 76.
1004. Judgment in *Sot. Lélos kai Sia EE and Others v. GlaxoSmithKline AEVE Farmakeftikon Proïonton*, Joined Cases C-468/06 to C-478/06, ECLI:EU:C:2008:504, paras 73 and 77.

Objective justifications relating to the negative impact that a duty to continue to supply may have on the innovation incentives or the ability to recoup investments of the dominant undertaking are not likely to be successful. After all, the existence of a voluntary prior course of dealing indicates there is no such risk.[1005]

One could argue that creating a separate cause of action for disruptions of supply may generate perverse incentives for dominant firms to refrain from supplying inputs to competitors in the first place out of fear that they may then be forced to deal with their rivals for as long as the latter require access to the inputs.[1006] However, the fact that a disruption of supply may give rise to a violation of Article 102 TFEU outside the conditions of the essential facilities doctrine does not mean that dominant firms are locked-in to their existing customers and can only terminate an existing business relationship by relying on an objective justification.[1007] The only prohibition that the three-part test proposed here imposes on dominant undertakings is that a disruption of supply cannot be based on a predatory strategy.[1008] The scope for competition law enforcement in this respect is thus limited to instances where a dominant undertaking disrupts existing levels of supply in order to drive a competitor off the market.

In the absence of a predatory strategy of the dominant firm, customers may rely on contract law to compel the latter to continue to supply or to obtain damages for the loss caused by the refusal to deal.[1009] Since the relationship between a firm and its customers primarily falls within the ambit of contract law, enforcement actions on the basis of competition law should remain limited to cases in which disruptions of supply are used by dominant undertakings as a pretext to exclude a competitor from the market.

While the European Commission and the General Court expressed the view that disruptions of supply should not be treated differently than absolute refusals to deal in,

---

1005. See also Communication from the Commission — Guidance on the Commission's enforcement priorities in applying Article 82 of the EC Treaty to abusive exclusionary conduct by dominant undertakings (Guidance Paper) [2009] OJ C 45/7, par. 84.

1006. In this light, see E. ELHAUGE, 'Defining Better Monopolization Standards', *Stanford Law Review* 2003, vol. 56, no. 2, (253), p. 314; C. AHLBORN, D.S. EVANS AND A.J. PADILLA, 'The Logic & Limits of the "Exceptional Circumstances Test" in *Magill* and *IMS Health*', *Fordham International Law Journal* 2004-2005, vol. 28, no. 4, (1109), p. 1146; C. RITTER, 'Refusal to Deal and "Essential Facilities": Does Intellectual Property Require Special Deference Compared to Tangible Property?', *World Competition* 2005, no. 28, (281), pp. 284-285 and H. HOVENKAMP, M.D. JANIS AND M.A. LEMLEY, 'Unilateral Refusals to License', *Journal of Competition Law and Economics* 2006, vol. 2, no. 1, (1), p. 30. This is also one of the criticisms expressed in response to the *TeliaSonera* judgment, as discussed in section 6.8.4 below, in which the Court of Justice made clear that a margin squeeze can be considered abusive in the absence of a duty to supply under the essential facilities doctrine.

1007. As argued by I. LIANOS, 'Competition Law and Intellectual Property Rights: Is the Property Rights' Approach Right?' in J. BELL AND C. KILPATRICK (eds.), *The Cambridge Yearbook of European Legal Studies. Volume 8*, 2005-2006, (153), pp. 165-166.

1008. See also D. GERADIN, 'Limiting the Scope of Article 82 EC: What Can the EU Learn from the U.S. Supreme Court's Judgment in *Trinko* in the Wake of *Microsoft*, *IMS*, and *Deutsche Telekom*?', *Common Market Law Review* 2004, vol. 41, no. 6, (1519), p. 1536 in the context of the *Commercial Solvents* reasoning.

1009. R. SUBIOTTO AND R. O'DONOGHUE, 'Defining the Scope of the Duty of Dominant Firms to Deal with Existing Customers under Article 82 EC', *European Competition Law Review* 2003, vol. 24, no. 12, (683), p. 684.

respectively, the Guidance Paper on exclusionary conduct under Article 102 TFEU and the *Microsoft* case, the Court of Justice still appears to distinguish with regard to the legal thresholds applicable to the two types of refusal to deal. In *Sot. Lélos v. GlaxoSmithKline*, a preliminary ruling case involving a refusal of a dominant pharmaceutical company to meet orders of existing customers in full with the aim of restricting parallel trade, the Court of Justice argued that '*established case-law of the Court shows that the refusal by an undertaking occupying a dominant position on the market of a given product to meet the orders of an existing customer constitutes abuse of that dominant position under Article [102 TFEU] where, without any objective justification, that conduct is liable to eliminate a trading party as a competitor*'.[1010] It is striking in this regard that the Court referred to the *Commercial Solvents* and *United Brands* judgments and not to the *Magill* and *IMS Health* judgments in which it established the stricter exceptional circumstances test. This may indicate that the Court of Justice still regards the *Commercial Solvents* reasoning as the applicable law for disruptions of supply.

Since the *Microsoft* judgment of the General Court was not appealed, the Court of Justice has not been given the opportunity to rule on the fact that the lower court applied the stricter exceptional circumstances test to Microsoft's termination of the previous level of disclosures of interoperability information. Its statements in the *Sot. Lélos v. GlaxoSmithKline* judgment may imply that the Court of Justice does not agree with the approach of the General Court in *Microsoft* and is of the view that the exceptional circumstances test of *Magill* and *IMS Health* should not be applied for determining the abusive nature of disruptions of supply.[1011] Instead, disruptions of supply may be assessed for their predatory character as the three-part test put forward here aims to do.

6.8.4 Discriminatory Refusals to Supply

Discriminatory refusals to supply can be considered as a third type of scenario next to absolute refusals to deal and disruptions of supply. Under Article 102(c) TFEU, a dominant firm is prohibited from '*applying dissimilar conditions to equivalent transactions with other trading parties, thereby placing them at a competitive disadvantage*'. In the refusal to deal context, this provision may capture situations in which a dominant firm treats a competitor differently from others by supplying this competitor on the basis of less favourable terms or by refusing to deal with this competitor while supplying (one of) the others. Such scenarios give rise to a constructive refusal to deal. A critical question in this regard is whether the exceptional facilities test has to be met in order for a form of discrimination with regard to the terms of supply to be abusive. The relevant issue is thus, in other words, whether discriminatory conditions of supply can be considered abusive in the absence of a duty to supply under the essential facilities doctrine.

1010. Judgment in *Sot. Lélos kai Sia EE and Others v. GlaxoSmithKline AEVE Farmakeftikon Proïonton*, Joined Cases C-468/06 to C-478/06, ECLI:EU:C:2008:504, par. 34.
1011. See also T. Käseberg, Intellectual Property, Antitrust and Cumulative Innovation in the EU and the US, Hart Publishing, 2012, pp. 222-223.

In *TeliaSonera*, the Court of Justice made clear that the conditions set out in *Bronner* do not '*necessarily also apply when assessing the abusive nature of conduct which consists in supplying services or selling goods on conditions which are disadvantageous or on which there might be no purchaser*'.[1012] The case concerned a so-called margin squeeze whereby a vertically integrated dominant firm sets its upstream and downstream prices to such a level to create a margin between them at which downstream competitors cannot generate a profit. The Court argued that a margin squeeze '*may, in itself, constitute an independent form of abuse distinct from that of refusal to supply*' that is not subject to the exceptional circumstances test.[1013] Otherwise, in the Court's view: '*before any conduct of a dominant undertaking in relation to its terms of trade could be regarded as abusive the conditions to be met to establish that there was a refusal to supply would in every case have to be satisfied, and that would unduly reduce the effectiveness of Article 102 TFEU*'.[1014]

The *TeliaSonera* case can be understood as meaning that once a dominant firm voluntarily decides to supply, it must do so on terms at which competitors can effectively compete even though no duty to deal can be established under the essential facilities doctrine.[1015] In that regard, *TeliaSonera* thus treats refusals to deal and margin squeezes, a form of constructive refusals to deal, differently. This approach adopted by the Court of Justice stands in contrast to the situation in the United States where the Supreme Court made clear in *linkLine* that no violation of Section 2 of the Sherman Act can be found for a margin squeeze in the absence of an antitrust duty to deal.[1016] One could argue that the creation of a separate form of abuse for margin squeezes leads to the perverse situation that a dominant firm is better off by refusing to give access to a non-indispensable input, for which no duty to deal exists under the exceptional circumstances test, to prevent the risk that the terms under which it would otherwise have supplied the input give rise to a margin squeeze.

According to the Court of Justice, its reasoning was in line with *Bronner* because it could not be inferred from the latter judgment that '*the conditions to be met in order to establish that a refusal to supply is abusive must necessarily also apply when assessing the abusive nature of conduct which consists in supplying services or selling goods on conditions which are disadvantageous or on which there might be no purchaser*'.[1017] In particular, the Court argued that in *Bronner* it was only called upon to interpret the conditions under which a refusal to supply may be abusive and therefore '*did not make any ruling on whether the fact that an undertaking refuses*

1012. Judgment in *Konkurrensverket v. TeliaSonera Sverige AB*, C-52/09, ECLI:EU:C:2011:83, par. 55.
1013. Judgment in *Konkurrensverket v. TeliaSonera Sverige AB*, C-52/09, ECLI:EU:C:2011:83, par. 56.
1014. Judgment in *Konkurrensverket v. TeliaSonera Sverige AB*, C-52/09, ECLI:EU:C:2011:83, par. 58.
1015. Coates suggests to look at the *TeliaSonera* case as a form of estoppel. See K. Coates, 'The Estoppel Abuse', *21st Century Competition: Reflections on Modern Antitrust*, 28 October 2013, available at http://www.twentyfirstcenturycompetition.com/2013/10/the-estoppel-abuse/.
1016. For a discussion of *linkLine*, see section 6.2.1 above.
1017. Judgment in *Konkurrensverket v. TeliaSonera Sverige AB*, C-52/09, ECLI:EU:C:2011:83, par. 55.

access to its home-delivery scheme to the publisher of a rival newspaper where the latter does not at the same time entrust to it the carrying out of other services, such as sales in kiosks or printing, constitutes some other form of abuse of a dominant position, such as tied sales'.[1018] Since the Court referred to 'any conduct of a dominant undertaking in relation to its terms of trade', the *TeliaSonera* judgment is also of relevance for types of conduct other than margin squeeze.[1019] In this sense, *TeliaSonera* may imply that discriminatory terms of supply can be abusive even in the absence of a duty to supply under the exceptional circumstances test.

In *Clearstream*, the European Commission did not apply the conditions of the exceptional circumstances test to a discriminatory refusal to deal but only assessed whether the difference in treating requests for the supply of primary clearing and settlement services in the context of securities transactions was justified by valid and objective reasons.[1020] However, the investigation targeted several access requests which were either refused or substantially delayed in comparison with other comparable customers in equivalent situations. The Commission did consider the conditions of indispensability and elimination of all effective competition with respect to the absolute refusals to deal. As made clear by the General Court on appeal, the Commission found that the absolute refusals to deal and the unjustified discrimination were two manifestations of the same course of conduct instead of two separate offences.[1021] Since the absolute and discriminatory refusals to deal were closely linked and considered together, no strong conclusions can be drawn from *Clearstream* as regards the applicable legal standards for assessing the abusive nature of discriminatory conditions of supply.

The fact that discriminatory conditions of supply constitute a self-standing form of abuse does not mean that a dominant firm should be obliged to deal with every similarly situated competitor once it has supplied one. The welfare effects of discrimination are more ambiguous than those of exclusionary conduct and may in many instances even be positive.[1022] Therefore, discriminatory refusals to deal should only be considered abusive if they have a substantial effect on competition. As regards an appropriate benchmark for assessing such substantial harm, the *BP* case is instructive. The case involved the allegedly abusive nature of BP's decision to reduce its supplies to ABG, an occasional customer, during the oil crisis to a much greater extent than in

---

1018. Judgment in *Konkurrensverket v. TeliaSonera Sverige AB*, C-52/09, ECLI:EU:C:2011:83, par. 57.
1019. The *TeliaSonera* judgment may even be considered to form another indication, in addition to the more specific statements of the Court of Justice in *Sot. Lélos v. GlaxoSmithKline*, that disruptions of supply should be subject to a different legal standard than absolute refusals to deal. See section 6.8.3 above.
1020. Case COMP/38.906 - *Clearstream*, 2 June 2004, par. 299.
1021. Judgment in Clearstream Banking AG and Clearstream International SA v. Commission, T-301/04, ECLI:EU:T:2009:317, par. 150.
1022. In the context of discrimination on the basis of price, see H.R. Varian, 'Price Discrimination and Social Welfare', *The American Economic Review* 1985, vol. 75, no. 4, (870) and M. Armstrong and J. Vickers, 'Competitive Price Discrimination', *RAND Journal of Economics* 2001, vol. 32, no. 4, (1) as quoted by R. Subiotto and R. O'Donoghue, 'Defining the Scope of the Duty of Dominant Firms to Deal with Existing Customers under Article 82 EC', *European Competition Law Review* 2003, vol. 24, no. 12, (683), p. 688.

relation to all its other customers. In this context, the Court of Justice referred to '*an obvious, immediate and substantial competitive disadvantage*' which might have jeopardised ABG's continued existence.[1023]

With respect to selective refusals to deal whereby a dominant undertaking is only willing to supply certain competitors and not others, it is important to note that Article 102 TFEU covers practices that cause harm to consumers and does not protect the position of particular competitors. As made clear by the Court of Justice in *Post Danmark I*, '*[c]ompetition on the merits may, by definition, lead to the departure from the market or the marginalisation of competitors that are less efficient and so less attractive to consumers from the point of view of, among other things, price, choice, quality or innovation*'.[1024] As a result, in the absence of damage to consumer welfare, the fact that a dominant firm excludes a particular competitor from the market by selectively refusing to supply this competitor does not violate Article 102 TFEU. For example, in cases where a large number of competitors already has access to the necessary input for providing certain products or services to consumers, not supplying the input to other competitors is unlikely to give rise to substantial consumer harm.[1025]

In conclusion, discriminatory refusals to deal should only be held abusive if the different treatment of competitors in similar situations results in substantial harm to competition and consumers that cannot be objectively justified.

6.9 CONCLUSION

The standards for the application of the essential facilities doctrine are different in the United States and the European Union. After the judgment of the US Supreme Court in *Trinko*, it is clear that the scope for antitrust liability is limited to instances where a monopolist foregoes short-term profits by terminating voluntary prior course of dealing. In the EU, absolute refusals to deal where the requested input has never been marketed before may also be found abusive under Article 102 TFEU.

Apart from these distinct legal standards, there is also an important difference in policy. Whereas US authorities and courts rely on the strength of the self-correcting mechanism of the market and emphasise the negative effects on innovation that may result from an interventionist approach, EU competition policy is characterised by its emphasis on keeping markets open and by the assumption that openness of markets is a prerequisite for innovation.

Essential facilities cases involve a trade-off between different interests. The trade-off that is made explicit in the EU decision-making practice and case law concerns the balance between the interest of essential facility holder on the one hand, and the interest in free competition on the other hand. EU cases remain silent on the underlying

---

1023. Judgment in Benzine en Petroleum Handelsmaatschappij BV and others v. Commission, Case 77/77, ECLI:EU:C:1978:141, paras 19-20.
1024. Judgment in *Post Danmark A/S v. Konkurrencerådet* (*Post Danmark I*), C-209/10, ECLI:EU:C:2012:172, par. 22.
1025. R. SUBIOTTO AND R. O'DONOGHUE, 'Defining the Scope of the Duty of Dominant Firms to Deal with Existing Customers under Article 82 EC', *European Competition Law Review* 2003, vol. 24, no. 12, (683), p. 688.

economic trade-off between competition *for* and competition *in* the market. The framework proposed in this chapter aims to contribute to the state of the art by providing a way to apply this economic trade-off in practice and to make it more objective, in particular in cases concerning absolute refusals to deal.

Instead of distinguishing between whether assets are protected by intellectual property law or not, the framework suggests to let the applicability of the new product condition depend on whether a market is characterised by external market failures. Considering that a competition law intervention cannot re-establish the race for competition *for* the market, caution is warranted in markets in which external market failures are absent. In these markets, the new product condition should be applied strictly because of the stronger self-correcting mechanism of the market which may make a competition law intervention to stimulate competition *in* the market less pressing.

In markets where external market failures are present, the new product requirement should be dropped to ensure that access seekers planning to introduce competition *in* the market can gain access to the necessary input. In these markets, there is a higher risk that the incumbent is able to extend its dominance in time and to prevent competitors from entering the market and competing on the basis price or quality which justifies a wider scope of liability for refusals to deal under Article 102 TFEU. In line with the approach in the US, the framework also provides for a different legal standard for disruptions of supply based on their potential predatory nature.

Considering that the proposed framework diverges from the existing legal standards in several ways, the question rises whether there is room for such a new approach towards the assessment of refusals to deal. From the way the exceptional circumstances test is phrased in *Magill* and *IMS Health*, it becomes clear that the existing conditions are not necessary for finding a violation of Article 102 TFEU but merely sufficient. In other words, the exceptional circumstances test is not exhaustive and the existing conditions may be complemented or even replaced by others.[1026] Statements of the Court of Justice in *Sot. Lélos v. GlaxoSmithKline* may suggest that it is of the view that disruptions of supply should be assessed under less strict standards than the current conditions of the exceptional circumstances test.

1026. It is interesting to note that, in the context of the seeking of injunctions on the basis of so-called 'standard essential patents' (SEPs), the European Commission explicitly stated in *Samsung* and *Motorola* that the list of exceptional circumstances in which the exercise of an intellectual property right can be held abusive under Article 102 TFEU is not exhaustive (Case AT.39939 – *Samsung - Enforcement of UMTS Standard Essential Patents*, 29 April 2014, par. 56 and Case AT.39985 – *Motorola - Enforcement of GPRS Standard Essential Patents*, 29 April 2014, par. 278). Similarly, the Court of Justice argued in *Huawei v. ZTE* that the exceptional circumstances of the latter case have to be distinguished from those giving rise to the refusal to deal case law. The Court made clear that a refusal by the proprietor of the SEP to grant a licence on FRAND terms may, in principle constitute an abuse within the meaning of Article 102 TFEU in the specific circumstances of the case where (1) the patent at issue was essential to a standard established by a standardisation body and (2) the patent at issue obtained SEP status only in return for the proprietor's irrevocable undertaking to the standardisation body in question that it was prepared to grant licences on FRAND terms (Judgment in *Huawei v. ZTE*, C-170/13, ECLI:EU:C:2015:477, paras 47-53).

It also remains to be seen whether the lower standards for the fulfilment of the exceptional circumstances tests as applied by the European Commission and the General Court in *Microsoft* will be upheld in future cases. This is especially relevant because the Court of Justice has not been given the opportunity to rule in the *Microsoft* case. One could argue in this regard that the Commission and the Court may have deliberately tailored the exceptional circumstances test to the particular market situation in the *Microsoft* case by lowering the applicable standards. If that is the case, there might be room for a framework in which the presence of external market failures is determinative for the strictness with which conditions have to be applied.

CHAPTER 7

Application of the Essential Facilities Doctrine to Data

7.1 INTRODUCTION

The essential facilities doctrine has been applied to physical infrastructures and intangible assets protected by intellectual property rights on several occasions. The question is if and how the essential facilities doctrine should be applied to user information on online platforms. Because of the personal nature of the data and the peculiar business model of online platform providers, the issue raises new concerns and may require a different analysis under the existing competition rules.

Section 7.2 discusses whether and to what extent the large collections of data of incumbent providers of search engines, social networks and e-commerce platforms give rise to a competitive advantage in the form of network effects and barriers to entry. In section 7.3, two scenarios with regard to refusals to give access to data on online platforms are identified based on whether a duty to deal leads to direct or indirect competition with the holder of the requested input. Afterwards, it is analysed how a relevant market for data can be defined in section 7.4, how market power with regard to data can be established in section 7.5 and how the abusive nature of refusals to deal involving data can be assessed in section 7.6.

7.2 DATA AS A COMPETITIVE ADVANTAGE[1027]

The role of data in the competitive process between online platforms and companies in the digital economy in general is a contentious issue that has started to attract attention

---

1027. The analysis in this section builds upon earlier work in I. GRAEF, 'Market Definition and Market Power in Data: The Case of Online Platforms', *World Competition* 2015, vol. 38, no. 4, (473), pp. 479-480 and 483-489.

from policy makers and scholars.[1028] Over the past years, a number of reports have been issued by government bodies and competition authorities in which the interaction between data and competition law has been discussed.[1029] Most notably, the Autorité de la concurrence (the French competition authority) launched a sector inquiry into the online advertising industry in May 2016 to gather information with a view to assessing the significance of data processing for competition in this sector.[1030]

One of the questions central to the debate is whether and to what extent the accumulation of data by incumbent online platforms gives rise to a competitive advantage. While it is uncontroversial that providers of search engines, social networks and e-commerce platforms employ a business model that relies on the acquisition and monetisation of user data, it is fiercely debated whether the effort required to collect the data necessary to be able to compete on equal footing with the incumbent amounts to a sustainable competitive advantage and barrier to entry.[1031]

Online platforms use algorithms to return the most relevant search results, suggested social network interactions and recommendations for future purchases to users. As more data on the behaviour and interests of users becomes available, the

---

1028. Scholars who have written on the topic include N. NEWMAN, 'Search, Antitrust, and the Economics of the Control of User Data', *Yale Journal on Regulation* 2014, vol. 31, no. 2, (401); A.V. LERNER, 'The Role of "Big Data" in Online Platform Competition', *SSRN Working Paper* August 2014, available at http://papers.ssrn.com/sol3/papers.cfm?abstract_id = 2482780; D.S. TUCKER AND H.B. WELLFORD, 'Big Mistakes Regarding Big Data', *The Antitrust Source* 2014, vol. 14, no. 2, (1); A.P. GRUNES AND M.E. STUCKE, 'No Mistake About It: The Important Role of Antitrust in the Era of Big Data', *The Antitrust Source* 2015, vol. 14, no. 4, (1); D.S. SOKOL AND R. COMERFORD, 'Does Antitrust Have A Role to Play in Regulating Big Data?' in R.D. BLAIR AND D.D. SOKOL (eds.), *Cambridge Handbook of Antitrust, Intellectual Property and High Technology*, Cambridge University Press, forthcoming, available at http://papers.ssrn.com/sol3/papers.cfm?abstract_id = 2723693; and D.A. BALTO AND M.C. LANE, 'Monopolizing Water in a Tsunami: Finding Sensible Antitrust Rules for Big Data', *SSRN Working Paper March 2016* available at http://papers.ssrn.com/sol3/papers.cfm?abstract_id = 2753249.
1029. See PRELIMINARY OPINION OF THE EUROPEAN DATA PROTECTION SUPERVISOR, 'Privacy and competitiveness in the age of big data: The interplay between data protection, competition law and consumer protection in the Digital Economy', March 2014; UK Competition & Markets Authority, 'The commercial use of consumer data. Report on the CMA's call for information', June 2015, pp. 74-96, available at https://www.gov.uk/government/uploads/system/uploads/attachment_data/file/435817/The_commercial_use_of_consumer_data.pdf; MONOPOLKOMMISSION, 'Competition policy: The challenge of digital markets', Special report No. 68, July 2015, pp. 27-36, available at http://www.monopolkommission.de/images/PDF/SG/s68_fulltext_eng.pdf; UK House of Lords Select Committee on European Union, 'Online Platforms and the Digital Single Market', 10th Report of Session 2015-16, 20 April 2016, paras 164-180, available at http://www.publications.parliament.uk/pa/ld201516/ldselect/ldeucom/129/129.pdf; and Autorité de la concurrence and Bundeskartellamt, 'Competition Law and Data', 10 May 2016, available at http://www.autoritedelaconcurrence.fr/doc/reportcompetitionlawanddatafinal.pdf.
1030. Press Release Autorité de la concurrence, 'The Autorité de la concurrence begins, at its own initiative, gathering information in order to assess data processing in the on-line advertising sector', 23 May 2016, available at http://www.autoritedelaconcurrence.fr/user/standard.php?id_rub = 630&id_article = 2780.
1031. For different views from a business perspective, see for instance T. MCGUIRE, J. MANYIKA AND M. CHUI, 'Why Big Data Is the New Competitive Advantage', *Ivey Business Journal* July/Aug 2012, vol. 76, no. 4, (1) and A. LAMBRECHT AND C.E. TUCKER, 'Can Big Data Protect a Firm from Competition?', *SSRN Working Paper* December 2015, available at http://papers.ssrn.com/sol3/papers.cfm?abstract_id = 2705530.

algorithm can be improved and will provide users with more relevant responses.[1032] The former Commissioner for Competition argued in this regard: '*the more people use a search engine the better it gets, because engineers need search data to refine their algorithms*'.[1033]

On the advertise side of the platform, the collected data is monetised to fund the usually free delivery of functionalities to users by giving advertisers the possibility to target their advertisements to specific groups of users. Under the pay-per-click advertising model that is most commonly employed on online platforms, advertisers only pay the provider once a user has actually clicked on an advertisement. By accumulating data about users, the provider is able to increase its revenues because with more user information available it will become better at displaying ads to users that are of such relevance that they will actually click on them. In addition, better targeting possibilities will also attract more advertisers to the platform because of the higher probability that a user buys the advertised product or service.[1034] This will again raise the revenues of the provider. This phenomenon can be referred to as economies of scale with regard to the monetisation of user data.[1035]

These economies of scale relating to data on the user[1036] and advertiser side of online platforms are argued to be subject to diminishing returns to scale.[1037] This implies that the value of having additional information declines as the amount of data

---

1032. See section 2.4.2 for a more detailed description of this process of machine learning and how it relates to the ability of a search engine to adapt to the constantly changing needs and intentions of users.

1033. Speech former Competition Commissioner Almunia, 'Competition in the online world', LSE Public Lecture London, 11 November 2013, SPEECH/13/905, available at http://europa.eu/rapid/press-release_SPEECH-13-905_en.htm. In this regard, see also Case No COMP/M.5727 – *Microsoft/Yahoo! Search Business*, 18 February 2010, par. 162: '*With larger scale, a search engine can run tests on how to improve the algorithm and ultimately implement corrections [...]With the higher "bandwidth" that comes with increased traffic volume, experimental traffic takes up a smaller proportion of overall traffic, and it is possible to experiment more, and faster*'.

1034. In the context of the *Microsoft/Yahoo* merger decision, Microsoft submitted that '*increased scale also impacts on the advertiser experience, since a higher degree of user engagement and a better ability of the platform to show relevant ads impacts on advertiser ROI [return on investment]. Higher query volume in turn generates ad inventory. A larger inventory translates into more opportunities for advertisers to reach and target their intended audience. More advertisers lead to more ads for the search engine to choose from for any given query. This, in turn, improves ad relevance and the likelihood that a user will click on an ad and ultimately convert his click into a purchase. As a result, the inventory becomes more valuable to advertisers who see their return on investment increase*' (Case No COMP/M.5727 – *Microsoft/Yahoo! Search Business*, 18 February 2010, par. 163).

1035. See the discussion in A.V. LERNER, 'The Role of "Big Data" in Online Platform Competition', *SSRN Working Paper* August 2014, pp. 41-44, available at http://papers.ssrn.com/sol3/papers.cfm?abstract_id = 2482780.

1036. The role of data on the user side of online platforms has also been characterised as constituting an indirect network externality or a learning economy. For a further discussion, see section 2.4.2 above.

1037. Lerner also argues that at a certain point a further increase in user volume may have the effect of lowering advertising prices because a rise in user queries on, for example, a search engine will lead to an increase in the supply of ad slots. According to basic economic principles, an increase in supply leads to a lower price, all else equal. In addition, Lerner states that monetisation is affected by other factors such as engineering efforts to improve the

rises. The strength of the benefits relating to large datasets would then depend on the volume at which the returns from extra data start to diminish.[1038] If the benefits of having additional information start to decline only at a very high amount of data, large volumes of data can give rise to, respectively, a competitive advantage for incumbent platforms and an entry barrier for new entrants and potential competitors.

One should note that it is not only the amount of data that matters but also its variety. In its *Google/DoubleClick* merger decision, the Commission argued that: '*Competition based on the quality of collected data thus is not only decided by virtue of the sheer size of the respective databases, but also determined by the different types of data the competitors have access to and the question which type eventually will prove to be the most useful for internet advertising purposes*'.[1039] In economic terms, economies of scope can be identified. By combining and linking data from different sources, a deeper and more detailed profile can be gained of users.[1040] In this regard, companies providing a number of related online services are in a better position because they have access to a wide variety of information enabling them to build a more comprehensive picture of consumer preferences.

For example, Newman argues with regard to Google:

> Whether a user is watching videos on YouTube, sending email from a Gmail account, checking for updates at Google News, checking their location on an Android phone, or buying a product through Google Offers, this data feeds the accumulating profile that Google has not only on the user as an individual, but on aggregated profiles of people like them that Google can package for its advertisers in ads broadcast on any and all of those products.[1041]

In addition, in a report commissioned by the Belgian Privacy Commission about Facebook's new privacy policy introduced in January 2015, concerns were expressed about the horizontal and vertical expansion of Facebook. In particular, it was observed that Facebook combines data from an increasingly wide variety of sources, including acquired companies, partnering platforms and websites or mobile applications that rely on Facebook for advertising or other services, and collects a growing variety of types of information by adding new functionalities.[1042]

The different economies of scale and economies of scope relating to data may reinforce each other and give rise to a so-called feedback loop. Users that appreciate

---

technologies for ad targeting. See A.V. LERNER, 'The Role of "Big Data" in Online Platform Competition', *SSRN Working Paper* August 2014, pp. 41-44, available at http://papers.ssrn.com/sol3/papers.cfm?abstract_id = 2482780.

1038. H.A. SHELANSKI, 'Information, Innovation, and Competition Policy for the Internet', *University of Pennsylvania Law Review* 2013, vol. 161, no. 6, (1663), p. 1681. See also section 2.4.2 above.

1039. Case No COMP/M.4731 – *Google/ DoubleClick*, 11 March 2008, par. 273.

1040. See OECD, 'Data-Driven Innovation. Big Data for Growth and Well-Being', 6 October 2015, p. 184, available at http://www.oecd.org/sti/data-driven-innovation-9789264229358-en.htm.

1041. N. NEWMAN, 'Search, Antitrust, and the Economics of the Control of User Data', *Yale Journal on Regulation* 2014, vol. 31, no. 2, (401), p. 431.

1042. B. VAN ALSENOY, V. VERDOODT, R. HEYMAN, ET AL., 'From Social Media Service to Advertising Network. A Critical Analysis of Facebook's Revised Policies and Terms', report commissioned by the Belgian Privacy Commission, 25 August 2015, p. 10.

relevant or personalised services will spend more time on the platform, which allows the provider to collect even more data, leading to better insights into consumer preferences, which can be used to further improve the quality of the services offered to users and advertisers, attracting even more users and advertisers. As the number of different applications, such as email, messaging, video and music, offered by a certain provider increases, a wider variety of information becomes available which can be linked together and used to deliver better services to users and advertisers.[1043]

When assessing to what extent the datasets to which incumbent providers have access may constitute a competitive advantage or an entry barrier, the economic characteristics of data should also be considered. Data is a so-called non-rivalrous good which means that the fact that a certain entity has collected a piece of data does not preclude others from gathering identical information. Consumers commonly provide general information such as their home address, phone number, gender and date of birth to many entities as a result of which the same data may be used by different firms at the same time.[1044]

Furthermore, the value of data often does not lie in the collected information itself but instead depends on the knowledge that can be extracted from it.[1045] This implies that different entities may generate the same knowledge by gathering distinct types of data. For example, a search engine provider may get to know the music preferences of a particular user by way of analysing the search queries that a user has inserted while a social network provider is able to gain the same knowledge by looking at the profile information that the user has shared on its platform.

Another important characteristic of data is its diversity in value. While some data including name and date of birth has lasting value and only has to be collected once by a specific entity, other types of data, such as the search queries that users have been looking for, are more transient in value and are relevant over a shorter period of time.[1046] The latter types of data lose value over time as a result of which firms have to continue to gather up-to-date information about the interests and preferences of users in order to be able to return relevant responses to users and to deliver targeted advertising services to advertisers. The control over these types of data may not in itself give rise to a durable barrier to entry.[1047] The Competition Commissioner argued in this

---

1043. OECD, 'Data-Driven Innovation. Big Data for Growth and Well-Being', 6 October 2015, p. 185.

1044. UK Competition & Markets Authority, 'The commercial use of consumer data. Report on the CMA's call for information', June 2015, par. 3.6. In its *Telefónica/Vodafone/Everything Everywhere* merger decision, the Commission noted that: '*Customers generally tend to give their personal data to many market players, which gather and market it. Therefore, this type of data is generally understood to be a commodity*' (Case No COMP/M.6314 – *Telefónica UK/Vodafone UK/Everything Everywhere/JV*, 4 September 2012, par. 543).

1045. G.A. Manne and R.B. Sperry, 'The Problems and Perils of Bootstrapping Privacy and Data into an Antitrust Framework', *CPI Antitrust Chronicle* 2015, vol. 5, no. 2, (1), p. 9.

1046. UK Competition & Markets Authority, 'The commercial use of consumer data. Report on the CMA's call for information', June 2015, par. 3.6 and D.S. Tucker and H.B. Wellford, 'Big Mistakes Regarding Big Data', *The Antitrust Source* 2014, vol. 14, no. 2, (1), p. 4.

1047. See also the speech given by UK Competition & Markets Authority Chief Executive Alex Chrisholm, at the UEA Centre for Competition Policy Annual Conference in Norwich, *Data and trust in digital markets: what are the concerns for competition and for consumers?*, 19 June 2015 stating that: '*Some data loses value over time, so it is hard to see how persistent,*

regard that: *'It might not be easy to build a strong market position using data that quickly goes out of date. So we need to look at the type of data, to see if it stays valuable'.*[1048]

One should thus note that it is not only essential for an online platform to have access to information on past events but also to be able to collect and process real-time data. A search engine, for example, has to keep gathering information to ensure that its search algorithm is constantly updated as the needs and intentions of users looking for information may change. An incumbent search engine provider is in a better position because of its established user base which enables it to quickly adapt to new consumer preferences.[1049] As a result, it seems to be a combination of factors which may result into strong market positions for incumbent providers of online platforms.

Markets in which online platforms compete are often by nature quite concentrated because the network effects crossing customer groups and the scale economies tend to limit the number of viable firms in a market.[1050] This is especially the case for multi-sided markets where users single-home and use only one provider for a specific service. Since users and advertisers expect to gain more value and are attracted to platforms with the largest group of customers on both sides, small and new firms may face difficulties in attaining a critical mass and in successfully launching their own platform.[1051]

The transient nature of some of the data that providers need to provide relevant services to users and advertisers arguably reinforces the operation of network effects. Because providers have to continue to gather real-time data about current preferences and interests of users, it is not sufficient to have a large dataset with varied information on past events and past behaviour of users. Even if potential competitors are able to purchase relevant data from data brokers and other market players, providers with an established user base are in a better position to update their databases and therefore have a competitive advantage over smaller platforms and new entrants which may be slower in adapting to the changing needs of users.

Arguments put forward for claiming that multiple providers of online platforms are easily able to collect relevant information include the alleged ubiquitous nature of data and low costs of data collection, storage and analysis.[1052] While some types of data such as basic contact and demographic information may indeed be purchased from data brokers and other companies, the information that search engines, social

---

unmatchable competitive advantage could be maintained. However some data has persistent value – for example in relation to customer transaction history on auction sites – and it is easier to see how the control of this data could become a barrier to entry'.

1048. Speech of Competition Commissioner Vestager, 'Competition in a big data world', DLD 16 Munich, 17 January 2016.
1049. For a further discussion, see section 2.4.2 above.
1050. D.S. EVANS, 'Competition and Regulatory Policy for Multi-Sided Platforms with Applications to the Web Economy', *SSRN Working Paper* March 2008, p. 13, available at http://papers.ssrn.com/sol3/papers.cfm?abstract_id = 1090368.
1051. UK COMPETITION & MARKETS AUTHORITY, 'The commercial use of consumer data. Report on the CMA's call for information', June 2015, par. 3.45 and 3.56.
1052. See D.S. TUCKER AND H.B. WELLFORD, 'Big Mistakes Regarding Big Data', *The Antitrust Source* 2014, vol. 14, no. 2, (1), p. 3.

networks or e-commerce platforms need to operate their services is specific and does not seem to be readily available on the market. As argued by Grunes & Stucke, providers of online platforms would not be investing considerable amounts of money in developing free services for users in order to collect and analyse relevant information if data was so widely and freely available as asserted.[1053] Claims about the wide availability of data therefore have to be nuanced considering that situations can be identified in which providers of online platforms will be able to exclude competitors by preventing or restricting access to information for which few or no substitutes are available.

Firms whose business model is built on the acquisition and monetisation of personal data feel the need for keeping their datasets to themselves. Some providers of online platforms try to shield data away from competitors: in the case of Facebook, for example, by prohibiting third parties in its general conditions from scraping content off its platform[1054] or, in the case of Google, by restricting the portability of advertising campaigns and by requiring websites to enter into exclusivity agreements for search advertisements.[1055] By engaging in such actions, these providers aim to reserve data to themselves and prevent competitors from making use of their data sources.[1056] In addition, as made clear in sections 5.3.2 and 5.3.3 above, providers of online platforms may rely on intellectual property and trade secret law to protect the data they have collected. With regard to the collection, storage and analysis of data, it is important to note that the costs involved in setting up the necessary tools for these activities are typically fixed whereas the marginal costs of increased production are low. As a result, economies of scale are created which may actually give rise to an entry barrier for small companies and new entrants.[1057]

One should recognise at the same time that in addition to relevant and recent data, engineering resources and a well-functioning underlying technology including an algorithm are required to successfully operate an online platform.[1058] The value of data is argued to be context dependent which means that the insights which can be extracted from it are determined by how the data is structured and analysed.[1059] But even though access to a large and up-to-date database is in itself no guarantee for the success of an online platform, data remains a necessary input of production for the

---

1053. A.P. GRUNES AND M.E. STUCKE, 'No Mistake About It: The Important Role of Antitrust in the Era of Big Data', *The Antitrust Source* 2015, vol. 14, no. 4, (1), p. 7.

1054. Under Facebook's Terms of Service on Safety, Facebook prohibits automatic collection of user content: '*You will not collect users' content or information, or otherwise access Facebook, using automated means (such as harvesting bots, robots, spiders, or scrapers) without our prior permission*', available at https://www.facebook.com/legal/terms.

1055. Speech former Competition Commissioner Almunia, 'Competition and personal data protection', Privacy Platform event: Competition and Privacy in Markets of Data Brussels, 26 November 2012, SPEECH/12/860.

1056. A.P. GRUNES AND M.E. STUCKE, 'No Mistake About It: The Important Role of Antitrust in the Era of Big Data', *The Antitrust Source* 2015, vol. 14, no. 4, (1), p. 7.

1057. UK COMPETITION & MARKETS AUTHORITY, 'The commercial use of consumer data. Report on the CMA's call for information', June 2015, paras 3.41-3.43.

1058. In the context of search engines, see A.V. LERNER, 'The Role of "Big Data" in Online Platform Competition', *SSRN Working Paper* August 2014, pp. 30-32, available at http://papers.ssrn.com/sol3/papers.cfm?abstract_id = 2482780.

1059. OECD, 'Data-Driven Innovation. Big Data for Growth and Well-Being', 6 October 2015, p. 186.

delivery of services to users and advertisers that are of the quality and relevance they expect. In this regard, a chief scientist of Google even suggested: *'We don't have better algorithms than anyone else. We just have more data'.*[1060]

Whether data gives rise to a barrier to entry depends on the factual circumstances of the case which means that it cannot be excluded at the outset that access to user data confers an economic advantage on an incumbent. If partial substitutes for the required data are available, the question is whether they are good enough for new entrants to attract at least a number of users to be able to reach the critical mass needed to successfully launch a new service. Beyond that point, it may not be necessary to have access to additional data. In such cases, a new entrant may be able to improve the service in another way and become a viable competitor to the incumbent.

In conclusion, it is submitted that the databases held by incumbent providers of online platforms may well give rise to a competitive advantage for incumbents and an entry barrier for potential competitors if two cumulative conditions are met: (1) data is an important input of production for the services provided on the online platform; and (2) the specific information necessary to compete on equal footing with the incumbent is not readily available to potential competitors.[1061] New entrants may get access to the required data by purchasing it elsewhere and substituting it with other existing data sources or by collecting the required information themselves. If the data necessary to provide good quality services is not readily available on the market and can only be gained through serving customers, it is clear that a barrier to entry exists. In that situation, empirical analysis is needed to establish the height of the entry barrier.

7.3 SCENARIOS WITH REGARD TO ACCESS TO DATA

Two main scenarios can be distinguished with respect to requests for access to data depending on the intention of the access seeker. The first scenario concerns the situation in which a potential competitor or new entrant needs access to data as an input for a product or service that does not stand in direct competition to the services that the provider offers to users and advertisers on its own platform. This is the usual

---

1060. See M. Asay, 'Tim O'Reilly: "Whole Web" is the OS of the Future', *CNET*, 18 March 2010, available at http://news.cnet.com/8301-13505_3-10469399-16.html.

1061. See UK COMPETITION & MARKETS AUTHORITY, 'The commercial use of consumer data. Report on the CMA's call for information', June 2015, paras 3.56 and 3.58. For similar views, see PRELIMINARY OPINION OF THE EUROPEAN DATA PROTECTION SUPERVISOR, 'Privacy and competitiveness in the age of big data: The interplay between data protection, competition law and consumer protection in the Digital Economy', March 2014, paras 66-68; H.A. SHELANSKI, 'Information, Innovation, and Competition Policy for the Internet', *University of Pennsylvania Law Review* 2013, vol. 161, no. 6, (1663), p. 1679; N. NEWMAN, 'Search, Antitrust, and the Economics of the Control of User Data', *Yale Journal on Regulation* 2014, vol. 31, no. 2, (401), p. 401; D. GERADIN AND M. KUSCHEWSKY, 'Competition Law and Personal Data: Preliminary Thoughts on a Complex Issue', *SSRN Working Paper* February 2013, p. 2, availabe at http://papers.ssrn.com/sol3/papers.cfm?abstract_id = 2216088; L. KIMMEL AND J. KESTENBAUM, 'What's Up with WhatsApp? A Transatlantic View on Privacy and Merger Enforcement in Digital Markets', *Antitrust Magazine* 2014, vol. 29, no. 1, (48), p. 52; A.P. GRUNES AND M.E. STUCKE, 'No Mistake About It: The Important Role of Antitrust in the Era of Big Data', *The Antitrust Source* 2015, vol. 14, no. 4, (1), pp. 7-8.

scenario in essential facilities cases, since the fact that the dominant undertaking can prevent indirect competition from occurring by refusing to deal points to the leveraging of dominance from the main or upstream market to a derivative or downstream market. An example of indirect competition in the context of online platforms is the use of data as an input to introduce statistical or analytics services.

The *PeopleBrowsr v. Twitter* case that occurred in the United States forms an illustration of such a scenario of indirect competition. PeopleBrowsr is a company that analyses Twitter data in order to sell information to clients about, for example, consumer reactions to products and services and identification of the Twitter users who have the most influence in certain communities. Twitter had informed People-Browsr (and several other third-party developers) that as from 30 November 2012 it would be losing its full access to the Twitter 'firehose' which is the entirety of tweets that are passing through Twitter on a second-by-second basis. Instead of having direct access to the Twitter data, PeopleBrowsr would have to approach one of Twitter's certified data resellers to gain access to the required data. PeopleBrowsr argued that it needed full firehose access to be able to deliver its services to customers.[1062] A San Francisco court mandated Twitter to temporarily continue providing PeopleBrowsr full access to its data by way of the imposition of a temporary restraining order.[1063] In April 2013, PeopleBrowsr and Twitter settled the dispute. The parties agreed that People-Browsr would have continued full firehose access until the end of 2013. As of 2014, PeopleBrowsr had to transition over to an authorised Twitter Data Reseller for getting access to Twitter data.[1064]

The facts of the *PeopleBrowsr* case point to the typical 'leveraging' behaviour whereby an undertaking seeks to extend its dominant position in the upstream market, the market for data relating to social networks or (more narrowly) microblogging services, to the downstream market, the market for data analytics services, by refusing to give access to the necessary input which in the present case amounted to Twitter's full firehose data.[1065] This way, Twitter may arguably have tried to foreclose competition in the downstream market in which its certified data resellers were already active by providing third parties access to a processed or analysed form of Twitter data.[1066] It could also be argued that Twitter refused to give access to its full firehose only after PeopleBrowsr demonstrated the existence of a lucrative market for analytics.[1067]

1062. *PeopleBrowsr, Inc. et al. v. Twitter, Inc. (PeopleBrowsr)*, No. C-12-6120 EMC, 2013 WL 843032 (N.D. Cal. 6 March 2013), at 1.
1063. See 'PeopleBrowsr Wins Temporary Restraining Order Compelling Twitter to Provide Firehose Access', 28 November 2012, available at http://blog.peoplebrowsr.com/2012/11/peoplebrowsr-wins-temporary-restraining-order-compelling-twitter-to-provide-firehose-access/.
1064. See 'PeopleBrowsr and Twitter settle Firehose dispute', 25 April 2013, available at http://blog.peoplebrowsr.com/2013/04/peoplebrowsr-and-twitter-settle-firehose-dispute/.
1065. It should be noted that in the US *PeopleBrowsr* case Twitter did not refuse PeopleBrowsr access to its data altogether. Instead, the case dealt with the conditions under which Twitter offered access.
1066. For a more detailed analysis, see I. GRAEF, S.Y. WAHYUNINGTYAS AND P. VALCKE, 'Assessing Data Access Issues in Online Platforms', *Telecommunications Policy* 2015, vol. 39, no. 5, (375), pp. 384-385.
1067. Z. ABRAHAMSON, 'Essential Data', *The Yale Law Journal* 2014, vol. 124, no. 3, (867), p. 874.

The second scenario involves a potential competitor or new entrant which seeks access to data on an online platform in order to launch a form of direct competition and to provide a rival platform to users and advertisers. In other words, the access seeker requests to have access to the user data collected by the incumbent provider to introduce its own search, social network or e-commerce platform which will compete with the platform offered by the incumbent in the same relevant product market. Data forms an important input for online services because it can be deployed as a means to improve, on the one hand, the possibilities of advertisers to engage in targeted advertising and, on the other hand, the relevance of, respectively, search results, purchase suggestions and social interactions. The imposition of such a duty to deal would have the effect of enabling an access seeker to compete with the provider at issue in a direct and horizontal way by introducing its own platform.

Figure 7.1   Comparing Possible Scenarios of Indirect and Direct Competition as Regards Access to Data

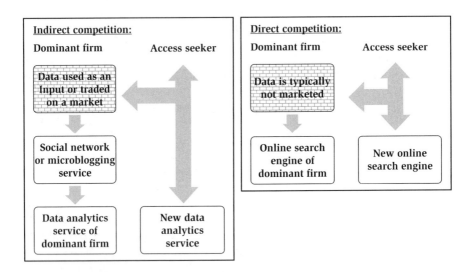

In addition to these situations in which competitors need data for being able to introduce their own services to users and advertisers, rival providers may also seek access to incumbent platforms in order to enable users to incorporate previously created and uploaded content into their own system or to bring profiles on different platforms together in one place. Since the sharing of content is at the core of their functionality, such disputes may particularly occur in the context of social networks. Two such cases have already occurred in the United States.[1068]

1068. These cases are also discussed in C.S. Yoo, 'When Antitrust Met Facebook', *George Mason Law Review* 2012, vol. 19, no. 5, (1147), pp. 1158-1160.

7.4 MARKET DEFINITION IN ESSENTIAL FACILITIES CASES RELATING TO DATA[1069]

Because the essential facilities doctrine targets the leveraging of market power from the main or upstream market in which the holder of the essential facility is dominant to a derivative or downstream market, two relevant markets have to be defined in refusal to deal cases. The downstream market comprises the derivative product or service that the access seeker will offer once given access to the required input which forms the upstream market.

After the introduction of the concept of hypothetical or potential markets by the Court of Justice in *IMS Health*,[1070] it is not necessary anymore for the requested input to have been already traded as an independent product by the dominant undertaking. The fact that online platform providers such as Facebook and Google have, unlike Twitter which actively licenses data to third parties, never marketed data separately before[1071] does therefore not preclude competition authorities or courts from imposing a duty to give their competitors access to the datasets these providers hold. While relevant markets are usually defined on the basis of concrete market experience by looking at supply and demand of products and services, the definition of a hypothetical or potential market can only be based on assumptions about how the market could be structured. Market definition in such cases thus amounts to a normative decision about how the market should look rather than constituting a reflection of market realities.[1072]

While Twitter licenses data to third parties and is thus active on a 'real' upstream market for data, other prevailing providers of search engines, social networks and e-commerce platforms do not sell or trade data. For the data held by those providers, only a hypothetical market can be defined. The key issue for determining the boundaries of a relevant market for data is the substitutability of different types of data. So far, the European Commission has not yet had to define a market for personal data or for any of its particular usages.[1073] In the *Facebook/WhatsApp* merger, the Commission did not investigate any possible market definition with respect to the provision of data or data analytics services, since neither of the parties involved was active in any such potential markets.[1074] The Commission does have experience in reviewing

---

1069. The analysis in this section is based on earlier work in I. GRAEF, 'Market Definition and Market Power in Data: The Case of Online Platforms', *World Competition* 2015, vol. 38, no. 4, (473), pp. 495-501.
1070. See section 6.8.1 above.
1071. Although Facebook and Google have each entered into specific partnerships with third parties for access to their platforms, both providers do not share data with advertisers and do not sell data to third parties.
1072. P. LAROUCHE, *Competition Law and Regulation in European Telecommunications*, Hart Publishing, 2000, pp. 207 and 212.
1073. Speech former Competition Commissioner Almunia, 'Competition and personal data protection', Privacy Platform event: Competition and Privacy in Markets of Data Brussels, 26 November 2012, SPEECH/12/860.
1074. Case No COMP/M.7217 – *Facebook/WhatsApp*, 3 October 2014, par. 72.

mergers between firms providing data-related services. These cases did not involve hypothetical or potential markets but 'real' markets where the data at issue was truly traded.

In 2008, the European Commission approved two mergers where markets relating to different types of data were defined. In *TomTom/Tele Atlas*, the Commission identified an upstream market for the provision of navigable digital map databases consisting of compilations of digital data typically including geographic information, additional information such as street names, addresses and speed limits, and display information. These digital map databases are sold to manufacturers and producers such as TomTom which integrates the databases it purchases from Tele Atlas into the navigation software and the navigation devices the company produces.[1075] The Commission concluded that the vertical integration of Tele Atlas into TomTom would not lead to a significant impediment of competition despite the duopoly market for navigable digital maps (in which only Tele Atlas and NAVTEQ were active) and TomTom's strong position in the market for portable navigation devices.

In the same year, the Commission cleared a merger between Thomson and Reuters raising competition concerns in the financial information industry only after accepting commitments requiring the parties to divest copies of the databases containing financial information products together with relevant assets as appropriate to allow purchasers of the databases and assets to quickly establish themselves as a credible competitive force in the marketplace in competition with the merged entity.[1076] The Commission also adopted a commitment decision in an abuse of dominance case against Thomson Reuters at the end of 2012 in which it argued that the latter had abused its dominant position in the worldwide market for consolidated real-time datafeeds by prohibiting its customers from using its so-called Reuters Instrument Codes to retrieve data from consolidated real-time datafeeds of other providers and by preventing third parties from creating and maintaining mapping tables incorporating Reuters Instrument Codes that would allow the systems of Thomson Reuters' customers to interoperate with consolidated real-time datafeeds of other providers.[1077]

In its appraisal of the joint venture between UK mobile operators Telefónica, Vodafone and Everything Everywhere in 2012, the Commission defined a market for data analytics services. It referred to the previous merger decisions *WPP/TMS* and *VNU/ACNielsen* in which related relevant markets where identified.[1078] In *WPP/TMS*, a merger in the sector for marketing communications services, the Commission defined a separate market for market research services aimed at measuring and understanding consumer attitudes and purchasing behaviour.[1079] In *VNU/ACNielsen*, the Commission identified the existence of different types of services related to marketing and audience measurement. These so-called marketing data services were further segmented into marketing information services, which consist of the provision of data (age, social

---

1075. Case No COMP/M.4854 – *TomTom/Tele Atlas*, 14 May 2008, paras 17-19.
1076. Case No COMP/M.4726 – *Thomson Corporation/Reuters Group*, 19 February 2008.
1077. Case AT.39654 – *Reuters Instrument Codes*, 20 December 2012.
1078. Case No COMP/M.6314 – *Telefónica UK/Vodafone UK/Everything Everywhere/JV*, 4 September 2012, paras 197-198.
1079. Case No COMP/M.5232 – *WPP/TNS*, 23 September 2008, paras 10-14.

group, etc.) on individual customers for direct marketing purposes, market research services, which are aimed at measuring actual purchasing patterns, and media measurement services, which are aimed at measuring the audience of specific media such as television and internet.[1080]

In *Telefónica/Vodafone/Everything Everywhere*, the Commission considered whether separate relevant markets had to be defined for the provision of data analytics services for static online advertising and mobile advertising. According to the vast majority of respondents to the market investigation, these two types of data analytics were considered as complementary and could not be substituted because the two services collect a different type of information and amount of consumer details. A market player submitted that the information collected via mobile data analytics is more personal, geo-located, and can be cross referenced with call behaviour, which cannot be offered by online data analytics to a comparable extent. While the Commission left the precise product market definition open, it argued that there were possibly separate relevant markets for online and mobile data analytics.[1081] As regards the data analytics activities of the joint venture, the Commission concluded that the operation was not likely to significantly impede effective competition since there would be various other players having access to a comparable set of data and offering services in competition with the joint venture.[1082]

Whereas brick-and-mortar undertakings such as retailers, telecom operators, banks and insurance companies also collect personal information, this data cannot necessarily be considered substitutable to the data gathered by providers of online platforms. Each of these entities is involved in a different activity and consequently has access to a particular kind of information about consumers such as transactional data, call data records and information relating to the financial position of consumers. These different types of data are clear supplements giving a more comprehensive picture of a specific consumer once brought together. But even though the information held by the different entities will overlap to a certain extent, the data gathered by any of the above mentioned brick-and-mortar companies may not in itself enable providers of online platforms to offer services to users and advertisers that are of the relevance they expect. The scope and specificity of information collected on the internet is not comparable to the data to which brick-and-mortar undertakings have access.

While offline retailers and online e-commerce platforms both gather information about the purchasing behaviour of consumers, a provider of an e-commerce platform is able to collect much more detailed information by analysing the behaviour of users on its platform. By looking at the product pages that a user viewed, the provider can easily find out which products a user has considered to buy before making his or her final purchase decision. A traditional retailer, to the contrary, might never know

---

1080. Case No COMP/M.2291 – *VNU/ACNielsen*, 12 February 2001, paras 10-12.
1081. Case No COMP/M.6314 – *Telefónica UK/Vodafone UK/Everything Everywhere/JV*, 4 September 2012, paras 199-203.
1082. Case No COMP/M.6314 – *Telefónica UK/Vodafone UK/Everything Everywhere/JV*, 4 September 2012, paras 557-558.

whether a shopper put a product back on the shelf before going to the check out.[1083] For this reason, it is doubtful whether the information held by brick-and-mortar retailers can serve as a substitute for the detailed data to which providers of e-commerce platforms have access. An analogy can be drawn with advertising where the European Commission held that separate relevant markets have to be defined for offline and online advertising because of the more precise targeting possibilities, measurement of effectiveness of ads and price mechanism applied to advertising.[1084] The Commission could apply a similar reasoning to distinguish separate relevant markets for data collected offline and online.

Within a potential market for online data, a further segmentation may be made between search data, social network data and e-commerce data as input for services offered on both the user and advertiser side of online platforms. Following the approach taken by the European Commission and suggested by economists to define separate relevant markets for each of the sides of online platforms,[1085] distinct relevant markets should also be defined for the data required to provide services on each of the sides of the platform in line with the purpose for which the data is used.

The data that a search engine needs to be able to offer a search functionality to users consists of the search queries that users have looked for and the links subsequently clicked on.[1086] This type of data is different from the information collected by a social network provider which includes profile information shared by users and the interactions in which users engage on the platform. E-commerce data, in turn, involves information about the purchasing behaviour of users, their virtual shopping cart and the items they have viewed, liked or rated. As a result, each of these online platforms needs a specific type of data as input to deliver good quality services to users thereby diminishing the substitutability of different kinds of data. With regard to social network data, a distinction may even be made between information collected by microblogging services such as Twitter and general social networking sites including Facebook.

In the context of the *PeopleBrowsr v. Twitter* case that occurred in the United States, PeopleBrowsr stated in a court document that Twitter data is a unique and essential input because tweets are *'contemporaneous reports on users' experiences that provide unique feedback regarding consumers' reactions to products and brands'*. In addition, it argued that the way Twitter enables users to respond to each other by retweeting each other's content or mentioning each other in their own tweets, forms a web of interactions that *'provides unique insight about which members of communities are influential'*. While data from social networking sites as Facebook may serve as a valuable complement, Twitter data can in PeopleBrowsr's view not be replaced by data

---

1083. H.A. SHELANSKI, 'Information, Innovation, and Competition Policy for the Internet', *University of Pennsylvania Law Review* 2013, vol. 161, no. 6, (1663), p. 1679.
1084. See section 4.2.3 above and in particular Case No COMP/M.4731 – *Google/ DoubleClick*, 11 March 2008, paras 45-46.
1085. See section 4.2.1 above.
1086. In the context of the US *Google/DoubleClick* merger decision, P.J. HARBOUR AND T.I. KOSLOV, 'Section 2 In A Web 2.0 World: An Expanded Vision of Relevant Product Markets', *Antitrust Law Journal* 2010, vol. 76, no. 3, (769), p. 784 refer to *'a possible market for "data gathered via search"'*.

from these sources. According to PeopleBrowsr, social networking sites '*do not provide the same rich set of public data regarding users' sentiments and influence*'.[1087] Because the parties settled their dispute, the competent US court did not have to express its opinion on the substitutability of Twitter data in the proceedings on the merits.

On the advertiser side of online platforms, a further market segmentation may also be made between different types of data. In merger cases such as *Google/DoubleClick*, *Microsoft/Yahoo* and *Facebook/WhatsApp*, and in the ongoing *Google* investigation, the European Commission considered the definition of separate relevant markets for search and non-search advertising. In *Facebook/WhatsApp* merger decision, the Commission even referred to the possibility of defining a specific relevant market for non-search advertising on social networking sites.[1088] If separate relevant markets are distinguished for these types of advertising, it would be logical to define separate relevant markets for the data that is used as input for providing different kinds of advertising services too. Whereas social network providers target advertisements on the basis of the information they have gathered about the demographics and interests of users, targeting of advertising on search engines and e-commerce platforms takes place on the basis of the intent of the user revealed by entering a search query or a product that he or she is interested in. The substitutability of the data needed to provide, on the one hand, social network advertising and, on the other hand, search advertising therefore seems limited.

Since providers of search engines and e-commerce platforms are both active in search advertising, the data they collect on their respective platforms may be considered interchangeable to a certain extent. However, the data of a provider of an e-commerce platform relates more specifically to the purchasing behaviour of users. In this regard, this data may only partially substitute the information to which a horizontal search engine needs access for being able to provide search advertising services on its platform where search queries not only consist of products or services a user is looking for.

Nevertheless, the Commission has not distinguished between different types of data in merger cases where the combination of the datasets of the merging parties were identified as a possible competition concern in markets for online advertising and data analytics services. In *Google/DoubleClick*, the Commission referred to portals, other major web publishers, internet service providers and Microsoft as players which '*have the ability to collect large amounts of more or less similar information that is potentially useful for advertisement targeting*'.[1089] The Commission argued that the combination of the information on search behaviour from Google and web-browsing behaviour from DoubleClick would not give the merged entity a competitive advantage that could not

---

1087. Declaration of John David Rich in support of plaintiff's application for a temporary restraining order in the case *PeopleBrowsr v. Twitter* in the Superior Court of the State of California, County of San Francisco, November 2012, paras 4-5, available at http://www.scribd.com/doc/114846303/Rich-Declaration-PB-v-TW-Restraining-Order-28-Nov-12.
1088. See section 4.2.3.
1089. Case No COMP/M.4731 – *Google/ DoubleClick*, 11 March 2008, paras 269-272.

be matched by competitors considering that such a combination of data was already available to a number of Google's competitors at the time of the proposed concentration.[1090]

In the context of its appraisal of the joint venture between UK mobile operators Telefónica, Vodafone and Everything Everywhere, the Commission assessed whether the joint venture would foreclose competing providers of data analytics services or advertising services by combining different types of data and by so creating a unique database that no competing provider would be able to replicate.[1091] The Commission concluded that the information available to the joint venture was *also available to a large extent to both existing and new market players such as Google, Apple, Facebook, card issuers, reference agencies or retailers*.[1092] Similarly, in its *Facebook/WhatsApp* merger decision the Commission referred to data collection across the web in general without differentiating between different types of advertising. The Commission considered Google, Apple, Amazon, eBay, Microsoft, AOL, Yahoo!, Twitter, IAC, LinkedIn, Adobe and Yelp as market participants that collect user data alongside Facebook and concluded that post-merger there would *continue to be a large amount of Internet user data that are valuable for advertising purposes and that are not within Facebook's exclusive control*.[1093]

The reasoning applied in these cases thus implies that the Commission regards the data collected by companies active on the internet as substitutable. However, important differences can be identified between the nature of the data gathered by, for example, search engines, social networks and e-commerce platforms. Furthermore, in *Telefónica/Vodafone/Everything Everywhere*, the Commission argued that separate relevant markets possibly existed for the provision of data analytics services for static online advertising, on the one hand, and mobile advertising, on the other hand, on the ground that these two services collect a different type of information and amount of consumer details.[1094] In that perspective, data collected through PCs may not be substitutable to data collected through mobile devices, because only the latter type of information contains sufficient details about the user's real-time location in order to provide mobile advertising services.[1095]

Such differences in the type of information seem to be even more substantial for search, social network and e-commerce data used as an input to provide targeted advertising possibilities. It thus remains to be seen if an all-encompassing market for

---

1090. Case No COMP/M.4731 – *Google/ DoubleClick*, 11 March 2008, paras 364-365.
1091. Case No COMP/M.6314 – *Telefónica UK/Vodafone UK/Everything Everywhere/JV*, 4 September 2012, par. 539.
1092. Case No COMP/M.6314 – *Telefónica UK/Vodafone UK/Everything Everywhere/JV*, 4 September 2012, par. 543.
1093. Case No COMP/M.7217 – *Facebook/WhatsApp*, 3 October 2014, paras 188-189.
1094. Case No COMP/M.6314 – *Telefónica UK/Vodafone UK/Everything Everywhere/JV*, 4 September 2012, paras 199, 200 and 202.
1095. The substitutability between different types of data in this regard has also been discussed in Autorité de la concurrence and Bundeskartellamt, 'Competition Law and Data', 10 May 2016, pp. 44-47.

internet data will be defined once the Commission is confronted with a case in which it has to determine the relevant market for personal data collected by a particular internet player.

The downstream or derivative market is defined around the product or service that the access seeker would like to introduce once given access to the required data. As discussed in the previous section, two possible scenarios can be distinguished depending on whether the access seeker is planning to introduce indirect or direct competition with the provider of the online platform. In the first scenario, the downstream market may consist of statistical or analytics services. In the second scenario, the access seeker will compete with the online platform provider in the same relevant market(s) for the functionality offered to users and/or the targeted advertising services delivered to advertisers.[1096]

7.5 MARKET POWER WITH REGARD TO DATA[1097]

In order to establish liability under Article 102 TFEU for a refusal to deal, the holder of the requested input has to be found dominant on the upstream market. Because of the alleged ubiquitous and non-rivalrous nature of information, it is argued that it is implausible for an undertaking to obtain market power with respect to user data.[1098] However, as discussed above in the context of the existence of entry barriers,[1099] such claims have to be nuanced. While an incumbent cannot prevent potential competitors or new entrants from gathering similar factual information such as the age, gender, profession and location of a user, the specific data that is necessary to compete on an equal footing with a prevailing search engine, social network or e-commerce platform provider may not be readily available to others. As an illustration, reference can be made to the argument of PeopleBrowsr in its court case against Twitter that Twitter data is not substitutable to user information from other social networks including Facebook. Particular types of user data may thus not be as widely available as claimed as a result of which it is not unlikely for an undertaking to have a dominant position in a certain market for data.

The question is how the existence of a dominant position in a market for data can be established and in particular how market shares should be calculated. The amount or quality of data that an undertaking controls do not seem to constitute adequate indicators for market power, because the datasets of different providers cannot be easily compared in this regard. It may be hard, if not impossible, to distinguish different pieces of information and attribute value to each of them. Factual information including the age and occupation of a particular user will normally have lower value

---

1096. For a discussion of how the relevant market for the user and advertiser side of online platforms may be defined, see sections 4.2.2 and 4.2.3.
1097. The analysis in this section builds upon earlier work in I. GRAEF, 'Market Definition and Market Power in Data: The Case of Online Platforms', *World Competition* 2015, vol. 38, no. 4, (473), pp. 501-504.
1098. D.S. TUCKER AND H.B. WELLFORD, 'Big Mistakes Regarding Big Data', *The Antitrust Source* 2014, vol. 14, no. 2, (1), p. 12.
1099. See section 7.2 above.

than data that is harder to get hold of such as information relating to the behaviour of a specific user on an online platform. Nevertheless, it seems challenging to quantify this difference in value.

A more objective way to measure the competitive strength of providers active in a market for data would be to look at their ability to monetise the collected information. The revenue gained by a provider through licensing of data to third parties and/or delivering targeted advertising services indicates how successful it is in the market. In a similar vein, the OECD proposed to look at the financial results of a company such as market capitalisation, revenues and net income on a per-user or per-record in order to estimate the monetary value of personal data.[1100] Since the value of a dataset depends on how it is employed by its owner and not only on its sheer volume, market shares can be calculated in a reliable way by looking at the share of the total profit earned by undertakings active in the relevant market for a specific type of data. This way the analysis of dominance does not only take into account the value of the dataset in itself but also the success of a provider in putting in place relevant resources and technologies for monetising the data. In this regard, it has been argued that the value of data is context dependent in the sense that the insights that can be extracted from it are determined by how the data is structured and analysed.[1101]

In case a particular market player does not offer paid products or services to customers on the basis of the collected data and does not monetise its dataset in another way, its dominance in a potential market for data cannot be established by following this approach. When the data is only used as an input for products or services for which no direct profits are realised, no data-related revenues can be identified and no value can be attributed to the data in this way. An example of a company which could be considered active in a potential market for data but which does not monetise the data by licensing it to third parties or by providing targeted advertising is WhatsApp. Since WhatsApp does not have any data-related revenues, its position in a potential market for data cannot be established by looking at its share of the turnover made by undertakings in this market. If possible competition problems cannot be sufficiently addressed in the 'real' relevant markets for the end product or service (in the case of WhatsApp possibly the relevant market for consumer communications services) and there is still a need to assess the competitive effects in a potential input market for data in the absence of any data-related revenues, competition authorities and courts could look at potential competition as a proxy for dominance.

Instead of merely calculating market shares, the European Commission is increasingly taking into account potential competition in its assessment of dominance in dynamic markets.[1102] In cases where the data has not yet been traded as a separate product and a 'real' market does not exist, it is particularly relevant to analyse the likelihood that other undertakings hold similar information or are able to collect

---

1100. OECD, 'Exploring the Economics of Personal Data: A Survey of Methodologies for Measuring Monetary Value', *OECD Digital Economy Papers*, No. 220, 2013, p. 20, available at http://dx.doi.org/10.1787/5k486qtxldmq-en.
1101. OECD, 'Data-Driven Innovation. Big Data for Growth and Well-Being', 6 October 2015, p. 186.
1102. See section 4.4.2 above.

the required data themselves thereby putting the incumbent under competitive pressure. If potential competition is absent, dominance will in such circumstances normally be established with the definition of a relevant market for the data to which access is requested. Since there are no readily available substitutes traded by others, potential competition is the only restraint to which the holder of the requested data can be subject.

The presence of the following non-exhaustive circumstances may in particular be considered to point towards market power in a market defined around data: (1) data is a significant input into the end products or services delivered on online platforms; (2) the incumbent relies on contracts or on intellectual property and trade secret law to protect its dataset as a result of which competitors cannot freely access the necessary data; (3) there are few or no actual substitutes readily available on the market for the specific information needed to compete on equal footing with an incumbent; (4) it is not viable for a potential competitor to collect data itself in order to develop a new dataset with a comparable scope to that of the incumbent (e.g., due to network effects or economies of scale and scope).[1103]

7.6 CHARACTERISTICS WHICH SET DATA APART FROM OTHER ASSETS PREVIOUSLY BEING CONSIDERED UNDER THE ESSENTIAL FACILITIES DOCTRINE

Several features can be identified that set data apart from other assets to which the essential facilities doctrine has been applied in previous cases. These characteristics may influence the assessment of the abusive nature of refusals to give access to data. As a non-rivalrous good, data can be used simultaneously by more than one entity. The fact that a certain entity has collected a piece of information does not preclude others from gathering the same data. The non-rivalrous nature of data may have an impact on the application of the essential facilities doctrine in two ways. Data that is truly non-rivalrous may not be found indispensable under the first condition of the essential facilities doctrine and may also not be liable to exclude effective competition on the downstream market under the second condition.

At the same time, data can be made exclusive by way of contracts or by relying on sui generis database protection and trade secret law. The peculiarity of these regimes is that they do not require the underlying subject matter of protection to be innovative. This is opposed to traditional forms of intellectual property protection such as patents and copyright which demand, respectively, an inventive step and originality for an invention or creation to benefit from protection. As discussed in section 6.7.3

1103. Circumstances (1) and (3) are also mentioned in UK COMPETITION & MARKETS AUTHORITY, 'The commercial use of consumer data. Report on the CMA's call for information', June 2015, par. 3.78 as market indicators suggesting a greater likelihood of competition concerns. In their joint report, the Autorité de la concurrence and the Bundeskartellamt refer to the scarcity or ease of replicability of data and whether the scale or scope of data collection matters to competitive performance as factors *'likely to be of much relevance when considering whether data can contribute to market power'* (Autorité de la concurrence and Bundeskartellamt, 'Competition Law and Data', 10 May 2016, p. 35).

above, sui generis database protection and trade secret law do not necessarily promote innovation because there are no such qualitative requirements concerning the subject matter of protection. In that context, there is more scope for competition problems to occur with regard to these regimes in the sense that a dominant player may solely rely on sui generis database protection or trade secret law to protect its market position and prevent competitors from entering the market.

It is worth recalling that the sui generis database right entitles a database maker to exclude others from re-utilising mere factual information and data. Single-source databases containing self-created data may attract protection despite the restrictive interpretation of the scope of the sui generis database right provided by the Court of Justice. If substantial investment has been made in either the verification or the presentation of the content of the database that can be differentiated from the investment in the creation of data, a database maker can still obtain sui generis protection for databases containing self-created data. In such situations, the holder of a sui generis database right can prevent others from re-utilising the self-generated information.

Trade secret law, on the other hand, only requires that commercially valuable information is kept secret. As a result, a trade secret holder may shield non-innovative information from competition for an unlimited period of time by refusing to deal in cases where independent discovery or reverse engineering is not successful. While trade secret law also played a role in *Microsoft*, the European Commission and the General Court did not explicitly consider the characteristics of trade secret protection when applying the conditions of the essential facilities doctrine. Although it does not seem to be necessary to set a new standard of intervention for refusals to deal involving sui generis database rights or trade secrets, it must be kept in mind that these forms of protection may lead to the control of information on which competitors are dependent for being able to enter a market.

A characteristic of data that would require competition authorities and courts to proceed with caution when mandating access to data is its value may go beyond the way it is currently used by its holder. In this regard, an access seeker may not only be able to use the requested data as an input to introduce a specific product that competes with or complements the product of the dominant firm but also to analyse it and extract further knowledge from it. Such knowledge could then potentially be used to identify trends and to develop new products for which consumer demand exists. In such cases, a duty to deal may have effects going beyond the relevant markets considered in the competition analysis. To prevent this, competition authorities and courts should limit the duty to deal to the type and amount of data that is necessary to remedy the negative effects of the refusal of the dominant firm on the downstream market.

With regard to possible objective justifications for refusals to deal, a dominant firm may try to show that it would not have invested in the creation of the requested input in the first place if it had known beforehand that it would have to share it with competitors. While any duty to deal imposed under the essential facilities doctrine may negatively affect ex ante investment incentives, there are reasons to believe that such an effect is more limited with regard to data collected by incumbent providers of online platforms as compared to other types of essential facilities. One could argue that the dataset established by a dominant provider of an online platform is a by-product of its past success. Even if the provider had known that it would later be required to share its data with competitors, it is unlikely that it would not have refrained from returning as relevant search results, social interactions or purchase suggestions as possible to users.[1104] Although the business models of most providers of online platforms nowadays revolve around data, the ownership of data was not what motivated initial entry in the markets that incumbents are currently dominating.[1105] Indeed, Google at first tried to gain revenue from licensing its search engine to other firms and Amazon's and eBay's initial business model was solely based on charging transaction fees.[1106] For these reasons, a duty to share data may only have a limited effect on ex ante innovation incentives which reduces the scope for ex ante efficiency defences to succeed.

With regard to possible ex post efficiency defences, the non-rivalrous nature of data may reduce the scope for objective justifications which refer to the costs that a duty to deal would pose for the dominant undertaking. In particular, a duty to give competitors access to data does not undermine the ability of the dominant undertaking to use its dataset to serve its own customers.[1107] In a similar vein, capacity constraints are unlikely to be accepted as objective justification for a refusal to give access to non-rivalrous data.[1108]

While the scope for objective justifications involving ex ante or ex post efficiency defences relating to data may be limited, dominant firms may instead rely on their obligations under data protection law to justify a refusal to give access to data. When a duty to deal requires a dominant undertaking to give access to information relating to identified or identifiable natural persons, competition authorities and courts also have to take into account possible considerations under data protection law. The interaction with the data protection regime in the context of objective justifications under the essential facilities doctrine is discussed in the next section.

7.7 ABUSIVE NATURE OF REFUSALS TO GIVE ACCESS TO DATA ON ONLINE PLATFORMS

Under the current standards of the EU essential facilities doctrine, four conditions are applicable to refusals to deal: indispensability, exclusion of all effective competition on the downstream market, prevention of the introduction of a new product and absence of an objective justification. In this section, guidance is given for each condition separately on how it may be applied and interpreted in the context of refusals to give access to data.

1104. C. ARGENTON AND J. PRÜFER, 'Search Engine Competition with Network Externalities', *Journal of Competition Law and Economics* 2012, vol. 8, no. 1, (73), p. 98.
1105. Z. ABRAHAMSON, 'Essential Data', *The Yale Law Journal* 2014, vol. 124, no. 3, (867), p. 876.
1106. See, respectively, sections 2.3.2 and 2.2.3 above.
1107. C. ARGENTON AND J. PRÜFER, 'Search Engine Competition with Network Externalities', *Journal of Competition Law and Economics* 2012, vol. 8, no. 1, (73), p. 98.
1108. Z. ABRAHAMSON, 'Essential Data', *The Yale Law Journal* 2014, vol. 124, no. 3, (867), pp. 877-878.

7.7.1 Indispensability of Data

With regard to the application of the indispensability requirement to user data, statements of the European Commission in merger decisions involving online advertising services are instructive.[1109] In *Google/DoubleClick*, the European Commission argued that the combination of information on search behaviour from Google and web-browsing behaviour from DoubleClick would not give the merged entity a competitive advantage that could not be matched by competitors thereby concluding that the data of Google and DoubleClick is not necessary or essential for providing advertising services in an online environment.[1110] The European Commission stated that similar data was already available to Google's competitors, including Microsoft and Yahoo!, and that the data could also be acquired from third parties and internet service providers.[1111]

In this regard, it is also instructive to refer to the statement of the United States Federal Trade Commission in *Google/DoubleClick*. The US Federal Trade Commission concluded that '*the evidence indicates that neither the data available to Google, nor the data available to DoubleClick, constitutes an essential input to a successful online advertising product*'.[1112] In particular, the US Federal Trade Commission was of the view that a number of Google's most significant competitors in the advertising intermediation market, namely Microsoft, Yahoo and Time Warner, had access to their own unique data stores containing information not available to Google. On this ground, the US Federal Trade Commission argued that all of these firms appeared to be well-positioned to compete vigorously against Google.[1113]

In *Telefónica/Vodafone/Everything Everywhere*, the European Commission assessed whether the joint venture between UK mobile operators Telefónica, Vodafone and Everything Everywhere would foreclose competing providers of targeted advertising services by creating a unique database of different types of information leading to a situation in which other providers might be dependent on the joint venture or might be unable to compete. After analysing which data the joint venture would possess, the European Commission concluded that the operation would not impede effective competition because similar information was available to other companies active in the market for targeted advertising and customers generally tend to give their personal data to many market players.[1114]

In the context of its approval of the acquisition of WhatsApp by Facebook, the European Commission similarly argued that even if Facebook were to start collecting

---

1109. See also I. Graef, S.Y. Wahyuningtyas and P. Valcke, 'Assessing Data Access Issues in Online Platforms', *Telecommunications Policy* 2015, vol. 39, no. 5, (375), p. 384.

1110. Case No COMP/M.4731 – *Google/ DoubleClick*, 11 March 2008, par. 366.

1111. Case No COMP/M.4731 – *Google/ DoubleClick*, 11 March 2008, par. 365.

1112. Statement of the Federal Trade Commission, *Google/DoubleClick*, FTC File No. 071-0170, 20 December 2007, p. 12, available at http://www.ftc.gov/system/files/documents/public_statements/418081/071220googledc-commstmt.pdf.

1113. Statement of the Federal Trade Commission, *Google/DoubleClick*, FTC File No. 071-0170, 20 December 2007, pp. 12-13.

1114. Case No COMP/M.6314 – *Telefónica UK/Vodafone UK/Everything Everywhere/JV*, 4 September 2012, paras 539-558.

and using data from WhatsApp users to improve targeted advertising on its social network the transaction would not raise competition concerns considering that *'there will continue to be a large amount of Internet user data that are valuable for advertising purposes and that are not within Facebook's exclusive control'*.[1115]

Although the outcome of these three merger cases indicates that data of incumbents will not easily be considered indispensable for providing targeted advertising services, this may be different with regard to the use of data for offering services of good quality to users in the form of, for example, the relevance of search results in online search engines, suggested social network interactions and purchase suggestions in e-commerce platforms. For the provision of these functionalities to users, a specific type of data is needed that may not be readily available on the market. For example, if the specific data needed to operate a search engine of good quality can only be obtained through serving customers, other data that is available from third parties will not form an adequate substitute for the search data of the incumbent search engine provider.

In addition, in line with the scenario involving indirect competition, third parties may need user data as an input for a product that is unrelated to the main services that the dominant provider offers such as statistical or analytics services. In its US court case against Twitter, PeopleBrowsr argued that Twitter data constituted an indispensable input for it to be able to provide its own customers with analytics services. In PeopleBrowsr's view, Twitter data could not substituted with information from other social networks.[1116]

The French and Belgian competition authorities have both already assessed the extent to which a dataset held by a dominant undertaking may be reproducible by competitors. In September 2014, the Autorité de la concurrence adopted an interim decision in which it found GDF Suez capable of taking advantage of its dominant position in the market for natural gas by using customer files it had inherited from its former monopoly status to launch offers at market prices outside the scope of its public service obligation. The Autorité de la concurrence made clear that the conformity of these practices with competition law depends on the conditions in which the company has established its customer base, as well as on the possibility for its competitors to reproduce such information. If the data has been acquired by the dominant undertaking in the context of a competition on the merits and can be reproduced by equally efficient competitors in the market at reasonable financial conditions and in a timely manner, the cross-use of a customer base does not constitute an abuse of dominance in the view of the Autorité de la concurrence.[1117]

When analysing the specific facts of the case, the Autorité de la concurrence found that the database of GDF Suez was a legacy of its former status as a monopolist in the market for the supply of gas and could not be regarded as the result of a particular innovation that GDF Suez had developed by its own merit. As regards the

---

1115. Case No COMP/M.7217 – *Facebook/WhatsApp*, 3 October 2014, paras 187-189.
1116. See section 7.4 above.
1117. Autorité de la concurrence, Décision n° 14-MC-02 du 9 septembre 2014 relative à une demande de mesures conservatoires présentée par la société Direct Energie dans les secteurs du gaz et de l'électricité, par. 146, available at http://www.autoritedelaconcurrence.fr/pdf/avis/14mc02.pdf.

reproducibility of the database, the Autorité de la concurrence followed the arguments of competitors which had stated that it was not reasonably possible for them to reproduce the advantage held by GDF Suez or to rely on other databases from which information could be retrieved that was effective for prospecting new customers in the market for the supply of gas.[1118] Against this background, the Autorité de la concurrence argued that the practices of GDF Suez could constitute abuse of dominance and foreclose potential competitors from the liberalised gas market and the electricity market.[1119]

To remedy such effects, the Autorité de la concurrence required GDF Suez by way of interim measures to share certain customer information with other market players having government authorisation to supply natural gas in order to enable them to contact potential new customers.[1120] Interim measures were necessary in the view of the Autorité de la concurrence to restore 'equality of arms' with regard to the prospecting of new customers in the liberalised market for gas and to prevent that GDF Suez would attract a substantial part of customers which may have had an irreversible impact on a market in transition.[1121] To ensure the effectiveness of the adopted measures, the Autorité de la concurrence also ordered GDF Suez to suspend its commercial activities relating to the supply of gas outside the scope of its public service obligation in case it had not made the required data available to competitors before a certain date.[1122]

In September 2015, the Belgian competition authority imposed a fine on the National Lottery for having abused its dominance in the Belgian market for public lotteries in which it has a legal monopoly. When entering the competitive market for sports betting in 2013, the National Lottery used the contact details of individuals contained in a database that it had established in the context of its legal monopoly in order to send a one-off promotional email for the launch of its new sports betting product Scooore!.[1123]

1118. Autorité de la concurrence, Décision n° 14-MC-02 du 9 septembre 2014 relative à une demande de mesures conservatoires présentée par la société Direct Energie dans les secteurs du gaz et de l'électricité, paras 147-154.

1119. Autorité de la concurrence, Décision n° 14-MC-02 du 9 septembre 2014 relative à une demande de mesures conservatoires présentée par la société Direct Energie dans les secteurs du gaz et de l'électricité, paras 169-174.

1120. Autorité de la concurrence, Décision n° 14-MC-02 du 9 septembre 2014 relative à une demande de mesures conservatoires présentée par la société Direct Energie dans les secteurs du gaz et de l'électricité, paras 290-296.

1121. Autorité de la concurrence, Décision n° 14-MC-02 du 9 septembre 2014 relative à une demande de mesures conservatoires présentée par la société Direct Energie dans les secteurs du gaz et de l'électricité, par. 285.

1122. Autorité de la concurrence, Décision n° 14-MC-02 du 9 septembre 2014 relative à une demande de mesures conservatoires présentée par la société Direct Energie dans les secteurs du gaz et de l'électricité, par. 297.

1123. Belgian Competition Authority, Beslissing n° BMA-2015-P/K-27-AUD van 22 september 2015, Zaken nr. MEDE-P/K-13/0012 en CONC-P/K-13/0013, *Stanleybet Belgium NV/Stanley International Betting Ltd en Sagevas S.A./World Football Association S.P.R.L./Samenwerkende Nevenmaatschappij Belgische PMU S.C.R.L. v. Nationale Loterij NV*, paras 44-48, available at http://www.mededinging.be/nl/beslissingen/15-pk-27-nationale-loterij.

In reference to the approach of the Autorité de la concurrence, the Belgian competition authority made clear that for establishing whether this practice amounts to abuse it was necessary to look at the circumstances in which the National Lottery had built the database as well as at the possibility for competitors to reproduce the database. In this regard, the Belgian competition authority concluded that the contact details used by the National Lottery were not acquired on the basis of a competition on the merits but resulted from its activities conducted in the framework of its legal monopoly. Moreover, given its nature and size, the data could not have been reproduced by competitors in the market at reasonable financial conditions and within a reasonable period of time in the view of the Belgian competition authority.[1124]

Even though the Belgian competition authority followed the Autorité de la concurrence as regards the criteria for assessing the reproducibility of the database of GDF Suez, it did not require the National Lottery to share the contact details obtained in framework of its monopoly status with competitors in the market for sports betting. This difference in approach could be explained by the fact that the National Lottery only made use of these contact details once when sending an email to promote the launch of its new sports betting product. In these circumstances, an obligation to share the contact details with competitors, as imposed on GDF Suez by the Autorité de la concurrence, may have been disproportionate.

Both of these national competition cases involved cross-use of data developed in the context of a monopoly[1125] and therefore do not have much similarity to a factual scenario centring around data gathered by a provider of an online platform. In addition, the data at issue in the two cases concerned contact details of customers instead of information valuable for advertising purposes or for offering relevant and good quality services to users on online platforms. Nevertheless, the reference made by both competition authorities to reasonable financial conditions and a reasonable period of time when assessing the possibility for competitors to reproduce a database may also be of relevance when assessing the economic viability of duplication in the context of the indispensability of a dataset in the online environment under the essential facilities doctrine.

7.7.2 Exclusion of All Effective Competition on the Downstream Market

The condition relating to the exclusion of effective competition is interpreted in previous EU essential facilities cases as requiring that the holder of the requested input is already active on the downstream market and reserves this market to itself by refusing to deal.[1126] This means that a dominant provider of an online search engine,

---

1124. Belgian Competition Authority, Beslissing n° BMA-2015-P/K-27-AUD van 22 september 2015, Zaken nr. MEDE-P/K-13/0012 en CONC-P/K-13/0013, *Stanleybet Belgium NV/Stanley International Betting Ltd en Sagevas S.A./World Football Association S.P.R.L./Samenwerkende Nevenmaatschappij Belgische PMU S.C.R.L. v. Nationale Loterij NV*, paras 69-70.

1125. These and a few other, similar competition cases that occurred in non-digital markets are also discussed in Autorité de la concurrence and Bundeskartellamt, 'Competition Law and Data', 10 May 2016, pp. 31-33.

1126. For a more elaborate analysis, see section 6.8.2.2 above.

social network or e-commerce platform cannot be forced to give access to its dataset to an access seeker that needs the data to start competing in a market in which the provider is not present. This is particularly relevant in the scenario of indirect competition where companies may seek access to data in order to introduce statistical, analytics or other products not directly related to the main services that providers of online platforms offer to users and advertisers.[1127] If the current interpretation of the requirement of exclusion of effective competition is upheld, a provider of an online platform can legitimately prevent access seekers from opening up new markets in which it is not active itself by refusing to give access to its dataset.

The conditions of indispensability and exclusion of effective competition overlap to a certain extent and can therefore be analysed in close connection. In *Microsoft*, the European Commission first considered what degree of interoperability was necessary to enable effective competition in the derivative market and then assessed whether the interoperability that Microsoft refused to disclose was indispensable to reach that degree of interoperability. In possible future cases involving access to data, a similar approach can be taken. The relevant issue that has to be assessed is whether potential competitors and new entrants need to be put on an equal footing with the incumbent and thus be given access to its dataset in order to ensure effective competition on the downstream market.

7.7.3   Prevention of the Introduction of a New Product

If the object to which access is sought is protected by intellectual property law, the new product condition also has to be met for a refusal to deal to be considered abusive under current Article 102 TFEU standards. As argued in section 5.3 above, user data may be protected under copyright, sui generis database protection and/or trade secret law as a result of which an access seeker would have to point to a new product that it would like to develop once given access to the required information. In the scenario of direct competition where the access seeker is planning to compete with the dominant provider by introducing rival services to users and advertisers, the new product requirement will not easily be considered met if the service to be introduced by the access seeker is similar to the existing service of the incumbent. For example, an access seeker will probably not succeed in its access request if it wants to set up its own online search engine in competition with that of the incumbent Google. Nevertheless, in *Microsoft* the European Commission and the General Court accepted that a mere technical development suffices to fulfil the new product condition.

As discussed in section 6.8.2.3 above, there is no convincing economic reason for treating refusals to license differently than refusal to deal involving non-intellectual property protected assets. In line with the proposed framework set out in the previous chapter, the applicability of the new product condition could instead be made

---

1127. Some providers of online platforms such as Google, Twitter and Amazon do provide analytics services on their own platform in the form of their Google Analytics, Twitter Analytics and Amazon Analytics products and can therefore be considered to be active on a market for analytics services.

dependent on whether a market is characterised by external market failures. In situations where a dataset is protected by strong network effects or economies of scale and scope, the fact that an incumbent remains dominant in the market may merely result from the market situation grown around the dataset instead of from its competitive success. It is submitted that a competition law intervention is warranted under less strict conditions in these cases to guarantee a certain level of competition *in* the market and to prevent an incumbent from artificially extending its dominance by refusing to give access to its dataset. This can be achieved by dropping the new product requirement.

For determining whether the new product condition should be applied to cases where data is the alleged essential facility, the extent to which a dataset gives rise to a competitive advantage for incumbents and an entry barrier for potential competitors would need to be established. If external market failures relating to the dataset of the dominant undertaking can be identified which prevent competitors from entering the market and from introducing their own products or services, the new product condition would not need to be met. As a result, an access seeker would not have to identify a new product that it wishes to introduce once given access to the data. This way, consumers will be able to benefit from sustaining innovations or products similar to that of the dominant undertaking in cases where external market conditions restrict the ability of potential competitors which do not have access to the necessary data to compete *in* the market.

Against this background, it is instructive that Argenton & Prüfer concluded in 2012 that there is a strong tendency towards market tipping and monopolisation in the market for online search engines due to the existence of indirect network externalities relating to the collected information on search queries and subsequent clicking behaviour of users.[1128] The results of their economic model of search engine competition showed that '*the rate of innovation, quality, consumer surplus, and total welfare are higher if search engines only compete with their actual algorithm*' and not on the basis of the amount of search data they hold.[1129] Even though they acknowledged that a dominant search engine provider could possibly face an obligation to share search data under the essential facilities doctrine, they proposed to introduce a universal data-sharing scheme requiring all search engines to share anonymised data on search queries.[1130] In their view, '*intense competition between search engines based alone on the merits of the search algorithm provides better incentives to the firms to produce high-quality products than the rent enjoyed by a dominant firm that exploits a competitive advantage created by network externalities*'.[1131]

1128. C. ARGENTON AND J. PRÜFER, 'Search Engine Competition with Network Externalities', *Journal of Competition Law and Economics* 2012, vol. 8, no. 1, (73), p. 76.
1129. C. ARGENTON AND J. PRÜFER, 'Search Engine Competition with Network Externalities', *Journal of Competition Law and Economics* 2012, vol. 8, no. 1, (73), p. 100.
1130. C. ARGENTON AND J. PRÜFER, 'Search Engine Competition with Network Externalities', *Journal of Competition Law and Economics* 2012, vol. 8, no. 1, (73), p. 96-99.
1131. C. ARGENTON AND J. PRÜFER, 'Search Engine Competition with Network Externalities', *Journal of Competition Law and Economics* 2012, vol. 8, no. 1, (73), p. 94.

Considering the possible existence of such external market failures as identified by Argenton & Prüfer, access seekers may rely on the essential facilities doctrine, in the absence of any regulatory initiatives, to get hold of the search data of the incumbent in order to launch their own search engine without having to fulfil the new product requirement (provided that the other conditions of the essential facilities doctrine are met). This would restore the ability of other market players to compete *in* the market with the incumbent.

In situations where the position of the dominant player is not protected by external market failures, the new product condition should be applied strictly. This to ensure that a competition law intervention only takes place if it results into substantial utility for consumers in the form of a new product. In this regard, the product to be introduced by the access seeker once given access to the requested data should have no or a relatively low degree of substitutability to the product already offered by the essential facility holder. Even though it is not necessary that the new product establishes a new market, it must be of such better quality or have such complementary features that it is not comparable to the existing product of the dominant firm from the perspective of consumers. Under this interpretation, the new product requirement is most likely to be fulfilled in a scenario of indirect competition whereby a refusal to give access to data would prevent an access seeker to introduce a value-added service such as data analytics.

7.7.4 Absence of an Objective Justification

An objective justification that a dominant provider may invoke to offset an alleged anticompetitive refusal to give access to data, can be based on its obligations towards its users under data protection law. The provider could argue that it will not be able to comply with these obligations anymore, since it cannot vouch for an adequate level of data protection if it is forced to share personal data of its users with third parties.[1132]

A comparison can be made in this regard with the so-called regulated conduct defence raised in the *Deutsche Telekom* case. Deutsche Telekom, the German incumbent telecom operator, tried to justify its potential abuse of dominance by relying on the fact that its behaviour was regulated by the German telecommunications regulator on the basis of sector-specific telecommunications regulation. Deutsche Telekom was obliged to provide competitors with local access to its network. The national regulatory authority had fixed the wholesale prices it could charge its competitors and the retail tariffs for end consumers were subject to a price cap.

In its 2003 decision, the European Commission concluded that Deutsche Telekom had abused its dominant position by charging prices to its competitors for wholesale access to its local loop network that were higher than its own retail tariffs to end consumers thereby preventing competitors from generating a profit from their retail

---

1132. For a further analysis of the interaction between competition and data protection law, see Part III.

services.[1133] The Court of Justice argued that, although wholesale prices were set by the German regulator, the margin squeeze was attributable to Deutsche Telekom, since it had sufficient scope to adjust the retail prices it charged to its end-users, notwithstanding the fact that those prices were subject to some form of regulation.[1134]

The *Deutsche Telekom* case thus makes clear that the fact that a sector is regulated does not mean that it is immune from competition law intervention as long as the applicable regulation leaves room for autonomous conduct. In analogy to the *Deutsche Telekom* case, it could be argued that as long as data protection law leaves room for autonomous conduct by a dominant provider an objective justification based on this legal regime will not be accepted by competition authorities.[1135]

7.8 CONDITIONS UNDER WHICH ACCESS TO DATA SHOULD BE GRANTED

An important issue relating to the imposition of a duty to deal under the essential facilities doctrine is under which conditions access should be granted to the requested input. For this purpose, reference can be made to the 2004 *Microsoft* decision in which the European Commission imposed an obligation on Microsoft to make the necessary interoperability information available on the basis of reasonable and non-discriminatory terms.

The Commission specified that Microsoft should not be allowed to render the duty to supply ineffective by imposing unreasonable conditions as regards the access to, or the use of, the interoperability information. With respect to the element of non-discrimination, the Commission noted that the disclosures should be made to any undertaking having an interest in offering work group server operating system products. While the Commission did not set the rate that Microsoft was allowed to charge for access to the protocols, it did state that the remuneration should not reflect the 'strategic value' stemming from Microsoft's market power in the market for client PC operating systems or in the market for work group server operating systems.[1136]

In February 2008, the Commission adopted a new decision imposing on Microsoft a penalty payment for non-compliance with its obligation in the 2004 decision to give access to the interoperability information on reasonable and non-discriminatory terms. By reference to the pricing scheme that Microsoft itself devised, the Commission made clear that in order to be considered reasonable the remuneration should allow interested third parties who implement the interoperability information to viably compete with Microsoft's work group server operating system and should not compensate Microsoft for the strategic value of the protocols stemming from its market power in the two markets at issue. In accordance with Microsoft's own remuneration scheme, the Commission stated that it was necessary to examine whether the protocols

---

1133. Case COMP/C-1/37.451, 37.578, 37.579 – *Deutsche Telekom AG*, 21 May 2003.
1134. Judgment in *Deutsche Telekom AG*, C-280/08 P, ECLI:EU:C:2010:603, par. 183.
1135. See S. VEZZOSO, 'The Interface between Competition Policy and Data Protection', *Journal of European Competition Law & Practice* 2012, vol. 3, no. 3, (225), p. 225.
1136. Case COMP/C-3/37.792 - *Microsoft*, 24 March 2004, par. 1005-1008.

concerned were Microsoft's own creations, to examine whether those creations constituted innovation and to take into account a market valuation of comparable technologies excluding the strategic value stemming from the dominant position of any such technologies.[1137]

After a factual assessment, the Commission concluded that the royalties demanded by Microsoft prior to 22 October 2007 were unreasonable. In particular, the Commission argued that in the absence of convincing evidence as to the innovative character of almost all of Microsoft's unpatented interoperability information and in view of a comparison with the pricing of similar interoperability information, including other technology made available by Microsoft itself, the remuneration scheme had to be considered unreasonable.[1138]

Microsoft lodged an appeal against this Commission decision before the General Court. In its 2012 judgment, the General Court rejected Microsoft's argument that the Commission was not entitled to impose a penalty payment for infringement of the 2004 decision before having made specific the obligations arising under it and, in particular, without having determined the rate of remuneration that it considered reasonable. The General Court made clear that even though several rates may be covered by the notion of 'reasonable remuneration rates', it was not for the Commission to impose upon Microsoft its own choice from among what are reasonable rates for the purpose of the 2004 decision.[1139] On that ground, the General Court held that the absence of a prior specification of a rate of remuneration which, in the Commission's view, would be reasonable did not stand in the way of the imposition of a penalty payment for a breach of the 2004 decision.[1140]

Following the General Court's endorsement of the Commission's approach in *Microsoft*, no remuneration rate has to be set by a competition authority when requiring a dominant undertaking to give access to its dataset under the essential facilities doctrine. It would suffice to lay down in the decision that the essential facility holder is obliged to share data with competitors on the basis of reasonable and non-discriminatory conditions. It is then for the essential facility holder to set the rate, keeping in mind, however, that it is not allowed to ask compensation for the strategic value of the data stemming from its dominant position in the market at issue.

It is instructive to note that the Autorité de la concurrence required GDF Suez in the interim decision discussed in section 6.8.2.1 above to give access to the required customer information at its own expense.[1141] This may be explained, however, by the fact that GDF Suez acquired the data in the framework of its former monopoly position and did not create the information itself. In this regard, it should also be noted that the data to be shared concerned merely factual information such as names, addresses, fixed telephone numbers and consumption profiles of customers. If a dataset to which

---

1137. Case COMP/C-3/37.792 - *Microsoft*, 27 February 2008, paras 116-118.
1138. Case COMP/C-3/37.792 - *Microsoft*, 27 February 2008, par. 280.
1139. Judgment in *Microsoft*, T-167/08, ECLI:EU:T:2012:323, par. 95.
1140. Judgment in *Microsoft*, T-167/08, ECLI:EU:T:2012:323, par. 100.
1141. Autorité de la concurrence, Décision n° 14-MC-02 du 9 septembre 2014 relative à une demande de mesures conservatoires présentée par la société Direct Energie dans les secteurs du gaz et de l'électricité, par. 290.

access is mandated under the essential facilities doctrine has been developed by the dominant player itself and contains innovative information, the holder should be entitled to ask for a reasonable remuneration rate.

Finally, technical issues need to be considered which may stand in the way of imposing a duty to supply data on dominant providers of online platforms. The fact that Microsoft's search engine Bing integrates data from a number of social networks such as Facebook, Twitter and Foursquare in its search results illustrates the technical feasibility of making datasets accessible to third parties for use in their own services.[1142] Reference can also be made to Twitter which gives developers access to its data via several types of application programming interfaces (APIs).[1143] API access seems particularly appropriate in situations where data runs stale quickly and access seekers need recent data to be able to offer their own services to customers. Data analytics would be an example of a service for which continuous access to a constantly updated database is necessary.

With regard to search data, it is instructive to note that Argenton & Prüfer suggest to require search engine providers to exchange anonymised data on search queries directly and bilaterally in order to implement their proposal for a universal data-sharing regime among online search engines.[1144] In addition to a body achieving standardisation of how search queries are reported, a compliance or monitoring regime would need to be set up to enable such a - in their view - relatively timely delivery of data.[1145] However, it should be kept in mind that their proposal goes beyond what can be achieved under the essential facilities doctrine considering that the data-sharing regime would apply to all search engine providers in the market.

7.9 CONCLUSION

Although the extent to which data can constitute a competitive advantage or a barrier to entry is subject to controversy, it cannot be excluded at the outset that the large and varied datasets of incumbent online providers give rise to an economic benefit. The specific data to which potential competitors or new entrants need access in order to provide services competing with or complementing the services offered by providers of online search engines, social networks and e-commerce platforms may not be readily available on the market or be reasonably reproducible.

With regard to possible cases involving refusals to give access to data on online platforms, two main scenarios can be identified based on whether an access seeker is planning to launch direct or indirect competition with the dominant provider. The finding of liability under Article 102 TFEU seems most likely in a scenario of indirect competition because this situation concerns the typical leveraging behaviour whereby an undertaking seeks to extend its dominant position in the upstream or main market

---

1142. See section 2.2.2 above.
1143. See https://dev.twitter.com/streaming/overview.
1144. As discussed in section 7.7.3 above.
1145. C. Argenton and J. Prüfer, 'Search Engine Competition with Network Externalities', *Journal of Competition Law and Economics* 2012, vol. 8, no. 1, (73), p. 95.

to the downstream or derivative market by refusing to give access to the necessary data. Nevertheless, after the *IMS Health* judgment it is not necessary for a product to have been traded on a market already as a result of which a duty to deal may also be imposed to enable an access seeker to compete with the holder of the requested input in a direct or horizontal way.

When assessing refusals to give access to data, competition authorities and courts should take into account the specific characteristics of data that set it apart from other assets to which the essential facilities doctrine has been applied in previous cases. While data is inherently non-rivalrous, it can be made exclusive. Sui generis database protection and trade secret law are of particular relevance in this regard. The peculiarity of these regimes is that they do not impose any qualitative requirements as regards the subject matter of protection. The fact that the sui generis database right and trade secret law protect, respectively, investment and secrecy should be taken into account in essential facilities cases as well as the higher probability of anticompetitive effects as compared to refusals to license traditional intellectual property rights.

At the same time, there is also reason for competition authorities and courts to proceed with more caution when mandating access to data. Because the value of data may extend beyond its current usages, duties to deal involving data should be limited to the specific data needed to remedy the competition problem caused by the refusal of the dominant firm. This way, possible effects outside the relevant markets at stake in a particular essential facilities case can be mitigated.

With regard to possible objective justifications for refusals to give access to data, the scope for ex ante and ex post efficiency defences seems limited. Instead, dominant firms may invoke obligations relating to the adequate protection of the personal data of users to justify a refusal to share data with competitors. If a duty to deal requires a dominant firm to give access to personal data of its users, competition authorities and courts should pay attention to the interaction of competition law with the data protection regime. The role of data protection interests in competition enforcement forms the focus of the third part of the book.

PART III

Data Protection Interests in Competition Enforcement

The emergence of personal data as an asset for market players does not only raise competition issues but also leads to data protection considerations. The increasing importance of data in the digital economy reveals links between these two fields of law. It is important to note that not all issues involving the use of personal data by dominant firms or parties to a merger raise data protection concerns. For example, questions of whether data constitutes a barrier to entry or whether a market for data has to be defined form part of the usual competition analysis relating to online platforms. While such questions may raise novel issues in terms of the application of existing competition tools to new situations, they can be adequately addressed by competition authorities and courts without having to consider data protection interests. Such 'mere' competition issues are discussed in Parts I and II and are not further explored here. The aim of Part III of the book is rather to identify how the field of data protection interacts with competition law and to what extent such interests can or should be integrated in competition analysis.

To that end, it is first discussed how data protection can be defined and how these interests have become relevant to competition enforcement. Afterwards, the interaction between competition and data protection law is discussed. Issues to which attention is paid include an analysis of key data protection principles in relation to competition law, the effect of data protection regulation on competition and potential conflicts between the two legal regimes. With regard to the question of how data protection issues may be incorporated into competition analysis, it is analysed whether data protection can constitute a non-price parameter of competition and to what extent it can be protected as non-efficiency concern in competition policy. While Chapter 8 takes a descriptive approach, the analysis in Chapters 9 and 10 provides more in-depth assessment of the potential for a greater role of data protection interests in competition cases.

How Data Protection Has Become Relevant to Competition Enforcement

8.1 INTRODUCTION

In the past years, the interaction of competition law with data protection gained prominence in policy debates. As the role of data in the digital economy keeps increasing, mergers and certain types of conduct of dominant undertakings seem to have as objective the collection of additional information about consumers. These issues may not only lead to competition problems but also give rise to data protection concerns. Against this background, data protection advocates have been pleading for a greater role of data protection considerations in competition cases.

In section 8.2, the notions of data protection and privacy are analysed against the background of the EU Charter of Fundamental Rights and the European Convention on Human Rights. Section 8.3 discusses how data protection started to attract attention in competition enforcement. The *Google/DoubleClick* and *Facebook/WhatsApp* mergers have played an important role in this regard. While the main focus is on the decisions of the European Commission in this chapter, the approach of the US Federal Trade Commission to these mergers is also discussed to allow for a comparative element in the analysis.

8.2 DISENTANGLING DATA PROTECTION AND PRIVACY

In Europe, data protection and privacy are protected under the Council of Europe's European Convention on Human Rights (ECHR)[1146] as well as under the Charter of Fundamental Rights of the European Union (EU Charter of Fundamental Rights).[1147]

1146. Council of Europe, European Convention for the Protection of Human Rights and Fundamental Freedoms, as amended, 4 November 1950.
1147. Charter of Fundamental Rights of the European Union [2012] OJ C 326/391.

Both legal instruments comprise a provision on privacy by providing for a right to respect for private and family life in Article 8 of the ECHR and in Article 7 of the EU Charter of Fundamental Rights. Whereas the Charter includes a separate right to data protection in Article 8, no such specific provision on data protection can be found in the ECHR. Nevertheless, by interpreting the right to privacy contained in Article 8 of the ECHR broadly, the European Court of Human Rights in Strasbourg has held this article to include a right to data protection as well.[1148]

In the EU legal order, the right to data protection is not only recognised as a fundamental right in the EU Charter of Fundamental Rights, which became legally binding as a source of primary EU law with the entry into force of the Lisbon Treaty in December 2009, but is also enshrined in Article 16 TFEU which was introduced in the Lisbon Treaty as the new legal basis for the adoption of secondary data protection legislation. The General Data Protection Regulation,[1149] which was adopted in April 2016 and which will replace the current Data Protection Directive,[1150] is based on Article 16 TFEU. The General Data Protection Regulation will apply from 25 May 2018 onwards.[1151]

In accordance with the wording of the right to privacy in the ECHR and the EU Charter of Fundamental Rights, the term privacy is used in this book to refer to the protection of one's 'private life'. In general, the notion of privacy is regarded as a concept that is difficult to define. Different descriptions of privacy can consequently be found in the literature.[1152] Most notably, Warren and Brandeis referred to privacy as 'the right to be let alone' in their seminal US law review article of 1890,[1153] whereas Westin defined privacy as the right to control personal information being communicated to others.[1154] The latter description of privacy can be considered a predecessor of the principle of informational self-determination which originates from a ruling of the German Federal Constitutional Court relating to personal information collected during the 1983 census.[1155] The right to data protection as contained in the EU Charter of

---

1148. See, for example, ECHR 16 February 2000, *Amann v. Switzerland*, No. 27798/95, ECLI:CE:ECHR:2000:0216JUD002779895, par. 65 and ECHR 4 May 2000, *Rotaru v. Romania*, No. 28341/95, ECLI:CE:ECHR:2000:0504JUD002834195, par. 43.

1149. Regulation (EU) No 2016/679 of the European Parliament and of the Council of 27 April 2016 on the protection of natural persons with regard to the processing of personal data and on the free movement of such data, and repealing Directive 95/46/EC (General Data Protection Regulation) [2016] OJ L 119/1.

1150. Directive 95/46/EC of the European Parliament and of the Council of 24 October 1995 on the protection of individuals with regard to the processing of personal data and on the free movement of such data (Data Protection Directive) [1995] OJ L 281/31.

1151. Article 99(2) of the General Data Protection Regulation.

1152. See for example, D.J. Solove, 'A Taxonomy of Privacy', *University of Pennsylvania Law Review* 2006, vol. 154, no. 3, (477), pp. 479-482.

1153. S.D. Warren and L.D. Brandeis, 'The Right to Privacy', *Harvard Law Review* 1890, vol. 4, no. 5, (193), p. 195.

1154. A.F. Westin, *Privacy and Freedom*, New York, Atheneum, 1967, p. 7.

1155. BVerfG 65, 1 - *Volkszählung*, 15 December 1983, available at http://openjur.de/u/268440.html.

Fundamental Rights, in its turn, requires that personal data be processed fairly for specified purposes and on the basis of the consent of the person concerned or another legitimate basis laid down by law.[1156]

Although the terms 'data protection' and 'privacy' are sometimes used inter-changeably, there are important differences between the two rights in terms of scope and substance. In general, the scope of the right to data protection is more limited than that of the right to privacy, since the right to data protection only comes into play if personal data is processed. The right to privacy, on the other hand, protects the private sphere of individuals irrespective of whether any processing of personal data is involved. At the same time, the scope of data protection is broader than the scope of privacy as far as the application of both rights to personal data is concerned. The right to data protection grants protection to all personal data and not only to data which is invasive of one's private life as protected under the right to privacy. Private life does not necessarily include all information relating to identified or identifiable natural persons which is the definition of personal data under EU data protection legislation.[1157]

Figure 8.1   Difference in Scope of the Rights to Data Protection and Privacy

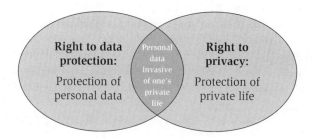

In this regard, the European Court of Human Rights appears to require an additional element to be present in order for personal data to be included in the scope of private life.[1158] In *Rotaru*, the European Court of Human Rights made clear that personal data

---

1156. Article 8(2) of the EU Charter of Fundamental Rights. This provision also explicitly provides for a right of access to personal data and a right to have personal data rectified.

1157. Article 2(a) of the Data Protection Directive defines 'personal data' as '*any information relating to an identified or identifiable natural person*', and specifies that '*an identifiable person is one who can be identified, directly or indirectly, in particular by reference to an identification number or to one or more factors specific to his physical, physiological, mental, economic, cultural or social identity*'. Article 4(1) of the General Data Protection Regulation similarly defines 'personal data' as '*any information relating to an identified or identifiable natural person*' and specifies that '*an identifiable person is one who can be identified, directly or indirectly, in particular by reference to an identifier such as a name, an identification number, location data, online identifier or to one or more factors specific to the physical, physiological, genetic, mental, economic, cultural or social identity of that natural person*'.

1158. As argued by J. KOKOTT AND C. SOBOTTA, 'The Distinction between Privacy and Data Protection in the Jurisprudence of the CJEU and the ECtHR', *International Data Privacy Law* 2013, vol. 3, no. 4, (222), p. 224.

concerning a person's distant past that is systematically collected and stored falls within the scope of private life.[1159] In the more recent *M.M.* case, the European Court of Human Rights argued that information about a criminal conviction or caution constitutes personal data but also becomes part of a person's private life '*as the conviction or caution itself recedes into the past*'. In the case at hand, the administration of the caution occurred almost twelve years beforehand.[1160]

With respect to their substance, one could regard the right to privacy as giving rise to a negative duty to refrain from unlawfully interfering in the private life of individuals, while the right to data protection can be considered to bring about a positive duty to take measures in order to process personal data in a legitimate way. In this perspective, the Data Protection Directive and the General Data Protection Regulation grant individuals (referred to as 'data subjects')[1161] whose personal data is being processed certain rights and lay down obligations of transparency, legitimate purpose and proportionality with which public authorities and private entities (known as 'controllers'[1162] or 'processors'[1163]) have to comply when processing personal data. Most activities relating to personal data such as its collection, storage and analysis qualify as acts of processing.[1164]

To prevent an interference with the right to data protection contained in Article 8 of the EU Charter of Fundamental Rights, personal data must be processed fairly, for specified purposes and on the basis of consent of the individual concerned or another legitimate legal basis. Yet, the act of processing of personal data may still be considered invasive of one's private life under Article 7 of the EU Charter of Fundamental Rights and Article 8 of the ECHR. With regard to the relationship between these two instruments, Article 52(3) of the EU Charter of Fundamental Rights makes clear that rights contained in the Charter corresponding with those in the ECHR must be

---

1159. ECHR 4 May 2000, *Rotaru v. Romania*, No. 28341/95, ECLI:CE:ECHR:2000:0504JUD00 2834195, par. 43.
1160. ECHR 13 November 2012, *M.M. v. the United Kingdom*, No. 24029/07, ECLI:CE:ECHR:2012: 1113JUD002402907, par. 188.
1161. Article 2(a) of the Data Protection Directive and Article 4(1) of the General Data Protection Regulation define a data subject as '*an identified or identifiable natural person*'. Hereafter, the terms 'data subject', 'individual', 'consumer' and 'user' are used interchangeably.
1162. Article 2(d) of the Data Protection Directive and Article 4(7) of the General Data Protection Regulation define a 'controller' as '*the natural or legal person, public authority, agency or any other body which, alone or jointly with others, determines the purposes and means of the processing of personal data*'.
1163. Article 2(e) of the Data Protection Directive and Article 4(8) of the General Data Protection Regulation define a 'processor' as '*a natural or legal person, public authority, agency or any other body which processes personal data on behalf of the controller*'.
1164. Article 2(b) of the Data Protection Directive defines 'processing of personal data' as '*any operation or set of operations which is performed upon personal data, whether or not by automatic means, such as collection, recording, organization, storage, adaptation or alteration, retrieval, consultation, use, disclosure by transmission, dissemination or otherwise making available, alignment or combination, blocking, erasure or destruction*'. Article 4(2) of the General Data Protection Regulation defines 'processing' as '*any operation or set of operations which is performed upon personal data or sets of personal data, whether or not by automated means, such as collection, recording, organisation, structuring, storage, adaptation or alteration, retrieval, consultation, use, disclosure by transmission, dissemination or otherwise making available, alignment or combination, restriction, erasure or destruction*'.

interpreted as having the same meaning and scope as those laid down by the ECHR.[1165] As a result, when applying the right to privacy as protected by Article 7 of the EU Charter of Fundamental Rights, regard should be had to the interpretation given to the corresponding Article 8 of the ECHR by the European Court of Human Rights.

If a form of processing of personal data relates to one's private life, there is an interference with the right to privacy which has to be justified in order to be lawful under the ECHR. A justification is examined in three steps under Article 8(2) of the ECHR: (1) the interference must be in accordance with the law (i.e., have a sufficient legal basis); (2) the interference must pursue a legitimate aim (i.e., one of the following admissible grounds mentioned in Article 8(2): national security, public safety or the economic well-being of the country, the prevention of disorder or crime, the protection of health or morals, or the protection of the rights and freedoms of others); and (3) the interference must be necessary in a democratic society (i.e., be proportional). Nevertheless, once an act of processing complies with the EU data protection rules, it is unlikely that a possible corresponding interference with the right to privacy cannot be justified.[1166] For this reason, the analysis in this book mainly focuses on the relationship between EU data protection legislation and competition law.

8.3 RISE OF ATTENTION FOR DATA PROTECTION IN COMPETITION ENFORCEMENT

The interaction of data protection with competition law started to gain attention from policy makers and academics after the announcement of Google's proposed acquisition of DoubleClick in 2007. The data protection concerns of the merger were in particular considered to relate to the concentration of user information in the hands of Google after the acquisition. Most notably, Peter Swire argued in his testimony to the US Federal Trade Commission Town Hall Meeting on behavioural advertising that the combination of 'deep' information from Google on search behaviour of individuals with 'broad' information from DoubleClick on web-browsing behaviour of individuals could significantly reduce the quality of Google's search engine for consumers with high privacy preferences.[1167]

Despite calls to oppose the *Google/DoubleClick* merger on the basis of privacy considerations,[1168] the Federal Trade Commission made clear that it lacks legal authority to attach conditions to a merger that do not relate to antitrust. In its view, the sole purpose of merger review is to identify and remedy transactions that harm

---

1165. The provision goes on to state that EU law is, however, not precluded from providing more extensive protection.

1166. J. Kokott and C. Sobotta, 'The Distinction between Privacy and Data Protection in the Jurisprudence of the CJEU and the ECtHR', *International Data Privacy Law* 2013, vol. 3, no. 4, (222), p. 226.

1167. P. Swire, 'Submitted Testimony to the Federal Trade Commission Behavioral Advertising Town Hall', 18 October 2007, p. 5, available at http://www.europarl.europa.eu/meetdocs/ 2004_2009/documents/dv/testimony_peterswire_/Testimony_peterswire_en.pdf.

1168. The term 'privacy' or 'information privacy' is used in the US instead of and in the meaning of the notion of 'data protection' as developed in the EU. For that reason, the terms 'privacy' and 'data protection' are used interchangeably in this book when referring to the US context.

competition. That said, the Federal Trade Commission still investigated the possibility that Google's acquisition of DoubleClick would adversely affect non-price attributes of competition including consumer privacy. It concluded, however, that the evidence did not support such a conclusion.[1169] In particular, Google and DoubleClick were found not to be able to significantly affect each other's prices or non-price product dimensions such as consumer privacy and service quality after the merger, because they were not regarded as competitors in the same relevant market.[1170]

The European Commission also argued that Google and DoubleClick were not exerting major competitive constraints on each other's activities as a result of which they could not be considered as competitors at the moment of the proposed transaction.[1171] Unlike the Federal Trade Commission, the European Commission did not refer to data protection as a non-price parameter of competition in this regard. Along similar lines to those of the Federal Trade Commission, the European Commission noted that its decision referred exclusively to the appraisal of the transaction with EU competition rules and was without prejudice to the obligations imposed on Google and DoubleClick by EU and national legislation in the field of data protection and privacy. In this regard, the European Commission expressly stated that: 'Irrespective of the approval of the merger, the new entity is obliged in its day to day business to respect the fundamental rights recognised by all relevant instruments to its users, namely but not limited to privacy and data protection'.[1172]

EU *Google/DoubleClick* merger decision

At the time of the proposed concentration, the two parties were engaged in the following relevant activities. Google operated an internet search engine, offered online advertising space on its own websites and provided intermediation services to publishers and advertisers for the sale of online advertising space on partner websites through its AdSense network. DoubleClick was mainly active in the sale of ad serving, management and reporting technology worldwide to website publishers, advertisers and advertising agencies.

The Commission's market investigation pointed out that Google and DoubleClick were not exerting a significant competitive constraint on each other's activities. Therefore, the merger did not seem to significantly impede effective competition with regard to the elimination of actual competition. While it could not be excluded that DoubleClick would, absent the merger, have developed into an effective competitor of Google in the market for online ad intermediation, it was rather likely in the Commission's view that a sufficient number of other competitors would be left in the market. As a result, sufficient competitive

---

1169. Statement of the Federal Trade Commission, *Google/DoubleClick*, FTC File No. 071-0170, 20 December 2007, pp. 2-3, available at http://www.ftc.gov/system/files/documents/public_statements/418081/071220googledc-commstmt.pdf.
1170. Statement of the Federal Trade Commission, *Google/DoubleClick*, FTC File No. 071-0170, 20 December 2007, p. 8 and footnote 7.
1171. Case No COMP/M.4731 – *Google/ DoubleClick*, 11 March 2008, par. 221.
1172. Case No COMP/M.4731 – *Google/ DoubleClick*, 11 March 2008, par. 368.

pressure would remain after the merger. On this basis, the Commission concluded that the elimination of DoubleClick as a potential competitor would not have an adverse impact on competition in that market.

The Commission also analysed the potential effects of non-horizontal relationships between Google and DoubleClick. Concerns expressed by third parties involved foreclosure scenarios based on DoubleClick's market position in ad serving, foreclosure scenarios based on Google's market position in search advertising and online ad intermediation services, and foreclosure scenarios based on the combination of DoubleClick's and Google's databases on customer online behaviour. The Commission found that such types of foreclosure would be unlikely to occur. Even if such scenarios did occur, they would not result in a significant impediment to effective competition according to the Commission. With regard to the possible combination of data of Google and DoubleClick after the merger, the Commission stated that this would be very unlikely to bring more traffic to AdSense so as to squeeze out competitors and ultimately enable the merged entity to charge higher prices for its intermediation services.

Case No COMP/M.4731 – *Google/ DoubleClick*, 11 March 2008, paragraphs 4-5, 192, 221-222, 278, 286-289, 329-332, 356-366.

In response to the decision of the majority to close the US investigation into the *Google/DoubleClick* merger, then-Commissioner Pamela Jones Harbour issued a dissenting statement in which she argued that the Federal Trade Commission could have relied on various theories to include privacy issues in its competition analysis of the transaction. She argued, for example, that consumer choice would decrease if network effects lead to a reduction in the number of competing search engines in the market. This would in turn diminish incentives of search engine providers to compete based on privacy protections.[1173] In addition, she stated that the Federal Trade Commission could have conducted a fuller analysis of the data-related issues of the merger through the definition of '*a putative relevant product market comprising data that may be useful to advertisers and publishers who wish to engage in behavioral targeting*'.[1174] She also suggested the Federal Trade Commission to mandate a firewall between the Google and DoubleClick data for some period of time to prevent potential anticompetitive effects.[1175] In a subsequent law journal article, Pamela Jones Harbour and her former advisor Tara Isa Koslov further advanced a new approach towards market definition in '*a Web 2.0 world*' which does not only rely on substitutability between existing products and technologies but also accounts for the emergence of new forms of

---

1173. Dissenting Statement of Commissioner Pamela Jones Harbour, *Google/DoubleClick*, FTC File No. 071-0170, 20 December 2007, p. 10 and footnote 25, available at http://www.ftc.gov/sites/default/files/documents/public_statements/statement-matter-google/doubleclick/071 220harbour_0.pdf.
1174. Dissenting Statement of Commissioner Pamela Jones Harbour, *Google/DoubleClick*, FTC File No. 071-0170, 20 December 2007, p. 9.
1175. Dissenting Statement of Commissioner Pamela Jones Harbour, *Google/DoubleClick*, FTC File No. 071-0170, 20 December 2007, footnote 23 on p. 9.

competition. In order to start the process of making privacy cognisable under competition law, they proposed to define relevant product markets either around data, separate from the markets for the services built on the data, or around privacy as a dimension of competition.[1176]

The debate about the role of data protection in competition analysis has continued since the *Google/DoubleClick* merger[1177] and attracted renewed attention from the competition law community in the context of Facebook's acquisition of WhatsApp in 2014. Both the US Federal Trade Commission and the European Commission approved the merger without obtaining any commitments from the parties. In the view of the European Commission, the acquisition of WhatsApp would not increase the amount of data potentially available to Facebook for advertising purposes because WhatsApp did not collect data valuable for advertising purposes at the time of the merger.[1178] The European Commission still investigated possible theories of harm relating to data concentration to the extent that it was likely to strengthen Facebook's position in the market for online advertising. In its *Facebook/WhatsApp* merger decision, the European Commission explicitly stated: '*Any privacy-related concerns flowing from the increased concentration of data within the control of Facebook as a result of the Transaction do not fall within the scope of the EU competition law rules but within the scope of the EU data protection rules*'.[1179]

EU *Facebook/WhatsApp* merger decision

The *Facebook/WhatsApp* investigation of the European Commission covered three areas: consumer communications services, social networking services and online advertising services. With regard to the relevant market for consumer communications services, the Commission found that Facebook Messenger and WhatsApp were not close competitors and that consumers would continue to have a wide choice of alternative communications apps after the transaction. The Commission did not take a final view on the existence and the still evolving boundaries of a potential market for social networking services and concluded that, irrespective of the exact market borders, Facebook and WhatsApp were only distant competitors given the differences between the functionalities and focus of their services. In the area of online advertising services, the Commission argued that the merger would not raise competition concerns even if Facebook would introduce targeted advertising on WhatsApp or start collecting data from

---

1176. P.J. HARBOUR AND T.I. KOSLOV, 'Section 2 In A Web 2.0 World: An Expanded Vision of Relevant Product Markets', *Antitrust Law Journal* 2010, vol. 76, no. 3, (769), pp. 773-774.

1177. See, most notably: R.H. LANDE, 'The Microsoft-Yahoo Merger: Yes, Privacy Is an Antitrust Concern', *FTC:WATCH* February 2008, no. 714, (1); J. BRILL, 'The Intersection of Consumer Protection and Competition in the New World of Privacy', *Competition Policy International* 2011, vol. 7, no. 1, (7); speech delivered to the American Bar Association Antitrust Section by US Senator Franken, 'How Privacy Has Become an Antitrust Issue', 30 March 2012, available at http://www.huffingtonpost.com/al-franken/how-privacy-has-become-an_b_1392580. html; and S. VEZZOSO, 'The Interface between Competition Policy and Data Protection', *Journal of European Competition Law & Practice* 2012, vol. 3, no. 3, (225).

1178. Case No COMP/M.7217 – *Facebook/WhatsApp*, 3 October 2014, par. 166.

1179. Case No COMP/M.7217 – *Facebook/WhatsApp*, 3 October 2014, par. 164.

WhatsApp users with a view to improving the accuracy of the targeted ads served on Facebook's social networking platform. In the Commission's view, there would continue to be a sufficient number of alternative providers to Facebook for the supply of targeted advertising after the merger, and a large amount of internet user data that are valuable for advertising purposes were not within Facebook's exclusive control.

Case No COMP/M.7217 – *Facebook/WhatsApp*, 3 October 2014, paragraphs 101-115, 146-158, 172-179 and 184-189.

The Federal Trade Commission did not address the data protection issues in its antitrust review of the merger either.[1180] Instead, the director of the Federal Trade Commission's Bureau of Consumer Protection urged Facebook in a letter to keep to WhatsApp's current privacy policy which gives users a higher level of protection with regard to the collection and use of their data than its own privacy statement. In addition, she made clear that both companies could be violating Section 5 of the Federal Trade Commission Act[1181] if WhatsApp fails to honour its privacy promises.[1182]

A final development that has moved forward the ongoing debate about the role of data protection in competition enforcement in the European Union, is the publication of a Preliminary Opinion on 'Privacy and competitiveness in the age of big data'[1183] by the EDPS[1184] in March 2014. The Preliminary Opinion and subsequent events organised by the EDPS[1185] have launched a more in-depth discussion of how the fields of data

---

1180. The statement of the Federal Trade Commission in *Facebook/WhatsApp* has not been published as a result of which the exact substance of the analysis under US antitrust standards remains unclear.

1181. Under Section 5 of the Federal Trade Commission Act (15 U.S.C. § 45), *'unfair methods of competition in or affecting commerce, and unfair or deceptive acts or practices in or affecting commerce'* are unlawful. Failure to keep promises made about data protection may constitute a deceptive practice and use of data in a manner inconsistent with promises made at the time the data was collected may qualify as an unfair practice. Both acts fall within the consumer protection competencies of the Federal Trade Commission.

1182. Letter From JESSICA L. RICH, Director of the Federal Trade Commission Bureau of Consumer Protection, to Erin Egan, Chief Privacy Officer, Facebook, and to Anne Hoge, General Counsel, WhatsApp Inc., 10 April 2014, available at https://www.ftc.gov/system/files/documents/public_statements/297701/140410facebookwhatappltr.pdf.

1183. PRELIMINARY OPINION OF THE EUROPEAN DATA PROTECTION SUPERVISOR, 'Privacy and competitiveness in the age of big data: The interplay between data protection, competition law and consumer protection in the Digital Economy', March 2014.

1184. The EDPS is the independent supervisory authority which oversees the data-processing activities of the EU institutions and provides the EU institutions with advice on data protection issues.

1185. In 2014 and 2015, several events were organised by or in collaboration with the EDPS (see https://secure.edps.europa.eu/EDPSWEB/edps/Consultation/big_data) including a workshop in the European Parliament on 'Privacy, Consumers, Competition and Big Data' on 2 June 2014; a Privacy Platform organised by Member of European Parliament Sophie in 't Veld on 'Privacy and Competition in the Digital Economy' on 21 January 2015; a seminar entitled 'Antitrust, Privacy & Big Data' organised by Concurrences and Cadwalader, Wickersham & Taft LLP on 3 February 2015; and a workshop held by the EDPS and the European Academy of Law entitled 'Competition Rebooted: Enforcement and Personal Data in Digital Markets' on 24 September 2015.

protection, competition law and consumer protection intersect in the digital economy. The initiative is hoped to stimulate a further dialogue between regulators and experts to explore the scope for closer coordination among the competent EU institutions in the three different areas of law.

8.4 CONCLUSION

In Europe, data protection and privacy are protected in the legal order of the Council of Europe as well as the European Union. Within the Council of Europe, the European Court of Human Rights in Strasbourg oversees the implementation of the ECHR which provides for a right to respect for private and family life in Article 8. This provision has been interpreted by the European Court of Human Rights to also comprise a right to data protection. In the European Union, privacy and data protection are included as separate rights in Articles 7 and 8 of the EU Charter of Fundamental Rights. In addition, the Lisbon Treaty introduced Article 16 TFEU which forms the new legal basis for the adoption of secondary data protection legislation on the EU level. While the Data Protection Directive is still applicable at the moment, it is going to be replaced by the General Data Protection Regulation that will apply from 25 May 2018 onwards. The rights to data protection and privacy are not identical as regards scope and substance. However, if a certain form of processing of personal data conforms to EU secondary data protection rules, a potential parallel interference with the right to privacy will likely be justifiable under the ECHR.

Despite calls from data protection advocates to consider data protection issues in the merger analysis of the *Google/DoubleClick* and *Facebook/WhatsApp* acquisitions, the US Federal Trade Commission as well as the European Commission made clear that merger review in principle takes place on the basis of the competition rules and that data protection-related concerns should rather be resolved under data protection law. Nevertheless, the debate about the proper role of data protection in competition cases is being continued at both sides of the Atlantic.

CHAPTER 9

Identifying the Interaction Between Competition and Data Protection Law

9.1 INTRODUCTION

Several links between competition and data protection law can be identified. Instead of focusing on procedural aspects, attention is paid in this chapter to how the two legal fields interact in terms of the substance of their respective obligations. The interface is examined from the viewpoint of competition law in the sense that the impact of the rise of attention for data protection concerns on competition enforcement forms the basis of the analysis.

In section 9.2, the main data protection principles and their enforcement are discussed by comparing them to relevant notions in competition law. Afterwards, the effect of data protection regulation on competition is analysed in section 9.3. Section 9.4 focuses on the question of whether and how data protection can be considered as constituting a non-price parameter of competition. Finally, potential conflicts between competition and data protection law are outlined in section 9.5.

9.2 KEY DATA PROTECTION PRINCIPLES AND THEIR ENFORCEMENT IN RELATION TO COMPETITION LAW

As an introduction to the more substantive analysis of how EU data protection and competition law interact, it is instructive to have a look at the key data protection principles and how they are enforced. This allows for a comparison with relevant concepts and enforcement mechanisms of EU competition law.

9.2.1 From Consent and Purpose Limitation to Substitutability

One of the main notions of EU data protection law is the principle of lawful processing which forms the first of the so-called data quality requirements contained in Article 6(1) of the current Data Protection Directive and Article 5(1) of the future General Data Protection Regulation. The principle of lawful processing requires that the processing of personal data has to take place on the basis of a legitimate ground.[1186] The most commonly used legal ground to lawfully process personal data in the context of digital services is by obtaining consent from the individual whose data will be processed. Article 2(h) of the Data Protection Directive defines consent as *'any freely given specific and informed indication of his wishes by which the data subject signifies his agreement to personal data relating to him being processed'*. Under Article 4(11) of the General Data Protection Regulation, consent is defined as *'any freely given, specific, informed and unambiguous indication of the data subject's wishes by which he or she, by a statement or by a clear affirmative action, signifies agreement to the processing of personal data relating to him or her'*.[1187] The application of such a key data protection concept as consent is difficult in concentrated markets where consumers are often confronted with take-it-or-leave-it offers and do not have a real choice but to accept the terms and conditions if they want to use a particular service.

Due to the existence of network effects, the markets in which online businesses compete are typically characterised by the presence of only a few firms that have a rather large market share. Individual control over personal data is becoming illusory when dominant companies are able to impose their practices on individuals by exploiting information asymmetries. Even though EU consumer protection legislation, in particular the Consumer Rights Directive, requires traders to provide consumers with relevant information on the main characteristics of a service before entering into a contract,[1188] consumers are often not fully aware to what extent and for what purposes the personal information they reveal by using a certain service is processed. This may result into an imbalance of power between individuals and providers of online services which calls into question the existence of a genuine choice for data subjects whether or not to give their consent to a particular form of processing of

---

1186. Article 7 of the Data Protection Directive and Article 6(1) of the General Data Protection Regulation specify the legal grounds for lawful processing of personal data.
1187. Article 7 of the General Data Protection Regulation lays down specific conditions for consent. For a detailed analysis of the concept of consent, see E. KOSTA, *Consent in European Data Protection Law*, Martinus Nijhoff Publishers, 2013.
1188. Directive 2011/83/EU of the European Parliament and of the Council of 25 October 2011 on consumer rights (Consumer Rights Directive) [2011] OJ L 304/64 requires traders to provide consumers in a clear and comprehensible manner with information on, for instance and as relevant for digital services: the main characteristics of the services (Article 6(1)(a)); the functionality, including applicable technical protection measures, of digital content (Article 6(1)(r)); and any relevant interoperability of digital content with hardware and software that the trader is aware of or can reasonably be expected to have been aware of (Article 6(1)(s)).

personal data.[1189] Since consent has to result from a free choice, its validity may be challenged when there is a limited number of providers in the market or when one provider is dominant.[1190]

The increased attention from data protection advocates for competition enforcement seems to stem from the concentrated nature of online markets which may reduce possibilities for users to exercise effective control over their personal data. Against this background, it is argued that strong competition enforcement could render data protection rules more effective by increasing competition in concentrated markets and by facilitating genuine consumer choice.[1191] However, a high level of concentration in itself is not a reason for competition authorities to intervene in a market. The application of competition law is only triggered in the presence of actual, proven competition problems.

Another concept that lies at the heart of EU data protection law is the so-called purpose limitation principle which sets the boundaries within which personal data collected for a particular purpose may be processed and put to further use. The principle of purpose limitation is designed to offer a balanced approach that aims to reconcile the need for predictability and legal certainty of data subjects on the one hand, and the need for some flexibility for controllers on the other hand.[1192] In accordance with Article 6(1)(b) of the Data Protection Directive and Article 5(1)(b) of the General Data Protection Regulation, the principle consists of two components: (1) personal data must be *collected for specified, explicit and legitimate purposes* (notion of purpose specification); and (2) once collected, personal data must not be *further processed in a manner that is incompatible with those purposes* (notion of compatible use).

The notion of purpose specification requires that the purpose of the processing activities be precisely identified and clearly revealed, explained or expressed to data subjects before the processing of personal data starts. In addition, the purpose must be legitimate. This requirement of legitimacy goes beyond the need to have a legal ground for processing under Article 7 of the Data Protection Directive and Article 6(1) of the General Data Protection Regulation. Legitimacy under the notion of purpose specification extends to other areas of law such as non-discrimination and has to be interpreted within the context of the processing which determines the reasonable expectations of

---

1189. PRELIMINARY OPINION OF THE EUROPEAN DATA PROTECTION SUPERVISOR, 'Privacy and competitiveness in the age of big data: The interplay between data protection, competition law and consumer protection in the Digital Economy', March 2014, par. 79.

1190. For a detailed discussion of the requirements that have to be met for consent to be valid, see ARTICLE 29 WORKING PARTY, 'Opinion 15/2011 on the definition of consent', WP 187, 13 July 2011, pp. 11-26. For example, the Article 29 Working Party has held that reliance on consent in the employment context where there may be a situation of subordination *should be confined to cases where the worker has a genuine free choice and is subsequently able to withdraw the consent without detriment*. See ARTICLE 29 WORKING PARTY, 'Opinion 8/2001 on the processing of personal data in the employment context', WP 48, 13 September 2001, p. 23.

1191. C. KUNER, F.H. CATE, C. MILLARD, ET AL., 'When Two Worlds Collide: The Interface between Competition Law and Data Protection', *International Data Privacy Law* 2014, vol. 4, no. 4, (247), p. 247.

1192. ARTICLE 29 WORKING PARTY, 'Opinion 03/2013 on purpose limitation', WP 203, 2 April 2013, p. 5.

the data subject. Purpose specification is a prerequisite for other data quality requirements including adequacy, relevance and proportionality of personal data (Article
6(1)(c) of the Data Protection Directive and Article 5(1)(c) of the General Data
Protection Regulation), accuracy of personal data (Article 6(1)(d) of the Data Protection Directive and Article 5(1)(d) of the General Data Protection Regulation) and the
requirement that personal data has to be kept in an identifiable form for no longer than
is necessary for the purposes for which the data was collected (Article 6(1)(e) of the
Data Protection Directive and Article 5(1)(e) of the General Data Protection Regulation).[1193] The General Data Protection Regulation adds a sixth data quality requirement
relating to integrity and confidentiality of personal data in Article 5(1)(f).

The notion of compatible use entails that in each situation where further
processing of personal data is considered, a distinction has to be made between
additional uses that are compatible with the original purpose, and other uses which are
incompatible and therefore unlawful.[1194] The fact that further processing of personal
data is allowed as long as it is not incompatible with the original purpose for which the
data was collected indicates that the legislator may have intended to provide for some
degree of flexibility with regard to further use. Compatibility is a complex issue which
needs to be assessed on a case-by-case basis taking into account all relevant circumstances.

Due to the lack of a harmonised interpretation, the notion of compatible use has
been applied in divergent ways in the different Member States.[1195] In order to reduce
inconsistencies, the Article 29 Working Party proposed some key factors that should be
considered when conducting a compatibility assessment such as the context in which
the personal data have been collected, the reasonable expectations of data subjects as
to the further use of their personal data, the nature of the personal data in question, the
impact of the further processing on data subjects and the safeguards adopted by the
controller to protect the data subject.[1196] Some of these factors have been codified in
Article 6(4) of the General Data Protection Regulation which lays down five specific
elements a controller should consider when ascertaining whether further processing is
compatible with the original purpose for which the data was collected. This provision
is applicable to situations where the processing is not based on the data subject's
consent or on a Union or Member State law which constitutes a necessary and
proportionate measure in a democratic society to safeguard certain objectives including
national security, defence and public security. In these cases, the controller should take
into account in its compatibility assessment: (a) any link between the purposes for

---

1193. ARTICLE 29 WORKING PARTY, 'Opinion 03/2013 on purpose limitation', WP 203, 2 April 2013,
    pp. 38-39.
1194. For a further analysis of the notion of compatible use as well as of the purpose limitation
    principle and the notion of purpose specification, see EUROPEAN UNION AGENCY FOR FUNDAMEN-
    TAL RIGHTS AND COUNCIL OF EUROPE, Handbook on European data protection law, 2014,
    pp. 68-70, available at http://www.echr.coe.int/Documents/Handbook_data_protection_
    ENG.pdf.
1195. ARTICLE 29 WORKING PARTY, 'Opinion 03/2013 on purpose limitation', WP 203, 2 April 2013,
    pp. 5 and 21.
1196. ARTICLE 29 WORKING PARTY, 'Opinion 03/2013 on purpose limitation', WP 203, 2 April 2013,
    pp. 23-27.

which the data has been collected and the purposes of the intended further processing; (b) the context in which the personal data has been collected, in particular regarding the relationship between data subjects and the controller; (c) the nature of the personal data, in particular whether special categories of personal data are processed or whether data related to criminal convictions and offences is processed; (d) the possible consequences of the intended further processing for data subjects; and (e) the existence of appropriate safeguards which may include encryption or pseudonymisation.

In its Preliminary Opinion on 'Privacy and competitiveness in the age of big data', the EDPS makes a link between the notion of compatible use in data protection law and the concept of substitutability as applied in competition cases to define relevant product markets. If a company collects personal data for the purpose of providing a service in one market and decides to further process the data in order to launch another service in a different market, this may, in the view of the EDPS, be an indication that the further processing is incompatible with the initial purpose for which the personal data was collected. In other words, if the two services are not substitutable from a competition law perspective and thus cannot be included in the same relevant market, it is argued that competition analysis would support the finding of a possible breach of data protection law.[1197] However, the notion of compatibility in data protection law seems wider than the concept of substitutability in competition law. While application of the competition law concept of substitutability may indicate that personal data are being processed for distinct purposes, this does not imply that the further processing is incompatible with the original purpose for which the personal data was collected. As the Article 29 Working Party makes clear, a change of purpose may be permissible and further processing of personal data may be considered compatible in situations where the expectations of society or of the data subjects themselves have changed about what additional use the data may be put to.[1198] A substitutability test in analogy to competition law thus cannot fully replace a compatibility assessment under data protection law. If the services are considered not to be substitutable from a competition law perspective, an additional analysis still has to be conducted in order to assess whether the further processing has to be deemed incompatible with the original purpose taking into account all relevant circumstances.

9.2.2 Comparing the Enforcement Mechanisms of EU Data Protection and Competition Law

Unlike the EU competition enforcement mechanism which consists in joint application and enforcement of the EU competition rules by the European Commission and

---

1197. PRELIMINARY OPINION OF THE EUROPEAN DATA PROTECTION SUPERVISOR, 'Privacy and competitiveness in the age of big data: The interplay between data protection, competition law and consumer protection in the Digital Economy', March 2014, paras 23 and 58.
1198. ARTICLE 29 WORKING PARTY, 'Opinion 03/2013 on purpose limitation', WP 203, 2 April 2013, p. 21.

national competition authorities,[1199] enforcement of data protection law solely takes place at the national level. Although the national data protection authorities of all Member States cooperate in the framework of the current Article 29 Working Party,[1200] each authority takes decisions on the basis of national data protection law that only take effect in its own territory. In accordance with Articles 22-24 of the Data Protection Directive, the Member States have set out appropriate remedies and sanctions in national law against unlawful processing of personal data and against any act incompatible with the national provisions adopted pursuant to the Directive. Since the Member States have been given a significant degree of discretion as regards applicable remedies, liability and sanctions when transposing the provisions of the Data Protection Directive into national law, there are considerable divergences among the Member States with regard to the enforcement mechanisms that are used to address violations of data protection principles in the EU.

As an illustration, reference can be made to the investigations into Google's privacy policy update announced in March 2012. After the French data protection authority started a preliminary investigation on behalf of all data protection authorities in the EU,[1201] several national authorities decided to launch national investigations on the basis of their own local data protection laws. These investigations have led to different outcomes. While the Dutch data protection authority imposed an incremental penalty payment on Google in December 2014 for combining personal data from different Google services without obtaining unambiguous consent from users to do so, the data protection authority from the United Kingdom did not impose a sanction but required Google to sign a formal undertaking to improve the information it provides to users about how it collects personal data.[1202] Even though national data protection authorities may join forces to investigate alleged data protection breaches of companies operating on an EU-wide basis, they still act as separate entities taking their own decisions as a result of which a company has to comply with individual recommendations from each Member State's data protection authority.

This is different in competition law which relies on joint enforcement of the EU competition rules by the European Commission and the national competition authorities through the European Competition Network. In this regard, Article 3(1) of

---

1199. Article 5 of Regulation 1/2003 states that the competition authorities of the Member States have the power to apply Articles 101 and 102 TFEU in individual cases.
1200. The Article 29 Working Party was set up under Article 29 of the Data Protection Directive and is composed of a representative from the national data protection authority of each EU Member State, a representative of the European Data Protection Supervisor (the independent supervisory authority that is responsible for ensuring that all EU institutions and bodies respect people's right to personal data protection and privacy when processing their personal data) and a representative of the European Commission.
1201. See Press Release Commission Nationale de l'Informatique et des Libertés (CNIL), 'Google's new privacy policy: incomplete information and uncontrolled combination of data across services', 16 October 2012, available at http://www.cnil.fr/english/news-and-events/news/article/googles-new-privacy-policy-incomplete-information-and-uncontrolled-combination-of-data-across-ser/.
1202. Press Release Information Commissioner's Office (ICO), 'Google to change privacy policy after ICO investigation', 30 January 2015, available at https://ico.org.uk/about-the-ico/news-and-events/news-and-blogs/2015/01/google-to-change-privacy-policy-after-ico-investigation/.

Regulation 1/2003[1203] provides that national competition authorities should also apply Articles 101 and 102 TFEU to, on the one hand, agreements, decisions by associations of undertakings or concerted practices which may affect trade between Member States and, on the other hand, abuses prohibited by Article 102 TFEU.[1204] With respect to the cooperation between the European Commission and the national competition authorities, Article 11(6) of Regulation 1/2003 states that the initiation of a competition law proceeding by the Commission relieves the competition authorities of the Member States of their competence to apply Articles 101 and 102 TFEU.

In addition, Article 13(1) of Regulation 1/2003 lays down that once one competition authority is dealing with a particular competition issue under Article 101 or 102 TFEU, this shall be sufficient grounds for the others to suspend proceedings or to reject a complaint against the same agreement, decision of an association or practice. In the area of merger review, a so-called one-stop-shop system is applied whereby the European Commission has exclusive competence to assess concentrations with a Community dimension.[1205] Article 21(3) of the EU Merger Regulation provides that no Member State shall apply its national competition rules to any concentration that has a Community dimension. Concentrations that fall below the Community dimension turnover thresholds are, in principle, subject to national merger control. However, if a concentration that does not have a Community dimension is capable of being reviewed under the national competition laws of at least three Member States, the undertakings concerned may request the European Commission to examine the merger. Once the Commission accepts to assess the concentration, it is deemed to have a Community dimension as a result of which the Member States are relieved of their competence to review the merger under their own national competition laws.[1206]

By laying down a single set of rules for the EU, the General Data Protection Regulation will bring about changes in the enforcement of data protection rules. Several new features are introduced by the Regulation which are expected to strengthen the enforcement of EU data protection law. Apart from setting out concrete measures to facilitate cooperation among national data protection authorities and to ensure consistency of application of EU data protection rules,[1207] the Regulation also provides for a one-stop-shop mechanism in cases where the controller or processor is established in more than one Member State. The objective of the one-stop-shop system

---

1203. Council Regulation (EC) No 1/2003 of 16 December 2002 on the implementation of the rules on competition laid down in Articles 81 and 82 of the Treaty (Regulation 1/2003) [2003] OJ L1/1.

1204. It is important to note that Member States are not 'precluded from adopting and applying on their territory stricter national laws which prohibit or sanction unilateral conduct engaged in by undertakings' under Article 3(2) of Regulation 1/2003. In other words, national competition law may diverge from the EU competition rules by having stricter national equivalents to Article 102 TFEU.

1205. Article 1(2) of Council Regulation (EC) No 139/2004 of 20 January 2004 on the control of concentrations between undertakings (EU Merger Regulation) [2004] OJ L 24/1 lays down the turnover thresholds that have to be met in order for a concentration to have a Community dimension.

1206. Article 4(5) of the EU Merger Regulation.

1207. Articles 60-67 of the General Data Protection Regulation.

is to increase the consistent application of EU data protection law and to reduce the administrative burden for controllers and processors.

In accordance with Article 56(1) of the General Data Protection Regulation, the national data protection authority of the main establishment or of the single establishment of the controller or processor is competent to act as lead supervisory authority for the cross-border processing of this controller of processor.[1208] As Article 4(23)(a) and (b) makes clear, cross-border processing of personal data means either *'processing of personal data which takes place in the context of the activities of establishments in more than one Member State of a controller or processor in the Union where the controller or processor is established in more than one Member State'* or *'processing of personal data which takes place in the context of the activities of a single establishment of a controller or processor in the Union but which substantially affects or is likely to substantially affect data subjects in more than one Member State'*. The lead supervisory authority will, in the wording of Article 56(6) of the General Data Protection Regulation, be *'the sole interlocutor of the controller or processor for the cross-border processing carried by that controller or processor'*.

Nevertheless, each national data protection authority is still competent to deal with a complaint lodged with it or to deal with a possible infringement of the Regulation in case the subject matter relates only to an establishment in its Member State or substantially affects data subjects only in its Member State.[1209] The national data protection authority at issue then has to inform the lead supervisory authority and may submit a draft for a decision which the latter has to take utmost account of when preparing the draft decision referred to in Article 60(3) of the General Data Protection Regulation.[1210] If the lead supervisory authority decides not to handle the case, the national data protection authority which informed the lead supervisory authority has to deal with it.[1211]

Where the lead supervisory authority decides to deal with the case, the cooperation procedure of Article 60 of the General Data Protection Regulation applies according to which the lead supervisory authority has to cooperate with the other concerned national data protection authorities in an endeavour to reach consensus.[1212] In

---

1208. According to Article 4(16)(a) and (b) of the General Data Protection Regulation, main establishment means: *'as regards a controller with establishments in more than one Member State, the place of its central administration in the Union, unless the decisions on the purposes and means of the processing of personal data are taken in another establishment of the controller in the Union and the latter establishment has the power to have such decisions implemented, in which case the establishment having taken such decisions is to be considered to be the main establishment'* and *'as regards a processor with establishments in more than one Member State, the place of its central administration in the Union, or, if the processor has no central administration in the Union, the establishment of the processor in the Union where the main processing activities in the context of the activities of an establishment of the processor take place to the extent that the processor is subject to specific obligations under this Regulation'*.

1209. Article 56(2) of the General Data Protection Regulation.

1210. Article 56(3) and (4) of the General Data Protection Regulation.

1211. Article 56(5) of the General Data Protection Regulation.

1212. Under Article 4(22) of the General Data Protection Regulation, a national data protection authority is concerned by a certain form of processing of personal data if *'(a) the controller or processor is established on the territory of the Member State of that supervisory authority;*

particular, in line with Article 60(4) of the General Data Protection Regulation, the consistency mechanism set out in Articles 63, 64 and 65 applies if any of the other concerned national data protection authorities expresses a relevant and reasoned objection[1213] to the draft decision of the lead supervisory authority and the latter does not follow the objection or is of the opinion it is not relevant and reasoned. The consistency mechanism requires that the European Data Protection Board (which will replace the current Article 29 Working Party) is given the opportunity to issue an opinion on such draft measures which the lead supervisory authority is considering to adopt.[1214] The European Data Protection Board will consist of the head of one national data protection authority of each Member State and of the EDPS.[1215] The European Commission will also designate a representative and has the right to participate in the activities and meetings of the European Data Protection Board without voting right.[1216] In case a national data protection authority has expressed a relevant and reasoned objection to a draft decision of the lead supervisory authority and the lead authority has rejected an objection as not being relevant and/or reasoned, the European Data Protection Board will adopt a binding decision.[1217] The lead supervisory authority will then adopt its final decision on the basis of the decision of the European Data Protection Board and notify it to the controller or the processor.[1218]

In principle, one single national data protection authority (the authority of the main establishment of the controller or processor (i.e., the lead supervisory authority)) will thus become competent under the General Data Protection Regulation for monitoring the processing of personal data and for taking the related decisions as far as the cross-border processing of personal data is concerned. At the same time, the General Data Protection Regulation gives each national data protection authority, other than

---

(b) data subjects residing in the Member State of that supervisory authority are substantially affected or likely to be substantially affected by the processing; or (c) a complaint has been lodged with that supervisory authority'.

1213. Article 4(24) of the General Data Protection Regulation defines 'relevant and reasoned objection' as *'an objection to a draft decision as to whether there is an infringement of this Regulation, or whether envisaged action in relation to the controller or processor complies with this Regulation, which clearly demonstrates the significance of the risks posed by the draft decision as regards the fundamental rights and freedoms of data subjects and, where applicable, the free flow of personal data within the Union'.*

1214. The consistency mechanism is also applicable whenever a competent national data protection authority intends to adopt one of the specific measures listed in Article 64(1) of the General Data Protection Regulation. In addition, as made clear in Article 64(2), any national data protection authority, the Chair of the European Data Protection Board or the European Commission may request that any matter of general application or producing effects in more than one Member State be examined by the European Data Protection Board with a view to obtaining an opinion.

1215. Article 68(3) of the General Data Protection Regulation.

1216. Article 68(5) of the General Data Protection Regulation.

1217. Article 65(1)(a) of the General Data Protection Regulation. In line with Article 65(1)(b) and (c), the European Data Protection Board will also adopt a binding decision where there are conflicting views on which of the concerned national data protection authorities is competent for the main establishment and where a competent national data protection authority does not request the opinion of the European Data Protection Board in the cases mentioned in Article 64(1) or does not follow the opinion of the European Data Protection Board issued under Article 64.

1218. Article 65(6) of the General Data Protection Regulation.

the lead supervisory authority, the competence to deal with complaints lodged with it or to take action against possible infringements only involving an establishment in its Member State or substantially affecting data subjects only in its Member State. In practice, controllers and processors may thus still have to deal with more than one national data protection authority which reduces the effectiveness of the one-stop-shop enforcement mechanism.

The main difference with the enforcement of EU competition law will persist after the entry into force of the General Data Protection Regulation, namely that the European Commission does not have the competence to take action and adopt measures under EU data protection law. However, the Commission is involved in the European Data Protection Board which, as discussed above, can take binding decisions in case of disagreement between national data protection authorities. Since it does not have a voting right in the European Data Protection Board, it remains to be seen to what extent the Commission can improve the uniformity in the application and strengthen the enforcement of the EU data protection rules after the entry into force of the General Data Protection Regulation.

Unlike the Data Protection Directive which left the exact scope of applicable enforcement mechanisms largely to the discretion of the Member States, the provisions of the General Data Protection Regulation are much more detailed as regards remedies, liability and sanctions. Particular attention deserves Article 83 which requires national data protection authorities to impose administrative fines on anyone who does not comply with any of the data protection obligations contained in the Regulation. Depending on the exact obligation that is violated, the fines amount to up to either EUR 10 million and in case of an undertaking up to 2% of the total worldwide annual turnover (whichever is higher), or EUR 20 million and in case of an undertaking up to 4% of the total worldwide annual turnover (whichever is higher).[1219] The maximum height of these fines is significantly lower than the ones applicable in EU competition cases where the European Commission is entitled to levy fines up to 10% of the total turnover for a breach of Article 101 or 102 TFEU.[1220] Nevertheless, the fact that fines can be imposed under the General Data Protection Regulation by national data protection authorities for data protection breaches is hoped to improve compliance with EU data protection rules.

9.3 EFFECT OF DATA PROTECTION REGULATION ON COMPETITION

When analysing the link between data protection and competition, it is also important to consider any possible competitive impact of data protection regulation. Since personal data is a vital input of production for many internet players, strict data protection rules place a burden on these market players. The imposition of further limits on the collection and use of personal information will restrict the freedom of internet companies to develop services building on user data as they wish and to gain

---

1219. Article 83(4), (5) and (6) of the General Data Protection Regulation.
1220. Article 23(2) of Regulation 1/2003.

revenue through the provision of targeted advertisements. As a result, such additional limits may force internet companies to charge consumers a monetary fee for the use of their services instead of letting them pay with their personal data.[1221] Since consumers have heterogeneous preferences with regard to data protection, an overly strict data protection regime may not only harm competition but also innovation by banning future products or services from the market that would have been valued by consumers who are less sensitive to data protection issues.[1222]

Although a higher level of data protection may benefit consumers by limiting possibilities for exploitation of personal information,[1223] an increase in protection may also weaken competition in the market. Assuming that new entrants need access to data in order to become viable competitors, stricter data protection rules relating to the purchase and use of personal information could increase barriers to entry.[1224] For instance, rules prohibiting the transfer or sale of personal information between companies would lead to the situation that each market player has to collect the necessary data organically. This may reduce the ability of new firms to successfully enter the market, since they would not be able to buy the data they need to compete with incumbents. In addition, data protection rules that only permit sharing and disclosure of personal information within a single company may create incentives for undertakings to circumvent such limits by vertically integrating their business and by engaging in acquisitions that would otherwise be unattractive.[1225] This will facilitate consolidation and favour large market players which potentially diminishes consumer choice.[1226]

On the one hand, strong data protection rules may harm consumer welfare by limiting firms in their ability to improve the quality of their services, by restricting possibilities to monetise user data and by letting advertisers forego potential cost reductions resulting from better targeting possibilities. Ultimately, the decrease in advertising costs ensuing from more effective targeting could directly benefit consumers in the form of lower prices for advertised products and services. On the other hand, weak data protection rules may harm consumer welfare because consumers have to incur the costs of disclosing their personal information and being tracked for

---

1221. Speech US FTC Commissioner Ohlhausen, 'Competition, Consumer Protection, and The Right [Approach] to Privacy', Premier Cercle Competition Summit 2013, Brussels, 6 December 2013, p. 10, available via https://www.ftc.gov/sites/default/files/documents/public_state ments/2013-premier-cercle-brussels-competition-summit/131206cerclebrussels.pdf.
1222. K. COATES, *Competition Law and Regulation of Technology Markets*, Oxford University Press, 2011, p. 365.
1223. Naive consumers who do not anticipate the use of personal data by firms are found to have a stronger need for protection because they are more likely to be harmed by exploitation of their personal data than rational consumers who are able to discipline firms that fail to protect their information. See C.R. TAYLOR, 'Consumer Privacy and the Market for Customer Information', *RAND Journal of Economics* 2004, vol. 35, no. 4, (631).
1224. J. BRILL, 'The Intersection of Consumer Protection and Competition in the New World of Privacy', *Competition Policy International* 2011, vol. 7, no. 1, (7), p. 18.
1225. R.C. PICKER, 'Competition and Privacy in Web 2.0 and the Cloud', *Nothwestern University Law Review Colloquy* 2008, vol. 103, (1), p. 10.
1226. Speech US FTC Commissioner Ohlhausen, 'Competition, Consumer Protection, and The Right [Approach] to Privacy', Premier Cercle Competition Summit 2013, Brussels, 6 December 2013, p. 10.

commercial purposes. Eventually, consumers may start to distrust internet services due to data protection concerns and reduce their online activities.[1227]

The overall effect of data protection regulation on consumer welfare thus remains ambiguous and can only be assessed on a case-by-case basis. Economic theory does not provide an answer to the issue of what level of data protection is optimal from a consumer welfare perspective in general. Economic findings to this end can only be used in individual cases.[1228] The only broad conclusion that can be drawn is that a balanced level of data protection regulation is necessary which addresses proven data protection harm while also providing consumers with the benefits of a competitive market.[1229] In other words, room should be made for differentiation, for example by providing consumers with a baseline level of data protection by way of regulation and enabling them to transact for additional data protection with individual market players.[1230]

A minimum level of data protection is particularly desirable for addressing possible externalities and persistent behavioural biases. Externalities are a form of market failure whereby an individual who reveals personal information does not take into account the positive or negative impact of his or her disclosure on other individuals (in case of shared preferences within a group of family or friends) or even on society at large (for instance by using data to improve existing services and develop new ones).[1231] In addition, due to behavioural biases consumers do not always act rationally and may make decisions that are not in their own long-term interest.[1232] Both of these phenomena justify a certain level of data protection regulation.[1233]

Since the ability to collect, analyse and monetise data is critical to the success of undertakings operating in the online environment, differences in data protection legislation between EU Member States and at the international level may result into competitive advantages for companies that are subject to less strict data protection rules. This is presuming that companies will use the opportunities available under data

---

1227. D.S. EVANS, 'The Online Advertising Industry: Economics, Evolution, and Privacy', *Journal of Economic Perspectives* 2009, vol. 23, no. 3, (37), pp. 57-58.
1228. See for example A.J. PADILLA AND M. PAGANO, 'Sharing Default Information as a Borrower Discipline Device', *European Economic Review* 2000, vol. 44, no. 10, (1951) and O. SHY AND R. STENBACKA, 'Investment in Customer Recognition and Information Exchange', *Information Economics and Policy* 2013, vol. 25, no. 2, (92) who assess the impact of different levels of data protection on consumer welfare.
1229. Speech US FTC Commissioner Ohlhausen, 'Competition, Consumer Protection, and The Right [Approach] to Privacy', Premier Cercle Competition Summit 2013, Brussels, 6 December 2013, pp. 10-11.
1230. As proposed by P. LAROUCHE, M. PEITZ & N. PURTOVA, 'Consumer Privacy in Network Industries', *CERRE Policy Report 25 January 2016*, pp. 6-7, available at http://www.cerre.eu /sites/cerre/files/160125_CERRE_Privacy_Final.pdf.
1231. P. LAROUCHE, M. PEITZ & N. PURTOVA, 'Consumer Privacy in Network Industries', *CERRE Policy Report 25 January 2016*, pp. 30-31.
1232. See, among others, A. ACQUISTI, L. BRANDIMARTE AND G. LOEWENSTEIN, 'Privacy and Human Behavior in the Age of Information', *Science* 2015, vol. 347, no. 6221, (509) and A. ACQUISTI, C. TAYLOR AND L. WAGMAN, 'The Economics of Privacy', *Journal of Economic Literature* 2016, vol. 54, no. 2, pp. 442-492.
1233. P. LAROUCHE, M. PEITZ & N. PURTOVA, 'Consumer Privacy in Network Industries', *CERRE Policy Report 25 January 2016*, p. 33.

protection law to collect and process personal data.[1234] Although competition to achieve a higher level of data protection is conceivable in theory and privacy-friendly alternatives for online services such as search engines are becoming increasingly available, the market for privacy-enhancing services in the digital economy in general remains rather undeveloped.[1235]

The General Data Protection Regulation is hoped to achieve a better level playing field between the different EU Member States. Differences in data protection standards across the EU enable companies to commercially exploit personal data to varying degrees and limit their market opportunities in different ways depending on the strictness of the rules that are applicable to them.[1236] As made clear in recital 7 of the Data Protection Directive and recital 9 of the General Data Protection Regulation, differences in the level of protection afforded to the processing of personal data in the Member States may constitute an obstacle to the pursuit of economic activities at the EU level and distort competition. The General Data Protection Regulation is expected to reduce legal fragmentation between Member States and to contribute to the functioning of the internal market by facilitating the free flow of personal data throughout the Union.[1237] Since the new EU data protection rules are contained in a Regulation instead of a Directive, they will be directly applicable in all Member States in accordance with Article 288 TFEU without the need for national implementing legislation. At the same time, the General Data Protection Regulation comprises a number of open-ended clauses and even provisions giving Member States the freedom to adopt specific provisions at the national level to apply the rules contained in the Regulation.[1238] For instance, according to Article 6(2) Member States may, for certain processing situations, maintain or introduce more specific provisions and other measures to ensure lawful and fair processing under the General Data Protection Regulation. To ensure that such provisions do not give rise to fragmentation between Member States and result into forum-shopping by controllers and processors of personal data, the role of the European Data Protection Board in developing a common approach towards the application and enforcement of the General Data Protection Regulation is vital.

As regards the level playing field between European and non-European countries, the General Data Protection Regulation is more likely to improve the status quo because of its wider geographic scope. The current Data Protection Directive applies to

---

1234. MONOPOLKOMMISSION, 'Competition policy: The challenge of digital markets', Special report No. 68, July 2015, par. 93, available at http://www.monopolkommission.de/images/PDF/SG/s68_fulltext_eng.pdf.

1235. See PRELIMINARY OPINION OF THE EUROPEAN DATA PROTECTION SUPERVISOR, 'Privacy and competitiveness in the age of big data: The interplay between data protection, competition law and consumer protection in the Digital Economy', March 2014, par. 14 and EUROPEAN DATA PROTECTION SUPERVISOR, 'Report of workshop on Privacy, Consumers, Competition and Big Data', 2 June 2014, p. 4, available at https://secure.edps.europa.eu/EDPSWEB/webdav/site/mySite/shared/Documents/Consultation/Big%20data/14-07-11_EDPS_Report_Workshop_Big_data_EN.pdf.

1236. MONOPOLKOMMISSION, 'Competition policy: The challenge of digital markets', Special report No. 68, July 2015, par. 164.

1237. See recital 9 of the General Data Protection Regulation.

1238. See also P. LAROUCHE, M. PEITZ & N. PURTOVA, 'Consumer Privacy in Network Industries', CERRE Policy Report 25 January 2016, pp. 51-52.

processing of personal data carried out in the context of a controller's EU establishment or, in case the controller is not established in EU territory, through the use of equipment situated in the EU.[1239] Yet, the future General Data Protection Regulation can also be applicable if neither the controller, nor its equipment is situated in the EU. The processing of personal data of data subjects who are in the EU is caught by the General Data Protection Regulation as soon as the processing activities are related to the offering of goods or services to such data subjects, irrespective of whether a payment of the data subject is required, or to the monitoring of their behaviour as far as their behaviour takes place within the European Union.[1240] As a result, online businesses active in the EU will be subject to EU data protection rules even though they are based outside the Union.

The General Data Protection Regulation thereby brings the geographic scope of application in line with that of EU competition law which can be determined on the basis of two doctrines: the doctrine of implementation and the effects doctrine. The doctrine of implementation has evolved from the *Woodpulp* cases in which the Court of Justice held that the decisive factor for the applicability of the EU competition rules is the place where the behaviour is implemented.[1241] In the *Gencor* case, the Court of Justice followed the effects doctrine by establishing that the application of EU competition law is justified when an immediate and substantial effect in the EU is foreseeable.[1242] In its 2014 *Intel* judgment, the General Court made clear that these two doctrines are alternative so that for the EU competition rules to apply, it is sufficient to establish either the qualified effects of the practice in the EU or that the practice was implemented in the EU.[1243] It follows that the place of establishment of a market player does not matter for jurisdiction to be assumed under EU competition law.

9.4 DATA PROTECTION AS A NON-PRICE PARAMETER OF COMPETITION

Instead of setting a monetary fee, providers of online platforms typically extract personal information from users as a means of payment for the delivery of their services. Since no price is charged, competition takes place on the basis of other dimensions. As discussed in Part I, the level of innovation and the relevance of the service are important parameters of competition in the online intermediary environment. In addition, the protection of personal data has emerged as a dimension of competition on the internet. The advent of privacy-related extensions for internet browsers forms an illustration of this phenomenon. An example is Ghostery which enables users to detect and control who is tracking their online behaviour.[1244] New

---

1239. Article 4(1)(a) and (c) of the Data Protection Directive.
1240. Article 3(2)(a) and (b) of the General Data Protection Regulation.
1241. Judgment in *Woodpulp*, Joined cases 89, 104, 114, 116, 117 and 125 to 129/85, ECLI:EU:C:1988:447, par. 16.
1242. Judgment in *Gencor*, T-102/96, ECLI:EU:T:1999:65, par. 90.
1243. Judgment in *Intel Corp. v. European Commission*, T-286/09, ECLI:EU:T:2014:547, paras 235-244.
1244. See https://www.ghostery.com/en/why-ghostery/for-individuals/.

firms have also entered existing markets by distinguishing themselves from incumbents through the provision of privacy-friendly alternatives for existing services. DuckDuckGo is an example of a search engine which does not collect personal information and does not track its users.[1245] The introduction of messaging applications specifically addressing data protection issues, such as Telegram[1246] and Threema,[1247] points to the increasing awareness among users of data collection by firms.[1248] It is instructive that data protection concerns seem to have led thousands of WhatsApp users to switch to these more secure apps after WhatsApp's acquisition by Facebook was announced in February 2014.[1249]

In line with these market developments, the European Commission and, in particular, the US Federal Trade Commission have started to refer to data protection as a potential dimension of competition. In its *Facebook/WhatsApp* merger decision, the European Commission argued that the main drivers of competitive interaction between consumer communications apps appear to be the functionalities offered and the underlying network or user base. With regard to functionalities, the Commission noted that, as indicated by the market investigation, privacy and security are becoming increasingly valued by users.[1250] The Commission also found that even though Facebook would in theory be able to introduce targeted advertising on WhatsApp, it may not have the incentive to do so as this *'could create dissatisfaction among the increasing number of users who significantly value privacy and security'*.[1251] Nevertheless, the European Commission did not specifically analyse the *Facebook/WhatsApp* transaction in this light, since privacy was only regarded as one of the many parameters of competition applicable to the case along with price, reliability of the communications service, the user base and perceived trendiness of the app.[1252]

In the context of the *TomTom/Tele Atlas* merger, the European Commission did assess the incentives of the merging parties to protect confidential information of customers and noted that *'confidentiality concerns can be considered as similar to product degradation'*.[1253] The confidentiality concerns assessed in the *TomTom/Tele Atlas* merger decision did not concern personal data of end consumers but information provided by customers of Tele Atlas who purchase the latter's navigable digital maps in the upstream market in order to integrate the maps into their portable navigation devices which are competing with those of TomTom in the downstream market.

1245. See https://duckduckgo.com/privacy.
1246. See https://telegram.org/privacy.
1247. See https://threema.ch/en.
1248. See also R. CASADESUS-MASANELL AND A. HERVAS-DRANE, 'Competing with Privacy', *Harvard Business School Working Paper 13-085* October 2013, p. 4, available at http://www.hbs.edu/faculty/Publication%20Files/13-085_95c71478-a439-4c00-b1dd-f9d963b99c34.pdf who state that '*[c]onsumers have access to a growing set of resources to learn about these [disclosure] practices, and privacy regulations increasingly require firms to inform prospective customers about their disclosure activities'*.
1249. As reported by the European Commission in Case No COMP/M.7217 – *Facebook/WhatsApp*, 3 October 2014, footnote 79 and par. 174.
1250. Case No COMP/M.7217 – *Facebook/WhatsApp*, 3 October 2014, paras 86-87.
1251. Case No COMP/M.7217 – *Facebook/WhatsApp*, 3 October 2014, par. 174.
1252. Case No COMP/M.7217 – *Facebook/WhatsApp*, 3 October 2014, paras 87-90.
1253. Case No COMP/M.4854 – *TomTom/Tele Atlas*, 14 May 2008, par. 274.

During the market investigation, concerns had been expressed that certain categories of confidential information, such as information on future competitive actions and technical information, that manufacturers of navigation devices provided to Tele Atlas could be shared with TomTom after the merger.[1254] The Commission argued that the perceived value of the digital maps for manufacturers of navigation devices would be lower if they feared that their confidential information could be revealed to TomTom. Since the map database of Tele Atlas could be regarded as relatively less valuable than that of its competitor NAVTEQ in such circumstances, confidentiality concerns could lead customers of Tele Atlas to consider switching to NAVTEQ. Because losing a customer in the upstream market would not be compensated by sufficient additional gains downstream, Tele Atlas would post-merger still have incentives to keep its current customers from switching to NAVTEQ in the view of the Commission. For that reason, the Commission concluded that the merged entity would continue to be incentivised to mitigate third-party concerns related to confidentiality after the merger and in particular by offering conditions to its customers that would make switching to NAVTEQ unattractive.[1255]

TomTom/Tele Atlas merger decision

The *TomTom/Tele Atlas* merger involved the vertical integration of Tele Atlas, a provider of navigable digital maps, into TomTom, which produces portable navigation devices. The European Commission assessed whether TomTom's acquisition of Tele Atlas would raise competition concerns in the light of the duopoly market for navigable digital maps (in which only Tele Atlas and NAVTEQ were active) and TomTom's strong position in the market for portable navigation devices.

Since navigable digital maps are essential inputs for portable navigation devices, the Commission focused on the ability and incentives of the merged entity to increase the costs for digital maps of other manufactures of navigation devices and to limit their access to these maps. The Commission concluded that the merged entity would be unlikely to pursue these strategies because its ability to restrict access to digital maps for other manufacturers of navigation devices would be limited by the presence of an upstream competitor, NAVTEQ. In addition, the merged entity would have no incentive to restrict access to digital maps considering that the sales of digital maps lost by Tele Atlas would not be compensated by additional sales of navigation devices by TomTom. On this basis, the Commission approved the transaction in May 2008.

Case No COMP/M.4854 – *TomTom/Tele Atlas*, 14 May 2008, paragraphs 193-237.

1254. Case No COMP/M.4854 – *TomTom/Tele Atlas*, 14 May 2008, paras 253 and 269.
1255. Case No COMP/M.4854 – *TomTom/Tele Atlas*, 14 May 2008, paras 273-276.

The *TomTom/Tele Atlas* merger dealt with sensitive information of commercial entities and not with personal data of end consumers. Yet, the Commission did recognise that the value of a product may decrease due to concerns relating to how customer information is used. This indicates that the level of protection applicable to information provided by customers and generated in the course of the use of a product can be seen as an aspect of quality in competition analysis. However, as is discussed below, the situation is more complex for personal data that is also used as an input to provide benefits to consumers in the form of more relevant and personalised services.

While the European Commission referred to privacy as one of the parameters of competition at stake in the *Facebook/WhatsApp* merger, it has to be noted that the protection of personal data has not yet been analysed in full as a dimension of competition in a competition case. Although the United States Federal Trade Commission addressed the potential effects of the *Google/DoubleClick* transaction on non-price attributes of competition including consumer privacy, there appeared to be no evidence of a privacy dimension of competition in the case because Google and Double-Click could not be regarded as competitors in the same relevant market.[1256] As a result, the Federal Trade Commission did not examine the application of this non-price parameter of competition to the case in more detail. Nevertheless, there seems to be consensus among US Federal Trade Commissioners that data protection may form a dimension of competition which has to be taken into account in competition cases in certain circumstances. Federal Trade Commissioner Brill argued in a 2014 speech that competition authorities would have to investigate the effects of a merger on the level of privacy in the future if there is evidence of significant pre-merger privacy competition between the merging parties.[1257] Similarly, in 2013 Federal Trade Commissioner Ohlhausen had already expressed the view that privacy, or the treatment of consumer data, should be included in a competition analysis where it represents a means of competition.[1258] When examining the protection of personal data as a non-price parameter of competition, several issues have to be kept in mind.

The 2010 US Horizontal Merger Guidelines explicitly recognise that anticompetitive effects *'can also be manifested in non-price terms and conditions that adversely affect customers, including reduced product quality, reduced product variety, reduced service, or diminished innovation'*.[1259] The EU Horizontal Merger Guidelines as well as the EU Non-Horizontal Merger Guidelines likewise acknowledge that firms may influence parameters of competition other than price by engaging in acts such as

---

1256. Statement of the Federal Trade Commission, *Google/DoubleClick*, FTC File No. 071-0170, 20 December 2007, pp. 2-3. See also section 8.2 above.

1257. Speech US Federal Trade Commissioner Julie Brill, 'Weaving a Tapestry to Protect Privacy and Competition in the Age of Big Data', European Data Protection Supervisor's Workshop on Privacy, Consumer Protection and Competition in the Digital Age, Brussels, 2 June 2014, p. 7, available at https://www.ftc.gov/system/files/documents/public_statements/313311/140602edpsbrill2.pdf.

1258. Speech US Federal Trade Commissioner Maureen K. Ohlhausen, 'Competition, Consumer Protection, and *The Right [Approach] to Privacy*', Premier Cercle Competition Summit 2013, Brussels, p. 6.

1259. United States Department of Justice and Federal Trade Commission, 'Horizontal Merger Guidelines', 19 August 2010, p. 2.

reducing output, choice or quality of goods and services, or diminishing innovation.[1260] While the notion of quality is put on equal footing with price as a dimension of competition in these instruments, a 2013 Policy Roundtable of the Organisation for Economic Co-operation and Development (OECD) on 'The Role and Measurement of Quality in Competition Analysis' indicated that in practice it has proven to be rather difficult to incorporate the assessment of quality in competition analysis.

According to the OECD, this is particularly the case because quality is difficult to define and to measure. Quality is a subjective concept in the sense that different consumers may value certain quality attributes to a different extent. Furthermore, quality is multidimensional in nature and thus comprises a variety of factors.[1261] The quality of a product may, for example, include both function and aesthetics. While a larger and more powerful watch battery will improve the reliability of a watch, it is likely to reduce its aesthetics at the same time. An assessment of quality is very complex if a trade-off has to be made between these quality dimensions and if consumers disagree as to the preference of one type of quality over the other.[1262]

These difficulties also apply when analysing data protection as a form of quality. Consumers have heterogeneous preferences in this regard. This is partly because firms often compensate for limited levels of data protection by setting a zero or very low price for the use of their services. Some consumers may be willing to provide their personal data and be targeted with personalised ads in exchange for free services, whereas others prefer to keep their personal information undisclosed and instead pay a monetary fee for the use of a service. In such cases, quality effects cannot be isolated from price. In addition, consumers may benefit from the data they provide or reveal by using a certain service in the form of, for example, more relevant and personalised search results.[1263] The relevance of a service and the level of data protection offered are thus different dimensions of quality that work in opposite directions. Consumers who decide not to share their information trade-off relevance as a quality attribute for the protection of their personal data, while consumers who prefer to have more relevant services give up (part of) their personal data.[1264] It has to be noted that the scope for

---

1260. Guidelines on the assessment of horizontal mergers under the Council Regulation on the control of concentrations between undertakings (EU Horizontal Merger Guidelines) [2004] OJ C 31/5, par. 8 and Guidelines on the assessment of non-horizontal mergers under the Council Regulation on the control of concentrations between undertakings (EU Non-Horizontal Merger Guidelines) [2008] C 265/6, par. 10.

1261. OECD POLICY ROUNDTABLES, 'The Role and Measurement of Quality in Competition Analysis', 28 October 2013, pp. 5-6, available at http://www.oecd.org/competition/Quality-in-competition-analysis-2013.pdf.

1262. G.A. MANNE AND R.B. SPERRY, 'The Problems and Perils of Bootstrapping Privacy and Data into an Antitrust Framework', *CPI Antitrust Chronicle* 2015, vol. 5, no. 2, (1), p. 3.

1263. J.C. COOPER, 'Privacy and Antitrust: Underpants Gnomes, the First Amendment, and Subjectivity', *George Mason Law Review* 2013, vol. 20, no. 4, (1129), pp. 1136-1137.

1264. See R. CASADESUS-MASANELL AND A. HERVAS-DRANE, 'Competing with Privacy', *Harvard Business School Working Paper 13-085* October 2013, p. 7, available at http://www.hbs.edu/faculty/Publication%20Files/13-085_95c71478-a439-4c00-b1dd-f9d963b99c34.pdf who argue that several empirical studies suggest that consumers take data protection issues into account when considering which firm to join and how much personal information to share. In a more recent study, Pew Research Center conducted a survey among Americans and found that there are a variety of circumstances under which many Americans would share personal

consumers to make such choices is more limited in communications services where consumers may suffer from social lock-in if their contacts are not willing to move to a new service.[1265]

To choose their preferred level of protection, consumers have to weigh the benefits derived from giving a firm access to their personal information against any data protection harm. As a result, the relationship between data protection and the quality of a service is subjective. While higher prices unambiguously harm all consumers, the welfare impact of a firm's decision to collect additional personal data or to retain stored data for a longer period depends on the preferences of individual consumers.[1266] Such acts will reduce the quality of the service in the eyes of consumers who are sensitive to data protection issues, but may at the same time improve quality in another dimension, notably in terms of the relevance and personalisation of the service, that is valued by other consumers.

Furthermore, even consumers who are sensitive to data protection issues may be willing to opt for lower data protection standards in exchange for a free service. By aligning an increase in data collection and use with worse overall quality, competition authorities would make assumptions about the preferences of consumers which do not match the reality of consumer heterogeneity. More importantly, it is not the task of competition authorities to impose a certain level of data protection on consumers but to maintain competitive conditions on the market thereby enabling consumers to transact with the companies providing the products and services of their own choice.[1267]

Figure 9.1   Trade-Off between Different Quality Dimensions and the Price of a Service

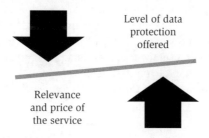

---

information in return for getting something of perceived value depending on the deal being offered and how much risk they face (see L. Rainie & M. Duggan, 'Privacy and Information Sharing', 14 January 2016, available at http://www.pewinternet.org/2016/01/14/privacy-and-information-sharing/). As a result, it is clear that consumers are, at least to a certain extent, aware of the commercial value of their personal data and make the trade-off discussed here in practice.

1265. For a discussion of the concept of social lock-in, see section 2.4.3 above.
1266. J.C. Cooper, 'Privacy and Antitrust: Underpants Gnomes, the First Amendment, and Subjectivity', *George Mason Law Review* 2013, vol. 20, no. 4, (1129), p. 1138.
1267. K. Coates, *Competition Law and Regulation of Technology Markets*, Oxford University Press, 2011, p. 394.

A prerequisite for consumers to make such choices is that they are adequately informed about what personal data is collected and how it is used, including the third uses to which their data may be put. By keeping consumers uninformed about the commercial use of their personal information, incumbents can create a so-called market for lemons and thereby impede other firms from convincing consumers to switch to more privacy-friendly services.[1268] For a well-functioning market, it is thus vital that the information requirements in consumer protection law and the conditions for valid consent in data protection law are strictly applied and enforced.

It is interesting to note in this regard that the Bundeskartellamt (the German competition authority) launched an investigation into Facebook's terms of service in March 2016 to examine whether consumers are sufficiently informed about the type and extent of personal data collected. The Bundeskartellamt suspects that Facebook's terms of service are in violation of data protection law and could thereby also constitute abuse of dominance under competition law by representing an abusive imposition of unfair conditions on users.[1269] Depending on how the investigation will evolve, the Bundeskartellamt may set a new precedent under which competition enforcement also has a role to play in preventing exploitation of consumers by dominant firms through the imposition of unfair conditions relating to the collection and use of personal data.

Two remarks need to be made to qualify the above. First, it is submitted that not all online services are characterised by the presence of different quality attributes that have to be traded off against each other. Relevance is an important dimension of quality in online search engines, social networks and e-commerce platforms which aim to provide users with the search results, social network interactions and purchase suggestions that best match their preferences. This is different, for example, for consumer communications apps which do not select the most relevant stories or content for a particular user but facilitate basic, instant real-time communication between users. Providers of these apps do not need access to personal information of users to make their service more relevant, since competition between communications apps is rather driven by the reliability of the communications service, the user base, price and perceived trendiness of the app.[1270] This may also explain why communications apps typically provide users with better data protection safeguards as compared to other online platforms that rely on user data as an input to provide services of good quality. Indeed, most consumer communications apps including WhatsApp currently

---

1268. In a similar vein, see N. NEWMAN, 'The Costs of Lost Privacy: Consumer Harm and Rising Economic Inequality in the Age of Google', *William Mitchell Law Review* 2014, vol. 40, no. 2, (849), p. 865 argues that '*if Google had less dominance of the online advertising field, there would be far greater pressure for Google to develop as sophisticated a market for users to be compensated for their privacy as the precision of the markets in which it resells that lost privacy to advertisers*'. See also P. LAROUCHE, M. PEITZ AND N. PURTOVA, 'Consumer Privacy in Network Industries', *CERRE Policy Report 25 January 2016*, pp. 66-67 recommending EU and national authorities to advocate in favour of certification schemes and trust marks in the field of data protection.

1269. Press Release Bundeskartellamt, 'Bundeskartellamt initiates proceeding against Facebook on suspicion of having abused its market power by infringing data protection rules', 2 March 2016, available at http://www.bundeskartellamt.de/SharedDocs/Meldung/EN/Pressemittei lungen/2016/02_03_2016_Facebook.html?nn=3591568.

1270. See Case No COMP/M.7217 – *Facebook/WhatsApp*, 3 October 2014, paras 86-90.

do not collect personal information about their users that is valuable for advertising purposes.[1271] The above statements on the trade-off between relevance and data protection as conflicting quality attributes therefore apply in particular to online platforms like search engines, social networks and e-commerce platforms that are characterised by relevance as an important parameter of competition.

Second, one should note that data protection rules limit the ability of firms to organise how they collect and use personal data as they deem fit. In this regard, the purpose limitation principle contained in Article 6(1)(b) of the Data Protection Directive and Article 5(1)(b) of the General Data Protection Regulation and the principle of data minimisation derived from Article 6(1)(c) of the Data Protection Directive and Article 5(1)(c) of the General Data Protection Regulation are of particular relevance. Under these principles, controllers have to limit the collection of personal data to what is necessary to accomplish a specified and legitimate purpose and cannot retain data any longer than necessary to fulfil that purpose. When collecting additional personal information or extending the retention period of stored data, firms have to act within these boundaries in order to prevent a breach of data protection law.

Next to consumer heterogeneity, another reason can be put forward why the analogy of data protection with quality does not work in all circumstances. A firm that decides to degrade the quality of its products will do so in order to cut costs and, consequently, make more profits. For example, a manufacturer that starts to use inferior car parts as inputs for its cars will, all else being equal, have lower manufacturing costs as a result of which its profit level increases. This while a degradation in quality in the form of the collection of additional personal data or the extension of existing data retention periods might actually raise costs because it requires a firm to collect, store and analyse additional data.[1272] The decision of a firm to lower data protection standards is thus not incentivised by the prospect of a decrease in costs, as in the usual case of product degradation, but should rather be seen as an investment in having better monetisation possibilities in the long term.

However, one can question whether this differentiation from the normal type of product degradation forms a strong impediment to regarding data protection as an aspect of quality under competition law. It is submitted that this difference in business strategy may be merely caused by the multi-sided nature of online platforms. By extracting additional personal data from users, a firm is able to improve the targeting of ads in the future. This may lead to extra advertising revenues through an increase in user clicks on ads (under the pay-per-click advertising model) and a growth in demand for ads to be displayed on its platform.[1273] The extra costs are thus recovered on the advertising side of the platform where the provider can make more profits by

---

1271. See Case No COMP/M.7217 – *Facebook/WhatsApp*, 3 October 2014, par. 71 and footnote 24 stating that WhatsApp only stores limited information about its users such as user name, picture, status message, phone number and the phone numbers in the user's phone book.
1272. G.A. MANNE AND R.B. SPERRY, 'The Problems and Perils of Bootstrapping Privacy and Data into an Antitrust Framework', *CPI Antitrust Chronicle* 2015, vol. 5, no. 2, (1), p. 4. At the same time, it should be noted that the costs of data storage keep diminishing.
1273. J.C. COOPER, 'Privacy and Antitrust: Underpants Gnomes, the First Amendment, and Subjectivity', *George Mason Law Review* 2013, vol. 20, no. 4, (1129), pp. 1135-1136.

monetising the additional personal information collected on the user side. Even though the link between a degradation of the level of data protection and extra profits is not as direct as in the usual case of product degradation, the motive of a provider of an online platform to collect additional data, and thereby degrade the quality of its service, seems the same as in other types of product degradation by one-sided firms.

Nevertheless, a parallel between an increase in data collection or data use and a degradation of quality on online platforms cannot be made if data protection correlates with price and other aspects of quality. As discussed above, a higher level of data protection is not necessarily valued by consumers in such circumstances. Although the analogy with quality breaks down in these cases, there are other ways of looking at data protection as a non-price parameter of competition. In this regard, it seems most appropriate to consider data protection as a form of consumer choice or product variety under competition law.[1274] While aligning the level of data protection with quality would endorse the incorrect belief that additional data collection and use is by definition harmful to consumers, this would not be the case when, instead, a parallel is made with consumer choice or product variety. Such an approach would take consumer heterogeneity towards data protection into account and merely recognise that consumers benefit from having the possibility to choose from products or services making a different trade-off between, on the one hand, the level of data protection, and, on the other hand, the relevance or price of the service. Enabling consumers to make such choices is the essence of competition.[1275]

By recognising data protection as a non-price parameter of competition in the form of consumer choice or product variety, the availability of products or services incorporating different levels of data protection and reflecting the consumer heterogeneity can be ensured. Even though, as discussed in section 9.3 above, externalities and behavioural biases may limit the ability of consumers to exercise a choice, these issues do not stand in the way of treating data protection as a form of choice or variety under competition law as long as consumer protection and data protection law provide, respectively, consumers and data subjects with a minimum level of protection in this regard. Competition, consumer protection and data protection law have to go hand in hand in order to create a well-functioning market. While competition law aims to ensure the availability of choice, consumer and data protection law should empower individuals to effectively exercise such a choice.

This way, data protection would become a dimension of competition to be considered in merger and abuse of dominance cases. Under merger control, the European Commission has to assess whether a proposed transaction would significantly impede effective competition as a result of the creation or strengthening of a dominant position.[1276] Such a form of increased market power may not only give firms the ability to profitably increase prices but also to reduce choice. Negative effects on

---

1274. See also R.H. LANDE, 'The Microsoft-Yahoo Merger: Yes, Privacy Is an Antitrust Concern', *FTC:WATCH* February 2008, no. 714, (1), p. 1 who makes a connection between consumer choice and privacy protection.
1275. K. COATES, *Competition Law and Regulation of Technology Markets*, Oxford University Press, 2011, p. 365.
1276. Article 2(2) and (3) of the EU Merger Regulation.

consumer choice or product variety may therefore form a reason to declare a transaction incompatible with the internal market. Similarly, conduct may be considered abusive under Article 102 TFEU if it is likely to harm consumer choice or product variety. The protection of effective competition under merger review and abuse of dominance rules may therefore include the protection of consumer choice in data protection. This does not mean, however, that competition enforcement is used to advance greater data protection. Instead, effective competition would require that consumers have a choice between higher and lower levels of data protection combined with either more or less relevant services and higher or lower prices.

A merger between, for example, two competing social network providers implementing different levels of data protection in their respective platforms is likely to raise competition concerns because the merger may result into a reduction of consumer choice as regards the different levels of data protection available in a potential relevant market for social networks. The new level of data protection in itself is not important; what matters is the fact that the merger has the effect of reducing options for consumers.[1277] Such a reduction in options would only lead to competitive harm and call for a competition enforcement action if data protection is a key parameter of non-price competition in the market.

9.5 POTENTIAL CONFLICTS BETWEEN COMPETITION AND DATA PROTECTION LAW

While data protection can be incorporated in competition analysis as a non-price parameter of competition, previous merger cases have also uncovered a way in which the regimes of competition and data protection law may conflict. In the context of the *TomTom/Tele Atlas* and *Microsoft/Yahoo* mergers, the parties put forward data-driven efficiencies as a defence to justify potential anticompetitive effects to which the respective transactions would give rise. In *TomTom/Tele Atlas*, the parties claimed that the acquisition of Tele Atlas by TomTom would bring about significant efficiencies due to the integration of feedback data from TomTom's large customer base to improve the map databases of Tele Atlas. In this light, the parties stated that the rationale of the merger was to allow the merged entity to produce better maps faster. While the European Commission argued that end-customers would certainly benefit from the more frequent and comprehensive map database updates made possible by the merger, it also made clear that such efficiencies are difficult to quantify. In the end, the Commission did not estimate the magnitude of the likely efficiencies because it concluded that the transaction lacked anticompetitive effects irrespective of the existence of efficiencies.[1278]

1277. See also G.A. MANNE AND R.B. SPERRY, 'The Law and Economics of Data and Privacy in Antitrust Analysis', *TPRC Conference paper* August 2014, pp. 12-13, available at http://papers .ssrn.com/sol3/papers.cfm?abstract_id = 2418779 on the distinction between a reduction in a choice and degraded data protection.
1278. Case No COMP/M.4854 – *TomTom/Tele Atlas*, 14 May 2008, paras 245-250.

In *Microsoft/Yahoo*, Microsoft argued that its strategic rationale in pursuing the transaction lay in the notion that success in search advertising and internet search is dependent on scale. By acquiring Yahoo, Microsoft expected to become a more credible alternative to Google because of the increased scale which, in its view, would have a positive effect on both users and advertisers. Microsoft argued, for instance, that the user and advertiser experience would improve because of the more relevant search results and better ad targeting possibilities resulting from a larger volume of search queries. While the Commission did not find conclusive evidence that higher scale is beneficial to users and advertisers, respondents to the market investigation confirmed that the merger would have procompetitive effects and would lead to more advantages than disadvantages. In addition, the large majority of advertisers and media agencies included in the market investigation believed that post-merger the new entity would be a stronger competitor to Google.[1279]

Microsoft/Yahoo merger decision:

Microsoft and Yahoo entered into several partnership agreements in 2009 that were approved under the EU Merger Regulation by the European Commission in February 2010. Under the agreements, Microsoft acquired an exclusive license to Yahoo's search technologies and the right to integrate Yahoo's search technologies into its existing search services. Microsoft became the exclusive internet search and search advertising provider used by Yahoo. In exchange, Microsoft paid a certain percentage of the search revenues generated on Yahoo's and its partners' websites to Yahoo.

The Commission concluded that Microsoft's and Yahoo's activities in internet search and online search advertising in the EEA were limited with combined market shares generally below 10% while Google was found to enjoy market shares of above 90% at the time of the merger. Microsoft argued that it would become a more credible alternative to Google and provide greater value to advertisers by acquiring Yahoo due to the increase of scale in search advertising. The investigation of the Commission had indicated that scale is indeed an important element to be an effective competitor in search advertising. With regard to the potential effects of the merger on the different market players, namely advertisers, users, online publishers and distributors of search technology, the Commission's investigation had shown that market participants did not expect the transaction to have negative effects on competition or on their business. They even expected it to increase competition in internet search and search advertising by allowing Microsoft to become a stronger competitor to Google.

1279. Case No COMP/M.5727 – *Microsoft/Yahoo! Search Business*, 18 February 2010, paras 160-176.

> Case No COMP/M.5727 – *Microsoft/Yahoo! Search Business*, 18 February 2010, paragraphs 4-6, 152-153, 112, 121-122, 200, 226, 237-238, 246.

Mergers giving rise to data-driven efficiencies may be incompatible with data protection law as such if personal data is involved. Although the integration or combination of data from previously separate entities can be beneficial from the perspective of economic efficiency, it is likely to raise data protection issues because, for instance, personal data is further processed for a purpose different than the original one. In such a situation, the new purpose must be specified and a legitimate basis for the new processing activities must be found. In case the lawfulness of the initial processing was based on consent, this consent must be renewed for every data subject that will be affected by the new processing activities. In order to comply with EU data protection rules, additional data protection measures thus may need to be implemented by the merged entity when data-driven efficiencies relate to personal data. Such efficiencies may not only play a role in merger review but also in the area of restrictive agreements. In that context, agreements whereby competitors cooperate and share personal data may be considered to give rise to efficiencies under Article 101(3) TFEU. Furthermore, such an agreement may not even be anticompetitive under Article 101(1) TFEU if it does not have an anticompetitive object or leads to anticompetitive effects, while the sharing of personal data with third parties is problematic from a data protection law perspective.

Such scenarios under Article 101 TFEU have a resemblance to other potential conflicts between the two legal regimes that may arise when data protection obligations are invoked to justify potential competition issues under EU merger review, Article 102 TFEU and Article 101 TFEU. In the area of merger review, a potential remedy to address data-related competition concerns may be to demand the merging parties to duplicate the relevant data to enable competitors to develop competing or complementary services on this basis.[1280] Precedent for such a remedy can be found in the context of the acquisition of Reuters by Thomson in 2008 where the Commission approved the merger on the condition that the merging parties would divest copies of their databases containing financial information.[1281] If personal data is included in the datasets, such a remedy would raise data protection issues which the merging parties may invoke in an attempt to prevent the remedy from being adopted by the Commission.

In the context of Article 102 TFEU, as discussed in section 7.7.4 above, a dominant firm may justify its refusal to give access to personal data by invoking an objective justification based on its obligations under data protection law. Data protection rules may also be invoked to justify a restriction of competition under Article 101(3) TFEU. For example, the implementation of the right to data portability as introduced by the General Data Protection Regulation may require data controllers to

---

1280. N.-P. Schepp and A. Wambach, 'On Big Data and Its Relevance for Market Power Assessment', *Journal of European Competition Law & Practice* 2016, vol. 7, no. 2, (120), p. 123.
1281. Case No COMP/M.4726 – *Thomson Corporation/Reuters Group*, 19 February 2008.

standardise their data formats and procedures for the processing and transmission of personal data. This while standardisation is liable to give rise to competition issues under Article 101(1) TFEU by limiting technical development through the foreclosure of innovative technologies.[1282]

However, such justifications are not likely to be accepted as long as data protection law leaves room for autonomous conduct to prevent a breach of competition law. With regard to the application of Article 101 TFEU to standardisation efforts for enabling data portability, the EU Horizontal Guidelines set out conditions relating to the procedure for adopting the standard and subsequent access to the standard under which standardisation agreements normally fall outside the scope of Article 101(1) TFEU.[1283] In the context of Article 102 TFEU and merger review, reference can be made to a case dealt with by the Autorité de la concurrence in September 2014 to illustrate how a dominant firm or the parties to a merger can implement a duty to share personal data with rivals in practice in a way that complies with data protection rules.

In response to a complaint of Direct Energie, the Autorité de la concurrence imposed interim measures on GDF Suez ordering it to give other market players with government authorisation to supply natural gas access to certain information about its customers. This duty concerned the customers who had a contract for the supply of gas with GDF Suez under the regulated tariffs which were only provided by GDF Suez as a result of its public service obligation. For these customers, GDF Suez was ordered to provide its competitors with personal data such as names, addresses, fixed telephone numbers and consumption profiles in order to enable them to contact potential new customers. Awaiting the investigation on the merits, the Autorité de la concurrence found GDF Suez capable of abusing its dominant position in the market for natural gas by using customer information it had obtained within the framework of its former monopoly status to launch offers at market prices outside the scope of its public service obligation.[1284]

In the operative part of its decision, the Autorité de la concurrence laid down how GDF Suez had to comply with its obligation to share customer information with rivals. In line with the recommendations made by the Commission Nationale de

---

1282. Communication from the Commission - Guidelines on the applicability of Article 101 of the TFEU to horizontal co-operation agreements (EU Horizontal Guidelines) [2011] OJ C11/1, par. 264.

1283. Communication from the Commission - Guidelines on the applicability of Article 101 of the TFEU to horizontal co-operation agreements (EU Horizontal Guidelines) [2011] OJ C11/1, paras 280-286. As stated in par. 280: 'Where participation in standard-setting is *unrestricted* and the procedure for adopting the standard in question is *transparent*, standardisation agreements which contain *no obligation to comply* [...] with the standard and provide *access to the standard on fair, reasonable and non-discriminatory terms* will normally not restrict competition within the meaning of Article 101(1)'.

1284. Autorité de la concurrence, Décision n° 14-MC-02 du 9 septembre 2014 relative à une demande de mesures conservatoires présentée par la société Direct Energie dans les secteurs du gaz et de l'électricité, paras 169-174, available at http://www.autoritedelaconcurrence.fr /pdf/avis/14mc02.pdf.

l'Informatique et des Libertés (CNIL), the French data protection authority,[1285] the Autorité de la concurrence specified that, in order to conform to data protection law, GDF Suez should send the respective customers a message either in the form of a letter, for customers who were receiving paper invoices, or in the form of an email, for customers who abandoned the paper invoices, to give them the possibility to oppose to the transmission of their personal data to third parties. More in particular, the Autorité de la concurrence stipulated that GDF Suez should request customers who did not want their personal data to be shared with other gas suppliers to fill out and return a form either by letter (for the first group of customers) or online (for the second group of customers).[1286] The Autorité de la concurrence also drafted the message that GDF Suez should send to its customers which included the following sentence: *'If you do not wish your data to be transmitted for marketing purposes to suppliers who have made a request to access the customer database of GDF Suez, please return the form. In the absence of opposition from you within the next 30 days, your data will automatically be made available to these suppliers [translation]'.*[1287]

Instead of requiring GDF Suez to obtain explicit consent from each affected customer, the Autorité de la concurrence imposed an opt-out system on GDF Suez whereby customers had to take action themselves to prevent that other gas suppliers would get access to their personal data. To assess whether this approach is in line with EU data protection law, the question has to be answered whether GDF Suez could have relied on a legitimate ground other than consent for sharing personal data of its customers with other gas suppliers. In this regard, the legitimate ground of Article 7(c) of the Data Protection Directive and Article 6(1)(c) of the General Data Protection Regulation is relevant.

Under these provisions, a legal obligation to which the controller is subject forms a legitimate ground for the processing of personal data. A duty to share personal data with third parties imposed on the basis of competition law would amount to such a legal obligation.[1288] In general, a competition law remedy to share personal data can thus not lead to a conflict with data protection rules as it forms a legitimate ground for processing in itself. Nevertheless, considering that the *GDF Suez* case concerned interim proceedings, one could argue that consent would have constituted a more appropriate ground for processing. If the finding of abuse is not upheld in the

---

1285. Autorité de la concurrence, Décision n° 14-MC-02 du 9 septembre 2014 relative à une demande de mesures conservatoires présentée par la société Direct Energie dans les secteurs du gaz et de l'électricité, paras 289 and 294.

1286. Autorité de la concurrence, Décision n° 14-MC-02 du 9 septembre 2014 relative à une demande de mesures conservatoires présentée par la société Direct Energie dans les secteurs du gaz et de l'électricité, pp. 52-53.

1287. Autorité de la concurrence, Décision n° 14-MC-02 du 9 septembre 2014 relative à une demande de mesures conservatoires présentée par la société Direct Energie dans les secteurs du gaz et de l'électricité, Article 6 on pp. 52-53.

1288. As regards examples of cases in which a legal obligation has been accepted as a legitimate ground for processing, EUROPEAN UNION AGENCY FOR FUNDAMENTAL RIGHTS AND COUNCIL OF EUROPE, *Handbook on European data protection law*, 2014, p. 82 makes reference to the legal duty of employers to process data about their employees for reasons of social security and to businesses to process data about their customers for reasons of taxation.

proceedings on the merits,[1289] the legal obligation for processing has deemed to have never existed. In that situation, the personal data of the customers of GDF Suez has already been shared with third parties in the absence of any legal obligation to that end.

It should also be noted that in addition to having a legitimate ground for processing, the other data quality requirements of Article 6(1) of the Data Protection Directive and Article 5(1) of the General Data Protection Regulation have to be met. In particular, in accordance with the notion of purpose specification, data subjects need to be informed that their personal data is shared with third parties and is thus processed for a new purpose.

Regardless of the lawfulness of the measures imposed on GDF Suez under data protection law, the Autorité de la concurrence may have overstepped its competences by interfering in the application of data protection rules to a specific case. It is submitted that it is not appropriate for a competition authority to outline specific measures that a firm should take in order to comply with data protection law. Even though the CNIL made recommendations about the case in an opinion addressed to the Autorité de la concurrence, it may have been more appropriate for the latter to have made a general statement that the duty to share customer information should be implemented in conformity with data protection law. The CNIL could then have monitored whether GDF Suez's approach was in line with the data protection rules or have provided GDF Suez with a concrete roadmap to be followed. If a duty to share personal data with third parties is imposed on the basis of competition law, it is desirable for a competition authority to actively involve the competent data protection authority in the implementation of the remedies. Since the sharing of personal data with third parties may raise considerable data protection issues, the cooperation should go beyond asking the data protection authority for possible recommendations. A closer cooperation between competition and data protection authorities in such cases would also benefit consumers by providing them with a more integrated form of protection in the two fields.

Although the duty to share personal data may not have been implemented in complete conformity with the data protection rules in the specific circumstances of the case, *GDF Suez* does illustrate that it is possible for a dominant undertaking to prevent a breach of data protection law as long as the right safeguards as required under the latter field are applied. In cases where it is not appropriate to rely on the competition law obligation as a legitimate ground for processing, a dominant firm may preclude a violation of data protection law by obtaining consent from customers to share their personal data with competitors or by anonymising personal data before third parties are granted access to it. One should note that anonymisation cannot form a solution in situations where competitors have to be granted access to the personal details of users, such as in the *GDF Suez* case where competitors needed certain specific information about individuals in order to contact potential new customers.

1289. The interim measure has been confirmed on appeal, according to Autorité de la concurrence and Bundeskartellamt, 'Competition Law and Data', 10 May 2016, footnote 67 on p. 31, available at http://www.autoritedelaconcurrence.fr/doc/reportcompetitionlawanddatafinal.pdf.

As soon as a piece of information cannot be linked to an identified or identifiable natural person anymore, it cannot be regarded as personal data and, as a consequence, EU data protection law is not applicable. In this regard, a difference has to be made between pseudonymised and anonymised data. The General Data Protection Regulation introduces a definition of pseudonymisation. According to Article 4(5) of the General Data Protection Regulation, pseudonymised data is personal data that is processed in such a way that the data can no longer be attributed to a specific data subject without the use of additional information.[1290] The Article 29 Working Party made clear that pseudonymisation should be seen as a useful security measure but not as a method of anonymisation.[1291] Data that has undergone pseudonymisation can still be attributed to a natural person by the use of additional information and therefore is considered as personal data to which the data protection rules fully apply.[1292] Nevertheless, recital 28 of the General Data Protection Regulation makes clear that the application of pseudonymisation to personal data can reduce the risks for data subjects and help controllers and processors to meet their data protection obligations.

Anonymised data, on the other hand, falls outside the scope of the data protection rules if the anonymisation is irreversible.[1293] It is important to keep in mind that the act of anonymising constitutes a form of processing of personal data in itself and therefore has to comply with all the data quality requirements of Article 6(1)(a) to (e) of the Data Protection Directive and Article 5(1)(a) to (f) of the General Data Protection Regulation. In April 2014, the Article 29 Working Party published an Opinion in which it analysed a number of anonymisation techniques and discussed their strengths and weaknesses.[1294]

In general, it seems difficult to create a truly anonymous dataset. In the context of the anonymisation of personal data in search engines, the Article 29 Working party referred to the possibility of indirect identification of users by combining anonymised information held by the search engine provider with information held by another stakeholder such as an internet service provider.[1295] In addition, data that did not relate to an identifiable person in the past might do so in the future because of new technological developments.[1296] Therefore, it is questionable whether a dominant firm can rightly claim that it has irreversibly anonymised personal data. In any case, it

---

1290. Article 4(5) of the General Data Protection Regulation defines 'pseudonymisation' as 'the processing of personal data in such a manner that the personal data can no longer be attributed to a specific data subject without the use of additional information, provided that such additional information is kept separately and is subject to technical and organisational measures to ensure that the personal data are not attributed to an identified or identifiable natural person'.
1291. ARTICLE 29 WORKING PARTY, 'Opinion 05/2014 on Anonymisation Techniques', WP 216, 10 April 2014, p. 20.
1292. Recital 26 of the General Data Protection Regulation.
1293. Recital 26 of the Data Protection Directive and the General Data Protection Regulation.
1294. ARTICLE 29 WORKING PARTY, 'Opinion 05/2014 on Anonymisation Techniques', WP 216, 10 April 2014.
1295. ARTICLE 29 WORKING PARTY, 'Opinion 1/2008 on data protection issues related to search engines', WP 148, 4 April 2008, p. 20.
1296. K. COATES, *Competition Law and Regulation of Technology Markets*, Oxford University Press, 2011, p. 373.

should consider the methods used to anonymise personal data carefully and perform them adequately in order to prevent a breach of data protection law.

9.6 CONCLUSION

Consent is one of the legitimate grounds on the basis of which personal data can be lawfully processed under EU data protection law. The notion of consent requires data subjects to have a genuine and free choice as to whether or not their personal data is to be processed for a particular purpose. However, such a form of control over data is lacking in concentrated markets where undertakings are able to impose their practices on individuals. Data protection advocates therefore seem to point to competition enforcement as a means to render data protection rules more effective.

In this regard, the General Data Protection Regulation is expected to strengthen the enforcement of data protection law in the European Union by introducing a one-stop-shop and a consistency mechanism. In practice, the application and enforcement of the data protection rules under the General Data Protection Regulation is likely to take place by way of a form of cooperation between the national data protection authorities of the Member States considering the competences given to the European Data Protection Board in the Regulation. The effectiveness of the new EU data protection rules therefore seems highly dependent on the future functioning of the European Data Protection Board. The General Data Protection Regulation also introduces a uniform regime for remedies, liability and sanctions which will enable national data protection authorities to impose fines for breaches of data protection obligations. Even though the height of the fines are not comparable to those usually imposed in competition cases, the compliance with EU data protection law is hoped to increase under the new sanctions regime.

The General Data Protection Regulation is aimed at contributing to a better functioning of the internal market by reducing the legal fragmentation that occurred under the Data Protection Directive. While the Regulation with its wider geographic scope is likely to increase the level playing field between European and non-European companies, it is more doubtful whether it will also lead to a true harmonisation of data protection rules throughout the European Union. This because of the room given for interpretation and additional legislation on the level of the Member States. As regards the impact of data protection regulation on competition in general, it can be concluded that in order to find a desirable level of protection a balance should be struck between addressing actual data protection concerns and giving firms the possibility to monetise their business and develop new services that bring benefits to consumers.

If data protection correlates with price and other aspects of quality, it is not desirable to regard it as a dimension of quality in competition analysis. In such situations, the analogy with quality breaks down because a stronger level of data protection is not necessarily valued by all consumers. This is particularly the case for online search engines, social networks and e-commerce platforms where the level of data protection, on the one hand, and the price as well as the relevance and personalisation of the services, on the other hand, are traded off against each other.

Data protection can still be integrated in competition analysis as a non-price parameter of competition in these industries by treating it as a form of consumer choice or product variety instead of as a dimension of quality. Such an approach would account for the heterogeneous consumer preferences towards data protection and enable consumers, with the help of an effective consumer and data protection regime, to make their own choices instead of requiring competition authorities to impose a preference for a certain level of data protection on consumers.

Even though competition and data protection law both aim to protect consumers, conflicts between the two fields may also arise. In particular, data-driven efficiencies in merger review and under Article 101 TFEU may be beneficial from an economic perspective but raise data protection issues if personal data is involved. In addition, a competition authority or court can impose a duty to share personal data in order to remedy a violation of Article 102 TFEU while the sharing of personal data is problematic from a data protection law perspective. In principle, a competition law decision has to be regarded as a legitimate ground for processing in itself as it constitutes a legal obligation to which the controller is subject. Remaining potential conflicts can be addressed by implementing the appropriate data protection safeguards in the form of specifying the new purpose of the processing activities, obtaining renewed consent from data subjects or through the anonymisation of personal data.

CHAPTER 10

Data Protection as a Non-efficiency Concern in Competition Policy

10.1 INTRODUCTION

Several theories have been proposed to incorporate data protection issues into competition law.[1297] As already discussed in section 9.4 above, data protection can be integrated into competition analysis as a non-price parameter of competition in case it is a key dimension of competition in the market. A more controversial question is whether data protection can be protected as a non-efficiency concern under competition law. This issue goes beyond the possible role of data protection as a non-price parameter of competition in the usual competition analysis. The question at stake is whether competition law can be used as a mechanism to advance better data protection standards. In this regard, it is important to keep in mind the inherent limitations of competition enforcement as a body of law mainly concerned with economic efficiency.

Before analysing the extent to which data protection interests can be integrated into merger and abuse of dominance cases, section 10.2 explores the objectives of EU competition law with the aim of examining whether room is made for the protection of non-efficiency considerations in current competition enforcement. While section 10.2 is based on a descriptive analysis of the current decision-making practice of the European Commission and the case law of the EU Courts, section 10.3 takes a more normative approach by discussing the scope for data protection interests in EU

1297. Classifications of these theories can be found in: P. Swire, 'Submitted Testimony to the Federal Trade Commission Behavioral Advertising Town Hall', 18 October 2007, pp. 2-6; G.A. Manne and R.B. Sperry, 'The Law and Economics of Data and Privacy in Antitrust Analysis', *TPRC Conference paper* August 2014, pp. 3-8, available at http://papers.ssrn.com/sol3/papers.cfm ?abstract_id = 2418779; and M.K. Ohlhausen and A.P. Okuliar, 'Competition, Consumer Protection, and the Right [Approach] to Privacy', *Antitrust Law Journal* 2015, vol. 80, no. 1, (121), pp. 134-136.

competition policy. Afterwards, more specific attention is paid to the potential role of data protection interests in, respectively, merger review in section 10.4 and abuse of dominance investigations in section 10.5.

10.2 EXPLORING THE OBJECTIVES OF EU COMPETITION LAW IN CURRENT DECISION-MAKING PRACTICE AND CASE LAW

When analysing to what extent data protection interests can be integrated in EU competition law, it is important to reflect on the objectives of the field. Protocol No. 27 on the internal market and competition, annexed to the Lisbon Treaty, makes clear that the internal market that the European Union is to establish in accordance with Article 3(3) of the Treaty on European Union[1298] includes *'a system ensuring that competition is not distorted'*.[1299] The EU competition rules are necessary for the functioning of the internal market and seek *'to prevent competition from being distorted to the detriment of the public interest, individual undertakings and consumers, thereby ensuring the well-being of the European Union'*.[1300] Although the exact scope of protection offered by EU competition law is the subject of recurrent debate,[1301] it is clear that the competition rules as currently enforced by the European Commission and the EU Courts predominantly seek to protect economic efficiency. This implies that non-efficiency concerns relating to, for instance, media pluralism, environmental protection, public health and also data protection are in principle protected through other laws and means to the extent that they cannot be translated into economic efficiency benefits. It is important to note that the notion of economic efficiency will comprise data protection if it forms a key factor on the basis of which companies compete in a particular market. However, the issue at stake here goes beyond the possible role of data protection as a non-price parameter of competition in the standard competition analysis. The point to be discussed is whether competition law should be used as an instrument to stimulate a higher level of data protection.

10.2.1 Article 101 TFEU

The current focus on economic efficiency is apparent in the three main branches of EU competition law. The prohibition of Article 101(1) TFEU on agreements between undertakings, decisions by associations of undertakings and concerted practices which

---

1298. Consolidated version of the Treaty on European Union [2012] OJ C 326/13.
1299. Protocol (No 27) on the internal market and competition [2012] OJ C 326/309.
1300. Judgment in *Konkurrensverket v. TeliaSonera Sverige AB*, C-52/09, ECLI:EU:C:2011:83, par. 22.
1301. For recent work, see for instance the contributions in D. ZIMMER (ed.), *The Goals of Competition Law*, Cheltenham, Edward Elgar, 2012. In the context of Article 101 TFEU, see B. VAN ROMPUY, *Economic Efficiency: The Sole Concern of Modern Antitrust Policy? Non-efficiency Considerations under Article 101 TFEU* in A. SUTTON (ed.) *International Competition Law Series*, Alphen aan den Rijn, Wolters Kluwer, 2012. In the context of Article 102 TFEU, see R. NAZZINI, *The Foundations of European Union Competition Law. The Objective and Principles of Article 102*, Oxford, Oxford University Press, 2011.

may affect trade between Member States and which have as their object or effect the prevention, restriction or distortion of competition within the internal market does not apply when the cumulative conditions of Article 101(3) TFEU are met. These conditions require that the restrictive practice at issue: (1) contributes to improving the production or distribution of goods or to promoting technical or economic progress; (2) allows consumers a fair share of the resulting benefit; (3) does not impose on the undertakings concerned restrictions which are not indispensable to the attainment of these objectives; and (4) does not afford such undertakings the possibility of eliminating competition in respect of a substantial part of the products in question. According to the Guidelines on the application of Article 101(3) TFEU, goals pursued by other Treaty provisions can be taken into account *'to the extent that they can be subsumed under the four conditions'*.[1302] Non-efficiency concerns had been integrated in the analysis conducted under Article 101(3) TFEU at instances before.

With respect to the protection of media plurality, reference can, for instance, be made to the *EBU/Eurovision* case in which the European Commission granted the Eurovision System an individual exemption under Article 101(3) TFEU on the ground that the Eurovision System benefitted consumers *'in that the System enables the members to show more, and higher-quality, sports programmes - both widely popular sports and minority sports - than they would be able to do without the advantages of Eurovision'*.[1303] However, the decision of the Commission was annulled by the General Court which has arguably limited the possibility to take non-efficiency concerns into account under Article 101(3) TFEU by requiring the analysis of indispensability of a restrictive practice to be made on an economic basis.[1304] The statement of the Commission in the Guidelines makes clear that goals pursued by other Treaty provisions will currently only be considered when they translate into economic benefits that satisfy the four conditions.[1305]

10.2.2 Merger Review

In the area of merger review, Article 21(4) of the EU Merger Regulation is instructive as regards the role of non-efficiency concerns in EU merger cases. On the basis of this provision, Member States are entitled to take appropriate measures to protect legitimate interests other than those taken into account by the EU Merger Regulation. The legitimate interests that are specified include public security, plurality of the media and prudential rules. Any other public interest must be communicated to the European

---

1302. Communication from the Commission — Notice — Guidelines on the application of Article 81(3) of the Treaty [2004] OJ C 101/97, par. 42.
1303. Case IV/32.150 - *EBU/Eurovision System* [1993] OJ L 179/23, par. 68.
1304. See in this regard P. LAROUCHE, 'EC competition law and the convergence of the telecommunications and broadcasting sectors', *Telecommunications Policy* 1998, vol. 22, no. 3, (219), pp. 234-238 and M. ARIÑO, 'Competition Law and Pluralism in European Digital Broadcasting: Addressing the Gaps', *Communications & Strategies* 2004, vol. 54, (97), pp. 107-108.
1305. L. KJOLBYE, 'The New Commission Guidelines on the Application of Article 81(3): An Economic Approach to Article 81', *European Competition Law Review* 2004, vol. 25, no. 9, (566), p. 570.

Commission by the Member State concerned after which its compatibility with the general principles and other provisions of Community law will be assessed by the Commission. Non-efficiency concerns raised by proposed concentrations may thus be dealt with at national level and in principle do not play a role in EU merger review. The *NewsCorp/BSkyB* merger can serve as an illustration in this regard.

The European Commission made clear in its merger decision that its analysis of the acquisition of BSkyB by NewsCorp was solely based on competition-related grounds under the EU Merger Regulation and was without prejudice to the media plurality review of the relevant UK authorities.[1306] While the European Commission approved the merger on the basis of a competition assessment, Ofcom, the regulatory and competition authority for the broadcasting, communications and postal industries in the UK, required remedies from NewsCorp to address media plurality issues.[1307] However, there are also EU merger cases in which concerns relating to media pluralism have been recognised and taken into account.

In its April 2012 merger decision involving the concentration by which Sony and Mubadala would acquire joint control of EMI Music Publishing, the European Commission explicitly stated in this regard that: '*According to Article 167 (4) of the TFEU, the Union shall take cultural diversity aspects into account in its actions under the other provisions of the Treaties, including the EU competition rules*'.[1308] It has to be noted, however, that the protection of cultural diversity or media plurality is mostly regarded as a side effect of the fact that competition will not be restricted by the proposed concentration.

Cultural diversity was also considered in the context of the acquisition of EMI by Universal which was approved by the European Commission in September 2012. As a condition for the clearance of the merger, Universal had to divest a number of assets including local EMI entities in certain Member States and EMI Recording Limited including EMI's iconic Parlophone label. The Commission was concerned that the proposed transaction, as initially notified, would harm consumers by increasing Universal's bargaining power and ability to impose onerous licensing terms on digital platforms, in particular small and emerging innovative music platforms. This would likely result in retail price increases for consumers, as well as a reduction in innovation and consumer choice. The Commission argued that, as a result, the proposed concentration would also have a negative impact on cultural diversity.[1309] The protection of

---

1306. Case No COMP/M.5932 – *News Corp/ BSkyB*, 21 December 2010, par. 309.
1307. In June 2011, it was reported that NewsCorp had reached an agreement with Ofcom to clear the takeover on the condition that it would spin-off BSkyB's dedicated news service Sky News into a separate company (see D. SABBAGH & J. DEANS, 'News Corp's BSkyB Bid: Jeremy Hunt Expected to Give Green Light Next Week', *The Guardian*, 23 June 2011, available at http://www.theguardian.com/media/2011/jun/22/news-corp-bskyb-jeremy-hunt). However, in July 2011 NewsCorp withdrew its bid to take ownership of BSkyB following a scandal over phone hacking at NewsCorp's UK newspaper group (see 'News Corp withdraws bid for BSkyB', *BBC News*, 13 July 2011, available at http://www.bbc.com/news/business-1414 2307).
1308. Case No COMP/M.6459 – *Sony/ Mubadala Development/ EMI Music Publishing*, 19 April 2012, par. 240.
1309. Case No COMP/M.6458 – *Universal Music Group/ EMI Music*, 21 September 2012, par. 666.

cultural diversity thus only seems to have played an ancillary role in the decision of the Commission to demand remedies from Universal, since the expected negative effect on cultural diversity is merely regarded as a consequence of the more economic impact of the concentration on innovation and consumer choice.[1310] Currently, the protection of non-efficiency concerns in EU merger review therefore typically forms an indirect result of competition rather than its aim.[1311]

10.2.3 Article 102 TFEU

Although Article 102 TFEU does not have a provision like paragraph 3 of Article 101 TFEU which renders the prohibition on abuse of dominance inapplicable when certain conditions are fulfilled, it is clear that abusive conduct can also be justified. In the Guidance Paper on exclusionary conduct under Article 102 TFEU, the European Commission specified that a dominant undertaking may do so either by demonstrating that its conduct is objectively necessary or by demonstrating that its conduct produces substantial efficiencies which outweigh any anticompetitive effects on consumers. In this context, the Commission will assess whether the conduct in question is indispensable and proportionate to the goal allegedly pursued by the dominant undertaking.[1312]

This approach of the European Commission has been endorsed by the Court of Justice in *Post Danmark I*. In its judgment, the Court of Justice argued that a dominant undertaking may justify its abusive behaviour by demonstrating '*either that its conduct is objectively necessary [...], or that the exclusionary effect produced may be counterbalanced, outweighed even, by advantages in terms of efficiency that also benefit consumers*'.[1313] In the last situation, '*it is for the dominant undertaking to show that the efficiency gains likely to result from the conduct under consideration counteract any likely negative effects on competition and consumer welfare in the affected markets, that those gains have been, or are likely to be, brought about as a result of that conduct, that such conduct is necessary for the achievement of those gains in efficiency and that it does not eliminate effective competition, by removing all or most existing sources of actual or potential competition*'.[1314]

As examples of efficiencies, the Commission refers to technical improvements in the quality of goods or reductions in the cost of production or distribution in the

---

1310. This can also be concluded from the wording that is used by the Commission in the merger decision such as that the proposed concentration would '*reduce consumer choice and innovation and* **hence** *cultural diversity as a consequence of the increased ability and incentive of the merged entity to shape the business model of digital customers and increase retail prices*' [emphasis added]. See Case No COMP/M.6458 – *Universal Music Group/ EMI Music*, 21 September 2012, par. 645.

1311. M. Ariño, 'Competition Law and Pluralism in European Digital Broadcasting: Addressing the Gaps', *Communications & Strategies* 2004, vol. 54, (97), p. 117.

1312. Communication from the Commission — Guidance on the Commission's enforcement priorities in applying Article 82 of the EC Treaty to abusive exclusionary conduct by dominant undertakings (Guidance Paper) [2009] OJ C 45/7, par. 28.

1313. Judgment in *Post Danmark A/S v. Konkurrencerådet* (*Post Danmark I*), C-209/10, ECLI:EU:C:2012:172, par. 41.

1314. Judgment in *Post Danmark A/S v. Konkurrencerådet* (*Post Danmark I*), C-209/10, ECLI:EU:C:2012:172, par. 42.

Guidance Paper on exclusionary conduct under Article 102 TFEU. Since only economic factors will point to such efficiencies, the scope to take into account other interests seems limited. With regard to justifications relating to the objective necessity of the conduct, the Commission made clear in its Guidance Paper that the question of whether conduct is objectively necessary must be determined on the basis of factors external to the dominant undertaking. In particular, the Commission noted that:

> *Exclusionary conduct may, for example, be considered objectively necessary for health or safety reasons related to the nature of the product in question. However, proof of whether conduct of this kind is objectively necessary must take into account that it is normally the task of public authorities to set and enforce public health and safety standards. It is not the task of a dominant undertaking to take steps on its own initiative to exclude products which it regards, rightly or wrongly, as dangerous or inferior to its own product.*[1315]

As a result, the European Commission will probably follow an approach similar to the one applied in the context of Article 101(3) TFEU, under which non-efficiency concerns are only considered if they lead to economic benefits for consumers.

10.2.4 Consumer Welfare Standard

The focus on economic efficiency is also apparent from the objectives of EU competition law as identified by the EU Courts and the European Commission. In its *Post Danmark I* judgment, the Court of Justice argued that *'[i]t is apparent from case law that Article [102 TFEU] covers not only those practices that directly cause harm to consumers but also practices that cause consumers harm through their impact on competition'*.[1316] Similarly, the General Court noted in *Intel* that *'[i]t is apparent from the case-law that Article [102 TFEU] is aimed not only at practices which may cause damage to consumers directly, but also at those which are detrimental to them through their impact on an effective competition structure'*.[1317] In *Post Danmark I*, the Court of Justice expressly stated that Article 102 TFEU does not *'seek to ensure that competitors less efficient than the undertaking with the dominant position should remain on the market'* and that *'not every exclusionary effect is necessarily detrimental to competition'*.[1318] In this regard, the Court noted that *'[c]ompetition on the merits may, by definition, lead to departure from the market or the marginalisation of competitors that are less efficient and so less attractive to consumers from the point of view of, among other things, price, choice, quality or innovation'*.[1319] Finally, in the Court's view,

---

1315. Communication from the Commission — Guidance on the Commission's enforcement priorities in applying Article 82 of the EC Treaty to abusive exclusionary conduct by dominant undertakings (Guidance Paper) [2009] OJ C 45/7, par. 29.
1316. Judgment in *Post Danmark A/S v. Konkurrencerådet* (*Post Danmark I*), C-209/10, ECLI:EU:C:2012:172, par. 20.
1317. Judgment in *Intel Corp. v. European Commission*, T-286/09, ECLI:EU:T:2014:547, par. 105.
1318. Judgment in *Post Danmark A/S v. Konkurrencerådet* (*Post Danmark I*), C-209/10, ECLI:EU:C:2012:172, par. 21-22.
1319. Judgment in *Post Danmark A/S v. Konkurrencerådet* (*Post Danmark I*), C-209/10, ECLI:EU:C:2012:172, par. 22.

Article 102 TFEU '*applies, in particular, to the conduct of a dominant undertaking that, through recourse to methods different from those governing normal competition on the basis of the performance of commercial operators, has the effect, to the detriment of consumers, of hindering the maintenance of the degree of competition existing in the market or the growth of that competition*'.[1320]

All these statements make clear that the main underlying goal of Article 102 TFEU as currently enforced by the EU Courts is to protect competition in order to enhance consumer welfare. As a result, a certain type of conduct which reduces competition is not necessarily abusive. What is decisive for the assessment under Article 102 TFEU is whether the reduction of competition caused by the behaviour of a dominant undertaking leads to consumer harm.[1321] In the Guidance Paper on exclusionary conduct under Article 102 TFEU, the European Commission also referred to the '*wider objective of achieving an integrated internal market*' and argued that effective enforcement of Article 102 TFEU is particularly important in this regard in order to make markets work better for the benefit of businesses and consumers.[1322]

The Court of Justice argued in *T-Mobile* and *GlaxoSmithKline* that '*Article [101 TFEU], like the other competition rules of the Treaty, is designed to protect not only the immediate interests of individual competitors or consumers but also to protect the structure of the market and thus competition as such*'.[1323] As such, the Court did not reject the notion of consumer welfare as an objective of Article 101 TFEU or EU competition law altogether but only seems to have placed it among several goals having equal importance. Nevertheless, a clear focus on the protection of consumer welfare is still apparent in the Guidelines on the application of Article 101(3) TFEU. The European Commission stated explicitly in the Guidelines that the objective of Article 101 TFEU is '*to protect competition on the market as a means of enhancing consumer welfare and of ensuring an efficient allocation of resources. Competition and market integration serve these ends since the creation and preservation of an open single market promotes an efficient allocation of resources throughout the Community for the benefit of consumers*'.[1324]

With regard to the objectives of EU merger review, the European Commission specified in the EU Horizontal Merger Guidelines and the EU Non-Horizontal Merger Guidelines that: '*Effective competition brings benefits to consumers, such as low prices, high quality products, a wide selection of goods and services, and innovation. Through*

1320. Judgment in *Post Danmark A/S v. Konkurrencerådet* (*Post Danmark I*), C-209/10, ECLI:EU:C:2012:172, par. 24.
1321. E. ROUSSEVA AND M. MARQUIS, 'Hell Freezes Over: A Climate Change for Assessing Exclusionary Conduct under Article 102 TFEU', *Journal of European Competition Law & Practice* 2013, vol. 4, no. 1, (32), pp. 41-42.
1322. Communication from the Commission — Guidance on the Commission's enforcement priorities in applying Article 82 of the EC Treaty to abusive exclusionary conduct by dominant undertakings (Guidance Paper) [2009] OJ C 45/7, par. 1.
1323. Judgment in *T-Mobile*, C-8/08, ECLI:EU:C:2009:343, par. 38. See also Judgment in *GlaxoSmithKline*, C-501/06 P, C-513/06 P, C-515/06 P and C-519/06 P, ECLI:EU:C:2009:610, par. 63.
1324. Communication from the Commission — Notice — Guidelines on the application of Article 81(3) of the Treaty [2004] OJ C101/97, par. 13.

its control of mergers, the Commission prevents mergers that would be likely to deprive customers of these benefits by significantly increasing the market power of firms'.[1325] The emphasis on the protection of consumers in EU competition law has led data protection advocates to query whether data protection considerations can be integrated into a broader consumer welfare standard to be pursued by EU competition law.[1326]

10.3 EXAMINING THE SCOPE FOR DATA PROTECTION INTERESTS IN EU COMPETITION POLICY

When examining the scope for data protection interests in EU competition policy, it is instructive to consider the underlying objectives of the two fields. While there is an overlap in goals, the means by which the objectives of EU competition and data protection law are pursued differ. Against this background, several pros and cons can be distinguished of integrating data protection interests in EU competition policy. In line with its elevation to a fundamental right after the entry into force of the Lisbon Treaty, three main ways are put forward of how data protection interests should be considered when applying and enforcing EU competition law.

10.3.1 Comparing the Objectives of EU Competition and Data Protection Law

There is a certain overlap between the goals of EU competition and data protection law. Both legal fields aim to protect the general public (either consumers more generally or individual data subjects, respectively) and to contribute to the functioning of the internal market. However, the means by which these objectives are pursued differ. EU data protection law aims to protect the fundamental right to data protection by giving data subjects control over their personal data and by setting limits on the collection and use of personal data. EU competition law, in turn, tries to enhance consumer welfare by intervening against restrictive practices, abusive behaviour and concentrations that significantly impede effective competition. Whereas EU data protection policy seeks to contribute to the functioning of the internal market through positive integration by adopting legislative instruments to harmonise national data protection law in the Member States, EU competition policy is based on negative integration by ensuring that undertakings do not inhibit effective competition to the detriment of consumer

---

1325. Guidelines on the assessment of horizontal mergers under the Council Regulation on the control of concentrations between undertakings (EU Horizontal Merger Guidelines) [2004] OJ C 31/5, par. 8 and Guidelines on the assessment of non-horizontal mergers under the Council Regulation on the control of concentrations between undertakings (EU Non-Horizontal Merger Guidelines) [2008] C 265/6, par. 10.

1326. See in particular PRELIMINARY OPINION OF THE EUROPEAN DATA PROTECTION SUPERVISOR, 'Privacy and competitiveness in the age of big data: The interplay between data protection, competition law and consumer protection in the Digital Economy', March 2014, par. 71: *'Given the reach and dynamic growth in online services, it may therefore be necessary to develop a concept of consumer harm, particularly through violation of rights to data protection, for competition enforcement in digital sectors of the economy'.*

welfare.[1327] In addition, EU data protection law follows a human rights-based approach, while EU competition enforcement takes place against the background of a more economic and effects-based analysis. This difference in approach can be explained by reference to the concept of data portability.

Table 10.1   Comparison Between the Objectives and Means of EU
Data Protection and Competition Law

	EU Data Protection Law	EU Competition Law
Objectives	- Protect individual data subjects	- Protect competition in order to enhance consumer welfare
	- Contribute to the functioning of the internal market	- Contribute to the functioning of the internal market
Means	- Human-rights based approach	- More economic and effects-based analysis
	- Positive integration	- Negative integration

As discussed in section 5.4.1 above, the General Data Protection Regulation introduces a right to data portability in EU data protection law. Article 20 of the Regulation gives a data subject the right to receive personal data concerning him or her, which he or she has provided to a controller, in a structured, commonly used and machine-readable format and to transmit this data to another controller without hindrance from the controller to which the personal data has been provided. This right applies where the processing is carried out by automated means and is based on consent or on a contract.[1328] Where technically feasible, the data subject also has the right to have the personal data transmitted directly from one controller to another.[1329] Irrespective of the applicability of the right to data portability under data protection law, data portability may also be enforced under competition law. If an undertaking is found to possess a dominant position on a given market, a refusal to ensure data portability which exploits consumers or excludes competitors and for which no objective justification exists would qualify as abusive conduct under Article 102 TFEU. In such a situation, the European Commission can impose a duty on the dominant provider to give users the possibility to transfer their data to a competitor. This can be illustrated by the *Google* case in which the Commission negotiated with Google about commitments which would force the search engine provider to stop imposing obligations on advertisers preventing them from moving their advertising campaigns to competing platforms.[1330] The difference with the General Data Protection Regulation in

---

1327. As explained by F. COSTA-CABRAL AND O. LYNSKEY, 'The Internal and External Constraints of Data Protection on Competition Law in the EU', *LSE Law, Society and Economy Working Papers 25/2015* 2015, p. 9, available at http://papers.ssrn.com/sol3/papers.cfm?abstract_id =2703655.
1328. Article 20(1) of the General Data Protection Regulation.
1329. Article 20(2) of the General Data Protection Regulation.
1330. Commitments of Google in Case COMP/C-3/39.740 *Foundem and others*, 3 April 2013, paras 27-31, available at http://ec.europa.eu/competition/antitrust/cases/dec_docs/39740/39740

this regard is that the proposal gives data subjects a right to data portability, while competition authorities can impose a duty on dominant providers to enable data portability in case their behaviour amounts to abuse under Article 102 TFEU.

In addition, the scope of application of the two regimes is different. The right to data portability only applies to transfers of personal data. Information that does not qualify as personal data falls outside the scope of the new right, while action under competition law can potentially be taken against a lack of portability of all data irrespective of whether it relates to an identified or identifiable natural person. The scope of application of competition law in this regard is thus much wider. However, action on the basis of Article 102 TFEU can only be taken if the restrictions on data portability qualify as abuse of dominance. In contrast, the right to data portability would apply generally to all forms of processing carried out by automated means and based on consent or on a contract.[1331] No dominance or abuse will have to be established in order for users to be able to transfer their data between services under the General Data Protection Regulation.[1332]

As the analysis in the previous section points out, even though non-efficiency considerations have at times been recognised in competition cases, current competition enforcement mainly focuses on protecting economic efficiency. Both the European Commission and the Court of Justice have already expressed views on the role of data protection concerns in EU competition law. Like discussed in section 8.2, the European Commission did not take into account data protection interests when assessing the *Google/DoubleClick* and *Facebook/WhatsApp* mergers. Prior to these merger decisions, the Court of Justice already made a statement in 2006 about the scope for data protection interests in EU competition policy in the context of a preliminary ruling case involving agreements between financial institutions for the exchange of customer solvency information. In its judgment in *Asnef-Equifax*, the Court noted that '*any possible issues relating to the sensitivity of personal data are not, as such, a matter for competition law, they may be resolved on the basis of the relevant provisions governing*

_8608_5.pdf. In October 2013, Google offered improved commitments to the Commission which included a new proposal providing stronger guarantees against circumvention of the earlier commitments regarding portability of advertising campaigns. See speech former Competition Commissioner Almunia, 'The Google antitrust case: what is at stake?', 1 October 2013, SPEECH/13/768, available at http://europa.eu/rapid/press-release_SPEECH-13-768_en.htm. In the US, the Federal Trade Commission closed its investigation into this issue when Google offered voluntary concessions to remove restrictions on AdWords that make it difficult for advertisers to manage advertising campaigns across multiple platforms (Press Release US Federal Trade Commission, 'Google Agrees to Change Its Business Practices to Resolve FTC Competition Concerns In the Markets for Devices Like Smart Phones, Games and Tablets, and in Online Search', 3 January 2013, available at http://www.ftc.gov/news-events/press-releases/2013/01/google-agrees-change-its-business-practices-resolve-ftc).

1331. These are the preconditions for the right to data portability to apply under Article 20(1)(a) and (b) of the General Data Protection Regulation.

1332. I. GRAEF, J. VERSCHAKELEN AND P. VALCKE, 'Putting the Right to Data Portability into a Competition Law Perspective', *Law. The Journal of the Higher School of Economics. Annual Review* 2013, (53), pp. 7-8, available at http://papers.ssrn.com/sol3/papers.cfm?abstract_id =2416537.

data protection'.[1333] As a result, the Court seems of the view that data protection issues should, in principle, be addressed under data protection legislation rather than under the competition rules.

At the same time, the wording used by the Court, i.e., that data protection is not *as such* a matter for competition law, is also interpreted by commentators as opening the door to the application of competition law to a set of facts to which data protection rules apply in parallel. In this regard, the Court's statement does not imply that data protection has no relevance to competition enforcement at all, but only seems to indicate that competition law should be applied in pursuit of the objectives underlying the discipline.[1334] In essence, this is what the European Commission did by leaving purely data protection-related interests aside and instead assessing possible competition concerns resulting from the combination of datasets in *Google/DoubleClick* and from data concentration in *Facebook/WhatsApp*. Irrespective of the fact that the European Commission and the Court of Justice are currently hesitant towards the inclusion of data protection interests in competition law, the more normative question can be raised whether the protection of this non-efficiency concern should be considered in the competition analysis.

10.3.2 Weighing Pros and Cons of Integrating Data Protection Interests in EU Competition Policy

In the literature, calls have been made upon the European Commission to give greater consideration to non-efficiency concerns in competition cases.[1335] The use of the relatively strong enforcement mechanism of EU competition law to foster other interests like media pluralism, public health or environmental protection is argued to result into a better protection of such non-efficiency concerns which are often safeguarded by legal regimes that lack the necessary force to be truly effective. In addition, the democratic legitimacy of competition law could increase when its scope of protection goes beyond preserving economic efficiency. At the same time, the protection of non-efficiency considerations by way of the application of competition law may create legal uncertainty and complicate the enforcement of the competition rules in individual cases. A similar weighing of pros and cons applies when considering the desirability of integrating data protection interests in EU competition policy.

On the one hand, there are reasons why competition policy would not be well-placed to serve as a mechanism to advance better data protection standards. As explained in section 9.4, data protection can form an aspect of quality but is often

---

1333. Judgment in *Asnef-Equifax v. Asociación de Usuarios de Servicios Bancarios*, C-238/05, ECLI:EU:C:2006:734, par. 63.
1334. A.J. Burnside, 'No Such Thing as a Free Search: Antitrust and the Pursuit of Privacy Goals', *CPI Antitrust Chronicle* 2015, vol. 5, no. 2, (1), pp. 3-4.
1335. See in particular B. Van Rompuy, *Economic Efficiency: The Sole Concern of Modern Antitrust Policy? Non-efficiency Considerations under Article 101 TFEU* in A. Sutton (ed.) *International Competition Law Series*, Rijn, Wolters Kluwer, 2012 and C. Townley, *Article 81 EC and the Public Policy*, Hart Publishing, 2009. For an opposing view, see O. Odudu, 'The Wider Concerns of Competition Law', *Oxford Journal of Legal Studies* 2010, vol. 30, no. 3, (599).

traded off against price and other quality dimensions such as relevance and personalisation. If data protection is not an isolated aspect of quality and interacts with other quality dimensions, consumer preferences for the product or service at issue will be heterogeneous. In such circumstances, competition authorities should not use their competences to impose a preference for strong data protection on consumers. Instead, it is the role of competition authorities to keep markets competitive in order to ensure that consumers can choose themselves between a variety of products and services with different characteristics.

A prerequisite for the existence of a well-functioning market is that consumer and data protection law are effectively applied to enable individuals to exercise a genuine and well-informed choice. Since data protection is valued differently by distinct groups of consumers, competition enforcement would become less predictable and transparent if its focus on economic efficiency were to be set aside at times in order to increase the level of data protection offered by a particular undertaking.[1336] It rather seems the task of the legislator to impose stricter data protection standards which also have a more general scope of application than the remedies adopted in individual competition cases. In this regard, the US Federal Trade Commission argued in its *Google/DoubleClick* statement that '*regulating the privacy requirements of just one company could itself pose a serious detriment to competition in this vast and rapidly evolving industry*'.[1337] Specific issues involving the protection of personal data are therefore best left to data protection authorities which have the necessary expertise to enforce data protection rules and to oversee activities relating to the processing of personal data.

Against this background, US Federal Trade Commissioner Ohlhausen and her Attorney Advisor Okuliar proposed to rely on a three screen test to select the most appropriate legal framework to deal with a particular concern by looking at (1) the type of harm; (2) its scope; and (3) the effectiveness of the available remedies. Harm caused by a reduction in economic efficiency is likely to be best tackled under competition law, while other types of more personal harm are more appropriately dealt with under data protection law. Whereas the latter legal field focuses on the protection of individual data subjects, competition law protects consumer welfare in a broader way. As a result, it is less appropriate to apply competition law as the scope of the respective data protection harm is more individualised. With regard to the available remedies, data protection law offers more effective remedies in response to data protection-related violations than competition law which only provides for remedies if there has also been harm to competition.[1338] As a side note, it is important to keep in mind that the rights granted to data subjects under EU data protection law apply irrespective of whether

1336. M.K. OHLHAUSEN AND A.P. OKULIAR, 'Competition, Consumer Protection, and the Right [Approach] to Privacy', *Antitrust Law Journal* 2015, vol. 80, no. 1, (121), p. 153.
1337. Statement of the Federal Trade Commission, *Google/DoubleClick*, FTC File No. 071-0170, 20 December 2007, p. 2.
1338. M.K. OHLHAUSEN AND A.P. OKULIAR, 'Competition, Consumer Protection, and the Right [Approach] to Privacy', *Antitrust Law Journal* 2015, vol. 80, no. 1, (121), pp. 123 and 153-156.

any harm to an individual is caused.[1339] In the EU context, it is therefore more appropriate to speak of the type of violation instead of the type of harm.

On the other hand, there are reasons why it would be desirable to integrate data protection interests in EU competition policy. Despite the delivery of several high-profile judgments by the Court of Justice such as *Google Spain*[1340] and *Schrems*,[1341] EU data protection law remains rather under-enforced to date while compliance is not as rigorous as one would like to believe.[1342] This begs the question of whether EU competition law with its strong enforcement mechanism should contribute to promoting data protection interests. The commonality in objectives of EU data protection and competition law may plead for such an integrated approach towards the protection of the interests of individuals.

10.3.3 Three-Layer Approach Towards the Integration of Data Protection Interests in EU Competition Policy

Irrespective of whether it is considered desirable to advance data protection interests through competition enforcement, it is important to note that nothing prevents competition law from being applied alongside data protection law in case a particular type of conduct or a proposed concentration also raises economic efficiency concerns.

1339. In *Google Spain*, the Court of Justice made clear that for the applicability of the right of a data subject to have information relating to him personally no longer be linked to his name by a list of results displayed in a search engine following a search made on the basis of his name, it is not necessary 'that the inclusion of the information in question in the list of results causes prejudice to the data subject' (Judgment in *Google Spain SL, Google Inc. v. Agencia Española de Protección de Datos, Mario Costeja González*, C-131/12, ECLI:EU:C:2014:317, par. 96).

1340. Judgment in *Google Spain SL, Google Inc. v. Agencia Española de Protección de Datos, Mario Costeja González*, C-131/12, ECLI:EU:C:2014:317. In *Google Spain*, the Court of Justice held that a search engine provider is responsible for the processing that it carries out of personal information which appears on web pages published by third parties. If, following a search made on the basis of a person's name, the list of results displays a link to a web page which contains information on the person in question, that person may approach the search engine provider directly and request, under certain conditions, the removal of that link from the list of results.

1341. Judgment in *Maximillian Schrems v. Data Protection Commissioner*, C-362/14, ECLI:EU:C:2015:650. In *Schrems*, the Court of Justice declared invalid the decision in which the European Commission found that the so-called US Safe Harbour scheme ensured an adequate level of protection as required by the Data Protection Directive for the transfer of personal data to third countries. One of the main reasons provided by the Court of Justice for declaring the decision of the Commission invalid was that the Safe Harbour scheme did not prevent interference by United States public authorities with the fundamental rights of persons whose personal data was or could be transferred from the European Union to the United States. On 2 February 2016, the European Commission and the United States agreed on a new framework for transatlantic data flows, the EU-US Privacy Shield, which is said to reflect the requirements set out by the Court of Justice in *Schrems* (Press Release European Commission, 'EU Commission and United States agree on new framework for transatlantic data flows: EU-US Privacy Shield', 2 February 2016, IP/16/216, available at http://europa.eu/rapid/press-release_IP-16-216_en.htm).

1342. See P. LAROUCHE, M. PEITZ & N. PURTOVA, 'Consumer Privacy in Network Industries', *CERRE Policy Report 25 January 2016*, p. 14 and B.-J. KOOPS, 'The Trouble with European Data Protection Law', *International Data Privacy Law* 2014, vol. 4, no. 4, 250 who argues that EU data protection law diverges from the reality of current data-processing practices.

As an illustration of such a situation in a different field, reference can be made to the state aid cases in the area of corporate taxation.

In parallel to the introduction of a number of legislative initiatives to improve the corporate tax environment in the EU, the European Commission declared the selective tax advantages granted to Fiat in Luxembourg and Starbucks in the Netherlands as well as a Belgian tax scheme illegal under EU state aid rules.[1343] These enforcement activities and ongoing investigations into tax rulings involving Apple in Ireland,[1344] Amazon in Luxembourg[1345] and McDonald's in Luxembourg[1346] should be seen against this broader background. The active role of the Commission as a competition authority in this sector has served as a lever to break open the gridlock around the ongoing reform of corporate taxation in the EU.[1347]

10.3.3.1 Protection of Economic Efficiency Also Furthers Data Protection Interests

In a similar way, the Commission could rely on the regimes of merger review and abuse of dominance under EU competition law in order to enhance the effectiveness of data protection law and help to achieve its goal of protecting data subjects. For example, by blocking a merger between two social network providers on the ground that it significantly impedes effective competition through its effect on the market for social networking services, the Commission can also prevent that previously separate datasets are combined and that personal data is used for incompatible purposes. In such a situation, competition law is applied to protect economic efficiency and at the same time achieves results that also foster data protection interests. This scenario has a resemblance with the acquisition of EMI by Universal as discussed in the previous section.

In its merger decision, the Commission took the negative effect on cultural diversity into account but merely as a consequence of the more economic impact of the concentration on innovation and consumer choice. In both cases, the protection of the

---

1343. Press Release European Commission, 'State aid: Commission decides selective tax advantages for Fiat in Luxembourg and Starbucks in the Netherlands are illegal under EU state aid rules', 21 October 2015, IP/15/5880, available at http://europa.eu/rapid/press-release_IP-15-5880_en.htm and Press Release European Commission, 'State aid: Commission concludes Belgian "Excess Profit" tax scheme illegal; around €700 million to be recovered from 35 multinational companies', 11 January 2016, IP/16/42, available at http://europa.eu/rapid/press-release_IP-16-42_en.htm.

1344. Press Release European Commission, 'State aid: Commission investigates transfer pricing arrangements on corporate taxation of Apple (Ireland) Starbucks (Netherlands) and Fiat Finance and Trade (Luxembourg)', 11 June 2014, IP/14/663, available at http://europa.eu/rapid/press-release_IP-14-663_en.htm.

1345. Press Release European Commission, 'State aid: Commission investigates transfer pricing arrangements on corporate taxation of Amazon in Luxembourg', 7 October 2014, IP/14/1105, available at http://europa.eu/rapid/press-release_IP-14-1105_en.htm.

1346. Press Release European Commission, 'State aid: Commission opens formal investigation into Luxembourg's tax treatment of McDonald's', 3 December 2015, IP/15/6221, available at http://europa.eu/rapid/press-release_IP-15-6221_en.htm.

1347. See A.J. BURNSIDE, 'No Such Thing as a Free Search: Antitrust and the Pursuit of Privacy Goals', CPI Antitrust Chronicle 2015, vol. 5, no. 2, (1), p. 6.

non-efficiency concerns at stake is not the aim of the measures taken by the Commission but rather their indirect result. In other words, competition law is applied in accordance with its inherent limitations as a body of law mainly concerned with economic efficiency.

Another situation in which the protection of competition will at the same time advance data protection interests occurs if data protection is an isolated aspect of product quality and a key parameter of competition in a market. A competition law intervention to address the anticompetitive effects of a type of behaviour or a merger will then at the same time foster data protection. Considering the status of data protection as a fundamental right in the EU legal order, it is submitted that EU competition policy may have to go further than indirectly protecting data protection interests in situations where certain conduct or a proposed concentration simultaneously raises economic efficiency concerns, or where data protection is a key parameter of competition.

10.3.3.2 Going beyond Protecting Economic Efficiency?

In this regard, one should note that the Lisbon Treaty brought about changes in the EU institutional framework as a result of which data protection cannot simply be regarded as any other non-efficiency concern.[1348] In particular, the Lisbon Treaty introduced the new Article 16 TFEU which has placed the right to data protection among the provisions having general application in the Treaty on the Functioning of the European Union. In conjunction with Article 7 TFEU, the EU institutions have to ensure consistency between different policies and activities which now also includes data protection.[1349] In addition, with the entry into force of the Lisbon Treaty, the EU Charter of Fundamental Rights became legally binding as a source of primary EU law and thereby elevated data protection to a fundamental right in the EU legal order.

It remains unclear how the changes introduced by the Lisbon Treaty may affect the application of competition law in concrete cases. Nevertheless, the existence of the EU Charter of Fundamental Rights and the new horizontal provision on data protection in the Treaty on the Functioning of the European Union would imply at least that competition policy cannot reach results contrary to the right to data protection. Even if it is not considered desirable for competition law to address non-efficiency concerns as such, the Lisbon Treaty may have laid the ground for a 'constitutionalisation' of EU law as a result of which fundamental rights cannot be disregarded anymore even in more economic-oriented policies. It would then be inevitable for the European Commission and the EU Courts to consider non-efficiency concerns to a certain extent in competition cases as well.

1348. See also F. FERRETTI, *EU Competition Law, the Consumer Interest and Data Protection. The Exchange of Consumer Information in the Retail Financial Sector*, Springer 2014, pp. 95-96.
1349. See also C. KUNER, F.H. CATE, C. MILLARD, ET AL., 'When Two Worlds Collide: The Interface between Competition Law and Data Protection', *International Data Privacy Law* 2014, vol. 4, no. 4, (247), p. 248.

In particular, Article 51(1) of the EU Charter of Fundamental Rights makes clear that the EU institutions are under a duty to respect and promote the application of the rights contained in the Charter. The EU therefore does not only have a negative duty to avoid violations (i.e., respect the fundamental rights) but also a positive obligation to take action to uphold (i.e., promote the application of) the fundamental rights. This implies that the European Commission is also bound by the fundamental rights of the Charter, including the right to data protection set out in Article 8, when acting in the field of EU competition law.[1350] In line with the wording used in Article 51(1) of the EU Charter of Fundamental Rights, a distinction can be made between a negative duty to respect the right to data protection and a positive duty to promote the application of the right to data protection.

10.3.3.3   Negative Duty to Respect the Right to Data Protection

As a fundamental right to be protected by the EU institutions, the right to data protection contained in Article 8 of the EU Charter of Fundamental Rights imposes limits on the application of EU competition law in terms of procedure as well as substance. As regards procedure, the European Commission has to implement safe-guards in its competition investigations to ensure that the right to data protection is respected.[1351] In this perspective, the question arises whether undertakings may invoke a violation of the right to data protection or the right to privacy in order to seek annulment of a measure or decision taken by a competition authority. However, as case law of the General Court suggests, not all acts taken by the Commission are challengeable in themselves and, additionally, companies may not have legal standing to bring claims based on a violation of their employees' right to privacy, as considered in *Nexans*, and the right to data protection, as explored in *Pilkington*.[1352]

In *Nexans*, the General Court made clear that '*the copying of each document and the asking of each question during an inspection are not to be regarded as acts separable*

1350. Article 51(1) of the EU Charter of Fundamental Rights makes clear that the provisions of the Charter are not only addressed to the institutions and bodies of the European Union but also to the Member States when they are implementing Union law. As a result, the national competition authorities of the Member States are also bound by the right to data protection when applying EU competition law.

1351. It is instructive to note that public authorities, including competition authorities, may benefit from exceptions or restrictions to the application of certain data protection principles in the Data Protection Directive and the General Data Protection Regulation. For instance, Article 13(1)(e) of the Data Protection Directive and Article 23(1)(e) of the General Data Protection Directive enable the adoption of legislative measures to restrict the scope of the data quality principles when such a restriction constitutes a necessary and proportionate measure to safeguard an important economic or financial interest of a Member State or of the European Union, including monetary, budgetary and taxation matters (public health and social security have been added to this list in the General Data Protection Regulation). Public authorities are thus in a privileged position as compared to companies regarding applicable data protection standards.

1352. For an analysis of the compatibility of the case law of the General Court in this regard with the case law of the European Court of Human Rights on dawn raids, see A. STEENE, 'Nexans, Deutsche Bahn, and the ECJ's Refusal to Follow ECHR Case Law on Dawn Raids', *Journal of European Competition Law & Practice* 2016, vol. 7, no. 3, (180).

from the decision under which the inspection was ordered but as measures implementing that decision'.[1353] Since the contested acts were considered to form part of the inspection decision, the applications for annulment of these acts were declared inadmissible.[1354] In the view of the General Court, two other options had been open to Nexans to bring claims against the Commission which would have affected the legality of its decisions. Nexans could either have waited until the Commission had adopted its final decision and have tried to challenge that decision on the ground of a violation of the right to privacy of its employees under Article 263 TFEU.[1355] It is important to note, however, that this would not have enabled Nexans to prevent the Commission from copying and reviewing documents potentially containing employees' personal data.[1356] Alternatively, Nexans could simply have refused to give access to the requested documents and to provide answers to the inspectors' questions during the inspection. If the Commission would afterwards have taken a decision on the basis of Article 23(1)(c) and (d) of Regulation 1/2003 imposing a fine for such refusals to cooperate, Nexans could have challenged this decision which would be distinct from the inspection decision and the final decision adopted by the Commission.[1357] However, by refusing to comply with the Commission's requests during the inspection, Nexans would have exposed itself to the risk of a fine in the hope that its reliance on the right to privacy would succeed in the end.[1358] As a result, these two other options do not seem to provide the same level of protection as if separate acts taken by the Commission during an inspection would be challengeable in their own right. As a third option and with regard to the copy that the Commission took of several computer files and of the hard drive of one of Nexans' employees, the General Court referred to the possibility of bringing an action against the Commission for non-contractual liability on the basis of Article 340 TFEU. However, as made clear by the General Court, such a remedy is not part of the system for the review of the legality of acts of the European Union.[1359] A claim for non-contractual liability thus suffers from the limitation that it does not affect the legality of the decisions of the Commission. One should keep in mind that such a claim is only of use for undertakings to claim damages for the harm suffered on account of the unlawful conduct on the part of the Commission.

Even in cases where the actions of the Commission are challengeable, the company concerned must still demonstrate that it has legal standing to raise claims relating to the protection of the privacy or personal data of its employees. After all, as

---

1353. Judgment in *Nexans France SAS and Nexans SA v. European Commission*, T-135/09, ECLI:EU:T:2012:596, par. 125.

1354. Judgment in *Nexans France SAS and Nexans SA v. European Commission*, T-135/09, ECLI:EU:T:2012:596, par. 134.

1355. Judgment in *Nexans France SAS and Nexans SA v. European Commission*, T-135/09, ECLI:EU:T:2012:596, par. 132.

1356. M. KUSCHEWSKY AND D. GERADIN, 'Data Protection in the Context of Competition Law Investigations: An Overview of the Challenges', *World Competition* 2014, vol. 37, no. 1, (69), p. 97.

1357. Judgment in *Nexans France SAS and Nexans SA v. European Commission*, T-135/09, ECLI:EU:T:2012:596, par. 126.

1358. M. KUSCHEWSKY AND D. GERADIN, 'Data Protection in the Context of Competition Law Investigations: An Overview of the Challenges', *World Competition* 2014, vol. 37, no. 1, (69), p. 97.

1359. Judgment in *Nexans France SAS and Nexans SA v. European Commission*, T-135/09, ECLI:EU:T:2012:596, par. 133.

an economic entity, a company cannot as such benefit from the protection offered by a fundamental right applicable to individuals. In *Pilkington*, a company brought an application for interim measures in order to prevent the publication of certain information by the Commission which would cause prejudice to the right to data protection of its employees who were allegedly involved in the implementation of a cartel. In this context, the General Court argued that *'the applicant cannot rely on the damage which its employees alone would suffer [...] rather the applicant must show that such damage is likely to entail – for itself – serious and irreparable personal harm'*.[1360] The General Court considered that Pilkington had not *'succeeded in establishing that the alleged damage to the interests of its employees would entail serious and irreparable harm for its undertaking as such'*. In particular, the General Court found that Pilkington had confined *'itself to a vague and speculative assertion'* and had not provided *'any details in that regard or substantiate[d] its assertion with any evidence'*. Similarly, Pilkington had failed to show, in the view of the General Court, that it would have been *'in the interests of the sound administration of justice for it to ensure the collective defence of the interests of the employees concerned on the ground that they cannot be required, because there are so many of them, to bring separate actions to secure protection of their personal data'*.[1361]

Considering the high standards set by the General Court in *Pilkington*, it will not be easy for companies in the future to show a level of harm to their own interests sufficient for giving them legal standing. At the same time, the General Court has put forward several ways in *Nexans* in which companies may successfully rely on the right to privacy or the right to data protection of their employees to attack the legality of decisions taken by the Commission.[1362] As a result, the Commission should be prepared to respect these fundamental rights in its competition investigations.

With respect to substance, competition law remedies have to be brought in line with the right to data protection in the sense that the European Commission cannot adopt measures that violate this fundamental right. For instance, when the Commission remedies a form of abuse under Article 102 TFEU by requiring a dominant undertaking to share personal data with competitors, it has to prevent that this form of processing breaches the principle of fair and lawful processing and the notion of purpose specification as laid down in Article 8(2) of the EU Charter of Fundamental Rights. As suggested in the context of the French *GDF Suez* case discussed in section 9.5

1360. Order in *Pilkington Group Ltd v. European Commission*, T-462/12 R, ECLI:EU:T:2013:119, par. 40. The Commission's appeal against the order has been dismissed in Order in *European Commission v. Pilkington Group Ltd*, C-278/13 P(R), ECLI:EU:C:2013:558.
1361. Order in *Pilkington Group Ltd v. European Commission*, T-462/12 R, ECLI:EU:T:2013:119, par. 41.
1362. See also M. Kuschewsky and D. Geradin, 'Data Protection in the Context of Competition Law Investigations: An Overview of the Challenges', *World Competition* 2014, vol. 37, no. 1, (69), p. 101 who plead for a system, based on the rule of law and the fundamental right to data protection, in which competition authorities would *'be prevented from relying on evidence which they have gathered in violation of data protection rules, similarly to the "fruit of the poisonous tree" doctrine in US law'*.

above, the Commission could comply with this negative duty by making a statement in its decision that the competition law duty to share data should be implemented in conformity with EU data protection law.

10.3.3.4 *Positive Duty to Promote the Application of the Right to Data Protection*

A more controversial issue is to what extent the Commission can be considered to be bound under the EU Charter of Fundamental Rights to take proactive measures to promote the application of the right to data protection. It should be noted at the outset that the principle of legality precludes the Commission from using its competences in the field of EU competition law to advance data protection interests in the absence of any economic efficiency concerns that trigger the application of Article 101 TFEU, Article 102 TFEU or the EU merger regime. In this regard, Article 51(2) of the EU Charter of Fundamental Rights explicitly states that the Charter does not establish any new power or task for the EU, or modify powers and tasks defined by the Treaties. However, when acting in its capacity as a competition authority to address identified violations of the competition rules, the Commission could guarantee the effectiveness of the right to data protection by adopting measures that actively promote data protection interests and go beyond what is necessary to protect economic efficiency concerns. The wording of Article 51(1) of the EU Charter of Fundamental Rights may even be argued to give rise to a duty for the Commission to take such positive action. While competition authorities cannot and should not use their competences to promote data protection interests if no violations of the competition rules can be identified, a better alignment between the two fields would benefit consumer welfare in situations where a competition law infringement interacts with data protection interests. To this end, the scope for the Commission to take such a proactive approach seems to be present in particular when requiring remedies from the parties to a merger[1363] and in commitment proceedings.[1364]

In both situations, undertakings find themselves at the mercy of the Commission to approve a merger or to abstain from adopting a prohibition decision and imposing a fine for a breach of Article 101 or 102 TFEU. This position gives the Commission scope to demand measures that do not only end the harm identified and restore competition but also reduce the risk of future violations. In the context of commitments proceedings, the Court of Justice made clear in *Alrosa* that while the principle of proportionality

---

1363. Articles 6(2) and 8(2) of the EU Merger Regulation give the Commission the competence to attach to its merger decision conditions and obligations intended to ensure that the undertakings concerned comply with the commitments they have entered into vis-à-vis the Commission with a view to rendering the concentration compatible with the common market.

1364. In a commitment decision, adopted on the basis of Article 9 of Regulation 1/2003, the European Commission does not establish an infringement of the competition rules but makes the commitments binding that have been offered by the undertaking concerned to meet the concerns expressed by the Commission. In a prohibition decision, on the other hand, having Article 7 of Regulation 1/2003 as legal basis, the Commission finds an infringement of Article 101 or 102 TFEU and requires the undertaking concerned to bring to an end to the infringement. The imposition of a fine usually forms an integral part of a prohibition decision.

applies to both prohibition and commitment decisions, the application of that principle nonetheless differs according to the nature of the procedure.[1365] In this regard, the Court of Justice stated that undertakings which offer commitments *'consciously accept that the concessions they make may go beyond what the Commission could itself impose on them'* in a prohibition decision.[1366] Considering that commitment decisions are typically not challenged in court, the Commission has some leeway to take a more proactive approach and facilitate the effectiveness of the right to data protection in a way that might otherwise not have been possible under EU data protection law.

Table 10.2   Three-Layer Approach Towards the Integration of Data Protection Interests in EU Competition Policy

Comparison with Other Non-efficiency Concerns	Character of the Obligation Incumbent on the European Commission as a Competition Authority	Effect on the Application of Competition Law
Data protection treated *as any other non-efficiency concern*	Protection of *economic efficiency* also furthers data protection interests	In accordance with the *inherent limitations* of competition law
Special status of data protection as a fundamental right in the EU Charter of Fundamental Rights	*Negative duty* to respect the right to data protection: - *procedural limits* in competition investigations; and - *limits on the substance* of competition law measures	Right to data protection *imposes limits* on how competition law can be applied
Special status of data protection as a fundamental right in the EU Charter of Fundamental Rights	*Positive duty* to promote the application of the right to data protection: *Scenario 1:* no economic efficiency concern found - legally impossible and undesirable to promote data protection on the basis of competition law *Scenario 2:* economic efficiency concern found - promote data protection when taking competition law measures	Take *proactive measures* on the basis of competition law to guarantee the effectiveness of the right to data protection

Despite the often expressed criticism that the use of remedies and commitments in this way will lead to an undue expansion of the Commission's competences and will

---

1365. Judgment in *European Commission v. Alrosa Company Ltd.*, C-441/07 P, ECLI:EU:C:2010:377, par. 47.
1366. Judgment in *European Commission v. Alrosa Company Ltd.*, C-441/07 P, ECLI:EU:C:2010:377, par. 48.

shift competition law towards a more regulatory model,[1367] such an approach can be beneficial from the perspective of consumers. In particular, it may lead to a more proper form of protection in a time where the boundaries between different legal fields are blurring and there is a need for coherent enforcement of EU law. Due to the elevation of data protection to a fundamental right, it could even be argued that the Commission does not have a choice anymore but rather an obligation stemming from the EU Charter of Fundamental Rights to actively take measures to guarantee the effectiveness of the right to data protection.[1368] Against this background, the interplay between data protection, on the one hand, and merger review and abuse of dominance, on the other hand, is discussed in the next two sections.

10.4 DATA PROTECTION INTERESTS IN MERGER REVIEW

This section outlines how the three-layer approach put forward above for integrating data protection interests into EU competition policy can be applied to merger review. In particular, it is discussed how data-related competition concerns in mergers should be assessed and to what extent there is room for positive action by the European Commission to integrate data protection considerations into its merger decisions.

10.4.1 Assessing Data-Related Competition Concerns in Merger Cases

In *Google/DoubleClick* and *Facebook/WhatsApp*, the European Commission explicitly stated that its merger analysis solely took place on the basis of EU competition rules and was without prejudice to obligations under data protection law. While the Commission did not assess the effect of the respective mergers on the protection of personal data and privacy as such, it did consider issues relating to data protection and privacy to the extent relevant for the competition analysis. In *Facebook/WhatsApp*, the Commission referred to privacy as one of the dimensions or parameters on the basis of which competition was taking place between providers of consumer communications apps. If data protection or privacy is a significant parameter of competition in a particular market, competition authorities have to take it into account in order to make a reliable analysis of the competitive situation. The Commission did not specifically analyse the *Facebook/WhatsApp* merger in the light of privacy as a dimension of competition, because it considered privacy to constitute only one out of several parameters of competition in the market for consumer communications apps.[1369]

With respect to the data-related competition concerns identified in the two merger cases, the Commission analysed the impact on the market of the combination

---

1367. See for instance, N. DUNNE, 'Commitment Decisions in EU Competition Law', *Journal of Competition Law and Economics* 2014, vol. 10, no. 2, (399).

1368. See also the analysis in F. COSTA-CABRAL AND O. LYNSKEY, 'The Internal and External Constraints of Data Protection on Competition Law in the EU', *LSE Law, Society and Economy Working Papers 25/2015* 2015, pp. 32-37, available at http://papers.ssrn.com/sol3/papers.cfm?abstract_id=2703655.

1369. See section 9.4 above.

of datasets in *Google/DoubleClick* and of data concentration in *Facebook/WhatsApp*. It is striking that the Commission has so far only assessed the effect of such competition concerns on the advertising side of the market. When assessing the competitive impact of the combination of the two data collections in *Google/DoubleClick*, the Commission referred to the possibility of the merged entity to use the combined dataset in order to better target ads to users.[1370] As regards the potential data concentration issues in *Facebook/WhatsApp*, the Commission analysed two theories of harm *'according to which Facebook could strengthen its position in online advertising'*, namely by introducing advertising on WhatsApp and/or using WhatsApp as a potential source of user data for the purpose of improving the targeting of Facebook's advertising activities outside WhatsApp.[1371] The Commission did not consider the effect of the data-related competition concerns on the user side of the market in these merger cases. This despite the important role of data in the process of optimising and personalising services provided to users.

In order to gain reliable insight into data-related competition concerns in merger cases, competition authorities should also reflect on the possible effects of the combination of datasets or data concentration on effective competition in the provision of services to users. In addition, the significance of data for the development of new products and services was not taken into account in *Google/DoubleClick* and *Facebook/WhatsApp*. The collection of data on users' behaviour and interests also enables undertakings to identify trends and changes in preferences which helps them to develop new products and services for which there is potential demand.[1372]

1370. Case No COMP/M.4731 – *Google/ DoubleClick*, 11 March 2008, par. 360.

1371. Case No COMP/M.7217 – *Facebook/WhatsApp*, 3 October 2014, par. 167.

1372. MONOPOLKOMMISSION, 'Competition policy: The challenge of digital markets', Special report No. 68, July 2015, paras 78 and 110. An additional issue relating to data-driven mergers as identified by the Monopolkommission in paras 454 and 459 is that the use of turnover thresholds to determine whether a merger has an EU dimension and thus has to be notified to the European Commission does not seem appropriate anymore due to the existence of other types of business models. An acquisition of a company having only a small turnover may still have a significant competitive impact, for example because the acquisition includes the transfer of valuable data, and thus deserves to be scrutinised by the Commission. To address this problem, the Monopolkommission proposes to include an additional notification requirement based on the agreed transaction volume (i.e., the purchase price) of the merger. For example, the *Facebook/WhatsApp* merger did not have an EU dimension because the turnover of WhatsApp did not meet the notification threshold. This while Facebook acquired WhatsApp for a purchase price of 19 billion dollar. The European Commission was only able to assess the merger under the EU Merger Regulation because the transaction was capable of being reviewed under the national competition laws of three Member States and Facebook had requested the Commission, on the basis of Article 4(5) of the EU Merger Regulation, to examine the merger (see Case No COMP/M.7217 – *Facebook/WhatsApp*, 3 October 2014, paras 4 and 9-12). Nevertheless, the Competition Commissioner seems hesitant to change the current notification thresholds considering her statement: *'Can we identify the right threshold, or would we be better off relying on cases being referred to us from the national authorities? After all, those referrals have already allowed us to see some important mergers that didn't meet our thresholds, not least the deal between Facebook and WhatsApp'* (Speech of Competition Commissioner Vestager, 'Refining the EU merger control system', Studienvereinigung Kartellrecht, Brussels, 10 March 2016, available at http://ec.europa.eu/commission/2014-2019/vestager/announcements/refining-eu-merger-control-system_en; see also the speech of Competition Commissioner Vestager, 'Competition: the mother of invention', European

In such circumstances, the competitive effects of a combination of datasets or greater data concentration caused by a merger go beyond existing markets. Such effects cannot be adequately considered when solely relying on a competition analysis in the relevant markets for the end products or services provided to users and advertisers. This problem can be solved by defining a potential market for data in addition to the existing relevant markets for the user and advertiser side of online platforms. The definition of such an additional market for data would enable competition authorities to more fully assess possible competition concerns relating to the asset that is used as an input to improve existing services and to develop new ones. In addition, it would allow for a more forward-looking stance towards market definition which does not merely rely on how data is currently used for the development of existing end products and services.[1373]

As regards merger review, the current distinction made between horizontal, vertical and conglomerate mergers does not always seem adequate to identify possible data-related competition issues. Even if a merger does not lead to a horizontal or vertical overlap or does not give rise to conglomerate effects in terms of the products and services that are offered by the merging parties, a combination of datasets may still have a competitive impact. In particular, it may give the merged entity a greater amount or variety of data to be used to improve existing services or to develop new ones. As proposed in Part I, even if data is not traded to third parties and no 'real market' exists in which supply and demand for data can be identified, a hypothetical or potential market for data could be defined by regarding data as a specialised asset in analogy to the EU Horizontal Guidelines.[1374]

At the same time, it is important to note that the fact that no market for the provision of data could be defined in *Facebook/WhatsApp* did not form a reason for the Commission to refrain from assessing potential data concentration issues.[1375] Nevertheless, by defining a potential market for data competition authorities would be able to undertake a more complete analysis of competition concerns relating to a combination of datasets or data concentration in merger cases. This would be a welcome development in merger review considering that acquisitions in the online environment are said to be increasingly motivated by the underlying dataset of the target undertaking.[1376] In a March 2016 speech, the Competition Commissioner stated in this regard that what makes a company an attractive merger partner is not always turnover: '*Sometimes, what matters are its assets. That could be a customer base or even a set of data*'. Even though the Competition Commissioner argues that '*our test is nimble*

Competition and Consumer Day, Amsterdam, 18 April 2016, available at http://ec.europa.eu /commission/2014-2019/vestager/announcements/competition-mother-invention_en).

1373. See also P.J. Harbour and T.I. Koslov, 'Section 2 In A Web 2.0 World: An Expanded Vision of Relevant Product Markets', *Antitrust Law Journal* 2010, vol. 76, no. 3, (769), p. 784.
1374. See in particular section 4.3.2 above.
1375. Case No COMP/M.7217 – *Facebook/WhatsApp*, 3 October 2014, par. 72.
1376. A.P. Grunes and M.E. Stucke, 'No Mistake About It: The Important Role of Antitrust in the Era of Big Data', *The Antitrust Source* 2015, vol. 14, no. 4, (1), p. 3.

enough to be applied in a meaningful way to the "new economy",[1377] the limitations of the current static approach to market definition in competition law have prevented the Commission from conducting a more forward-looking assessment in its *Google/ DoubleClick* and *Facebook/WhatsApp* merger decisions. While, respectively, Google and DoubleClick as well as Facebook and WhatsApp might not have been close competitors in the relevant markets for the services they offered to consumers, it is likely that the Commission would have been able to identify current or foreseeable future competitive constraints relating to data as an input for Google's and Facebook's services. Regardless of whether such constraints would have called for additional remedies or even for a prohibition of the mergers, these issues would have been worth an assessment by the Commission.[1378]

The added value of conducting an additional competition analysis of a potential relevant market for data can also be illustrated by reference to the acquisition of Nest by Google in early 2014.[1379] Nest, a producer of smart home devices such as thermostats and smoke detectors, was not competing with Google in any relevant product market when it was acquired by Google. Nevertheless, this move of Google has reinforced its position with regard to access to data about the behaviour of consumers.[1380] The acquisition of Nest has arguably not only impacted Google's ability to improve the relevance of existing services offered to users and advertisers on its search platform, but may also enable Google to develop new products on the basis of the new insights gained by analysing the additional data from Nest and combining it with its own information. The US Federal Trade Commission, which cleared the deal in February 2014,[1381] would have been able to assess such concerns in more detail had it defined an input market for data.[1382]

The EDPS has criticised the analysis of the European Commission in *Google/ DoubleClick* on a different basis. In its Preliminary Opinion on 'Privacy and competitiveness in the age of big data', the EDPS argued that the Commission due to its *'purely economic approach to the case [...] neglected the longer term impact on the welfare of millions of users in the event that the combined undertaking's information generated by search (Google) and browsing (DoubleClick) were later processed for incompatible*

1377. Speech of Competition Commissioner Vestager, 'Refining the EU merger control system', Studienvereinigung Kartellrecht, Brussels, 10 March 2016, available at http://ec.europa.eu/ commission/2014-2019/vestager/announcements/refining-eu-merger-control-system_en.
1378. For a detailed analysis of market definition and market power with regard to data in the context of essential facilities cases, see section 7.4 and 7.5 above.
1379. As discussed in I. GRAEF, 'Market Definition and Market Power in Data: The Case of Online Platforms', *World Competition* 2015, vol. 38, no. 4, (473), pp. 493-494.
1380. N. Newman, 'Why Antitrust Authorities Should Block Google's Takeover of Nest's 'Smart Home' Business', *Huffington Post*, 15 January 2014, available at http://www.huffingtonpost .com/nathan-newman/why-antitrust-authorities_b_4603053.html.
1381. US Federal Trade Commission, *Early Termination Notice 20140457: Google Inc.; Nest Labs, Inc.*, 4 February 2014, available at https://www.ftc.gov/enforcement/premerger-notification -program/early-termination-notices/20140457.
1382. See also the analysis in I. GRAEF, 'Market Definition and Market Power in Data: The Case of Online Platforms', *World Competition* 2015, vol. 38, no. 4, (473), pp. 492-495.

purposes' under data protection law.[1383] Although it does not add a conclusion to its reasoning, the EDPS seems to suggest the Commission to use its competences under merger control to advance data protection interests irrespective of the existence of any economic efficiency concerns. In the extreme, such an approach may lead to the situation that a merger which does not significantly impede effective competition is blocked on the sole basis that it may give rise to future data protection issues.

The Commission finds itself at the other side of the spectrum considering its statements in *Google/DoubleClick* and *Facebook/WhatsApp* that its merger analysis was without prejudice to the obligations imposed on the parties by data protection legislation and that privacy-related concerns do not fall within the scope of EU competition law. While the approach of the EDPS is too blunt and would require the European Commission to go beyond the competences granted to it as a competition authority, the Commission is submitted to be too conservative by denying any role for data protection interests in competition law. In order to develop a more refined approach towards the integration of data protection considerations in merger review, two scenarios can be distinguished in line with whether a merger is found to significantly impede effective competition or not.

10.4.2   Scenario 1: The Merger Does Not Significantly Impede Effective Competition

If a proposed transaction does not significantly impede effective competition, the European Commission has to declare the merger compatible with the common market in accordance with Articles 6(1)(b) and 8(1) of the EU Merger Regulation. In those situations, the Commission does not have the competence to impose any remedies or even block the merger because it might raise data protection issues. Even if the European Commission were to block a merger for the mere reason that the resulting combination of datasets or the increased concentration of data might give rise to data protection concerns, this may actually have the perverse effect of providing incentives to the parties to structure their transaction in a way which would avoid triggering the application of the merger control rules. The merging parties could, for example, decide to share data through licensing agreements.[1384] The integration of data protection issues into merger analysis in such a way therefore does not seem to constitute an adequate means to foster data protection interests on a long-term basis.

Since merger review is without prejudice to the obligations of the parties under data protection law, the approval of a transaction under the EU Merger Regulation does not prevent national data protection authorities from initiating their own parallel investigation to examine whether the concentration raises any data protection issues. In order to achieve a better coordination between the European Commission as a

---

1383. PRELIMINARY OPINION OF THE EUROPEAN DATA PROTECTION SUPERVISOR, 'Privacy and Competitiveness in the Age of big data: The interplay between data protection, competition law and consumer protection in the Digital Economy', March 2014, par. 64.
1384. M.K. OHLHAUSEN AND A.P. OKULIAR, 'Competition, Consumer Protection, and the Right [Approach] to Privacy', *Antitrust Law Journal* 2015, vol. 80, no. 1, (121), p. 155.

competition authority and the national data protection authorities in this regard, Article 21(4) of the EU Merger Regulation may be relied upon by Member States. As discussed in the context of the *NewsCorp/BSkyB* merger in section 10.2 above, this provision enables Member States to take appropriate measures to protect public interests other than those considered in merger review. Data protection is not explicitly mentioned as a legitimate interest, unlike public security, plurality of the media and prudential rules. This means that a Member State has to notify data protection as a public interest to the Commission before it is entitled to take appropriate measures to this end on the national level. The Commission then has to decide whether data protection can be recognised as a legitimate interest on the basis of its compatibility with the general principles and other provisions of Community law.

Since the right to data protection is mentioned among the principles of general application in Article 16 TFEU and is protected under the EU Charter of Fundamental Rights, the Commission does not seem to have much room to reject data protection as a legitimate interest under Article 21(4) of the EU Merger Regulation when invoked by a Member State. Nevertheless, data protection is different than the public interests that are explicitly mentioned in the provision because it is not an issue solely subject to national law.[1385] After all, the right to data protection is recognised as an EU fundamental right. At the same time, even though the General Data Protection Regulation is directly applicable in the Member States and does not need national implementing legislation, the enforcement of EU data protection law will continue to take place at the national level.[1386] One could therefore argue that there is no reason why a Member State should not be able to invoke data protection as a legitimate interest under Article 21(4) of the EU Merger Regulation. In case questions would arise about which national data protection authority is best placed to take action, it is submitted that the new one-stop-shop mechanism could be applied which prescribes that the national data protection authority of the main establishment of the controller or processor is competent.

It is important to note that the analysis conducted by a Member State under Article 21(4) takes place on the basis of national law and outside the framework of EU merger review. If a new public interest such as data protection will indeed be accepted by the Commission as a legitimate basis for adopting measures to protect non-efficiency considerations at the national level, the Member State may, on the basis of national law, subject a merger to additional conditions and may even block it if

---

1385. For an overview of national interests that have been invoked by Member States under Article 21(4) of the EU Merger Regulation, see A. JONES AND J. DAVIES, 'Merger Control and the Public Interest: Balancing EU and National Law in the Protectionist Debate' in B.E. HAWK (ed.), *International Antitrust Law and Policy: Fordham Competition Law 2014*, Juris Publishing, 2015, (63), pp. 102-109.

1386. Under Article 60(7), (8) and (9) and Article 65(6) of the General Data Protection Regulation, the national data protection authorities adopt the final decisions and notify them to the controllers or processors at issue even in cases of disagreement among the authorities where the European Data Protection Board takes a binding decision. In addition, Article 60(10) of the General Data Protection Regulation requires controllers or processors to inform the relevant national data protection authority about the measures taken for complying with the decisions notified to them.

prohibiting the transaction altogether is proportionate in order to protect the public interest concerned. However, since EU data protection law does not provide national data protection authorities with the possibility to adopt any prospective or structural measures, it does not seem possible for a national data protection authority to subject a merger to any conditions, let alone block it, if it does not give rise to data protection issues at the time the merger is approved by the Commission under the EU Merger Regulation. Merger analysis is forward-looking by nature and the EU Merger Regulation explicitly provides for the possibility to block mergers which are incompatible with the common market. This while the current Data Protection Directive and the future General Data Protection Regulation only provide for behavioural remedies by enabling national data protection authorities to sanction companies after they have infringed data protection law and to require changes in the way they process personal data. These instruments do not enable data protection authorities to take action in order to prevent certain market developments from occurring that might have a detrimental effect on data protection interests in the future.

By criticising the Commission in *Google/DoubleClick* for not taking into account the possibility that Google would start to use the combined data for incompatible purposes, the EDPS seems to attempt to lay the ground for the adoption of measures in merger cases that prevent possible data protection problems from arising. Even if a Member State had relied on Article 21(4) of the EU Merger Regulation in order to examine the merger in the light of its impact on data protection, its national data protection authority would not have been competent to impose any conditions on the transaction because the acquisition of DoubleClick by Google did not in itself breach data protection law. The sole possibility that a violation of data protection law might occur in the future if, for example, the combined data of Google and DoubleClick would be used for incompatible purposes, had not given a national data protection authority the competence to take pre-emptive measures in order to protect the data protection interests of users. Allowing the fields of data protection and competition law to blend in such a way would jeopardise legal certainty and create the situation that remedies or conditions will be imposed on a transaction which actually complies with both the applicable competition and data protection rules but not with the mix of the two that is put forward by data protection advocates such as the EDPS.[1387]

A national data protection authority would thus only be entitled to impose conditions to a merger under Article 21(4) of the EU Merger Regulation if the transaction in and of itself infringes data protection rules. If a national data protection authority merely anticipates that certain data protection issues might occur at some point in the future after the merger has been finalised, its only option is to monitor whether the merged entity continues to comply with its data protection obligations. Once there are indications that the merged entity is breaching data protection rules, it may start an investigation on its own initiative on the basis of data protection law and thus outside the framework of Article 21(4) of the EU Merger Regulation. The

---

1387. R. CRAIG, 'Big Data and Competition – Merger Control Is Not the Remedy for Data Protection Issues', *Taylor Wessing*, July 2014, available at http://united-kingdom.taylorwessing.com/ globaldatahub/article_big_data_competition.html.

procedure under the latter provision therefore only seems to have relevance for mergers that at the time of their notification to the Commission under EU merger review already raise data protection issues.

One should note, however, that the General Data Protection Regulation introduces new requirements for controllers which will enable national data protection authorities to monitor risky processing activities more proactively. Under Article 35(1) of the General Data Protection Regulation, controllers must, prior to the processing, carry out an assessment of the impact of the envisaged processing operations on the protection of personal data where a type of processing is likely to result in a high risk for the rights and freedoms of individuals. Article 36(1) of the General Data Protection Regulation requires the controller to consult the competent national data protection authority prior to the processing of personal data in situations where the data protection impact assessment indicates that the processing would result in a high risk in the absence of measures taken by the controller.

It is submitted that the obligation of a controller to conduct a data protection impact assessment would also apply in case a merger gives rise to a combination of previously separate datasets which contain personal data. Because of the risk that personal data will be processed for incompatible purposes after the merger, the merged entity may have to take mitigation measures and consult the national data protection authority before the start of the processing activities. In this way, the data protection authority can closely monitor how personal data is processed after the merger and give advice to the controller even though no violation of EU data protection law could be identified at the time the merger had been notified to the European Commission under EU merger review.

In addition, the principle of accountability, which is explicitly mentioned and plays a significant role in the General Data Protection Regulation, may enable national data protection authorities to act in a more proactive way. The principle of accountability implies that the controller is responsible for and able to demonstrate compliance with EU data protection rules.[1388] For instance, Article 24(1) of the General Data Protection Regulation requires controllers to implement appropriate technical and organisational measures to ensure and be able to demonstrate that the processing of personal data is performed in compliance with the rules. Upon request of a data protection authority, controllers thus have to be able to show that adequate measures are in place to ensure that their processing activities comply with EU data protection law.

10.4.3   Scenario 2: The Merger Significantly Impedes Effective Competition

When a proposed transaction is found to significantly impede effective competition, the merging parties typically offer remedies to the European Commission to address the identified competition concerns with a view to rendering the concentration compatible

---

1388. See Article 5(2) of the General Data Protection Regulation in the context of the data quality requirements.

with the common market. In accordance with Articles 6(2) and 8(2) of the EU Merger Regulation, the Commission attaches conditions and obligations to its decision intended to ensure that the merging parties comply with the commitments they have entered into vis-à-vis the Commission in this regard. Because the merging parties are dependent on the discretion of the Commission to prevent the merger from being blocked, the Commission has scope to require remedies that go beyond ending the identified competition concerns and that have a more structural impact. As discussed in the previous section, the scope for prospective analysis under EU data protection law is limited. In particular, the current Data Protection Directive and the future General Data Protection Regulation do not give national data protection authorities the competence to adopt structural measures to prevent possible future data protection issues from occurring. By imposing conditions to a merger, the Commission may be able to overcome this limitation. Conditions could be adopted which not only address economic efficiency concerns but also guarantee the effectiveness of the right to data protection in a way that would otherwise not have been available to national data protection authorities when enforcing data protection law.

For example, if the combination of datasets is considered to strengthen the position of the merged entity in a particular relevant market in such a way as to significantly impede effective competition, the Commission could require the merging parties to keep their datasets separate. In this light, former US Federal Trade Commissioner Pamela Jones Harbour suggested in her dissenting statement regarding the *Google/DoubleClick* merger that it may have been desirable to mandate a firewall between the data of Google and DoubleClick for some period of time to prevent any anticompetitive effects.[1389] In line with the positive duty of the Commission to promote the application of the right to data protection included in the EU Charter of Fundamental Rights, it could involve the competent national data protection authority in the implementation of the merger remedies.

In this regard, it is instructive to note that the establishment of a firewall between the datasets of the merging parties would also prevent personal data from being used for incompatible purposes under EU data protection law. This way, a remedy designed to address economic efficiency concerns could be extended to include commitments with regard to how the merged entity will handle personal data after the merger. To ensure that the merged entity indeed keeps the datasets separate as committed to the Commission, the competent national data protection authority could be put in charge of monitoring whether personal data is not exchanged between previously distinct services. This would also enable the data protection authority to require the merged entity to take pre-emptive measures to prevent that personal data is being combined and, as a consequence, used for incompatible purposes. A breach of the notion of compatible use would imply a violation of the conditions imposed by the Commission in the merger decision. In accordance with Article 14(2)(d) of the EU Merger Regulation, the Commission may then impose fines up to 1% of the aggregate turnover of the

---

1389. Dissenting Statement of Commissioner Pamela Jones Harbour, *Google/DoubleClick*, FTC File No. 071-0170, 20 December 2007, footnote 23 on p. 9.

undertakings concerned if they intentionally or negligently fail to comply with one of the conditions included in the merger decision.

The question can be raised whether a further cooperation between competition and data protection authorities should be realised in general. In this regard, the current EDPS Buttarelli[1390] suggested competition authorities to inform data protection authorities when investigating a merger or an alleged anticompetitive practice in the digital sector.[1391] While it is indeed desirable for the two types of authorities to exchange views on cases that are under parallel investigation by competition and data protection authorities, it should be kept in mind that the cause of concerns is different in the two legal fields. Unlike competition law, data protection law is not concerned with scale as such in the sense that a breach of data protection rules can be equally damaging to the interests of individual data subjects irrespective of the market position of the firm and the size of the dataset or the processing activities.[1392] Data protection authorities should thus not limit their resources to investigate cases that are notified to them by competition authorities if such a collaboration between the two types of authorities would be established in the future.

1390. By joint decision, the European Parliament and the Council appoint a European Data Protection Supervisor and an Assistant Supervisor who are assigned as members of the institution for a period of five years (Article 42(1) of Regulation (EC) No 45/2001 of the European Parliament and of the Council of 18 December 2000 on the protection of individuals with regard to the processing of personal data by the Community institutions and bodies and on the free movement of such data [2001] OJ L 8/1). Both the institution and the person appointed to head the institution are thus referred to as 'EDPS'. When reference is made to the head of the EDPS instead of the institution in this book, this will be made explicit. Giovanni Buttarelli and Wojciech Wiewiórowski, the current EDPS and Assistant Supervisor, took office on 4 December 2014.

1391. Speech European Data Protection Supervisor Buttarelli, 'Privacy and Competition in the Digital Economy', Privacy Platform event: The Digital Economy, Competition and Privacy Brussels, 21 January 2015, p. 5, available at https://secure.edps.europa.eu/EDPSWEB/we bdav/site/mySite/shared/Documents/EDPS/Publications/Speeches/2015/15-01-21_speech_GB_EN.pdf.

1392. However, the General Data Protection Regulation does take into account the level of risk of a certain form of processing in such a way that more detailed obligations will apply to controllers where the risk of processing is higher. For example, 'the risks of varying likelihood and severity for the rights and freedoms of natural persons' play a role in determining to what extent the controller must implement appropriate technical and organisational measures to ensure and be able to demonstrate that the processing of personal data is performed in compliance with the applicable rules under Article 24(1) of the General Data Protection Regulation. In addition, the Court of Justice referred to the ubiquity of online search engines in *Google Spain* when determining the effect of the interference caused by Google's processing of personal data with the fundamental rights to privacy and data protection of the data subject at issue (Judgment in *Google Spain SL, Google Inc. v. Agencia Española de Protección de Datos, Mario Costeja González*, C-131/12, ECLI:EU:C:2014:317, par. 80). While no formal distinction is made on the basis of scale or size under EU data protection law, the risk that particular processing activities may bring about and the ubiquitous nature of a data controller can thus be considered as relevant factors in establishing, respectively, the scale of its obligations under the General Data Protection Regulation and the impact of its processing activities on the rights of the data subject.

10.5 DATA PROTECTION INTERESTS AND ABUSE OF DOMINANCE

Data protection is also becoming of relevance to competition enforcement in the area of Article 102 TFEU. In this context, data protection may play a role in assessing dominance as well as in establishing abuse. It is argued that a serial disregard for the privacy interests of consumers forms an indication that an undertaking has the power to behave independently in the market and thus possesses a dominant position.[1393] The fact that, for example, a company can make its terms and conditions less privacy-friendly without losing a significant number of customers is alleged to point to the existence of dominance.[1394] Such a reasoning would only be valid in markets where data protection in itself, instead of price or variety of services, is a key parameter of competition.

As explained in section 9.4 above, no competition case has yet been fully analysed in the light of the protection of personal data or privacy as a dimension of competition. In its Guidance Paper on exclusionary conduct under Article 102 TFEU, the European Commission did make a reference to how decisions of undertakings to influence non-price parameters of competition could point to the existence of a dominant position. In this regard, the Commission stated that an undertaking which is capable of profitably increasing prices above the competitive level for a significant period of time can generally be regarded as dominant. The Commission made clear that the expression 'increase prices' is used in this context *as shorthand for the various ways in which the parameters of competition - such as prices, output, innovation, the variety or quality of goods or services - can be influenced to the advantage of the dominant undertaking and to the detriment of consumers'*.[1395] Ironically, the ability to set a very low or zero price in order to limit the scope for potential competitors to offer more privacy-friendly services against a monetary fee may form an indication of the existence of dominance in online markets.

However, it should be kept in mind that a decrease in data protection is not necessarily detrimental to consumer welfare if privacy forms only one aspect of quality and is traded off against other product characteristics such as price and relevance. A continuous disregard for the privacy of consumers can therefore not form an indication of dominance if a decrease in data protection leads to better prices or to more relevant end products or services. Nevertheless, if data protection is an isolated aspect of quality and does not interrelate with price or other product dimensions,[1396] a serial disrespect for the privacy of consumers may indeed indicate that the undertaking at issue is

---

1393. A.J. BURNSIDE, 'No Such Thing as a Free Search: Antitrust and the Pursuit of Privacy Goals', *CPI Antitrust Chronicle* 2015, vol. 5, no. 2, (1), p. 6.

1394. See S.W. WALLER, 'Antitrust and Social Networking', *North Carolina Law Review* 2012, vol. 90, no. 5, (1771), p. 1792 who refers to Facebook's privacy policy updates which at times have caused fierce opposition on the part of the users without, however, affecting the growth of its social network.

1395. Communication from the Commission — Guidance on the Commission's enforcement priorities in applying Article 82 of the EC Treaty to abusive exclusionary conduct by dominant undertakings (Guidance Paper) [2009] OJ C 45/7, par. 11.

1396. As discussed in section 9.4 above, consumer communications apps may be an example of a product which is characterised by data protection as an isolated dimension of quality.

dominant. In these circumstances where data protection is the main parameter of competition, an undertaking may lower data protection guarantees to its own advantage and to the detriment of consumers.

With regard to the role of data protection in establishing abuse, the EDPS Buttarelli stated in a 2015 speech that '*[w]e should be prepared for potential abuse of dominance cases which also may involve a breach of data protection rules*'.[1397] In 2012, the then-Commissioner for Competition Almunia already referred to the possibility that '*[a] single dominant company could of course think to infringe privacy laws to gain an advantage over its competitors*'.[1398] By collecting personal data beyond the consent of data subjects, a company can get more insight into the preferences of individuals and thereby create better services for users as well as advertisers. In this regard, the excessive extraction of personal data of users has been identified as a potential form of abusive conduct under Article 102 TFEU.[1399] Since personal data replaces price as a type of currency in the online environment, exploitative abuse may relate to the excessive collection of information about consumers instead of to the monetary price charged for a product or service. The question then arises what amount of data is to be considered as excessive.

With regard to excessive pricing, the Court of Justice argued in *United Brands* that '*a price which is excessive because it has no reasonable relation to the economic value of the product supplied*' is abusive under Article 102 TFEU.[1400] In its Preliminary Opinion on 'Privacy and competitiveness in the age of big data', the EDPS seems to rely on this statement in *United Brands* by stating that exploitative abuse may occur if '*the "price" paid through the surrender of personal information [is] to be considered excessive in relation to the value of the service consumed*'.[1401] In order to establish whether the price charged for the Chiquita bananas in *United Brands* were of an excessive nature, the Court suggested to make a comparison between the selling price and the production costs which would then disclose the profit margin. If this difference is indeed excessive, it would still need to be determined, in the Court's view, whether

---

1397. Speech European Data Protection Supervisor Buttarelli, 'Keynote speech at Joint ERA-EDPS seminar', workshop Competition Rebooted: Enforcement and personal data in digital markets Brussels, 24 September 2015, p. 3, available at https://secure.edps.europa.eu/EDPSWEB/ webdav/site/mySite/shared/Documents/EDPS/Publications/Speeches/2015/15-09-24_ERA _GB_EN.pdf.

1398. Speech former Competition Commissioner Almunia, 'Competition and personal data protection', Privacy Platform event: Competition and Privacy in Markets of Data Brussels, 26 November 2012, SPEECH/12/860.

1399. See Autorité de la concurrence and Bundeskartellamt, 'Competition Law and Data', 10 May 2016, p. 25; UK House of Lords Select Committee on European Union, 'Online Platforms and the Digital Single Market', 10th Report of Session 2015-16, 20 April 2016, par. 180, available at http://www.publications.parliament.uk/pa/ld201516/ldselect/ldeucom/129/129.pdf; Monopolkommission, 'Competition policy: The challenge of digital markets', Special report No. 68, July 2015, paras 326 and 329; and A.J. Burnside, 'No Such Thing as a Free Search: Antitrust and the Pursuit of Privacy Goals', *CPI Antitrust Chronicle* 2015, vol. 5, no. 2, (1), p. 6.

1400. Judgment in *United Brands v. Commission*, Case 27/76, ECLI:EU:C:1978:22, par. 250.

1401. Preliminary Opinion of the European Data Protection Supervisor, 'Privacy and competitiveness in the age of big data: The interplay between data protection, competition law and consumer protection in the Digital Economy', March 2014, p. 29.

the price is unfair in itself or when compared to competing products.[1402] The Court made clear that next to this method, alternative ways may be devised of determining whether a price is excessive.[1403]

It seems difficult to apply such an economic test to assess whether the collection of personal data by a particular firm is excessive. Even though surveys and experiments may be held to determine the willingness of consumers to reveal certain information in exchange for being provided with a particular service,[1404] it will be hard to prove a form of exploitative abuse relating to the extraction of personal data. As explained by the Monopolkommission, an independent expert committee which advises the German government and legislature in the area of competition policy, the services provided in the online environment may be so complex or user-specific that they require a situation- or user-dependent evaluation of the value of the service in question.[1405] In addition, the heterogeneous preferences of consumers towards data protection may ask for a user-specific analysis. While some consumers will not regard a particular form of data collection as excessive because they value the higher level of relevance and personalisation that it brings about, this may be different for consumers who are more sensitive to data protection issues.[1406]

Another approach that has been proposed to assess whether a certain form of data collection is excessive under Article 102 TFEU involves the use of data protection principles as a benchmark against which the existence of abusive behaviour can be tested.[1407] For example, the purpose limitation principle contained in Article 6(1)(b) of the Data Protection Directive and Article 5(1)(b) of the General Data Protection Regulation and the principle of data minimisation derived from Article 6(1)(c) of the Data Protection Directive and Article 5(1)(c) of the General Data Protection Regulation could be applied. Under these principles, controllers have to limit the collection of personal data to what is necessary to accomplish a specified and legitimate purpose and cannot retain data any longer than necessary to fulfil that purpose. In other words, if a firm extracts personal data beyond what is necessary to achieve a particular purpose or keeps it for a period longer than necessary to fulfil this purpose, it is violating the data minimisation and purpose limitation principles of the Data Protection Directive and the General Data Protection Regulation.

A similar analogy can be made with regard to principles used in consumer protection law. In speeches, the EDPS Buttarelli also referred to non-negotiable and

---

1402. Judgment in *United Brands v. Commission*, Case 27/76, ECLI:EU:C:1978:22, paras 251-252.
1403. Judgment in *United Brands v. Commission*, Case 27/76, ECLI:EU:C:1978:22, par. 253.
1404. See OECD, 'Exploring the Economics of Personal Data: A Survey of Methodologies for Measuring Monetary Value', *OECD Digital Economy Papers*, No. 220, 2013, pp. 29-32, available at http://dx.doi.org/10.1787/5k486qtxldmq-en.
1405. MONOPOLKOMMISSION, 'Competition policy: The challenge of digital markets', Special report No. 68, July 2015, par. 329.
1406. See the analysis in section 9.4 above.
1407. See also F. COSTA-CABRAL AND O. LYNSKEY, 'The Internal and External Constraints of Data Protection on Competition Law in the EU', *LSE Law, Society and Economy Working Papers 25/2015* 2015, pp. 20-21, available at http://papers.ssrn.com/sol3/papers.cfm?abstract_id=2703655.

misleading privacy policies as constituting a potential form of abuse of dominance.[1408] It seems hard to determine at what point a (change in) privacy policy should give rise to competition law liability under Article 102 TFEU. Article 6(1) of the Unfair Commercial Practices Directive[1409] may be of assistance in this regard. According to this provision, a commercial practice has to *'be regarded as misleading if it contains false information and is therefore untruthful or in any way, including overall presentation, deceives or is likely to deceive the average consumer, even if the information is factually correct'* in relation to one or more of the elements specified in subsections (a) to (g) such as the nature of the product or its main characteristics.

By using principles from these legal regimes as benchmarks for assessing abuse of dominance, data protection and consumer protection interests can be integrated in the competition analysis conducted under Article 102 TFEU. If a particular practice of a dominant firm does not comply with, for example, the purpose limitation or data minimisation principle as contained in the Data Protection Directive and the General Data Protection Regulation, or qualifies as misleading under the Unfair Commercial Practices Directive, this may be taken as an indication of the existence of abuse of dominance. Reference can be made in this regard to the *AstraZeneca* and *Allianz Hungaria* judgments in which the Court of Justice recognised that the breach of one area of law can be a factor in deciding that there has been a violation of competition law as well.

The *AstraZeneca* case involved a pharmaceutical group which was fined by the European Commission for having committed two abuses of a dominant position. One of these abuses consisted in the provision of misleading representations to patent offices which was alleged to form part of an overall strategy designed to prevent or delay market entry of competing generic products. The Court of Justice endorsed the finding of the General Court that representations designed to unlawfully obtain exclusive rights constitute an abuse if it is established that they are actually liable to lead the public authorities to grant the exclusive right applied for.[1410] Since AstraZeneca's misleading representations enabled it to obtain exclusive rights either to which it was not entitled or to which it was entitled only for a shorter period, the Court of Justice confirmed the abuse identified by the Commission and upheld by the General

---

1408. Speech European Data Protection Supervisor Buttarelli, 'Privacy and Competition in the Digital Economy', Privacy Platform event: The Digital Economy, Competition and Privacy Brussels, 21 January 2015, p. 5 with respect to non-negotiable privacy policies; and speech European Data Protection Supervisor Buttarelli, 'Keynote speech at Joint ERA-EDPS seminar', workshop Competition Rebooted: Enforcement and personal data in digital markets Brussels, 24 September 2015, p. 3 as regards misleading privacy policies.

1409. Directive 2005/29/EC of the European Parliament and of the Council of 11 May 2005 concerning unfair business-to-consumer commercial practices in the internal market and amending Council Directive 84/450/EEC, Directives 97/7/EC, 98/27/EC and 2002/65/EC of the European Parliament and of the Council and Regulation (EC) No 2006/2004 of the European Parliament and of the Council (Unfair Commercial Practices Directive) [2005] OJ L 149/22.

1410. Judgment in *AstraZeneca AB and AstraZeneca plc v. European Commission*, C-457/10 P, ECLI:EU:C:2012:770, par. 106.

Court.[1411] In this way, the *AstraZeneca* judgment makes clear that the misuse of regulatory procedures is to be regarded as abuse of dominance where such conduct has a potential anticompetitive effect.[1412]

The *Allianz Hungaria* case dealt with agreements between insurance companies, on the one hand, and individual car repairers and a car repairers' association, on the other hand. The agreements related to the hourly charge to be paid by the insurance company to car dealers in their capacity as repair shops. Since the charge was increased in accordance with the number and percentage of insurance contracts that the dealer sells for that insurance company, the agreements linked the remuneration for the car repair service to that for the car insurance brokerage. The Court argued that *'while the establishment of such a link between two activities which are in principle independent does not automatically mean that the agreement concerned has as its object the restriction of competition, it can nevertheless constitute an important factor in deter-mining whether that agreement is by its nature injurious to the proper functioning of normal competition'*.[1413] In addition, the Court stated that the agreements at issue could in particular amount to a restriction of competition by object where *'domestic law requires that dealers acting as intermediaries or insurance brokers must be independent from the insurance companies'*.[1414] The Court thus put weight on the breach of domestic insurance law in identifying a restriction of competition by object under Article 101 TFEU.[1415] One could argue that, in line with this reasoning of the Court of Justice in *AstraZeneca* and *Allianz Hungaria*, a breach of data protection or consumer protection law may be of relevance in assessing a violation of competition law.[1416]

In March 2016, the Bundeskartellamt announced the opening of proceedings against Facebook on suspicion of having abused its possible dominant position in the market for social networks. In particular, the Bundeskartellamt suspects that Facebook's terms of service are in violation of data protection law and thereby also represent an abusive imposition of unfair conditions on users. If a connection can be identified between the alleged data protection infringement and Facebook's possible dominance, the use of unlawful terms and conditions by Facebook could, in the view of the Bundeskartellamt, also be regarded as an abuse of dominance under competition

---

1411. Judgment in *AstraZeneca AB and AstraZeneca plc v. European Commission*, C-457/10 P, ECLI:EU:C:2012:770, paras 107-113.
1412. With regard to the issue of whether the misleading representations could be found to be such as to restrict competition, the Court of Justice stated that *'although the practice of an undertaking in a dominant position cannot be characterised as abusive in the absence of any anti-competitive effect on the market, such an effect does not necessarily have to be concrete, and it is sufficient to demonstrate that there is a potential anti-competitive effect'* (Judgment in *AstraZeneca AB and AstraZeneca plc v. European Commission*, C-457/10 P, ECLI:EU:C:2012:770, par. 112).
1413. Judgment in *Allianz Hungária Biztosító Zrt*, C-32/11, ECLI:EU:C:2013:160, par. 41.
1414. Judgment in *Allianz Hungária Biztosító Zrt*, C-32/11, ECLI:EU:C:2013:160, par. 47.
1415. A.J. Burnside, 'No Such Thing as a Free Search: Antitrust and the Pursuit of Privacy Goals', *CPI Antitrust Chronicle* 2015, vol. 5, no. 2, (1), p. 5.
1416. European Data Protection Supervisor, 'Report of workshop on Privacy, Consumers, Competition and Big Data', 2 June 2014, p. 3.

law.[1417] The Bundeskartellamt thus appears to rely on data protection law as a benchmark for assessing whether certain exploitative behaviour of a dominant firm should be considered anticompetitive under Article 102 TFEU.

The investigation in fact forms a first attempt by a competition authority to integrate data protection interests into competition analysis. A possible intervention by the Bundeskartellamt on the basis of competition law could thereby also help alleviate data protection concerns. It is worth noting that the investigation does not seem to relate to the excessiveness of data collection but rather to the question of whether consumers are sufficiently informed about the type and extent of personal data collected. The specific benchmark relied upon by the Bundeskartellamt to establish anticompetitive exploitation of consumers under abuse of dominance would then be the validity of consent under data protection law. In particular, the main focus of the investigation seems to be whether the consent given by Facebook users is sufficiently informed as required by Article 2(h) of the current Data Protection Directive and Article 4(11) of the future General Data Protection Regulation.

Considering that the finding of a competition law infringement would become partly dependent on the application of rules from another legal regime, it is worth analysing if the *ne bis in idem* principle imposes any limitations in this regard. According to this general principle of law laid down in Article 50 of the EU Charter of Fundamental Rights and Article 4 of Protocol No. 7 to the European Convention of Human Rights, legal proceedings cannot be instituted twice for the same cause of action. As regards the application of the *ne bis in idem* principle in the context of EU competition law, the Court of Justice made clear that it is subject to the threefold condition of identity of the facts, unity of offender and unity of the legal interest protected. In other words, the same defendant cannot be sanctioned more than once for a single unlawful course of conduct designed to protect the same legal asset.[1418]

In her Opinion in *Toshiba*, Advocate General Kokott argued that, in line with the interpretation of the *ne bis in idem* principle in areas of EU law other than competition law and in the case law of the European Court of Human Rights, account should only be taken of the identity of the facts which necessarily includes the unity of the offender.[1419] The only relevant criterion for the application of the principle in the view of Advocate General Kokott is identity of the '*material acts, understood as the existence of a set of concrete circumstances which are inextricably linked together*'.[1420] However, under current law, identity of the legal interest protected is still one of the conditions for the application of the *ne bis in idem* principle. Because of the difference in their

---

1417. Press Release Bundeskartellamt, 'Bundeskartellamt initiates proceeding against Facebook on suspicion of having abused its market power by infringing data protection rules', 2 March 2016, available at http://www.bundeskartellamt.de/SharedDocs/Meldung/EN/Pressemittei lungen/2016/02_03_2016_Facebook.html?nn = 3591568.
1418. Judgment in *Aalborg Portland and Others v. Commission*, C-204/00 P, C-205/00 P, C-211/00 P, C-213/00 P, C-217/00 P and C-219/00 P, ECLI:EU:C:2004:6, par. 338; and Judgment in *Roquette Frères v. Commission*, T-322/01, ECLI:EU:T:2006:267, par. 278.
1419. Opinion of Advocate General Kokott in *Toshiba Corporation and Others*, C-17/10, ECLI-:EU:C:2011:552, paras 116-123.
1420. Opinion of Advocate General Kokott in *Toshiba Corporation and Others*, C-17/10, ECLI-:EU:C:2011:552, par. 124.

underlying legal interest, this general principle of law would not stand in the way of launching an investigation on the basis of competition law in addition to a parallel procedure under the data protection or consumer protection rules for the same facts.

Another way by which the use of principles from data protection or consumer protection law to establish a competition law infringement may be opposed is by questioning whether competition law is an appropriate instrument to address potential abusive commercial patterns relating to the exploitation of individual data subjects or consumers. In this respect, the former Commissioner for Competition Almunia argued: '*When unfair or manipulative commercial practices become pervasive in a market to the detriment of consumers and users the matter is best resolved with regulation*'.[1421] It is also important to note that the European Commission has not provided any guidance relating to abusive exploitative conduct while its Guidance Paper on exclusionary conduct under Article 102 TFEU was published in 2009. In fact, competition authorities rarely challenge behaviour that directly harms individuals and instead focus on addressing conduct of dominant firms leading to the foreclosure of competitors. This may be explained by the fact that it remains complicated to establish at what point a certain type of exploitative behaviour becomes anticompetitive.

By using principles from data protection or consumer protection law as benchmarks for analysing whether abuse of dominance under competition law exists, these difficulties may be overcome. Such an approach could enrich the traditional toolkit of competition authorities to address new forms of anticompetitive behaviour in the online environment. At the same time, caution is required to avoid outcomes whereby any law infringement by a dominant firm automatically becomes of relevance to competition enforcement. For that reason, commercial manipulation of personal data and privacy policies should remain an issue first and foremost tackled by data protection and consumer protection authorities. Nevertheless, if a strong link can be identified between a violation of data protection or consumer protection law and the dominant position of the infringer in the relevant market, there is no reason why a breach of one of these legal regimes cannot be a relevant factor for considering an independent violation of Article 102 TFEU.[1422]

10.6   CONCLUSION

Even though the European Commission and the Court of Justice currently seem reluctant to take data protection concerns into account when enforcing competition law, it is submitted that greater consideration should be given to data protection in competition cases in accordance with its status as a fundamental right in the EU legal

---

1421. Speech former Competition Commissioner Almunia, 'Competition and personal data protection', Privacy Platform event: Competition and Privacy in Markets of Data Brussels, 26 November 2012, SPEECH/12/860.

1422. In the context of the abuse of dominance investigation against Facebook as announced by the Bundeskartellamt in March 2016, see I. GRAEF & B. VAN ALSENOY, 'Data Protection Data Protection through the Lens of Competition Law: Will Germany Lead the Way?', *LSE Media Policy Project blog*, 23 March 2016, available at http://blogs.lse.ac.uk/mediapolicyproject/2016/03/23/data-protection-through-the-lens-of-competition-law-will-germany-lead-the-way/.

order. In this regard, the role of data protection in EU competition policy has to go beyond the way the Commission has occasionally addressed other non-efficiency considerations in previous cases. A distinction can be made between three approaches by which the Commission and national competition authorities, when applying the EU competition rules, could or even should, following the wording of Article 51(1) of the EU Charter of Fundamental Rights, advance data protection interests through competition enforcement.

First, by adopting remedies in order to address economic efficiency concerns, competition authorities may at the same time foster data protection interests and prevent, for instance, that personal data is processed for incompatible purposes after a merger. Second, competition authorities are under a negative duty to respect the right to data protection as contained in the EU Charter of Fundamental Rights. In this context, the right to data protection imposes limits on how competition law can be applied in terms of procedural safeguards to be followed in competition investigations and limits as regards the substance of competition law measures. Third, competition authorities are subject to a positive duty to promote the application of the right to data protection in cases where a breach of the competition rules is found. While it may be considered controversial to require competition authorities to take proactive measures to guarantee the effectiveness of the right to data protection, one could argue that the Commission has leeway to negotiate remedies that go beyond merely ending the identified economic efficiency concern in merger and commitment decisions.

In the context of Article 102 TFEU, data protection interests can be integrated into competition analysis by using the purpose limitation or data minimisation principle as a benchmark to establish whether a certain form of data collection by a dominant undertaking is excessive and qualifies as abuse of dominance. In its *Facebook* investigation, the Bundeskartellamt seems to rely on the validity of consent under data protection law in order to establish a possible form of anticompetitive exploitation of consumers in the market for social networks. Similarly, the definition of a misleading practice in the Unfair Commercial Practices Directive can be used to identify whether a privacy policy should give rise to competition law liability under Article 102 TFEU. Support for the approach whereby a breach of another legal regime is considered relevant for determining whether competition law has also been violated can be found in the *AstraZeneca* and *Allianz Hungaria* judgments of the Court of Justice.

With regard to enforcement, a closer cooperation between competition and data protection authorities is desirable in order to provide consumers with a more unified form of protection. To that end, Article 21(4) of the EU Merger Regulation could be interpreted in such a way as to give data protection authorities a legal ground to review proposed concentrations on the basis of their impact on data protection. Since EU data protection law does not provide for the possibility to adopt structural or prospective remedies, this provision does not make national data protection authorities competent to block mergers on the basis of data protection considerations or to impose remedies to address possible future data protection issues. However, the principle of accountability and the introduction of data protection impact assessments for risky processing activities in the General Data Protection Regulation may enable data protection authorities to take more proactive measures in the future even if a concrete violation of the EU data protection rules cannot yet be identified. In addition, the Commission could involve the competent national data protection authority in the implementation or even the monitoring of merger remedies which also affect data protection interests.

While there is scope for more collaboration between the two types of authorities, it should be kept in mind that competition and data protection law are distinct legal regimes having a different cause of concerns and requiring a specific kind of expertise. This implies that pure data protection issues should remain to be mainly addressed by the competent data protection authority. Nevertheless, considering that the use of personal data as an asset by market players may conflict with the data protection interests of individuals, it is submitted that the Commission has a certain level of responsibility to respect and promote the application of the right to data protection when acting in its capacity as a competition authority.

CHAPTER 11
Conclusion

11.1 THREEFOLD RELEVANCE OF DATA FOR COMPETITION POLICY

Against the background of the emergence of data as an asset for market players operating in the online environment, the relevance of data for competition enforcement is submitted to be threefold: (1) as personal data is replacing price as a currency on the internet, theories of harm relating to price may be converted to data; (2) data may constitute a necessary input for products and services to be introduced by competitors of incumbent providers of online platforms; and (3) by analysing data, an incumbent may be able to detect trends and changes in consumer preferences enabling it to develop new products and services possibly giving rise to new markets. Each of these possible roles of data in competition policy relates to one of the three parts of the book.

In the light of the value of data as an asset, the underlying objective of mergers and behaviour of dominant undertakings may be to collect additional information about consumers. Theories of harm applicable to firms operating in the digital economy should therefore consider the role of data. When it comes to personal data, not only the economic value for market players has to be taken into account but also the link with the right to data protection of individuals as protected by the European Convention on Human Rights and the EU Charter of Fundamental Rights as well as under EU secondary data protection legislation. In this context, the possible role of data protection considerations in merger review and abuse of dominance cases have been discussed in Part III.

Part II revolved around the issue of whether and to what extent data forms a necessary input for products and services to be launched by competitors of a dominant online platform provider. To answer this question, a normative analysis of the essential facilities doctrine has been undertaken resulting in a proposed framework which may lay the ground for a more coherent application of the doctrine in future cases.

In line with the role of data in identifying possible future products and services for which consumer demand exists, it has been proposed in Part I to take a more forward-looking approach to competition analysis in merger and abuse of dominance cases. In the context of market definition and the assessment of dominance relating to online platforms, it seems desirable to consider a form of potential competition whereby providers do not only compete in the relevant product markets for the specific services offered to users and advertisers but also in a broader market for data.

11.2 TWO GENERAL OBSERVATIONS

Two general observations can be made that are valid for all three parts of the book. As is outlined in more detail below, one can observe from the analysis in each part that existing competition concepts are still fit for purpose, provided that their application is adapted to the peculiarities of online platforms. Even though the necessary tools are available, competition authorities and courts have to be willing to employ them in such a way as to ensure that the competition analysis reflects the competitive reality of the markets in which providers of online platforms compete. For each dimension of the threefold relevance of data to competition enforcement, a lack of willingness can be identified on the part of the European Commission and the EU Courts to use existing concepts and tools in a way enabling them to reliably assess possible data-related competition issues. In this context, recommendations are provided to these institutions in the next sections for bringing the application of competition law in line with the demands of dynamic markets and for adequately protecting consumer welfare in the online environment.

While the book focuses on a specific issue that is at the heart of current competition law debates, the relevance of the analysis is not confined to the role of data in competition analysis. Broader insights can be obtained from each of the three parts that go beyond the particular setting of the book and that may still be relevant when the attention shifts to other competition issues. Against this background, the results from the analysis in the three parts of the book are presented in the following sections and put in a broader perspective by outlining their wider relevance for competition policy in general.

11.3 SUMMARISING THE RESULTS FROM THE ANALYSIS IN PART I

In Part I of the book, the economic characteristics of online platforms have been outlined with the aim of analysing how the existing competition concepts of market definition and dominance can be applied to online search engines, social networks and e-commerce platforms. Relevant economic characteristics include the multi-sided nature of the business models of currently predominant providers and network economy features such as economies of scale, network effects, switching costs and entry barriers. Another peculiarity of online platforms is that due to the fact that services are typically provided free of charge to users, innovation instead of price is the predominant parameter of competition. While online platforms raise new challenges for competition enforcement, the tools that are used to define relevant markets and to assess dominance are sufficiently apt to be adequately applied to these new services.

With regard to market definition, the approach of the Commission in the ongoing *Google* abuse of dominance investigation and the *Facebook/WhatsApp* merger to define separate relevant markets for the user and advertiser side of an online platform seems most appropriate. If only one relevant market for the entire platform would be defined, it is not possible to consider potential competitive constraints imposed by businesses that are not active on both sides of the platform but only compete with the provider on one side. One should note in this regard that multi-sided platforms may also compete with one-sided undertakings and with multi-sided businesses that have an overlap with the respective platform on only one side. These forms of competitive pressure can only be taken into account when defining separate relevant markets for the user and advertiser side of the platform.

Because of the fast-moving nature of competition in the online environment, market boundaries are under a constant rate of change. To reflect the dynamic process of competition in new economy industries, it would be desirable for competition authorities and courts to define relevant markets more loosely. Even though the European Commission and the General Court acknowledged in the *Microsoft/Skype* merger in the framework of online consumer communications services that potential competition forms a better indicator of dominance than market shares, such a willingness to apply existing competition concepts more in line with the dynamic nature of competition cannot be observed with regard to market definition. Statements made by the Commission in the context of the *Google* case and its merger decisions in *Microsoft/Yahoo*, *Microsoft/Skype* and *Facebook/WhatsApp* indicate that relevant product markets are still defined narrowly on the basis of the functionality offered to users.

A specific recommendation that has been made in Part I in this regard is for competition authorities and courts to define and analyse a potential market for data in addition to the narrow relevant product markets for the services provided to users and advertisers. This would result into a more forward-looking approach to competition analysis. By considering possible competitive constraints in a potential market for data, the significance of data for the development of new products and services can be taken into account. In this context, it is proposed to rely on the existing notion of competition in innovation as developed within the framework of Article 101 TFEU and to regard user data as a specialised asset in analogy to the EU Horizontal Guidelines. Even if user data is not traded to third parties and no supply and demand for data can be identified under current competition law standards, it is submitted that it would still be desirable for competition authorities and courts to define a potential market for data in order to make competition analysis more conducive to innovation.

The analysis of a potential market does not only seem desirable for data-related competition issues but also for other cases in the context of digital markets where market players experience competitive pressure beyond relevant markets for existing products and services. By defining relevant markets narrowly, the Commission implicitly chooses to favour sustaining innovation within existing markets over disruptive innovation in new markets. This while market players in the new economy typically compete by introducing new services instead of by substituting or improving existing services. Such a static approach therefore risks overlooking potential competitive constraints from related or future services. This can be overcome by defining a potential market in addition to the specific relevant product markets. Although this would require competition authorities and courts to go beyond current competition law standards in the sense that a market has to be defined in the absence of supply and demand, existing concepts used in the area of Article 101 TFEU could be relied upon. This way, a more dynamic approach towards competition analysis can be developed which better reflects the competitive reality of current digital markets.

11.4 SUMMARISING THE RESULTS FROM THE ANALYSIS IN PART II

As a new tool for data subjects to exercise effective control over their personal data in the online environment, the right to data portability as introduced in the General Data Protection Regulation is to be welcomed. While this new right may also impact the level of competition in the market, potential competitors and new entrants will still have to rely on competition law in order to get access to data of an incumbent online platform provider. In Part II, two scenarios have been distinguished with regard to refusals to give access to data on online platforms. The usual scenario in essential facilities cases concerns the situation in which a market player needs access to an input for a product or service to be launched in a downstream market. An example in the context of online platforms would be the use of data for the introduction of a statistical or analytics service. The other scenario would involve the use of data as an input to launch a form of direct competition with the dominant firm and to provide a rival search, social network or e-commerce platform to users and advertisers.

It is submitted that competition authorities and courts have to make a trade-off between competition *for* and competition *in* the market when deciding whether to impose a duty to deal under the essential facilities doctrine. Competition *in* the market comprises competition on the basis of price and output in established markets, whereas competition *for* the market attacks existing market structures and leads to the development of new markets. Although innovation is a complex process that may have unpredictable outcomes, competition *for* the market is generally argued to provide stronger incentives for disruptive innovation, whereas competition *in* the market primarily stimulates sustaining innovation.

The trade-off to be made in essential facilities cases amounts to a choice between giving competitors access to the required input, which would enable them to create products complementary to that of the dominant firm, or denying access as a result of which competitors would be mainly incentivised to develop substitutes competing with the product of the dominant firm. While the first option provides stronger incentives for competition *in* the market and sustaining innovation, the second option will primarily stimulate competition *for* the market and disruptive innovation. Considering that both types of competition and innovation bring value to society albeit in a different way, the decision to give preference to one over the other amounts to a policy issue.

The framework proposed in Part II aims to contribute to the state of the art by providing a way to apply this economic trade-off in practice and to make the application of the essential facilities doctrine more coherent. Taking the trade-off fully into account would require a tool that differentiates on the basis of the type of competition or innovation that is at risk in a particular market situation. The new product requirement is by its very nature capable of implementing such an exercise under the essential facilities doctrine because it determines what level of innovativeness the product or service to be introduced by the access seeker has to bring about. Even though the new product condition forms an adequate tool to make the trade-off between competition *for* and competition *in* the market more transparent in essential facilities cases, the Commission and the EU Courts have so far been unwilling to explicitly consider incentives for competition *for* the market in decisions and judgments. While it is a valid choice of the Commission and the EU Courts to favour competition *in* the market, this does not mean that incentives for competition *for* the market should be disregarded. In order to make the trade-off visible, it is submitted that incentives for competition *for* the market should be openly analysed in essential facilities cases even if preference is given to competition *in* the market.

In this context, an adapted version of the new product condition has been put forward that accounts for differences in market characteristics. Instead of distinguishing between whether assets are protected by intellectual property law or not, the proposed framework suggests to let the applicability of the new product condition depend on whether a market is characterised by external market failures. External market failures such as the presence of strong network effects and switching costs, which to a certain extent also characterise the markets in which online search engines, social networks and e-commerce platforms operate, could make it commercially unviable for competitors to introduce a new product. If, for instance, consumers are locked-in to a particular standard, a requirement that access seekers have to introduce a new product is of no relevance because consumers are not willing to switch to a different system. It is important to note that external market failures may enable the incumbent to extend its dominance in time irrespective of whether the requested input is protected under intellectual property law. Since there is no convincing economic rationale for treating intellectual property rights differently than other types of assets under the essential facilities doctrine, it is proposed to focus instead on the presence of external market failures as a way to determine whether the new product condition should be met in order to hold a refusal to deal abusive under Article 102 TFEU.

Considering that a competition law intervention cannot re-establish the race for competition *for* the market, caution is warranted in markets in which external market failures are absent. In these markets, the new product condition should be applied strictly because of the stronger self-correcting mechanism of the market. As a result, a competition law intervention to encourage competition *in* the market risks unnecessarily lowering incentives for competition *for* the market in this situation. Incentives for competition *for* the market are best preserved by avoiding government interference in the market and thereby maintaining the prospect of dominance for new entrants. In markets where external market failures are present, the new product requirement should be dropped to ensure that access seekers planning to introduce competition *in* the market by introducing sustaining innovations or products similar to that of the dominant undertaking can gain access to the necessary input. In these markets, there is a higher risk that the incumbent is able to extend its dominance in time and to prevent competitors from entering the market and competing on the basis price or quality which justifies a wider scope of liability for refusals to deal under Article 102 TFEU. Therefore, if the market is locked-in due to the presence of strong network effects or switching costs and the essential facility holder has had a stable dominant position for some time, competition authorities should be able to impose a duty to deal even if the access seeker is not able to indicate a new product that it would like to introduce once given access to the requested input. This provided that the other conditions of the essential facilities doctrine are met which require, respectively: indispensability of the requested input, exclusion of all effective competition on the downstream market and absence of an objective justification.

When assessing the abusive nature of refusals to give access to data, attention has to be paid to the characteristics which set data apart from other assets previously being considered under the essential facilities doctrine. These features include its inherently non-rivalrous nature which may, however, be lost when the data is made exclusive by way of contracts or by protecting it under the sui generis database right and trade secret law, and the possible personal nature of data as a result of which the EU data protection regime would become applicable.

One of the main issues for the application of the essential facilities doctrine will be to establish the indispensable nature of the requested data. In this regard, the question has to be answered whether the data is objectively necessary for being able to compete on the downstream market and whether economically viable substitutes are available. Even though the statements of the Commission in the *Google/DoubleClick*, *Telefónica/Vodafone/Everything Everywhere* and *Facebook/WhatsApp* mergers may indicate that data of incumbents will not easily be considered indispensable for providing targeted advertising services, this may be different with regard to the use of data for offering services of good quality to users in the form of, for example, the relevance of search results in online search engines, suggested social network interactions and purchase suggestions in e-commerce platforms. For the provision of these functionalities to users, a specific type of data is needed that may not be readily available on the market. For example, if the specific data needed to operate a search engine of good quality can only be obtained through serving customers, other data that is available from third parties will not form an adequate substitute for the search data of the incumbent search engine provider. With regard to the economic viability of duplication of the required data, the interventions by the French and Belgian competition authorities in, respectively, the national energy and lottery markets are instructive. Both national competition cases concerned the cross-use of data developed in the context of a monopoly and therefore do not have much similarity to a factual scenario centring around data gathered by a provider of an online platform. Nevertheless, the reference made by both competition authorities to reasonable financial conditions and a reasonable period of time when assessing the possibility for competitors to reproduce a database may also be of relevance when assessing the economic viability of duplication in the context of the indispensability of a dataset in the online environment.

As an answer to the main research question, it can be concluded from the analysis in Part II that the essential facilities doctrine can be adequately applied to potential refusals to give access to data on online platforms as long as the peculiarities of data are taken into account. Whether new regulation is necessary beyond the application of the essential facilities doctrine under Article 102 TFEU, is essentially a policy issue. A regulatory intervention may be considered desirable in situations where horizontal competition in a market is limited due to external market failures. Reference can be made here to Argenton & Prüfer's proposal to require all search engine providers to share data on search queries so that market players only compete with their algorithms and not on the basis of the information they hold about previous searches on their platform.[1423] It would, however, be challenging to adequately devise such a new form of regulation. Apart from any problems relating to the practical implementation and enforcement of such an obligation, it may prove difficult to establish to which entities the duty to share data should apply. In this regard, it has to be kept in mind that search functionality also plays a role in social networks. E-commerce platforms, in their turn, can be regarded as vertical search engines. As a result, it seems arbitrary to limit the scope of application of a potential data-sharing scheme to a particular class of market players. In addition, the expected short-term increase of competition in the market has to be weighed against possible negative effects of a regulatory intervention on competition and innovation in the long term. Moreover, there are strong reasons to adhere to the case-by-case assessment under Article 102 TFEU. In particular, the application of the essential facilities doctrine enables competition authorities and courts to take into account all specific factual circumstances. Since the extent to which data may constitute a competitive advantage or an entry barrier differs depending on the particular setting, it is difficult to make generalisations about the circumstances in which data should be shared with competitors. While data may be an important input of production that cannot be easily duplicated in some scenarios, the assessment may be different in other situations where data cannot be made exclusive.

With regard to possible limitations that data protection legislation puts to the mandated sharing of data with third parties under Article 102 TFEU, it should be noted that, in principle, a competition law obligation in itself constitutes a legitimate ground for processing of personal data under the EU data protection regime. Any remaining potential conflicts between competition and data protection law can be adequately addressed by requiring the dominant firm to implement appropriate data protection safeguards in the form of specifying the new purpose of the processing activities, obtaining renewed consent from affected data subjects or through the anonymisation of personal data.

Even though Part II focuses on refusals to deal as a specific type of behaviour of dominant firms, several elements of the analysis have a wider relevance. In particular, the way the relevant market for data is defined and dominance is assessed in essential facilities cases may illustrate how a competition analysis of a potential market for data in other abuse and merger cases in the online environment, as proposed in Part I, can be undertaken. After the introduction of the concept of hypothetical or potential markets by the Court of Justice in *IMS Health*, it is not necessary anymore for the

---

1423. C. ARGENTON AND J. PRÜFER, 'Search Engine Competition with Network Externalities', *Journal of Competition Law and Economics* 2012, vol. 8, no. 1, (73), p. 91. See also section 7.7.3 above.

application of the essential facilities doctrine that the requested input is already traded as an independent product by the dominant undertaking. In such cases where the alleged essential facility has not been marketed before, market definition amounts to a normative decision about how the market should look and does not reflect 'real' supply and demand of products and services. Such a hypothetical or potential market for data, in essential facilities as well as in other abuse and merger cases, can be defined by looking at the substitutability of different types of data and in particular at the functionality which can be offered with a specific set of data as input. In this way, separate relevant markets can possibly be defined for offline and online data and, as further sub-segmentations within the latter market, for search, social network and e-commerce data. As regards market power in data, one needs to find an objective manner to attribute value to data. The turnover generated by a provider through the monetisation of data by licensing information to third parties, delivering targeted advertising services or offering other paid products and services to customers on the basis of the collected data, may form an indication of its competitive strength in a potential market for a particular type of data. In the absence of any data-related revenues, potential competition may form an adequate proxy for dominance in relevant markets defined around data.

The relevance of the analysis relating to the economic trade-off between competition *for* and competition *in* the market also extends beyond the specific setting of the essential facilities doctrine. One could argue that, to some extent, competition authorities have to make a choice between encouraging competition *for* or competition *in* the market when determining whether to intervene in a market to remedy other types of exclusionary conduct under Article 102 TFEU as well. Enforcement actions against tying or bundling strategies of dominant firms, for example, also have as their objective to restore competition *in* the market but may at the same time reduce incentives for competition *for* the market by taking away the prospect of dominance for new entrants. In this regard, the existence of external market failures could also form a guiding principle for determining the scope for competition law liability in other abuse of dominance cases.

11.5 SUMMARISING THE RESULTS FROM THE ANALYSIS IN PART III

Part III of the book revolved around the role of data protection interests in competition enforcement. The relevance of data protection for competition enforcement started to gain attention in the context of the *Google/DoubleClick* merger in 2007 which led to the combination of information from Google on users' search behaviour with information from DoubleClick on users' web-browsing behaviour. The current interest from data protection advocates in competition enforcement seems to stem from the concentrated nature of online markets which may reduce possibilities for users to exercise effective control over their personal data. The application of key data protection concepts such as consent is difficult in concentrated markets where undertakings may be able to impose their practices on individuals. One should note, however, that the application of competition law is only triggered in case of a real, identified competition problem. A high level of concentration in itself does not form a reason for competition authorities to intervene in a market.

Considering that differences in data protection standards among EU Member States may lead to a distortion of competition within the internal market, the possible role of the new General Data Protection Regulation in achieving a better level playing field in the EU is worthy of attention. By posing limits to the freedom of market players to collect and use personal data as they deem fit, data protection regulation may also have a competitive impact. Even though the new data protection rules are contained in a Regulation and will therefore be directly applicable without the need for national implementing legislation, the General Data Protection Regulation leaves room for interpretation and additional legislation at the national level which may give rise to fragmentation between Member States. Because of its responsibility in ensuring the uniformity in the application of EU data protection law, the functioning of the future European Data Protection Board seems of vital importance in this regard. The main difference with the enforcement of EU competition law will persist under the General Data Protection Regulation, namely that the European Commission does not have the competence to act under EU data protection law. While the European Data Protection Board, in which the Commission is involved without having a voting right, can take binding decisions in case of disagreement between national data protection authorities, the adoption of the final decisions as addressed to controllers and their enforcement will continue to take place at the national level.

When considering whether data protection may constitute a non-price parameter of competition, it is submitted that a difference should be made between situations in which data protection forms an isolated aspect of quality and situations in which data protection correlates with price and other aspects of quality. In the latter case, it is not desirable to regard data protection as a dimension of quality in competition analysis because a stronger level of data protection is not necessarily valued by all consumers. This is particularly the case for online search engines, social networks and e-commerce platforms where the level of data protection, on the one hand, and the price as well as the relevance and personalisation of the services, on the other hand, are traded off against each other. Data protection can still be integrated in competition analysis as a non-price parameter of competition in these industries by treating it as a form of consumer choice or product variety instead of as a dimension of quality.

While data protection can be integrated as a non-price parameter of competition in the usual competition analysis if it is a key dimension of competition in the market, a more controversial question is whether data protection should be protected as a non-efficiency concern under competition law. Despite calls from data protection advocates, including the EDPS, for a greater role of data protection considerations in competition cases, the European Commission and the Court of Justice have so far been reluctant to integrate data protection into competition analysis as a non-efficiency concern. In *Asnef-Equifax*, the Court of Justice stated that issues relating to the sensitivity of personal data are not a matter for competition law as such. In its *Google/DoubleClick* and *Facebook/WhatsApp* merger decisions, the Commission made clear that its analysis was without prejudice to the obligations imposed on the parties by data protection legislation and that privacy-related concerns do not fall within the scope of EU competition law.

Considering the status of data protection as a fundamental right in the EU legal order as protected by the EU Charter of Fundamental Rights, it is submitted that data protection deserves greater consideration in competition analysis than the way the Commission has occasionally addressed other non-efficiency concerns in competition cases. In this regard, a three-layer approach has been put forward for integrating data protection interests in EU competition policy. First, by adopting remedies to address economic efficiency concerns, competition enforcement may at the same time achieve results that also foster data protection interests. For example, by blocking a merger or by imposing merger remedies to address economic efficiency concerns, a competition authority can also prevent that personal data is processed for incompatible purposes after the merger. Second, competition authorities are under a negative duty to respect the right to data protection in terms of procedural safeguards to be followed in competition investigations and as regards the substance of competition law measures that can be adopted. Third, competition authorities are subject to a positive duty to promote the application of the right to data protection in line with Article 51(1) of the EU Charter of Fundamental Rights in cases where a breach of the competition rules is identified. While competition authorities cannot and should not use their competences to promote data protection interests if no violation of the competition rules can be found, there is scope for the Commission to take a more proactive approach in particular in the context of merger and commitment proceedings. In these cases, undertakings find themselves at the mercy of the Commission to approve a merger or to abstain from adopting a prohibition decision for a breach of Article 101 or 102 TFEU. This position gives the Commission room to demand measures that do not only end the competitive harm identified and restore competition but also facilitate the effectiveness of the right to data protection in a way that might otherwise not have been possible under EU data protection law.

The three-layer approach may not only have relevance for the right to data protection but also for the other fundamental rights contained in the EU Charter of Fundamental Rights. In this regard, data protection may form a case study of how the European Commission and national competition authorities can take the protection of fundamental rights into consideration when enforcing EU competition law. Even though the Commission and the Court of Justice have until now been unwilling to do so, the EU Charter provides these institutions with the opportunity to take a more coherent approach towards the protection of the interests of individuals by creating room for the integration of fundamental rights in EU policies including competition policy. Considering the elevation of the EU Charter to a source of primary EU law with the entry into force of the Lisbon Treaty, one could argue that the EU institutions do not only have the ability but even a legally binding obligation to promote the application of the fundamental rights contained in the EU Charter when acting in the field of EU competition law.

11.6 OUTLOOK

The fact that the European Commission and the EU Courts have so far been unwilling to make use of the available means to adequately adapt the application of competition law to the realities of online and, more generally, dynamic markets is especially problematic in a time where competition enforcement in this sector is experiencing increasing political pressure. In the context of the *Google* investigation, reference can be made to the resolution on the digital single market that the European Parliament adopted in November 2014 calling upon the Commission '*to enforce EU competition rules decisively*' and '*to consider proposals aimed at unbundling search engines from other commercial services*'.[1424] In addition, within the framework of the Digital Single Market Strategy of the Commission, the introduction of regulation for online platforms beyond the application of competition law in specific cases is currently being considered.[1425]

Against this background, the need for competition authorities and courts to use existing competition concepts and tools in a way conforming to the demands of new market developments seems pressing. More transparency about how competition law is applied could help making politicians and policymakers aware of the trade-off that has to be made when deciding whether or not to intervene in a particular market. Even though regulation may increase competition and innovation in the short term, possible economic effects on the long term should also be considered. Since politicians and policymakers are inherently more incentivised to address short-term concerns leading to observable results more quickly, it is all the more important to raise attention for how a regulatory intervention may negatively affect the innovation incentives of the targeted incumbents as well as of other market players in the long term. The analysis involving the economic trade-off between competition *for* and competition *in* the market in essential facilities cases can thereby also provide input for the broader policy debate on openness in digital markets in general.

With regard to the integration of data protection interests in competition cases, it would be beneficial for the democratic legitimacy of competition enforcement to give more consideration to data protection in competition analysis. By going beyond strictly protecting economic efficiency concerns, criticisms can be addressed that competition law ignores other dimensions of consumer welfare. In addition, such an approach

---

1424. European Parliament resolution of 27 November 2014 on supporting consumer rights in the digital single market, 2014/2973(RSP), par. 15, available at http://www.europarl.europa.eu/sides/getDoc.do?pubRef = -//EP//TEXT + TA + P8-TA-2014-0071 + 0 + DOC + XML + V0//EN.
1425. A public consultation on the regulatory environment for platforms, online intermediaries, data and cloud computing and the collaborative economy was launched in September 2015 and closed in January 2016. See the Synopsis Report on the public consultation on the Regulatory environment for Platforms, Online Intermediaries and the Collaborative Economy, 25 May 2016, available at https://ec.europa.eu/digital-single-market/en/news/full-report-results-public-consultation-regulatory-environment-platforms-online-intermediaries and the Communication from the Commission to the European Parliament, the Council, the European Economic and Social Committee and the Committee of the Regions. Online Platforms and the Digital Single Market. Opportunities and Challenges for Europe, COM(2016) 288 final, 25 May 2016.

would give consumers a more integrated form of protection in a time where there is a need for a coherent enforcement of EU law. Competition authorities and courts should be prepared to tackle mergers and behaviour of market players that transcend narrow relevant product markets and blur the boundaries between distinct legal fields. A more dynamic competition analysis and a wider interpretation of the scope of protection offered by the competition rules are vital to adequately protect the interests of consumers in the digital economy.

Bibliography

Books

BAUMOL, W.J., PANZAR, J.C. AND WILLIG, R.D., *Contestable Markets and the Theory of Industry Structure*, Harcourt Brace Jovanovich, 1982.

BORK, R.H., *The Antitrust Paradox. A Policy at War with Itself*, The Free Press, 1993.

BROWN, I. AND MARSDEN, C.T., *Regulating Code: Good Governance and Better Regulation in the Information Age*, MIT Press, 2013.

CHRISTENSEN, C.M., *The Innovator's Dilemma. When New Technologies Cause Great Firms to Fail*, Boston, Harvard Business School Press, 1997.

CHRISTENSEN, C.M. AND RAYNOR, M.E., *The Innovator's Solution: Creating and Sustaining Successful Growth*, Harvard Business School Press, 2003.

COATES, K., *Competition Law and Regulation of Technology Markets*, Oxford University Press, 2011.

EUROPEAN UNION AGENCY FOR FUNDAMENTAL RIGHTS AND COUNCIL OF EUROPE, *Handbook on European Data Protection Law*, 2014, available at http://www.echr.coe.int/Documents/Handbook_data_protection_ENG.pdf.

FERRETTI, F., *EU Competition Law, the Consumer Interest and Data Protection. The Exchange of Consumer Information in the Retail Financial Sector*, Springer, 2014.

FREEMAN, C., *Technology and Economic Performance: Lessons from Japan*, Pinter, 1987.

GERBER, D.J., *Law and Competition in Twentieth Century Europe: Protecting Prometheus*, Clarendon Press, 1998.

KÄSEBERG, T., *Intellectual Property, Antitrust and Cumulative Innovation in the EU and the US*, Hart Publishing, 2012.

KOSTA, E., *Consent in European Data Protection Law*, Martinus Nijhoff Publishers, 2013.

LAROUCHE, P., *Competition Law and Regulation in European Telecommunications*, Hart Publishing, 2000.

LUNDVALL, B.-Å. (ed.), *National Innovation Systems: Towards a Theory of Innovation and Interactive Learning*, Pinter, 1992.

MAYER-SCHÖNBERGER, V. AND CUKIER, K., *Big Data: A Revolution That Will Transform How We Live, Work and Think*, John Murray, 2013.

MOTTA, M., *Competition Policy. Theory and Practice*, Cambridge University Press, 2004.

NAZZINI, R., *The Foundations of European Union Competition Law. The Objective and Principles of Article 102*, Oxford University Press, 2011.

NEALE, A.D., *The Antitrust Laws of the United States*, 2nd edn, 1970.

ORGANISATION FOR ECONOMIC CO-OPERATION AND DEVELOPMENT (OECD), *Supporting Investment in Knowledge Capital, Growth and Innovation*, OECD Publishing, 2013.

PALFREY, J. AND GASSER, U., *Interop: The Promise and Perils of Highly Interconnected Systems*, Basic Books, 2012.

PURTOVA, N., *Property Rights in Personal Data. A European Perspective* in HUGENHOLTZ, P.B. (ed.) *Information Law Series*, Kluwer Law International, 2011.

ROUSSEVA, E., *Rethinking Exclusionary Abuses in EU Competition Law*, Hart Publishing, 2010.

SCHUMPETER, J.A., *Capitalism, Socialism and Democracy*, Routledge, 1942 (version published in 2003).

SHAPIRO, C. AND VARIAN, H.R., *Information Rules. A Strategic Guide to the Network Economy*, Harvard Business School Press, 1999.

SHY, O., *The Economics of Network Industries*, Cambridge University Press, 2001.

STIGLER, G.J., *The Theory of Price*, Macmillan 1966.

STIGLER, G.J., *The Organization of Industry*, Richard D. Irwin, 1968.

SURBLYTE, G., *The Refusal to Disclose Trade Secrets as an Abuse of Market Dominance - Microsoft and Beyond* in DREXL, J. (ed.) *Munich Series on European and International Competition Law*, 28, Berne Stämpfli Publishers Ltd., 2011.

TIROLE, J., *The Theory of Industrial Organization*, MIT Press, 1988.

TOWNLEY, C., *Article 81 EC and the Public Policy*, Hart Publishing, 2009.

VAN ROMPUY, B., *Economic Efficiency: The Sole Concern of Modern Antitrust Policy? Non-efficiency Considerations under Article 101 TFEU* in SUTTON, A. (ed.) *International Competition Law Series*, Wolters Kluwer, 2012.

VAN ROOIJEN, A., *The Software Interface Between Copyright and Competition Law. A Legal Analysis of Interoperability in Computer Programs* in HUGENHOLTZ, P.B. (ed.) *Information Law Series*, Kluwer Law International 2010.

WESTIN, A.F., *Privacy and Freedom*, Atheneum, 1967.

ZIMMER, D. (ed.), *The Goals of Competition Law*, Edward Elgar, 2012.

Articles and Book Chapters

ABRAHAMSON, Z., 'Essential Data', *The Yale Law Journal* 2014, vol. 124, no. 3, 867-881.

ACQUISTI, A., BRANDIMARTE, L. AND LOEWENSTEIN, G., 'Privacy and Human Behavior in the Age of Information', *Science* 2015, vol. 347, no. 6221, 509-514.

ACQUISTI, A., TAYLOR, C. AND WAGMAN, L., 'The Economics of Privacy', *Journal of Economic Literature* 2016, vol. 54, no. 2, pp. 442-492.

AGHION, P., BLOOM, N., BLUNDELL, R., ET AL., 'Competition and Innovation: An Inverted-U Relationship', *Quarterly Journal of Economics* 2005, vol. 120, no. 2, 701-728.

AGHION, P., BLUNDELL, R., GRIFFITH, R., ET AL., 'The Effects of Entry on Incumbent Innovation and Productivity', *The Review of Economics and Statistics* February 2009, vol. 91, no. 1, 20-32.

AGHION, P., HARRIS, C., HOWITT, P., ET AL., 'Competition, Imitation and Growth with Step-by-Step Innovation', *Review of Economic Studies* 2001, vol. 68, no. 3, 467-492.

AHLBORN, C., EVANS, D.S. AND PADILLA, A.J., 'Competition Policy in the New Economy: Is European Competition Law Up to the Challenge?', *European Competition Law Review* 2001, vol. 22, no. 5, 156-167.

AHLBORN, C., EVANS, D.S. AND PADILLA, A.J., 'The Logic & Limits of the "Exceptional Circumstances Test" in *Magill* and *IMS Health*', *Fordham International Law Journal* 2004-2005, vol. 28, no. 4, 1109-1156.

ALEXANDROV, A., DELTAS, G. AND SPULBER, D.F., 'Antitrust And Competition In Two-Sided Markets', *Journal of Competition Law and Economics* 2011, vol. 7, no. 4, 775-812.

ANDREANGELI, A., 'Interoperability as an "Essential Facility" in the Microsoft Case - Encouraging Competition or Stifling Innovation?', *European Law Review* 2009, vol. 34, no. 4, 584-611.

AREEDA, P., 'Essential Facilities: An Epithet in Need of Limiting Principles', *Antitrust Law Journal* 1989, vol. 58, no. 3, 841-853.

ARGENTON, C. AND PRÜFER, J., 'Search Engine Competition with Network Externalities', *Journal of Competition Law and Economics* 2012, vol. 8, no. 1, 73-105.

ARIÑO, M., 'Competition Law and Pluralism in European Digital Broadcasting: Addressing the Gaps', *Communications & Strategies* 2004, vol. 54, 97-128.

ARMSTRONG, M., 'Competition in Two-Sided Markets', *RAND Journal of Economics* 2006, vol. 37, no. 3, 668-691.

ARMSTRONG, M. AND VICKERS, J., 'Competitive Price Discrimination', *RAND Journal of Economics* 2001, vol. 32, no. 4, 1-27.

ARROW, K.J., 'Economic Welfare and the Allocation of Resources for Invention' in GROVES, H.M. (ed.), *The Rate and Direction of Inventive Activity: Economic and Social Factors*, National Bureau of Economic Research, 1962, 609-626.

AUER, D. AND PETIT, N., 'Two-Sided Markets and the Challenge of Turning Economic Theory into Antitrust Policy', *The Antitrust Bulletin* 2015, vol. 60, no. 4, 426-461.

BAIN, J.S., *Barriers to New Competition: Their Character and Consequences in Manufacturing Industries*, Harvard University Press, 1956.

BAKER, J.B., 'Beyond Schumpeter vs. Arrow: How Antitrust Fosters Innovation', *Antitrust Law Journal* 2007, vol. 74, no. 3, 575-602.

BALTO, D.A. AND LANE, M.C., 'Monopolizing Water in a Tsunami: Finding Sensible Antitrust Rules for Big Data', *SSRN Working Paper March 2016* available at http://papers.ssrn.com/sol3/papers.cfm?abstract_id=2753249.

BAUMOL, W.J., 'Contestable Markets: An Uprising in the Theory of Industry Structure', *American Economic Review* 1982, vol. 72, no. 1, 1-15.

BERNERS-LEE, T., 'Long Live the Web: A Call for Continued Open Standards and Neutrality', *Scientific American* December 2010, vol. 303, no. 6, 80-85.

BÖHM, F., EUCKEN, W. AND GROSSMANN-DOERTH, H., 'The Ordo Manifesto of 1936' in PEACOCK, A. AND WILLGERODT, H. (eds.), *Germany's Social Market Economy: Origins and Evolution*, MacMillan, 1989, 15-26.

BOONE, J., 'A New Way to Measure Competition', *The Economic Journal* 2008, vol. 118, no. 531, 1245-1261.

BORK, R.H. AND SIDAK, J.G., 'What Does the Chicago School Teach About Internet Search and the Antitrust Treatment of Google?', *Journal of Competition Law and Economics* 2012, vol. 8, no. 4, 663-700.

BOWER, J.L. AND CHRISTENSEN, C.M., 'Disruptive Technologies: Catching the Wave', *Harvard Business Review* 1995, vol. 73, no. 1 (January-February), 43-53.

BOYD, D.M. AND ELLISON, N.B., 'Social Network Sites: Definition, History, and Scholarship', *Journal of Computer-Mediated Communication* 2008, vol. 13, no. 1, 210-230.

BRACHA, O. AND PASQUALE, F., 'Federal Search Commission? Access, Fairness, and Accountability in the Law of Search', *Cornell Law Review* 2008, vol. 93, no. 6, 1149-1210.

BRESNAHAN, T.F., 'The Mechanisms of Information Technology's Contribution to Economic Growth' in TOUFFUT, J.P. (ed.), *Institutions, Innovation and Growth. Selected Economic Papers*, Edward Elgar Publishing, 2003, 116-141.

BRILL, J., 'The Intersection of Consumer Protection and Competition in the New World of Privacy', *Competition Policy International* 2011, vol. 7, no. 1, 7-23.

BRIN, S. AND PAGE, L., 'The Anatomy of a Large-Scale Hypertextual Web Search Engine', 8 Appendix A, available at http://infolab.stanford.edu/pub/papers/google.pdf.

BRODER, A., 'A Taxonomy of Web Search', *Special Interest Group on Information Retrieval (SIGIR) Forum* 2002, vol. 36, no. 2, 3-10.

BROOS, S. AND MARCOS RAMOS, J., 'Google, Google Shopping and Amazon: The Importance of Competing Business Models and Two-Sided Intermediaries in Defining Relevant Markets', *SSRN Working Paper* November 2015, available at http://papers.ssrn.com/sol3/papers.cfm?abstract_id = 2696045.

BURNSIDE, A.J., 'No Such Thing as a Free Search: Antitrust and the Pursuit of Privacy Goals', *CPI Antitrust Chronicle* 2015, vol. 5, no. 2, 1-8.

BUTTS, C., 'The Microsoft Case 10 Years Later: Antitrust and New Leading "New Economy" Firms', *Northwestern Journal of Technology and Intellectual Property* Spring 2010, vol. 8, no. 2, 275-291.

CAILLAUD, B. AND JULLIEN, B., 'Competing Cybermediaries', *European Economic Review* 2001, vol. 45, no. 4-6, 797-808.

CAILLAUD, B. AND JULLIEN, B., 'Chicken & Egg: Competition among Intermediation Service Providers', *RAND Journal of Economics* 2003, vol. 34, no. 2, 309-328.

CANNARELLA, J. AND SPECHLER, J.A., 'Epidemiological Modeling of Online Social Network Dynamics', *ArXiv* 2013, 1-11.

CARLTON, D.W., 'A General Analysis of Exclusionary Conduct and Refusal to Deal - Why *Aspen* and *Kodak* are Misguided', *Antitrust Law Journal* 2001, vol. 68, no. 3, 659-683.

CARRIER, M.A., 'Refusals to License Intellectual Property after *Trinko*', *DePaul Law Review* 2006, vol. 55, no. 4, 1191-1209.

CASADESUS-MASANELL, R. AND HERVAS-DRANE, A., 'Competing with Privacy', *Harvard Business School Working Paper 13-085* October 2013, available at http://www.hbs.edu/faculty/Publication%20Files/13-085_95c71478-a439-4c00-b1dd-f9d963b99c34.pdf.

CAUWELS, P. AND SORNETTE, D., 'Quis Pendit Ipsa Pretia: Facebook Valuation and Diagnostic of a Bubble Based on Nonlinear Demographic Dynamics', *The Journal of Portfolio Management* 2012, vol. 38, no. 2, 56-66.

CHIRITA, A.D., 'Google's Anti-Competitive and Unfair Practices in Digital Leisure Markets', *The Competition Law Review* 2015, vol. 11, no. 1, 109-131.

COASE, R.H., 'The Problem of Social Cost', *The Journal of Law & Economics* October 1960, vol. 3, 1-44.

CONDE GALLEGO, B., 'Unilateral Refusal to License Indispensable Intellectual Property Rights – US and EU Approaches' in DREXL, J. (ed.), *Research Handbook on Intellectual Property and Competition Law*, Cheltenham, Edward Elgar Publishing, 2008, 215-238.

COOPER, J.C., 'Privacy and Antitrust: Underpants Gnomes, the First Amendment, and Subjectivity', *George Mason Law Review* 2013, vol. 20, no. 4, 1129-1146.

COSTA-CABRAL, F. AND LYNSKEY, O., 'The Internal and External Constraints of Data Protection on Competition Law in the EU', *LSE Law, Society and Economy Working Papers 25/2015* 2015, available at http://papers.ssrn.com/sol3/papers.cfm?abstract_id = 2703655.

DAVISON, M.J. AND HUGENHOLTZ, P.B., 'Football Fixtures, Horseraces and Spin Offs: The ECJ Domesticates the Database Right', *European Intellectual Property Review* 2005, vol. 27, no. 3, 113-118.

DERCLAYE, E., 'Abuses of Dominant Position and Intellectual Property Rights: A Suggestion to Reconcile the Community Courts Case Law', *World Competition* 2003, vol. 26, no. 4, 685-705.

DERCLAYE, E., 'Databases Sui Generis Right: Should We Adopt the Spin-Off Theory?', *European Intellectual Property Review* 2004, vol. 26, no. 9, 402-413.

DERCLAYE, E., 'The Court of Justice Interprets the Database Sui Generis Right for the First Time', *European Law Review* 2005, vol. 30, no. 3, 420-430.

DEVINE, K.L., 'Preserving Competition in Multi-Sided Innovative Markets: How Do You Solve a Problem Like Google?', *North Carolina Journal of Law & Technology* 2008, vol. 10, no. 1, 59-117.

DOHERTY, B., 'Just What Are Essential Facilities', *Common Market Law Review* 2001, vol. 38, no. 2, 397-436.

DREXL, J., 'IMS Health and Trinko - Antitrust Placebo for Consumers Instead of Sound Economics in Refusal-to-Deal Cases', *International Review of Intellectual Property and Competition Law* 2004, vol. 35, no. 7, 788-808.

DREXL, J., 'Abuse of Dominance in Licensing and Refusal to License: A "More Economic Approach" to Competition by Imitation and to Competition by Substitution' in EHLERMANN, C.D. AND ATANASIU, I. (eds.), *European Competition Law Annual 2005: The Interaction between Competition Law and Intellectual Property Law*, Hart Publishing, 2007, 647-664.

DREXL, J., 'Refusal to Grant Access to Trade Secrets as an Abuse of Market Dominance' in ANDERMAN, S. AND EZRACHI, A. (eds.), *Intellectual Property and Competition Law. New Frontiers*, Oxford University Press, 2011, 165-185.

381

DREXL, J., 'Anticompetitive Stumbling Stones on the Way to a Cleaner World: Protecting Competition in Innovation Without a Market', *Journal of Competition Law and Economics* 2012, vol. 8, no. 3, 507-543.

DUNNE, N., 'Commitment Decisions in EU Competition Law', *Journal of Competition Law and Economics* 2014, vol. 10, no. 2, 399-444.

EASTERBROOK, F., 'The Limits of Antitrust', *Texas Law Review* 1984, vol. 63, no. 1.

ECONOMIDES, N., 'The Economics of Networks', *International Journal of Industrial Organization* 1996, vol. 14, no. 6, 673-699.

EDLIN, A.S. AND HARRIS, R.G., 'The Role of Switching Costs in Antitrust Analysis: A Comparison of Microsoft and Google', *Yale Journal of Law and Technology* 2013, vol. 15, 169-213.

ELHAUGE, E., 'Defining Better Monopolization Standards', *Stanford Law Review* 2003, vol. 56, no. 2, 253-344.

EVANS, D.S., 'The Antitrust Economics of Multi-Sided Platform Markets', *Yale Journal on Regulation* 2003, vol. 20, no. 2, 325-381.

EVANS, D.S., 'Competition and Regulatory Policy for Multi-Sided Platforms with Applications to the Web Economy', *SSRN Working Paper* March 2008, available at http://papers.ssrn.com/sol3/papers.cfm?abstract_id = 1090368.

EVANS, D.S., 'The Economics of the Online Advertising Industry', *Review of Network Economics* September 2008, vol. 7, no. 3, 359-391.

EVANS, D.S., 'Antitrust Issues Raised by the Emerging Global Internet Economy', *Northwestern University Law Review Colloquy* 2008, vol. 102, 285-306.

EVANS, D.S., 'The Online Advertising Industry: Economics, Evolution, and Privacy', *Journal of Economic Perspectives* 2009, vol. 23, no. 3, 37-60.

EVANS, D.S., 'The Antitrust Economics of Free', *Competition Policy International* 20 May 2011, vol. 7, available at http://papers.ssrn.com/sol3/papers.cfm?abstract_id = 1813193.

EVANS, D.S., 'Two-Sided Markets', in *Market Definition in Antitrust. Theory and Case Studies*, ABA Section of Antitrust Law 2012, Chapter XII, available at http://papers.ssrn.com/sol3/papers.cfm?abstract_id = 1396751&download = yes.

EVANS, D.S., 'Attention Rivalry Among Online Platforms', *Journal of Competition Law and Economics* 2013, vol. 9, no. 2, 313-357.

EVANS, D.S. AND NOEL, M., 'Defining Antitrust Markets When Firms Operate Two-Sided Platforms', *Columbia Business Law Review* 2005, vol. 2005, 101-134.

EVANS, D.S. AND NOEL, M.D., 'The Analysis of Mergers that Involve Multisided Platform Businesses', *Journal of Competition Law and Economics* 2008, vol. 4, no. 3, 663-695.

EVANS, D.S. AND PADILLA, A.J., 'Designing Antitrust Rules for Assessing Unilateral Practices: A Neo-Chicago Approach', *The University of Chicago Law Review* 2005, vol. 72, no. 1, 73-98.

EVANS, D.S. AND SCHMALENSEE, R., 'Some Economic Aspects of Antitrust Analysis in Dynamically Competitive Industries' in JAFFE, A.B., LERNER, J. AND STERN, S. (eds.), *Innovation Policy and the Economy, Volume 2*, MIT Press, 2002, 1-49.

EVANS, D.S. AND SCHMALENSEE, R., 'The Industrial Organization of Markets with Two-Sided Platforms', *Competition Policy International* 2007, vol. 3, no. 1, 151-179.

EVANS, D.S. AND YANHUA ZHANG, V., 'The Qihoo v. Tencent Landmark Decision', *Competition Policy International* 9 April 2013.

FARRELL, J. AND KLEMPERER, P., 'Coordination and Lock-In: Competition with Switching Costs and Network Effects' in ARMSTRONG, M. AND PORTER, R. (eds.), *Handbook of Industrial Organization, Volume 3*, Elsevier, 2007, 1967-2072.

FARRELL, J. AND SHAPIRO, C., 'Antitrust Evaluation of Horizontal Mergers: An Economic Alternative to Market Definition', *The B.E. Journal of Theoretical Economics: Policies and Perspectives* 2010, vol. 10, no. 1, 1-39.

FARRELL, J. AND SALONER, G., 'Standardization, Compatibility, and Innovation', *RAND Journal of Economics* 1985, vol. 16, no. 1, 70-83.

FARRELL, J. AND SALONER, G., 'Installed Base and Compatibility: Innovation, Product Preannouncements, and Predation', *American Economic Review* 1986, vol. 76, no. 5, 940-955.

FILISTRUCCHI, L., GERADIN, D. AND VAN DAMME, E., 'Identifying Two-Sided Markets', *World Competition* 2013, vol. 36, no. 1, 33-59.

FILISTRUCCHI, L., GERADIN, D., VAN DAMME, E., ET AL., 'Market Definition in Two-Sided Markets: Theory and Practice', *Journal of Competition Law and Economics* 2014, vol. 10, no. 2, 293-339.

FOX, E.M., 'Monopolization, Abuse of Dominance, and the Indeterminacy of Economics: The U.S./E.U. Divide', *Utah Law Review* 2006, vol. 2006, no. 3, 725-740.

FREEMAN, C., 'The "National System of Innovation" in Historical Perspective', *Cambridge Journal of Economics 1995, 19, 5-24* 1995, vol. 19, no. 1, 5-24.

GALLOWAY, J., 'Driving Innovation: A Case for Targeted Competition Policy in Dynamic Markets', *World Competition* 2011, vol. 34, no. 1, 73-96.

GEBICKA, A. AND HEINEMANN, A., 'Social Media & Competition Law', *World Competition* 2014, vol. 37, no. 2, 149-172.

GERADIN, D., 'Limiting the Scope of Article 82 EC: What Can the EU Learn from the U.S. Supreme Court's Judgment in *Trinko* in the Wake of *Microsoft, IMS*, and *Deutsche Telekom*?', *Common Market Law Review* 2004, vol. 41, no. 6, 1519-1553.

GERADIN, D., 'Loyalty Rebates after Intel: Time for the European Court of Justice to Overrule Hoffman-La Roche', *Journal of Competition Law and Economics* 2015, vol. 11, no. 3, 579-615.

GERADIN, D. AND KUSCHEWSKY, M., 'Competition Law and Personal Data: Preliminary Thoughts on a Complex Issue', *SSRN Working Paper* February 2013, available at http://papers.ssrn.com/sol3/papers.cfm?abstract_id = 2216088.

GERBER, D.J., 'Rethinking the Monopolist's Duty to Deal: A Legal and Economic Critique of the Doctrine of "Essential Facilities"', *Virginia Law Review* 1988, vol. 74, no. 6, 1069-1113.

GEROSKI, P.A., 'Competition in Markets and Competition for Markets', *Journal of Industry, Competition and Trade* 2003, vol. 3, no. 3, 151-166.

GHIDINI, G. AND AREZZO, E., 'On the Intersection of IPRs and Competition Law With Regard to Information Technology Markets' in EHLERMANN, C.D. AND ATANASIU, I. (eds.), *European Competition Law Annual 2005: The Interaction between Competition Law and Intellectual Property Law*, Hart Publishing, 2007, 105-118.

GILBERT, R., 'Looking for Mr. Schumpeter. Where Are We in the Competition-Innovation Debate?' in JAFFE, A.B., LERNER, J. AND STERN, S. (eds.), *Innovation Policy and the Economy*, The MIT Press, 2006, 159-215.

GILBERT, R.J., 'Competition and Innovation' in COLLINS, W.D. (ed.), *Issues in Competition Law and Policy*, Volume I, Chapter 24, American Bar Association Antitrust Section, 2008, 577-300, available at http://eml.berkeley.edu/~gilbert/wp/competition_and_innovation.pdf.

GILBERT, R.J. AND NEWBERY, D.M.G., 'Preemptive Patenting and the Persistence of Monopoly', *American Economic Review* June 1982, vol. 72, no. 3, 514-526.

GILBERT, R.J. AND SUNSHINE, S.C., 'Incorporating Dynamic Efficiency Concerns in Merger Analysis: The Use of Innovation Markets', *Antitrust Law Journal* 1995, vol. 63, no. 2, 569-601.

GOLDFARB, A. AND TUCKER, C., 'Privacy and Innovation' in LERNER, J. AND STERN, S. (eds.), *Innovation Policy and the Economy*, University of Chicago Press, 2012, 65-89.

GOULD, E.D., PASHIGIAN, B.P. AND PRENDERGAST, C.J., 'Contracts, Externalities, and Incentives in Shopping Malls', *Review of Economics and Statistics* 2005, vol. 87, no. 3, 411-422.

GRAEF, I., 'Tailoring the Essential Facilities Doctrine to the IT Sector: Compulsory Licensing of Intellectual Property Rights after *Microsoft*', *Cambridge Student Law Review* 2011, vol. 7, no. 1, 1-20.

GRAEF, I., 'How Can Software Interoperability Be Achieved under European Competition Law and Related Regimes?', *Journal of European Competition Law & Practice* 2014, vol. 5, no. 1, 6-19.

GRAEF, I., 'Sneak Preview of the Future Application of European Competition Law on the Internet?: Cisco and Messagenet', *Common Market Law Review* 2014, vol. 51, no. 4, 1263-1280.

GRAEF, I., 'Mandating Portability and Interoperability in Online Social Networks: Regulatory and Competition Law Issues in the European Union', *Telecommunications Policy* 2015, vol. 39, no. 6, 502-514.

GRAEF, I., 'Market Definition and Market Power in Data: The Case of Online Platforms', *World Competition* 2015, vol. 38, no. 4, 473-506.

GRAEF, I., VERSCHAKELEN, J. AND VALCKE, P., 'Putting the Right to Data Portability into a Competition Law Perspective', *Law: The Journal of the Higher School of Economics. Annual Review* 2013, 53-63, available at http://papers.ssrn.com/sol3/papers.cfm?abstract_id=2416537.

GRAEF, I., WAHYUNINGTYAS, S.Y. AND VALCKE, P., 'Assessing Data Access Issues in Online Platforms', *Telecommunications Policy* 2015, vol. 39, no. 5, 375-387.

GREAVES, R., 'Magill Est Arrivé...RTE and ITP v Commission of the European Communities', *European Competition Law Review* 1995, vol. 16, no. 4, 244-247.

GRILICHES, Z., 'The Search for R&D Spillovers', *Scandinavian Journal of Economics* 1992, vol. 94 Supplement, S29-S47.

GRIMMELMANN, J., 'The Structure of Search Engine Law', *Iowa Law Review* 2007, vol. 93, no. 1, 1-63.

GRUNES, A.P. AND STUCKE, M.E., 'No Mistake About It: The Important Role of Antitrust in the Era of Big Data', *The Antitrust Source* 2015, vol. 14, no. 4, 1-14.

HAGIU, A., 'Pricing and Commitment by Two-Sided Platforms', *RAND Journal of Economics* 2006, vol. 37, no. 3, 720-737.

HAGIU, A., 'Merchant or Two-Sided Platform?', *Review of Network Economics* 2007, vol. 6, no. 2, 115-133.

HAGIU, A. AND WRIGHT, J., 'Marketplace or Reseller?', *Management Science* January 2015, vol. 61, no. 1, 184-203.

HAGIU, A. AND WRIGHT, J., 'Multi-sided Platforms', *International Journal of Industrial Organization* November 2015, vol. 43, 162-174.

HARBOUR, P.J. AND KOSLOV, T.I., 'Section 2 In A Web 2.0 World: An Expanded Vision of Relevant Product Markets', *Antitrust Law Journal* 2010, vol. 76, no. 3, 769-797.

HAY, G.A., 'Innovations in Antitrust Enforcement', *Antitrust Law Journal* 1995, vol. 64, no. 1, 7-17.

HEIDEMANN, J., KLIER, M. AND PROBST, F., 'Online Social Networks: A Survey of a Global Phenomenon', *Computer Networks* 2012, vol. 56, no. 18, 3866-3878.

HOERNER, R.J., 'Innovation Markets: New Wine in Old Bottles?', *Antitrust Law Journal* 1995, vol. 64, no. 1, 49-73.

HOPPNER, T., 'Defining Markets for Multi-Sided Platforms: The Case of Search Engines', *World Competition* 2015, vol. 38, no. 3, 349-366.

HOU, L., 'The Essential Facilities Doctrine – What Was Wrong in Microsoft?', *International Review of Intellectual Property and Competition Law* 2012, vol. 43, no. 4, 451-471.

HOVENKAMP, H., JANIS, M.D. AND LEMLEY, M.A., 'Unilateral Refusals to License', *Journal of Competition Law and Economics* 2006, vol. 2, no. 1, 1-42.

HUGENHOLTZ, P.B., 'Abuse of Database Right: Sole-Source Information Banks under the EU Database Directive' in LÉVÊQUE, F. AND SHELANSKI, H.A. (eds.), *Antitrust, Patents and Copyright: EU and US Perspectives*, Edward Elgar, 2005, 203-219.

IBÁÑEZ COLOMO, P., 'Intel and Article 102 TFEU Case Law: Making Sense of a Perpetual Controversy', *LSE Legal Studies Working Paper No. 29/2014* November 2014, available at http://papers.ssrn.com/sol3/papers.cfm?abstract_id = 2530878& rec = 1&srcabs = 2567628&alg = 1&pos = 3.

JANSEN, B.J., BOOTH, D.L. AND SPINK, A., 'Determining the Informational, Navigational, and Transactional Intent of Web Queries', *Information Processing and Management* 2008, vol. 44, 1251-1266.

JIANG, T., 'The Qihoo/Tencent Dispute in the Instant Messaging Market: The First Milestone in the Chinese Competition Law Enforcement?', *World Competition* 2014, vol. 37, no. 3, 369-390.

JONES, A. AND DAVIES, J., 'Merger Control and the Public Interest: Balancing EU and National Law in the Protectionist Debate' in HAWK, B.E. (ed.), *International Antitrust Law and Policy: Fordham Competition Law 2014*, Juris Publishing, 2015, 63-114.

KAGAN, J., 'Bricks, Mortar, and Google: Defining the Relevant Antitrust Market for Internet-Based Companies', *New York Law School Law Review* 2010/11, vol. 55, no. 1, 271-292.

KALLAUGHER, J., 'Existence, Exercise, and Exceptional Circumstances: The Limited Scope for a More Economic Approach to IP Issues under Article 102 TFEU' in

ANDERMAN, S. AND EZRACHI, A. (eds.), *Intellectual Property and Competition Law. New Frontiers*, Oxford University Press, 2011, 113-139.

KAPLOW, L., 'Why Ever Define Markets?', *Harvard Law Review* December 2010, vol. 124, no. 2, 437-517.

KAPLOW, L., 'Market Definition: Impossible and Counterproductive', *Antitrust Law Journal* 2013, vol. 79, no. 1, 361-379.

KATZ, M.L. AND SHAPIRO, C., 'Network Externalities, Competition, and Compatibility', *American Economic Review* 1985, vol. 75, no. 3, 424-440.

KATZ, M.L. AND SHAPIRO, C., 'Technology Adoption in the Presence of Network Externalities', *Journal of Political Economy* 1986, vol. 94, no. 4, 822-841.

KATZ, M.L. AND SHAPIRO, C., 'Antitrust in Software Markets' in EISENACH, J.A. AND LENARD, T.M. (eds.), *Competition, Innovation and the Microsoft Monopoly: Antitrust in the Digital Marketplace*, Kluwer Academic Publishers, 1999.

KATZ, M.L. AND SHELANSKI, H.A., '"Schumpeterian" Competition and Antitrust Policy in High-Tech Markets', *Competition* 2005, vol. 14, 47.

KERN, B.R., 'Innovation Markets, Future Markets, or Potential Competition: How Should Competition Authorities Account for Innovation Competition in Merger Reviews?', *World Competition* 2014, vol. 37, no. 2, 173-206.

KILLICK, J., '*IMS* and *Microsoft* Judged in the Cold Light of *IMS*', *The Competition Law Review* 2004, vol. 1, no. 2, 23-47.

KIMMEL, L. AND KESTENBAUM, J., 'What's Up with WhatsApp? A Transatlantic View on Privacy and Merger Enforcement in Digital Markets', *Antitrust Magazine* 2014, vol. 29, no. 1, 48-55.

KJOLBYE, L., 'The New Commission Guidelines on the Application of Article 81(3): An Economic Approach to Article 81', *European Competition Law Review* 2004, vol. 25, no. 9, 566-577.

KOKOTT, J. AND SOBOTTA, C., 'The Distinction between Privacy and Data Protection in the Jurisprudence of the CJEU and the ECtHR', *International Data Privacy Law* 2013, vol. 3, no. 4, 222-228.

KOOPS, B.-J., 'The Trouble with European Data Protection Law', *International Data Privacy Law* 2014, vol. 4, no. 4, 250-261.

KOSTA, E., 'Peeking into the Cookie Jar: The European Approach towards the Regulation of Cookies', *International Journal of Law and Information Technology* 2013, vol. 21, no. 4, 380-406.

KRATTENMAKER, T.G. AND SALOP, S.C., 'Anticompetitive Exclusion: Raising Rivals' Costs to Achieve Power over Price', *Yale Law Journal* 1986, vol. 96, no. 2, 209-293.

KUNER, C., CATE, F.H., MILLARD, C., ET AL., 'When Two Worlds Collide: The Interface between Ccompetition Law and Data Protection', *International Data Privacy Law* 2014, vol. 4, no. 4, 247-248.

KUSCHEWSKY, M. AND GERADIN, D., 'Data Protection in the Context of Competition Law Investigations: An Overview of the Challenges', *World Competition* 2014, vol. 37, no. 1, 69-102.

LAMBRECHT, A. AND TUCKER, C.E., 'Can Big Data Protect a Firm from Competition?', *SSRN Working Paper* December 2015, available at http://papers.ssrn.com/sol3/papers.cfm?abstract_id = 2705530.

LANDE, R.H., 'The Microsoft-Yahoo Merger: Yes, Privacy Is an Antitrust Concern', *FTC:WATCH* February 2008, no. 714, 1-2.

LANGENFELD, J., 'Intellectual Property and Antitrust: Steps Toward Striking a Balance', *Case Western Reserve Law Review* 2001, vol. 52, no. 1, 91-110.

LAO, M., '*Aspen Skiing* and *Trinko*: Antitrust Intent and "Sacrifice"', *Antitrust Law Journal* 2005, vol. 73, no. 1, 171-208.

LAROUCHE, P., 'EC Competition Law and the Convergence of the Telecommunications and Broadcasting Sectors', *Telecommunications Policy* 1998, vol. 22, no. 3, 219-242.

LAROUCHE, P., 'The European Microsoft Case at the Crossroads of Competition Policy and Innovation', *Antitrust Law Journal* 2008, vol. 75, no. 3, 601-631.

LAROUCHE, P. AND SCHINKEL, M.P., 'Continental Drift in the Treatment of Dominant Firms: Article 102 TFEU in Contrast to Section 2 Sherman Act' in BLAIR, R.D. AND SOKOL, D.D. (eds.), *The Oxford Handbook of International Antitrust Economics. Volume 2*, Oxford University Press, 2015, 153-187.

LE, N., 'What Does "Capable of Eliminating All Competition" Mean?', *European Competition Law Review* 2005, vol. 26, no. 1, 6-10.

LEE, R.S., 'Vertical Integration and Exclusivity in Platform and Two-Sided Markets', *American Economic Review* 2013, vol. 103, no. 7, 2960-3000.

LEMLEY, M.A., 'Private Property', *Stanford Law Review* 2000, vol. 52, no. 5, 1545-1557.

LERNER, A.P., 'The Concept of Monopoly and the Measurement of Monopoly Power', *Review of Economic Studies* June 1934, vol. 1, no. 3, 157-175.

LERNER, A.V., 'The Role of "Big Data" in Online Platform Competition', *SSRN Working Paper* August 2014, available at http://papers.ssrn.com/sol3/papers.cfm?abstract_id=2482780.

LESSIG, L., 'The Architecture of Privacy', *Vanderbilt Journal of Entertainment Law & Practice* 1999, vol. 1, no. 1, 56-65.

LÉVÊQUE, F., 'Innovation, Leveraging and Essential Facilities: Interoperability Licensing in the EU Microsoft Case', *World Competition* 2005, vol. 28, no. 1, 71-91.

LEVIN, R.C., COHEN, W.M. AND MOWERY, D.C., 'R&D Appropriability, Opportunity, and Market Structure: New Evidence on Some Schumpeterian Hypotheses', *The American Economic Review* May 1985, vol. 75, no. 2, 20-24.

LI, J., 'Is Online Media a Two-Sided Market?', *Computer Law and Security Review* 2015, vol. 31, no. 1, 99-111.

LIANOS, I., 'Competition Law and Intellectual Property Rights: Is the Property Rights' Approach Right?' in BELL, J. AND KILPATRICK, C. (eds.), *The Cambridge Yearbook of European Legal Studies* 2005-2006, vol. 8, 153-186.

LIEBOWITZ, S.J. AND MARGOLIS, S.E., 'Are Network Externalities a New Source of Market Failure?', *Research in Law and Economics* 1995, vol. 17, 1-22.

LIEBOWITZ, S.J., AND MARGOLIS, S.E., 'Network Externalities (Effects)' in *The New Palgraves Dictionary of Economics and the Law*, Palgrave Macmillan, 1998, available at http://wwwpub.utdallas.edu/~liebowit/palgrave/network.html.

LIPSKY, A.B. AND SIDAK, J.G., 'Essential Facilities', *Stanford Law Review* 1999, vol. 51, no. 5, 1187-1248.

LUCHETTA, G., 'Is the Google Platform a Two-Sided Market?', *Journal of Competition Law and Economics* 2014, vol. 10, no. 1, 185-207.

LUND, J., 'Property Rights to Information', *Northwestern Journal of Technology and Intellectual Property* 2011, vol. 10, no. 1, 1-18.

MACKENRODT, M.-O., 'Assessing the Effects of Intellectual Property Rights in Network Standards' in DREXL, J. (ed.), *Research Handbook on Intellectual Property and Competition Law*, Edward Elgar, 2008, 80-103.

MANNE, G.A. AND SPERRY, R.B., 'The Law and Economics of Data and Privacy in Antitrust Analysis', *TPRC Conference paper* August 2014, available at http://papers.ssrn.com/sol3/papers.cfm?abstract_id = 2418779.

MANNE, G.A. AND SPERRY, R.B., 'The Problems and Perils of Bootstrapping Privacy and Data into an Antitrust Framework', *CPI Antitrust Chronicle* 2015, vol. 5, no. 2, 1-11.

MANNE, G.A. AND WRIGHT, J.D., 'Google and the Limits of Antitrust: The Case Against the Case Against Google', *Harvard Journal of Law & Public Policy* 2010, vol. 34, no. 1, 171-244.

MANNE, G.A. AND WRIGHT, J.D., 'Innovation and the Limits of Antitrust', *Journal of Competition Law and Economics* 2010, vol. 6, no. 1, 153-202.

McGUIRE, T., MANYIKA, J. AND CHUI, M., 'Why Big Data Is the New Competitive Advantage', *Ivey Business Journal* July/August 2012, vol. 76, no. 4, 1-4.

MURPHY, R.S., 'Property Rights in Personal Information: An Economic Defense of Privacy', *Georgetown Law Journal* 1996, vol. 84, no. 7, 2381-2417.

NEWMAN, J.M., 'Antitrust in Zero-Price Markets: Foundations', *SSRN Working Paper* July 2014, available at http://papers.ssrn.com/sol3/papers.cfm?abstract_id = 2474874&download = yes.

NEWMAN, N., 'The Costs of Lost Privacy: Consumer Harm and Rising Economic Inequality in the Age of Google', *William Mitchell Law Review* 2014, vol. 40, no. 2, 849-889.

NEWMAN, N., 'Search, Antitrust, and the Economics of the Control of User Data', *Yale Journal on Regulation* 2014, vol. 31, no. 2, 401-454.

NIHOUL, P., 'The Ruling of the General Court in Intel: Towards the End of an Effect-Based Approach in European Competition Law?', *Journal of European Competition Law & Practice* 2014, vol. 5, no. 8, 521-530.

ODUDU, O., 'The Wider Concerns of Competition Law', *Oxford Journal of Legal Studies* 2010, vol. 30, no. 3, 599-613.

OHLHAUSEN, M.K. AND OKULIAR, A.P., 'Competition, Consumer Protection, and the Right [Approach] to Privacy', *Antitrust Law Journal* 2015, vol. 80, no. 1, 121-156.

PADILLA, A.J. AND PAGANO, M., 'Sharing Default Information as a Borrower Discipline Device', *European Economic Review* 2000, vol. 44, no. 10, 1951-1980.

PALLIS, G., ZEINALIPOUR-YAZTI, D. AND DIKAIAKOS, M.D., 'Online Social Networks: Status and Trends' in VAKALI, A. AND JAIN, L.C. (eds.), *New Directions in Web Data Management 1. Studies in Computational Intelligence*, Berlin Heidelberg, Springer, 2011, 213-234.

PARDOLESI, R. AND RENDA, A., 'The European Commission's Case Against Microsoft: Kill Bill?', *World Competition* 2004, vol. 27, no. 4, 513-566.

PARKER, G.G. AND VAN ALSTYNE, M.W., 'Two-Sided Network Effects: A Theory of Information Product Design', *Management Science* 2005, vol. 51, no. 10, 1494-1504.

PETIT, N., 'Intel, Leveraging Rebates and the Goals of Article 102 TFEU', *European Competition Journal* 2015, vol. 11, no. 1, 26-68.

PICKER, R.C., 'Competition and Privacy in Web 2.0 and the Cloud', *Northwestern University Law Review Colloquy* 2008, vol. 103, 1-12.

RAMSEY, F.P., 'A Contribution to the Theory of Taxation', *Economic Journal* 1927, vol. 37, no. 145, 47-61.

RAPP, R.T., 'The Misapplication of the Innovation Market Approach to Merger Analysis', *Antitrust Law Journal* 1995, vol. 64, no. 1, 19-47.

RATLIFF, J.D. AND RUBINFELD, D.L., 'Is There a Market for Organic Search Engine Results and Can Their Manipulation Give Rise to Antitrust Liability?', *Journal of Competition Law and Economics* 2014, vol. 10, no. 3, 517-541.

RATNER, J.R., 'Should There Be an Essential Facility Doctrine?', *University of California, Davis Law Review* 1988, vol. 21, no. 2, 327-382.

REES, C., 'Tomorrow's Privacy: Personal Information as Property', *International Data Privacy Law* 2013, vol. 3, no. 4, 220-221.

REINGANUM, J.F., 'Uncertain Innovation and the Persistence of Monopoly', *American Economic Review* September 1983, vol. 73, no. 4, 741-748.

REY, P. AND VENIT, J.S., 'An Effects-Based Approach to Article 102: A Response to Wouter Wils', *World Competition* 2015, vol. 38, no. 1, 3-30.

RIDYARD, D., 'Compulsory Access under EC Competition Law - A New Doctrine of "Convenient Facilities" and the Case for Price Regulation', *European Competition Law Review* 2004, vol. 25, no. 11, 669-673.

RITTER, C., 'Refusal to Deal and "Essential Facilities": Does Intellectual Property Require Special Deference Compared to Tangible Property?', *World Competition* 2005, no. 28, 281-3.

ROCHET, J.C. AND TIROLE, J., 'Cooperation among Competitors: Some Economics of Payment Card Associations', *RAND Journal of Economics* 2002, vol. 33, no. 4, 549-570.

ROCHET, J.C. AND TIROLE, J., 'Platform Competition in Two-Sided Markets', *Journal of the European Economic Association* 2003, vol. 1, no. 4, 990-1029.

ROCHET, J.-C. AND TIROLE, J., 'Two-Sided Markets: A Progress Report', *RAND Journal of Economics* 2006, vol. 37, no. 3, 645-667.

ROUSSEVA, E., 'The Concept of "Objective Justification" of an Abuse of a Dominant Position: Can it Help to Modernise the Analysis under Article 82 EC?', *The Competition Law Review* 2006, vol. 2, no. 2, 27-72.

ROUSSEVA, E. AND MARQUIS, M., 'Hell Freezes Over: A Climate Change for Assessing Exclusionary Conduct under Article 102 TFEU', *Journal of European Competition Law & Practice* 2013, vol. 4, no. 1, 32-50.

RYSMAN, M., 'The Economics of Two-Sided Markets', *Journal of Economic Perspectives* 2009, vol. 23, no. 3, 125-143.

SALOP, S.C., 'Avoiding Error in the Antitrust Analysis of Unilateral Refusals to Deal', *statement to the Antitrust Modernization Commission* 21 September 2005.

SAMUELSON, P., 'Privacy As Intellectual Property?', *Stanford Law Review* 2000, vol. 52, no. 5, 1125-1173.

SAMUELSON, P., VINJE, T. AND CORNISH, W., 'Does Copyright Protection under the EU Software Directive Extend to Computer Program Behaviour, Languages and Interfaces?', *European Intellectual Property Review* 2012, vol. 34, no. 3, 158-166.

SCHEPP, N.P. AND WAMBACH, A., 'On Big Data and Its Relevance for Market Power Assessment', *Journal of European Competition Law & Practice* 2016, vol. 7, no. 2, 120-124.

SCHERER, F.M., 'Market Structure and the Employment of Scientists and Engineers', *The American Economic Review* June 1967, vol. 57, no. 3, 524-531.

SCHMALENSEE, R., 'Sunk Costs and Antitrust Barriers to Entry', *American Economic Review* May 2004, vol. 94, no. 2, 471-475.

SCHMIDT, C. AND KERBER, W., 'Microsoft, Refusal to License Intellectual Property Rights, and the Incentives Balance Test of the EU Commission', *SSRN Working Paper* November 2008, available at http://papers.ssrn.com/sol3/papers.cfm?abstract_id = 1297939.

SCHWARTZ, P.M., 'Property, Privacy, and Personal Data', *Harvard Law Review* 2004, vol. 117, no. 7, 2056-2128.

SHAPIRO, C., 'Competition and Innovation: Did Arrow Hit the Bull's Eye?' in LERNER, J. AND STERN, S. (eds.), *The Rate and Direction of Inventive Activity Revisited*, NBER, 2012, 361-404.

SHELANSKI, H.A., 'Unilateral Refusals to Deal in Intellectual and Other Property', *Antitrust Law Journal* 2009, vol. 76, no. 2, 369-395.

SHELANSKI, H.A., 'Information, Innovation, and Competition Policy for the Internet', *University of Pennsylvania Law Review* 2013, vol. 161, no. 6, 1663-1705.

SHY, O. AND STENBACKA, R., 'Investment in Customer Recognition and Information Exchange', *Information Economics and Policy* 2013, vol. 25, no. 2, 92-106.

SIDAK, J.G. AND TEECE, D.J., 'Dynamic Competition in Antitrust Law', *Journal of Competition Law and Economics* 2009, vol. 5, no. 4, 581-631.

SILVESTRI, F., 'Mining Query Logs: Turning Search Usage Data into Knowledge', *Foundation and Trends in Information Retrieval* 2010, vol. 4, no. 1-2, 1-174.

SOKOL, D.D. AND COMERFORD, R., 'Does Antitrust Have A Role to Play in Regulating Big Data?' in BLAIR, R.D. AND SOKOL, D.D. (eds.), *Cambridge Handbook of Antitrust, Intellectual Property and High Technology*, Cambridge University Press, forthcoming, available at http://papers.ssrn.com/sol3/papers.cfm?abstract_id = 2723693.

SOLOVE, D.J., 'A Taxonomy of Privacy', *University of Pennsylvania Law Review* 2006, vol. 154, no. 3, 477-560.

SPULBER, D.F., 'Unlocking Technology: Antitrust and Innovation', *Journal of Competition Law and Economics* 2008, vol. 4, no. 4, 915-966.

STALLIBRASS, D. AND PANG, S., 'Clash of Titans: How China Disciplines Internet Markets', *Journal of European Competition Law & Practice* 2015, vol. 6, no. 6, 418-423.

STEENE, A., 'Nexans, Deutsche Bahn, and the ECJ's Refusal to Follow ECHR Case Law on Dawn Raids', *Journal of European Competition Law & Practice* 2016, vol. 7, no. 3, 180-193.

SUBIOTTO, R. AND O'DONOGHUE, R., 'Defining the Scope of the Duty of Dominant Firms to Deal with Existing customers under Article 82 EC', *European Competition Law Review* 2003, vol. 24, no. 12, 683-694.

SWIRE, P. AND LAGOS, Y., 'Why the Right to Data Portability Likely Reduces Consumer Welfare: Antitrust and Privacy Critique', *Maryland Law Review* 2013, vol. 72, no. 2, 335-380.

TAYLOR, C.R., 'Consumer Privacy and the Market for Customer Information', *RAND Journal of Economics* 2004, vol. 35, no. 4, 631-650.

THÉPOT, F., 'Market Power in Online Search and Social Networking: A Matter of Two-Sided Markets', *World Competition* 2013, vol. 36, no. 2, 195-221.

TROY, D.E., 'Unclogging the Bottleneck: A New Essential Facility Doctrine', *Columbia Law Review* 1983, vol. 83, no. 2, 441-487.

TUCKER, D.S. AND WELLFORD, H.B., 'Big Mistakes Regarding Big Data', *The Antitrust Source* 2014, vol. 14, no. 2, 1-12.

ULLRICH, H., 'Intellectual Property, Access to Information, and Antitrust: Harmony, Disharmony, and International Harmonization' in DREYFUSS, R.C., ZIMMERMAN, D.L. AND FIRST, H. (eds.), *Expanding the Boundaries of Intellectual Property. Innovation Policy for the Knowledge Society*, Oxford University Press, 2001, 365-402.

VANBERG, A.D., 'From Archie to Google - Search Engine Providers and Emergent Challenges in Relation to EU Competition Law', *European Journal of Law and Technology*, vol. 3, no. 1, 1-18.

VAN LOON, S., *The Power of Google: First Mover Advantage or Abuse of a Dominant Position?* in LOPEZ-TARRUELLA, A. (ed.) *Information Technology and Law Series*, Google and the Law. Empirical Approaches to Legal Aspects of Knowledge-Economy Business Models, T.M.C. Asser Press, 2012.

VARIAN, H.R., 'Price Discrimination and Social Welfare', *The American Economic Review* 1985, vol. 75, no. 4, 870-875.

VENIT, J.S., 'Case T-286/09 Intel v Commission—The Judgment of the General Court: All Steps Backward and No Steps Forward', *European Competition Journal* 2014, vol. 10, no. 2, 203-230.

VERHAERT, J., 'The Challenges Involved with the Application of Article 102 TFEU to the New Economy: A Case Study of Google', *European Competition Law Review* 2014, vol. 35, no. 6, 265-273.

VEZZOSO, S., 'The Incentives Balance Test in the EU Microsoft Case: A Pro-innovation "Economics-Based" Approach?', *European Competition Law Review* 2006, vol. 27, no. 7, 382-390.

VEZZOSO, S., 'The Interface between Competition Policy and Data Protection', *Journal of European Competition Law & Practice* 2012, vol. 3, no. 3, 225-225.

WAHYUNINGTYAS, S.Y., 'Interoperability for Data Portability between Social Networking Sites (SNS): The Interplay between EC Software Copyright and Competition Law', *Queen Mary Journal of Intellectual Property* 2015, vol. 5, no. 1, 46-67.

WALLER, S.W., 'Antitrust and Social Networking', *North Carolina Law Review* 2012, vol. 90, no. 5, 1771-1806.

WALLER, S.W. AND TASCH, W., 'Harmonizing Essential Facilities', *Antitrust Law Journal* 2010, vol. 76, no. 3, 741-767.

WANG, B., 'Survival and Competition among Social Networking Websites. A Research Commentary on "Critical Mass and Willingness to Pay for Social Networks" by J. Christopher Westland', *Electronic Commerce Research and Applications* 2010, vol. 9, no. 1, 20-22.

WARREN, S.D. AND BRANDEIS, L.D., 'The Right to Privacy', *Harvard Law Review* 1890, vol. 4, no. 5, 193-220.

WAUTERS, E., DONOSO, V. AND LIEVENS, E., 'Optimizing Transparency for Users of Social Networking Sites', *info* 2014, vol. 16, no. 6, 8-23.

WERDEN, G.J., 'The Law and Economics of the Essential Facility Doctrine', *Saint Louis University Law Journal* 1987, vol. 32, no. 2, 433-480.

WERDEN, G.J., 'The Relevant Market: Possible and Productive', *Antitrust Law Journal Online* April 2014, 1-7.

WESTLAND, J.C., 'Critical Mass and Willingness to Pay for Social Networks', *Electronic Commerce Research and Applications* 2010, vol. 9, no. 1, 6-19.

WEYL, E.G., 'A Price Theory of Multi-Sided Platforms', *American Economic Review* 2010, vol. 100, no. 4, 1642-1672.

WHINSTON, M.D., 'Tying, Foreclosure, and Exclusion', *American Economic Review* 1990, vol. 80, no. 4, 837-859.

WHISH, R., 'Intel v Commission: Keep Calm and Carry on!', *Journal of European Competition Law & Practice* 2015, vol. 6, no. 1, 1-2.

WILBUR, K.C., 'A Two-Sided, Empirical Model of Television Advertising and Viewing Markets', *Marketing Science* 2008, vol. 27, no. 3, 356-378.

WILS, W., 'The Judgment of the EU General Court in Intel and the So-Called More Economic Approach to Abuse of Dominance', *World Competition* 2014, vol. 37, no. 4, 405-434.

WRIGHT, J., 'One-sided Logic in Two-sided Markets', *Review of Network Economics* 2004, vol. 3, no. 1, 44-64.

YOO, C.S., 'When Antitrust Met Facebook', *George Mason Law Review* 2012, vol. 19, no. 5, 1147-1162.

ZANFIR, G., 'The Right to Data Portability in the Context of the EU Data Protection Reform', *International Data Privacy Law* 2012, vol. 2, no. 3, 149-162.

ZINGALES, N., 'Regulating Search: Competition Policy and Data Protection at the Crossroad', *Media Laws* 10 September 2012, available at http://www.medialaws .eu/regulating-search-competition-policy-and-data-protection-at-the-crossroad/.

ZINGALES, N., 'Product Market Definition in Online Search and Advertising', *The Competition Law Review* March 2013, vol. 9, no. 1, 29-47.

Speeches

Speech former Competition Commissioner Almunia, 'Statement of Commissioner Almunia on the Google antitrust investigation', Press room Brussels, 21 May

2012, SPEECH/12/372, available at http://europa.eu/rapid/press-release_
SPEECH-12-372_en.htm.

Speech former Competition Commissioner Almunia, 'Competition and personal data protection', Privacy Platform event: Competition and Privacy in Markets of Data Brussels, 26 November 2012, SPEECH/12/860, available at http://europa.eu/rapid/press-release_SPEECH-12-860_en.htm.

Speech former Competition Commissioner Almunia, 'Abuse of dominance: a view from the EU', Fordham's Competition Law Institute Annual Conference New York, 27 September 2013, SPEECH/13/758, available at http://europa.eu/rapid/press-release_SPEECH-13-758_en.htm.

Speech former Competition Commissioner Almunia, 'The Google antitrust case: what is at stake?', 1 October 2013, SPEECH/13/768, available at http://europa.eu/rapid/press-release_SPEECH-13-768_en.htm.

Speech former Competition Commissioner Almunia, 'Competition in the online world', LSE Public Lecture London, 11 November 2013, SPEECH/13/905, available at http://europa.eu/rapid/press-release_SPEECH-13-905_en.htm.

Speech former Competition Commissioner Almunia, 'Competition, innovation and growth: an EU perspective on the challenges ahead', Third BRICS International Competition Conference New Delhi, 21 November 2013, SPEECH/13/958, available at http://europa.eu/rapid/press-release_SPEECH-13-958_en.htm.

Speech former Competition Commissioner Almunia, 'Intellectual property and competition policy', IP Summit 2013 Paris, 9 December 2013, SPEECH/13/1042, available at http://europa.eu/rapid/press-release_SPEECH-13-1042_en.htm.

Speech former Competition Commissioner Almunia, 'Looking back at five years of competition enforcement in the EU', Global Antitrust Enforcement Symposium (Georgetown) Washington, 10 September 2014, SPEECH/14/588, available at http://europa.eu/rapid/press-release_SPEECH-14-588_en.htm?locale = en.

Speech former Competition Commissioner Almunia, 'Presenting the Annual Competition Report', 23 September 2014, SPEECH/14/615, available at http://europa.eu/rapid/press-release_SPEECH-14-615_en.htm.

Speech US Federal Trade Commissioner Julie Brill, 'Weaving a Tapestry to Protect Privacy and Competition in the Age of Big Data', European Data Protection Supervisor's Workshop on Privacy, Consumer Protection and Competition in the Digital Age, Brussels, 2 June 2014, available at https://www.ftc.gov/system/files/documents/public_statements/313311/140602edpsbrill2.pdf.

Speech European Data Protection Supervisor Buttarelli, 'Privacy and Competition in the Digital Economy', Privacy Platform event: The Digital Economy, Competition and Privacy Brussels, 21 January 2015, available at https://secure.edps.europa.eu/EDPSWEB/webdav/site/mySite/shared/Documents/EDPS/Publications/Speeches/2015/15-01-21_speech_GB_EN.pdf.

Speech European Data Protection Supervisor Buttarelli, 'Keynote speech at Joint ERA-EDPS seminar', workshop Competition Rebooted: Enforcement and personal data in digital markets Brussels, 24 September 2015, available at https://secure.edps.europa.eu/EDPSWEB/webdav/site/mySite/shared/Documents/EDPS/Publications/Speeches/2015/15-09-24_ERA_GB_EN.pdf.

Speech delivered to the American Bar Association Antitrust Section by US Senator Franken, 'How Privacy Has Become an Antitrust Issue', 30 March 2012, available at http://www.huffingtonpost.com/al-franken/how-privacy-has-become-an_b_1392580.html.

Speech former Director-General for Competition Italianer, 'Innovation and competition policy in the IT sector: the European perspective', Conference on Innovation, Competition Policy and Online Service Providers in Beijing, 26 June 2012, available at http://ec.europa.eu/competition/speeches/text/sp2012_04_en.pdf.

Speech former Director-General for Competition Italianer, 'Prepared remarks on: Level-playing field and innovation in technology markets', Conference on Antitrust in Technology, Palo Alto (US), 28 January 2013, available at http://ec.europa.eu/competition/speeches/text/sp2013_01_en.pdf.

Speech former Director-General for Competition Italianer, 'Competition Policy in the Digital Age', 47th Innsbruck Symposium - 'Real sector economy and the internet – digital interconnection as an issue for competition policy', 7 March 2014, available at http://ec.europa.eu/competition/speeches/text/sp2014_01_en.pdf.

Speech of former Consumer Commissioner Kuneva at the Roundtable on Online Data Collection, Targeting and Profiling, 31 March 2009, SPEECH/09/156, available at http://europa.eu/rapid/press-release_SPEECH-09-156_en.htm.

Speech Director-General for Competition Laitenberger, 'Competition and Innovation', CRA Annual Conference Brussels, 9 December 2015, available at http://ec.europa.eu/competition/speeches/text/sp2015_04_en.pdf.

Speech US FTC Commissioner Ohlhausen, 'Competition, Consumer Protection, and The Right [Approach] to Privacy', Premier Cercle Competition Summit 2013, Brussels, 6 December 2013, available via https://www.ftc.gov/sites/default/files/documents/public_statements/2013-premier-cercle-brussels-competition-summit/131206cerclebrussels.pdf.

Speech Competition Commissioner Vestager, 'Statement by Commissioner Vestager on antitrust decisions concerning Google', STATEMENT/15/4785, 15 April 2015, available at http://europa.eu/rapid/press-release_STATEMENT-15-4785_en.htm?locale = en.

Speech of Competition Commissioner Vestager, 'Competition in a big data world', DLD 16 Munich, 17 January 2016, available at https://ec.europa.eu/commission/2014-2019/vestager/announcements/competition-big-data-world_en.

Speech of Competition Commissioner Vestager, 'Refining the EU merger control system', Studienvereinigung Kartellrecht, Brussels, 10 March 2016, available at http://ec.europa.eu/commission/2014-2019/vestager/announcements/refining-eu-merger-control-system_en.

Speech of Competition Commissioner Vestager, 'Competition: the mother of invention', European Competition and Consumer Day, Amsterdam, 18 April 2016, available at http://ec.europa.eu/commission/2014-2019/vestager/announcements/competition-mother-invention_en.

Reports, Studies and Other Official Documents

ARTICLE 29 WORKING PARTY, 'Opinion 8/2001 on the processing of personal data in the employment context', WP 48, 13 September 2001.
ARTICLE 29 WORKING PARTY, 'Opinion 4/2007 on the concept of personal data', WP 136, 20 June 2007.
ARTICLE 29 WORKING PARTY, 'Opinion 1/2008 on data protection issues related to search engines', WP 148, 4 April 2008.
ARTICLE 29 WORKING PARTY, 'Opinion 15/2011 on the definition of consent', WP 187, 13 July 2011.
ARTICLE 29 WORKING PARTY, 'Opinion 03/2013 on purpose limitation', WP 203, 2 April 2013.
ARTICLE 29 WORKING PARTY, 'Opinion 05/2014 on Anonymisation Techniques', WP 216, 10 April 2014.
ARTICLE 29 WORKING PARTY, 'Opinion 9/2014 on the application of Directive 2002/58/EC to device fingerprinting', WP 224, 25 November 2014.
AUTORITÉ DE LA CONCURRENCE AND COMPETITION & MARKETS AUTHORITY, 'The economics of open and closed systems', 16 December 2014, available at http://www.autoritedelaconcurrence.fr/doc/economics_open_closed_systems.pdf.
AUTORITÉ DE LA CONCURRENCE AND BUNDESKARTELLAMT, 'Competition Law and Data', 10 May 2016, available at http://www.autoritedelaconcurrence.fr/doc/reportcom petitionlawanddatafinal.pdf.
Commitments of Google in Case COMP/C-3/39.740 Foundem and others, 3 April 2013, paras 27-31, available at http://ec.europa.eu/competition/antitrust/cases/dec_docs/39740/39740_8608_5.pdf.
Communication from the Commission. EUROPE 2020. A strategy for smart, sustainable and inclusive growth, COM(2010) 2020, 3 March 2010.
Communication from the Commission to the European Parliament, the Council, the European Economic and Social Committee and the Committee of the Regions. Europe 2020 Flagship Initiative. Innovation Union, COM(2010) 546 final, 6 October 2010.
Communication from the Commission to the European Parliament, the Council, the European Economic and Social Committee and the Committee of the Regions. Measuring innovation output in Europe: towards a new indicator, COM(2013) 624 final, 13 September 2013.
Communication from the Commission to the European Parliament, the Council, the European Economic and Social Committee and the Committee of the Regions. A Digital Single Market Strategy for Europe, COM(2015) 192 final, 6 May 2015.
Communication from the Commission to the European Parliament, the Council, the European Economic and Social Committee and the Committee of the Regions. Online Platforms and the Digital Single Market. Opportunities and Challenges for Europe, COM(2016) 288 final, 25 May 2016.

A. DE STREEL AND P. LAROUCHE, 'Disruptive Innovation and Competition Policy Enforcement', *Note for OECD Global Forum on Competition*, DAF/COMP/GF(2015)7, 20 October 2015, available at http://www.oecd.org/officialdocuments/publicdisplaydocumentpdf/?cote = DAF/COMP/GF(2015)7&docLanguage = En.

DG Competition discussion paper on the application of Article 82 of the Treaty to exclusionary abuses, December 2005.

EUROPEAN COMMISSION, XXVth Report on Competition Policy 1995, COM(96)126 final.

EUROPEAN COMMISSION, 'DG Internal Market and Services Working Paper. First evaluation of Directive 96/9/EC on the legal protection of databases', 12 December 2005, available at http://ec.europa.eu/internal_market/copyright/docs/databases/evaluation_report_en.pdf.

EUROPEAN COMMISSION, 'Innovation Union Scoreboard 2015', available at http://ec.europa.eu/growth/industry/innovation/facts-figures/scoreboards/files/ius-2015_en.pdf.

PRELIMINARY OPINION OF THE EUROPEAN DATA PROTECTION SUPERVISOR, 'Privacy and competitiveness in the age of big data: The interplay between data protection, competition law and consumer protection in the Digital Economy', March 2014.

EUROPEAN DATA PROTECTION SUPERVISOR, 'Report of workshop on Privacy, Consumers, Competition and Big Data', 2 June 2014, p. 4, available at https://secure.edps.europa.eu/EDPSWEB/webdav/site/mySite/shared/Documents/Consultation/Big%20data/14-07-11_EDPS_Report_Workshop_Big_data_EN.pdf.

EUROPEAN DATA PROTECTION SUPERVISOR, Opinion 7/2015 Meeting the challenges of big data. A call for transparency, user control, data protection by design and accountability, 19 November 2015.

List of events about the interaction between data protection, competition law and consumer protection organized in 2014 and 2015 by or in collaboration with the EDPS: https://secure.edps.europa.eu/EDPSWEB/edps/Consultation/big_data.

European Parliament resolution of 27 November 2014 on supporting consumer rights in the digital single market, 2014/2973(RSP), available at http://www.europarl.europa.eu/sides/getDoc.do?pubRef = -//EP//TEXT + TA + P8-TA-2014-0071 + 0 + DOC + XML + V0//EN.

FTC REPORT, 'Protecting Consumer Privacy in an Era of Rapid Change. Recommendations for Business and Policymakers', March 2012, available at https://www.ftc.gov/sites/default/files/documents/reports/federal-trade-commission-report-protecting-consumer-privacy-era-rapid-change-recommendations/120326privacyreport.pdf.

P. LAROUCHE, M. PEITZ AND N. PURTOVA, 'Consumer Privacy in Network Industries', *CERRE Policy Report 25 January 2016*, available at http://www.cerre.eu/sites/cerre/files/160125_CERRE_Privacy_Final.pdf.

MONOPOLKOMMISSION, 'Competition policy: The challenge of digital markets', Special report No. 68, July 2015, par. 93, available at http://www.monopolkommission.de/images/PDF/SG/s68_fulltext_eng.pdf.

OECD, 'Exploring the Economics of Personal Data: A Survey of Methodologies for Measuring Monetary Value', *OECD Digital Economy Papers*, No. 220, 2013, available at http://dx.doi.org/10.1787/5k486qtxldmq-en.

OECD Policy Roundtables, 'The Role and Measurement of Quality in Competition Analysis', 28 October 2013, available at http://www.oecd.org/competition/ Quality-in-competition-analysis-2013.pdf.

OECD, 'Data-Driven Innovation. Big Data for Growth and Well-Being', 6 October 2015, available at http://www.oecd.org/sti/data-driven-innovation-9789264229358- en.htm.

Letter From Jessica L. Rich, Director of the Federal Trade Commission Bureau of Consumer Protection, to Erin Egan, Chief Privacy Officer, Facebook, and to Anne Hoge, General Counsel, WhatsApp Inc., 10 April 2014, available at https://www .ftc.gov/system/files/documents/public_statements/297701/140410facebookw hatappltr.pdf.

Study for the ECON Committee of the European Parliament, 'Challenges for Competition Policy in a Digitalised Economy', July 2015, available at http://www. europarl.europa.eu/RegData/etudes/STUD/2015/542235/IPOL_STU(2015)5422 35_EN.pdf.

Study on Trade Secrets and Confidential Business Information in the Internal Market, prepared for the European Commission, April 2013, available at http://ec.europa .eu/internal_market/iprenforcement/docs/trade-secrets/130711_final-study_en .pdf.

P. Swire, 'Submitted Testimony to the Federal Trade Commission Behavioral Advertising Town Hall', 18 October 2007, available at http://www.europarl.europa.eu /meetdocs/2004_2009/documents/dv/testimony_peterswire_/Testimony_peter swire_en.pdf.

Synopsis Report on the public consultation on the Regulatory environment for Platforms, Online Intermediaries and the Collaborative Economy, 25 May 2016, available at https://ec.europa.eu/digital-single-market/en/news/full-report- results-public-consultation-regulatory-environment-platforms-online-intermedia ries.

UK Competition & Markets Authority, 'The commercial use of consumer data. Report on the CMA's call for information', June 2015, available at https://www.gov.uk /government/uploads/system/uploads/attachment_data/file/435817/The_com mercial_use_of_consumer_data.pdf.

UK House of Lords Select Committee on European Union, 'Online Platforms and the Digital Single Market', 10th Report of Session 2015-16, 20 April 2016, available at http://www.publications.parliament.uk/pa/ld201516/ldselect/ldeucom/129/1 29.pdf.

UK Office of Fair Trading, 'Online Targeting of Advertising and Prices - A market study', May 2010, available at http://webarchive.nationalarchives.gov.uk/2014 0402142426/http:/www.oft.gov.uk/shared_oft/business_leaflets/659703/OFT1 231.pdf.

B. VAN ALSENOY, V. VERDOODT, R. HEYMAN, ET AL., 'From Social Media Service to Advertising Network. A Critical Analysis of Facebook's Revised Policies and Terms', report commissioned by the Belgian Privacy Commission, 25 August 2015, available at http://www.law.kuleuven.be/citip/en/news/item/facebooks-revised-policies-and-terms-v1-3.pdf.

WORLD ECONOMIC FORUM, 'Personal Data: The Emergence of a New Asset Class', January 2011, available at http://www3.weforum.org/docs/WEF_ITTC_PersonalData NewAsset_Report_2011.pdf.

Press Releases

European Commission

Press Release European Commission, 'Antitrust: Commissioner Kroes takes note of MasterCard's decision to cut cross-border Multilateral Interchange Fees (MIFs) and to repeal recent scheme fee increases', 1 April 2009, IP/09/515, available at http://europa.eu/rapid/press-release_IP-09-515_en.htm?locale = en.

Press Release European Commission, 'Antitrust: Commission probes allegations of antitrust violations by Google', 30 November 2010, IP/10/1624, available at http://europa.eu/rapid/press-release_IP-10-1624_en.htm.

Press Release European Commission, 'Antitrust: Commission seeks feedback on commitments offered by Google to address competition concerns', 25 April 2013, IP/13/371, available at http://europa.eu/rapid/press-release_IP-13-371_en.htm.

Press Release European Commission, 'Antitrust: Commission obtains from Google comparable display of specialised search rivals', 5 February 2014, IP/14/116, available at http://europa.eu/rapid/press-release_IP-14-116_en.htm.

Press Release European Commission, 'State aid: Commission investigates transfer pricing arrangements on corporate taxation of Apple (Ireland) Starbucks (Netherlands) and Fiat Finance and Trade (Luxembourg)', 11 June 2014, IP/14/663, available at http://europa.eu/rapid/press-release_IP-14-663_en.htm.

Press Release European Commission, 'State aid: Commission investigates transfer pricing arrangements on corporate taxation of Amazon in Luxembourg', 7 October 2014, IP/14/1105, available at http://europa.eu/rapid/press-release_IP-14-1105_en.htm.

Press Release European Commission, 'Antitrust: Commission sends Statement of Objections to Google on comparison shopping service; opens separate formal investigation on Android', 15 April 2015, IP/15/4780, available at http://europa.eu/rapid/press-release_IP-15-4780_en.htm.

Press Release European Commission, 'Antitrust: Commission sends Statement of Objections to MasterCard on cross-border rules and inter-regional interchange fees', 9 July 2015, IP/15/5323, available at http://europa.eu/rapid/press-release_IP-15-5323_en.htm.

Press Release European Commission, 'State aid: Commission decides selective tax advantages for Fiat in Luxembourg and Starbucks in the Netherlands are illegal under EU state aid rules', 21 October 2015, IP/15/5880, available at http://europa.eu/rapid/press-release_IP-15-5880_en.htm.

Press Release European Commission, 'State aid: Commission opens formal investigation into Luxembourg's tax treatment of McDonald's', 3 December 2015, IP/15/6221, available at http://europa.eu/rapid/press-release_IP-15-6221_en.htm.

Press Release European Commission, 'State aid: Commission concludes Belgian "Excess Profit" tax scheme illegal; around €700 million to be recovered from 35 multinational companies', 11 January 2016, IP/16/42, available at http://europa.eu/rapid/press-release_IP-16-42_en.htm.

Press Release European Commission, 'EU Commission and United States agree on new framework for transatlantic data flows: EU-US Privacy Shield', 2 February 2016, IP/16/216, available at http://europa.eu/rapid/press-release_IP-16-216_en.htm.

Press Release European Commission, 'Antitrust: Commission sends Statement of Objections to Google on Android operating system and applications – Factsheet', MEMO/16/1484, 20 April 2016, available at http://europa.eu/rapid/press-release_MEMO-16-1484_en.htm.

National Authorities

Press Release Autorité de la concurrence, 'The Autorité de la concurrence begins, at its own initiative, gathering information in order to assess data processing in the on-line advertising sector', 23 May 2016, available at http://www.autoritedela concurrence.fr/user/standard.php?id_rub = 630&id_article = 2780.

Press Release Bundeskartellamt, 'Bundeskartellamt initiates proceeding against Facebook on suspicion of having abused its market power by infringing data protection rules', 2 March 2016, available at http://www.bundeskartellamt. de/SharedDocs/Meldung/EN/Pressemitteilungen/2016/02_03_2016_Facebook. html?nn = 3591568.

Press Release Commission Nationale de l'Informatique et des Libertés (CNIL), 'Google's new privacy policy: incomplete information and uncontrolled combination of data across services', 16 October 2012, available at http://www.cnil.fr/english /news-and-events/news/article/googles-new-privacy-policy-incomplete-inform ation-and-uncontrolled-combination-of-data-across-ser/.

Press Release Information Commissioner's Office (ICO), 'Google to change privacy policy after ICO investigation', 30 January 2015, available at https://ico.org.uk/ about-the-ico /news-and-events / news-and-blogs /2015/01/google-to-change-pri vacy-policy-after-ico-investigation/.

Other

Amazon Press Releases, 'Amazon Marketplace a Winner for Customers, Sellers and Industry; New Service Grows over 200 Percent in First Four Months', 19 March 2001, available at http://phx.corporate-ir.net/phoenix.zhtml?c = 176060&p = irol -newsArticle&ID = 502691&highlight = .

Press Release IBM, 'Twitter and IBM Form Global Partnership to Transform Enterprise Decisions', 29 October 2014, available at http://www-03.ibm.com/press/us/en/pressrelease/45265.wss.

Press Release IBM, 'IBM and Facebook Team Up to Deliver Personalized Brand Experiences Through People-Based Marketing', 6 May 2015, available at http://www-03.ibm.com/press/us/en/pressrelease/46760.wss.

Press Release US Federal Trade Commission, 'Google Agrees to Change Its Business Practices to Resolve FTC Competition Concerns In the Markets for Devices Like Smart Phones, Games and Tablets, and in Online Search', 3 January 2013, available at http://www.ftc.gov/news-events/press-releases/2013/01/google-agrees-change-its-business-practices-resolve-ftc.

Other Sources

Amazon, 'Amazon Advertising Preferences', available at http://www.amazon.com/gp/dra/info.

Amazon, 'Amazon Product Ads. Frequently Asked Questions', available at http://services.amazon.com/product-ads-on-amazon/faq.htm?ld = NSGoogleAS.

Amazon, 'Sell on Amazon', available at http://www.amazon.com/gp/seller-account/mm-product-page.html?topic = 200274770.

Amazon.com Privacy Notice, 'Does Amazon.com Share the Information It Receives?', available at https://www.amazon.com/gp/help/customer/display.html?nodeId = 468496#GUID-A2C397AB-68FE-4592-B4A2-7550D73EEFD2__SECTION_3DF6 74DAB5B7439FB2A9B4465BC3E0AC.

http://www.amazon.com/gp/help/customer/display.html?nodeId = 537806.

M. Asay, 'Tim O'Reilly: "Whole Web" Is the OS of the Future', *CNET*, 18 March 2010, available at http://news.cnet.com/8301-13505_3-10469399-16.html.

M. Bergen, 'AT&T Gives Discount to Internet Customers Who Agree to Be Tracked. Customers Must Pay $29 More to Avoid Targeted Ads', *Ad Age*, 18 February 2015, available at http://adage.com/article/digital/t-u-verse-ad-tracking-discount-subscribers/297208/.

Bing, 'Bing Social Updates Arrive Today: For Every Search, There is Someone Who Can Help', *Bing Blogs*, 17 January 2013, available at http://www.bing.com/blogs/site_blogs/b/search/archive/2013/01/17/bing-social-updates-arrive-today-for-every-search-there-is-someone-who-can-help.aspx.

Bing, 'Comment and Like Stuff on Facebook Directly from Bing', *Bing Blogs*, 10 May 2013, available at http://www.bing.com/blogs/site_blogs/b/search/archive/2013/05/10/comment-and-like-stuff-on-facebook-directly-from-bing.aspx.

Bing blogs, 'Updates to Bing Privacy', 19 January 2010, available at http://www.bing.com/blogs/site_blogs/b/search/archive/2010/01/19/updates-to-bing-privacy.aspx.

K. Coates, 'The Estoppel Abuse', *21st Century Competition: Reflections on Modern Antitrust*, 28 October 2013, available at http://www.twentyfirstcenturycompetition.com/2013/10/the-estoppel-abuse/.

J. CONSTINE, 'Facebook Finally Lets Its Firehose Be Tapped for Marketing Insights Thanks to DataSift', *TechCrunch*, 10 March 2015, available at http://techcrunch .com/2015/03/10/facebook-topic-data/#.lvtbsd:KVhL.

J. CONSTINE, 'Facebook Climbs to 1.59 Billion Users and Crushes Q4 Estimates with $5.8B Revenue', *TechCrunch*, 27 January 2016, available at http://techcrunch. com/2016/01/27/facebook-earnings-q4-2015/.

R. CRAIG, 'Big Data and Competition – Merger Control Is Not the Remedy for Data Protection Issues', *Taylor Wessing*, July 2014, available at http://united-kingdom .taylorwessing.com/globaldatahub/article_big_data_competition.html.

Declaration of John David Rich in support of plaintiff's application for a temporary restraining order in the case PeopleBrowsr v. Twitter in the Superior Court of the State of California, County of San Francisco, November 2012, available at http://www.scribd.com/doc/114846303/Rich-Declaration-PB-v-TW-Restraining-Order-28-Nov-12. https://joindiaspora.com/

J. DREXL, 'Droit de la concurrence et propriété intellectuelle à l'ère du numérique', *A quoi sert la concurrence?* September 2014, available at http://aquoisertla concurrence.org/articles/droit-de-la-concurrence-et-propriete-intellectuelle-a-le re-du-numerique/

DuckDuckGo, 'Advertising and affiliates', available at https://duck.co/help/company /advertising-and-affiliates.

DuckDuckGo, 'Privacy', available at https://duckduckgo.com/privacy.

eBay, 'Data that delivers', available at http://advertising.ebay.nl/home.

eBay, 'Privacy Policy', 11 September 2013, available at eBay, 'Standard selling fees', available at http://pages.ebay.com/help/sell/fees.html.

http://pages.ebay.com/help/feedback/scores-reputation.html

http://pages.ebay.com/help/policies/privacy-policy.html

https://ello.co/wtf/about/ello-manifesto/

Email from Facebook to Max Schrems, 28 September 2011, available at http://www. europe-v-facebook.org/FB_E-Mails_28_9_11.pdf.

EuroPriSe, 'European Privacy Seal for Ixquick and Startpage', available at https:// www.european-privacy-seal.eu/EPS-en/Ixquick-startpage.

Facebook for Business, 'News Feed FYI: A Window Into News Feed', available at https://www.facebook.com/business/news/News-Feed-FYI-A-Window-Into-News-Feed.

Facebook for Business, 'Reach all the right people', available at https://www.facebook .com/business/products/ads/ad-targeting/.

Facebook for Business, 'Topic Data: Learn What Matters to Your Audience', available at https://www.facebook.com/business/news/topic-data.

Facebook, 'An Update to Facebook Ads', 9 January 2014, available at https://www. facebook.com/notes/facebook-and-privacy/an-update-to-facebook-ads/643198 592396693/.

Facebook, 'Download Your Info', available at https://www.facebook.com/help/1311 12897028467.

Facebook, 'How News Feed Works', available at https://en-gb.facebook.com/help/3 27131014036297/.

Facebook, 'Payments Terms', 1 January 2015, available at https://developers. facebook.com/policy/payments_terms/.

Facebook, 'Platform Policy. 6. Things you should know', available at https:// developers.facebook.com/policy.

Facebook, 'Sponsored Stories for Marketplace', 20 October 2011, available at http:// www.facebook.com/ads/stories/SponsoredStoriesGuide_Oct2011.pdf.

Facebook, 'Statement of Rights and Responsibilities. Sharing Your Content and Information', available via https://en-gb.facebook.com/legal/terms.

Facebook, 'What are partner categories and how are they different from Facebook categories?', available at https://en-gb.facebook.com/business/help/298717656 925097.

Facebook Help Centre, 'Does Facebook sell my information?', available at https:// www.facebook.com/help/152637448140583.

Facebook's Terms of Services on Safety, available at https://www.facebook.com/legal /terms.

http://search.fb.com/

C. FARIVAR, 'Fueled by Snowden and Apple, Private Search Engine DuckDuckGo Rapidly Grows', *Ars Technica*, 25 June 2015, available at http://arstechnica.com /business/ 2015/06/ fueled-by-snowden-and-apple-private-search-engine-duckd uckgo-rapidly-growing/.

S. FRIER, 'Twitter Reaches Deal to Show Tweets in Google Search Results', *Bloomberg*, 5 February 2015, available at http://www.bloomberg.com/news/articles/2015-02-05/twitter-said-to-reach-deal-for-tweets-in-google-search-results.

http://ftc.gov/opa/2013/01/google.shtm

Gartner IT Glossary, 'Big data', available at http://www.gartner.com/it-glossary/big-data/.

https://www.ghostery.com/en/why-ghostery/for-individuals/

Google, 'Privacy Policy', 19 August 2015, available at http://www.google.com/intl/en -GB/policies/privacy/.

'Google Takeout' service, available at https://support.google.com/takeout/answer/2 508459?hl = en&ref_topic = 2508503.

Google, 'Terms of Service', 11 November 2013, available at http://www.google.com/ intl/en/policies/terms/changes/.

Google Inside AdWords, ' + Post ads now available to all advertisers and support Hangouts on Air', 16 April 2014, available at http://adwords.blogspot.nl/2014/ 04/post-ads-now-available-to-all.html.

Google Privacy, 'Is Google using my data? What for?', available at https://support. google.com/googleforwork/answer/6056650?hl = en.

https://www.google.com/intl/en/about/company/

I. GRAEF & B. VAN ALSENOY, 'Data Protection Data Protection through the Lens of Competition Law: will Germany Lead the Way?', *LSE Media Policy Project blog*, 23 March 2016, available at http://blogs.lse.ac.uk/mediapolicyproject/2016/03/23 /data-protection-through-the-lens-of-competition-law-will-germany-lead-the-way/.

402

S. Hargreaves, 'Twitter Forecasts Slowing Sales and User Growth', *CNN Money*, 6 February 2014, available at http://money.cnn.com/2014/02/05/technology/social/twitter-earnings/.

R. Hof, 'Amazon's Ad Business Suddenly Looks Real', *Forbes*, 5 June 2013, available at http://www.forbes.com/sites/roberthof/2013/06/05/amazons-ad-business-suddenly-looks-real/.

Z. Hofer-Shall, 'Working Directly with the Twitter Data Ecosystem', *Gnip Company Blog*, 10 April 2015, available at https://blog.gnip.com/twitter-data-ecosystem/.

IBM Big Data & Analytics Hub, 'The Four V's of Big Data', available at http://www.ibmbigdatahub.com/infographic/four-vs-big-data.

Ixquick, 'FAQ. Q: Is Ixquick free? How does Ixquick generate its income?', available at https://ixquick.com/eng/company-faq.html.

Ixquick, 'Ixquick Protects Your Privacy!', available at https://www.ixquick.com/eng/what-makes-ixquick-special.html.

Ixquick, 'Our Privacy Policy', available at https://ixquick.com/eng/privacy-policy.html.

A. Lamadrid de Pablo, 'A Comment on Case T-79/12 Cisco Systems and Messagenet v European Commission (Microsoft/Skype)', *Chillin'Competition*, 12 May 2014, available at http://chillingcompetition.com/2014/05/12/a-comment-on-case-t-7912-cisco-systems-and-messagenet-v-european-commission-microsoftskype/.

K. Liyakasa, 'Amazon's Q1 Sheds (More) Light On Ad Revenues', *AdExchanger*, 23 April 2015, available at http://adexchanger.com/ad-exchange-news/amazons-q1-reveals-ads-business-may-bank-1-billion-a-year/.

J.P. Mangalindan, 'Amazon's Recommendation Secret', *Fortune*, 30 July 2012, available at http://fortune.com/2012/07/30/amazons-recommendation-secret/.

https://mewe.com/faq

D. Meyer, 'Facebook Beware? EU Antitrust Chief Warns over Data Portability', 27 November 2012, available at http://www.zdnet.com/facebook-beware-eu-antitrust-chief-warns-over-data-portability-7000007950/.

Microsoft Corporation, 'The European Commission's Decision in the Microsoft Case and its Implications for Other Companies and Industries', April 2004, available at http://www.microsoft.com/presspass/download/legal/EuropeanCommission/CommentonECMicrosoftDecision.pdf.

G. Moody, 'Facebook Says Some of Your Personal Data Is Its "Trade Secrets or Intellectual Property"', *Techdirt*, 12 October 2011, available at https://www.techdirt.com/articles/20111011/12190216306/facebook-says-some-your-personal-data-is-its-trade-secrets-intellectual-property.shtml.

S. Nair, 'Must-Know: Assessing Facebook's Revenue Sources', *Market Realist*, 15 January 2014, available at http://marketrealist.com/2014/01/facebook-revenue-advertising/.

'News Corp withdraws bid for BSkyB', *BBC News*, 13 July 2011, available at http://www.bbc.com/news/business-14142307.

N. NEWMAN, 'Why Antitrust Authorities Should Block Google's Takeover of Nest's "Smart Home" Business', *Huffington Post*, 15 January 2014, available at http://www.huffingtonpost.com/nathan-newman/why-antitrust-authorities_b_4603053.html.

K. O'TOOLE, 'Susan Athey: How Big Data Changes Business Management. The Stanford Economist Explains How Troves of Digital Data Will Reshape Competition', *Insights by Stanford Business*, 20 September 2013, available at http://www.gsb.stanford.edu/insights/susan-athey-how-big-data-changes-business-management.

'PeopleBrowsr Wins Temporary Restraining Order Compelling Twitter to Provide Firehose Access', 28 November 2012, available at http://blog.peoplebrowsr.com/2012/11/peoplebrowsr-wins-temporary-restraining-order-compelling-twitter-to-provide-firehose-access/.

'PeopleBrowsr and Twitter settle Firehose dispute', 25 April 2013, available at http://blog.peoplebrowsr.com/2013/04/peoplebrowsr-and-twitter-settle-firehose-dispute/.

N. PETIT, 'Antitrust and The Challenge of Policing "Moligopolists"', Keynote at Ninth CLEEN Workshop, 28-29 May 2015, Tilburg, available at http://orbi.ulg.ac.be//handle/2268/182226.

L. RAINIE & M. DUGGAN, 'Privacy and Information Sharing', 14 January 2016, available at http://www.pewinternet.org/2016/01/14/privacy-and-information-sharing/.

D. SABBAGH & J. DEANS, 'News Corp's BSkyB Bid: Jeremy Hunt Expected to Give Green Light Next Week', *The Guardian*, 23 June 2011, available at http://www.theguardian.com/media/2011/jun/22/news-corp-bskyb-jeremy-hunt.

https://telegram.org/privacy

https://threema.ch/en

Twitter, 'Never miss important Tweets from people you follow', 10 February 2016, available at https://blog.twitter.com/2016/never-miss-important-tweets-from-people-you-follow.

Twitter, 'Promoted Promotions', available at https://blog.twitter.com/2010/promoted-promotions.

Twitter, 'What are Promoted Trends?', available at https://support.twitter.com/articles/282142.

Twitter, 'What are Promoted Tweets?', available at http://support.twitter.com/articles/142101-what-are-promoted-tweets.

https://dev.twitter.com/streaming/overview

https://partners.twitter.com/about

A. WHITTEN, 'Updating Our Privacy Policies and Terms of Service', *Google Official Blog*, 24 January 2012, available at http://googleblog.blogspot.be/2012/01/updating-our-privacy-policies-and-terms.html.

Yahoo, 'Data Storage and Anonymisation', available at https://policies.yahoo.com/ie/en/yahoo/privacy/topics/datastorage/index.htm.

M. Yglesias, 'The Justice Department Was Absolutely Right to Go After Microsoft in the 1990s', *Slate*, 26 August 2013, available at http://www.slate.com/blogs/ moneybox/2013/08/26/microsoft_antitrust_suit_the_vindication_of_the_justice _department.html.

Table of Cases

Court of Justice

General Court

Opinions Advocates General

European Court of Human Rights

US Supreme Court

Lower US Courts

US Federal Trade Commission

National Competition Authorities

Table of Legislation

EU Legislation

Regulations and Accompanying Documents

Official Documents Relating to the General Data Protection Regulation

Directives

US Federal Trade Commission

Index

INTERNATIONAL COMPETITION LAW SERIES

1. Ignacio De Leon, *Latin American Competition Law and Policy: A Policy in Search of Identity*, 2001 (ISBN 90-411-1542-0).
2. Wim Dejonghe & Wouter Van de Voorde (eds), *M & A in Belgium*, 2001 (ISBN 90-411-1594-3).
3. Yang-Ching Chao, Gee San, Changfa Lo & Jiming Ho (eds), *International and Comparative Competition Law and Policies*, 2001 (ISBN 90-411-1643-5).
4. Martin Mendelsohn & Stephen Rose, *Guide to the EC Block Exemption for Vertical Agreements*, 2002 (ISBN 90-411-9813-X).
5. Clifford A. Jones & Mitsuo Matsushita (eds), *Competition Policy in the Global Trading System: Perspectives from the EU, Japan and the USA*, 2002 (ISBN 90-411-1758-X).
6. Christian Koenig, Andreas Bartosch, Jens-Daniel Braun & Marion Romes (eds), *EC Competition and Telecommunications Law*. Second Edition, 2009 (ISBN 978-90-411-2564-4).
7. Jürgen Basedow (ed.), *Limits and Control of Competition with a View to International Harmonization*, 2002 (ISBN 90-411-1967-1).
8. Maureen Brunt, Economic Essays on Australian and New Zealand Competition Law, 2003 (ISBN 90-411-1991-4).
9. Ky P. Ewing, Jr., *Competition Rules for the 21st Century: Principles from America's Experience*, Second Edition, 2006 (ISBN 90-411-2477-2).
10. Joseph Wilson, *Globalization and the Limits of National Merger Control Laws*, 2003 (ISBN 90-411-1996-5).
11. Peter Verloop & Valérie Landes (eds), *Merger Control in Europe: EU, Member States and Accession States*, Fourth Edition, 2003 (ISBN 90-411-2056-4).
12. Themistoklis K. Giannakopoulos, *Safeguarding Companies' Rights in Competition and Anti-dumping/Anti-subsidies Proceedings*, Second Edition, 2011 (ISBN 978-90-411-3404-2).
13. Marjorie Holmes & Lesley Davey (eds), *A Practical Guide to National Competition Rules across Europe*, Second Edition, 2007 (ISBN 978-90-411-2607-8).
14. Sigrid Stroux, *US and EU Oligopoly Control*, 2004 (ISBN 90-411-2296-6).
15. Tzong-Leh Hwang and Chiyuan Chen (eds), *The Future Development of Competition Framework*, 2004 (ISBN 90-411-2305-9).

16. Phedon Nicolaides, Mihalis Kekelekis and Maria Kleis, *State Aid Policy in the European Community: Principles and Practice,* Second Edition, 2008 (ISBN 978-90-411-2754-9).

17. Doris Hildebrand, *Economic Analyses of Vertical Agreements: A Self- Assessment,* 2005 (ISBN 90-411-2328-8).

18. Frauke Henning-Bodewig, *Unfair Competition Law: European Union and Member States,* 2005 (ISBN 90-411-2329-6).

19. Duarte Brito & Margarida Catalão-Lopes, *Mergers and Acquisitions: The Industrial Organization Perspective,* 2006 (ISBN 90-411-2451-9).

20. Nikos Th. Nikolinakos, *EU Competition Law and Regulation in the Converging Telecommunications, Media and IT Sectors,* 2006 (ISBN 90-411- 2469-1).

21. Mihalis Kekelekis, *The EC Merger Control Regulation: Rights of Defence. A Critical Analysis of DG COMP Practice and Community Courts' Jurisprudence,* 2006 (ISBN 90-411-2553-1).

22. Mark R. Joelson, *An International Antitrust Primer: A Guide to the Operation of United States, European Union and Other Key Competition Laws in the Global Economy,* Third Edition, 2006 (ISBN 90-411-2468-3).

23. Themistoklis K. Giannakopoulos, *A Concise Guide to the EU Anti-dumping/ Anti-subsidies Procedures,* 2006 (ISBN 90-411-2464-0).

24. George Cumming, Brad Spitz & Ruth Janal, *Civil Procedure Used for Enforcement of EC Competition Law by the English, French and German Civil Courts,* 2007 (ISBN 978-90-411-2471-5).

25. Jürgen Basedow (ed.), *Private Enforcement of EC Competition Law,* 2007 (ISBN 978-90-411-2613-9).

26. Jung Wook Cho, *Innovation and Competition in the Digital Network Economy: A Legal and Economic Assessment on Multi-tying Practices and Network Effects,* 2007 (ISBN 978-90-411-2574-3).

27. Akira Inoue, *Japanese Antitrust Law Manual: Law, Cases and Interpretation of the Japanese Antimonopoly Act,* 2007 (ISBN 978-90-411-2627-6).

28. René Barents, *Directory of EC Case Law on Competition,* 2007 (ISBN 978-90-411-2656-6).

29. Paul F. Nemitz (ed.), *The Effective Application of EU State Aid Procedures: The Role of National Law and Practice,* 2007 (ISBN 978-90-411-2657-3).

30. Jurian Langer, *Tying and Bundling as a Leveraging Concern under EC Competition Law,* 2007 (ISBN 978-90-411-2575-0).

31. Abel M. Mateus & Teresa Moreira (eds), *Competition Law and Economics – Advances in Competition Policy and Antitrust Enforcement,* 2007 (ISBN 978-90-411-2632-0).

32. Alberto Santa Maria, *Competition and State Aid: An Analysis of the EC Practice,* 2007 (ISBN 978-90-411-2617-7).

33. Barry J. Rodger (ed.), *Article 234 and Competition Law: An Analysis,* 2007 (ISBN 978-90-411-2605-4).

34. Alla Pozdnakova, *Liner Shipping and EU Competition Law,* 2008 (ISBN 978-90-411-2717-4).

35. Milena Stoyanova, *Competition Problems in Liberalized Telecommunications: Regulatory Solutions to Promote Effective Competition*, 2008 (ISBN 978-90-411-2736-5).

36. *EC State Aid Law/Le Droit des Aides d'Etat dans la CE. Liber Amicorum Francisco Santaolalla Gadea*, 2008 (ISBN 978-90-411-2774-7).

37. René Barents, *Directory of EC Case Law on State Aids*, 2008 (ISBN 978-90-411-2732-7).

38. Ignacio De Leon, *An Institutional Assessment of Antitrust Policy: The Latin American Experience*, 2009 (ISBN 978-90-411-2478-4).

39. Doris Hildebrand, *The Role of Economic Analysis in EU Competition Law: TheEuropean School*, Fourth Edition, 2016 (ISBN 978-90-411-6245-8).

40. Eugène Buttigieg, *Competition Law: Safeguarding the Consumer Interest. A Comparative Analysis of US Antitrust Law and EC Competition Law*, 2009 (ISBN 978-90-411-3119-5).

41. Ioannis Lianos & Ioannis Kokkoris (eds), *The Reform of EC Competition Law: New Challenges*, 2010 (ISBN 978-90-411-2692-4).

42. George Cumming & Mirjam Freudenthal, *Civil Procedure in EU Competition Cases before the English and Dutch Courts*, 2010 (ISBN 978-90-411-3192-8).

43. A.E. Rodriguez & Ashok Menon, *The Limits of Competition Policy: The Shortcomings of Antitrust in Developing and Reforming Economies*, 2010 (ISBN 978-90-411-3177-5).

44. Mika Oinonen, *Does EU Merger Control Discriminate against Small Market Companies? Diagnosing the Argument with Conclusions*, 2010 (ISBN 978-90-411-3261-1).

45. Eirik Østerud, *Identifying Exclusionary Abuses by Dominant Undertakings under EU Competition Law: The Spectrum of Tests*, 2010 (ISBN 978-90-411-3271-0).

46. Marco Botta, *Merger Control Regimes in Emerging Economies: A Case Study on Brazil and Argentina*, 2011 (ISBN 978-90-411-3402-8).

47. Jürgen Basedow & Wolfgang Wurmnest (eds), *Structure and Effects in EU Competition Law: Studies on Exclusionary Conduct and State Aid*, 2011 (ISBN 978-90-411-3174-4).

48. George Cumming (ed.), *Merger Decisions and the Rules of Procedure of the European Community Courts*, 2012 (ISBN 978-90-411-3671-8).

49. Eduardo Molan Gaban & Juliana Oliveira Domingues (eds), *Antitrust Law in Brazil: Fighting Cartels*, 2012 (ISBN 978-90-411-3670-1).

50. Giandonato Caggiano, Gabriella Muscolo & Marina Tavassi (eds), *Competition Law and Intellectual Property: A European Perspective*, 2012 (ISBN 978-90-411-3447-9).

51. Ben Van Rompuy, *Economic Efficiency: The Sole Concern of Modern Antitrust Policy? Non-efficiency Considerations under Article 101 TFEU*, 2012 (ISBN 978-90-411-3870-5).

52. Liyang Hou, *Competition Law and Regulation of the EU Electronic Communications Sector: A Comparative Legal Approach*, 2012 (ISBN 978-90-411-4047-0).

53. Barry Rodger, *Landmark Cases in Competition Law: Around the World in Fourteen Stories*, 2012 (ISBN 978-90-411-3843-9).
54. Andreas Scordamaglia-Tousis, *EU Cartel Enforcement: Reconciling Effective Public Enforcement with Fundamental Rights*, 2013 (ISBN 978-90-411-4758-5).
55. Bernardo Cortese (ed.), *EU Competition Law: Between Public and Private Enforcement*, 2014 (ISBN 978-90-411-4677-9).
56. Barry Rodger (ed.), *Competition Law: Comparative Private Enforcement and Collective Redress across the EU*, 2014 (ISBN 978-90-411-4559-8).
57. Nada Ina Pauer, *The Single Economic Entity Doctrine and Corporate Group Responsibility in European Antitrust Law*, 2014 (ISBN 978-90-411-5262-6).
58. Urška Petrovčič, *Competition Law and Standard Essential Patents: A Transatlantic Perspective*, 2014 (ISBN 978-90-411-4960-2).
59. David Telyas, *The Interface between Competition Law, Patents and Technical Standards*, 2014 (ISBN 978-90-411-5418-7).
60. Katerina Maniadaki, *EU Competition Law, Regulation and the Internet: The Case of Net Neutrality*, 2014 (ISBN 978-90-411-4140-8).
61. Horacio Vedia Jerez, *Competition Law Enforcement and Compliance across the World: A Comparative Review*, 2015 (ISBN 978-90-411-5815-4).
62. Kadir Baş, *The Substantive Appraisal of Joint Ventures under the EU Merger Control Regime*, 2015 (ISBN 978-90-411-5816-1).
63. Alberto Santa Maria, *Competition and State Aid: An Analysis of the EU Practice*, Second Edition, 2015 (ISBN 978-90-411-5818-5).
64. Lúcio Tomé Feteira, *The Interplay between European and National Competition Law after Regulation 1/2003: "United (Should) We Stand?"*, 2016 (ISBN 978-90-411-5663-1).
65. Giovanni Pitruzzella & Gabriella Muscolo(eds), *Competition and Patent Law in the Pharmaceutical Sector: An International Perspective*, 2016 (ISBN 978-90-411-5927-4).
66. Małgorzata Cyndecka, *The Market Economy Investor Test in EU State Aid Law: Applicability and Application*, 2016 (ISBN 978-90-411-6102-4).
67. Damiano Canapa, *Trademarks and Brands in Merger Control: An Analysis of the European and Swiss Legal Orders*, 2016 (ISBN 978-90-411-6717-0).
68. Inge Graef, *EU Competition Law, Data Protection and Online Platforms: Data as Essential Facility*, 2016 (ISBN 978-90-411-8324-8).